Energy, the State, an

Energy, the State, and the Market

British Energy Policy since 1979

Revised Edition

DIETER HELM

OXFORD
UNIVERSITY PRESS

*This book has been printed digitally and produced in a standard specification
in order to ensure its continuing availability*

OXFORD
UNIVERSITY PRESS

Great Clarendon Street, Oxford OX2 6DP

Oxford University Press is a department of the University of Oxford.
It furthers the University's objective of excellence in research, scholarship,
and education by publishing worldwide in

Oxford New York

Auckland   Cape Town   Dar es Salaam   Hong Kong   Karachi
Kuala Lumpur   Madrid   Melbourne   Mexico City   Nairobi
New Delhi   Shanghai   Taipei   Toronto
With offices in
Argentina   Austria   Brazil   Chile   Czech Republic   France   Greece
Guatemala   Hungary   Italy   Japan   South Korea   Poland   Portugal
Singapore   Switzerland   Thailand   Turkey   Ukraine   Vietnam

ISBN 978-0-19-927074-3

PREFACE

This book has taken much longer to write than intended. It started out as an account of the market approach to energy gradually introduced after the 1979 general election when the Conservative Party came to power. The new policy was articulated by Nigel Lawson in 1982, and led on to the privatizations of the gas and electricity industries. The ramifications continue to be felt over a decade later. The coal crises of 1992/93 and 1997/98, the break-up of British Gas and the liberalizations of domestic markets were all consequences of the market approach and conditioned by the privatizations. Not until the end of Labour's first term in office could a semblance be seen of what a post-privatization and part-liberalization energy policy might look like.

In British political, regulatory, and corporate life, individuals have been able to exert powerful influences and shape events. The delegation of public-interest powers to individual regulators, the two-party system, the comparative absence of judicial oversight, and the liberal approach to corporate governance have all contributed to a more enhanced role for personalities than in Europe or the United States.

Necessarily, therefore, any study of the energy sector must pay due attention to the chairmen of the nationalized industries, the Cabinet ministers and the regulators, and these people figure highly in what is inevitably a particularly personalized account of energy policy since 1979. Many of these I have had the privilege to get to know and, in some cases, to work with over the last two decades. The list of influences on my analysis is consequently a considerable one though none of course is responsible for the analysis or any errors and omissions. I have had the privilege of being a member of the Department of Trade and Industry's (DTI) Energy Advisory Panel since its inception in 1993 to its demise in 2003, and, though members have come and gone, Michael Parker, Tony White, Alex Kemp, Peter Lehmann, David Green, Paul Jefferiss, Tony Cooper, Peter Nicholls, and Nigel Evans have all helped to shape my views. Among current and former officials at the DTI, Charles Henderson, Anna Walker, Jon Bird, Rupert Steele, and Adrian Gault have all been important influences. I was also a member of the steering group of the UKAEA quinquennial review in 2002, and benefited from the debates and discussions with Gordon MacKerron and Stephen Spivey.

Then there have been colleagues in the Academic Panel of the Department of the Environment, the Department of the Environment, Transport and the Regions, and then the Department for Environment, Food and Rural Affairs, which I now chair. David Newbery, Chris Riley, and Wilfred Beckerman have all been important to this book.

In the regulatory field, I have greatly benefited from discussions over the years with the late Michael Beesley, Callum McCarthy, Richard Morse, Eileen Marshall, Clare Spottiswoode, Ian Byatt, Douglas McIldoon, Penny Boys, Derek Morris, David Currie, James Strachan, Stephen Littlechild, James McKinnon, Malcolm Keay, Doug Andrews, Chris Bolt, and Joanna Whittington. In the wider regulatory circles, I would also like to acknowledge discussions with Colin Robinson, Christopher Foster, Colin Mayer, Tim Jenkinson, Graham Mather, George Yarrow, Richard Green, David Pearce, Dan Corry, and Geoff Norris.

I also owe a considerable debt of gratitude to a large number of people in the industries themselves—too often treated by academic economists as mere managers. I could not possibly list them all, but Edmund Wallis, John Baker, David Varney, David Jefferies, John Roberts, Ian Robinson, John Wybrew, John Harris, Robin Jeffrey, Hugh Collum, Norman Askew, David Jackson, David Tolley, Ian Russell, and John Collins have all been particularly helpful.

In addition to all the general help and support I have received, a number have been kind enough to read and comment on drafts. Michael Parker read most of the book and commented extensively. Other chapters have been read by Les Hannah, Robin Smale, Cameron Hepburn, Gareth Davies, Tim Tutton, John Guinness, Stuart Anderson, David Jefferies, Adrian Gault, Geoff Horton, Martin Donnelly, Patrick Law, Robin Jeffrey, John Harris, Stephen Littlechild, James McKinnon, Malcolm Keay, Chris Bolt, Jon Bird, Tony Cooper, and Roger Witcomb.

In the political field, David Howell, Nigel Lawson, Peter Walker, Michael Spicer, Ian Lang, Peter Mandelson, Tim Eggar, Cecil Parkinson, and Dan Corry have all read and commented on drafts.

At OXERA, of which I have been a director for most of the period, numerous colleagues have influenced me, notably Nick Hartley, Luis Correia da Silva, Helen Jenkins, Martin Brough, Derek Holt, Alan Horncastle, Robin Smale, Gareth Davies, Fod Barnes, Leon Fields, Chris Jenkins, Patrick Lane, and Phil Gray. The OXERA Energy Group has been a major forum for the discussion of many of the issues covered in this book.

Among my colleagues at New College, I have had the chance to talk through many of the more general aspects of the book, notably with Roger Elliott, Chris Allsopp, Martin Ceadel, and David Wiggins.

I have had the great benefit of Cate Dominian's excellent production of the book, correcting my many mistakes and generating numerous drafts. Vicky Hibberd has provided research assistance, as did Emily Clark. Anne Warner has also provided wonderful support throughout. I am also grateful to Alison Gomm for her invaluable assistance in the early days of the project.

Finally, all books take their toll on families, and this is no exception. I would like to thank my wife, Susie, for constant support, and Laura and Oliver for their forbearance, and dedicate the book to them.

D.H.

PREFACE TO PAPERBACK EDITION

Since publication in February 2002, the government has produced its long-awaited and much delayed White Paper, 'Our Energy Future—Creating a Low Carbon Economy'. Although all the main themes were anticipated, I have taken the opportunity of this paperback edition to add a new chapter which critiques the White Paper, noting the change in policy direction it acknowledges, but also pointing to the disconnect between its bold aspirations and its weakness in terms of delivery.

There have been other developments in energy policy during 2003 which have also required recognition, notably the faltering of British Energy, the Draft Nuclear Sites and Radioactive Substances bill, new draft guidance to Ofgem on social and environmental matters, and the little noticed contracting by National Grid Transco for the output of the Drax power station. The nuclear developments have been added to Chapter 10, 'Nuclear Privatization and the End of the Nuclear Dream'; the guidance and contracting have been covered in the new chapter on the energy White Paper (Chapter 22). Finally, the power cuts in the USA, together with the problems experienced across Europe in summer and autumn 2003, cannot be left without mention.

This edition also allows me to make a number of comparatively minor corrections and revisions to the main text. In doing so, I have had the great benefit of a number of reviews and comments; and am particularly grateful to Roger Barnard, Tim Eggar, Adrian Gault, David Green, Jonathan Green, Malcolm Grimston, Alex Henney, and Rob Wright.

Finally, Cate Dominian has once again provided excellent production support, for which I am most grateful.

D.H.

CONTENTS

LIST OF FIGURES

LIST OF TABLES

GLOSSARY OF TERMS

AA	Automobile Association
AEP	American Electric Power
AGR	advanced gas-cooled reactor
ARA	Amsterdam–Rotterdam–Antwerp (coal price)
ASLEF	Associated Society of Locomotive Engineers and Firemen
BACM	British Association of Colliery Management
bbl	barrel (of oil)
BETTA	British energy trading and transmission arrangements
BGC	British Gas Corporation
BGT	British Gas Trading
BNFL	British Nuclear Fuels Ltd
BNOC	British National Oil Company
BRTF	Better Regulation Task Force
BSC	Balancing and Settlement Code
BST	bulk supply tariff
CAPEX	capital expenditure
CBI	Confederation of British Industry
CCA	current-cost accounting
CCGT	combined-cycle gas turbine
CCL	Climate Change Levy
CEB	Central Electricity Board
CEGB	Central Electricity Generating Board
CHP	combined heat and power
CND	Campaign for Nuclear Disarmament
CO_2	carbon dioxide
CSW	Central and South West Corporation
DEFRA	Department for Environment, Food, and Rural Affairs
DETR	Department of the Environment, Transport, and the Regions
DG TREN	Directorate-General for Energy and Transport
DGFT	Director General of Fair Trading
DTI	Department of Trade and Industry
EDF	Electricité de France
EEC	Energy Efficiency Commitment
EESOP(s)	Energy Efficiency Standard(s) of Performance

EFL	external financial limit
EST	Energy Saving Trust
FBR	fast-breeder reactor
FERC	Federal Energy Regulation Commission
FFL	Fossil Fuel Levy
FGD	flue-gas desulphurization
FPN	final physical notification
FT	*Financial Times*
GDP	gross domestic product
GEC	General Electric Company
GW	gigawatt
GWh	gigawatt hour
HMSO	Her Majesty's Stationery Office
HMT	Her Majesty's Treasury
IEA	Institute of Economic Affairs
IIP	Incentives and Innovation Project
IPCC	Intergovernmental Panel on Climate Change
IPP	independent power producer
IPPR	Institute of Public Policy Research
kW	kilowatt
kWh	kilowatt hour
LCPD	Large Combustion Plants Directive
LDZ	local distribution zone
LIC	large industrial customer
LNG	liquefied natural gas
LOLP	loss of load probability
LRMC	long-run marginal cost
Magnox	magnesium alloy graphite moderated gas-cooled uranium oxide reactor
MALC	market abuse licence condition
Manweb	Merseyside and North Wales Electricity Board
MAR	market-to-asset ratio
MMC	Monopolies and Mergers Commission
MOX	mixed oxide (fuel)
MTFS	Medium Term Financial Strategy
MW	megawatt
MW	megawatt hour
NACODS	National Association of Colliery Overmen, Deputies, and Shotfirers
NAO	National Audit Office
NAPAG	National Academies Policy Analysis Group

NATO	North Atlantic Treaty Organization
NCB	National Coal Board
NDA	Nuclear Decommissioning Authority
NEA	Nuclear Energy Agreement
NEDO	National Economic Development Office
NETA	new electricity trading arrangements
NFFO	Non Fossil Fuel Obligation/Order
NGC	National Grid Company
NGT	National Grid Transco
NIE	Northern Ireland Electricity
NICs	National Insurance Contributions
NORWEB	North Western Electricity Board
NOx	oxides of nitrogen
NTS	National Transmission System (for gas)
NUCG	Nuclear Utilities Chairmens Group
NUM	National Union of Mineworkers
NUR	National Union of Railwaymen
O&M	operations and maintenance
Ofcom	Office of Communications
Offer	Office of Electricity Regulation
Ofgas	Office of Gas Supply
Ofgem	Office of Gas and Electricity Markets
Ofreg	Office for the Regulation of Electricity and Gas
OFT	Office of Fair Trading
Oftel	Office of Telecommunications
Ofwat	Office of Water Services
OPEC	Organization of Petroleum Exporting Countries
OPEX	operating expenditure
OPM	overall project manager
OTC	over-the-counter
OXERA	Oxford Economic Research Associates
PES	public electricity supplier/public electricity supply
PIU	Performance and Innovation Unit (part of the Cabinet Office)
PPA	power purchase agreement
PPP	Pool purchase price
ppmv	parts per million of volume
PPT	private purchase tariff
PRT	petroleum revenue tax
PSBR	public-sector borrowing requirement
PWR	pressurized-water reactor

R&D	research and development
RAB	regulatory asset base
RCEP	Royal Commission on Environmental Pollution
REC	regional electricity company
RETA	review of electricity trading arrangements
RO	Renewables Obligation
ROC	Renewables Obligation Certificate
RPI	retail price index
$RPI - X$	retail price index minus X per cent
RRR	required rate of return
SEEBOARD	South Eastern Electricity Board
SGHWR	steam-generating heavy water reactor
SMP	system marginal price
SRO	Scottish Renewables Obligation
SO	system operator
SO_2	sulphur dioxide
SPRU	Social Policy Research Unit
SRMC	short-run marginal cost
SSEB	South of Scotland Electricity Board
SWALEC	South Wales Electricity Board
SWEB	South Western Electricity Board
TGWU	Transport and General Workers' Union
THORP	thermal oxide reprocessing plant
TPA	third-party access
TO	transmission operator
TUC	Trades Union Congress
UDM	Union of Democratic Mineworkers
UKAEA	United Kingdom Atomic Energy Authority
VAT	value-added tax
VOLL	value of loss of load
WPD	Western Power Distribution

1

Introduction

Energy has always been treated as 'special'. Energy supplies have played a major part not only in national economic development, but also in defence and security. Japan and Germany both ran out of oil in the Second World War, and France's ambitious nuclear programme has been motivated in large measure by the search for national self-sufficiency. The US's foreign policy is in significant measure dictated by the politics of oil and oil dependency.

In economic matters, it is hard to overestimate the role of fossil fuels in facilitating and sustaining the industrialization of the twentieth century. Global energy consumption has increased more than tenfold—indeed, it could be called the energy century. Had Marx observed the twentieth, rather than the nineteenth, century, he might have more accurately focused on an energy rather than a labour theory of value. The implicit energy which is required to make most of the goods we consume is very great—from mineral extraction, to machinery manufacture, the manufacturing process, and, of course, transport to final customers. The service sector, too, requires heat, light, and power.

For Britain the role of energy is especially great. Its industrialization was based upon water power and then coal. From the 1970s onwards, Britain became a major oil and gas producer, saving it from balance-of-payment crises and providing tax revenues in the 1980s and 1990s to prop up its public finances. Such energy abundance has enabled Britain to make the economic adjustments necessary to keep pace with its energy-poor European neighbours.

For most politicians in the post-war period, the importance of energy has naturally translated into the assumption that governments need to control its production and distribution. Until the 1980s, it was a conventional wisdom of the post-war years that markets are hopelessly inadequate in providing appropriate energy supplies. State-owned companies were deemed to be so natural that they were made *statutory* monopolies, and it was assumed that regulation was inevitable. Mainstream Conservatives never challenged the nationalized status of the electricity, coal, and later gas industries in the 1950s, 1960s, and 1970s. Indeed, such was the consensus that their privatization was not even included in Margaret Thatcher's manifesto in 1979.

Throughout this period, the overwhelming objective was to produce as much energy as possible (domestically) to keep pace with the demand of what has become known as the 'golden age' of the British economy. Building enough coal power stations to keep pace with economic growth, and developing civil nuclear power which might be 'too cheap to measure' dominated energy policy. Indeed, by 1970, the chairman of the Central Electricity Generating Board (CEGB), Sir Stanley Brown, could look forward to a capacity of over 100 GW in 25 years' time (1995), on the simple basis that 2–3 per cent growth in the economy implied a 7 per cent growth in electricity demand (Brown 1970). (In fact, only just over half that amount was needed in 1995.)

By the mid-1980s, the post-war model had been turned on its head. In place of nationalization and statutory monopoly, privatization and competition became the driving forces of energy policy. Security of supply would no longer be driven by government, but instead would be the outcome of market forces. The job of government was limited to setting the framework within which the scope of market forces would be maximized.

The political rhetoric belied a much more muddled and gradual shift in policy priorities. Thatcher's agenda was always more complex and confused than the simple expositions given by her ministers for energy. Whilst Nigel Lawson set out a neat theoretical vision of the 'market for energy', Thatcher's battle with the miners led her along a path which at one stage promoted a new nuclear programme of up to ten more pressurized-water reactors (PWRs), and bolted on to the privatized structures a set of contracts for coal and protected revenues for nuclear. She left the gas monopoly intact, postponed domestic competition in electricity for almost a decade, held out no prospect at all for domestic gas competition, and took no effective steps to privatize coal.

The history of the energy sector in the 1990s was largely that of transition from monopoly to competition in the context of abundant, cheap supplies. In the case of electricity, this was the unfolding of the eight-year transition to domestic competition provided in the Electricity Act 1989. In the case of gas, the Gas Act 1995 put it on a fast track to full competition in 1998 alongside electricity. In both cases, the process was often tortuous, and inevitably full of surprises. At the high level, it was one of closing down most of the coal industry, a significant increase in the role of gas in electricity generation, and the break-up of British Gas as a single integrated monopoly. There was also a major increase in regulation. At the level of detail, a new model for the energy sector gradually emerged, based upon spot markets, financial risk spreading, and novel business structures. The political fallout from the transitions in electricity and gas was considerable, for competition was radical in rooting out the cross-subsidies which the monopoly structures had tolerated. Under competitive pressures, profit-seeking firms set prices in relation to costs; the costs of generating from coal were challenged by gas; and the costs of supplying poorer and rural customers were exposed when new entrants began to chase the fatter margins of the more affluent. The consequences for the miners and the poor proved too much for the incoming Labour government in 1997 to bear, with the result that, before the transition to the full competitive model was completed, Labour began to intervene in an attempt to marry the political imperatives with the market.

The coal crisis of 1997/98 forced the new government into an unplanned policy shift, set out in Peter Mandelson's 1998 White Paper on energy sources. To hide the protection of the miners, it argued that a moratorium on new combined-cycle gas turbines (CCGTs) was necessary to buy time during which the 'distortions' in the market would be corrected. These distortions, it claimed, had placed coal at a disadvantage and, once removed, the market would again be king. Although the case was largely spurious (in that the market had in fact been rigged with special contracts to hold *up* both the price and volume of coal), the energy sources White Paper began a more serious debate about the economic and political boundaries between the market and the state in energy. It claimed that, henceforth, energy policy would set competitive markets in the context of security of supply, diversity and sustainable development. How these sometimes conflicting objectives were to be achieved proved a much tougher matter, and yet another review of energy policy was announced in the summer of 2001, just after the general election. When it reported in February 2002, it added little to the political problem of trading off low prices against fuel poverty and environmental constraints. The subsequent White Paper, 'Our Energy Future—A Low Carbon Economy', published in February 2003, set ambitious long-term carbon targets, but added little concrete guidance as to how these might be achieved. Labour proved good at adding more and more objectives, but not at resolving the resultant tensions within its very broad political umbrella. Periodic shocks and crises, such as those affecting California, Enron and British Energy, brought these tensions out into the open.

In attempting this task, which was much more complicated than that of the Conservatives (to whom competition and privatization provided a clear ideological and practical steer), history provides some salutary lessons. As so often happens in the history of energy policy, politicians seek solutions to yesterday's problems. After the 1960s, cheap energy assumptions left government floundering when the OPEC shocks came along. In the 1970s, the government assumed that the oil price would go on rising and backed the 'Plan for Coal' and the development of more nuclear reactors. In the 1980s, the collapse of oil prices and the discovery of natural gas undermined the case for constructing nuclear power stations, and heralded the 'dash for gas' in the 1990s. The 1999 oil shock changed the position again.

These presumptions about the underlying fuel prices and supply conditions in world markets dogged not just the British government, but those throughout the industrial world too. They will almost certainly surprise them again. But looking forward, the key change in the background conditions in the coming decades looks like being driven by environmental considerations. With the increasing acceptance amongst scientists that global warming is taking place, and that the burning of fossil fuels for electricity production and in transport is a major cause, environmental concerns threaten to fundamentally change the nature of energy policy. It is apparent that the current energy (and transport) sectors are designed on very different assumptions: that fossil fuels are abundant and cheap; that market forces will ensure that supply meets demand; and that pragmatic, gradualist policy adjustments will deal with the environmental problems.

It is true that, between 1990 and 2000, the United Kingdom managed to reduce its emissions of carbon dioxide (CO_2) and thereby easily met its target of stabilization by 2000. (It is also true that the sulphur dioxide (SO_2) objectives have largely been met.) This, however, can be of little comfort to a government which in 1997 embraced a unilateral target of reducing its CO_2 emissions by 20 per cent from the 1990 levels by 2010, and which faces even bigger challenges in the first half of the twenty-first century having now committed itself to a 60% reduction by 2050 from the current levels. The reductions in the 1990s were largely due to the rapid contraction of the coal industry, the associated dash for gas, increases in the output from nuclear stations, and the economic recession of the early 1990s. It would be rash to assume that such benign scenarios are likely to be replicated in the next two decades. Ominously, after 2000 CO_2 emissions started to *rise*.

The new environmental objectives will not be achieved without a significant shift in policy. This is one of the themes of this book. However, the design of policy depends upon the context, and, as indicated above, the energy sector onto which such policies need to be grafted is very different from that which has dominated almost all of the post-war period. The competitive model—of open markets, physical and financial—will behave differently from the old one of monopoly, planning and 'picking winners', and hence environmental policies will need to be designed with the new model in mind. The traditional regulatory levers in the economic and environmental context will not produce the required results.

The structure of the book is rather different from conventional analyses of energy policy. It is neither an economics text, nor a history of the sector. Rather it tries to blend the two together. Whereas, in other industries, the future can be very disjointed from the past, that is not so in the energy sector. Many of the assets in place now were built a long time ago, and new assets may last for decades to come. Many of Britain's coal-fired power stations operating in the 1990s and into the twenty-first century were constructed in the 1960s; the gas network was built in the 1970s and 1980s, and will remain beyond the middle of the next century; and the Sizewell B nuclear reactor will probably still be generating in 2030. The waste from nuclear generation will be with us for centuries. In an important sense, the energy sector is a prisoner of its past. Policy, too, evolves from its history.

But history is not enough to guide us in designing future energy policy. The ways in which markets function—a central theme of modern economics— are well researched, and the industrial economics literature has much to offer by way of insights into the emerging model of the sector. Economics, too, has much to say about the control of pollution—how to measure costs and benefits, and how to design regulation, taxes, and subsidies.

Energy policy needs to blend its historical legacy with the potential of markets and market forces to deliver what governments cannot—or will not—do. To this blend must be added a third component: the political and institutional structures. Throughout the twentieth century, energy has been 'political', in the sense that the issues it raises have a collective resonance. Its oligopolistic and monopoly structures necessitate regulation; its public-good networks require a national coordination and an element of strategic planning. And, because it constitutes such a significant component of the budget of companies and households, governments are inevitably interested in its efficiency and costs, and in the distributional burdens these impose across social groups.

Finally, though often forgotten in times of excess supply such as the 1980s and 1990s, energy is a complementary good to the rest of the economy. The twentieth century was built on the conversion of fossil fuels into the primary means of production, and any failures in its supply bring widespread disruption. The Yom Kippur War, the miners' strikes of 1972, 1974, and 1984, and the more recent petrol delivery interruptions in 2000 are reminders of our vulnerability. Internationally, the Gulf War in 1990, the Russian invasion of Chechnya in 1994, the events of 11 September 2001 and its aftermath, and the Iraqi War in 2003 are reminders of global dependency. Power cuts and the energy crisis in California in 2001 and across the US and Europe in 2003 have illustrated the costs of such failures. In the twenty-first century, North Sea gas and oil will gradually run out, making Britain more like its European neighbours, where politics has required a broad international set of contracts to underpin national economic performance—be it France's opting for nuclear, or Germany's détente with Russia (and Ruhrgas's linkages with Gazprom). As long as fossil fuels are the engine of the economy, security of supply will remain an important concern of government. It never has been, and never will be, solely a matter for competitive markets.

It would be trite to observe that there are no easy and simple answers to the design of energy policy, if it were not for the fact that so many have claimed that there are. Those who argued that nationalization would solve the problem, because private and social interests would no longer be in conflict, have been thoroughly and convincingly confuted by the evidence of labour monopoly and inefficiency. So, too, have the ideological privat-izers, who thought that private ownership and competition were suffi-cient, rather than at best necessary conditions. Environmentalists who have seen energy efficiency and renewables (but not, of course, nuclear) as panaceas have had no convincing explanation to offer as to how people's aspirations for economic growth can be reconciled with the implied costs of their solutions. Protests over petrol prices in autumn 2000 provided a salutary reminder.

But the complexity of the problems does not mean that there are no answers. Some energy policy measures are obviously better than others. Some have, by and large, 'worked'; others have comprehensively 'failed'. A distinguishing feature has been the ability to adapt to circumstances— to go with the flow of technology and market developments, and so respond to new political and practical concerns. None of the policies of the past is ideally suited to a future in which information technology has transformed the workings of markets, in which new technologies for extracting and delivering energy are emerging, and in which environ-mental constraints are biting harder. We can learn from the past, but we must not be blinkered by it. The past provides constraints, and it provides numerous examples of mistakes and errors which, with hindsight, we can see. In the future, more mistakes will be made, but we should at least avoid repeating past ones.

The period since 1979 has been a distinct one for many reasons. Its politics were a clear break from those of the post-war consensus between the parties, called 'Butskellism' after the names of the two figures most associated with it: Butler and Gaitskell.[1] Its economics were different too—the OPEC years gave way to gradually lower inflation and much lower oil prices. The 1980s was the first full decade of large-scale North Sea oil and gas production. The year 1979 was therefore—with hindsight—a big enough discontinuity in this history of the energy sector.

But our period can no more escape its past than any other, and, hence, Chapter 2 begins with a summary of the legacy left by nationalization and the OPEC years. The immediate enthusiasm for public ownership gave way to a struggle to find ways of regulating these great monopolies within the public sector. The nuclear programme, the gradual development of financing and pricing rules, and the response to OPEC are part of its history.

Our period gets properly under way in Chapter 3, with the first steps towards the market philosophy. It was a period of caution and gradualism in practice, but also one in which the principles of energy policy were rewritten, notably after Nigel Lawson moved to the Department of Energy. His restatement of energy policy in his speech on 'The Market for Energy' in 1982 can be seen, in retrospect, as a defining moment. A new philosophy was set out, motivating much of what followed. His rejection of planning and many of the activities then going on within the Department of Energy was revolutionary at the time, and it haunts much of what follows.

Only after the 1983 Conservative election victory, facilitated by the Falklands War, did the central battle of the Thatcher years take place—the miners' strike and her trial of strength with Arthur Scargill. Avoiding Heath's fate of being defeated by the miners (and breaking up the monopolies which supported the National Union of Mineworkers, NUM) was her prime objective, as Chapter 4 explains. Only in this context can the inconsistency between upholding competition over monopoly *and* proposing a big expansion of nuclear power be understood (the subject of Chapter 5). That these were incompatible within a market framework—which is what Lawson had in mind—was not to become apparent until electricity privatization after the 1987 election victory.

Before that came the privatization of British Gas in 1986, as an integrated monopoly (the subject of Chapter 6). History has not been kind to this privatization—its structures have not survived, nor was its regulation smooth. At the time, there were two big constraints: first, that the key players, Peter Walker and Denis Rooke (respectively, Secretary of State for Energy and Chairman of British Gas), opposed any break-up; and, second, that no

---

[1] Notwithstanding Edward Heath's brief flirtation in 1970 with what we would now call Thatcherism.

privatization on this scale had ever been tried out on financial markets.

Chapter 7 addresses the most daring and complex privatization of all—electricity. There has been much myth-making about what actually happened at the time, about the 'failures' to introduce sufficient competition, the 'rigged' contracts, and the 'shortcomings' of the Electricity Pool of England and Wales.[2] Many mistakes were undoubtedly made, as the chapter spells out, but the radical nature of the proposals—both politically and economically—should not be forgotten. It took the United States, France, and Germany another ten years to even begin to catch up, by which time the fundamentals of supply and demand in world energy markets were rather different.

Chapter 8 looks at the transition to competition in the electricity market, the controversies over the Pool and market abuse, and new entry into electricity generation. Ensuring security of supply and making sure that more decentralized markets 'worked', in the sense that the lights stayed on and gas flowed through the pipes, were major tasks successfully fulfilled in the 1990s within the new framework, against many dire warnings to the contrary. There were no Californian-style blackouts, and no obvious lack of investments in the North Sea or in new power stations. Indeed, on the contrary, there was a 'dash for gas'.

Chapters 9 and 10 deal respectively with the privatizations of the coal and much of the nuclear industry. Chapter 9 analyses the coal crisis that confronted Michael Heseltine in 1992 after the general election and did much to dent his political reputation, and examines the aftermath of break-up and sale. Chapter 10 looks at the 1994 nuclear review and the subsequent sale of some of the nuclear reactors, leaving only the Magnox stations with British Nuclear Fuels (BNFL) (which also took much of the nuclear contractual risk for the new British Energy, as well as having responsibility for the THORP reprocessing plant and the Sellafield site).

Throughout much of the 1990s, regulation was of major political and media interest. The newly privatized companies were seen to be making lots of money, creating 'fat cats' as the visible face of what some might consider Thatcherite economic greed. Chapter 11 looks at the regulation of the regional electricity companies (RECs), and the conduct of the Office of Electricity Regulation (Offer). The repeated interventions—the two attempts at the 1994/95 periodic review, as well as the subsequent payouts from the flotation of the National Grid Company (NGC), and then the

---

[2] Henceforth referred to as the Pool.

windfall tax—represented not only 'regulatory failures', but also served to undermine the credibility of the price-cap RPI − X regime.

Chapters 11 and 12 look at how the corporate market responded to the new private-sector freedom: to restructure, diversify, and merge. The takeover mania after the 1994/95 periodic reviews of the RECs, the multi-utility models, and vertical integration created a new industrial structure, reflecting the search both for more efficient business forms to respond to changes in underlying costs, and for market power. Chapter 12 focuses on the RECs and electricity generators, and Chapter 13 considers how the combination of the collapse of gas prices and regulatory pressures led to the dismemberment of British Gas.

Chapter 14 provides an overview of the introduction of full retail competition into electricity and gas, finally breaking the traditional link between investors in longer-term fixed and sunk costs and customers. The process itself proved (not surprisingly) a fraught one, but its longer-term consequences, as investors wrestled with the speculative nature of new power plants and take-or-pay contracts, were largely ignored.

Chapters 15 and 16 focus on the many areas of policy debate and reform in the run-up to, and after, the 1997 Labour election victory: Chapter 15 looks at regulation and regulatory reform; Chapter 16 critiques Mandelson's 1998 White Paper, which tried to both promote competition and support coal. It was a triumph of 'spin' over substance, and the ban on gas entry inevitably failed. Labour struggled to come to terms with the Conservative legacy, embracing competition within its 'modernizing', 'new' agenda, but without appreciating how radically different markets could be. It wanted a predictable and fair regulatory regime which lowered the cost of capital, but also one which promised the delivery of social and environmental objectives. It wanted a competitive generation market, but also one which protected the coal industry. Not surprisingly, neither its regulatory reform agenda, nor Mandelson's White Paper provided much by way of answers. In both cases, the gap between aspiration and reality turned out to be rather large.

Whilst Labour in power attempted to grasp the bigger energy policy issues, the regulators, who now determined much of the practical policy, continued to consolidate the Conservative model. The new electricity trading arrangements (NETA) and their gas counterpart were designed and introduced without much understanding by the politicians and civil servants as to their radical effects. Price caps were reset, pushing down prices and further sweating the network assets. Chapters 17 and 18 detail these developments and their consequences for energy policy more generally. In many respects, they represent a last gasp of what had been so revolutionizing in the 1980s and what had now become the conventional wisdom. Competition, competitive spot markets, unbundling and downward pressure on prices had become the new panaceas of energy policy. But, as the nationalized monopoly structures of the 1970s had failed the test of the falling fossil-fuel prices and abundant supplies of the 1980s and 1990s, by the turn of the century the agenda had shifted again. New environmental constraints implied higher prices and a scarcity of non-carbon supplies, just when the Office of Gas and Electricity Markets (Ofgem) and the Department of Trade and Industry (DTI) were bent on ever-lower prices, and the abundant domestic sources of North Sea gas were giving way to a future reliance on imported gas from Norway and Russia, where long-term, take-or-pay contracts, not spot energy trading, would be the key vehicle for supply. As the North Sea supplies begin to run out, Britain is joining its European neighbours with their traditional concerns of reliance on external supplies, and the creation of European, rather than national, energy policy. Chapters 19 and 20 address these two new forces in energy policy.

By 2001, the Labour government had realized that there were serious risks with its complacent acceptance of the Conservative legacy. The report in 2000 by the Royal Commission on Environmental Pollution (RCEP) suggested that a 60 per cent reduction in CO_2 emissions might be required by 2050, and that could not be squared with low prices, supported by coal- and gas-fired generation. The prospect of nuclear was once again raised. The switch to imported gas posed a challenge too, especially when Germany and France could contract long-term on the basis of substantial *de facto* domestic market power, whilst Britain's fragmented industry had no such security for contracting. The Cabinet Office's Performance and Innovation Unit's report published in February 2002 recognized some of the problems, but provided few answers. Chapter 21 reviews its findings and critiques the report.

A year later, the government produced a White Paper, 'Our Energy Future—A Low Carbon Economy' (DTI, 2003a) which adopted the RCEP's target, and proposed to deliver this through renewables and energy efficiency *aspirational* targets for 2020. The nuclear option was to be kept open, but only just, and the government accepted the inevitability of joining the European emissions trading scheme, making a virtue of its market-based approach. Although security of supply was gradually moving up the political agenda, the White Paper added little by way of concrete substance here, and indeed the commitment to wind energy, combined with the phasing-out of nuclear and the lack of any countervailing strategy to ever greater dependence on imported gas, will have exacerbated the problems. Chapter 22 dissects the White Paper.

Finally, Chapter 23 concludes by drawing together the themes of the book, and suggests a policy framework to address the multiple market failures—of monopoly, of externalities, and of public goods. Neither the state nor the market alone can deliver a secure and sustainable energy supply. Both are needed, which requires an intelligent role for the state in the design of infrastructures, institutions, and regulation. Competition is a means, not an end, and competitive markets require rules, regulation and institutional structures. These need to be robust enough to adjust to tomorrow's agenda, rather than struggling to reconcile the market to yesterday's one.

The starting point for reinventing energy policy is to be clear about the objectives. Energy policy has a necessary political element, both because economic efficiency is not the sole criterion and because many decisions about the weights to be attached to different market failures are inevitably collective. The interests of the fuel poor need to be weighed against those of richer customers, and the importance of the environment inherited by future generations needs to be traded against the immediate interests of today's consumers. Markets cannot decide such things: governments have to do this.

The role of the state extends to that of risk bearing too. It is not just that societies cannot function if energy supplies fail, and that energy is too important to be left purely to market forces, but that many of the sorts of investments required have a political context. The risks in nuclear plants are an obvious example, but gas pipelines, renewables technologies, and even coal mines function in a regulated context, relying on governments to provide rules and stability for investors. Tearing up long-term contracts, stranding assets and changing the rules on climate change objectives are examples of the sorts of exposure investors can face in the energy sector.

Regulation, then, is not an afterthought to energy policy, as the architects of the privatizations thought, but an inherent part of the framework provided by the state within which the market functions. Rules need to be defined not only to limit abuse, but also to provide protection to investors. Regulation is not something that can 'wither away' or be completely 'independent' of politics and political control. It is the crucial instrument for the functioning of energy markets. Long-term contracts—very much the substance of energy security of supply and the stability of markets—require just such a political context.

But because regulation is the means of translating the objectives into outcomes through the market process, it does not follow that it needs to be all-pervasive. It depends how regulation is done. In the state-owned monopolies, the Department of Energy and its predecessors *planned* the conduct of the industries. Regulation by the civil servants involved pick-ing winners, and arguably that was a prime reason for its failure. But such detailed planning is not an inevitable part of energy policy: the reliance on market-based instruments can provide a mechanism for correcting the market failures without having to make choices about technologies. A carbon tax or a properly designed emissions trading scheme would allow the demand and supply sides of the market to adjust and bring forth new technological options. The requirement to over-provide to insure against the consequences of supply failure to the economy as a whole can be reflected in a premium for such services. The intelligent use of market instruments thereby helps to bring the various market failures together with some consistency.

But market-based instruments are not always the best route, and some-times more direct regulation is needed. The energy industries have system properties which require a view to be taken of the whole, as well as setting the incentives for the parts. Investment in wind farms in the Outer Hebrides or offshore influences the design of the grid as a whole, and new gas-fired power stations have an impact on the gas transmission system as a whole.

This necessitates an element of sectoral coordination which can be done in a variety of ways. At present, it is done by the NGC and Transco (and now merged into National Gas Transco), but with Ofgem and DTI over-sight. Privatization did not abolish this coordination function, it merely transferred its location. And, whereas in the 1980s and 1990s not much infrastructure investment was strictly needed, in periods of substantive change—such as dictated by the new environmental and gas import agen-das—what is needed is a coherent vision of the network as a whole. This is not planning in the sense of picking winners, but it does require some form of integrated design. It is a function that cannot be performed by markets—unless by collusion—and it is not well done by the so-called independent regulators. The networks are long-term sunk investments, capable of being stranded and reliant upon the framework of government policy. Only government can provide the stability.

The institutions and the way such intervention is carried out matter greatly. Pure market solutions do not work, but neither does the record of direct ministerial control have much to recommend it. The network and regulatory functions need to be carried out *between* the state and the mar-ket. The economic regulators were the creation of those who believed in keeping politics out of the energy sector and whose faith in markets was often almost unbounded. A new balance is needed, taking some functions out of ministers' hands towards a more specialist energy agency, and creating an element of consistency between the treatment of the different kinds of market failure, rather than the overwhelmingly dominant focus on monopoly which pervaded Offer and Ofgas, and now pervades Ofgem. Though they served their purpose, such bodies are now a hindrance to the reinvention of energy policy.

Energy policy is then a continuous process of ensuring that there is a framework of contracts and networks capable of meeting objectives which often conflict, but the trade-offs between which need to be defined. That process has an inevitable—and permanent—regulatory context, and because it extends well beyond the problem of monopoly, it needs to be set in an appropriate institutional context. That the nationalized system failed to satisfy these requirements led the Conservatives in the 1980s and 1990s to the belief that if only private ownership and competition were introduced, markets would solve the problems without the need for much intervention. Markets would commoditize energy, would create sufficient diversity and security of supply, and energy could become like any other commodity market. Labour, in 1997, embraced this message. However, as the problems have mounted, so it has gradually been recognized that energy policy is altogether more complicated to design and implement, and that energy markets, though typically the best way of allocating resources, can only function well when set in a framework of policy. The British experiment in the 1980s and 1990s changed the landscape of the sector, but it did not solve the fundamental problems of energy policy, nor indeed did it abolish them.

2

The Inheritance—State Ownership, Monopoly, and Planning

Monopoly, in all its forms, is the taxation of the industrious for the support of indolence, if not plunder. (John Stuart Mill, *Principles of Political Economy*, 1909)

There should be no insuperable difficulty in arranging that current estimates of relative long-run costs are adequately reflected in prices... There is also the major task of ensuring that, in their *interpretation* of these figures, and in their actions based upon them, decision-makers come together in a forum. What better forum than the committee room of the bank that provides their finance—provided that the bank is well-informed, and has its own secretariat, with knowledge, skills and experience? Despite many recent complaints, I remain of the view that the Whitehall machine, with vigorous and consistent political leadership, is capable of providing that service. (Michael Posner, *Fuel Policy*, 1973, p. 347)

For most of the post-war period, the energy sector was run by the state through integrated monopolies. The nationalized coal industry dug coal primarily for the nationalized electricity industry, which built enough power stations to secure supply. Customers, with nowhere else to go, paid the costs. When North Sea oil and gas were discovered, the Gas Council (and the British Gas Corporation, BGC, as it became) built the National Transmission System (NTS), converted households to natural gas and signed long-term contracts for gas to flow through its planned network. The British National Oil Company (BNOC) completed the picture, set up in 1976 to give the state a direct hand in the North Sea, complementing the oil interests of British Gas.

To most Labour and Conservative politicians, at least until 1979, this industrial structure seemed 'normal'. Energy was part of the planned economy, and the task of government was to improve its performance within that overall structure. Energy *policy* was designed to map out the demands and supplies, and to ensure that they were balanced, so that the post-war economic boom could be facilitated. The idea that all this could have been left to market forces was simply beyond the pale, in the sense that it did not enter into the framework of public policy debate.

Planning meant much more than setting prices and outputs. It had a part to play in macroeconomic management.[1] The energy sector also had an important social role to play. It was 'special', in the sense that access to affordable heating and lighting was necessary to sustain a minimum standard of living, and to participate in society. The sector therefore had a distributional role, and the building out of networks without charging the full costs to outlying areas and poorer customers was part of the policy framework: energy policy was social as well as economic.

It was this planned approach to energy policy that created the assets inherited in the 1980s and 1990s. Most of the nuclear and coal power stations were built within this framework, as well as the electricity grid and the gas transmission and distribution networks. The only significant assets added as a result of investment decisions since 1979 have been the combined-cycle gas turbines (CCGTs), the Sizewell B nuclear power station, and some upgrading and addition of electricity and gas interconnectors with the Continent and within the United Kingdom.[2] Everything else was essentially a legacy asset. The period since 1979 has, in consequence, been one focused on sweating inherited assets, not creating them.

To do justice to all the twists and turns of energy policy in the period 1945–79 is well beyond the remit of this book;[3] nor is it necessary for the development of the main arguments. In picking and choosing between the mass of day-to-day detail, there are several themes which survive the passage of time, and which serve to illustrate the wider issues.

The first of these is ownership, and more particularly, the *obsession* with ownership. What did Labour politicians think nationalization would achieve? Why should the Labour Party's Clause 4 on public ownership be so pertinent to the energy sector? Since Margaret Thatcher was much later to share this obsession—albeit drawing the opposite conclusion—it is worth reminding ourselves of the rationale for nationalization. For Labour after the war, nationalization had associated with it a view about how the great state enterprises should be managed—how the social good was to be integrated into the fabric of the boardroom. Regulation was largely from the inside. The *regulation of nationalized industries*, and its failures is the second theme.

---

[1] The 1944 White Paper on Employment Policy (HMSO 1944) suggests that varying local authority and public utility investment should be one of the methods of supplementing monetary policy (see Skidelsky 2000: 282).

[2] The electricity interconnector with France, initially carrying 160 MW, went on line in 1961, but the substantial upgrade to 1,988 MW took effect in 1986.

[3] See Hannah (1982) on electricity and Ashworth (1986) on coal.

The third theme is the *integration of structures*: the creation of single companies to span industries and to be locked together through the planning process. This integration is closely bound up with monopoly, and, in particular, *statutory* monopoly. Competition was not just inferior: it could be positively harmful, and hence, had to be made *illegal*. The monopoly structure facilitated two further dimensions of policy: long-term contracts, and cross-subsidies for distributional and industrial policy reasons. It also facilitated union power and, with it, over-production and low productivity.

The cult of the engineer is the fourth theme: how the nationalized industries concentrated on ever bigger and more technical investments, manifest, most noticeably, in the development of the nuclear industry. Free from the constraints of competitive markets, engineers could plan a nuclear future that would create energy 'too cheap to measure'. Although the nuclear enthusiasm was driven as much by politicians as it was by managers, the nationalized industries provided a framework which privatization did not, as Labour would discover when it began to think about building more nuclear stations in 2002 and 2003. Whereas engineers ran the nationalized industries, their role was greatly reduced in the 1980s and 1990s.

The engineers' priorities—propped up by state ownership and monopoly—proved insufficient to guarantee a satisfactory financial outcome, and this led successive governments to grapple with the economic principles which ought to underpin prices, outputs, and investments. Efforts to 'solve' these problems began in the early 1960s, with the attempt to regulate within the public sector. The owner proved incapable of credibly committing to binding constraints. This is the fifth theme: *the financial costs and the failure of the Treasury's attempts to control them*.

But if financial control was poorly exercised within the public sector, at least it might be claimed that the framework of energy policy ensured that the lights stayed on. Sadly, as the OPEC experience and the miners' industrial action in the 1970s showed, quite the contrary was the case. Our sixth theme is that, far from protecting the nation from supply interruptions, *the combination of state ownership and monopoly provided the very conditions to endanger security of supply*, by providing a basis for the growth and sustaining of union power, notably in the form of the National Union of Mineworkers (NUM). Apart from the crisis of 1947, and some local distribution problems, only the miners dimmed the lights in post-war Britain.

The final theme is a more positive one: *the role of energy policy in developing North Sea oil and gas*. Here, in the investment stage of new industries (natural gas and oil exploration and development), state guarantees of contracts helped underpin major investments in new technology at the margins of profitability. North Sea oil could only pass the economic test as a result of OPEC holding up the price above Middle Eastern costs. That the industry developed so rapidly is, in part, the result of the state's involvement.

The consequences of state ownership are thus numerous and complex. There is no simple answer to the question: 'Did it work?' Indeed, the question itself is naive. What, however, is not in doubt is that it bequeathed the assets which formed the basis for the privatization and competition policy in the 1980s and 1990s. This legacy was real.

The Obsession with Ownership

With the exception of France, few countries have been quite so obsessed as Britain has with the idea that the ownership of industries is crucial to their performance. Mixed ownership has pervaded much of Europe, with a complex web of municipal, regional, and state holdings (Helm and McGowan 1989). It is an issue that has its roots in ideology. On the Right is the concept of the sanctity of property as a bulwark against revolution (the Conservative tradition honed by the reaction to the French revolution), and as the foundation of liberalism and the free-market economy. On the Left, socialism has defined itself in terms of equality, and hence, redistribution, as well as the instrumental theory that public ownership is more efficient as a vehicle for the achievement of the public rather than the private good.

By the 1930s, all of these positions had become part of the fabric of political debate, as they had across Europe. But, unlike most of Europe, they remained the central ones in British political debate into the 1980s. It was natural that the energy sector—as such a dominant part of the economy—would prove a test bed for these conflicts of principle. To the Labour government after the war, and to Thatcher's second and third governments, these were defining themes. To the former, nationalization would bring about a transformation in the energy sector; to the latter, privatization was the answer.

The result of this obsession with ownership is that, in the period 1945–51, most of the energy sector was nationalized, and then, since the late 1970s, most of it has been privatized, with the exception of British Nuclear Fuels (BNFL) and the Magnox nuclear power stations. The election of the Labour government in 1997 made little difference, in that the new status quo has not been significantly changed. Like the Conservatives in the 1950s, Labour in the 1990s and 2000s has settled for trying to regulate what it has inherited, rather than returning to the ideological battleground. There might be 'wobbles' with the railways, the Post Office, British Energy and BNFL, but, by the end of the 1990s, there was a wide consensus that private was generally better than public (Table 2.1).

Labour's nationalization policy brought together the two wings of the party. On the one hand, the Marxist tradition on the Left regarded public ownership as a distributional matter. The means of production should be owned by those who produced. These were the working classes. Their surplus—the difference between the cost of labour and the price of output—should be distributed to them, and not to the parasitic capitalists. Those on the Marxist Left differed only on the questions of timing and the extent to which intervention should precede what was regarded as the inevitable

TABLE 2.1 Ownership changes

	Pre-war ownership	Nationalized	Privatized[a]
Coal	Private	National Coal Board (1947)	RJB Mining and others (1995)
Electricity	Central Electricity Board, municipalities, and private companies	Central Electricity Authority (1948) and then the Central Electricity Generating Board, Area Boards, and the Electricity Council (1957)	National Power, PowerGen (1990) National Grid Company (1990) Regional electricity companies (1990) Scottish Power and Scottish Hydro-Electric (1991)
Gas	Municipalities and private gas undertakings	Area Boards and the Gas Council (1948), and then British Gas Corporation (1972)	British Gas (Gas Act 1986)
Oil	Anglo-Iranian Oil Company	BP (partial), British National Oil Company (1977)	BP final sale (1987) Britoil (1982) Enterprise Oil (1984)
Nuclear	None	United Kingdom Atomic Energy Authority (1954), British Nuclear Fuels (1971), Nuclear Electric (1990), Scottish Nuclear (1990)	British Energy (1996)

[a] Dates refer to Vesting of assets, except BP.

crisis and collapse of capitalism. The economic woes of the 1930s had, to many, been just such a collapse of capitalism, and the Second World War completed the transition from nineteenth century laissez faire towards collectivism. And, like Lenin in Russia, the prospect of waiting for the inevitable course of history to exhaust itself and give rise to the dawn of communist nirvana was not one which appealed to men of action, especially if they had just won an historic electoral victory.

On the other hand—and the dominant one—the old Left-Liberal tradition in the Labour Party, which had gradually transferred from the Asquith wing of the Liberal Party (spurred on by rejection of Lloyd George's interwar policies), was concerned not just with the distributional questions but also with efficiency. Many in this tradition believed that the 1930s had demonstrated—both politically and through the development of economic theory—that public enterprise could be more efficient than private. From the rationale of the Beveridge welfare state, through to the case for statutory monopoly, the economic theories of Lange, Lerner, and Keynes provided a pragmatic underpinning to an enlarged collective state. To the belief that the battle of ideas had been lost by Hayek and other free-market thinkers was added the evidence of the war effort and its success in mobilizing the workforce, so much of which had been idle in the 1930s.

The nationalization programme was implemented remarkably quickly and in very difficult general economic circumstances. Whereas the Thatcher governments took a decade to privatize the electricity industry (and it was to take another five years to privatize parts of the nuclear and coal industries), Attlee's government nationalized coal, electricity, and gas within a five-year Parliament. The practicalities which faced Labour in 1945 were, however, rather different from those Thatcher faced. Much of the sector had been under effective state control throughout the war, and some of it (such as the Central Electricity Board, CEB) was already in state hands. Much of the rest of the electricity industry was controlled by local authorities. Furthermore, nationalization involved the state legislating and then buying out private interests, whereas privatization required ministers not only to legislate, but also to write prospectuses which boards would sign, and to persuade private investors to part with their money. Nationalization was compulsory; privatization required the voluntary cooperation of managers and potential shareholders.

The economic backdrop for Labour did not, however, make nationalization easy. It is often said nowadays that governments could not afford to renationalize. John Prescott, for example, told Labour's conference in 1997 that Railtrack could not be brought back into public ownership for the serious reason that Labour had other, more pressing, calls on its resources (and for the more bizarre reason that it would make 'the fat cats fatter'). But the comparison between 1997 and 1945 could not be starker. Labour's strong economic inheritance in 1997 was markedly different from a government which faced international bankruptcy at the end of the war.

As Cairncross has demonstrated,[4] the winter of 1947 was not only extremely cold, but the country got within spitting distance of running out of coal and foreign reserves, and faced the prospects of power cuts on a large scale. Some of the problem with coal stocks was undoubtedly due to Manny Shinwell's weakness as Minister for Fuel and Power. As Ashworth (1986) concluded in his history of this period of the coal industry, Shinwell 'showed little capacity for the coherent treatment of the industry as a whole' (p. 28), and responded far too slowly to the labour recruitment problems already obvious in 1946. The broad underlying economics were, by any measure, extremely demanding, and in these circumstances it is remarkable that it did not seriously occur to ministers that nationalization could not be afforded—as, for example, it did over the creation of the National Health Service. The fact that the operating surpluses of the industries could finance the interest on government bonds might have facilitated this, had Treasury capital been freely available. But having to finance nationalization inevitably limited other calls on public investment.

The nationalization Acts were essentially facilitation instruments. They provided for the government to purchase assets from private owners and expropriate those owned by local government. Parliamentary debate over coal was a limited affair; there were few who wanted to defend the record of the private mine owners, and, among Conservatives, the middle way advocated by Macmillan in the 1930s found a strong resonance with Churchill (who had crossed the House), Eden and Butler. Conservatives wanted to distance themselves from the General Strike in 1926 and the bitterness in the mines in its aftermath.

Electricity nationalization was more complex. Here, the case for nationalization went beyond that of mere ownership change for its own sake, and required a substantial element of rationalization. (The words 'nationalize' and 'rationalize' have a similar ring about them, catching the view that the Left's approach was more rational and, in the terms of the 1940s, more modern.) A host of local undertakings was therefore combined on a regional basis, but with economic control exercised from the top down

---

[4] See Cairncross (1985), Chapter 6 on the convertibility crisis and Chapter 13 on the coal crisis.

through the Central Electricity Authority (and subsequently the Electricity Council and the Central Electricity Generating Board (CEGB) in 1957), rather than driven by local distribution interests.

With these two industries under state ownership, that left only gas—which was town gas then—and oil. The Gas Act 1948 nationalized the 1,046 gas companies and undertakings, and rationalized the structure into twelve Area Boards and an overarching Gas Council, which had advisory functions to government, as well as assisting the Area Boards with borrowing and research and development. It was to be further rationalized into a single BGC with the Gas Act 1972. The government's oil interests were more diffuse, and necessarily international. BP had, in its very early days, played a special role as national champion when the state took a 50 per cent stake in 1913 in its precursor, the Anglo Persian Oil Company, under Churchill's encouragement to provide fuel for the navy. But for much of the post-war period it acted largely as if it were a private and international oil company.

Managing Nationalized Industries: 'Good Chaps' in Charge

Nationalization was, for many in the Labour Party, an end in itself. It was the fulfilment of the purposes for which Labour had been founded: to control the means of production through common ownership. The Coal and Electricity Acts in the 1940s applied Clause 4 of its constitution to arguably the two most important industries in Britain. More than one million people became state employees. But it soon transpired that ownership would not automatically produce the end that some had assumed, but was merely an imperfect means. It is what is done as a result of the control that ownership confers which matters. Having assumed nationalization to be sufficient, Labour found itself with very little idea of how to manage its new empire. It needed to devise a set of incentives, rules and supporting institutions that could render nationalization a vehicle for economic success.

What Labour had in the 1940s was a very simplistic—and, it transpired, naive—solution to these challenges. Nationalization had placed ownership, control and regulation within a single framework, and hence internalized them. The linchpin of the system was management under the control of ministers. In the original blueprint for the industries devised by Herbert Morrison, they would have boards comprising executive managers, who would run the businesses on day-to-day commercial lines, and non-executive directors, who would ensure that the company pursued the public interest. This was modelled on his experience of London's transport and electricity industries in the interwar years, and subsequently as

Minister of Transport (1929–31) in Ramsay MacDonald's government (see Donoughue and James 1973: chs 9 and 10). Morrison used this experience as the basis for his *Socialism and Transport* (1933). He wanted monopoly, but under democratic control. The public corporation had to reconcile economic efficiency with a wider socialist concern.

The owners of the industries would exercise control through their non-executive directors. These directors would pursue social rather than private returns, in an environment free from competitive pressures, and hence there would be no need to add an additional layer of regulation. By definition, the managers would pursue the public interest—that, after all, was the *point* of nationalization. The bitter industrial relations conflicts of the inter-war years would be replaced by a harmony of interests between governments, managers, and workers. The elimination of competition meant that investment could be planned on a long-term basis, for the good of the economy as a whole, so that a rational planning system would ensure that there was a sufficient supply of energy to match demand.

Although the nationalized industry structure did indeed manage to keep supply in line with demand through the golden years of British post-war economic growth, its failures were already becoming apparent during the 1950s, and, by the 1970s, serious cracks were beginning to appear. Not surprisingly, the way in which it was supposed to operate and the practical reality began to diverge rapidly after the war. The idea that managers, sitting around a boardroom table, would pursue the public interest turned out to be as optimistic as it was seductive. (Advocates of stakeholder boards for the privatized industries were to make similar mistakes in the late 1990s—see Chapter 15.) The non-executives were political appointees, with particular agendas of their own, while the lack of any detailed definition of the financial targets the industries were supposed to achieve meant that, in practice, surplus cash flow translated into investment and wages. As the 1950s progressed, the industries became increasingly producer-driven, providing customers with the services and prices that suited political and managerial interests.[5] For the politicians, the time horizon was especially short, while, for managers, technological priorities tended to dominate other objectives. And for the workers, the monopoly structure strengthened their hand as against the fragmented pre-war industries. A strike in a nationalized monopoly industry could be

---

[5] Not surprisingly, the managers themselves saw things differently, and many—Denis Rooke, Derek Ezra, and Walter Marshall in particular—were to become staunch defenders of the Morrisonian structures: 'Had the Morrisonian principle been properly applied I have no doubt that things would have turned out differently and that, in the case of the energy sector, there would have been a much more consistent and sustained strategy' (Ezra 1993: 392).

altogether more credible, a point which was to cost Edward Heath his premiership and which was not missed by Thatcher.

Once the nationalized industries are put into a positive analytical context, it is possible to sort out the consequences that might be expected to follow from the incentive structure in the public sector. Assuming that managers' salaries were largely independent of financial performance (which they were), that they would attempt to pursue their own interests, and that labour interests were important in the decision-making process, it was to be expected that the nationalized industries would tend to hold output above the competitive market level, and hence hold prices down, and that, at the margin, they would employ more labour at somewhat higher wages than their private-sector counterparts. It was also likely that managers would gain personal satisfaction from technological leadership, and that, in practice, the industries could be expected to be dominated by engineers rather than the more financial orientation of private-sector firms for which dividends were an objective rather than a constraint.[6]

To these managerial incentives must be added those of politicians. Their interests can be considered as more short term, focused on winning elections over a four- to five-year timespan. Thus, on pricing, politicians can be expected to avoid price increases, especially close to elections, and, with the luxury of monopoly, to use the price system to benefit particular political interest groups. Cross-subsidy to the benefit of rural customers and discounts to large industrial companies might be encouraged. It is also likely that the size and timing of pricing and investment decisions might be designed to take account of wider macroeconomic concerns, and that the location of investments would be influenced by constituency and lobby interests. Finally, in the search for votes, politicians have an addiction to being perceived as 'modern' and a desire to be associated with science and progress. In the energy sector, for much of the post-war period, the 'white heat of technology' meant nuclear power.

All these predictions arise from the economist's assumption of the pursuit of narrow self-interest, rather than the public good: in other words, the rejection of the assumption at the heart of Labour's approach—that is, that 'good chaps' (the non-executives) with the 'right outlook' (the public interest) would pursue the public good. What the precise incentives of the main actors were is a matter for biography. In general, the evidence broadly tends to support the theoretical predictions rather than the ideology, and the legacy of nationalization includes inappropriate price levels

---

[6] On price below marginal costs, see Posner (1972: 252–4). Rees (1989) develops a model along these lines.

and structures, as well as significant technical bias in the assets. The detailed evidence to support these claims is beyond the scope of this book, but it can be found in the various official studies,[7] notably Monopolies and Mergers Commission (MMC) investigations into the CEGB, Area Boards, National Coal Board (NCB), and aspects of the gas industry which were produced in the early 1980s, together with the 1976 study by the National Economic Development Office (NEDO). Academic studies, notably by Pryke (1981), Hannah (1982), and Foreman-Peck and Millward (1994), lend support too.[8]

Monopoly, Vertical Integration, and Planning

Morrison's 'good chaps' were protected from the day-to-day shocks of normal commercial life by *statutory* monopoly. Competition was made illegal. This enabled long-term planning and contracting so that the industries would not be vulnerable to the short-term opportunism of rivals, and, hence, had little risk of loss of market share. In addition, costs could be certain to be recovered from customers whose demand was inelastic. The 'cement' provided by these contractual arrangements, under the umbrella of common public ownership, made the energy sector even more concentrated.

With hindsight, the prohibition on competition seems, at best, misguided, and, at worst, an invitation to inefficiency. By 1997 even Labour was singing the virtues of competition, endorsing the liberalization of the domestic electricity market, and soon to be even giving encouragement to competition in the water industry. But, at the time, the backdrop was very different: namely the perceived destructive and short-term competition of the 1930s. Competition was perceived as anarchic, and the greed of capitalists widely considered to have contributed to the mass unemployment of the 1930s—a theme which was to be echoed in the 'fat cats' demonization of utility directors in the 1990s. Curiously, politicians were thought to be less short-termist and more benevolent than those in business.

There was a further, more energy-focused, reason for limiting competition. In the electricity sector, the growth of numerous local distribution networks created significant coordination problems (as had also occurred

---

[7] These are described in Chapter 3.

[8] Pryke's 1981 study was particularly influential, especially since he had changed his mind from his earlier study (Pryke 1971), which had been much more favourable to the nationalized industries. Lawson, in particular, drew on Pryke's work (Lawson 1992: 202).

with regional railways). Coordination required common standards for voltages and frequencies. Although, in principle, private companies could voluntarily cooperate, in practice each had important assets at stake, which could be stranded if other standards were adopted. Monopoly would assist in standardization. Standardization, in turn, allowed economies to be reaped. The post-war period saw the capacity of power stations increase, with access to the market through more integrated networks. The networks themselves were also moving to higher voltages. A monopoly could ensure that these two technical trends were interlinked. Indeed, the British and French electricity systems stood in a much superior position to the more fragmented system of Germany, where a process of gradual evolution was preferred. Without the spur of nationalization, progress proved much slower elsewhere.

The networks, in turn, raised an important economic issue about pricing. Network economics are complex, but there are two broad features relevant to this discussion. First, the difference between marginal and average cost is typically large; second, the customer benefits from the *system* characteristics, rather than from individual lines, and hence costs cannot easily be disaggregated. Under monopoly, pricing is a matter of policy choice, given that overall demand is inelastic. Under competition, where networks are in common ownership with generation and supply, the pricing system of the network may be an important deterrent to entry.

Monopoly also reduces risks to the investor, although not necessarily to the customer. This implies a lower cost of capital, as there is little risk in investing if the costs are bound to be recovered from captured customers. At the time, this cost of capital effect of monopoly was submerged within the more general question of the cost of government borrowing versus the private rate. With the low risk of Treasury gilts, it might follow that, *in general*, public ownership would be superior to private ownership, particularly for capital-intensive industries. Although this debate is clearly important (and one which would resurface in the 2000s with Network Rail and Welsh Water), the risk itself is not dissipated by public ownership. Within nationalized monopolies, there is a *choice* of tax bases to allocate the risk of failures: either the Treasury can subsidize more, or customers' bills can rise. If it is the latter then monopoly transfers risk from the investor (the government) to the customer.

Risk could also be reduced through vertical integration. Vertical integration allowed the electricity and coal industries to be linked together throughout the post-war period—indeed until at least 1998. The electricity industry would take coal output, and the NCB could then develop its assets on the basis of an assured customer, who would absorb the NCB's costs and then pass these through to electricity customers. Similarly, later on, British Gas was able to enter into long-term contracts for the North Sea on a take-or-pay basis, reducing the risk—and hence the cost of capital—for the offshore oil and gas companies as fields were developed (Fig. 2.1).

Vertical integration facilitated planning. The government (in practice, its civil servants) had taken on the role of the market in coordinating demand and supply. The ministry would prepare demand forecasts (it would *predict*) and then determine the investment path to satisfy demand (and hence *provide*). The planning process worked in two directions. Demand forecasting looked at industrial and retail customers, and was coordinated through the electricity industry—eventually through the Electricity Council. Supply worked backwards from coal (which was assumed to be elastic, in the sense that the miners would extract what was required), to generation capacity and transmission and distribution systems. A formal process was put in place, resulting in several 'Plans for Coal', joint undertakings, and so on. In theory, responsibility for the coordination of planning lay with the Ministry of Fuel and Power and then the Department of Energy, using its formal energy modelling capability, with input from other planning bodies, such as the Department of Economic Affairs (in the 1960s) and NEDO. In practice, the dominant role was taken by the Treasury, which rationed capital and therefore had the final say on the investment plans of the nationalized industries, but at least the Department of Energy could support its bids for public funds with detailed technical analysis—something many other competing departments could not.

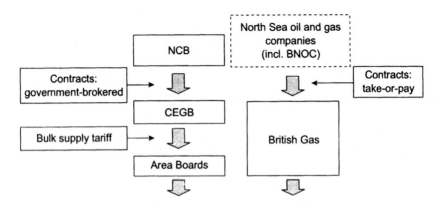

FIG. 2.1   Vertical integration between nationalized industries

The Technical Fix: Engineers, Planning, and Nuclear Power

All the ingredients—public ownership, monopoly, and vertical integration—were present for the age of rational planners to build a better energy sector. The overriding objective was, in practice, to maximize output to meet the demands of the post-war boom. Their job was to secure sufficient supplies to meet demand, and that meant a programme of building new power stations, and later building the natural gas network. It was a period of creating, rather than sweating, assets.

Demand for electricity rose during the 1950s and 1960s at a rate of around 7 per cent per year, and, in response, the electricity industry built new power stations to keep up with this growth. Investment was at the forefront of the industries' objectives, and it is hardly surprising that they were dominated by engineers.[9] There is an obvious relationship in the nationalized industries between the decisions taken and the characteristics of those who made them, free from the discipline of the stock market. In a normal competitive market, investment is dictated by the growth of demand, the conduct of rivals and the willingness of investors to provide finance. In electricity (and later in gas), there were no rivals and no stock-market constraints. Investment levels were what managers and government agreed. As long as customers and taxpayers would pick up the bills, the nationalized industries' managers favoured more investment over less, and larger units rather than smaller ones. The average size of coal-fired power stations rose from 330 MW in 1950 to 1,482 MW in 1974 by the time Drax was constructed. This increasing scale was backed by the argument that thermal efficiency was correlated to size. While there is much technical argument to justify this scale economy, it was a happy coincidence that it matched the incentives; and, if larger stations could use exciting new technology, so much the better, especially if this was nuclear.

Britain's love affair with nuclear technology had its origins in the Second World War, and the development of the nuclear deterrent. It was always military first, before civil considerations applied. Magnox would not have been possible had not nuclear power been developed by the military, and it would be pushed forward because uranium was thought to be in short supply and the military needed plutonium (Gowing 1974: vol. 2, ch. 19). It provided an example of the spin-off from defence spending, turning swords into ploughshares. (Concorde was to be another

---

[9] Hannah's classic industry study for the period is aptly entitled, *Engineers, Managers, and Politicians* (1982).

unhappy example.) Being military in origin, Magnox was also constrained by its design. The early nuclear reactors were relatively small-
scale, and developed ahead of most industrial countries. Chapel Cross
and Calder Hall had capacities of 196 and 192 MW, respectively.
Interestingly, both were still functioning at BNFL's sites at the turn of the
millennium.[10] The technology was given an additional spur by the Suez
Crisis in 1956, when the government of the day became concerned about
possible interruptions in supply from the Middle East. Some seventeen
years later, the OPEC shock would give nuclear a further boost across
Europe, giving rise to the massive French pressurized-water reactor
(PWR) programme, the German expansion, as well as that in Britain.[11]

Throughout most of its history, nuclear power has been regarded as
modern and technically advanced, as well as sinister and frightening. It was
beyond the powers of most politicians and civil servants to understand it,
and, as a result, advice from scientists and the electricity industry was often
unchecked. Its mathematics and physics might capture the brightest scientists, but ordinary politicians could neither grapple with the concepts nor see
the result. The technological dream, together with the awesome psycholo-
gical image of atomic explosions, captured politicians, and their advisers.
The 1955 White Paper 'A Programme of Nuclear Power' presented that
optimistic vision (Ministry of Fuel and Power 1955). 'Nuclear energy is the
energy of the future', it boldly proclaimed. It continued: 'Whatever the
immediate uncertainties, nuclear energy will in time be capable of producing power economically. Moreover, it provides a source of energy potentially
much greater than any that exist now. The coming of nuclear power therefore marks the beginning of a new era.' It was no less than 'our duty to establish this new industry', the final reward for which 'will be immeasurable'.

With hindsight, what is so striking about the 1955 White Paper is the
crudeness of the economic analysis and what it left out. In the three pages
devoted to 'The Probable Cost of Nuclear Power', the estimates are simplistic, and derived from a combination of actual costs for the Calder Hall
reactor and optimism on load factors. The assumptions were broadbrush,
with enormous ranges.[12] Risk analysis, if considered at all, appeared to be

---

[10] In June 2002, BNFL announced the closure of both (BNFL 2002).

[11] The 1999/2000 oil shock again excited interest in nuclear—see Chapter 21.

[12] The assumptions were: capital cost at or below £10–£20 million, output of 100–150 (or
even 200) MW, a load factor of 80%, and life of plant as 10–20 years; and a ballpark figure of
£5 million was given for the initial charge of fabricating uranium, recurring every three to
five years: 'On these assumptions a rough figure for the annual overhead cost for each unit
of output can be calculated. The works and operating costs, excluding fuel costs, can be
estimated from the experience of operating coal-fired power stations and military reactors
at Windscale.'

all on the upside: 'Developments in reactor design...should gradually lead to much higher heat ratings, without much increase in capital costs. This would reduce still further the capital cost per kilowatt and thus reduce the overheads.'

On the waste-fuel side, the plutonium by-product was seen as positively advantageous, for which a credit in the costs was added. The fast-breeder reactor (FBR) was already explicitly envisaged, and, with this in mind, 'the early reactors will be producing not only electricity but also the capital equipment (i.e. the initial charge of fissile material) for future power stations.' Though this credit could not be easily valued, the White Paper concluded that 'the effect on the net cost of electricity could be considerable.' Taking all these factors into account, the cost from the first Magnox stations was expected to be about the same as from new coal-fired stations.

The paper then proposed a ten-year programme to provide a capacity of 1,500–2,000 MW to satisfy 25 per cent of electricity needs at a total cost of £300 million (£4,593 million in 2002 prices). Beyond 1965 it was envisaged that the nuclear option would be cheaper than the coal one, as well as providing some insurance against the coal industry.

On safety and decommissioning, the White Paper has just three paragraphs, which, again with hindsight, give an impression of complacency. It states that the 'disposal of radioactive waste products should not present a major difficulty'. On decommissioning costs, the White Paper is silent.[13]

None of the core assumptions turned out to be correct and, as a consequence, there were many changes to the initial programme—first in 1957, following on from the Suez Crisis, to triple the programme, and then in 1960, to slow it down. By 1964, the White Paper on 'The Second Nuclear Power Programme' (Department of State and Official Bodies and Ministry of Power 1964) began the process of choosing the next technology: picking nuclear winners, and particularly those which would be 'made in Britain'. The advanced gas-cooled reactor (AGR) was the preferred model. The fact that the costs of the Magnox stations had turned out to be higher than expected was acknowledged, but still the 1964 paper remained optimistic,

---

[13] In the 1959 White Paper on 'The Control of Radioactive Waste' (Radioactive Substances Advisory Committee 1959), this complacency was enshrined in official policy. Industrial solid wastes, such as that from uranium works at Springfields, and other materials were to be 'dumped in a disused quarry at Whittle Hill, near Preston. When full, it will be covered with earth and trees planted' (para 44). With regard to other waste: 'We consider that there need be no public health hazard in disposing of the materials of the [Windscale] reactor which will constitute a solid radioactive waste' (para 63). The Windscale fire of 1957 had reduced confidence in leaving nuclear safety to the industry, and led to the Nuclear Installations Act 1959. This resulted in regulation of the new nuclear stations, although interestingly *not* Windscale or other UKAEA sites. This was done much later.

stating that: 'Detailed studies show that nuclear power is likely to have an economic place in the British electricity system by the early 1970s and suggest that, thereafter, it will become cheaper than conventional power for the generation of baseload' (para 8). As a result, a further 5000 MW was planned to be commissioned during 1970–75, which was revised upwards in 1965 to 8000 MW (Ministry of Fuel and Power 1965: paras 69–71).

Having opted in 1965 for the AGR, by 1974 the steam-generating heavy water reactor (SGHWR) was preferred for the third nuclear programme, only for that technology to be rejected by Tony Benn in 1978 in favour of a switch back to the AGR, this time as opposed to PWRs. After 1979, the new Conservative government amended this policy yet again in July 1981 (House of Commons Select Committee on Energy 1981*b*). While supporting the new AGR programme of 1978, it moved closer to the PWRs for the next programme (see Chapter 3).

The Financial Costs of Nationalization and the Treasury's Attempt to Impose Financial Discipline

There is a striking resemblance in experience after nationalization and that after privatization. Just as Labour found itself in 1997 having to sort out the consequences of privatization as it tried to create a more stable regulatory regime, so, too, did the Conservative governments after 1951 struggle to tame the nationalized industries inherited from Labour. With both nationalization and privatization, regulation proved an afterthought.[14]

The regulatory problem after nationalization was multifaceted. The ambitions of politicians extended well beyond narrow economic efficiency. Nationalization was as much about workers' rights in the land fit for heroes returning from the war. The bitter industrial relations battles of the 1930s in the mines were to be solved by internalizing them within the new industrial structures. If the workers' party was in power, and if it chose the bosses, how could the workers be exploited?

Nationalization had distributional ambitions too. The nationalized industries played a part in the overall welfare state. The Beveridge concept that a decent society provided for a minimum of basic social primary goods had a plurality of manifestations. Education and health were to be directly provided. Income supplements would take care of food, which was also rationed. The energy industries could play their part in providing

---

[14] In considering coal nationalization, Shinwell (quoted on p. 629 of Supple 1987) wrote that, as Minister of Fuel and Power, 'I found that nothing practical and tangible existed ... I had to start on a clear desk'. This was somewhat overstated.

heating and light (see Dilnot and Helm 1987). This distributional role had two practical consequences: cross-subsidies and comprehensive or universal service. By virtue of the statutory monopoly, charging for electricity became very much a tax-collecting activity, and Labour exploited this to ensure that tariffs included a notion of ability to pay. Cost-reflective transmission, distribution and supply tariffs were typically modified for distributional reasons. In the 1990s, the removal of monopoly and the introduction of retail competition directly challenged this distributional element, and not surprisingly (except perhaps to the Conservative architects of the policy) caused major political problems, right through to the Utilities Act 2000, with its associated social guidance.

A further consequence of the distributional objective was to place priority on the inclusiveness of energy (and especially electricity and later gas) supply. A cohesive society provided the basic social primary goods not only regardless of the ability to pay, but also regardless of location. To the extent that rural customers were too expensive to justify connection, they were to be paid for by the urban masses. Connecting up the Scottish Highlands, rural Wales and other upland areas was subsidized by revenues from central locations, and, perhaps more significantly, transmission and distribution charges tended to be averaged. Again, as with the welfare element, the consequences were pricing policies that could not easily survive the transition to a competitive market.

Until 1979, for both Labour and Conservatives, these distributional concerns were largely taken for granted, and they did not receive much public comment, except where they affected local constituency matters. Rather, public debate focused on economic performance, and particularly on output. As already noted, in the immediate post-war period, the challenge in the energy sector was to keep supply in line with demand. That meant recruiting enough miners to dig coal and pursuing the nuclear option. Provided that the industries managed to keep their demands on the Treasury within reasonable bounds (and, hence, tapped their monopoly customers to finance investment), the question of regulation hardly arose.

These assumptions were perhaps easily made against a background of the planned war economy. However, they were naive, as experience was soon to dictate. The primary focus for regulation was the Treasury, and its concerns with public finance, in which the nationalized industries had assumed a major role. This can be seen in two ways: the proportion of government activities which the nationalized industries as a whole comprised; and, with respect to the energy sector in particular, the deteriorating operating performance and rising demands for capital investment.

The causes of this deteriorating position were many and various. At the core was a deep confusion about objectives. Though the non-executives were supposed to pursue the public interest, nobody made it clear exactly what this meant. There had been numerous attempts to set objectives for the energy sector, but these invariably conflicted, and, in any event, presented only a partial picture of the full political agenda. It is in this context that the first serious attempt at regulation—the 1961 White Paper (HMT 1961)—should be seen. This was a *Treasury* paper, which was designed to provide a financial constraint. The rule proposed was break-even, over the medium term. The simplicity of the approach was reflected in the fact that the White Paper was only three pages long.

The practical impact was to act as a constraint on the setting of the bulk supply tariff (BST), which determined the price of electricity. Such a crude control offended traditional economic thought and the dictates of welfare economics. The pricing methodology handed down from the 1930s gave precedent to the idea that the correct approach was to set prices at long-run marginal cost (LRMC). In industries characterized by declining average costs (which would now be termed 'natural monopolies'), it was inevitable that the consequences of LRMC would be losses. These losses were 'efficient', but hardly palatable to a Treasury whose primary task related to controlling—and limiting—public expenditure.[15]

The high watermark of the economists' influence on nationalized industry pricing came in the 1967 White Paper on Nationalized Industries (HMT 1967) (and its associated White Paper on Fuel Policy, HMSO 1967), which explicitly endorsed efficient pricing, and proposed that investment should be evaluated on a project-by-project basis, subject to a test discount rate, though its economic purity was rather spoilt by its over-determination (the pricing and investment rules turned out to be incompatible). But it was only a paper victory because the devaluation crisis of the same year led to a Treasury squeeze in the name of macroeconomic imperatives. Roy Jenkins' post-devaluation policies aimed at reducing public demand to address the deficit on the current account of the balance of payments—an objective which was eventually

---

[15] At this stage, the distinction between the *network* natural monopoly and the generation and supply activities was rarely made, the industry being regarded as an integrated whole. Conventional thinking was represented by the Simon Committee report on domestic fuel policy (Ministry of Fuel and Power 1946) and the Ridley Committee 1952 report on national fuel policy. In a classic critique, Little (1953) argued that the price of coal was too low, failing to reflect the *rising* marginal costs of coal. Little also argued that second-best considerations should not unduly undermine marginal cost principles because coal, gas, and electricity are 'producer' and not 'consumer' goods (pp. xi–xii).

achieved in 1970.[16] Any notion that the 1967 White Paper (HMT 1967) could allow the energy industries to avoid Treasury restraint was quickly dispelled. After 1970, regulation became more overtly political, as energy matters rose to the top of the political agenda. The miners' strikes in 1972 and 1974, the OPEC shock in 1973 and inflation meant that day-to-day regulatory decisions were replaced by direct Cabinet involvement.

In time, the 1967 White Paper on Nationalized Industries became suspect on economic theory grounds too. Its architects had been principally concerned with welfare—with what *ought* to happen. They had paid less attention to what actually happens—to the incentives and behaviour of the incumbent managers and their political masters. This more sceptical approach provides a rationale for the 1978 White Paper (HMT 1978) drafted by Ian Byatt (who much later became the water regulator in 1989), and pushed through the Cabinet by Denis Healey on the nod. Though it became the principal mechanism for regulating nationalized industries for the next two decades, at the time it was paid little more than passing interest. In the new post-1976 climate, monetary targets had been adopted, and the government had accepted that public expenditure had to be constrained as part of the 1976 International Monetary Fund Letter of Intent.[17] Cash limits—mirroring the cash basis for measuring the public-sector borrowing requirement (PSBR)—were already the *de facto* method of controlling nationalized industries' budgets. However, given the subsequent importance of the 1978 White Paper, it is worth rehearsing its main components, and considering how they fit in with the positive approach to managers' behaviour.

The key features of the 1978 White Paper were short- and medium-term sets of financial constraints. These broadly reflected the controls thought to be exercised by the capital market for private-sector firms. In the short term, the industries would be subject to external financial limits (EFLs)—crudely, the subsidy or profit that the business would target over the year in cash terms, set for some years ahead.[18] In the medium term, investment would be subject to a required rate of return (RRR), set over projects as a whole rather than individually. This approximated a cost of capital to a company and was initially set at 5 per cent (on the assumption that this is what the private sector typically earned). It was raised to 8 per cent in the 1980s. Broadly speaking, the EFLs would encourage static efficiency (the best use

---

[16] See Jenkins 1991, Chapter 12 for a description of the context and the post-devaluation budget.

[17] The 1976 International Monetary Fund letter led directly to pressure on British Gas to raise prices to provide revenue. See British Gas annual report and accounts, 1976/77.

[18] EFLs had already been introduced in 1976 as cash limits.

of existing resources) and the RRR would ensure dynamic efficiency by encouraging the appropriate level of investment (see Heald 1980).

Viewed from a welfare economic perspective, the 1978 White Paper was seriously flawed. There could be no assumption that prices would equal LRMC, nor that investment would exhaust all positive net present value projects. The cost of capital in the public sector was not the same as that in the private sector—nor, indeed, was risk equivalent across public-sector projects, from the reprocessing plant THORP to hospitals and railways. However, from a positive perspective, the effect of the two constraints would be to push prices up and to limit investment, thereby reducing pressures on the PSBR. In practice the RRR calculation proved 'too difficult' for the Department of Energy, and the EFLs dominated. Whether this would improve efficiency depends on the starting point: whether prices were too low and investment too great. Neither of these assumptions was tested.

The 1978 White Paper did, however, survive the test of time, though its central omission—the determination of the value of assets to which a rate of return should be applied to derive the EFL—was left to Ian Byatt to subsequently sort out. This was the agenda for the Byatt Committee, discussed below in Chapter 3.

Keeping the Lights On: OPEC and the Miners

Strictly speaking, the OPEC oil shock in 1973 was not the first such shock. That status is reserved for the Suez Crisis, which in 1956 led to the political enthusiasm for nuclear and a trebling of the original nuclear programme announced in the 1955 White Paper (Ministry of Fuel and Power 1955). However, Suez proved temporary and arose in a period of much less dependence on oil in the total energy demand. The rise in oil prices in the early 1970s was a 'shock' of an altogether different magnitude, and it was sufficient to invert the conventional assumptions which underpinned energy policy. For most of the history of the oil industry, real prices had remained remarkably constant. Supply was elastic to demand, with any potential rise in prices leading to greater exploration and production. Early reserves in the United States and in Russia were augmented by discoveries in the Far East and Iran. The discoveries in Iran proved the base for the Anglo–Iranian Oil Company, which later became BP. These reserves were in turn bolstered by the further extraordinary Middle Eastern discoveries.[19]

---

[19] See Yergin (1991) for a popular account of the history of the oil industry.

By the 1960s, oil was in plentiful supply. Demand did not remotely exceed supply, and the Middle East was not the political hotbed that it subsequently became. Cheap petrol stimulated the automobile market, and oil was rapidly displacing coal as the engine of heavy industry. Oil was even used in power stations. The official view, set out in the 1967 White Paper, 'Fuel Policy', confirmed this, concluding that 'there are a number of reasons for expecting [oil prices] not to increase' (HMSO 1967: para 53). As Posner (1973: 57) pointed out, 'from the moment that the words of the White Paper were written, oil prices moved rapidly upwards.'

However, the benefit of hindsight does reveal that, while a shock, the increase in prices was not entirely a surprise. Commodity prices generally began to edge upwards in the 1960s. Demand continued to rise throughout the period, and the industrialized nations became more dependent on oil—particularly from the Middle East—losing the diversity that had provided the long-term insurance against interruptions in supplies. The golden economic age of the 1950s and 1960s had (like that of the 1980s and 1990s) been fuelled by cheap oil, and it was easy in both periods to assume that cheap oil was the norm.

These demand-side changes would not, in themselves, have brought about the dramatic price movements. Actions on the supply side proved critical. Any successful cartel between self-interested nations requires a series of conditions to be fulfilled. The product needs be homogeneous, costs should be broadly similar, output should be easy to monitor, so that cheating can be detected, and credible threats should be available to deter cheats. The oil market in 1972 met only some of these conditions. OPEC did not control all the oil resources, and cheating could occur without effective sanction.

So why did OPEC work? The control Saudi Arabia exercised as a swing producer was overwhelmingly dominant and, as the supply–demand balance tightened, it exercised its market power. But to exercise such power, it needed a broader political protection, and this was provided by the Arab political unity, which temporarily overcame the inherent economic instability of the cartel. But such a coincidence of market power and politics was to prove transient, though few realized at the time just how weak it would be. The cartel was only likely to last as long as the political will remained.

The political catalyst was war—as it was to be in every subsequent oil shock until 1999. In 1973 it was the Israel–Arab war (the Yom Kippur War). The military strike by Egypt and Syria on Israel was initially successful. However, within days, a reversal took place. The Arabs responded with the oil weapon. The pretext was the US decision to resupply the Israeli Air Force. Saudi Arabia responded by cutting output by 25 per cent, and an embargo against the United States. OPEC raised its price from $3.00 per barrel to $5.11, and subsequently to $11.65. Suddenly, the post-war assumptions looked very shaky.

As would again happen at the end of the 1990s, the oil shock exposed the failures of energy policy in the 1960s and led to a series of policy innova-tions that were to set the framework for the Conservatives' inheritance in 1979. Faced with the quadrupling of oil prices, the British government's benign neglect of energy policy ended. The conventional wisdom was now reversed. Oil prices were *assumed* to be on a (permanently) rising trend—though there was some debate as to whether this was necessarily a 'bad thing', given the North Sea oil and gas prospects. This simple assumption triggered a more pro-coal strategy, more nuclear power, and more intense North Sea oil exploration. These 'solutions' to the problem of high and rising fossil-fuel prices were to outlast this rationale—long after oil prices collapsed in the 1980s.

Faced with an energy crisis, the Conservative government signalled its intent by setting up a new Department of Energy in 1974 to carry through the management of the immediate OPEC crisis and to pursue the drive for diversity.[20] Peter Carrington, a close colleague of Heath, then Prime Minister, was appointed its first Secretary of State. These immediate object-ives were soon to be forgotten, as the Department quickly became dogged by industrial disputes and industry capture. The miners' strike rapidly took central stage, with the Department's energies being diverted from the longer-term policy issues to the more immediate imperative of keeping the lights on in the face of miners' hostility. As Nigel Lawson was to later remark: 'The Department of Energy could more aptly be described as the Department of Nationalized Industries' (Lawson 1992: 131). Its 20-year history has not been covered in glory. It sanctioned the Plan for Coal, fur-ther AGRs, Sizewell B, preserved British Gas as an integrated monopoly, and, if some within it had had their way, the CEGB might still be intact. In terms of overall contribution, it was the Treasury which reined back the Department's more grandiose schemes, provided some semblance of regulatory rules, and pushed the privatization and competition agenda.

The obvious answers to Britain's energy needs at this stage were diver-sification out of OPEC into non-OPEC supplies; out of energy imports into domestic self-sufficiency in coal and nuclear electricity; and faster development of the North Sea. The object of energy policy was to create diversity as part of state planning. Of these options, coal forced itself immediately onto the agenda.

---

[20] Until 1969, there had been a Ministry of Fuel and Power. In 1969 this was integrated into the Ministry of Technology, which in turn was incorporated into the Department of Industry in 1970 (see Hennessey 1989: 242 and 432).

The Miners Threaten Security of Supply

The problem with coal was that the miners' union, the NUM, appeared to threaten the nation's energy supplies to an even greater extent than Sheikh Yamani's OPEC did. The miners were the vanguard of the trade unions' opposition to the Heath government's incomes policy. They first went on strike in 1972, and, through the corporatist style of dispute resolution, were awarded their wage claim in full by the hastily set-up Wilberforce Inquiry. They put in another large claim in summer 1973 (a wage increase of 31 per cent) in a direct challenge to the government's incomes policy. Overtime was banned from November, which eventually led to a national strike in February 1974. This in turn led to the three-day week, the February 1974 election, and finally a minority Labour government.

After the Conservatives' defeat, Labour quickly settled with the miners, who got what they wanted: the wage increases, and what they thought would be a guaranteed future. This 'guaranteed future' rested on the Plan for Coal—in reality, a series of different Plans, to be much disputed from their inception through to the 1984 strike (see Chapter 4). In essence, the Plan comprised a coal policy designed to hold up output, and then worked back to the investment required to finance it. As Michael Parker (2000: 2–8), who was intimately involved at the NCB as Head of Economics, stated: 'when compared to the original "Plan for Coal" submitted to the Conservative government, the final Plan had acquired, in various subtle ways, a greater emphasis on volume targets, with less economic and financial rigour.'

For the mining unions at least, the endorsement of the Plan for Coal represented an 'unconditional political commitment to the expansion of the industry' (ibid.: 7). Not only had energy policy become a coal expansion policy, but it was also now effectively on what John Hicks, for the economy as a whole, had described as 'the Labour standard'.[21] The NUM set the terms, and electricity customers and the Treasury paid the bill. The costs would only become apparent when the oil price collapsed, and, with it, the headroom for the coal industry and the miners' pay.

Yet More Nuclear

The second diversification option was more investment in nuclear power. This appealed to many industrialized countries, and spurred the nuclear programmes in France, the United States, and Germany, as well as Britain. The programmes themselves have all had their problems, and all have, with the benefit of hindsight, so far been uneconomic. However, it is probable that

---

[21] Hicks (1955) famously suggested that the post-war period had moved to the Labour standard, playing an analogous role to the gold standard of the 1930s.

Britain's record is amongst the worst, and this was dictated by the decision to opt for AGR technology over the PWR, and by the form that the investment programme took.

The decision-making process was complicated by disputes which raged within the Department of Energy, and the peculiar political position of its Secretary of State, Tony Benn, who was widely thought to have been 'exiled' there by James Callaghan to limit his influence on policy more generally. Opting for a continuation with AGR technology was a decision reluctantly taken by Benn in 1978, against the advice of the Chief Scientific Officer, Walter Marshall, and under pressure from Callaghan who wanted the matter settled. Benn opted for British technology at a time when the world was turning to the PWR.[22]

The decision was not taken in ignorance of the problems with AGRs, which were already all too apparent. The scale of the error was compounded by the piecemeal build programme, which was spread over a long period. The timescale meant that economies of scale in construction were not fully exploited, technical changes created new 'first-of-a-kind' costs with each new station, and the planning approval process proved more complex than anticipated. As a result, the economic performance, at least until the 1990s, was dismal. At worst, Dungeness B took some 22 years to produce a spark of electricity, and load factors for the AGRs were around 40 per cent. The lack of transparent public-sector accounts for the nuclear industry will, however, make any definitive assessment virtually impossible. As Chapter 7 details, the legacy of the 1970s' and early 1980s' stations was eventually to be sorted out through the privatization of the electricity industry, though even after British Energy was privatized, the deep-seated problems would remain, and create another crisis in 2002.

Drilling in the North Sea

The third plank of the new post-OPEC energy policy focused on the North Sea, following on from the discovery of the Dutch Groningen field in the late 1950s. Significant gas reserves had been discovered in the North Sea in the mid-1960s.[23] Oil discoveries followed, spurred on by the higher prices which OPEC had delivered. The costs of exploration— assumed to be in excess of $10/bbl—were now worth the risk (against an

---

[22] See Chapter 5 for the detail of the AGR programme, the decision-making process and Benn's position.

[23] The first round of licences was issued in 1964, and BP found significant resources in West Sole in 1965.

OPEC production cost of $2–$3/bbl). Oil companies throughout the world began to search for new supplies.[24]

As with coal and electricity, state monopolies and planning were central to energy policy in the North Sea. The two vehicles were the Gas Council (after 1972, the BGC) and BNOC. The Continental Shelf Act 1964 gave monopoly powers to the Gas Council, and the Council was empowered in the Gas Act 1965 'to manufacture gas, to get or acquire gas in or from Great Britain or elsewhere, and to supply gas in bulk to any area board', and it used these powers to sign long-term contracts with North Sea companies. These powers were monopoly ones, and in two senses: the Gas Council had a monopoly in purchasing (strictly a monopsony), and it had a monopoly of customers. The latter underwrote its risks in contracting; as long as there was no competition, customers would always pay the Gas Council's costs. Moreover, as it could *therefore* enter long-term contracts, it provided the basis for fixed-price contracts to those developing the North Sea fields. This was a happy circumstance for the gas industry, to the extent that costs were recovered, although there was much dispute about the price.[25] It would eventually come unstuck in the 1990s.

The Gas Act 1972 created the British Gas Corporation as a fully integrated company, which was to continue the monopoly activities. But it was to do much more: it would build the integrated natural gas transmission and distribution system, and it would branch out downstream into appliances and showrooms, and upstream into oil. These diversifications were eventually to be ended by the Oil and Gas (Enterprise) Act 1982, discussed in Chapter 3.

The offshore oil industry was much more heterogeneous than onshore coal, gas, and electricity. It was an international business dominated by multinationals. The government could not hope to monopolize all of its activities or finance the scale of investment required from the public purse. BP had always been treated as a private company, and the government's stake had almost always been passive, and would continue to be so. BNOC was invented as the next best thing, to 'manage' the development of fields and to play a part by gaining the pick of the licences. It was a classic confusion of producer, regulator, and agency of government.

The origins of BNOC go back to the early 1970s, and the realization that the British government had little direct control over the industry.

---

[24] Along with the North Sea, Alaska proved a fertile ground. BP discovered the Prudhoe Bay field in 1969, and this was to prove its backstay for the next decade. For a detailed account of BP's hot-and-cold strategy in Alaska, see Bamberg (2000: 191–5).

[25] BP's initial contract was set at just over 2 pence/therm, and subsequent deals were even tougher (see Corti and Frazer 1983: ch. 3).

In its 1973 report following an inquiry into how much the government was getting out of the North Sea, the Public Accounts Committee exposed accounting practices amongst oil companies that enabled 'losses' to be claimed through transfer pricing, whilst at the same time the auction of some of the licences in the fourth round had revealed a surprisingly high willingness to pay by the same companies (House of Commons Committee of Public Accounts 1973).

It was left to the incoming Labour government in 1974 to sort out North Sea policy, and with the full implications of the OPEC price hike in mind. The key distinction from an energy policy perspective was between the extraction of rents and the control of supplies, given the threat of an embargo. Labour's solution to the former was taxation (but not auctioning licences), and to the latter, BNOC.

BNOC's initial rationale was to take a controlling stake in North Sea oil, but, as Corti and Frazer (1983) pointed out, the undertaking by government that companies would be 'no better or worse off' meant that its participation in licences would have to take the form of an option to purchase at 'market' price, rather than nationalization. BNOC's approach had to be one of negotiation, and each case was treated differently in a process which took the rest of the decade to complete. Once achieved, however, Britain could ensure that in the event of a supply interruption of the kind threatened in the early 1970s, oil would be landed in Britain for the home market.

The establishment of options was most fraught for licences which had already been granted in the fourth and earlier rounds. In subsequent licensing rounds, BNOC could take a more proactive role, and it had a privileged and preferred status, allowing further equity to be built up in the company. Because the negotiations were long and often tortuous, events conspired to alter early plans—including the collapse of Burmah and the financial difficulties of some of the smaller players yielding equity stakes—whilst the extension of options made BNOC an important price setter in the market place, a role it would continue to perform in the 1980s even after its assets had been floated off in Britoil.

Whether control was necessary for security of supply, and whether BNOC could have achieved this without moving to equity, is debatable. These functional issues were further complicated by the fact that Benn was Secretary of State, and, as noted, that he had been transferred from the Department of Industry to Energy to marginalize his political role. The ideas of planning, control, and ownership had been confused in the approach he adopted at the Department of Industry, and they were to be no clearer at Energy. It was a confusion which the Conservatives were to deal with as one of their early energy policy priorities, but which Labour itself also began to come to terms with: it was Labour (and Denis Healey in particular) which began to *sell* its stake in BP (at 48 per cent) at the same time as BNOC was *acquiring* more stakes in the North Sea.

The Legacy

The nationalized framework created the industry structure which the Conservatives inherited in 1979, almost all of which they subsequently privatized. This endeavour proved much harder and more complex than the main architects imagined. The reasons were partly related to their own confused objectives, but, more fundamentally, they related to the nature of the legacy and its political and economic consequences.

This inheritance comprised the assets, the price levels and structures, and the public expectations of these industries. Although it is interesting to speculate what the energy sector would look like if its assets were designed on a blank piece of paper to meet current market conditions, in practice they are almost always built under very different assumptions and conditions. Asset lives are often very long and, in consequence, a small number of power stations are under construction at any one time relative to the total number; gas and electricity transportation and trans-mission systems are mature; and oil and gas field development in the North Sea is incremental. The inherited assets would have turned out 'sub-optimal' *ex post*, even without the added shortcomings of nationalization.

From this observation, there follows an important consequence: the test of privatization in the early years was largely about the ability of the pri-vate sector to operate a set of assets that were sub-optimal. The way in which the outputs from these assets were managed and priced would in turn influence the investment climate for future capacity. Thus, if the pri-vatized electricity generators attempted to maximize short-run profits from old coal-fired stations, it is likely that entry by new CCGTs would be faster than if a longer-term pricing strategy were pursued. Indeed, this is not merely a hypothetical example: as we shall see in Chapter 8, the pric-ing behaviour by PowerGen and National Power has been a key determin-ant of the dash for gas.

In the case of gas, it is not just assets that have been inherited from the public sector, it is also contracts. In order to cover the risk of developing North Sea assets, British Gas in the public sector entered into contracts averaging twenty-five years on a take-or-pay basis. These contracts could be signed because British Gas had a statutory monopoly downstream with its customers. It could pass the costs through. When that monopoly was abolished, first in the business market in the late 1980s and then in retail through the Gas Act 1995, British Gas found that, in the face of falling spot prices, it could no longer guarantee to recover its contract costs. The result was that supply competition developed much faster, as customers switched to new entrants, and, as we shall see in Chapter 13, British Gas eventually had to break itself up and write off its Morecambe Bay field against the stranded contracts.

Some of the legacy assets were more important than others, both in scale and their economic viability in current and future energy markets. At the high level, arguably the most significant were the coal and nuclear industries. Whereas, in 1990, Britain's electricity generation comprised around 75 per cent coal, 20 per cent nuclear and 5 per cent other (oil, etc), it was rapidly apparent after privatization that, for *new* generating plant, CCGTs were much more cost effective than either coal or nuclear, and that, without government assistance, no new coal or nuclear plant would be built. Much of the problem of the post-privatization transition to competition has been about the speed with which these two once dominant industries have declined.

Policy responses have been *ad hoc*, often designed to put off the day of reckoning. The new era of low fossil-fuel prices only gradually sunk into government thinking. In the case of coal, the privatization of the electricity industry provided a cushion through uneconomic contracts with British Coal, holding up output and prices for the period 1990–93 (i.e. until after the next general election). When the likely scale of the industry decline on the expiry of these contracts became apparent in autumn 1992, the great 'coal crisis' almost ended Michael Heseltine's political career, and led to another set of artificial contracts for the period 1993–98 (i.e. until after the *next* general election). Labour was to try to do the same again in 1998.

In the case of nuclear, early optimism about privatizing these assets and their liabilities in 1988 proved unfounded, and the assets had to be left in the public sector. In addition, electricity customers were forced to pay a levy (around 10–11 per cent of electricity bills) to cover the decommissioning costs. When the AGR and PWR assets were eventually sold in 1996, much of their costs were effectively written off and much of the nuclear risks were effectively largely passed back to the public sector through contracts with the still state-owned BNFL. Even then British Energy found it hard to survive in the new competitive environment.

In sum, then, the Conservatives inherited a largely uneconomic coal industry, Magnox stations nearing the end of their economic lives ready for decommissioning, AGRs which did not work very well, and a large stock of coal power stations. To this was added a well-developed electricity transmission and distribution system, and a developing natural gas network. Finally, it inherited the prize of North Sea oil and gas.

The legacy assets came with price levels, structures, and contracts. These were designed not purely to maximize efficiency, but rather to meet wider political and social objectives. The relationship between price and cost—the *sine qua non* of a competitive market—was, at best, tenuous. Gas was too cheap, coal was too expensive, and electricity prices did not recover the costs of the (often inefficiently built and operated) power stations. Customers simply paid the costs which the monopolies passed through.

These prices, in turn, came with a set of public expectations of the energy industries, which in large measure conflicted with those proposed by economists. The public had been led to expect nationalized industries to take a wide account of the public interest—to include concepts of fairness to their workers and customers, to subsidize worthy causes, and to provide a public service. This meant showrooms in every town in Britain, sponsorship of research and development, and contributing to macro- as well as microeconomic objectives. The electricity industry even found itself as a 'commanding height' contributing to counter-inflation policies. The unwinding of these distortions has created the main difficulties of the transitions to more competitive conditions in the private sector, and the impacts will continue to live with us in the twenty-first century.

3

First Steps Towards the Market Philosophy

> I do *not* see the government's task as being to try to plan the future shape of energy production and consumption. It is not even primarily to try to balance UK demand and supply for energy. Our task is rather to set a framework which will ensure that the market operates in the energy sector with a minimum of distortion and energy is produced and consumed efficiently. (Nigel Lawson, 1982)

The Myths and Realities of 1979

With hindsight, the 1979 general election represented a turning point in British politics which compares with that of 1945. At the time, however, the clarity of hindsight was far from obvious. Margaret Thatcher's rhetoric was similar to that of Edward Heath's in the first years in office in the 1970s. 'Selsdon Man', named after the Conservatives' conference at Selsdon Park, would have been an ardent Thatcherite. But, as with Heath's U-turn, the ideology of capitalist individualism might easily have wilted under the everyday pressures of events. And even had Thatcher wished to unleash a new market-orientated beginning, her Cabinet was far from onside, and many of the policies which would subsequently be associated with her name were yet to be developed from crude academic blueprints. With the hindsight of twenty years of privatization, and its acceptance by Labour after 1997, the early years were timid ones, but, at the time, privatization and competition in core utilities were regarded as fanciful academic ideas by all but the most die-hard marketeers. The first Thatcher government was, inevitably, to feel its way gradually towards policies that would reach fruition after the second and third election victories.

Although private ownership was to be preferred *in principle* to nationalization, its initial application was to be to the myriad of industrial and commercial public-sector holdings. Denis Healey had taken the opportunity to sell off a stake in BP in the late 1970s,[1] but there was no mention of

---

[1] See Cairncross (1994: 85) and Foreman-Peck and Millward (1994: 331) for the background.

privatization in the Conservative manifesto in 1979. Furthermore, to the extent that the Conservatives quickly sold off a number of small holdings in companies already in competitive markets, these had little to do with the major state enterprises.

The first Conservative government was more concerned to avoid a confrontation with the miners, and, in particular, Thatcher was obsessed with avoiding Heath's fate in 1974. To this end, an early dispute in 1981 led to concessions, and policy was directed to building coal stocks for what many (but not all) regarded as the eventual showdown. There was no recognition at this stage that the problem of the miners would ultimately be solved by breaking up and privatizing the electricity industry. Instead, trade union reform and coal stocks were seen as the necessary steps. (Thatcher's battle with Arthur Scargill is the subject of Chapter 4.)

The first Conservative Secretary of State for Energy was one of those who held to 'the faith' in the opposition years. David Howell had transformed himself in the second half of the 1970s into one of the inner core of Thatcher's team ('one of us'), and she thought that he could be relied upon to take a robust, if not more market-orientated, line with the nationalized energy companies. The immediate issues that faced him were the consequences of the second oil shock in 1978/79, and the legacy of Tony Benn's North Sea oil policies. The 1978/79 shock was regarded as capable of producing a rerun of 1973/74, with all the associated problems of energy shortages, petrol queues and gas supply interruptions. At the Department of Energy, despite the change of government, the sense of continuity is what emerges from Howell's term of office, 1979–81: a focus on security of supply; adapting to a world of ever-higher oil prices; and managing the North Sea. The 'solutions' were: higher gas prices; more nuclear power stations; sustaining the coal industry; and a faster extraction rate of oil. To this should be added the political dimension: managing the threat from the National Union of Mineworkers (NUM).

Whatever his own prejudices, Howell's approach to his twin challenges of the consequences of the second OPEC shock and the threat from the miners was to prove the last throw of the conventional dice. He did little to reform the traditional planning approach to energy policy within the Department, and he was further hampered by the fact that the underlying assumptions of planning for the 1980s—that oil prices would stay high and demand for energy would continue on its upward trend—were wrong. But this is to rush ahead. We need to step back and look forward from the perspective of 1979, to see Howell's canvas and begin with the immediate problem of gas prices, and the fear that supply would not meet demand.

Changing the Prices

The first step was to change the prices, which the incoming government considered to be too low. As we saw in Chapter 2, there were good reasons for this view: the nationalized industries tended towards output rather than profit maximization, resulting in prices which may be considered to be below, perhaps well below, marginal costs. But, as is inevitable with such general propositions, the position in the various industries differed considerably. In 1979, the coal industry was much engaged with the Plan for Coal, which the 1978/79 oil shock had reinforced. Oil prices had obviously risen, being market-determined, while gas and electricity prices lagged. Thus the main focus of attention was these latter two cases; although, as we shall see in due course, both were subsequently to be subject to downward pressure—gas, because oil prices collapsed in the mid-1980s, and electricity because of the massive excess supply consequent on the 1980–82 recession, and, in particular, the collapse of manufacturing output.

None of this, of course, was foreseen in the brighter days of 1979, following the May general election victory. Indeed, it was not to be obvious to Nigel Lawson, who succeeded Howell as Energy Secretary in the 1981 reshuffle. Howell started the process off with a three-year plan to increase domestic gas prices by the retail price index (RPI) + 10 through to 1982. The rationale for the increase was that oil prices had risen sharply, but not gas, and, in consequence, the demand for gas might exceed supply 'without increases in price of the size proposed'. Howell told the House of Commons on 11 February 1980, 'for the coming year there would be a clear possibility of supply interruption.'[2] But this was not the only reason: 'The sort of profit we are talking about for the coming year is needed and is in line with the colossal investment required to put in the new transmission lines and meet the vast backlog of those who wish to have gas.'

This second reason was strange economics—current customers would pay for future investment—but then much of the economics behind the British Gas Corporation (BGC) was strange. The company comprised three main parts: a set of long-term take-or-pay contracts with North Sea producers; the transmission and distribution assets; and a number of (as it turned out, ill-thought-out) ancillary activities, from oil in the North Sea to showrooms selling gas appliances. It was not obvious that the long-term contract prices should be linked to spot (oil) prices for customers;[3] it was

---

[2] HC Deb (session 1979–80) vol. 978, col. 1046 fifth series. The 1978 Energy Policy Green Paper had predicted that gas would run out in the 1990s (Department of Energy 1978).

[3] How far prices to domestic customers ought to follow spot (oil prices) is a fraught question. It was to dog British Gas again in the 1990s, when oil prices were low, but gas in excess supply, and then again its successors in 2000/01 when oil prices rose sharply.

not clear what valuation underlay the network assets; and the other activities were hard to evaluate because they were bundled together in aggregate accounts. Just what the 'right prices' were was very hard to estimate.

As noted in Chapter 2, the Continental Shelf Act 1964 and the Gas Act 1965 had given the Gas Council monopoly rights which allowed it to determine long-term contract prices with North Sea companies—first BP, and then others. These contracts could in principle have been market-related, to oil prices or in relation to town gas. Indeed, as Corti and Frazer (1983) report, there was some expectation that this might be the case. In practice, the Gas Council sought cost-based prices, and it was these prices which were not only arguably inefficiently low at the time, but became ever more so as the oil price marched up. In effect, supplies were rationed by the description of gas as a 'premium fuel', since demand was inflated by the low prices. The contracts also provided for significant variation in field-take, enabling the Gas Council to use the fields, rather than its network, to act as 'storage' to manage its load.

Whatever the 'right answer' was, it was apparent that the prices at the time were clearly wrong, and by a very wide margin. It was a view held not only by the Department of Energy, but also the Price Commission (which had just been abolished). And, in 1979, the Department was not to know that a very sharp recession was about to change the supply–demand balance. The impact of Howell's price increases, which tried to close the gap between gas and oil prices, against fixed-supply contracts, went straight to the bottom line, and Labour opposition MPs were quick to see this as milking the nationalized industries.

The price of electricity was even less market-driven than that of gas and Howell instigated a review of the bulk supply tariff (BST) in July 1980.[4] The BST was not the product of supply and demand in the market place, but the aggregation of costs passed through from the coal industry and the Central Electricity Generating Board (CEGB). With coal the dominant input cost, the price was determined by the *joint understanding* between the National Coal Board (NCB) and the CEGB, which, in turn, passed its costs through the BST to Area Boards. The BST had an energy component (largely coal) and a capacity component (the power stations and the grid, then owned by the CEGB). The Area Boards added on their distribution costs, to arrive at the final price. The 'variables' in this cost pass-through were the accounting items (how much the assets were worth, and what return ought to be earned), and the level of investment (to which we return below).

---

[4] The review was eventually published as 'Electricity Supply Industry in England and Wales' (The Electricity Council 1981).

The coal position was political, and set in the context of a long campaign which many thought would eventually end in a strike. This is the subject of Chapter 4. The government increased its support for the coal industry and assumed that, in the context of the OPEC oil shock, output would have a more important role to play, with the new nuclear programme meeting the *additional* energy demands, rather than displacing coal. A 'joint understanding', which passed for a contract in the public sector, agreed in October 1979 that the CEGB would take up to 75 million tonnes a year for five years, at prices pegged to inflation—that is, RPI − 0. While such a fixed-price, fixed-output arrangement looked very like a conventional take-or-pay contract, it was based on the assumptions of 1979, not those of 1980–82, when the recession bit hard.

The problems over gas and electricity prices reflected a much more general concern over the ability of the Department of Energy to ever get them 'right'. Immediate and large errors, such as those in gas, and the problems of costs in coal and electricity, all reflected the monopoly basis of the industries, and, hence, the absence of market prices for comparative purposes. The underlying asset values were, until the 1980s, based on historical costs which were largely meaningless for long-lived assets, and where the assets themselves were inefficiently created. In the 1970s, inflation made any tangency with reality that historical costs might have had redundant.[5]

Efficiency and Resource Allocation

The early Thatcher period was marked by an attempt to use whatever levers were available to address these resource allocation, efficiency, and pricing issues. This second initiative was largely confined to weakening the monopoly status, and opening up the industries' accounting and management practices. The Competition Act 1980 had two main effects: to abolish the statutory monopoly and to open up the nationalized industries to scrutiny by the Monopolies and Mergers Commission (MMC). The first of these points had limited immediate effect, and it would require the Oil and Gas (Enterprise) Act 1982 and the Energy Act 1983 to begin to address the underlying issues of pricing and access to networks, introduced by Howell's successor, Lawson. Competition required competitors, and after more than thirty years of statutory monopoly, only a small fringe of self-generators existed.

The MMC was extensively used by the government to audit efficiency across the energy sector, but with an important proviso. The MMC could

---

[5] See Edwards *et al.* (1987: Chs 5 and 6) and the Byatt report (HMT 1986), discussed below.

look at costs, but could not consider 'any question relating to the appropriateness of any financial obligations or guides to financial objectives (however expressed) imposed on or given to the person in question by or under any enactment, or otherwise by a Minister' (Competition Act 1980, Section 11(8)). In other words, matters relating to the new tough regime of external financial limits (EFLs) were out of bounds. These would be a separate part of nationalized industry policy within the broader macroeconomic framework of the Medium Term Financial Strategy (MTFS).

The MMC was, in practice, to carry out 'fishing' exercises, bringing companies 'into play'. Each raised particular issues, but in the process began to paint a more general picture of inefficiency, which eventually formed part of the justification for the much more radical privatizations and competition policies which followed at the end of the 1980s. There were MMC reports on the CEGB (MMC 1981) and on a number of electricity Area Boards (MMC 1983*a,c*, 1984, 1985*a,b*, 1986). Coal, of course, was also subject to an inquiry (MMC 1983*b*). These studies were very professional, and revealed to the public a wealth of information about the conduct of the state-run companies.

From the detail, a number of core conclusions were distilled, and it is worth reviewing the main findings for each of the stages in the vertical chain, from coal and power generation to electricity distribution and sales. The MMC report on the NCB was eventually published in June 1983 (it was referred in March 1982) and noted the financial weakness of the NCB: 'On the information available to us, there is little possibility that the NCB will be able to operate without a deficit grant, let alone generate sufficient funds to finance any significant part of its own capital investment, before the end of the decade' (MMC 1983*b*: para 19.6, 364).

Demand had not risen as anticipated, nor had closures been at the expected rate since the Plan for Coal was agreed in 1974. The MMC was critical of the NCB for nevertheless pushing on with the 1974 Plan to add 40 million tons of new and modernized capacity. The MMC was therefore: 'concerned that these appear to have taken precedent over the statutory obligation to adopt a policy directed to securing that the revenues shall not be less than sufficient for meeting all the outgoings properly chargeable to the revenue account on an average of good and bad years' (ibid.: para 19.9, 365).[6]

It found that the NCB's aims were 'vague', and that the industry was characterized by over-capacity and high-cost pits. A 10 per cent capacity cut was suggested. Moreover, the problem was urgent: 'the longer the problems are left the worse they will become' (ibid.: para 19.22, 369).

---

[6] The relevant statutory reference is the 1946 Coal Industry Nationalization Act, Section 1(4)(c).

In the context of the subsequent disputes with the NUM, the report gave the government the stamp of approval for a policy of containment on which it had already embarked, as described in Chapter 4.

Whereas the NCB report largely set out what was already known, the 1981 MMC report on the CEGB was perhaps the most significant because it provided a first glimpse at the even less transparent decision-making processes behind the development of coal and nuclear capacity in the 1970s. The report made depressing reading for those whose faith rested in the nationalized industry model. Its principal conclusions were that the government's financial targets would push up prices; that industry demand forecasting had been seriously inaccurate and had led to premature orders for new plant which had increased costs; that the generation security standard was overgenerous and led to higher costs; that the assumptions relating to coal price and availability 'did not satisfy the MMC as plausible or mutually consistent'; and that plant construction costs did not take proper account of market information. In other words, the central planks of a planned electricity industry—demand forecasting, input costing and investment decision-making—were in this case seriously flawed. To these inefficiencies and bias in the planned industrial structure was added the allocative distortion caused by the overriding effect of government pricing. Only the basic functions of merit-order despatch escaped serious criticism, which is hardly surprising because it is in this area that the gains from centralized control might be expected to be greatest—as indeed they continued to be, through the compulsory Pool system developed at privatization. (It should also be borne in mind that the information technology on which the Pool, and now its replacement NETA, relies was in its infancy in 1981.)

The MMC reports into the electricity Area Boards concentrated on various aspects of their businesses. The 1983 reports on London and Yorkshire looked, respectively, at the 'direction and management... of its business of retailing domestic electrical goods, spare parts and ancillary goods'; and efficiency and costs (MMC 1983a,b). The report in 1984 on South Wales was also on efficiency and costs (MMC 1984), as were those on Scottish Hydro-Electric in 1985 (MMC 1985b) and South of Scotland in 1986 (MMC 1986).

A 1985 report investigated the revenue-collection systems of the East Midlands, North Eastern, South Eastern, and South Western Area Boards (MMC 1985a). In the case of gas, the 1980 report looked at domestic gas appliances and provided much of the ammunition that Lawson needed to try to divest these activities from British Gas (MMC 1980).

What did these reports demonstrate? The first, and obvious, point was that any naive optimism about the efficiency of the nationalized industry system—of monopoly and state control—was misplaced. On the contrary, these industries displayed many of the hallmarks that the positive theories of managerial state enterprise predicted: excess output, keeping pits open and building too many power stations; financial laxity in planning and project execution; prices set at artificially low levels relative to costs; and labour bias and overstaffing. Add to these the familiar problem of shorter-term political interference (usually done in private, rather than in terms of any direction through published guidance), and it is remarkable that their Morrisonian structure had lasted so long. By the early 1980s, the nationalized industries had built up sufficient inefficiencies to warrant more radical surgery. The MMC reports largely confirmed the government's prejudices, and provided important ammunition for the arguments to come.

None of this was new, especially to the Treasury. The 1978 White Paper on nationalized industries had explicitly set out to tackle these well-known problems through a regulatory solution (HMT 1978). The task was to design ever more effective constraints, as well as address the managerial incentives through the appointment of more commercial management. More flesh was eventually added to the financial aspects of regulating nationalized industries by the Byatt Committee, set up in September 1984 (though it did not publish its report until 1986). This recommended the adoption of current-cost accounting, which had the effect of increasing asset valuation, and thereby giving a rationale for raising prices (HMT 1986). But the 1978 White Paper, and its subsequent development, was a largely technical exercise in conduct regulation, and, as such, a stopgap. Many Conservatives thought that the problems were more systematic, and looked to the central pillars of the framework: the prohibition on competition and public ownership.

Howell's Nuclear Programme

The third major initiative in the Howell period as Secretary of State for Energy was the decision to start building a family of pressurized-water reactors (PWRs). He told the House of Commons on 18 December 1979 that: 'Even with full exploitation of coal and conservation, and with great efforts on renewable energy sources, it would be difficult to meet this country's long-term energy needs without a sizeable contribution from nuclear power.'

The aim was to start building the first PWR in 1982, and Howell went on to say that he accepted the electricity industry's advice that there was a need to build one PWR a year for the decade from 1982. This was 'a reasonable prospect against which the nuclear power plant industry can plan.' Not only that, but 'the size of the programme I have announced would still leave a major and expanding need for coal in our economy.'

None of Howell's PWRs would see the light of day for a decade, and only Sizewell B would make it to generation. The Sizewell Inquiry would take until 1987 to report (Department of Energy 1987), and, by then, the prospect of privatization would loom, as we shall see in Chapter 5. The extraordinary feature of Howell's commitment, however, was not the choice of nuclear over coal, or PWRs over advanced gas-cooled reactors (AGRs), but rather the capacity forecasts on which it was based. As both the Select Committee on Energy (1981*a*) and the MMC (1981) noted, the demand for electricity was not growing very quickly, even before the recession bit, and there was a surplus of supply. The peak demand to be met reflected the absence of any serious attempt to load-manage, and it would eventually turn out that *no* more stations were needed for the whole of the 1980s.

What the curious gulf between the facts and Howell's decision reflected was the degree of capture by the industry over the Department and its ministers. The electricity industry (previously the CEGB) predicted and the government provided. That the projected nuclear stations would displace coal was a supplementary reason for building them, and one which did not escape Thatcher: 'if we had spent more on nuclear power, as the French had done, our electricity would have been cheaper—and, indeed, our supplies more secure', she reflected (somewhat erroneously) in reviewing the coal crisis which confronted her government in 1981 (Thatcher 1995: 140).

She shared with the CEGB a curious blind spot when it came to the economics of the nuclear industry and its poor record, which contrasted strongly with her scathing criticisms of the NCB, its management and the NUM. It would take the hard constraints of privatization for the true costs to emerge, and for her nuclear ambitions to be buried. But perhaps, given the Heath legacy and the intransigence of the increasingly militant NUM, her bias was, at least politically, understandable.

Bailing Out Coal: The 1981 Crisis

The three initiatives—on prices, the MMC and nuclear—were largely overshadowed by the fourth feature of Howell's period: the coal crisis in 1981, and the retreat that had to be made to avoid a strike. The background to the 1981 crisis was a complex one, comprising a mixture of national energy policy to support coal as an alternative to oil and oil dependency, the particular investment legacy of the Plan for Coal (first discussed by the Heath government, and carried through by Labour after the general election in February 1974), the peculiar economics of the coal industry, its dependency on the electricity industry, and the union monopoly.

In sorting out these various strands, it is important to distinguish between the economic fundamentals and the political practicalities. As will be discussed in further detail in Chapter 4, the coal industry faced a range of economic factors which would have made life very difficult even for an efficient industry, which the British coal industry in 1981 most certainly was not. Imports were cheaper than deep-mine coal, as was opencast. Production exceeded demand, and costs exceeded the market price. The industry was propped up by the monopoly–monopsony deal with the CEGB, which could, in turn, use its monopoly to pass through the excessive costs, and by the government which subsidized the NCB's investment and operating losses. And underneath all this superstructure lay the NUM and its stranglehold on fuel supplies to power stations.

Howell did not inherit a principled policy, but only a pragmatic tradition of negotiating between the parties, which the Department of Energy had managed since its origins in the first oil shock. As Michael Parker correctly pointed out in his history of the coal industry under Thatcher: 'There is no evidence that the new government came into power in 1979 with a clearly thought out long-term master plan designed to effect radical change in the coal industry' (Parker 2000: 9).

Yet the absence of a master plan did not mean a free hand for the NCB. Excess production resulted in stocks for which there was no market, and the high costs of deep mines produced losses which landed at the Treasury's door, just as the recession worsened the government's financial position. The answer was twofold: pit closures and pressure to reduce imports.

These economic fundamentals cut no ice with the NUM, and, in particular, Arthur Scargill, soon to be elected its leader. A strike loomed, and at this stage the government was in no position to resist. Thatcher blamed the Department and the NCB management. There had been, she was to later claim, 'no forward thinking in the Department of Energy about what would happen in the case of a strike' (Thatcher 1995: 141). Although written in a triumphalist style ten years later, there is little reason to doubt her assessment: 'I was appalled to find that we had inadvertently entered into a battle which we could not win...It became very clear that all we could do was to cut our losses and live to fight another day, when—with adequate preparation—we might be in a position to win...Defeat in a coal strike would have been disastrous' (pp. 140–1).

Whether the fault lay entirely with the Department and the management is a matter for debate, since the Treasury had an important role to play in squeezing the NCB's EFL and limiting the financing of coal stocks, but Howell was left to carry the blame and to give a humiliating statement of the extent of the climbdown to the House of Commons on 19 February 1981. The statement is quoted at length in Chapter 4.

There were many lessons to be learnt from the experience of 1981, if it was to be the last time the NUM would hold the upper hand. Thatcher believed she would need a new Secretary of State (Lawson), and he, in turn, believed he would need new management in the nationalized industries. The long war of attrition would work through the building of coal stocks, the reform of trade union law (especially on secondary picketing), and contingency planning in the CEGB. There was no certainty when the strike threat would re-emerge, only that some form of confrontation would come in the end.

Blown Away by the Recession

What is striking about the early Conservative years in the energy sector is how little recognition of the underlying economic reality pervaded the Department of Energy and policy thinking. The underlying assumptions were 1970s' ones: oil prices would continue on their rising trend; coal would continue to dominate electricity generation; and gas would remain a scarce, premium fuel. Prices therefore had to be pushed up, and investment would need to be at a high level to support demand. The nuclear dimension needed to be addressed, as it was assumed that it would become economic.

Much of this conventional wisdom was understandable in the context of the early 1980s. Thatcher's rhetoric might be bellicose, but the government comprised a majority of 'wets'. Until the Falklands War in 1982, it was not unreasonable to expect her government to be a one-term event. But the foundations of the old-style energy policy were being rapidly undermined. The oil price turned out to be at a peak which would not be attained again until 1999, except for the brief blip during the Gulf War in 1991. Demand was about to take a nosedive, and the ready availability of public funds to underwrite the losses and finance the investments was about to cease. Recession and monetary policy proved a powerful catalyst for change, making the Plan for Coal *and* the PWR programme both unnecessary and unsustainable.

Although Healey had adopted monetary targets, the newly elected Conservative government announced a more comprehensive monetary and fiscal policy framework: the MTFS. Targets were set for a broad measure of money (called sterling M3), and corresponding rules were set for the public-sector borrowing requirement (PSBR) and the share of GDP accounted for by the state sector. The government would control inflation by reducing the money supply, borrowing would be constrained, and the scope for private initiative and enterprise would be increased by reducing that of the state.

This simple framework, which owed much to Milton Friedman and Friedrich von Hayek,[7] was applied to a British economy which was fast becoming a major oil exporter, and in the context of a world recession following the OPEC oil shock. The consequences were dramatic: the exchange rate rose from around US$1.50 to a peak of US$2.40; and manufacturing output, priced out of export markets and facing low domestic demand, fell some 25 per cent. Unemployment began its continuous rise, peaking at over three million in 1986.

There was much debate at the time as to whether the recession which followed—the sharpest since the 1930s—was *caused* by oil or by the MTFS, or indeed world events. Forsyth and Kay (1980) took the view that the exchange-rate rise was the inevitable consequence of the oil revenues. It was 'simply the market's mechanism'. 'The contraction of manufacturing output and an increase in domestic absorption of imported manufacturers are [the] only means by which the British economy can benefit from the North Sea.' This was a very different view to that which had pervaded Labour thinking, notably in the White Paper, 'Challenge of North Sea Oil' (HMSO 1978). Forsyth and Kay estimated that the resulting gains would be at least 10 per cent of national income by the mid-1980s. This view was quickly challenged by the Bank of England (1982), and then comprehensively rebutted by Allsopp and Rhys (1989), on the grounds that the core assumption—that North Sea oil should be treated as a windfall in the context of a fully employed economy—was incorrect.

Three factors intervened to create a very different macroeconomic outcome. First, unemployment rose rapidly so that the full-employment model of adjustment was replaced by one of excess domestic capacity in the capital and labour markets. Second, the exchange rate—the mechanism by which the rewards would be gained—collapsed, reaching almost parity with the dollar in 1985. Third, the oil price fell sharply, reducing the value of the windfall.

---

[7] Both had advised Thatcher in the early years. Friedman's work on monetary policy and the market advocacy in his popularist *Free to Choose* (Friedman and Friedman 1980, the subject of a television series in 1980), together with Hayek's famous post-war *The Road to Serfdom* (1944) and the summary of his approach in *The Constitution of Liberty* (1960) were core components of the thinking of the new right.

These macroeconomic changes had a microeconomic corollary. As the costs of unemployment rose, so did the PSBR. Higher nominal interest rates also had a serious impact on the PSBR, as the cost of financing public debt increased. There was, in effect, little or no money for the public sector. The rules for pricing and investment may have been set out in the 1978 White Paper (HMT 1978), described in Chapter 2, but the reality was that nationalized industry prices were increased more with an eye to the desperate need for revenue, and investment plans were scaled down or curtailed.

This public spending constraint had within it the seeds of much of the policy which was to follow: nationalized industry prices had to rise, their costs had to fall, and the private sector would increasingly have to finance new investment.[8] Under *any* government, as Healey had begun to realize, there were limits to the share of government in the economy, and that meant that the private sector would have to play a greater role in financing investment. All European governments faced this constraint, though it took over a decade for European governments and the Labour Party in Britain to recognize the implications.

The recession did much to destroy the corporatist architecture built up from coal to electricity. The demand for electricity fell, and suddenly the policy assumption behind the PWR programme—namely, excess demand—translated into excess supply throughout the vertical chain.[9] The excess production of coal could only lead to mounting stockpiles, while the capacity margins in the electricity industry reached 40 per cent. New power stations were no longer needed, and, indeed, no more coal stations and only one nuclear station were to be built. The arrival of the combined-cycle gas turbine (CCGT) in the 1990s led to many more stations, but largely to displace coal, and they added to the surplus capacity— eventually substantially contributing to the collapse of electricity prices at the end of the 1990s.

In the mid-1980s, the oil price would collapse, knocking out a further prop to the Howell policies. The gas pricing policy and the economic case for PWR nuclear stations were both rendered questionable, and, in the 1990s, the gas prices would eventually follow oil down, and the PWR programme would be abandoned.

These major changes in background conditions meant more than simply that Howell and the Department of Energy had been mistaken.

---

[8] An early casualty was British Gas's plan for a North Sea gas-gathering pipeline, which, after a search for private finance failed, the Treasury vetoed in 1981.

[9] The demand forecasting of the Department of Energy was, in any event, subject to bias towards over-investment, as the MMC (1981) had shown. See also Robinson (1992).

More fundamentally, their energy policy itself was flawed. The task of the 1980s was to design a policy focused on running the existing system as cheaply as possible—sweating the assets—and not on the post-war agenda of investment. Planning suited the former; competition and markets suited the latter. And, although Howell had very gradually edged towards a more market-orientated position, he had little coherent idea about energy policy *per se*. Asked in the House of Commons on 29 October whether the government's approach to energy policy was not to have one, Howell revealingly replied that:

I sometimes think that there is a tendency to confuse energy policy with merely writing down in hope a great many targets and figures for the future and imagining that one thereby has a strategy to meet them. That is not so. Our energy strategy consists of tackling vigorously, by a number of means, all the problems relating to energy matters... (HC Deb. (session 1979–90), vol. 972, col. 814)

What Howell had not quite realized was that this exercise in 'targets and figures' was inevitable in a state-run energy sector: only markets could start to chip away at this increasingly hopeless task.

Lawson's Market for Energy

The logic of the position was explicitly recognized by Lawson, who was appointed Energy Secretary in the Cabinet reshuffle of September 1981, having been a key player at the Treasury in designing the MTFS.[10] Lawson's appointment marks the real turning point in post-war energy policy, and he began immediately with the Oil and Gas (Enterprise) Act 1982, with its focus on privatizing Britoil (the plans for which were already well advanced) and introducing competition into the gas industry. Electricity was to be dealt with during the 1982/83 Parliament, in the Energy Act 1983.

The philosophy behind this new approach was set out in Lawson's speech in June 1982, entitled 'The Market for Energy'—perhaps, with hindsight, one of the most significant expositions of energy policy in the post-war period. The central idea was the rejection of planning in favour of a more market-orientated framework. Lawson said: 'I do *not* see the government's task as being to try to plan the future shape of energy production and consumption. It is not even primarily to try to balance UK demand and supply for energy. Our task is rather to set a framework which will ensure

---

[10] Howell's demotion to Transport followed his disagreement with Thatcher over her desire to placate the miners (see Lawson 1992: 131–2). Howell claims that he had a wider disillusion with the Treasury and what he called 'punk monetarism'.

that the market operates in the energy sector with a minimum of distortion and energy is produced and consumed efficiently' (1982).

The speech went on to suggest that energy prices should, wherever possible, be set by markets, and where this was not possible, by the costs of supply. Thus he rejected deliberate policies to husband North Sea oil, and instead welcomed the use of market forces and an open licensing regime. In this area, the implication was also a rejection of the BGC's approach to pricing gas below cost, but this was left unsaid.

Wherever possible, competition was to be welcomed: 'the key lies in increasing the responsiveness of these industries to the forces of the market place.' Energy, Lawson asserted, was 'a traded good'. Yet, he found room for a (very) positive statement about nuclear power, and recognized the need to carry on taking decisions about new investments in power stations. The job of government is, he argued, now very different from the past. Instead of planning to bring supply and demand together: 'the way to bring the two sides together and to ensure that they act consistently is to give them the same information and the same realistic signals.' This meant setting the right economic prices and improving information flows. But this was a temporary necessity, given, in particular, the monopoly nature of the electricity industry and the instantaneous requirement on matching supply and demand. 'But above and beyond all this, the main spur must be competition.'

Lawson already recognized the structural issues relating to the combination of natural monopoly networks and potentially competitive activities within single monolithic nationalized industries. 'It is time', he said, 'to question both the extent of the natural monopoly, and, where it can be shown to exist, the most effective means of regulation. State ownership is neither a universal necessity nor the only means of regulation.'

Two decades later, there is little to disagree with in all this: it has itself become the conventional wisdom. But, back in 1982, it was *radical*. Lawson did not pull his punches. Most of the sacred cows of the Department of Energy were attacked—what had been so clearly set out in the 1967 White Paper on fuel policy (HMSO 1967), analysed in Posner's book with the same title, *Fuel Policy* (1973) and set out in the 1978 Green Paper on Energy Policy (Department of Energy 1978). The calculation of resource costs, the coordination of investment decisions, and the central planner role in price setting were all rejected. Only the faith in nuclear power survived the Lawson attack, which, given Thatcher's strong views on the subject, was probably politically wise.

The Lawson doctrine had its ambiguities, and it is easy with hindsight to imbue it with more rigour, and more personal originality than deserved (or, indeed, claimed by Lawson himself). In particular, the 'framework' was ill-defined, and was never confined purely to competition, though, with excess supply, the other elements could be at least temporarily ignored. But such academic niceties could not disguise its intent, which was radically different from all that had made up the post-war energy consensus. It changed the *functions* of the state in the energy sector, making room for market forces where monopoly planners had been in the ascendancy since the war. It was, in reality, the culmination of a quiet intellectual revolution within not just the Conservative Party, but a more widely based arena of theorists, policy-makers and commentators. Lawson was not entirely free of Keynes' doctrine of politicians being slaves of defunct economists. His slavery had strong Friedmanic and Hayekian foundations within what was, at the time, described as the 'new right', but it also carried with it the pragmatic, market-based Conservatism which had developed from the eighteenth and nineteenth centuries.[11]

This approach has a variety of rather diffuse, and not always consistent, origins. It took the preference for free-market solutions from Friedman; the more tolerant view of monopoly from Schumpeter, who believed that monopoly profits provided the incentives of entrepreneurs and were typically transitory, and the desire for a strong framework for property rights from Hayek. These views were reinforced by the much more critical approach to government failure and the costs of regulation, which ultimately derived from Popper, and was much influenced by von Mises' informational work.[12]

Amongst the architects in Britain of the practical policy implications of these intellectual currents were a remarkably small and tight-knit group of economists, associated with the Institute of Economic Affairs (IEA), together with political theorists who stressed the link between free markets and individual liberty. The most influential were British economists Michael Beesley, Colin Robinson, Eileen Marshall, and Stephen Littlechild, all of whom were to figure significantly in the energy sector over the next two decades.

This IEA group had championed the so-called Austrian approach.[13] Most had gone through the Economics and Commerce Department at the University of Birmingham. Beesley had taught Littlechild; Marshall

---

[11] See Lawson (1980), particularly on Hayek's influence.

[12] See Friedman and Friedman (1980), Schumpeter (1943), Hayek (1948), Popper (1945, 1957), and von Mises (1949).

[13] On the political aspirations and history of the IEA, and the role that Hayek's ideas played in shaping the approach, see Cockett (1994), Chapters 4 and 5.

worked under Littlechild; Marshall published with Robinson. With Robinson at the University of Surrey, all were outside the mainstream of academic economics, and all preferred policy to theory and had little faith in detailed mathematical, statistical, and econometric analysis. Indeed, one of the attractions of the Austrian approach was that it denied the possibility of empirically testing many of its claims: the superiority of markets over governments and regulation was at best a theoretical proposition, and at worst an *assumption* (Helm 1986).

These ideas had a particular and timely resonance on governmental thinking in general, and considerable coincidence with Thatcher's and Lawson's own philosophies in particular. Their political prejudices (antagonism towards the state, to unions and to direct taxation, and an emphasis on individuals and on consumers rather than producers), the economic necessities of public expenditure control, and the excess supply conditions fitted rather neatly with the IEA position. It was a policy revolution waiting to happen. Suddenly what had been a fringe institute producing interesting papers became mainstream. Littlechild's 'Ten Steps to Denationalization' (1981*b*) had raised the game from incentives within the public sector to privatization directly, while Beesley advised the Department of Trade and Industry.[14]

Thus Lawson's radical departure took place against a fertile intellectual background, and although the full force of the new doctrine would take about two decades to be realized, and there would inevitably be setbacks and counterforces (such as the planning required to see off Scargill and the seductive attractions of nuclear power), the solid theoretical (and ideological) foundations were to carry it through, conveniently proselytized by the IEA. It was not capture as such, nor did the IEA economists determine policy, but they were influential nonetheless. And it is remarkable that some of the principal figures were to hold regulatory office for most of the 1990s. Marshall did not retire from Ofgem until 2003, and Littlechild returned in 2001 as an adviser.

If the broad theory was well developed for Lawson to draw upon, execution was more difficult. Whatever the merits of the market-based philosophy, the facts were those of state ownership and monopoly. The steps Lawson took in his two years at the Department of Energy were therefore heavily constrained—by the cloud that the NUM cast over the whole of the government, by the interlocking monopolies between the NCB, the CEGB and the Area Boards, and by the dominance of the BGC and its contractual stranglehold on gas supplies.

[14] On Beesley's influence, see Littlechild (2002).

In his two years, Lawson took an evolutionary approach, chipping away at the foundations, following the lines of his broad philosophy, but with only limited success. He began, as noted above, with oil and gas. His first piece of legislation, the Oil and Gas (Enterprise) Act 1982, had two parts: the (predominant) structural separating out of Britoil and Enterprise Oil (from, respectively, the British National Oil Company, BNOC, and BGC); and starting the (very) long process of opening up the gas network to competition.[15]

Structurally, British Gas had extended its influence well into the North Sea. As discussed in Chapter 2, it provided long-term contracts to oil companies which, in effect, underwrote the (sunk) investment costs of developing gas fields. These were a form of vertical integration, and made sense at the time,[16] although much later the collapse of gas prices in the mid-1990s and the coming of competition were to turn these contracts into significant liabilities. But BGC had not been content to stick to gas transportation, distribution and supply. It also expanded its range of interests into oil, both where oil and gas were joint products from fields, and more generally.

The 1982 Act put an end to such expansions of BGC's empire, and reiterated a little noticed, but important regulatory rule in the public sector: 'thou shalt not diversify'. The practical effect was the formation of Enterprise Oil and its flotation. Steps had already been taken in 1981 to dispose of BGC's Wytch Farm oil development under the powers in the Gas Act 1972 (see House of Commons Select Committee on Energy 1982). The further (more substantive) splitting out of Enterprise Oil merely completed the process in respect of oil,[17] but not, of course, gas, and BGC was to retain offshore interests in Rough and Morecambe Bay.

[15] Early energy privatizations and sales of holdings

Date	Company	Proceeds (£m)
November 1979	BP	290
June 1981	BP	15
November 1982	Britoil	549
September 1983	BP	566
May 1984	Wytch Farm	80
June 1984	Enterprise Oil	392
August 1985	Britoil	449
October 1987	BP	5727

[16] Interestingly, a similar contractual set of relationships has been emerging in the 2000s between Gazprom and Western European counterparts, such as Ruhrgas—see Chapter 21.

[17] Enterprise Oil was eventually taken over by Shell in May 2002.

The 1982 Act also dealt with BNOC and the legacy of Benn's state sponsorship of North Sea development. Although government ownership of oil interests was the rule rather than the exception, with rights over the seabed and its mined wealth, as well as a substantial long-term stake in BP, BNOC represented an active attempt to participate in production along the lines of the traditional nationalized industry model. It was an example of Bennite 'socialism' which Lawson was keen to eliminate.

The Act provided for the disposal of BNOC's production activities, and hence for the creation of Britoil. In introducing the Second Reading of the Bill on 19 January 1982, Lawson gave three main reasons why oil exploration and production should be put in the private sector.[18] First, 'no industrial corporation should be owned and controlled by the State unless there is a positive and specific reason for such an arrangement.' The state's role was one of regulation, not duplication through regulation *and* ownership. Second, 'privatization will be in the best interests of BNOC itself', since it could expand in the private sector free from political constraints and competition against other claims on the public purse. Third, 'we believe that the British people should have a much better opportunity to share directly in the country's oil wealth "through share ownership, not symbolic ownership"'. BNOC could not, however, be completely privatized; important pricing and trading functions remained, as well as contractual rights, and it was to limp on as a rump organization for some time.

The second part of the 1982 Act addressed BGC's supply monopoly. The rationale was focused on the incentives to explore and develop new gas reserves, where BGC's monopsony provided a barrier. Its control of the pipes as well as supplies, and its ability to discriminate in the industrial contracts market, continued to allow it to see off almost all comers.[19] There was no independent regulator (though, in the Second Reading debate, this point was raised and Lawson expressed sympathy with it), and none of the substantive issues of access regulation was provided for. This was liberalization without regulation, and its failure was to be almost total.

It is easy to argue that the 1982 Act ought to have gone further but for the parliamentary practicalities and the fact that there was little experience to draw upon. Yet, rereading the parliamentary debate twenty years later, it is striking how many of the subsequent difficulties were foreseen, and by actors who were to assume a more central role in the debates to come. Peter Rost (a key backbench advocate of competition)

---

[18] HC Deb (Session 1981–82), vol. 16, cols. 169–252.

[19] The Act provided for others to build their own pipelines to bypass BGC's system, although, again, BGC saw off the challenge.

questioned BGC's concerns that the gas may run out, and claimed that 'one of the main reasons why British Gas is opposed to this legislation is that it is afraid that so much gas will come forward from the incentive that will be provided that it will undermine the long-term contracts that it has with Norway',[20] a point that would not, in fact, be recognized until the mid-1990s, to disastrous effect on the company. Tim Eggar (a future Energy Minister) welcomed the breaking up of BGC's monopoly, though it was to be over a decade before he could preside over the completion of the job Lawson had started.

The Energy Act

The Energy Act 1983 was more ambitious than the 1982 Act, and represented a serious attempt to address the entry conditions in the electricity industry—going beyond liberalization to require the incumbent Area Boards to purchase electricity from entrants challenging the CEGB's monopoly. It tried, and failed, to facilitate competition within the context of an incumbent state-owned integrated monopoly. In many ways, the attempts by the European Commission to liberalize electricity markets in Europe at the end of the 1990s are similar, as discussed in Chapter 20. The CEGB in 1983 bore many features in common with Electricité de France (EDF): its monopoly extended from generation through to despatch and transmission. The Area Boards provided a bit more management diversity, but, in practice, as we saw in Chapter 2, the CEGB set the prices and the Area Boards acted as its agents.

The aims of the Act were to facilitate competition in generation, transmission, and supply, although these distinctions were not sharply drawn. There were three major changes to the statutes. First, it abolished the monopolies, dating back to the Electric Lighting Act 1909, which had prohibited persons other than the Electricity Boards from supplying or distributing electricity, and the Electricity (Supply) Act 1911, which had restricted generation. Second, the Act required the Area Boards to publish 'private purchase tariffs' (PPTs) at which they would purchase electricity from private producers, and, subject to technical feasibility, it required them to purchase power offered by private producers. Third, the Act required the industry to allow private producers to make use of its transmission and distribution system in order to supply electricity directly to final customers and to publish a schedule of charges for such 'use of the system'.

[20] See HC Deb (session 1982–83), vol. 16, para 203, 19 December 1982.

In the only detailed analysis of the application of the Act and, in particular, of the PPTs and their relation to the BST, Hammond et al. (1986) considered two hypotheses: that entry did not take place because the industry was more efficient than the entrants; and that entry barriers were effective deterrents. They showed that the Act was flawed, in that it left the incumbent industry with effective control of prices and entry conditions. The level of the PPTs, based upon 'avoidable costs', the uncertainty about future rates, and the fact that they were set annually, made it hard for new entrants to contemplate the risk of sinking capital into new generating capacity. In practice, the main effect of the Act was on the prices received by already existing private suppliers, notably the combined-heat-and-power (CHP) scheme at Slough Estates. PPTs tended towards short-run marginal cost (SRMC), rather than the LRMC in the BST, and failed to reward the full costs of electricity generation (notably the absence of a capacity and system service charges), with the result that the CEGB could price-discriminate between its own and private electricity supplies.

A further distortion that the 1983 Act failed to address was the relative cost of capital between the CEGB and private entrants. Not only were private producers faced with short-term contracts—and hence, could not easily hedge future price risk—but they also had to borrow at private rates considerably higher than those of the Treasury. Furthermore, the vertically integrated monopoly could invest, in the knowledge that final monopoly customers would foot the bill—a luxury which new entrants would not have. It was not a level playing field.

In retrospect, the gap between the ambitions of the Act and its practical consequences was enormous. It lacked effective safeguards and regulatory oversight. The monolithic structure of the industry, and the corresponding absence of clear disaggregated cost data, inevitably made entrants tiny Davids in taking on the Goliath. If it were not, as noted above, that the European Commission was to adopt a similar approach to EDF, and was also to fail (but, in its case, with the benefit of hindsight of the failures of the British Energy Act 1983 to draw upon), it would be tempting to regard Lawson's efforts as naive.

Hindsight, however, is not always fair. In 1983, no major utility had been privatized, nor indeed been contemplated for privatization. The Act served to provide the incentive for subsequent ministers to push on—to recognize that public ownership and dominant integrated structures could not be compatible with the promotion of competition. The legacy of the Energy Act 1983 was to provide the rationale for the restructuring and privatization of the electricity industry. Tinkering at the edges of monopoly was seen for what it was.

Finding the Right 'Chaps'

Although professing a faith in competitive markets, Lawson, like Thatcher, put particular emphasis on choosing the right individuals to carry out his policies. He wanted to find managers who were 'one of us'. Gone were the days when consensus figures would be chosen, to represent the wider public interest along Morrisonian lines. Lawson wanted partisan people, and the executives were to be chosen with a mind to the political objectives as much as their managerial competence.

The first opportunity arose when Glyn England, Chairman of the CEGB, came up for reappointment in May 1982. Lawson declined to extend his term, and made one of his deputies, Fred Bonner, acting Chairman while a suitable replacement was sought. As Lawson put it: 'I was looking not merely for the right man in the run-up to a likely coal strike and for the strike itself, but also someone who would take a fresh look at this highly secretive organization so set in its ways' (Lawson 1992: 153).

Lawson chose Walter Marshall, then Chairman of the UKAEA, and former Chief Scientific Advisor to Benn until Marshall's dismissal over the choice of reactors. Marshall had the added advantage of being very close to Thatcher, especially with regard to nuclear power. At the NCB, Derek Ezra was not reappointed in 1982. Ezra had been first appointed by Heath in 1971 and reappointed by Benn in 1977, and was held partly responsible for the debacle in 1981 over the threatened strike (see Chapters 2 and 4). For one year, Norman Siddall was made Chairman (but was forced to retire owing to poor health), then Ian MacGregor was appointed in September 1983. Marshall (the scientist) and MacGregor (the businessman) would be the team who would take on Scargill, and neither would 'wobble' under the pressures, as England and Ezra might have done (or at least that was what Thatcher and Lawson expected).

Ironically, with this team in place, Thatcher chose someone of a very different persuasion to lead the political side. Peter Walker, almost the last of those known as the 'wets' in Thatcher's Cabinet, became Energy Secretary after the 1983 election victory. He had come to political prominence under the Heath government. His career spanned finance and politics.[21] His outlook, like that of his like-minded colleague, Michael Heseltine, was solidly corporatist. Big business held few fears for him,

---

[21] He was part of Slater–Walker set up in the late 1960s, until the 1970 election. Slater–Walker subsequently collapsed in 1975. See Walker (1991: 66–72) for his account of his involvement.

and he had little taste for the radical competitive model that Lawson—and his IEA supporters—advocated. It was, however, a politically astute choice: Walker could ensure that both wings of the Conservative Party were 'on board' for the strike; he would present a more human face once the strike was under way; and he was every bit as anti-NUM and Scargill as Thatcher and Lawson were. His was a different sort of capitalism, but capitalism nonetheless.[22]

The politics of coal overshadowed everything the Department of Energy did, and until this set piece of the 1980s was resolved, little else could be achieved. Neither of Lawson's Acts produced much competition, and what immediate success they had was largely confined to the divestment of assets. Littlechild (1981b) had predicted as much: 'creating smaller organisational structures and introducing competition where possible will yield useful benefits, but to ensure that the industries have the incentive and freedom to operate efficiently requires a transfer to private ownership'. The time, however, was not politically right. First British Telecom would test the water, and the miners had to be beaten. But if the Acts themselves achieved little, they did at least start the process of implementing the market approach, and, when the election was called, Britain had a new energy policy thanks to its innovative Energy Secretary. The government knew where it wanted to go, and the 1983 manifesto reflected this: 'In the next Parliament, the interests of the whole country require Britain's massive coal industry, on which we depend for the overwhelming bulk of our electricity generation, to return to economic viability' (Conservative Party 1983).

---

[22] See Walker (1991) for his explanation of the reasons for his appointment.

4

Thatcher and Scargill—Getting off the Labour Standard

It should not be necessary to remark that a coal theory of value, though more modern, is even less acceptable than a labour theory of value: and that neither provides a reasonable basis for making policy.
(Ian Little, *The Price of Fuel*, 1953, p. ix)

One of the post-war events which shaped Margaret Thatcher's political outlook had been the defeat of Edward Heath's government by the miners. To her, the miners had come to represent not just a threat to her own government, but much that was wrong with Britain. She regarded the trade union militancy of the National Union of Mineworkers (NUM) in general and Arthur Scargill in particular as the embodiment of a socialism she was determined to consign to history. These were what she subsequently described as 'the enemy within'.

On the Labour side, the miners represented the heart and soul of the Labour Party. They personified the working class, and their unions' battles in the 1930s were heroic acts. Mining constituencies were solidly Labour. Socialism was in an important sense identified with the miners. They had seen off Heath, and now they would see off Thatcher too. The political roots went deep, as Labour was to find in the coal crisis in 1997, long after the number of miners had fallen to an insignificant level. No aspiring Labour MP could speak against the coal interest.

The battle with the miners thus represented far more than a problem of subsidy and the management of nationalized industries or energy policy. It became a symbolic struggle for the Conservative administration as a whole. The 1984 miners' strike and the government's triumph were a defining moment when Thatcherism shifted from its uneasy compromises with the Left of the Conservative Party to a more outright philosophy of competition and privatization. Although this was by no means the last gasp of the coal industry—there were to be further important convulsive spasms in 1992/93, in 1997/98, and in 2000—it was the decisive one.

The Seeds of Conflict in the 1970s

The miners' strike in 1984 was the product of both the politics and the economics of the 1970s. The politics derived from the battle with the Heath government, and the attempt to curtail union power and its associated wage inflation. The economics derived from the OPEC oil shock of 1973 and the Plan for Coal. A quadrupling of oil prices was likely to create severe economic dislocation in any industrialized country. As noted in Chapter 2, for Britain it could not have come at a worse time. Just when oil prices rose, the Heath government became locked in its struggle with the coal miners, which ultimately led to the three-day week and electoral defeat.

The 1970–74 Conservative government faced two miners' strikes in its term of office. There were several causes of the unrest in the coal industry. First, during the 1960s, the industry had undergone massive contraction, as reflected in the falls in coal production, employment, and the number of pits in operation. Second, conditions for those left in the industry had not improved in terms of pay and security of employment. The Wilberforce Inquiry, set up by the government to examine the causes and circumstances of the 1971–72 dispute, reported that miners' earnings had fallen well behind those of other workers (Department of Employment 1972). Last, the propensity to sustain the fight was fuelled by the widely held belief that the industry would soon be in a position to exploit an improved market status, with rises in oil prices making coal suddenly much more competitive. The wage claims were supported by arguments that the enhanced position depended on attracting 'young and skilled manpower'.[1]

The 1971–72 dispute followed a spate of unofficial strikes in 1970 and early 1971, leading to two crucial conference decisions in July: the first was to reduce the majority required before an official strike could be declared; the second called for a major pay claim. This was received coolly by the National Coal Board (NCB), which offered increases slightly less than the preceding year and the miners responded with an overtime ban from 1 November 1971. Following a ballot at the end of the month, the NUM announced a national strike to begin on 9 January 1972. Last-minute pay offers by the NCB before the strike began were unacceptable because the Board was constrained by the government's pay policy (as it would be until the change of government in 1974).[2]

---

[1] *Coal News*, October 1971, p. 6; quoted in Jackson (1974: 134).
[2] By the end of 1972, this took the form of a 'Statutory Prices and Pay Standstill', followed in 1973 by a 'Price and Pay Code'.

The initial confidence of the government based on coal stockpiles amassed at the power stations was soon dispelled when the relatively new phenomenon of secondary picketing prevented access to these, and the power workers threatened a dispute of their own. A state of emergency restricted consumption of electricity by large industrial consumers, and on 16 February the Department of Employment admitted that, due to the restrictions, 1.2 million workers had been 'laid off' (Jackson 1974: 139). Eventually, the government was forced to capitulate, and accept the terms set out by the Wilberforce Inquiry. The report of the Inquiry broadly supported the position of the miners, which was regarded as a 'special case' deserving special treatment. It emphasized the deteriorated position of the miners in terms of pay relativities, and the particular unpleasantness and danger associated with the work. The settlement negotiated between the Prime Minister and the NUM Executive on 19 February was to cost £100 million (NCB 1972: 35).

The second coal strike of 1973/74 was set in the context of the Heath government's macroeconomic U-turn in 1971/72 and the sharp increases in oil prices from October 1973. Having set out on the path of market-led policies (which was strongly mirrored by those of Thatcher a decade later), Heath and his Chancellor, Antony Barber, reflated the economy to address rising unemployment, and opted for voluntary income policies to contain inflation. 'Beer and sandwiches' at No. 10 had been turned into an art form by Harold Wilson in the late 1960s: Heath tried to follow a similar path in much more difficult circumstances without much success.

The 1973/74 strike began gradually and, as with so many British industrial disputes, was marred by confusion, complex bargaining, and much rewriting of history after the event. By 1973/74, optimism about the future of the industry among those within the industry itself (and, indeed, in government circles) had heightened, with increases in demand from nearly all markets. The oil price hike, which gave coal sold to power stations a significant advantage over oil,[3] seemed to provide a strong political argument for government support of the industry. From the alternative angle, however, recent industrial unrest undermined the case made for security of supply from a domestic fuel reserve. Moreover, coal was not the only domestic energy resource and would have to be competitive against other fuels, and, indeed, imported coal.[4]

---

[3] This was of the order of around £5.50 per ton in the central coalfields and between £2 and £3 elsewhere (Ashworth 1986: 330).

[4] At this stage, gas was not seen as a competitor in the power station market, and even international trade in steam coal was poorly developed.

The coal dispute of 1973/74 was again sparked off by wage demands. Inflation tends to create uncertainty about future living costs and provoke economy-wide demands for large increases in money wages. The yearly scramble for higher pay awards quickly outdated the Wilberforce settlement, and, as Ashworth points out, resulted in anomalies in wage differentials between industries (1986: 331). The claim, announced at the NUM's July 1973 conference, amounted on average to about 31 per cent, which far exceeded the incomes policy ceiling. The NCB offered what was permissible within the framework of its counter-inflation strategy: a general 7 per cent wage increase, improvements in holiday pay, and a 'threshold' agreement which added an extra 40 p per week if the cost of living rose by 7 per cent, and a further 40 p for each additional percentage point rise.

After negotiations with the Prime Minister collapsed, from which Heath won nothing but accusations of partiality, the NUM organized an overtime ban in November 1973 which developed into a national strike in the New Year. A state of emergency was declared soon after the overtime ban which was designed to restrict consumption of coal and electricity, and which enforced a three-day week for industry. In view of the deadlock that endured into 1974, the Trades Union Congress (TUC) intervened by offering that if the government waived its incomes policy stipulations in the 'special case' of the miners, no other union would invoke the settlement in support of their own claims. The government did not buy this. The NCB exploited loopholes on payments for unsociable hours, and for time spent waiting or bathing in order to increase the offer to 17 per cent, but could not secure the support of the NUM.

Notice of strike action was met by the government with the announcement of a general election to be fought on the question 'Who Governs Britain'? This was somewhat odd, given the government's working majority, and the arrangements it had already made for resolving the relativities dispute.[5] The question had been referred to the Pay Board, which reported shortly after the election, confirming that average weekly earnings of male manual workers in mining had fallen from 105.6 per cent of those in manufacturing industries in 1972 to 102.3 per cent the following year (Berkovitch 1977: 182). Moreover, it supported the contention of the NCB that higher relative pay was necessary to attract and retain sufficient workers to counter the industry's decline, especially with respect to underground workers for whom pay differentials remained important, despite the NUM's insistence on narrowing differentials (Pay Board 1974).

---

[5] See Walker (1991: 122–3) for the deal agreed between Walker and Gormley on the reference to the Relativities Board.

The Pay Board report appeared after the election results, which gave no party a clear majority.[6] The Labour Party came into office upon the Conservatives' failure to form a coalition with the Liberals, and the new Secretary of State for Employment, Michael Foot, resolved that a settlement would proceed without reference to the previous government's pay policy restrictions.

Labour Settles with the Miners: The Plan for Coal

The coal miners won much more than their wage increase when the Heath government fell and Wilson's minority government took office. In the short term, they gained a commitment to coal as Britain's solution to the oil crisis. After 20 years of decline, the prospect arose of an end to job losses and contracting output. Coal was to play a key part in solving Britain's energy problem. Although the origins lay with the NCB submission to the Conservative Secretary of State in November 1973, the Plan for Coal was given official status by Labour. But, in the longer term, the Conservatives had learned a lesson: the new party leadership, under Margaret Thatcher and Keith Joseph, was determined to prevent a recurrence. To the Conservatives, coal, although domestic and abundant, was not a secure source of supply, and energy policy had to be directed towards weaning the electricity industry off it.

The basis of the settlement was the Plan for Coal.[7] Following the 1973 submission, a revised version was prepared to be presented to the Department of Energy in mid-February 1974. The general election delayed submission, and the NCB made further changes before finally laying its proposals before the new Secretary of State, Eric Varley,[8] in April. The Plan was considered as part of the Tripartite Discussions (known as the Coal Industry Examinations) that devised the settlement to the coal dispute, and was accepted in June as a long-term strategy for the industry, subject to annual review.

---

[6] The results were: Labour 301, Conservative 296, Liberal 14, and others 24.

[7] The final settlement of the 1973/74 strike was estimated to cost £103 million (Ashworth 1986: 339–40). New minimum wage rates were negotiated of £31 a week for surface workers, £36 a week for underground men, and £45 a week for faceworkers. In addition, the NCB agreed to a premium of 19 p per hour for 'anti-social' hours worked at night, increased holiday pay, an increase in the lump sum to those voluntarily retired, and improved death-in-service benefits.

[8] Varley was Secretary of State for Energy from March 1974 to June 1975, when he was swapped with Benn to become Secretary of State for Industry.

Output was to be stabilized and then increased as far as possible towards 150 million tons by 1985. This required the creation of 42 million tons of new capacity, half of which would be found from improvements in existing mines and the other half from new ones, including the exploitation of the new Selby coalfield, and the expansion of opencast production. The cost of the Plan to 1985 was estimated at £600 million in 1974 prices. To finance the expansion, the borrowing powers of the NCB were extended to 1976, and the government was empowered to issue grants to finance stocks of coal and coke, to protect the industry from fluctuations in demand (Hall 1981: 223). The report concluded:

> We welcome the establishment of a financial framework for the industry which will give it the objective of long term competitiveness while covering its costs of production and contributing towards financing the new investment, but at the same time, recognising the special burdens of the past, the need to provide safeguards against short term fluctuations in the prices of competing fuels, and the need to take appropriate action if other public policies prevent commercial pricing or impose exceptional burdens on the Board. (Department of Energy 1974)

Implementing the Plan was hindered by various difficulties. Forward planning was subject to much uncertainty in the context of floating exchange rates which caused fluctuations in the relative prices of fuels from different sources. There were, as a result, repeated forecast revisions and postponements of the Plan. A major review was undertaken in 1976, by which time inflation had increased the Plan's capital costs by 74 per cent. Moreover, half the output from the new collieries would not be available until 1985. However, a decision was made to press forward with the Plan, and almost half the capital projects set out in it had been approved by September 1976 (Ashworth 1986: 363).

In early 1979, the Department of Energy published 'Coal for the Future—Progress with "Plan for Coal" and Prospects to the Year 2000' (Department of Energy 1979). This document was the high watermark of coal optimism, and its assumptions and forecasts were to contrast starkly with the reality that unfolded. The NCB forecasts encouraged it to advocate the objective of adding 4 million tons of new capacity *per annum* from 1985 to 2000, half to replace exhaustion, half as new capacity. Fortunately, 'Plan 2000', as it was known, was not endorsed by the government, and indeed its status within the NCB was very dubious.[9]

By now, Tony Benn had become Secretary of State for Energy, in a move widely interpreted as an attempt by Harold Wilson, Prime Minister, to

---

[9] Private correspondence with Michael Parker.

marginalize him.[10] The Bennite Department of Energy produced an energy Green Paper (Department of Energy 1978), which assumed that power station coal demand would increase to, and stabilize at around, 80 million tons per annum up to 2000, which was broadly in line with Plan 2000. (In the event, it would be less than half that number.) But, whereas Benn and the NCB/NUM might agree with each other, the political as well as the economic tide was turning. Benn could issue a Green Paper, but the Treasury held the purse strings, and the 1978 White Paper on Nationalized Industries (HMT 1978) produced a set of financial constraints which meant that Benn's arithmetic would not (and could not) add up. As detailed in Chapter 2, while Benn might dream of taking control of the commanding heights of the economy, and instituting social planning, Denis Healey had discovered monetary targets, and had been forced into a policy of fiscal rectitude and even privatization to raise money. In fact, ever since the International Monetary Fund Letter of Intent in 1976, and the cash limits which followed, the era of state subsidies for grandiose plans had been drawing to a close. Politics—and, in particular, the need to keep the Labour Left of Foot and Benn on board—had merely dictated a slower transition to a harder market test.

Phase One: Preparing for the Main Event

There can be little doubt that much of what happened in energy policy after the Conservative election victory in 1979 was a long preparation for the main event—a trial of strength between Thatcher and Scargill—although in what sense and at what stage Thatcher actually 'wanted' a strike is far from clear, and Walker claimed that he tried to avoid a strike by ensuring that there would be no successful ballot (1991: 166–9). That Scargill did is beyond reasonable doubt, as Routledge's biography makes abundantly clear (Routledge 1993). Although both were more complex characters, and occasionally more flexible, than popular history has tended to paint them, they had fundamentally different philosophical approaches. Coal provided the battleground: it was highly unionized, its union had acquired political power, it was a monopoly, it was a nationalized industry, and it made losses. Trade union reform and financial discipline demanded action against an industry that was, in economic terms, technically and allocatively inefficient. It was a matter of credibility, at a

---

[10] James Callaghan, on succeeding Wilson in 1976, left Benn at the Department of Energy, where he was 'effectively isolated or neutralized' (Morgan 1997: 480). For Benn's interpretation, see Benn (1989: 389–95).

time when it was widely predicted that the Thatcherite approach would soon produce a U-turn, as Heath had to do in the early 1970s.

The preparations were long, tortuous, and often opportunistic. Thatcher could not be seen to court a strike, nor did she want to provoke one when she might lose; she frequently told colleagues that she did not want one. The first years after 1979 were not easy ones: in Cabinet, she was in a minority with the 'wets'—including William Whitelaw, Ian Gilmour, Peter Walker, and Jim Prior—and the initial focus on the Medium Term Financial Strategy (MTFS) created a straitjacket within which the exchange rate rose to unprecedented levels, industrial output fell sharply, and unemployment rose. Up until the Falklands War in 1982, her government was among the most unpopular ever recorded by opinion pollsters, and it was a common assumption that her only hope of winning in 1983 or 1984 was that the Labour Party led by Foot would prove too extremist. So it was to prove: its manifesto was indeed referred to as the 'longest suicide note in history', but by then the Falklands War was over, and the economy was beginning to turn (except for unemployment, which kept on rising until 1986). The opportunity to return the coal industry to 'economic viability'—promised in the 1983 Conservative manifesto—had arrived.

As detailed in Chapter 3, the first steps were understandably cautious. The external financial limits (EFLs) were tightened, rendering the rationale of the original Plan for Coal redundant. The recession—and particularly the decline of large-scale intensive energy users—reduced demand further, thereby increasing the stranglehold of the EFLs. The peak demand for electricity in 1979/80 was not to be significantly exceeded for the next two decades. The Coal Industry Act 1980 required all grants, except social ones and some interest relief, to cease by 1983/84, and thereafter the NCB was to break even. The era of subsidy was to cease. As Ashworth put it, 'the financial provisions...were so drawn as to make it almost impossible to operate the industry in the way it had been operating until then' (1986: 352). The 'almost' was superfluous. The effect was to put the NCB in an impossible position: it therefore decided in February 1981 that it would be necessary to accelerate the rate of colliery closures.[11] The NUM responded by threatening to call a strike ballot, and the miners in South Wales jumped the gun and went on strike.

---

[11] There is some debate about whether this was an attempt by the NCB (and its chairman Derek Ezra in particular), to provoke a U-turn, in the knowledge that the government could not withstand a strike, or merely the logic of the position in which it found itself.

Thatcher ordered a climbdown—what Ashworth describes as a 'unilateral political decision' (1986: 417)—and the cumbersome Colliery Review Procedure, which the NCB's decision had bypassed, was reinstated. The accelerated closure programme was withdrawn, and more money was pumped in. The Coal Industry Act 1982 facilitated the new subsidy arrangements.

It fell to David Howell, as Secretary of State, to announce the humiliating terms of the climbdown following the Tripartite Group meeting on 18 February 1981. He told the House of Commons that:

As the House knows, there was a tripartite meeting of the coal industry yesterday. This had been called at the industry's request to discuss the situation which had arisen following the meeting in London on February 10th between the NCB and the unions. At that meeting the NCB had outlined its approach to the current problems facing the industry. It had put forward a four-point plan for bringing the supply and demand for coal back into the balance, whilst maintaining investment for the future. The plan included an accelerated programme for the closure of older capacity approaching the end of its productive life. This was to be discussed in detail in the areas. The Board believed its plan to be reasonable and acceptable. However, fears and anxiety among the work force arose through rumoured and distorted impressions of what was being proposed.

It was against this background that yesterday's meeting took place. At the meeting three main points were raised—closures, financial constraints and coal imports. I said that the Government were prepared to discuss the financial constraints with an open mind and also with a view to movement. The chairman of the National Coal Board said that in the light of this the Board would withdraw its closure proposals and re-examine the position in consultation with the unions. I accordingly invited the industry to come forward with new proposals consistent with 'Plan for Coal'.

As regards imports, I pointed out these would, in any case, fall this year from their 1980 levels. The industry representatives said that they wished to see this figure brought down to its irreducible minimum. I said that the Government would be prepared to look, with a view to movement, at what could be done to go in this direction.

I welcome the decision of the national executive committee of the NUM today and hope that its lead will be followed. I will be meeting the industry again next Wednesday.[12]

The government gave the miners more money, endorsed the continuation of investment under the Plan for Coal, and restricted imports.[13] There can be

---

[12] This statement is reproduced in MMC (1983*b*), vol. 2, Appendix 2.2, p. 2.

[13] Even contracted import cargoes had to be sold, at a loss of £18 million, for which the CEGB was compensated (Ledger and Sallis 1994: 96).

few examples of such a rapid U-turn in the face of industrial muscle. Thatcher had proved a softer touch than Heath. She was, however, to have another bite at the cherry.

The climbdown was seen at the time for what it was. Nicholas Ridley and others on the right had, back in the 1970s, begun to plan for coal stocks to be increased to be better prepared to face the miners.[14] At the Institute of Economic Affairs (IEA), Littlechild was already proposing a structural break-up of the NCB into twelve separate subsidiaries, with commercially viable ones to be sold to the miners at reduced cost. He also suggested the NCB should be shorn of its right to mine unexploited reserves, which would then be auctioned to the highest bidder (Littlechild 1981*b*). These ideas were to take another decade to become mainstream in the policy debate, but indicate a more radical undercurrent already circulating in governmental circles. Eileen Marshall and Colin Robinson pursued a similar line in a stream of publications.[15]

There were three steps necessary to prevent any repeat of the events of early 1981: changing the people, changing the rules for strikes, and building up stocks.

Changing the People

Changing the people was a priority for Thatcher, who had always regarded the 'one of us' test as key to getting her economic and political philosophy implemented. Her main move was to place Nigel Lawson at the Department of Energy in September 1981. He, in turn, set about replacing Derek Ezra at the NCB and Glyn England at the Central Electricity Generating Board (CEGB) with Norman Siddall (and then Ian MacGregor) and Walter Marshall, respectively. These changes are described in Chapter 3.

Both Thatcher and Lawson were very clear in their contempt for existing management. It was not just that they regarded England, and particularly Ezra, as lacking commercial expertise, but there was a more general perception of too cosy a relationship between the management and the

---

[14] Ridley's ideas, prepared for Keith Joseph, were leaked to *The Economist* and published in 'Appomattox or Civil War' on 27 May 1978, p. 21. *The Economist* claimed that the annex to the Ridley report proposed building maximum coal stocks, drawing up contingency plans for imports, encouraging recruitment of non-union lorry drivers, and encouraging dual coal- and oil-firing of power stations to deal with any 'political threat' from 'the enemies of the next Tory government'.

[15] In Robinson and Marshall 1985, the authors proposed that coal be liberalized and privatized *before* electricity. See also, Robinson (1981).

unions. Not that this should have come as the surprise Lawson claimed it was: it had become normal (as, indeed, it had been *intended* back at the time of nationalization) for the union leaders and board management to 'agree' on major decisions. Across the nationalized industries, the workers were, after all, expected to be partners, and it was therefore hardly surprising that they should behave in that way—especially after the experiences of industrial militancy in the 1970s. That Thatcher considered Ezra an appeaser (Thatcher 1995: 342), and Lawson thought that genuine business management was 'largely unknown' in the coal industry (Lawson 1992: 154–5), reflects as much a desire to break the corporatism which had pervaded the post-war consensus on the appropriate way to run the commanding heights of the economy, as the particular failings of the individuals.[16]

A major trial of strength could not be won unless the leaders were 'up to it', and both Thatcher and Lawson were probably correct in wanting more robust chairmen. Indeed, given the fiction had to be maintained that it was the NCB and not the government that was proposing the closure programme, it was essential that this was the case. When the strike came, had the Chairman of the NCB 'wobbled' under pressure, it could have been very embarrassing for the government.

On the other side, the NUM Executive was also tightening its grip on power, and stiffening its resolve. The more moderate Joe Gormley had (successfully) led the NUM through the wage claims of the 1970s and the Plan for Coal, keeping both his communist deputy, Mick McGahey, and the majority of the members on-side. In doing so with considerable skill, Gormley had made the miners arguably the most powerful union in British industrial history. Entering the 1980s, there were still bitter rivalries between 'Gormleyite moderates' and 'Scargillite militants', but the latter had consolidated their power—though, as it would turn out, never to the extent that they could command a majority in a strike ballot in 1984/85. However, the NUM commanded a sufficiently unified set of troops to humiliate Thatcher in 1981, and had solidified the Plan for Coal, on the back of rising oil prices. Despite the continued internal strife, the position at least *looked* strong.

Myths and realities, class theory and the demands of practical politics all got muddled up in the NUM. This was the period of the Bennite struggle

---

[16] Whether, by this stage, the NCB saw itself as a partner with the NUM is a debatable point. Some within the NCB clearly saw this as a more limited relationship, to avoid a strike, rather than act as genuine coequals. Others, however, probably carried over the ethos of the 1970s, with which Benn was particularly associated.

in the Labour Party, which almost saw Benn beat Healey for the deputy leadership. As party leader, Foot was seen as a 'friend' of the miners after his role in conceding to their demands in 1974. To many on the Left, one last push would see a Left-wing Labour government in office in 1983/84, and socialism entrenched in the commanding heights. With this set of spectacles, the militants in the NUM began their own preparations by electing Scargill to its leadership—a man who provided the antithesis to Thatcher. Scargill's beliefs are well documented, and were well known at the time. He had been a communist, held a somewhat crude Marxist theory of the class struggle, and believed that the NUM was a key instrument for establishing a socialist society. These broader ideological views were married with a practical proposition that he held with impressive tenacity—that pits should never be closed on economic grounds, but only when exhausted. This issue, rather than Gormley's focus on wages and working conditions, had the great merit of forcing confrontation. Whereas, in the 1970s, conflicts could be bought off through higher wages, in Scargill's NUM only surrendering to the economics would meet his demands. For Scargill, coal *output* was a given, and it was the job of government to ensure that the economy was organized so that it was burnt.

Scargill's grip on the NUM was bolstered by both his reputation and the loyalty of his men (particularly in Yorkshire), and the mastery of the internal politics of the union. Scargill could claim to have almost single-handedly invented the 'flying picket' in the 1970s, and conveniently made himself the hero of the Saltley Coking secondary picketing action in 1972.[17] There can be little doubt that some in the union adored him, and others hated him. Few had lukewarm personal feelings about him. But loyalty would not have been enough, and Scargill had internal support too. The moderate wing lost all the main union offices. Peter Heathfield replaced Lawrence Daly as General Secretary in 1984, defeating the candidate of the moderates, John Walsh.

Scargill therefore presented a formidable opponent to Thatcher. He had an ideology—Marxism; he had a principle—no pit closures; he had a firm grip on his union; and he had close-knit, like-minded union officers. Thatcher had a strongly held ideology too—a belief in capitalism; an economic principle of market-determined output; and, after 1983, a subset of Cabinet ministers who thought likewise.

---

[17] Interestingly, as Routledge documents (1993: 77), these coking supplies in Birmingham were not critical, but it was the symbolism, not the physical implications, of the closing of the gates which counted (and not just to the NUM, but also to the 1979 Conservative government).

Changing the Rules

Changing the rules was part of a wider agenda to reduce trade union power generally, but the miners were also part of the target. In the early days, Prior was in charge of Employment and was decidedly Heathite in his approach, to be replaced in 1981 by Norman Tebbit. The strategy was a cautious one of attrition: one piece of legislation after another. From the perspective of the miners, the three key changes were: the outlawing of secondary picketing, the requirement to ballot members, and the exposure of unions' assets to attack with the removal of legal immunity. The main pieces of legislation were the Employment Acts 1980 and 1982 (introduced by Prior), and the Trade Union Act 1984 (often referred to as Tebbit's Law).

Restrictions on secondary picketing were aimed at stopping the types of action which had occurred in the 1973/74 strike in the coal industry and the notorious Grunwick dispute with the print unions in 1977. More specifically, the concern was that the monopoly in coal could be linked to that in transporting coal by railways, and its burning by the CEGB. The real threat, which even Heath had avoided in 1973/74, was a concerted strike by all three groups of workers. Even the support of railwaymen would be very serious. For Scargill, the history of the Triple Alliance in the General Strike of 1926 was a potent one, and if one lesson he drew was that the TUC could not be relied upon, the other was that class solidarity meant a more general strike to bring down the Thatcher government.

A second target was balloting, which had long been on the union reform agenda, and it was to prove crucial in defeating the NUM. The wild cat strikes of the 1970s, with the infamous 'show of hands', were to be replaced by compulsory ballots. The assumption was that the need for a full ballot would give moderates in the NUM the upper hand. It was not, at this stage, envisaged that the NUM leadership might simply bypass a ballot, with the result that, eventually, the union itself split.[18] The break-away Union of Democratic Mineworkers (UDM) was still a long way off.

The third target was the legal immunity enjoyed by unions since the famous Taff Vale case in 1901.[19] By making unions responsible for the consequences of their actions, particularly when they broke the law, the government was in effect forcing compliance with the first two changes on secondary action and balloting. This was to cost the NUM dear and to place some of Scargill's actions outside the law.

---

[18] Peter Walker worked on the assumption that there would be no majority, and *hence* no strike (1991: 169).

[19] In 1901, the House of Lords upheld the Taff Vale Judgement, which ruled that a trade union could be sued and compelled to pay for damages inflicted by its officials.

Building the Stocks

The third strand in the Thatcherite armoury was the building of (uneconomically high) coal stocks at the power stations (rather than the pithead).[20] Unlike the 1970s, some features of the position played into the government's hands. The one commodity not in short supply was coal. The climbdown in 1981 meant pits that ought to have been closed on economic grounds were kept open. Uneconomic coal was piling up at pitheads. As Ledger and Sallis pointed out: 'It is ironic that the NUM's success in prevailing on the government to keep the pits open in 1981 made it inevitable that any future NUM industrial action would be disadvantaged by the high coal stockpiles that the continuing overproduction made necessary' (1994: 99).

The stocking position was increased from the pre-1981 policy of 17 million tonnes at the end of October, and 11 million tonnes in March, to a Department of Energy target set in February 1982 of 24 million tonnes for October 1982, the expected physical limit.[21] This was increased to 26 million tonnes as more space was realized (ibid.: 102). The target was achieved and by November 1983 the total exceeded 30 million tonnes. The battle lines were drawn, ready for the NUM overtime ban.[22]

The Causes of the Strike

Before setting out the course of the strike, it is important to keep a grip on the fundamentals. Much has been written about how close-run the strike was and how Scargill 'nearly won'; and much recrimination has been vented on both the UDM men who worked, and on the NUM leadership who failed to hold a proper ballot. But behind the detail, sight should not be lost of the economic hopelessness of Scargill's cause. The central question of the 1984 strike was very simple: should at least some of the uneconomic pits be closed? The case for the prosecution was overwhelming. Demand had failed to grow at the rates projected in the Plan for Coal.

---

[20] Other supplies to keep power stations operational were also important, but we focus here on coal.

[21] Henceforth, the references in the book to coal capacity refer to metric tonnes, as opposed to imperial tons.

[22] Frank Ledger led the contingency planning activities in the CEGB, supported by Edmund Wallis, who, more than any other individual, made his mark in the build-up and conduct of the strike, eventually to emerge as Chief Executive of PowerGen. The detailed planning is described in Ledger and Sallis (1994: Ch. 9). Their account of the strike is inevitably partial, both to the CEGB's role and performance, and that of Ledger. The lack of other published sources limits the ability to provide a more balanced view.

Supply continued at roughly the expected level. The consequence was coal stocks piling up alarmingly. Imports and exports made very little difference, with exports slightly exceeding imports in the early 1980s.

As Parker (2000) has conclusively demonstrated, this imbalance was already evident in the late 1970s, placing the NCB in a very different position. Scargill's 'no pit closures' position would, in the end, have meant subsidized exports. But what made matters so much worse was the structural changes to the British industry wrought by the recession in the early 1980s and the associated high exchange rates. The real underpinning of the coal industry lay in the demand for electricity. The 1980–82 recession decimated heavy industry, and, thereafter, the structure of the economy changed to one in which economic growth no longer needed ever more electricity generation. The old equation of 2–3 per cent economic growth implying about 7 per cent extra electricity generation no longer held. From now on, economic growth could be sustained by a roughly *constant* electricity generating capacity. These broad trends meant that the numbers simply did not add up, and the mounting stocks, in turn, meant even greater subsidies.

Already the long-term NUM case was being lost: investment in existing and new mines was not a sensible use of government monies; imports were getting cheaper; and the NCB's customers were, in any event, all trying to diversify away to other sources of supply, and other fuels. Faced with this arithmetic, it was never going to be easy for Scargill to argue that the pits should be kept open until exhaustion. Sympathetic academics tried to create arguments that the full economic costs of closure created a case for keeping the pits going to avoid unemployment and other social costs. But such arguments were both partial (in that they omitted from the calculations the additional external, environmental and other *costs* of mining), and were running against the tide of improving economic conditions.

A cost–benefit calculation of this type was produced by Glyn (1984), who considered the trade-off between the value of the coal and the costs of unemployment. Even if the marginal costs exceeded the average price, the revenue might still be better than the unemployment and other social benefits, set against no revenue. Such partial analyses failed to include the environmental and health costs of coal production (both of which have turned out to be very large), and to explain how this arrangement might work if applied to the economy as a whole. Miners might be less mobile in the jobs market than other groups of workers, and mining communities might be more vulnerable because of their overwhelming economic dependency on pits, but some credit still needed to be put into the account for adjustments within the labour market. Glyn's analysis did not include the implications of the financing of the resulting losses and the distortions this might cause. Within the MTFS, more subsidy for miners would mean less money for other, desirable causes. To be fair, neither Glyn nor the Scargill faction would have accepted these constraints, but then it is important to distinguish the case for and against pit closures *within* a broadly market-based economy, and the case in a planned social-ist system.[23]

Whereas, in 1981, the macroeconomic position looked dire, by the time of the strike, the economy was well on the way towards the boom of the mid- to late 1980s, productivity elsewhere was improving, and the dark days of collapsing manufacturing of 1980–82 had passed. The Conservatives were re-elected in 1983 with a large majority, and were now sufficiently confident to push on to tax cuts and wider privatization proposals. British Telecommunications was sold in 1984, the first major utility to be privatized. The strike arose in the context of what was increasingly seen at the time as a renaissance in the British economy, with a decisive electoral endorsement for market-orientated policies. Scargill's claims looked like—and more importantly could be characterized as—a throwback from the 'bad old days' of the 1970s, out of tune with the modern economy. The NUM's case, then, had little economic rationale, but much political content, and it was on these shaky foundations that it—or rather its officials—chose to fight its corner.

Phase Two: The Overtime Ban

To the NUM, the 1981 climbdown was only a temporary reprieve. Even the most hardened Left-wing unionist could see the arithmetic. There was simply too much coal being produced at loss without a market. Nor were the unions fooled by the climbdown itself: Thatcher's real interests were never much in doubt. If there was complacency on the union's side, it derived from two political sources: the belief that Thatcher would prove a temporary aberration, to be banished by a Foot–Benn government by 1983/84; and the associated view that socialist (union) solidarity would render the efforts of the CEGB to hoard coal stocks pathetically inad-equate as a more general strike loomed. It is too often forgotten that the unbroken eighteen-year history from 1979 of Conservative rule was not something which contemporaries expected. Labour was considered by many to be the dominant party, and the period of history that contempor-aries had in mind was 1963 onwards, with Heath's brief experiment with market economics ending in tears. It was not irrational to assume that

---

[23] See also Glyn (1984), Glyn and Machin (1997), and Cooper and Hopper (1988).

Thatcher's fate would be a similar one, especially given the recession it was believed to have caused, and that then Labour would return as the 'natural party of government'.

To the NUM, balloting for strike action of one form or another was everyday union politics. That is, what happened around the annual conference. Strike ballots took place before Scargill took over from Gormley, and two more around the overtime ban. It was how the Left engaged with the moderates. The July conference in 1983 voted unanimously to authorize another ballot as and when appropriate, and pay negotiations in the autumn failed to make much progress. It was naturally assumed—especially by the moderates—that this would be called before any all-out strike was initiated. An overtime ban from 31 October was agreed at the special NUM conference on 21 October. Hostilities had begun—just two months after MacGregor took up the NCB Chairmanship.[24]

Given everything that was to follow, it is important to recognize that, from the start, the NUM deliberately fought on a wide canvas, even if the real core of the dispute was narrow. The special conference wanted a better wages deal, but it also agreed 'to reaffirm the union's opposition to all pit closures other than on grounds of exhaustion', and furthermore 'to fight any further reductions in manpower levels'. With such an intransigent position, it meant that one side had to lose. Despite all the subsequent attempts at mediation and negotiation, no form of words could ever bridge this gap.

The ban on overtime was a device that suited the NUM Executive. It did not create too much hardship for the members, and it did not require an immediate ballot. (The earlier summer call for such a ballot did not say *when* it should be called.) Pressure could be exerted on the other coal union, NACODS, and it could be varied in effect through the impact on maintenance and safety. It also gave the NUM flexibility: it could see how the battlefield developed, before committing itself further. By choosing October to get started, the winter would take its toll. Perhaps it was even envisaged that the NCB, and therefore the government, would back down before the winter was out.

NACODS was not so cooperative as might have been hoped, and this was an important portent for the future. However, losses were inflicted on the NCB, stocks at power stations were reduced, though not by any serious degree (despite Ledger and Sallis's more alarmist tone, 1994)—and

---

[24] Ledger and Sallis (1994) provide a detailed account of the way the overtime ban worked and how the CEGB coped.

the National Union of Railwaymen (NUR) pledged support by January. The NUM itself had also hardened internally with the election of Peter Heathfield as Scargill's deputy.

Phase Three: The Strike

The overtime ban left both sides bruised, but still ready for the fight. The CEGB had tested its coal management policies, the NCB had seen some evidence of cracks in the NUM's position (in particular, signs that the strike would not be total), and the government had survived the 1983/84 winter with its position intact, ready to face the summer with time on its hands.

Indeed, a process began to impose itself on the battlefield. The NCB produced on cue its budget for 1984/85. The pit closure programme resurfaced, with Cortonwood in South Yorkshire providing the test case. Polmaise provided the Scottish flashpoint.[25] The NUM response was automatic: its position at the start of the overtime ban was no closures, except on exhaustion grounds. The two pits were in the Left's traditional strongholds. The red rag had thereby been waved, and the NUM responded predictably. But in doing so, it made two tactical errors, both of which were probably unavoidable, short of a humiliating climbdown. The strike began at the worst time of the year—March—with the summer ahead during which its members would lose wages, without much prospect of immediate victory. And it began without a ballot—which it probably would not have won. Whether the NCB deliberately triggered the strike at this point in time and in this manner is a matter of considerable dispute, but the effect is not. If it did, it was to turn out tactically astute.

The NUM did not call the strike; the NUM Executive merely decided to make any strike action by the regions official.[26] Within a week more than 100,000 miners were on strike. Flying pickets intimidated those more reluctant to join the fight. One miner died at Ollerton in Nottinghamshire, where the bitterness of the divisions between the moderates and the militants (mostly from Yorkshire) was at its most intense. Nottinghamshire NUM balloted and, on 18 March, declared a large anti-strike majority. From now on, the miners' divisions were explicit, and the television screens would be filled with images of battalions of police officers facing ugly scenes at working pits.

---

[25] MacGregor's role in determining the start of the strike is not clear. Walker had little regard for his tactical or presentational skills. He had 'inherited him' and questioned his political skills (1991: 173–6).

[26] The device used was the NUM's Rule 41, under which each area could call a local strike and then ask for national backing.

The NUM's tactics in Nottinghamshire badly backfired. First, intimidation failed to produce a pro-strike ballot result. The NUM Conference then called on all areas to join the strike. This was followed by the local NUM declaring that anyone on strike was officially so, and the NUM at national level then declared that this meant that the Nottinghamshire area had an 'official' strike. It was only to be a matter of time before the NUM's tactics, and the everyday hatred which divided striking miners from those they termed 'scabs', led to a formal split in the union. The UDM would not formally come into existence until 1985, but from March there were effectively two unions.

The CEGB response was multifaceted, but an important point was the increasing use of oil, right from the start. The flexibility of the CEGB's system was at last being tested, and it proved able to switch fuels within a considerable amount of its capacity. Just as the threat of competitors in markets tests the ingenuity of managers, so the threat to supplies tested Marshall's management team. Burning oil might be costly, but it conserved the precious coal stocks for the winter—especially those already at power stations. These stocks were all the more precious because ASLEF and the NUR told their members not to cross the miners' picket lines. Railwaymen also obstructed oil deliveries where these were by rail, and the Transport and General Workers' Union (TGWU) declared support for the NUM. The option that remained was road haulage, particularly in the Midlands area, using the smaller, less unionized haulage companies. A third response was to use the inherent features of an integrated transmission system, and the CEGB's Systems Operations Board, run by Edmund Wallis, coordinated this. Other responses included maximizing nuclear output by avoiding summer shutdowns.

Parker provides a calculation of the various factors which contributed to meeting the underlying coal demand in 1984/85 (assuming that this would have been the same as 112 million tonnes of coal which had been consumed in 1983/84), as shown in Table 4.1.

TABLE 4.1 How underlying coal demand was met during the Great Strike

Factor	Million tonnes
Continued working of 'moderate' coal fields and opencast	42
Switch from coal to fuel oil in power stations	38
Net stock lift	13
Net imports	10
All other factors	9
Total	**112**

Source: Reproduced from Parker (2000: 48, Table 2.16).

If these figures are right—and the net coal lift was only 13 million tonnes—then it was inevitable that the NUM's position would gradually weaken as the winter approached. Although it might hope that cold weather and peak demand would save the day, the clock was also ticking on it and its members. Scargill had chosen to take on the full might of the state, which was prepared to spend whatever was necessary to defeat him. The new laws had begun to bite, and real hardship for striking miners' families beckoned.

As noted above, the reforms of trade union law were always intended to be relevant to the NUM, and legal action started to have a serious impact on the NUM's ability to persevere with the strike in the summer. It was to take two main forms. The first was to mobilize the police to protect working miners and to keep pits clear of pickets. The second was direct action against the NUM and its assets. (There were also many violent acts, notably at Orgreave, and, most notoriously, the dropping of a concrete block off a bridge on the M4 motorway.)

The picketing position was the one which was most graphic to the general public, who witnessed the police convoys on the motorways and the television news pictures from outside the pits. The legal action against the NUM's assets took longer to bring, and led to a merry-go-round of monies moved to offshore jurisdictions. At the time, it was a complex web of intrigue, but its net effect was to demonstrate that union monopoly had been brought within the law, and that the law would be upheld in the face of a major union strike—unlike the conventional view in the 1970s.

The process began early on, and took on considerable significance through the action brought by working miners, with a ruling that the national strike was unlawful in Derbyshire, and, consequently, stopping 'official' picketing. Scargill rejected this intervention, putting himself in contempt which he would eventually have to purge. But this would not come until the end of the strike. The more immediate effect was fines: £100,000 for the union, and £1,000 for Scargill. By the end of October, the entire assets of the NUM were sequestrated.

There was only one serious fright for the government before the drift back to work began to erode the strike. This was the vote by NACODS to strike, which led in turn to major concessions by the NCB, including those in relation to the closure programme and the associated procedures. But for this exception, the war of attrition was being won and there was a gradual drift back to work before Christmas. By January, the strike was effectively over. By the beginning of March, nearly 100,000 miners were back at work. The second great miners' strike of the post-war period had failed, where its predecessor had brought down the government in 1974.

An Inevitable Defeat

Parker has described the defeat of the strike as 'in many respects, a lucky victory which owed less to careful pre-planning by government, and more to the folly of the NUM leadership' (2000). He claims that 'above all, the defeat of the Great Strike flowed from the attempts of Scargill and his militant associates in the NUM to launch a national strike without a national ballot, and to prosecute the strike by mass picketing at those collieries opposed to the strike' (p. 206). On this view, it was indeed a lucky victory.

While it is true that Scargill played his hand badly, it is hard to see that he had any other hand to play. The reason why Rule 41 was used, and a delegate conference was used instead of a ballot, is that the NUM leadership knew they would not get a sufficient majority. Hence the stark choice, faced with MacGregor's closure programme, was either to capitulate and accept what the NUM had resolutely opposed since the late 1970s, or to fight as best as they could, given the circumstances. Neither was very promising.

Moreover, while it is far from clear that the government did deliberately engineer a strike in early 1984, it had made very careful preparations ever since the humiliation of 1981. In choosing to face up to the economic realities of the coal industry and the necessity to reduce excessive output, a strike was probably inevitable. The EFLs were tightened, and hence the Treasury squeeze could only force closures. Scargill's position was precisely that there should be *no* closures on economic grounds. Without the new labour laws, without the stocking policies, without the more gentle treatment of what became UDM areas (especially over Belvoir) (see Lawson 1992: 144–6), and without the generous redundancy packages, it would have been more close-run. Parker is perhaps therefore rather too taken by the mistakes of NUM strategy (of which there were undoubtedly many) in explaining the outcome, and gives insufficient credit to the gradual but firm government strategy. Thatcher and Lawson had played a much better hand, and victory for the NUM, with hindsight, was very unlikely. Luck played a part, but one of the arts of politics is to know how to exploit the opportunities provided by opponents.

What had been achieved by the defeat of the strike went well beyond the ability to close excess capacity in the coal industry and increase productivity. The battle with Scargill was a symbolic victory for Thatcherism which has only the Falklands War as a comparator. Britain had finally left the 'labour standard': the cost pass-through from the wages that unions could extract in the nationalized industries was at an end, and henceforward prices would be determined with more of an eye to markets, with output and ultimately employment adjusting. It would take the break-up of the coal monopoly and the creation of competition in electricity generation to complete the process, and the need to prop up the coal industry would go through at least another decade of special deals and fixes. But if Lawson's speech in 1982 marked the decisive shift in philosophy, 1985 marked the real turning point in the application of the new energy policy. Thereafter, it was a matter of a (politically) managed decline, and the price of electricity could begin to be determined by the market, by supply and demand, rather than by producers and unions. The new Lawsonian 'market for energy' entailed the defeat of all that Scargill and the NUM had stood for.

In achieving this victory, the major post-war threat to security of supply—industrial action—had been removed. From 1985 onwards, threats to security of supply would remain remote for the rest of the century, and, when they emerged as a serious possibility again, they would be largely external (the supply of imported gas), environmental or caused by contractual and regulatory failures, which encouraged asset-sweating rather than investment. The only other threat came from customers, rather than workers, in the fuel price protest of autumn 2000.

5

The Nuclear Option in the 1980s—Security of Supply and National Energy Independence

[nuclear power is] a cheaper form of electricity generation than any known to man. (David Howell, HC Deb. (Session 1979–80) cols 287–304, 18 December 1979)

There should be no commitment to a large programme of nuclear fission power until it has been demonstrated beyond reasonable doubt that a method exists to ensure the safe containment of long-lived highly radioactive waste for the indefinite future (Royal Commission on Environmental Pollution, 'Nuclear Power and the Environment', 1976)

Victory in the miners' strike might have opened the way for a more full-blooded market philosophy in energy policy, but there remained ambiguities within the Conservative government over how far energy could be left *entirely* to market forces. This ambiguity was reflected not only in the differing priorities of Peter Walker from those of his predecessor, Nigel Lawson, but also between Lawson and Margaret Thatcher. The desire to weaken the grasp of the miners combined with a curious inconsistency in Thatcher's apparent faith in markets. Breaking union power was her priority: competition and markets were one means amongst many, including nuclear power and the break-up of monopolies, to create smaller companies and hence reduce the chance of national strikes.

Her soft spot for nuclear had a complexity of motives. In part, it was connected with her wider views of the military use of nuclear power as a deterrent. Opposition to the Campaign for Nuclear Disarmament (CND) and her determination to pursue the Trident programme formed part of her background. In part, it reflected a desire to emulate France, with the nationalism that underpinned its own pressurized-water reactor (PWR) programme. It probably also had something to do with her scientific background. From this complexity emerged a strong desire to promote nuclear power.

The Conservatives did not, however, inherit a void into which a new nuclear programme could simply be planted. More than perhaps any other technology, nuclear has the habit of making any minister the prisoner of past decisions. Nuclear assets last a long time and automatically create problems for subsequent governments by bequeathing them with nuclear waste and decommissioning costs. The Conservatives in the 1980s inherited the Magnox and advanced gas-cooled reactor (AGR) programmes from their predecessors. Any future choice of technique was constrained by past choices, and, in retrospect, these had turned out less well than anticipated in the heady days of the 1950s and 1960s.

Made in Britain: The AGR Inheritance

Of the various energy policy responses to the OPEC crises of the 1970s, one was the renewed impetus given to nuclear power. The shadow of energy supply interruptions and price hikes was, eventually, to leave not only a new power station, Sizewell B, but also the THORP reprocessing plant, and eventually the mixed oxide (MOX) plant. To understand the PWR decision that resulted from the Sizewell inquiry, the history of the technological changes of the 1960s and 1970s needs to be rehearsed, as well as the wider energy context, since these form the backdrop which shaped ministers' perceptions and what were in hindsight their (almost totally) erroneous decisions in the 1980s.

Magnox technology was, by the end of the 1960s, dated. The scramble began for the next generation of stations. There were basically three options: the AGR, the steam-generating heavy water reactor (SGHWR) and the PWR. The choice between these was of considerable importance: whichever technology was chosen, there would then need to be a period of sustained technical development, followed by a series of orders over which to spread these development costs. As noted in Chapter 2, Britain made the wrong choice: it was to prove probably one of the biggest investment mistakes since the Second World War. Reasons for this mistake go to the heart of British energy policy, and it is therefore worth looking at the decision in some depth, in order to inform nuclear decision-making in the current energy policy debate.

In the 1960s, it had been policy to maintain three separate groups competing for nuclear orders. However, in the light of the collapse of the consortium constructing Dungeness B (Atomic Power Constructions), and evidence that the competitive environment had not succeeded in keeping down capital costs, the government agreed in 1973 to amalgamate the whole reactor-building industry into one consortium, the National Nuclear Corporation. Management of the consortium was placed in the hands of the private General Electric Company (GEC), which held 50 per cent of the shares in the Corporation; 35 per cent was held by other private interests; and 15 per cent by UKAEA. (GEC reduced its holding to 35 per cent after the government's 1974 announcement regarding the future of the industry.)

In the mid-1960s, the Central Electricity Generating Board (CEGB) and the government adopted the AGR,[1] and orders for five sites were placed in 1970 after an exhaustive contracting round—at Hinkley, Hunterston, Heysham and Hartlepool, as well as Dungeness (see Ministry of Fuel and Power 1965). Long-term plans for a British-led reactor technology lay with the liquid metal fast-breeder reactor (FBR).[2] The 250 MW prototype fast reactor at Dounreay was ordered in 1966, became operational in 1974, and in 1977 reached its full thermal power output. The attraction of this design was that the FBR could use the plutonium, produced as a by-product of the civil and military nuclear programmes, and could extract up to 60 times more energy from available uranium (Department of Energy 1978: para 10.6). However, this project was pre-empted by the French Phénix FBR, commissioned in 1973, and the commercial market upon which further plans would have been based was not forthcoming.

In 1971, Edward Heath's government set up the Vinter Committee under the Deputy Secretary at the Department of Trade and Industry (DTI) to investigate the choice of the next reactor. The Committee completed its work in 1972, having reached few conclusions other than deciding that the UKAEA should keep investigating and developing all its current projects. With respect to the American PWRs, the Committee suggested that the objective should be to achieve 'assurance about questions that have arisen as to safety'.

Despite the tentative recommendations of the Vinter Committee's report for limited change, and the enthusiasm of the CEGB and the GEC for PWRs, it was to take the miners' strike of 1972 and the subsequent oil price rises to illustrate the vulnerability of an energy policy based upon fossil fuels. Before the oil price rises, the CEGB declared its conversion from the gas-cooled technology to PWRs. Arthur Hawkins, the new Chairman of the CEGB, announced in 1973 that the CEGB needed to order nine new nuclear power stations between 1974 and 1979, and nine more between 1980 and 1983—in effect, a plan on a par with that of the French.[3]

---

[1] The Minister for Power, Fred Lee, said: 'I am quite sure we have hit the jackpot this time.' Hansard, Official Report, 25 May 1965, Vol 173, Cols 237–8.

[2] Elliot *et al.* (1978) note that the FBR had been an ambition of the British nuclear programme from its early days. Gowing notes that, in the period from 1948 to the early 1950s: 'The only point on which there was general agreement throughout all these years was on the long term future—on the ultimate and overriding importance of breeder reactors' (1974: vol. 2, p. 266).

[3] This plan represented a considerable *volte face* from Hawkins' reluctance to concede even one extra nuclear station in 1972 on the basis of scaled-down demand forecasts.

But if the CEGB was in favour, opposition to the PWR scheme comprised an impressive and diverse list, including, notably: the Select Committee on Science and Technology, which comprised long-standing heavy-water enthusiasts; Lord Hinton; Frank Tombs, Chairman of the South of Scotland Electricity Board (SSEB) (who said he would not put a PWR on the Scottish grid); the Institution of Professional Civil Servants; and Friends of the Earth. Arguments against the programme centred around the safety of PWRs, specifically the integrity of the pressure vessel. The Select Committee said plainly, 'it is, in our opinion, for the proponents of light water technology to prove its safety beyond all reasonable doubt, rather than for their opponents to prove the contrary' (House of Commons Select Committee on Science and Technology 1974: para 19).[4] There were also concerns about the effect on the balance of payments of imported components, and the accuracy of demand forecasts upon which the programme depended (Patterson 1983: 145).

In view of the controversy (which was not dispelled until favourable reports by the Nuclear Installations Inspectorate and Walter Marshall in the late 1970s), the third nuclear programme, announced in July 1974 by the new Labour Energy Secretary, Eric Varley, was based on the SGHWR. Authorization was given for six 660 MW reactors: four for the CEGB and two for SSEB. This was a controversial decision given the views of the opposition to the design. Varley's decision went against the wishes of the CEGB, the UKAEA, the National Nuclear Corporation, and the thinking of the Department of Energy. In its defence, the government claimed that the SGHWR would 'provide power reliably, and we can proceed to order it quickly'.

With implacable opposition from the CEGB, the SGHWR was probably doomed. By 1976, its expected cost had in any event escalated to an embarrassing level, and in July, the Varley Plan was postponed as part of the round of public spending cuts resulting from the financial crisis and the International Monetary Fund Letter of Intent. The UKAEA and the CEGB urged the government to cancel the programme. As lower CEGB forecasts of between 3.4 and 1.3 per cent demand growth per year emerged, Hawkins was able to declare 'we do not need any new capacity.' The expense and the unlikelihood of exports were added as reasons to urge cancellation. However, few figures were produced by the main opponents—Hawkins and Marshall—and, if the SGHWRs were unexportable, then so was the PWR, as contracts were unlikely to be won by anyone but the market leaders—the Americans. Eventually the government gave way to the relentless pressure of its immediate advisers, and, in

---

[4] The Three Mile Island accident in 1979 was later to refocus attention on PWR safety in the US.

January 1978, announced the cancellation of the project, mindful of the warning given by Hawkins:

governments should involve themselves with the principles, but should be careful not to get into technology and say which particular route we should use to harness nuclear, otherwise they are taking on sometimes a little more than they fully understand. (quoted in Hall 1986: 129)

Although the government decided to discontinue work on the SGHWR, it was obliged to decide upon an alternative, if not for extra capacity (indeed the CEGB and the SSEB had too much spare capacity), then to avert crisis in the power station construction business. By the late 1970s, two major boiler-makers and two turbine manufacturers were on the brink of collapse without further orders. In contrast to the 2 GW a year estimated by the CEGB to be necessary to replace plant and meet demand, the government estimated 5–6 GW of work a year would be needed for wider industrial policy reasons.[5]

The government's decision, after much dithering, announced on 28 January 1978[6] was set out in the 1978 Green Paper on energy policy:

The CEGB and the SSEB were authorized to begin work immediately, with a view to ordering one AGR station each as soon as possible. The government also announced their view that our thermal reactor strategy should not at this stage be dependent upon an exclusive commitment to any one reactor system, and that, in addition to the AGR, we should develop the option of adopting the PWR system in the early 1980s. (Department of Energy 1978: para 10.5)

Behind the decision lay a furious dispute pitting Tony Benn, Secretary of State for Energy, against his own civil servants. The PWR lobby drew support from the National Nuclear Corporation on the basis of cost advantages, although they recognized that the AGR might provide a stop-gap, given that construction of a PWR could not begin until 1980. Similarly, the CEGB wished to order an AGR as soon as possible, and a PWR at a later date. Perhaps more significant, however, was the stance that the Department of Energy appeared to take. In the midst of the debate before the 1978 statement, Permanent Secretary, Jack Rampton, recommended the construction of £20 billion worth of PWRs.[7] His argument contrasted the operating experience of the American design with the commercially unproven AGRs, which he regarded as unexportable. Alex Eadie, Junior Minister for Atomic Energy, suggested that such a fate

---

[5] The total was to include a second coal unit at Drax B as well as the AGRs (see Patterson 1983: 188).   [6] HC Deb. (session 1977–78) col. 1392.
[7] There was also a plan to cooperate with Iran to build twenty PWRs, but this was apparently conditional on Britain building PWRs too (see Benn 1990: 140).

might await a PWR built to meet British requirements which would render it unique, and quite unsuited to compete in the international market—a suggestion which was to prove all too accurate.

Benn, whose view remained steadfastly that it was wrong to build an American-designed PWR, said of the episode that he was subject to 'a greater use of pressure...than I have seen in almost any other issue I have had anything to do with', and had involved a 'systematic attack upon British technology'.[8] Given his antipathy to PWRs and his views on the role of government in fostering British technologies which he had developed in the Wilson government of the 1960s as Minister of Technology, it was remarkable that Benn suffered Marshall (Chairman of the UKAEA, and a committed PWR man) as his Chief Scientific Adviser, for as long as he did: Marshall was dismissed in 1977. Benn's attitude to Marshall is summed up in his diary entry of 31 March 1977, 'He is a self-satisfied and pompous man with poor political judgement' (Benn 1990: 100; see also the entry of 20 June 1977: 171). Benn claimed that there was 'something a bit unhealthy about the relationship' between Westinghouse, the American PWR company, and the British nuclear interests, as represented by Weinstock of the GEC, Marshall, and the then Permanent Secretary to the Department of Energy, Rampton. Benn, and his Parliamentary Private Secretary, Brian Sedgemore, were highly suspicious of the control exercised by non-elected commercial interests over the choice of thermal reactor options.

Benn's isolation at the Department of Energy meant that his influence on decisions was marginal. He was also given a moderate, Dick Mabon, as Minister, who was frequently in conflict with Benn. But, notwithstanding his isolation, he did have an important point about lobbying and vested interests. British governments have proved particularly inept at making scientific and engineering decisions. 'Picking winners' has been widely viewed as disastrous. But within the planned integrated set of energy monopolies which existed in the 1970s, technological choices did have to be made, and there is no evidence to suggest that their managers were unbiased. Benn confronted an industry, important elements of which campaigned *against* the PWR and *in favour* of the PWR. The CEGB kept changing its mind. The only point on which it seemed agreed was the rejection of the SGHWR. A lesson which was not learned from this episode was that the machinery of government needed to be reformed if

---

[8] HC Deb. vol. 942, cols. 1391–408. In his *Diaries* (Benn 1990), he states that 'only the AGR can meet our needs... We have 22 years' experience of the AGR, it is publicly acceptable, it is licensed, and there is planning permission.'

more sensible 'winners' were to be 'picked'. Interestingly, as we shall see, governments proved similarly inept when it came to renewables two decades later.[9]

The upshot was that two more AGRs were ordered in 1980, and were built at the Heysham site (Heysham II) and at a greenfield site south-east of Edinburgh, called Torness. Although more successful in terms of programme and budget, neither was to add much to the already tarnished record of the AGR technology, although performance would eventually improve in the 1990s in the run-up to privatization.[10]

Early Thoughts on Waste

The problems of nuclear waste and its disposal remain as inimitable as they have always been throughout the history of the nuclear industry. The Magnox plants generated large quantities of waste—a point Marshall was to emphasize at the end of the 1980s (see Marshall 1989)—and some solution would be needed, eventually. Military waste would also need to be dealt with.

The first review of waste management resulted in the 1959 White Paper, 'The Control of Radioactive Wastes' (Radioactive Substances Advisory Committee 1959). As noted in Chapter 2, this treated the waste problem rather like other industrial cases, recommended the use of disused quarries, and dumping on the sea bed, and a relaxed attitude to emissions to air. The first serious attempt to tackle the problem was not until 1976, when the Royal Commission on Environmental Pollution (RCEP), chaired by Sir Brian Flowers, came up with a series of practical recommendations as to how waste problems should be dealt with (RCEP 1976). Specifically, it proposed that a statutory body, the Nuclear Waste Management Advisory Committee, should be set up to advise the Secretary of State on technical matters, and that a separate Nuclear Waste Disposal Corporation should have the responsibility of dealing with the waste, financed by an industry levy. The Flowers Report was based on a fundamental functional principle: that the advice of *how* to deal with the problem should be separated from the carrying out of the chosen waste handling and disposal policy. That, in turn, would separate science, politics, and economics from delivery. (It was a principle which might have helped to avoid the problems of the choice of reactor, too.)

---

[9] See Chapter 19 on the definitional issue of renewable technologies in policy design.

[10] Additional uncertainty in the choice of reactor design was added by the Three Mile Island accident in Pennsylvania in March 1979.

In this fundamental principle, Flowers was right, and over two decades later, that judgement was again confirmed by the House of Lords Select Committee on Science and Technology 1999 report on the 'Management of Nuclear Waste'. Being 'right' is not, however, any guarantee of being implemented, and the Labour government of the 1970s chose instead to create a flawed organizational structure, focused on the Radioactive Waste Management Advisory Committee (RWMAC) in 1978. To this, the Conservatives added the Nuclear Industry Radioactive Waste Management Executive, which became a limited company, Nirex, in 1985.[11]

At each stage, politicians have sought to combine the perception of action with the practice of inaction. No Secretary of State would want to take a decision on matters such as a deep depository if it could be reasonably postponed. In the 1990s and 2000s, John Gummer, for the Conservatives, and Michael Meacher, for Labour, would each defer a decision.[12] A series of *ad hoc* decisions replaced a clear strategy (House of Lords Select Committee on Science and Technology 1999: 10). The creation of Nirex was one such example—intended to think about a solution, rather than implement a decision. Indeed, as we shall see in Chapter 10, despite radical plans for a new Nuclear Decommissioning Authority, no decision on the disposal of long-lived waste has yet been made, nor indeed is it likely to be made in the near future.

THORP

THORP, the nuclear reprocessing plant at Sellafield, was a component within the more general nuclear strategy. Whilst the CEGB concerned itself with Magnox, AGRs, and PWRs, from the early post-war years, the FBR had been the goal to which nuclear technology strove. The idea of almost limitless energy from a plant which would literally breed its own fuel was one which captured the imagination of nuclear engineers and politicians (including, notably, Thatcher). The experimental plant at Dounreay was one step towards this goal; THORP would provide the plutonium.

---

[11] Nirex's history was not to be a happy one. In the late 1990s, its advocacy of a deep depository proposal was subject to considerable criticism. Indeed, its own internal investigation revealed: 'The overall process for developing proposals for a deep waste depository at Sellafield adopted by Nirex in the nineties was damagingly unclear... Lack of clarity about the relationship between scientific investigations and the decision to introduce the concept of an underground rock laboratory within the programme...the site selection process leading to Sellafield was not transparent' (Nirex 2001: 7).

[12] This was not a uniquely British exercise in dithering. The US Nuclear Waste Policy Act 1982 directed its Department of Energy to research sites for a deep repository, but only in 2002 was the choice of the Yucca Mountain brought to the decision point.

THORP, however, did much more than manufacture an input—it 'dealt' with nuclear waste. It could solve two problems in one plant. With the oil price hikes in the 1970s (assumed to be a permanent feature of the energy landscape for decades to come), with the eventual run down of oil supplies, and with militant (and expensive) miners, the *general* case for nuclear was much enhanced. To add the specifics of an even better technology *and* a 'solution' to waste management provided what many in the nuclear industry, and quite a lot of politicians too, thought was a cast-iron case. Indeed, some continued to believe in it as virtually all the background trends moved against nuclear in the 1980s and 1990s—low prices, abundant supplies of fossil fuels and the demise of the threat from the National Union of Mineworkers (NUM).

As we saw in Chapter 2, the nuclear lobby had rarely bothered too much with economics, and its vision of a nuclear power base for the British economy extended far beyond that of conventional reactors. At its heart were the FBR, THORP, and plutonium. Conventional reactors, such as the PWRs, would be needed now, providing spent fuel to be reprocessed, which would then be burnt in the FBR. This vision had a concrete reality, with the Windscale Inquiry chaired by Mr Justice Parker, which reported in 1978 (Department of the Environment 1978), giving the green light to THORP, and with UKAEA building the prototype FBR at Dounreay on the far north coast of Scotland (see Williams 1980: ch. 11). It was one complete vertically integrated chain, from the CEGB's supply monopoly, through conventional nuclear power stations, to THORP and then the FBR—a planner's vision of perfection.

Such a bold plan, and its associated vast and inevitably very uncertain costs, required a political commitment to be sustained over several decades—perhaps even centuries. The nuclear economy required acceptance by the governing class, with consensus providing a secure investment environment. It could not be delivered flexibly, since flexibility would inevitably undermine the sunk costs and create uncertainty, raising the cost of capital to the ancillary industries. The private sector would not buy into this level of risk—either a government guarantee or long-term contracts with customers would be needed, like Ulysses, to bind the country to the mast of the nuclear future, and for a very long time to come.

At least four countries looked capable of making such political commitments: the United States, France, Japan, and Britain. Three of these were military nuclear powers, and hence had, for defence reasons, an involvement in nuclear technology which would in any event be binding for decades to come. France and Japan had no significant natural resources, and hence were exposed to oil price shocks and embargoes, which the OPEC episode in the early 1970s had painfully reminded them of. All had pretentions to become nuclear technology leaders. (Others, like Germany, Belgium, and Sweden would follow a nuclear path, but without reprocessing and FBRs.)[13]

The major difference amongst this group of leading nations was the political culture and the nature of the political system. Only Britain had a powerful anti-nuclear group, CND, and a political Left which was anti-nuclear. Any investor in British nuclear power in the 1970s and 1980s had to contemplate a government sometime in the future which might contain a Foot, Benn, or Kinnock. Although Labour politicians had signed up to nuclear power in the 1970s (notably Benn, who was once a strong advocate), the politics had always been volatile. How could their compliance be relied upon into the future?

This ambiguity was to prove part of the programme's undoing. But Britain's overall approach to industrial policy played a part too, as did its civil servant culture and the role of the Treasury. The inherent ability to pick holes in large-scale plans, and to avoid large-scale public commitments, were features of British policy formulations, which have their echoes in more recent debates about rebuilding the railways and the London Underground (Helm 2001a). As France and Japan were to demonstrate, the costs of nuclear are such that probably only a full-blown programme could reap sufficient economies of scale. In an important sense, nuclear is an all-or-nothing technological option. The cost of flexibility (one-at-a-time, different technologies, keeping options open) might suit politicians as expedient, but was to prove the most expensive way forward. Walker (1999) has argued that THORP in particular provided an example of 'policy entrapment', and the flexibility should have been built in throughout the programme's development. However, this is to misconstrue the nature of commitment in public policy: in reality, to follow Walker's approach would have been very costly. The right thing to do was to commit or not. As it turned out, at the end of the 1970s, 'not' would probably have been the right answer.

THORP was the child of the 1970s, based upon assumptions about fossil-fuel price escalation, a shortage of uranium, and technological optimism over the FBR. These assumptions were set out in the Windscale Inquiry (Department of the Environment 1978). Like the Plan for Coal of the same period, all the main assumptions turned out to be wrong. But at

---

[13] Sweden's commitment to nuclear power was undermined by a referendum endorsing closure, and from 1998 Germany's Red–Green alliance also adopted a phase-out policy, though in both cases the implementation has not been pursued as a matter of urgency.

least the uncertainties were recognized in THORP's case, and the sunk-cost nature of the project was clearly underwritten by contracts with its three main customers: Japan, Germany, and Britain's domestic nuclear industry. These contracts covered an initial operating period and allowed the capital costs to be recovered once the plant became operational. For Japan especially, but also for Germany, THORP represented an option. It bought time whilst their own waste strategies were developed—in Japan's case by building its own reprocessing facility and in Germany's case in searching for an acceptable storage solution.

But whether or not the contracts recovered the sunk costs, it remains far from clear that the Windscale Inquiry properly evaluated the proposal. Walker (1999) provides an excellent summary of the decision-making process which followed the Inquiry—the absence of serious parliamentary consideration of the issues of substance, the secrecy of the project, and the determination of the nuclear establishment to see the project delivered. None of these would provide reinforcement for the commitment that would need to be made for decades to come, helping to weaken it subsequently, as was to be revealed in late 2003 in the political debate on THORP's closure. But, for the time being (i.e. the early to mid-1980s), it seemed that Britain could deliver on the next generation of nuclear power, even if it did not, to Thatcher's regret, quite have the stomach for the French-style large-scale commitment to PWRs.

Switching to the PWR: The Plan for Ten

While Britain persisted with the AGR, the French had opted for the American-designed PWR.[14] Very much with the French model in mind, the politicians and the CEGB moved belatedly to embrace the PWR too. As described in Chapter 3, the incoming Conservative government's policy on nuclear power was set out in a statement to Parliament made by Secretary of State for Energy, David Howell, on 18 December 1979.[15] The statement formalized plans which Howell had put before the Cabinet in October, and announced a substantial nuclear programme of thermal reactors amounting to 15 GW of capacity, or ten power stations. One power station a year was scheduled from 1982, and, although no clear decision on reactor type was made, the PWR design was broadly favoured because it passed safety requirements. Howell expressed his confidence that nuclear power was 'a cheaper form of electricity generation than any other known

[14] See Price (1990: 47–61) for an overview of the French programme and key decisions.
[15] HC Deb. (session 1979–80) cols. 287–304.

to man'. The Cabinet minutes show that the security of supply provided by an extended nuclear programme was regarded as a potential weapon against the miners in the event of a strike: 'A nuclear programme would have the advantage of removing a substantial portion of electricity production from the dangers of disruption from industrial action by coal miners or transport workers' (O'Riordan *et al.* 1988: 3).

Almost as soon as the vast programme was announced, the Energy Select Committee held hearings in 1980 on the policy statement, reporting in February 1981 (House of Commons Select Committee on Energy 1981*a*, see especially paras 11–13), and this was followed in May by the investigation by the Monopolies and Mergers Commission (MMC) into the CEGB's record in making decisions about investment (MMC 1981).[16] The Committee's report recognized a strong economic case for cancellation of the two second-generation AGRs: Heysham and Torness. This opinion was informed by evidence of falling demand, by suggestions that the SSEB had 73 per cent excess capacity (to which Torness could only add), and by escalating construction costs due to additional safety features and high bids for supplying materials. (The additional costs of constructing an AGR were estimated at 25 per cent in the year to April 1980.) The report was also highly critical of the CEGB's demand forecasting and investment analysis. It concluded:

In view of the inevitable uncertainties of the Board's key assumptions, the obscurity of the presentation of much of the relevant information, and the Board's less than satisfactory attitude to cost comparisons, we remain unconvinced that the CEGB and the government have satisfactorily made out the economic and industrial case for a programme of the size referred to by the Secretary of State. (House of Commons Select Committee on Energy 1981*a*: para 71, p. 43)

The MMC was also critical of over-optimistic appraisal techniques, reporting that:

A large programme of investment in nuclear power stations, which would greatly increase the capital employed for a given level of output, is proposed on the basis of investment appraisals which are seriously defective and liable to mislead. We conclude the Board's course of conduct in this regard operates against the public interest. (MMC 1981)

The case made by the CEGB in defence of the programme was based on constantly shifting sands: its own demand forecasts. Given the duty to supply—which was to play such a role in the debate over nuclear within electricity privatization—the CEGB could essentially 'predict and provide'.

---

[16] See also Henderson (1981: 15–19) for a critique of Howell's statement and nuclear policy more generally.

Since it argued (erroneously) that nuclear was cost-competitive (and, correctly, that it added diversity), the demand forecasts determined the nuclear investment requirement. Nuclear enthusiasts—then as now—too often argued from the conclusion to the evidence, not the other way around.

The forecast that prompted Howell's statement estimated a peak demand in the winter of 1986/87 of 52 GW. This had fallen by 7 per cent within seven weeks. By 1980–81, the CEGB's Development Review projected a level of electricity demand that would be met by 24 GW (reduced from 35 GW) of nuclear capacity by the year 2000 (Hall 1986: 176). The comparison of nuclear power against other fuels was also based on questionable predictions of the value of key variables. For instance, the CEGB assumed that the price of coal would increase by 50 per cent in real terms before the end of the century, excluding the possibility of fixed-price contracts. Moreover, the calculations were also questionable regarding load factors and completion times for construction.

By 1981 the government had scaled down the nuclear commitment in the face of the criticisms outlined above. The Under Secretary of State, John Moore, said on 1 February 1982 during a debate on the Committee's report, 'the government are not in the business of a 15 GW, ten year programme.'[17] The Select Committee report, 'The Government's Statement on the New Nuclear Power Programme', indicated that any new power station ordered would now have to be justified on its own merits (House of Commons Select Committee on Energy 1981a). The government's indecision reflected the absence of assurances on costs from the PWR advocates where progress had been hampered by design adjustments 'to meet British needs', rendering the project far more expensive than predicted. Marshall was brought back in from the cold in April 1981 to put the programme back on track, and, in July 1982, he became Chairman of the CEGB, partly in order to present the case for the British PWR at the Sizewell Inquiry.

The Sizewell Inquiry

The Sizewell Inquiry was unprecedented for its length, beginning on 11 January 1983 and ending in March 1985 with the report delivered to the Energy Secretary on 5 December 1986, cost (over £25 million), complexity and the length of the Inspector's report (3,000 pages).[18] The terms of reference were vague: indeed, it seemed that the government almost

---

[17] HC Deb. (session 1981–82), vol. 17, col. 98.

[18] Decision-making for large capital projects through the public inquiry route was not, however, abandoned after Sizewell: the Heathrow Terminal 5 inquiry was to replicate many of the problems fifteen years later.

wanted guidance from the inquiry in order to determine its policy priorities (O'Riordan *et al.* 1988: 4). In answer to a question about the terms, Howell replied:

On the information so far available to me it appears the following points are relevant:

(a) the CEGB's requirement for the power station in terms of the need to secure an economic electricity supply and having regard to the government's long term energy policy;
(b) the safety features relevant to the design, construction and operation of the station and in particular the view of the Nuclear Installations Inspectorate as the licensing authority;
(c) the arrangement for waste management, in the light of the views of the authorising department;
(d) the implication of the proposed development (including both construction and operation) for agriculture and fisheries, local employment, water supply and disposal, transport requirements, coast protection, housing and public services generally, and local amenities and in particular areas of special landscape value of nature conservation interest. (HC Deb. col. 128, 22 July 1981)

Although this statement did not represent a formal specification of the terms of the inquiry, it did indicate that ministers were prepared to concede a broad remit to the Inspector, Sir Frank Layfield QC,[19] in the hope that it would provide a generic judgement on the PWR technology, thereby smoothing the path for subsequent proposed stations. Questions that fell under the scrutiny of the inquiry therefore included the future of the coal industry, the role of electricity supply in the government's overall energy strategy, the disposal of nuclear waste, the problem of decommissioning nuclear power stations, and the CEGB's costing methodology—in other words, much of *energy policy*. Although subject to much criticism, Layfield deserves some credit for largely confining the inquiry to the arguments for and against a major shift in Britain's electricity generation to an American-designed nuclear technology, implying the abandonment of the British nuclear tradition which Benn had trumpeted.

The CEGB, under Marshall's leadership, took the lead. It had to demonstrate the need for additional capacity and then show that the PWR was the best option (CEGB 1982). Once it had shown that demand would exceed supply, its duty to supply implied investment. Its role was that of

---

[19] Layfield was a leading planning barrister, whose previous experience included the Greater London Development Plan (1970–73) and as counsel to the Town and Country Planning Association at the Windscale Inquiry.

an advocate, not an impartial servant of the public interest in the Morrisonian mode. There was no separation of technical advice from industry interests. Its role was not to present balanced evidence, but rather to gather all the arguments in favour, and rubbish the opposition. Its resources relative to the opponents were overwhelming, and it is remarkable that it failed to convince quickly and decisively. The case presented by the CEGB in favour of the PWR made much of alleged cost advantages relative to coal, the only serious alternative considered—combined-cycle gas turbines (CCGTs) did not figure. The CEGB claimed that it could build a PWR in seven years, compared with the minimum nine years taken by the Americans. Not surprisingly, given the recent history of nuclear power station construction, this was received with some scepticism. Sir Alistair Frame, who had been involved in the UKAEA's earlier construction programmes, said that he found nothing in the CEGB's track record which would lead him to believe that the project could be completed to time or to cost. Moreover, the projections for nuclear costs and the estimates of the costs of alternatives (largely coal), as well as its fuel price predictions, were questioned. The 1981 MMC inquiry, discussed in Chapter 3, had cast serious doubt on the CEGB's forecasting and planning. Independent criticisms, notably from MacKerron (summarized in MacKerron 1984) and Odell, who argued that oil prices would fall towards the end of the century (the CEGB predicted an increase), further undermined the CEGB's case.[20] Others took a much more benign view. Notable amongst these were Evans, who argued that 'there is a 60 per cent chance that Sizewell B will prove to be justified on economic grounds. More importantly . . . the expected value of the project turns out to be large and positive' (1984: 288).[21]

Notwithstanding the major flaws in the CEGB's case and the Chernobyl explosion which occurred on 26 April 1986 in the Ukraine in a Soviet-designed RBMK reactor towards the end of the Inquiry, Layfield eventually found in favour of Sizewell B. The burden of proof in practice lay with the opponents. On 12 March 1987, Walker announced his decision to give the go-ahead to Sizewell B on the grounds that construction of the power station was undoubtedly in the nation's interest, and that there was no practicable alternative to construction,[22] notwithstanding that by then oil prices had in fact collapsed.

[20] See the Layfield Report (Department of Energy 1987), and O'Riordan *et al.* (1988: ch. 6) for a summary of the economic case. See also Pryke (1987).

[21] All these estimates were before the arrival of gas and CCGTs as the alternative, and Evans was to take a very different view in the 1990s and, in particular, in the 1994 nuclear review.

[22] HC Deb. (Session 1986–87) vol. 112, col. 475. Walker was strongly pro-nuclear—see his account of the Sizewell decision (1991: 117–18 and 198).

The Economics of Nuclear and the Lessons from the Sizewell Inquiry

What strikes one in retrospect about the Sizewell Inquiry and the subsequent decision by Walker is how intelligent people, confronted with literally feet of evidence, could get the answer so badly wrong. Sizewell B, as a sole PWR, was to prove every bit as expensive as its critics suggested, and to run into many of the problems its predecessors had done. There was a whole history of past mistakes to draw upon. Not once since the first White Paper in 1955 (Ministry of Fuel and Power 1955) had nuclear delivered what was promised. Nuclear power was not 'too cheap to measure', but it certainly was difficult to ascertain its true costs. The industry had absorbed many of Britain's best brains and engineering skills, much of its primary research budget, and an unquantified (and probably unquantifiable) subsidy from customers' bills.

As noted above, the AGR programme had been fraught with difficulties. The generally poor performance of the AGRs was augmented by stark and poignant examples. In the 1965 White Paper on 'Fuel Policy' (Ministry of Fuel and Power 1965), Dungeness B costs[23] compared very favourably with the Drax coal power station project and even oil at Pembroke. These encouraging estimates had led the government to give the go-ahead for a new nuclear programme, starting with Dungeness B. The project turned out to be a disaster—so much so indeed that Thatcher and Lawson bet on the apparently oft-repeated Department of Energy claim that it would be on stream 'within six months' (Lawson 1992: 167). It was, in the end, to take 22 years to come on stream.

It is worth rehearsing the 'mistakes' made in the Sizewell report. These included the limiting of the choice of technology to that between coal and PWRs, and the associated failure to anticipate the move to gas and the CCGTs (which would begin before privatization in 1990—just two years after the Sizewell decision). The report lacked serious consideration of environmental problems, and had little by way of a detailed examination of the waste issues and the related THORP and MOX consequences, relying instead on the assumption that THORP would provide a viable waste-management option. The significant first-of-a-kind costs were not fully appreciated, despite the evidence of Magnox and AGRs. This was in part due to the further assumption that Sizewell B would be followed by other PWRs. Finally, and crucially, as noted above, the assumptions about fuel prices were flawed, despite the fact that, by the time Layfield had finished, the oil price had collapsed.

[23] These were estimated assuming a 7.5% discount rate, a 75% load factor, and a 20-year life.

In practice, no new coal stations were to built in the 1980s or 1990s, and almost all new capacity was to be gas. As already remarked, peak demand in 1980 was not significantly different from that in 2000. Thus, overarching all the above failures, it turned out that, not only was Sizewell uneconomic compared with the alternatives, but very little new capacity was needed *at all*—whether coal, nuclear or gas. Rarely has a decision been taken upon such an erroneous view of the next decade—especially when virtually all the key investment decisions depended upon government and regulatory policy.

What Sizewell illustrates most graphically is how hopeless both the government and the planning processes are at adjudicating between technologies. Here was Layfield, a lawyer, presiding over a fundamental investment decision at a time when the conventional assumptions underlying post-war energy policy were collapsing around him. The context for Sizewell had been the oil shocks of the 1970s, not the collapse of the mid-1980s and the coming on stream of large quantities of cheap gas which could be burnt in CCGTs. The energy world of the early 1990s would have been a foreign one to the conventional wisdoms of the Sizewell team. The best argument for Sizewell B—climate change—was not given much prominence either.

The most plausible explanation of the Sizewell decision is that it is exactly what one would expect given the interests and relative informational and resource advantages and disadvantages of the participants. The case for Sizewell B was supported by the government generally and the Department of Energy in particular. The Department of Energy had, in turn, long been captured by the CEGB, which was determined to pursue the PWR route. Industry-based ministries—whether energy, agriculture, or transport in their various post-war guises—all ended up being the advocates of producer interests, and the Department of Energy's dependency on coal and nuclear interests is analogous to the agriculture department's dependency on the National Farmers' Union.

The CEGB behaved at the Sizewell Inquiry as would be predicted of a monopoly state-owned industry. As discussed in Chapter 2, the incentives on such industries are to maximize output, and to promote managerial interests in new, large-scale technologies. The CEGB did what its top managers wanted (and Marshall in particular, for whom science always had priority over economics, and for whom the future was nuclear)—it presented scenarios that put the PWR in the best possible light.[24] It argued that capacity was needed to fulfil its obligation to secure supplies; it

---

[24] Marshall was to tell the Energy Select Committee in February 1990: 'I have tried for a quarter of a century to persuade this country to build reactors that work' (House of Commons Select Committee on Energy 1990: 8).

argued a high oil price scenario. The Morrisonian ideal of nationalized industries pursuing the public interest had been subverted to the interests of the few.

The planning process allowed the CEGB to take the lead, and its resources enabled it to train the best minds on arguing its interests, and attacking its critics. It did this with considerable skill and would do so again at the Hinkley C Inquiry which followed shortly afterwards.[25] The real lesson from the Sizewell Inquiry was that energy policy questions, such as the Sizewell one, should not be left to planning inquiries to determine, and, as long as there was a Department of Energy and a monopoly CEGB (rather than an independent energy agency or similar body), decisions would reflect their producer and managerial interests. It is notable that, since both have been dismantled, neither the privatized successors to the CEGB nor the DTI pushed for the building of PWRs in the 1990s. Only in the 2000s did British Energy start to campaign for new stations to be built, and then only when its financial position had become precarious and its British diversification strategy had failed. Similarly, it was not until 2002 that a DTI minister—Brian Wilson—was again supportive of its ambitions to build more PWRs and this probably cost him his job and found little support in the 2003 energy White Paper.

The Nuclear Legacy at Electricity Privatization

But perhaps the most enduring lesson of the Sizewell episode is that any energy policy which requires governments to pick and choose between competing technologies is extremely vulnerable to changes in market fundamentals. Then, as now, energy policy tends to assume that the technological options are *given*, and that the paths of fossil-fuel prices and consumer demand can be predicted. The Sizewell process assumed the options were coal or nuclear, failing to anticipate the dash for gas, and that fossil-fuel prices would rise not fall. Other technologies, such as fuel cells, hydrogen and solar, which might have a significant role in the first half of the twenty-first century, were effectively dismissed. What the nuclear dimension added in policy terms was not only the technical winner, but also the peculiar economics which made a large-scale nuclear programme more economic than the one-of-a-kind piecemeal approach. Britain, unlike France, lacked the political framework and consensus to carry through such a large-scale and long-term commitment. It turned out to be more like Sweden and Germany—subject, in other words, to doubts.

---

[25] The Hinkley C Inquiry was set up on 21 March 1988 and reported in 1990 (HMSO 1990).

With competition and liberalization as its driving principles, as we shall see in Chapter 7, the privatization of the electricity industry was to spell the end of the civil nuclear programme in Britain in the 1990s. Confronted with the test of writing a prospectus which set the assets next to the liabilities, it would eventually be revealed just how uneconomic successive nuclear programmes had been. No new nuclear power stations could withstand the economic requirements of a purely private market, and it was to be one of the major contributions of the privatization of the electricity industry that the nuclear lobby would be confronted with the economic realities rather than the illusory world view presented to the Sizewell Inquiry. Compulsory take-or-pay contracts, and liabilities support and insurance would all be needed if the nuclear option was to be reactivated.[26]

---

[26] In the United States, the 1957 Price–Anderson Act placed the risk of liability for nuclear accidents with the state beyond an initial threshold, and the disposal of waste is a state responsibility. Thus, the role of the private sector is as builder and operator only. In effect, the US nuclear industry risk therefore is not in the private sector.

6

Missed Opportunity—British Gas Privatization

> in the gas case the initial legislation and authorization were so anti-competitive that Ofgas and the MMC will find it difficult to substantially improve matters. (George Yarrow, 'Does Ownership Matter?', 1989)

It has become a conventional wisdom that the privatization of British Gas was a victory for old-guard monopolists, and that the failure to break it up and create the structural conditions for a competitive market was a missed opportunity. The doctrine of national champions won the political debate, such as it was. Peter Walker, then Secretary of State for Energy, and Denis Rooke, then Chairman of British Gas, saw off the challenge from Nigel Lawson, Chancellor of the Exchequer, and supporters of his market for energy.

With hindsight, this conventional wisdom is almost certainly correct, and the fraught history of the struggle between British Gas's directors and the regulators was the direct consequence. It was to take three Monopolies and Mergers Commission (MMC) inquiries and a further Gas Act to undo the mistakes made in 1985 and 1986, with the gradual emergence of a structure over the subsequent fifteen years, at least some of which could have been put in place back in 1985. Only in 2001 was the final part of the restructuring—the break-up of Transco into the National Transmission System (NTS) and the local distribution companies—to be considered, but only partially achieved through regulation in 2002. It is therefore likely that the years of excess supply—when a disaggregated structure would have best 'sweated the assets'—will have been those where an integrated monopoly dominated, whereas facing the prospect of imports and problems in ensuring sufficient supplies in the coming two decades will be ones in which the fragmented structure will dominate, notwithstanding the subsequent merger in 2002 of Lattice, the owner of Transco, and the National Grid Company, and Centrica's piecemeal vertical integration.

Yet history has tended to simplify and gloss over the real difficulties that faced officials and ministers at privatization. Back in 1985, when the debate took place, the ideas of full retail competition, and of the complete separation of supply from transmission and distribution, were still largely confined to economic theory and think-tanks. The information technology to support customer switching had not yet been invented. Then, too, the idea of floating off several new companies created out of the monopoly was a daunting one. With hindsight, capital markets were subsequently to prove able to absorb transactions on a massively larger scale, culminating in mergers and takeovers in excess of £100 billion in the 1990s. But this was after the bull market had really got going and the full consequences of financial liberalization had emerged. There was also the important matter of parliamentary and election timetables. Getting British Gas privatized ahead of the 1987 election restricted the scope for radical surgery. A break-up would have taken at least a couple of years to effect, and bring to the market—as electricity was subsequently to demonstrate.

This chapter reviews the main factors that contributed to this policy 'mistake'—how the monopolists won the battle in 1985. (Chapter 13 explains how they eventually lost the war in the 1990s.) The background to privatization, and, in particular, the monopolistic nature of the creation of the natural gas industry and its North Sea contracts, are set out. There then follows an account of the break-up debate, and the ways in which the arguments for competition were squeezed out by a combination of political manoeuvring, ambiguity over national champions, and managerial influence. The privatization itself shaped many of the attitudes towards the subsequent programme of asset sales, and this legacy is described. Finally, the initial structure of regulation is set out, which set the scene for so much subsequent conflict.

The Background to Privatization

British Gas was the most modern of the energy industries, being largely a result of the North Sea discoveries of natural gas. Its origins, however, lay in town gas, in the conversion of other fossil fuels (mainly coal). Town gas was, as its name implied, a local affair, with gas holders as the familiar manifestation in the skyline of many urban areas. It was an industry with a very limited market, and an even more limited future. For the gas industry, the traditional, coal-based foundation provided a constraint which it needed to break out of, and before the advent of natural gas from the North Sea, options were already under consideration. These boiled down to just three: new methods of coal conversion (new plant technology); oil feedstock substitution for coal; or liquefied natural gas (LNG) suppliers (see Corti and Frazer 1983: ch. 1).

The latter was the serious option and one which other developed countries without their own natural gas supplies were to adopt. The Canvey Island terminal began taking Algerian supplies in 1964, with a pipeline taking supplies to Leeds and elsewhere. In the absence of domestic supplies, and because it could be stored, LNG provided a realistic way of not only augmenting supplies, but managing peak demand.[1]

The discovery of British supplies of natural gas transformed the industry. Surveys of the east coast began in 1962, and the first round of drilling licences were allocated in 1964, with BP making the first discovery in 1965—West Sole, off Humberside. By the late 1960s a clear opportunity arose to break out of the industry's post-war straitjacket. Management grasped this, and a highly successful conversion programme began in the late 1960s (HMSO 1967). It required a new pipeline network and the replacement of domestic appliances and commercial boilers because the calorific values were quite different. It required an overall vision, the commitment of capital and a coordinated engineering effort. The public sector could carry the risk on the back of the monopoly and the guarantee of the Treasury. The project took almost a decade, and, as an example of the planned creation of a new infrastructure, only the building of the national electricity grid in the late 1920s and 1930s rivals its achievement.[2] A public good was constructed according to an integrated plan with common specifications, at a reasonable cost of capital.

In addition to the delivery network, the other main components of the modern British Gas were the gas contracts and the relationship with the North Sea producers. Here, state ownership played a critical part too. Not only did the government own the Gas Council, which had the benefit of Section 9 of the Continental Shelf Act 1964, giving it first option to buy all the gas landed, but it also held the licences which the oil companies needed, and control of taxation of the oil companies' profits. Therefore, the companies had to negotiate for licences, and for contracts with the Gas Council, and deal with the Treasury over taxation. It required a relationship to be developed and, in effect, made *ex post* revision a fact of life, since, if the companies made too much money, they could be taxed, and, if they did not cooperate, their position in future licence rounds might be compromised. And, of course, they had the bigger oil position to consider. But the government also needed the companies, and recognized their need to make a return. Energy policy therefore involved a process of continual bargaining with the private sector and was played out through the multiple points of interaction, using the Gas Council as one of its instruments.

---

[1] As discussed in Chapter 21, when the United Kingdom becomes a significant importer of gas in the next couple of decades, it may again prove a useful component of energy supply (and security).

[2] See Hannah (1979: ch. 4) for a detailed description of the development of the national grid.

The government's objectives, in common with all its successors, were to get the oil and gas produced as quickly as possible; to ease the chronic balance-of-payments constraints; and to raise money for the Exchequer.[3] The Gas Council was not only the monopsonist, but in the uniquely powerful position of having its owner—the government—able to manipulate the oil companies into contracting with it on favourable terms. The Gas Council needed to recover its total costs, but was under no obligation to charge market prices to its customers. Indeed, there was no market price, since there was no real market. In consequence, the Gas Council had lots of power to discriminate, which it did aggressively, and was to continue to do so, to the considerable concern of the MMC in 1988, as we shall see below.

The contractual structure put in place through the Gas Council is of more than historical interest since its legacy bedevilled the subsequent privatization, and, more importantly, the introduction of competition in the second half of the 1990s. The core elements were the rationale for *long*-term contracts on a take-or-pay basis and the price.[4] Take-or-pay contracts were more than simply a method of ascertaining future prices: they transferred risk from producers to consumers, via the Gas Council. In turn, the oil companies could be certain of the price component, and, hence, the economics of field development turned on the recoverable reserves, as against the costs. It is inconceivable that North Sea gas could have been developed in the late 1960s and 1970s on the basis of short-term contracts, analogous to the position of Russian gas and Gazprom in the 2000s. The risk to *any* developer of oil or gas *anywhere* would have been great, raising its cost of capital. However, in the North Sea context, there was only one country to land the gas, and it would have been largely worthless had the Gas Council not set about building the network. That, in turn, could not have been contemplated unless there were customers to pay for it. Hence, the monopoly the Gas Council enjoyed provided the means of committing customers to the longer-term sunk investments in the gas

[3] The Gas Levy Act 1981 imposed a levy on all UK Continental Shelf (UKCS) gas purchased by British Gas under all contracts entered into before 1 July 1975 (and therefore exempt from the UK petroleum revenue tax, PRT), which was at a rate of 4 pence per therm at privatization, and, under the Gas Act 1986, it could not be increased before 1992.

[4] The details of the contracts remained private, but the privatization prospectus stated that most British Gas purchase contracts provide for an initial term of approximately 25 years, and gave a broad indication of the price structure, as follows: 'The price payable for the gas is generally for the whole length of the contract by reference to a base price and the operation of price variation provisions. In addition, each contract commits British Gas to pay for annual or daily quantities, whether gas is taken or not. However there is flexibility in most contracts for gas paid for, but not taken, to be taken or credited in later years' (NM Rothschild 1986).

pipes onshore and the gas fields offshore. In modern terms, the contracts formed the basis of a massive public–private partnership.

The price element was more contentious, and, in what was, at the time, an important critique of nationalized industries, Richard Pryke (1981) summarized the pricing muddle that resulted. He showed that British Gas's marginal price—the price of gas supplies from Frigg—bore little relationship to its charging policy, with the result that imbalances between supply and demand had to be managed. ICI was to benefit from a very low price, and, although the British Gas Corporation (as the Gas Council had become) made a substantial surplus in its accounts (some £430 million in 1978–79), this was more to do with the low price it was paying for North Sea gas. As Pryke states: 'if it had had to pay a price equal to that of Frigg gas, the Corporation would have incurred a net loss of approximately £830 million, which is another way of saying that prices were too low' (1981: 18).[5]

Pryke is clearly correct in his criticism of the disconnection between the marginal price in the North Sea and final prices to customers. Economic theory dictates that the price of marginal supplies (the most expensive source necessary to meet demand) signals the true resource costs. However, the fundamental question is what price ought to have been paid to the oil companies in the first place. Should it have been set at the marginal costs of the particular contracted field, or the marginal costs of the marginal field necessary to meet the system's demand, as theory dictated? These are two different numbers, and the difference represents the economic rent. To encourage oil companies to develop a field requires that its costs are recovered and that profits justify the risk. The rest is for the owner of the resource—the government. In oil, PRT, introduced in 1975, was designed to extract this rent, but, in gas, the benefits of the rent accrued to a considerable degree to customers, through lower prices, until gas prices were increased in the early 1980s.

However, all this depends on knowing the marginal costs—which in the early 1960s were far from obvious. Whereas Pryke—and, indeed, David Howell and Lawson—in the early 1980s had enough information to reconsider prices on the basis of the *facts* of a developed natural gas industry, both offshore and onshore, in 1964, when licences were first allocated, and in subsequent negotiations with oil companies, the 'facts' were far from certain. The government therefore needed to strike prices without much information, and hence it is hardly surprising that it started

---

[5] Pryke argued that North Sea gas licences should have been auctioned, and then the marginal price fed through into the contracts.

high to encourage the others. Consequently, the first, BP, received a good deal, but prices subsequently fell. For the Gas Council, the important point was that the price was below that of coal-based manufactured gas and LNG. The next contracts were much lower, calculated on a cost-plus-margin basis—what might be regarded as an approximation to a crude rate-of-return approach.

The more radical option—of simply auctioning the licences—was considered, but at the time such a process would have been fraught with difficulties. There were a limited number of bidders, a monopsony buyer and companies with multiple relationships with the government. The theoretical prerequisites for an efficient auction were largely absent. Much later, in the 1990s, auctions were to become more fashionable, but, with experience, some of the drawbacks also became apparent.[6]

Negotiating tough contracts with oil companies was not the only form of pressure. The Gas Council (and also to a limited extent the National Coal Board, NCB) took a direct stake through the licensing regime. Indeed, by the second round of licences, 'any proposals which may be made for facilitating participation of public enterprise in the development and exploitation of the resources of the Continental Shelf' were to be favoured (Corti and Frazer 1983: 45). These stakes gave the Gas Council not only a vertical integration, but also information which, in turn, helped its negotiating strategy—a tactic to be repeated through British National Oil Company (BNOC) in dealings with oil.

Whether or not the Gas Council was right to strike cost-plus deals with oil companies, the price to be passed on to customers was a separate question. The problem was that, although the system marginal cost was very hard to establish, once the cheaper Southern basin fields' gas-only sources were augmented by other more complex sources, the marginal cost was clearly rising, as Pryke (1981) had noted. And, as demand rose to reflect the prices actually being charged, there was a real danger that demand would exceed supply, as Howell recognized in the early 1980s (see Chapter 3). It was for this reason that prices were ramped up considerably and the Gas Levy Act 1981 imposed a levy payable on all UK Continental Shelf gas purchased by British Gas under contracts entered into before 1 July 1975. Eventually these prices were to prove vulnerably high in the much lower fossil-fuel price era in the 1990s once competition in supply arrived. But, with a monopoly position, British Gas's finances were

---

[6] The most famous example is the third-generation mobile licences. See Klemperer (1999) for a survey of the main theoretical insights. The problems of applying auctions to the gas network are discussed in Chapter 18.

always artificial, based on the difference between the initial contract legacy and the prices it chose to set.[7] The Oil and Gas (Enterprise) Act 1982, discussed in Chapter 3, did little to disturb the contractual structure of the gas industry, and it was the role as long-term contractor for gas supplies which the management of British Gas had in mind when the industrial structure was debated in 1985.

The Rooke–Walker Position

The privatization of the gas industry, as with any other, had to be carried through with the support of the incumbent management. In the case of British Gas, that meant Denis Rooke, who dominated its board. He was a gas man, through and through, having joined the industry in 1949. He was the full-time member of the Gas Council in 1966 for production and supply, playing a key role in negotiating the long-term, take-or-pay contracts. By 1972 he was Deputy Chairman, and Chairman from 1976, a post he combined with membership of BNOC from 1976 to 1982.

Rooke's supremacy was backed up by other gas industry lifers. Robert Evans, his successor, joined in 1950, and Cedric Brown, Chief Executive from 1992 to 1996, had joined in his teens. Only Martin Jacomb from the City, and Leslie Smith from BOC, were outsiders on the board—both Lawson appointments. It would have been incredible had British Gas's board endorsed any model other than the integrated monopoly. A radical change in the board would have been necessary first, along the lines adopted in New Zealand's privatizations, and this would have taken several years to effect.[8]

But the industry had little to fear from the Energy Secretary, Peter Walker. He fought off Lawson's arguments for a competitive, regional model. In his autobiography, Walker dismisses competition based on a structural break-up on the grounds that 'the distribution of gas in London was entirely different from in Cornwall' (1991: 189), and therefore comparisons were meaningless. Break-up of British Gas would be 'lunacy'. Walker 'wanted a powerful British company which could compete round the world' (p. 190)—as would the Germans with Ruhrgas. With this, Rooke could agree. Whereas Lawson had divested British Gas of its North Sea assets, Walker believed that 'any sizeable gas industry in the world

---

[7] The failure to separate out network from supply costs, or to provide a proper asset value further confused the accounts.

[8] In New Zealand's privatizations in the 1980s, boards were restructured *before* privatizations proceeded.

would do gas exploration as well as gas distribution' (p. 192). So great was the commonality of views that Walker regarded Rooke as 'the best nationalized industry chairman I met' (p. 192). They only seem to have disagreed about the Sleipner deal for gas imports from Norway.[9]

Lawson's views of Rooke were rather different. He blamed him for the depletion policy which treated gas as a 'premium fuel', and for the cheap domestic gas pricing policy. He described British Gas as 'Rooke's empire' (Lawson 1992: 174), and Rooke as 'my most formidable opponent'. Rooke, Lawson claimed, 'dominated British Gas and regarded the Energy Department as the principal obstacle to his plans for the gas industry, and indeed for the economy as a whole, treating ministers and officials alike with a mixture of distrust, dislike and contempt' (1992: 213–14).

Lawson and Walker represented very different wings of the Conservative Party, and it was inevitable they would clash on gas privatization. Their views on energy policy could not have been more distinct. Lawson wrote that Walker's 'views on the privatization of British Gas were as different from mine as was his attitude on most other issues', and that 'my former officials told me it was almost as if there had been a change of government at Thames House'[10] (Lawson 1992: 215).

It was in this context of personal animosity between Lawson and Rooke, deep ideological differences between Lawson and Walker, and almost complete personal and philosophical agreement between Walker and Rooke, that the debate about the privatization of British Gas took place. It was a debate that Walker and Rooke would win, but it was to be a temporary victory, and when Walker joined the board of British Gas,[11] he was to witness the pressures that the regulators would bring to bear on the integrated monopoly.

The Break-up Case

Mindful of all that subsequently happened, it is remarkable that so little public discussion of the structural options took place in 1985. In part this

[9] In February 1984 British Gas and Statoil agreed provisional terms for the sale of gas from the Sleipner field, but in February 1985 Walker rejected the draft contract (see HC Deb. (session 1984–85), vol. 73, col 27, sixth series), on the basis that reserves in the British North Sea had increased. In doing so, he also rejected exports from the British sector, something which Tim Eggar had urged upon him. It is also worth noting that Rooke estimated that British Gas would be short of supplies in the 1990s.

[10] Thames House was the location of the Department of Energy.

[11] The obvious problem of being the Secretary of State who privatized the company and then joined its board seems to have caused Walker few difficulties. In his autobiography, he gives as a reason that the British Gas board would believe that 'I had gone elsewhere for more money', had he declined (Walker 1991: 227).

reflected the immature nature of the debate (and the supporting literature) on utilities and regulation, and, in part, it was a reflection of the political reality. Back in 1985, the two radical ideas which were eventually to become central to the economic argument—the separation of natural monopoly from potentially competitive parts of the industry, and full retail competition in supply—were yet to surface. Despite the failures of Lawson's two Acts, there was little understanding of the difficulties that would face entrants from a large incumbent monopoly armed with a comprehensive set of long-term contracts.

All this was in the future. Privatization itself was seen as a difficult enough objective. Stephen Littlechild had suggested in his 'Ten Steps to Denationalization' (1981*b*) that British Gas should be sold as a 'single private company', on the understandable but erroneous argument that: 'gas is subject to sufficient competition from other fuels to make its potential monopoly power under private ownership not a major source of concern. The problem lies on the supply side, where the legal monopsony (sole buying) of the Gas Corporation enables it to extract "rent" from the North Sea oil companies.'

Littlechild advocated the ending of this monopsony, allowing oil companies to contract directly with major users—a right that was granted under the Oil and Gas (Enterprise) Act 1982, but to little effect. More radically, he also anticipated subsequent regulatory intervention in proposing the auctioning-off of rights to existing North Sea gas fields.

The sole academic article proposing that British Gas be broken up was by Hammond, Helm, and Thompson (1985). The authors argued for a structure along the lines of the electricity industry, in that there should be a series of local gas companies, analogous to the regional electricity companies. They also argued that the NTS should be a separate entity, anticipating the case for splitting the national grid out of the Central Electricity Generating Board (CEGB).

There was no serious suggestion at this stage that this disaggregation should be accompanied by a further separation of supply. In the mid-1980s, the experience with supply competition was extremely limited and confined to the industrial market. Furthermore, all the contracts were in the hands of British Gas. The Hammond, Helm, and Thompson break-up proposal was designed to improve the incentives for efficiency *within* a regulated monopoly context, not to create competition. As the authors put it, 'although appealing in theoretical terms, the complete vertical separation of the sale of gas from ownership of the distribution system appears impractical at least as far as supply to domestic customers is concerned.' It is ironic that, as it turned out, the separation of supply was to come first, in 1997 with the final demerger of Centrica, and that it was not until 2001 that Lattice, the owner of Transco, was finally to contemplate (though not necessarily carry out) implementing parts of the Hammond, Helm, and Thompson model.[12]

Although nobody was to bother to reply publicly to the break-up proposal, there was a powerful, pragmatic case against it, which served as a defence of the status quo. Its main components were: efficiency and transactions costs, security of supply, the practicality of flotation, and the legislative timetable.

There is a long, detailed and respectable case for vertical integration in utilities, based upon risk minimization and transaction costs. The vertically integrated structure allowed the coordination of the network to be effected under a common set of objectives, reducing the costs of the market transactions that would have had to achieve this, and allowing an important element of flexibility. The risk inherent in such transactions, and the scope for *ex post* opportunism, reneging on contractual agreements, would have increased the cost of capital. Where new sunk investments might be required, these risks would have been particularly expensive. In the creation of the British Gas infrastructure and the development of North Sea fields, it is likely that the vertically integrated structure was the efficient one. By 1985, however, much of this investment phase was over, and the challenge was moving to the efficient exploitation of the now created assets in a world of more abundant supply. But such a view is only clear with hindsight—in 1985 it was reasonable to at least *argue* that the additional costs of a disaggregated structure might not be worth paying, and that such risks might threaten the overarching duty to secure supply in conditions of rising demand.

Politically, too, British Gas represented a risk. Although the government in the end recruited an army of shareholders, called 'Sids' after the character in the promotional advertising, the idea that virtually any scale of operation could be privatized caught on largely *as a result* of the British Gas sale, not in advance of it. Thus, it is hardly surprising that the government trod carefully in preparing gas for privatization. Add to this that the existing management had strong objections to break-up and had behind them the successful development of the NTS of the 1970s and early 1980s, there were good political reasons for the government to opt for a 'minimum change' approach, transferring an intact monopoly to the private sector. If politics is 'the art of the possible' then it was reasonable for the government in 1985 to stick with the status quo.

---

[12] See (Ofgem 2002, Ofgem 2002e and Ofgem 2002f) on separate price formulae for each of the local distribution companies. In 2003, NGT began to take active steps with a view to selling up to four local distribution companies.

Yet, bearing all these in mind, the privatization of the gas industry was a missed opportunity which it would take years to rectify. By 2000, Centrica was on a par with Transco, and supply competition considered quite normal and taken for granted, and it is clear that the monopolists in 1985 had been wrong, not only about competition, but also about shareholders' interests. A regulatory war of attrition was probably the worst outcome. On the one hand, had British Gas been broken up then, the next fifteen years of excess supply might have been managed more efficiently; on the other, had British Gas remained intact throughout that period, it would now be able to take a leading role in the European gas market, as Ruhrgas has done, especially with Gazprom. The end result is a fractured structure which has finally emerged *at the end of* a period of excess supply, when a new investment phase may be required.

Privatization and the Practicalities of Floating so Large a Company

British Gas was privatized for many different reasons, reflecting a mix of ideology, economics and political interests, and pragmatic opportunism.[13] Despite many of the criticisms at the time, it is, at best, naive to assume that governments have clear and well-defined objectives that easily translate into policy.

An extensive literature grew up in the middle to late 1980s on the 'rationale of privatization'. Economists focused on the questions of ownership, competition, and regulation, and this reflected a curious idea prevalent in much of the literature that 'ownership didn't much matter.' For example, Yarrow (1989) wrote that 'there is little in theory or evidence to suggest that regulated private monopoly is a particularly attractive industrial structure.' In the case of gas privatization, he concluded that 'a competitive and regulatory framework was established that might almost have been designed to show private ownership in its least favourable light.' The models of industrial structure in economics had (at least up until the 1980s) focused more on the disciplines of the market place—the selection mechanisms of competition in rooting out firms which did not maximize profits by minimizing costs—than on ownership and the takeover mechanism. It was competing firms and the threat of entry that mattered most: competition might even be *sufficient* to enforce efficiency.

---

[13] John Moore, Financial Secretary, set out the main political arguments in a speech on 'The Success of Privatization' (HMT 1985).

The problem with this argument was that, for the utilities, competition did not exist by virtue of actual or *de facto* monopoly, and that *parts* of the monopoly were natural. Hence, the question of policy strategy arose: would creating a competitive market be enough, or was private ownership necessary? And for the natural monopoly, would private ownership under regulatory scrutiny be better than public ownership in creating bankable incentives, even if it raised the cost of capital?[14]

The 'right' answer for the potentially competitive bits, as argued above, is creating *both* competition *and* private ownership, since the former introduces the discipline of the product market, and the latter, the capital market. Moreover, the incentive to compete is the possibility of extra economic rents, which the private sector can keep, but the public sector cannot. Where these rents occur in the public sector, they are often dissipated on inflated costs and over-investment, or taken by the Treasury. For the natural monopoly, the ownership question is more difficult, and, given that British Gas had a substantive natural monopoly and that the supply business would retain very great market power, the ownership issues were more complex. As long as it was to be the Rooke–Walker national champion, the case for privatization looked weaker.

In practice, many ownership issues competed to facilitate the sale. The owners—the government—sold the company to enhance its political grip on the electorate, through the creation of an economic interest in equity—the share-owning democracy argument. This could be matched up with the practical difficulty of what, at the time, was so large a flotation. Recruiting an army of Sids was one way in which a big enough market for the shares could be created. This, in turn, suited the Rooke–Walker axis: if a large swathe of the electorate owned shares, they would have an interest in the monopoly profits, and hence provide a bulwark against subsequent attempts to introduce more competition and break up the business.

The owners, too, had an interest in realizing their assets, even if the revenue from the sale arose at a time of an improving budget position. Some have claimed that, because of this, the government did not need the money, and therefore 'selling the family silver' was not in fact the rationale. While it is true that the financial pressures were more lax, this conclusion does not follow. It also depends on the counterfactual of what the taxation/spending position would have been without the sale proceeds which the Treasury had targeted. It depends, too, on the hindsight of knowing how macroeconomic conditions turned out in 1987, in the run-up

---

[14] These issues were to arise again with the Post Office and Network Rail in 2002.

to the election. Finally, since British Gas was loaded with a significant element of debt, the flexibility to call upon this debt, as and when it might be needed, was of some benefit to the Treasury.

A final argument for privatization is that it separated functions—in particular, the interests of ownership from those of regulation. This probably figured somewhat lower as a rationale at the time, though already the effect of separation had begun to become important in the telecommunications case. It was, however, to prove decisive in the years to come: the introduction of competition and the eventual break-up of the company in the 1990s would have been much harder—and perhaps impossible—to achieve under state ownership.

The politics of gas privatization were thus complex and much more the messy stuff of party coalitions of interests and ideology than a reflection of the purity of economic models. The break-up case was lost and the government sought to make the maximum political capital out of the populist sale. The bill passed through the parliamentary process in a fairly predictable fashion. With Royal Assent in July 1986, the privatization itself went into full swing: with an initial debt of £2.5 billion, £750 million maturing on 31 March 1987, and the rest in instalments to 1992.

Regulation: An Afterthought

The Gas Act 1986 facilitated the privatization. British Gas was to be the sole licensee for an initial period of 25 years, then subject to ten years' notice from the Secretary of State, and obligations were placed upon it to ensure supplies. It was to be regulated by James McKinnon, a new Director General of Gas Supply (appointed in August 1986 for three years in the first instance), supported by a new regulatory body, the Office of Gas Supply (Ofgas).

It is fair to say that little attention was paid during the flotation process to Ofgas, and the incumbent management clearly regarded it as more of an irritant than a serious threat. The general duties of the Director General appeared vague and unspecified, whilst the initial price cap was regarded as more than adequate to ensure that the business could comfortably meet the prospectus estimates of returns. Ofgas would, in any event, be tiny—just twenty staff at the outset. The new army of Sids could rest easy in the knowledge that their monopoly returns were safe.

This complacency was, eventually, to prove British Gas's downfall (as we shall see in Chapter 13). McKinnon, the regulator, became the focus for lobbying and complaints to which he was sympathetic, and quickly used his powers to promote competition in the commercial market. By 1988

British Gas found itself at the MMC. That set off a chain of events that were only finally resolved a decade later.

The regulatory regime set up at privatization carried on the tradition that had been established for BT—that is, light-handed, with an RPI − X price cap and a regulator charged with general duties. The price cap was imposed on the tariff excluding the gas purchase costs (which were passed on in full), and set at RPI − 2 from 1 April 1987 running through to 1 April 1992. The cap applied to the 'tariff sector', comprising 70 per cent of total sales revenue and made up predominantly of domestic customers, but also including 480,000 commercial and 76,000 industrial customers. The 'contract sector' (24,000 premises, 30 per cent of total sales revenue) was left to negotiated contracts, on either a firm or an interruptible basis. The contract sector was not subject to price control, but British Gas published maximum prices, and the prospectus stated that these would be charged 'until further notice'. The prospectus went on to state that 'British Gas has also indicated its intention, subject to certain qualifications, to limit increases in published maximum firm contract prices for a period of three years to about the rate of inflation' (NM Rothschild 1986: 13).

This light-handed framework contained virtually all the seeds of the regulatory morass that embroiled British Gas for the next decade and a half. The basis for calibrating the initial formula was not defined, so the regulator had to create the building blocks after privatization at the first periodic review. All that existed were the opening prices, and the accounting basis described in the prospectus. These accounts were integrated (and not focused on the separate elements of the business). They were based on current-cost accounting (CCA), and current-cost depreciation was used.[15] As the prospectus stated, 'British Gas charges the cost of replacing certain categories of fixed assets against the profit and loss account' (NM Rothschild 1986: 5, note 4). The CCA depreciation was, however, offset by a target rate of return on the CCA valuation of only 4 per cent, set in 1983 to run through to the end of March 1987. This was supported by further financial targets—12 per cent reduction in net trading costs per therm over the same period, and short-term cash targets (external financial limits, EFLs). It was these three targets which provided the financial and cost position at the time of privatization, and RPI − 2 + Y was, in effect, the rolling forward of this framework. (Y is the pass-through of gas purchase costs.)

---

[15] The use of a CCA approach was consistent with the findings of the Byatt Committee (HMT 1986) and could be linked back to Howell's case for increasing gas prices in 1980 (see Chapter 3).

The valuation was around £16 billion in CCA terms and £6 billion in historical costs, and the scale of the trade-off between the CCA valuation and depreciation, on the one hand, and the low 4 per cent return, on the other, can be seen in the flotation value of around £8 billion.[16] The three key numbers—the CCA value, the market value and the rate of return—were then set, and provided the basis for the subsequent contentious periodic review, described in Chapter 13.

The lack of any effective regulation of the industrial market left British Gas with a powerful monopoly position, which it did not hesitate to exploit. Finally, the long-term, take-or-pay contracts meant that, when the spot price collapsed in the mid-1990s, British Gas faced serious financial problems. The legacy of these features of British Gas at privatization would eventually undermine the company itself. The accounting and market power problems would exercise the MMC in 1988, 1993, and 1996/97. The contracts overhang would lead British Gas to break itself up into two separate companies.

The Unwinding of the Privatization Structure

Although these MMC inquiries will be dealt with more extensively in Chapter 13, it is worth rehearsing the main features here. The 1988 MMC report led to the gas release scheme, whereby British Gas would relinquish gas supply contracts to its rivals, and to a series of undertakings on conduct. In 1991, it fell to the Office of Fair Trading (OFT)—whose duty it was to police the undertakings—to review progress. The OFT proposed radical structural action. In effect, it argued that, although British Gas had fulfilled all the terms of the undertakings, there was nevertheless not enough competition. Simultaneous with this OFT action, Ofgas came up with new price-control proposals for the pipeline business.

---

[16] Asset valuation, 31 March 1986 (£ million)

Form	CCA	Historical cost accounting
Land and buildings	1,190	363
The pipeline system	13,778	4,111
Gas and oil fields	1,609	1,420
Other	188	156
Total	16,765	6,050

Source: NM Rothschild (1986: p. 23).

Deadlock was reached, and the management of British Gas decided to use the good offices of its non-executive director, Walker, to persuade his erstwhile colleague, Michael Heseltine, by now President of the Board of Trade, to make a broad Fair Trading Act 1973 reference of British Gas to the MMC. Simultaneously, British Gas rejected the new price control, automatically bringing this to the MMC as well.

British Gas clearly thought that a full-scale MMC inquiry would sort out the regulatory mess into which the company had got embroiled. The MMC rose to this challenge, and found that there was an inherent conflict of interest between ownership of the natural monopoly transmission and distribution network, and the supply business. It crafted a neat solution which it thought might succeed: British Gas was to be broken in two: the costs of break-up would be reflected in a softer price cap (RPI − 4 rather than RPI − 5); and domestic competition would not be introduced until around 2002, and then only after a further careful analysis.

The upshot was that British Gas fought break-up, proposing instead to accept a fast track to competition in 1998, and accounting separation to overcome the conflict of interest. Ministers at the time, in particular Tim Eggar, could not believe their luck. British Gas would cooperate in delivering the vision of full competition on a fast track, and the government would not be seen to be dismantling British Gas.

The next step was the Gas Act 1995, which effected the removal of the monopoly. The scale of British Gas's mistake then became apparent. It had signed up long-term contracts with North Sea suppliers on the basis that the costs could be passed to final customers and in fulfilment of its statutory duty to ensure security of supply. Now customers could desert to cheaper spot-priced gas. The 1995 Act completed a process that had already begun in the commercial market of stranding British Gas's contracts.

All this was, however, in the future and unforeseen in 1985 and 1986. The lessons for energy policy of the privatization were that the interface between the politics and the economics is much more complex and significant than either one thought through in isolation. The monopoly model was arguably the only politically possible one in 1985 if the industry was to be privatized before the next general election, but it was also the least attractive in terms of economic efficiency. With hindsight—and the 1987 majority—taking a little longer to address the structure would have been a better policy.

The board of British Gas and the Secretary of State, Walker, probably thought that the privatization structure was the end of the matter. British Gas would be a private-sector national champion, in much the same way as BP was regarded. Privatization had removed the Treasury's grip and hence now allowed British Gas to take on the world. The future was bright, with international expansion providing the growth as the North Sea matured. British Gas would take its place alongside the Dutch, German, and French national champions. Energy policy could continue to be conducted through the company so that, with BP, the CEGB and a much chastened NCB, British Gas would remain a commanding height. It might even be able to go back into oil and expunge the memory of the sale of Enterprise Oil, which Nigel Lawson had forced upon it through the Oil and Gas (Enterprise) Act 1982.

That it turned out that there would be little or no energy policy to make in the 1990s, and that the focus would be largely in the opposite direction—reducing prices, low investment and staff reductions—did not feature in either Walker's or Rooke's vision of the future. Nor did it occur to British Gas that the most significant player would not be itself, but rather the regulators it so obviously disregarded. There was no monopoly on misreading the future. The coal miners could do it, the nuclear industry could do it, and so, too, could the gas industry.

7

Electricity Privatization

The Government's proposals will end the effective monopoly in generation and give more influence to the distribution companies and their customers. Every part of the industry will become properly accountable to its shareholders. The Government is determined to make electricity a better industry, by introducing competition and new customer rights, and by building on its existing strengths. Not just the industry, but the economy too, will benefit. ('Privatising Electricity', HMSO, 1988)

The Early Ideas

Once gas had been privatized, it was only a matter of time before electricity would follow, provided of course that the Conservatives remained in office. The election victory of 1987 appeared to give recognition that privatization had become mainstream, allowing the Thatcher government to proceed with both water and electricity. In addition, the old guard on the Left of the party could now be discarded. Accordingly, Margaret Thatcher gave Cecil Parkinson the energy job, having moved Peter Walker to the Welsh Office. With Nigel Lawson still at the Treasury, the two key ministers were all of one mind about the desirability of privatization based upon a more competitive model than gas had been. Michael Spicer, as Parkinson's supporting minister, was also on-side. Agreement on the exact form of the privatization would be more difficult to achieve, but the argument would be within a politically agreed framework, not outside.

As with gas privatization, it is difficult now to appreciate how daunting the task seemed at the time. Electricity provided at least three core problems: the sheer scale of the sale; the nuclear component; and the challenge of introducing competition into a traditional monopoly industry without prejudicing security of supply or technical efficiency. Any one of these alone would have been a major challenge for government to overcome; together, they represented (and still do) the toughest privatization nut to crack. Even the complexity of rail privatization—which was modelled on electricity—was much easier to effect, requiring contracts, but little competition and no Pool.

The scale dwarfed previous privatizations. Whereas British Gas had been valued at around £8 billion, the current-cost assets of the Central

Electricity Generating Board (CEGB) were around £32 billion in the public accounts, and there were the twelve Area Boards and the two Scottish
companies too. In the heady days after British Gas was privatized, there
seemed no limits on the appetite of the stock market for privatizations,
but the crash in autumn 1987, with the BP flotation caught right in the
middle, introduced an element of caution.

The nuclear dimension brought out many of the contradictions in
Thatcher's approach to industrial policy, as well as raising new complex-
ities to valuations. Its economics, as we saw in Chapter 5, were very
uncertain, and in the end nuclear *risk* (as opposed to nuclear assets) was
substantially transferred to British Nuclear Fuels (BNFL), and would
prove difficult to privatize, even a decade later.

Finally, in the debate over competition, electricity privatization raised
fundamental questions about its feasibility. Could electricity be traded
like any other commodity, or was it special? Did the nature of the risks in
generation and the need for security of supply at every point in time, and
through time, mean that the competitive model would lead to instability
and even the lights going out? Were long-term contracts and vertical integration essential for price stability and security of supply, or simply unfortunate consequences of state ownership and monopoly? Back in the late
1980s, these were very real questions on which not just interested parties
and lobby groups could disagree. The 1998 White Paper, 'Conclusions of
the Review of Energy Sources for Power Generation and Government
Response to Fourth and Fifth Reports of the Trade and Industry
Committee' (DTI 1998b), with its emphasis on diversity and security of
supply, the 2002 Performance and Innovation Unit report, 'The Energy
Review' (PIU, 2002) and then the 2003 White Paper, 'Our Energy Future'
(DTI 2003a) are salutary reminders that these questions are yet to be fully
resolved. California's price shock and power shortages in 2001, and the
major failures of the network in the north-east of the US and Canada in
August 2003, and subsequently the power cut in London, illustrate that
such concerns have a substantive foundation.

These three factors—scale, nuclear, and the feasibility of competition—
exercised the Department of Energy and its advisers. They also exercised
the management of the industry, particularly its towering figure, Walter
Marshall. From the start, the government had to tread a careful path
between Marshall's belief in the integrity of the CEGB, its planning system, its nuclear programme, and its control of the grid; and the more radical elements led by Lawson and Parkinson. Marshall shared many of the
assumptions of the French, with Electricité de France (EDF) the comparator to emulate. It is not too strong to say that he *believed* in nuclear power,
and, rightly, recognized that it had little future in a competitive model of

the industry. Like Denis Rooke at British Gas, Marshall saw himself as the architect of the national interest, and, proud of both the CEGB's technology and its record during the miners' strike, he had little real sympathy with the free-market approach, and the army of accountants, investment bankers and commercial strategists which it brought. His, ultimately, was the world of rational scientific planning and technology, and his cast of mind was mathematical. It was one of intellectual conviction, not mere prejudice or ideology.[1]

Parkinson and his team had to come up with a solution that kept the management on board, as well as solved the mountain of problems in the practical design of a new electricity industry structure. The development of this, ultimately successful, exercise is not just one which has shaped the energy sector, but also reveals much about the interaction between the often crude exercise of political power, the subtlety of the way in which the civil service deals with business, and the ways in which the City moulds political ambitions into saleable packages.

This chapter sets out the history of electricity privatization and the compromises over the various often conflicting objectives, some of which had to be unwound over the subsequent transitionary years. It begins with the structural debate and the nuclear dilemma, and its influence on the privatization White Paper (HMSO 1988), through to the gradual withdrawal of Magnox, advanced gas-cooled reactors (AGRs) and the Sizewell B pressurized-water reactor (PWR). The treatment of coal and the coal contracts is discussed, with the deliberate design of the post-privatization transitionary period. That transition provided the framework in which the 1998 problems with full liberalization of supply, debates about Pool reform and the two coal crises that followed in 1992 and 1997 were set, and is discussed in Chapter 8.

The White Paper: The Structural Debate

After various broad options had been canvassed, the debate about the White Paper turned upon two styled models, grounded in very different conceptions of industrial policy: those of the Fabian planners, with their national champions; and the competitive marketeers. The first was led by Marshall, but with some support from the Walker–Heseltine wing of the

---

[1] As the *Times* obituary (23 February 1996) put it: 'For more than two decades, Walter Marshall was the most eloquent spokesman and principal cheerleader for nuclear power in Britain. A rationalist who fell among politicians and emerged bruised, he never quite understood why his arguments so often fell on deaf ears. But he remained unbowed, the epitome of the scientist-engineer who believes that all things are possible.' See also Fishlock and Roberts (1998).

Conservative Party; with Parkinson, Nicholas Ridley and, most importantly, Lawson on the other. Thatcher's position was deeply ambiguous—but decisive—in the debate which ensued.

The two schools of thought that emerged were a modified monopoly model and a competition model. The former would, as with gas privatization, have left the existing structure largely intact, but permitted the freedom of entry. The CEGB would then be able to use its monopoly power to carry the nuclear programme, backed up with the duty to supply. Costs, nuclear and otherwise, would then have been passed through to the regional electricity companies (RECs), and, hence, customers. The bulk supply tariff (BST) would have remained the mechanism. This was Marshall's preferred structure, and one which he thought Thatcher endorsed. (It is also the one which EDF managed to maintain throughout the 1990s, enabling it to become one of the top three companies dominating the European market.)

The competition model built on Lawson's market for energy, and the economic ideology of the more radical Thatcherites: the creation of a competitive market structure, and then the promotion of competition as the main duty of the regulator, in effect commoditizing electricity. This model would have seen the CEGB broken up into at least five generating companies, a separate grid, and the twelve Area Boards in England and Wales, with supply competition being opened up. It was a model that Parkinson tended towards, and which Lawson, now Chancellor, preferred.

The difference between the two models was not simply the structure of the generation market. It also turned on whether the grid could be split off from generation, and whether distribution could be separated from supply within the Area Boards. Supply competition would have the effect of driving the industry towards the consumer rather than the producer perspective. There could be no cost pass-through and no BST in the competition model. Customers would no longer be tied to any particular generator or supplier.

Generation and the Nuclear Problem

The case for a break-up was conducted on relatively simplistic grounds: that competition needed competitors, and that the experience of the Energy Act 1983 suggested that entry would not be expected to make much difference to the market power of the incumbents for several years to come. Thus a pre-emptive break-up would deliver competition now, rather than waiting for the liberalized consents policy for new power stations to have its effects. Splitting up the generation capacity into a number of competing companies (probably five) was the preferred route of the advocates of competition. The number 'five' was based upon the old regional structure of the CEGB (which had been scrambled in the mid-1980s, in part, possibly, to head off the option).

Market theorists favoured this structural approach, which would have the merit of reducing the need for *ex post* conduct regulation. It had an added political attraction, which was that the break-up of the CEGB would further reduce union power. Given the trade union reforms of the 1980s, unions in one firm could not support strike action in another. Hence, the prospects of an industry-wide power strike would be much diminished. Break-up would also bear down on the coal industry, in that the National Coal Board (NCB) would have a set of contracts of different durations and terms, and that competitive generators would not be able simply to pass through the NCB's costs. This consequence of break-up appealed to Thatcher, and complemented her instinctive distrust of large corporate entities, national champions and the corporatist philosophy which she associated with Walker and Heseltine. The more radical and individualistic philosophy of competition fitted with her mission of reversing Britain's relative economic decline.

The case against break-up came from two directions: the problem of passing through the higher costs of nuclear (a bulwark against the miners); and the practical difficulty of selling break-up to both Marshall and the workforce. Of these, the former proved the most resistant.

Nuclear power and competitive markets do not easily mix. A nuclear power station is a long-term bet: its construction costs dominate its running costs, and therefore it is extremely sensitive to the discount rate used.[2] Once the investment is committed, it is sunk, and changes in assumptions in the thirty or forty years of its subsequent operation can undermine its economics. The French PWRs, for example, were planned when oil prices were high and expected to remain so, but then turned out to be low in the late 1980s and 1990s. But, by the 2000s, oil prices were again high, and climate change gave the nuclear power stations a significant environmental advantage. Whereas the state might take such risks, private investors would need contract security to protect the investment from becoming stranded. But long-term, take-or-pay contracts do not sit easily with competitive generation or supply markets, where customers can switch to cheaper sources. Indeed, stranded assets in the nuclear sector were to

---

[2] On the discount-rate debate, see the exchange of letters in the *Financial Times* in April and May 1988 (Helm 28 April 1988; Jones 9 May 1988; Mobbs 9 May 1988; Helm 16 May 1988). The core issue was whether the discount rate should be more than 10%.

become a major policy problem, not only in Britain but also in the United States, Spain, and Germany in the early stages of the introduction of competition.

In the early debates on privatization, the sustaining of the nuclear programme was part of the unwritten objectives of the exercise, and Thatcher's role in this was critical. She could never quite make up her mind about nuclear power and energy policy. Her nationalistic tendencies encouraged an admiration of the French nuclear programme and EDF, especially in the darker moments during the miners' strike. As noted in Chapter 5, nuclear power held a fascination for her: as a scientist, for its technical achievements; as an advocate for a strong defence policy; and, as an opponent of the miners, in the form of an insurance policy.[3] As so often in energy policy, advisers sought a compromise which would *both* promote competition *and* provide support for nuclear power, and, as with so many compromises, it created a mess. In this case, that mess took a decade to sort out.

The compromise was to break up generation into two competing companies: National Power and PowerGen. National Power was to be given enough market power to carry all the nuclear costs, while PowerGen would be given a big enough market share to keep an element of competitive pressure on National Power. Entry would then gradually erode the market shares of the dominant incumbents, but nuclear would be protected through a nuclear tax—the Fossil Fuel Levy, discussed in Chapter 10.[4] This compromise eventually emerged in the 1988 White Paper (HMSO 1988), but did have a considerable number of hoops to get through: in Cabinet, with management, and with the unions. But before the twists and turns of the politics are set out, the other structural component needs to be dealt with—splitting off the grid.

The CEGB management originally argued that plant despatch had to be coordinated by generators, and, hence, if the grid was not to be part of a unified CEGB, it should at least be controlled by generators and not by distributors.[5] The RECs—and presumably their financial advisers—argued

---

[3] 'The trouble with [the more radical option] was that it was difficult to see any of these companies being large enough to keep up the very costly development of nuclear power, which I regarded as essential, both in order to ensure security of power supply, and for environmental reasons' (Thatcher 1995: 683). Whether she really considered the environmental question in 1987/88 in the context of privatization, or whether it seemed more appropriate when she wrote in 1995, is open to question.

[4] On the controversy in the run-up to the White Paper and Electricity Bill, see Helm (1987c, 1988).

[5] See, for example, John Baker's exposition of the CEGB's views in 'How Best to Give Power to the People', *Financial Times* (25 November 1987). He stated that 'separating the grid from the bulk of the power stations in an untried system would be less secure, for there is a dynamic interaction between generation and transmissions which, if got wrong, leads to voltage collapse and blackouts.' See also Helm (1987b) and Electricity Consumers' Council (1987).

that the grid could not be floated as a stand-alone business, so ought to be 'bundled up' within the REC flotations. Behind these two positions lay the history of antagonism between Marshall at the CEGB and Philip Jones at the Electricity Council (see below). The CEGB argued that it was not feasible to ensure the lights stayed on under the Pool, whilst the RECs argued that a purely debt-financed grid company was not a financially viable option. Ironically, both turned out to be wrong, but, in the event, the RECs won the political argument, and the National Grid Company (NGC) was to be owned by the RECs in rough proportion to their current-cost accounting value, through a holding company. There was, in addition, to be a golden share held by the Secretary of State. NGC was, through its articles of association, given a measure of operational independence from the holding company. Within NGC, its transmission business was separated from its other activities—settlements, interconnections, ancillary services, and its pumped-storage generation business in north Wales—and the transmission licence prevented cross-subsidy.

The Debate over the Pool

Although the concept of a pool based on prices rather than costs is now commonplace in electricity markets—and, more generally, energy spot markets too—in the middle to late 1980s the concept was a novel one. There were no markets in associated financial instruments for electricity, and there was a widespread belief that, because electricity was not generally storable, and because security of supply in the short and medium term was essential, markets could not cope. Despatch and scheduling had to be centrally directed through a 'command-and-control' mechanism, one that had served the industry well throughout the post-war period across the developed world.

The case for centralized control over despatch had several parts. It was argued that, in order to ensure that plant were despatched on the basis of least-cost, only a single monopoly would have both the relevant information *and* the appropriate incentives to ensure the efficient operation of a 'merit' order. Conversely, for a set of competing generators, information was necessarily diffuse, and there could be no guarantee that the separate and independent decisions of the many would translate into the optimal system solution. Their individual profit-maximizing incentives (perhaps short-term in focus) would not necessarily coincide with the interests of the system as a whole. In normal commodity markets, stocks could cope with mistakes; in electricity, the costs of insufficient supply were very great. It was therefore better to be sure of supply, even if this cost a little inefficiency, than to be efficient but risk supply interruptions.[6]

Experience with the Central Electricity Board in the 1930s, and with the development of the high-voltage network, and the preoccupation with ensuring that enough power stations were built to meet the post-war economic boom, added a longer-term dimension to the argument. Even if the market could ensure some sort of approximation to the efficient merit order, the prospect of investment being either sufficient or correctly located under a market system seemed remote to the CEGB managers. Who would take responsibility for ensuring that enough supply of the correct type, and in the right location, was forthcoming? Individual incentives might not lead to the social optimum.[7]

It was against this background that the architects of the Pool set to work. They had to design a market solution that would approximate efficient scheduling (the merit order); to provide effective incentives to ensure enough capacity was available to meet demand peaks; and to facilitate enough investment. The Pool needed to ensure that prices would approximate the system marginal cost (for efficient despatch); availability payments would need to be sufficient to keep a reserve margin of plant; and prices would need to be high enough to tempt investors to build more plant in a timely fashion.

The Pool was a valiant—and inevitably flawed—attempt to approximate the merits of a planned system. Yet its architects were lucky: the circumstances were particularly favourable. The recession at the beginning of the 1980s had radically reduced industrial demand, and the overall low growth had further contributed to the excess supply of plant in the late 1980s. Put simply, the problem for the 1990s was not investment: it was how to run existing plant as efficiently as possible. There was little chance of a threat to security of supply, since there was plenty of plant to keep the lights on. What mattered was cost minimization, and here the advocates of the market approach could point to the costs of monopoly: the inefficiency of plant operating costs. The CEGB might have been able to construct a merit order from internal cost information, but it was on the basis of costs which were argued at the time to be (and, it subsequently transpired, were) excessive. Even if the market turned out to be less good at getting a merit order, the gains in efficiency should be balanced against this possible detriment.

---

[6] Weitzman's seminal article on prices and quantities is relevant here (1974). At the margin, if demand exceeds supply, the damage function is very steep relative to the cost function, and hence it makes sense to ensure sufficient *quantity* of capacity, even at the expense of the extra costs.

[7] This argument, though self-serving, turned out to have some theoretical foundation (see Castro-Rodriguez *et al.* 2002).

How could the merit order be replicated so that the lights stayed on? The answer which the Department of Energy came up with in the late 1980s was an ingenious one, and it was in two parts: the unified Pool; and the rules which the participants were obliged to obey (the 'Pool rules'). It was not an answer which immediately gained acceptance: a 'two pool' system (called the D system) provided an early alternative model, and then there was a debate between various types of unified pools. Agreement was not formally reached until well after the 1988 White Paper. In practice, the differences between the two models were less than the protagonists imagined: the market had to fulfil both an energy and a capacity function. The D system had two separate markets for these functions: the unified Pool, as its name dictated, brought the two functions under one framework.

The Pool replaced the merit order based upon internal costs with prices. Although surrounded by other complex details,[8] the essential principles were quite simple. Generators bid a day ahead the price at which they would be willing to supply electricity, and their availability. In a *competitive* market, these prices would be equal to the station's short-run marginal cost (SRMC). However, they would be paid the market clearing price, which, in theory, would be the SRMC of the last (most expensive) station needed to equate supply and demand—to keep the lights on. This was the system marginal price (SMP) equal to the system marginal cost. But, although the SMP would reward the station's marginal costs and make some contribution towards its fixed costs (the difference between the station's SRMC and the system's SMP), the total return would be insufficient to encourage the availability of sufficient capacity to deal with demand peaks (the 'insurance' problem). Thus an extra—availability— payment was needed, given that electricity cannot normally be economically stored in sufficient quantities to instantaneously balance the system.

The architects of the Pool here took a theoretical, correct, line: capacity was to be rewarded through the calculation of the value of the loss of load (VOLL) multiplied by the loss of load probability (LOLP). The practical problem was informational. The market did not provide a mechanism to reveal what the VOLL would be, and, hence, it was set exogenously. The probability was not easy to estimate, since in theory it depended on the expectations created in what was expected to be a competitive market. These aspects of the Pool were designed to fulfil two functions simultaneously: to provide a mechanism to reward the capacity margin;

---

[8] For an exposition, see OXERA (1999).

and to signal when investment would be needed. (In practice, it would over-provide for the former, and give little guidance to the latter.)[9]

Whereas the capacity payment was designed as a forward-looking investment signal, an additional *uplift* element was added to the Pool purchase price (PPP) to obtain the Pool selling price (PSP), which suppliers pay for electricity bought from the Pool (PSP = PPP + uplift). Uplift represented the additional costs of reserve, availability and ancillary services for capacity that is not used, and it applied only in times of higher demand.[10] Uplift turned out to be a significant component of PSP, at up to 10 per cent. These charges rose sharply after privatization, despite the dash for gas and the surplus capacity margin.[11]

The final main component of costs carried over from the integrated CEGB was the use-of-system charge for the grid. This was set on a zonal basis, with a per-kW charge designed to reflect the marginal costs of investment and maintenance to meet peak demand. It was designed with little reference to the charges for the NTS operated by British Gas (and hence took no account of the distortions to plant location created by inconsistency in the prices and costs of transporting gas and transmitting electricity), and was subsequently to come under severe criticism, although the radical solutions, such as auctions, proposed in 2001/02 were to fail to resolve the issues (see Chapter 18).

A crucial feature of the Pool was that participation by generators was *compulsory*. All plant over 100 MW had to be despatched through this mechanism, and any supplier could buy at the Pool price. At the time, compulsion was seen as a mechanism for ensuring that the merit order was replicated and security of supply (and system control) was maintained. But this element was to have further advantages that the critics failed to take properly into account when NETA replaced the Pool at the end of the decade. Compulsion made the Pool transparent and liquid, and it made discrimination by generators between suppliers much more difficult. When

[9] The capacity payment was paid to unconstrained scheduled plant as LOLP (VOLL – SMP). LOLP was determined every half-hour, varying between zero and one. VOLL is the maximum level quoted by any public electricity supply or second-tier supply licence. All these licences specify the VOLL = £2/kWh in 1990/91 prices, upgraded by the RPI. VOLL – SMP therefore is an attempt to approximate the consumer surplus lost in the event of a failure to supply.

[10] Technically, periods were divided into *Table A* and *Table B*. In Table A (higher demand), SMP covers the full costs of the marginal generating set, including 'no load' and start-up costs. In Table B periods, when there is considerable spare capacity available, SMP covers only marginal costs.

[11] The 1997 NGC price control attempted to create appropriate incentives to address this problem (Offer 1996).

supply competition was fully opened up, and when the generators were allowed to vertically integrate, these advantages were to prove more important than the Pool architects imagined. The Pool's liquidity and transparency should also have helped the development of futures markets, although the market power of the incumbents was to prove a major obstacle. The Pool provided a standardized spot contract on which long-term contracts could be written.[12]

With hindsight, it can be seen that the original Pool had considerable merits and demerits, many of which were, not surprisingly, not well understood at the time. The SRMC/system marginal cost market was beset by problems of market power, while the availability mechanism was subject to significant gaming. The capacity element never provided a serious mechanism for investment. These defects were to be revealed after privatization. Indeed, the exercise of market power revealed through the Pool led many of its critics—in particular the Labour government after 1997—to reject the Pool mechanism itself, rather than recognize its subsequent strengths in encouraging supply competition, preventing discrimination between customers and exposing generator conduct. But this is the subject for Chapter 17 and the debate about the Pool successor, NETA.

At the time, however, there were considerable doubts even among its architects, and the Pool was buttressed by a number of 'protective' measures to support its operation, and to provide a safety net to make sure that supply equalled or exceeded demand. Many advocated an explicit duty on the grid to ensure security of supply. That was rejected (though the RECs would, in practice, partially have this obligation). Instead, NGC would have reserve powers to override the Pool, and would produce a 'Seven Year Statement' indicating the likely course of supply over a period considered sufficiently long for new build to be triggered and completed.[13]

The faith in the LOLP/VOLL mechanism and the rejection of the planning model[14] were reinforced by the taking of decisions about the location of power stations away from the grid, and placing them firmly in the hands of generators. Thus, a prospective generator could require the grid to connect it to the network, at a pre-set rate of return for the connection investment. The grid then became the facilitator of the plans of generators,

---

[12] The importance of contracts to the Pool's behaviour is described in Helm and Powell (1992).

[13] Strictly, the Statement was not NGC's view, but the aggregation of plans which were formally notified to it by the generators.

[14] There was to be a brief interest in 1990 in least-cost planning to address the demand side of energy markets, led by Ofgas (see Ofgas 1990). The E factor was one element of this, see Chapter 15.

and this was given substance through the formal duty *on the grid*, rather than merely the regulator, to facilitate competition. Such a reactive view was to lead to difficulties not foreseen at the time. The combination of inconsistent pricing between the electricity and gas networks and the effective duty to connect led to significant inefficiency in locations of new plant—to which we return in Chapter 8.

Finally, in case it all went wrong, the Secretary of State was given extensive powers to intervene. The general duties under the Electricity Act 1989 were placed upon *both* the Secretary of State *and* the Director General. Under Section 36 of the Act, the Secretary of State had the power to grant consents for the construction, extension or operation of any power station over 50 MW, could impose conditions on such consents, and could direct that planning provision should be deemed to have been granted. These were extensive powers, and Section 36 was to prove the instrument for imposing the gas moratorium in 1997/98 and to require consideration of 'good quality' combined heat and power (CHP) (see Chapter 16).[15]

Although many predicted that the combination of the Pool, the associated supporting requirements on the grid, and the general powers would not be enough to entertain taking such a risk, the case had sufficiently convinced the Department of Energy to separate the grid from generation. The natural conclusion was a separate grid company. That, however, ran into the two objections referred to above: the first, practically, that investors would not want to invest in such a novel company; and second, politically, the desire by the Area Boards (and the Electricity Council) to wrest power from the CEGB, and hence integrate the transmission system with distribution.

The practical arguments were financial: it was not considered feasible to float off the grid as a saleable entity, and in particular it had no track record and the model of a purely debt-financed company was rejected. Although statutory water companies had long had this status, the cult of equity dominated the late 1980s, both at the Treasury and in financial markets. It was only much later, after the death of inflation in the late 1990s, that equity would gradually be replaced by debt through special dividends, share buy-backs, securitization and debt finance of new investment.

The politics arose out of the fierce rivalry between the CEGB and the Area Boards, and in particular, between Marshall, Chairman of the CEGB,

---

[15] The Secretary of State also held powers under Section 14(3) of the 1976 Energy Act with regard to notice of new stations and gas contracts, and powers in these circumstances 'if he thinks it expedient having regard to current energy policies'.

and Jones, Chairman of the Electricity Council.[16] Marshall had turned the national partnership between all parts of the industry at the Electricity Council into a neutered forum for agreeing the BST, based upon the CEGB's costs. In a production-driven industry, with the overriding security-of-supply rationale for new investment, the interests of domestic customers (and their representatives, the Area Boards) were never able to break the monopoly on decision-making which mirrored the monopoly of generation—until privatization came along.

These two factors—the practicalities and the internal industry politics—led to a compromise. The grid would be an independent company, separate from generation, but it would be owned by the Area Boards. Marshall therefore not only lost the grid, but had to see it pass into the hands of the distribution businesses. It was a structure which could be lived with. However, were it not for the managerial skill with which its first Chairman, David Jefferies, managed to divide the RECs after privatization and hence prevent them exercising effective control, it might not have played such an independent and important role in bedding down the new structure. The grid was never to be accused of discriminating in favour of either the generators or the RECs.

How Many RECs?

Having split off the grid and placed it into the hands of the RECs, there was a further debate about how many RECs there ought to be. The debate turned around two magic numbers: twelve, based upon the existing Area Boards, and five. The case for consolidation was not strong, but at the time it was seriously argued that it would be easier for financial markets to absorb larger entities. The Area Boards that were thought to be particularly 'weak' in financial terms were SWEB, South Wales Electricity and Manweb. Such financial arguments were more pertinent in the late 1980s than they would be now, but even then they were hard to sustain. Balance sheets and price formulae could be adapted accordingly and, as with the bundling of nuclear within National Power, a problem is not 'solved' through amalgamation *per se*. Since there was no *evidence* produced at the time to suggest that larger RECs would be more efficient in distributional terms, any gains would be in terms of market power in the purchase and sale of electricity, and this was in any event to be dealt with through contracts set in advance

---

[16] Jones was appointed in October 1982 by Lawson, despite pressure from Thatcher on the grounds that he was a Department of Energy civil servant rather than a businessman (see Lawson 1992: 135–6). As a result, Kenneth Couzens became Permanent Secretary.

and price caps on supply. The only vulnerability in the first three years lay in the over 1 MW market.

By international standards, British Area Boards were already very large, since nationalization after the war had eliminated local government ownership and consolidated the numerous independent distributors. No convincing econometric evidence was produced to show that scale, scope or density economies continued to increase efficiency above a certain threshold. Indeed, although the application of information technology in the 1990s to networks might have been expected to yield greater economies of scale, the case for REC consolidation remains to be proven (and is discussed in Chapter 12). Of more immediate importance was the fact that some chairmen and directors of the existing Area Boards which would be amalgamated had a great deal to lose, were the government to opt for consolidation. Early on in the privatization, the chairmen formed their own group, and it was this lobby that commissioned work to prove the case for twelve.[17] Provided that the financial objections could be overcome, *politically* it would have been very difficult to proceed with privatization with the chairmen's active hostility. And, even if these managerial objections could be overcome, the *process* of merging some of the companies would have taken time, and a track record would not have been in place in 1990 ready for privatization ahead of the next election. The case for five (or at least some consolidation) would have to wait a decade, and even then was initially to take the rather messy form of joint operations on the distribution side. In 1987, supply competition and supply integration between the RECs were distant thoughts. They began after the golden shares expired in 1995, and really got going in earnest only when Callum McCarthy became regulator under Labour and the anti-merger stance was relaxed.

Scotland and Northern Ireland

Reflecting the pragmatic approach, the different circumstances in Scotland led to an integrated model. Two companies, Scottish Hydro-Electric and ScottishPower, were created, comprising generation, joint ownership of the transmission system, distribution and supply—a structure which mirrored the German system, and to which the system in England and Wales would, in due course, approximate (except, of course, in transmission).

---

[17] A report was produced for the Area Board chairmen to support their position in November 1987 (London Economics 1987).

Vertical integration was accepted for reasons of scale and cross-subsidy. It was assumed that, with a total population of around seven million, two companies were the maximum that could serve the market whilst being large enough to attract investors. Furthermore, the geography of northern Scotland and the islands required an element of cross-subsidy to ensure that everybody could have access to the network, and afford electricity. A secure monopoly basis was required to facilitate these cross-subsidies. Finally, the large-scale dependency on nuclear power in Scotland and the special features of hydro sources reduced the scope for a more radical competitive structure.[18]

Although there was little discussion about the general structure of the proposed solution, there were at the time a number of examples of small countries with challenging geography. New Zealand was then in the process of adopting a more radical model, and Northern Ireland was subsequently broken up into several generators separate from the transmission, distribution and supply functions. Neither the New Zealand nor the Northern Ireland model, however, was to demonstrate significant competition in practice: New Zealand, because of the small number of critical price-setting plants set in the context of significant hydro; and Northern Ireland because of the long-term contracts.

Northern Ireland's generation capacity (2 GW) was vested in March 1992 into four separate companies, independent of Northern Ireland Electricity (NIE), which would control transmission, distribution, and supply. The four generating companies were sold by competitive tender in April 1992, together with long-term power purchase agreements (PPAs) covering availability, output and emissions for the lifetime of the plant.[19]

This was competition *for* a market, rather than competition within a market: once the PPAs were set, there was little to compete for, and, in any event, one plant (Ballylumford) had almost half the total market. Longer term, the competitive threat would come from interconnection—with Scotland through the 250 MW interconnector, granted permission in 1998, and, eventually, possibly through links with the Republic of Ireland to the south.

---

[18] A special Hydro Benefit was created, which provided for a subsidy from generation (including cheap hydro power) to distribution and transmission to meet the higher costs of the more remote and sparsely populated north of Scotland (see Industry Department for Scotland 1988; MMC 1995).

[19] Three owners acquired the four generating plants and associated contracts. These were Premier Energy Holdings (British Gas)—Ballylumford, 1,069 MW; Nigen (AES–Tractebel)—Kilroot 578 MW and Belfast West 240 MW; and a management buy-out of Coolkeeragh 358 MW.

Protecting UDM Mines: The Coal Contracts

A central political purpose of restructuring the electricity industry—
especially for Thatcher—was to break up union power, in both the
electricity industry and in coal. By introducing competition, workers
would face the hard constraint of the market: bidding up wages would
lead to a loss of market share for the generators, and hence unemployment. Strike action would be more difficult outside the protection of a
monopoly, and workers in one generator could not strike in support of
those in another. Finally, other sources of cheaper coal would be sought
for competitive advantage.

That intent created tensions. The privatization itself would have been
more politically difficult if a significant contraction of the coal industry
had been immediately effected. There was a strong political desire to protect miners in the Union of Democratic Mineworker (UDM) areas—those
who had carried on working through the great strike (in 1984), and hence
helped to provide Thatcher with her great victory. The policy problem
was therefore: how could a competitive market be combined with some
protection for the UDM miners? The answer was contracts: the generators
would take into the private-sector obligations to purchase coal in higher
volumes and at higher prices than dictated by the market, for an initial
period, 1990–93.[20] The year 1993 was chosen because it was conveniently
after the next general election. If the Conservatives won in 1992 then the
coal output would be determined by market forces; if Labour won (as was
widely expected) then it would have to negotiate with private-sector electricity companies and pay for the consequences of supporting coal. What
was not expected was that the Conservatives would be the party that
propped up coal after 1993, and that the seeds of a coal crisis for the
Conservatives had been sown. As we shall see in Chapter 8, it was a crisis which did much to undermine the Conservative government.

Buying Off the Large Users

The final interest group which the political process of privatization
needed to satisfy were the large industrial customers (LICs). This group—
led in public debates by ICI—was one of the leading supporters of
restructuring, and there was clearly the assumption that privatization
would lead to lower prices. Such support had already been tested when
Parkinson announced the 15 per cent increase in electricity prices over

---

[20] See Parker (2000: 90–2) on the detail of these contracts.

two years in November 1987. There had been a strong reaction from the Confederation of British Industry (CBI), culminating in a report prepared by Helm and Mayer (1988) which argued that the prices should reflect the SRMCs of the system, and that, in the presence of excess supply, prices should be expected to fall, rather than be increased.[21]

The LICs had cause for further concern, in that the compulsory, transparent Pool meant that there could be no discrimination between LICs and retail customers, since the RECs were on equal footing. LICs argued that they should receive cheaper power because of the size of their demand, but they were in fact smaller than RECs. To buy off these concerns, the government offered two concessions: a LICs' scheme and early access to competitive supply for over 1 MW customers.

The LICs' scheme ran for an initial period of one year (1990–91) and its provisions ensured that their prices rose by no more than the rate of inflation. With this scheme, and a number of RECs falling over each other to try to match the generators in supplying these customers in the early years, this lobby was at least temporarily bought off, although, as we shall see in the next chapter, they were to agitate for regulatory action against the generators and for bilateral contracts outside the Pool for the next decade.

The Electricity Act 1989

The Electricity Act 1989 facilitated the new structure by giving the Secretary of State the powers to carve up the industry, creating the role and defining the functions of the Director General of Electricity Supply, and establishing the consumers' committees. The Director General was given primary duties *concurrent* with the Secretary of State to secure that all reasonable demands for electricity are satisfied; to secure that licence-holders are able to finance the activities which they are authorized by their licences to carry on; and, subject to a cross-subsidy requirement for Scotland, to promote competition in the generation and supply of electricity.

Crucially, and this was to be extremely important in later controversies, the Director General and the Secretary of State had *secondary* duties to protect consumers' interests; promote efficiency and economy in supply and transmission, and in the use of electricity; promote R&D; protect the public from dangers arising from the industry; and to secure health and safety. In other words, if the promotion of competition conflicted with consumer interests, competition should come first. That the regulator

---

[21] There was much press coverage, and a high-profile CBI meeting with Parkinson. See *Financial Times* editorial, 'Fair Pricing of Electric Power', 22 February 1988.

(and the government) claimed that the best way to protect consumers' interests was to promote competition did not obviate the ranking of these objectives, and it was always open to others to dispute this equation, particularly since the Act grouped all consumers together.

The debates on the Act were curiously devoid of much excitement, particularly given that Tony Blair was shadow minister at the time, and led the opposition in the debates. The minister in charge, Michael Spicer, agreed with Blair that the Labour Party's key points would be accepted, and, in response, Labour did not obstruct the Bill's progress through Parliament. The unions, led by John Lyons, were also muted, but then their interests with regard to pensions and other rights were well taken care of.[22]

The White Paper Revised

From the first discussions of the new generation structure, doubts were raised about nuclear. The fix—competition from PowerGen, but enough monopoly power for National Power—was always hard to maintain, and it rapidly became apparent that investors would not easily subscribe to these arrangements. The accounts presented in political memoirs are that, after the White Paper was published, new information became available about the nuclear costs.[23] Although this has an element of truth, in that obviously the process would lead the officials and their advisers to trawl through the accounts, this new information only added confirmation to what was already well known—of the three types of reactors, the Magnox decommissioning was extremely uncertain in cost terms (and relatively imminent); the AGRs, as we saw in Chapter 5, had an appalling economic record; and the costs of Sizewell B were, at best, likely to exceed official estimates.

A tactical retreat was necessary, and it was among Parkinson's last acts in July 1989 as Secretary of State for Energy to withdraw the Magnoxes before being shifted sideways to Transport. It fell to John Wakeham, Thatcher's 'fixer', to complete the withdrawal by taking out the rest of the nuclear assets from National Power and the Scottish companies in November 1989, and creating Nuclear Electric and Scottish Nuclear.

---

[22] In public, the Engineers and Managers Association took an anti-privatization and anti-competition position. See Lyons (1987, 1988).

[23] See Parkinson (1992: 274–5), Lawson (1992: 168–9), and Thatcher (1995: 685). These *ex post* rationalizations are particularly questionable in Parkinson's case. He told the House of Commons on 12 December 1988 that the decommissioning costs were currently funded and—most interestingly—that any increases caused by changes in public policy would continue to be underwritten by the taxpayer—inviting the response from Blair that this would be a 'nuclear tax' (HC Deb., session 1988–89, col. 684).

With nuclear withdrawn, the assets of the non-nuclear generators were ready for the market. The fact that the rationale for creating just two main competitors (the nuclear plant was baseload and therefore played little part in price-setting) had thereby evaporated was conveniently ignored, especially given the timetable for flotation ahead of the election. With hindsight, a further break-up after the withdrawal of nuclear would have avoided many of the difficulties that emerged with the exercise of market power, but privatization would then have been put back to at least 1991, and may well have not been completed until after the general election. Many thought that it would be won by the Labour Party, and the privatization would have been shelved for the foreseeable future. As with gas, there was a trade-off between, on the one hand, speed and certainty of a change of ownership, and, on the other, the creation of a competitive structure. For the Conservative governments, ownership was always more important.

The Licences and the Regulatory Arrangements

Almost all the main political debates about privatization focused on the structure of the industry. Like telecommunications and gas before in the 1980s, the regulatory framework was somewhat of an afterthought, and, like these earlier examples, it was left to the regulator to develop much of the detail *ex post*. Ministers talked of 'light-touch' regulation and a staff at the Office of Electricity Regulation (Offer) in the low hundreds.[24]

A number of key questions could not, however, be avoided. What sort of licences were needed? Who needed them? How might they be revised? In providing answers, it should be remembered that, at the time, the architects of the new arrangements thought that generation would quickly become competitive, and hence *light* regulation would be sufficient. Only subsequent experience taught that competition needed to be proactively promoted through regulation. None of the architects foresaw a day when generation would be subject to a price cap; that there would need to be repeated investigations; that further plant disposal would be required; or that, in 2000, a 'good behaviour' licence condition would be debated. The generation licence therefore provided only that all available generation sets over 100 MW would be available for despatch by NGC, and that ancillary services would be provided to NGC on request.

NGC needed a licence too, in addition to its special duties, providing for its price caps, the grid code and other miscellaneous conditions. The

---

[24] See, for example, *The Sunday Times*, 27 November 1988, p. D10.

RECs had an overarching (public electricity supply, PES) licence which incorporated both supply and distribution (Department of Energy 1989*a*), only to be split formally in the Utilities Act 2000. They were, however, treated as *de facto* separated from the start. Suppliers were licensed as either first-tier (i.e. monopoly) or second-tier (i.e. competitive) activities. The supply aspects of the RECs' licences focused on the price caps, economic purchasing (Condition 5), own generation (Condition 6, relaxed in 1995) and security of supply (Condition 10). The distribution licence terms were focused on the price cap and the distribution code (Condition 11). Given that the initial PES licence *combined* both supply and distribution, a number of conditions fell across both—such as the standards of performance (Condition 12, later important for energy efficiency) and the efficient use of fuels (Condition 22).

Vesting, the New Companies, and New Faces

The new structure created a number of new companies, but in practice it was much more evolutionary than it might at first have appeared. The RECs were managed by the same people as the Area Boards: NGC was chaired by Jefferies, who had played a key role in the Electricity Council; National Power took over most of the senior CEGB management; and PowerGen's leadership came from the CEGB's next level, led by Edmund Wallis. Thus, the privatized industry was to be run largely by people whose experience was that of operating under monopoly and planning. Very few had any experience of dealing with equity markets or diversifications.

Among the new companies, National Power carried the CEGB ethos and legacy forward. Indeed, as we have seen, the original 1988 White Paper model gave National Power a dominance reminiscent of the role BT had in relation to Mercury in the telecommunications privatization in the early 1980s. Its two key people at the outset—Marshall and John Baker—were both opposed to the break-up of the CEGB. Marshall, as we saw above, believed that the duty to supply was necessary, both for the coherence of the overall structure and to carry through a new nuclear programme. He was forced to resign with the withdrawal of the rest of the nuclear stations, and was replaced by Sir Trevor Holdsworth in July 1990, formerly of GKN. Baker had joined the CEGB as Secretary in 1979. Together, the National Power management team had, as UBS Phillips & Drew calculated, 118 years of experience in the electricity supply industry, out of a total of 262 years of work (UBS Phillips and Drew 1991).

PowerGen had a sharper management focus from the outset, although, ironically, its first outside Chairman, Robert Malpas, did not find it easy to adapt to the challenges of the negotiations with the Treasury over the debt injection and the prospect of a trade sale to Hanson (see below). He was not to survive long, being quickly replaced by Graham Day in November 1990.

The management of the grid had to be constructed from scratch, and, again, the leadership initially came from within the industry. As noted, David Jefferies was Chairman, and the dominant figure on NGC's board, having previously held posts at Southern Electric, the CEGB, as Chairman of London Electricity, and, immediately prior to privatization, as Deputy Chairman of the Electricity Council—the winning side of the battle with the CEGB and Marshall, over control of the grid. Bill Kerss was Chief Executive, again with experience in the Area Boards and the CEGB.

Among the Area Boards, it was 'business as usual'.[25] James Smith (Eastern) and John Harris (East Midlands) had the highest profile. David Jones and then Roger Urwin were, in due course, to play a significant role in NGC, and in Urwin's case later in NGC–Lattice. Together, the RECs' chairmen played a powerful role in privatization negotiations, with very considerable experience, and in a position to thwart challenges to their interests. Not surprisingly, the RECs got an extremely good deal; distribution price caps were actually positive, whereas hindsight demonstrates they should have been negative; gearing was low; and they were able to begin gradual vertical integration. They were to do very well personally out of privatization too, with considerably higher salaries and share options. It was also not surprising that, given virtually none had any experience of acquisitions and diversifications, and their negotiations had left the companies strongly cash-positive, some of the cash was spent on badly focused and expensive acquisitions of new businesses. Chapter 12 documents this large-scale waste of shareholders' assets.

Curiously, the one area where industry knowledge was not greatly represented at privatization was at Offer. The new Director General of

---

[25] The leading cast of figures comprised James Smith, Chairman and Chief Executive of Eastern (incumbent since 1982); John Harris, Chairman and Chief Executive of East Midlands (again, since 1982); John Wilson, Chairman, and Roger Urwin, Managing Director at London (the former since 1982, the latter since 1990, but also an industry insider); Bryan Wilson, Chairman, and John Roberts, Chief Executive, of Manweb (later Chief Executive of United Utilities); Bryan Townsend, Chairman of Midlands (since 1986); David Morris, Chairman of Northern (since 1989); George Squair, Chairman and Chief Executive of SEEBOARD (since 1983); Duncan Ross, Chairman and Chief Executive of Southern (since 1984); Wynford Evans and David Jones (both insiders), Chairman and Managing Director respectively of SWALEC; William Nicol and John Seed, respectively Chairman and Managing Director of SWEB (both insiders); and James Porteous, Chairman and Chief Executive of Yorkshire (since 1984).

Electricity Services, Stephen Littlechild, was an academic with virtually no commercial experience (unlike James McKinnon at Ofgas) and not much specialist knowledge of electricity accounting or even electricity economics. Likewise, his team was made up of outsiders, with Penny Boys, a civil servant, managing the office (and later attempting to provide a link to government in the coal crisis in 1992/93). If the asymmetry of information between the regulators and the industry is a core problem for effective regulation, the sides were extremely unevenly matched.[26]

The Strange Case of Lord Hanson and PowerGen

While, in public, the government continued with the plans for flotation of the industry, in private, the incumbent managements of the companies to be privatized were putting up a good fight. Their interests lay in the early years *after* privatization, not in maximising the proceeds to their existing owner—the government. Armed with all the inside information, and, as we have seen, years of experience in the industry, the companies and their advisers set about lowering expectations about future cost savings, revenues, and, hence, profits. The value of the companies—the outcome of the valuation exercise which the market would impose at flotation—was a variable.

Incumbent management wanted, other things being equal, a low valuation (since shares and share options would then rise), ungeared balance sheets (since this would improve their free cash flow), weak price caps (in the case of the distribution businesses of the RECs, so that they could outperform), and weak regulation of generation (coupled with a generous gap between the price of coal in the British Coal contracts), and of the sale contract for electricity to the RECs (in the case of National Power and PowerGen). REC supply businesses wanted a soft supply price cap to maximize profits and the scope to pass through the costs of investments in new gas power stations.

In almost all these areas, the incumbent management outplayed the Department of Energy and the Treasury. As we shall see, the companies were eventually privatized with a much more benign contractual and regulatory framework than they could reasonably have hoped for. But, on one issue, the Treasury and the Department of Energy decided to fight—the debt on the balance sheets of the generators.

---

[26] The counter-argument was that what the industry needed was 'outside' thinking to break the traditional planning approaches.

Despite Treasury pressure, PowerGen in particular proved very resistant to carrying *any* debt, and, faced with intransigent opposition, the Secretary of State for Energy, Wakeham, just happened out of the blue to receive an expression of interest from Lord Hanson to purchase PowerGen, which Wakeham announced in a statement to the House of Commons on 23 July 1990.[27] Hanson was permitted sole access to relevant information about PowerGen for a month, with a view to making a formal offer, which would then be subject to open competitive bidding from any other interested parties. Just how serious Hanson was, and how seriously the government really considered a trade sale to Hanson, is hard to judge. However, once Wakeham had made his statement, he then had to make a reasonable defence both of Hanson and the possibility of a trade sale rather than a flotation.

Hanson posed several difficulties for Wakeham. The opposition, led now by Shadow Secretary of State, Frank Dobson (Blair having moved to Employment in 1989) homed in on two issues: the tax status of Hanson and the tax implications of acquiring PowerGen; and Hanson's donations to the Conservative Party and his close personal relations with Thatcher. Dobson told the House of Commons that 'the Hanson Trust is not fit to own it [PowerGen]' and, more interestingly, that 'the next Labour government will hold it, like any other shareholders, to a maximum share ownership of 15 per cent.' Other MPs were more prescient: Robert Sheldon questioned whether other bidders would really come forward (with the recent Rover sale to BAe very much in mind); Alan Williams referred to Hanson's formidable reputation as a 'bid-and-break-up machine', and asked for assurances against 'massive asset-stripping'; while Peter Rost suggested that a trade sale might 'increase genuine competition by reducing the risk of a cosy dependency'.

But the real political threat in the opposition challenge came with the allegations that discussions with Hanson had been going on since May, with the implication that the interest was not 'out of the blue'. Ian Bruce, in the debate, pointed out that 'the electricity industry has been trying regularly to talk down the value of its assets' and Wakeham responded that 'competitive tendering can do nothing other than demonstrate clearly the proper value of the company', and he went further in saying he would also entertain an approach for National Power.

In the end, the government got the best out of the Hanson affair. Hanson went away, but the generators suddenly became much more compliant

---

[27] See *Hansard*, 23 July 1990 for the statement by Wakeham, and the ensuing debate.

about balance sheets. And the Hanson episode was to have two further consequences for PowerGen. First, it led to the removal of its Chairman, who was perceived as weak in responding to what its board saw as a threat. Second, PowerGen's incumbent management, inherited from the industry, had to think through what the application of Hanson's cost-cutting strategy would mean; and the experience of the Hanson approach provided the basis for its subsequent superior cost-reduction strategies, when compared with National Power. PowerGen's corporate objective became that of being the 'lowest-cost producer' (Powergen Annual Report 1990), and, in effect, it implemented much of what Hanson would have done.

The Rolling Flotation: RECs, National Power and PowerGen, and Scotland

The scale of the asset sales meant that there would have to be a rolling process to flotation: the RECs in November 1990, and then National Power and PowerGen, 60 per cent of which was sold in March 1991 (the remaining 40 per cent in March 1995 at a much higher price), and finally the Scottish companies in June 1991. Golden shares in each were retained at the time for the purpose of preventing national strategic assets falling into foreign hands. Much later, in the generators' case, these were to give the government significant bargaining power (see Chapter 12).

The RECs, incorporating NGC, had an issue price of £2.40 per share. The proceeds of the 100 per cent sale were around £8 billion (£5.1 billion for the shares, and £2.8 billion in debt), and therefore on a par with those from the privatization of British Gas. The shares, payable in instalments, went to an immediate premium of 49 p, against a 15 p target used by the Department of Energy. The National Audit Office (NAO) attributed 30 p of the 49 p to 'the general upward movements in the market which began after the offer was priced' (NAO 1992a: 4), and pointed to the recommendations of the Department's advisers against a 100 per cent sale, which the government ignored, given its overriding objectives of completing the sale ahead of the election (ibid.: 6).

The generators were sold next for 175 p per share, and the offer was five times oversubscribed (1.9 million applications for shares were received). The shares rose to a first-day premium of 213 p.

The value of the 60 per cent of the two companies amounted to just under £3 billion (£2.1 billion for the shares and £0.8 billion debt). It was a far cry from the £22.6 billion replacement cost of the power stations, which had formed the basis of the price increases in early 1988, themselves the outcome of the application of the Byatt Committee's report but the NAO's report on the sale nevertheless found very little to criticize (NAO 1992*b*).

By the time the government came to sell the Scottish companies, ScottishPower and Scottish Hydro-Electric, the process of 'learning-by-selling' was well advanced. £3.5 billion was raised (£2.9 billion in shares and £0.6 billion in debt), and £1 billion of National Loan Fund debt was written off. The initial premia were very much smaller than for the RECs or the generators, and the companies were to trade close to the offer price for some time. Not surprisingly, the NAO concluded that 'the Department carried out the sale...on favourable terms for the taxpayer, securing proceeds which were as high as could have been expected' (NAO 1992*c*: 5). For the companies, the lack of a premium was to make it harder to grow their businesses through acquisition, and it is all the more remarkable that ScottishPower was to lead the way with its bid for Manweb on 24 July 1995, as we shall see in Chapter 12.

A Qualified Success

Although electricity privatization has been much criticized, within the political parameters it was much more successful than that of gas. Against managerial opposition, the CEGB was broken up, and the principle of competition in generation and supply was accepted. Compared with the snail's pace of reform in much of Europe, British electricity privatization was well ahead of the other European Member States and the European Commission.

The creation of the Pool was at the centre of the new model: without it, supply competition would have been much weaker, and the generators' duopoly behaviour much harder to monitor and bear down upon. To create such a market from scratch, and one which was up and running within a short period of time, and which actually worked, was a major achievement for the small team at the Department of Energy. It stands in strong contrast to the costs and delays associated with the NETA programme a decade later, and, despite the subsequent assertions that it was 'a flawed market' (as detailed in Chapter 17), the failures in the generation market had more to do with the structure of the industry, and the politically engineered coal contracts, than the Pool's design.

As with all large-scale political initiatives, electricity privatization involved the trade-off of numerous conflicting objectives. It had not only to meet the tests of economic efficiency, but also to recognize the interests of miners, the nuclear industry, electricity workers, incumbent management, and customers. And there was only one Parliament in which to complete the process—ahead of what the opinion polls predicted would be a Labour victory in 1992.

Of course, it could all have been done much better. The nuclear confusion determined that serious mistakes would be made with the structure, and the UDM miners' position dictated the initial vertical contracts. Incumbent management leveraged its position, which resulted in excess returns immediately after privatization. An initial break-up of the CEGB into five firms would have given competition in generation a better start, and the liberalization of coal first would have provided more efficient cost signals, and probably headed off more of the first round of the dash for gas.

Compared with other liberalization experiments abroad, the feature that stands out in the British exercise is the 'solution' to the stranded costs in nuclear and coal. In the former, by (eventually) keeping the assets (and liabilities) in the public sector for the first five years after privatizing the rest of the industry, taxpayers could take most of the hit without affecting pricing, and customers could be taxed through the Fossil Fuel Levy without distorting supply competition. (In Scotland, contracts also played a role.) In the case of coal, the main asset write-down was completed ahead of privatization of the electricity industry, and, although initial contracts protected the industry, a three-year transition to full market competition was not entirely unreasonable, given the history of the subsidy. Had either nuclear or coal assets been in private hands, the government's freedom of manoeuvre would have been heavily curtailed. The examples of Spain and Germany, for nuclear stranded assets, as well as the United States, illustrate how much harder the problem is to solve when the liberalizer (the government) does not own the stranded assets.

In terms of its lasting effects, privatization facilitated a substantial reduction in costs on a scale quite unanticipated at the time. It allowed regulators to promote competition against private companies, which could no longer call on ministers to defend them at the despatch box, and it broke the element of capture that existed between the industry and the department. State-owned industries (such as EDF in France) have proved far more effective in their resistance to competition.

But the most important consequences have been in relation to the fuel mix and investment. Privatization was bad news for the nuclear industry, unable to compete in the capital markets against coal or gas technologies. The heady days when Howell could project forward one PWR a year for a decade, and Thatcher could enviously contemplate following France's lead were over. Marshall was surely right when he claimed that, once the CEGB lost the duty to supply, the nuclear dream was over. The gradual erosion and then removal of the supply monopoly made it worse. Even if the CEGB had been kept intact, after privatization, more nuclear investment would have been impossible without direct government support. After privatization, the nuclear industry was forced to concentrate on sweating its assets, not building more of them. Any eventual return in the 2000s would require major surgery, or subsidy, to the electricity market. (In the event, British Energy could not survive without government assistance.)

Electricity privatization also doomed the coal industry, since it let gas into the market on a basis with which coal could not compete. No new coal stations were to be built in the next decade, and it was to fall from overwhelming dominance (about 75 per cent of generation) almost to second place with gas within a decade. While it could have been protected at a greater level, privatization made the assistance required look more explicitly like state aid, and, as competition in supply emerged, customers could bypass such expensive options. Though, as we shall see in Chapter 8, the causes were complex, the dash for gas was only possible on a large scale and at such a speed because the coal contracts kept the price high—a fact that was to be conveniently ignored by Peter Mandelson in his 1998 White Paper (DTI 1998*b*), when he blamed the generators' abuse of market power, and the Pool as the vehicle for its exercise.

So the overriding result was that existing assets were used much more efficiently, and the nuclear and coal industries were reduced to the status of declining fuel sources. Privatization converted an industry for which coal and nuclear were the dominant fuels into one in which they were increasingly marginal. It was not the change of ownership alone which caused this to happen, but its contribution in conjunction with the transition to competition, which it facilitated. As with gas privatization—which was much worse in design—the change in ownership facilitated the encroachment of competition. The catalyst was, in both cases, the regulator, who after privatization had a much more powerful effect on privately owned companies. Neither McKinnon nor Littlechild had to regulate nationalized industries,[28] although the government itself, through residual ownership (the 40 per cent stake in the generators and continued ownership of the coal industry), would provide some difficult moments. The most infamous was the coal crisis in 1992/93, the first real test of the government's commitment to its planned transition to a fully liberalized fuel and electricity supply market.

[28] The difficulties which Postcomm faced in 2002 in trying to open up the state-owned company, the Post Office, provide a strong contrast.

8

The Transition to Competition in the Electricity Industry

Competition is essentially a process of the formation of opinion: by spreading information, it creates that unity and coherence of the economic system which we presuppose when we think of it as one market. It creates the views the people have about what is best and cheapest, and it is because of it that people know at least as much about possibilities and opportunities as they in fact do. It is thus a process which involves a continuous change in the data and whose significance must therefore be completely missed by any theory which treats these data as constant. ('The Meaning of Competition', Friedrich von Hayek, 1948, p. 106)

The Transitional Programme

Privatization is never a clean and simple matter. Carefully designed policies enshrined in ideal structures cannot realistically be expected. Although economists might concentrate on the promotion of competition to ensure efficiency, the social-welfare function is much more complex. Politicians are routinely attacked for the inevitable compromises and trade-offs between social and economic objectives, but these are what the electorate demands. In order for privatization to take place at all, a majority in Parliament is needed, and ever more sophisticated models of industrial structure inevitably take time to introduce. Any privatization is thus a reflection of the peculiar mix of politics, ideology, and economics, welded together by the particular individuals with power at the time. In the case of electricity, the key individuals were, as we saw in Chapter 7, decidedly more pro-competition than those who oversaw gas privatization. But although Cecil Parkinson was able to break up the structure of the Central Electricity Generating Board (CEGB), he was not able to make it fully competitive. That had to be a post-privatization policy, and therefore had to rely on a regulator who would execute this policy.

In addition to the matter of timing, there were several additional reasons why a transitionary period would be required. The legal prohibition on burning gas in power stations was about to be lifted,[1] and hence the coming of combined-cycle gas turbines (CCGTs) in generation was more a prospect than a reality (even though Roosecote was already contracted). The challenge of gas to PowerGen and National Power would unfold after privatization.

Supply competition was an even more distant prospect in 1990. Although a number of developed countries had already introduced a competitive element for large industrial customers (as, indeed, had Britain in the Energy Act 1983), nobody had much idea of how supply competition for smaller companies and domestic customers might actually work. The necessary metering and information technology infrastructure for domestic switching was largely absent. While a number of smaller countries in the Nordic region, as well as New Zealand and Chile, had toyed with radical notions, none had addressed the issues raised by a country the size of Britain.

In an important sense, the concept and design of the transition to full retail competition was an article of faith rather than a well worked-out plan. A series of milestones was laid down, to which all participants would adjust. These milestones were remarkably simple, as Fig. 8.1 illustrates.

It was a plan which was to provide the momentum for change in the industry throughout the 1990s. It was also to provoke a series of crises for

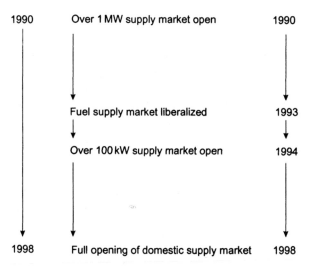

FIG. 8.1 The transitionary milestone

---

[1] EC Directive 75/404/EEC was repealed in March 1991 (Council of the European Communities 1975). In fact, the Department of Energy discovered that CCGTs could be legal in 'special' circumstances, and the Department used the loophole to begin the dash for gas before privatization.

all the players: in coal, in generation, for the regional electricity companies (RECs) and at each stage for Offer (and subsequently Ofgem) and the
government. Only the 1994 date was met, and that caused considerable
chaos. The 1998 liberalization was expensive, late, and fairly chaotic. Coal,
even in 2002, was still not yet fully open to competition.

Why, then, did its architects pick such a rigid timetable in ignorance of
its practicality? Although there was inevitably a strong dose of cynicism
in fixing dates which were carefully designed to be beyond the successive
general elections, there was a clear rationale behind the plan and, as with
much in the Conservatives' market approach, there was a strong dose of
Austrian economics. The central idea is that competition is a process of
discovery. In a world of imperfect information, the competitive process
allows entrepreneurs to test out new ideas. Some of these fall by the way-
side, the victims of a market equivalent of a Darwinian struggle. Others
thrive and succeed. For electricity supply, the task was to liberalize, to let
markets work. What would then happen could not strictly be predicted.
But not to try would be to waste all the innovation and opportunities
which only the market could reveal.

To this faith in markets was added a further observation. The job of
business is not to create competition, but rather monopolies, and, once
established, to protect them. British Coal fought to protect its monopoly
by handicapping gas and nuclear, and by encouraging monopolistic contracts with the generators. Generators had a duopoly and, without checks,
would be likely to collude to hold up prices and deter entry. The RECs
already had a statutory monopoly in supply, and it would be odd to
expect them to volunteer to give it up. It would be like turkeys voting for
Christmas. Hence, a powerful regulator was required to apply the necessary pressure, and deadlines needed to be set.

The role of the deadlines is to give companies (and regulators) targets.
Like other transitionary programmes (such as monetary union), one can
either wait until conditions are right, and then take the final step, or decide
when the players must be ready and work backwards to ensure implementation. Given the (lack of) incentives on the RECs to open up their
markets to supply competition, the preset deadlines were a better route.
The industry then had to be bound to the mast of an ever more liberalized
market, with companies, regulators, and government forced to come up
with solutions, or face the criticism which inevitably follows delay.

Preset deadlines do, however, need to be translated into practical implementation plans, and it is here that a major part of Austrian economics was
largely ignored. For Hayek, the role of the state (and, in this case, regulators) was to define the rules within which individuals and firms would

cooperate and compete. Competition did not arise spontaneously, but only in the context of the framework for markets, and this involved prescribing the rules. Then contracts and trades could be defined and, more importantly, enforced through law.

The most competitive markets are usually ones in which rules are clearly defined. The Stock Exchange is an obvious example, where rules define who can trade, what constitutes a trade, and how a trade is settled. Such market rules can be set by the players or outside regulators. In electricity supply, they could only be set by outsiders, since the incumbents had little incentive to make the market work. This crucial link in the transition to competition was not one that the Director General of Electricity Supply, Stephen Littlechild (or, indeed, subsequent ministers), put much emphasis on. It was considered to be enough to place the responsibility on the RECs to open up their supply markets and expect them to deliver. The result should not be surprising, and this fundamental mistake was to be repeated again much later in the early design of NETA to replace the Pool.

Fuel Sources: The Failure to Liberalize Coal

The link between the coal industry and electricity generation had been a tight one throughout the post-war period, as we saw in Chapter 2. Coal output was planned to meet power station demand, and power stations were built to burn coal. This planning model had reached its rationalistic apex in the planning approach of the 1960s and 1970s. Its economics were set out in Posner's *Fuel Policy* (1973). The result was that Britain's electricity capacity ended up overwhelmingly coal-fired and dependent on the National Coal Board (NCB) (reinforced when the oil price jumped in th/ 1970s). It was a relationship which Margaret Thatcher had been dete mined to break since 1979.

For Thatcher, the problem of coal was identified with the miners her strategies had been to break the power of the National Un' Mineworkers (NUM). Victory over the miners' strike achieved described in Chapter 4. But to ensure the victory was entren/ dependency on coal was to be further undermined by policies to reduce its market share. Among these policies, building mc capacity was an early ambition. However, only Sizewell B got ahead (Hinkley C subsequently got planning permission but built), and the privatization process itself had revealed the ov/ cost obstacles to her dream of a French-style pressurized-w (PWR) programme. There remained three further options against the miners: importing coal, switching to gas, and br/

electricity and coal industries through privatization. Her government, and its Conservative successors, were to encourage all three.

The timing of the transition to competition had to have regard to the initial contracts between British Coal and the two generators, National Power and PowerGen for the period 1990–93. The end date was deliberately chosen: the expiry at the end of March 1993 meant that coal prices and volumes would be held up artificially until safely after the last possible date for the next general election. In consequence, those pits employing the Union of Democratic Mineworkers (UDM) miners who had helped Thatcher to her victory over Arthur Scargill in the great strike in 1984/85 would have some protection, and coal could be 'parked' off the political agenda for the rest of the Parliament. Then either Labour would have to explicitly backtrack on competition, or a new Conservative mandate could provide the basis for the completion of the transition.

To complete this contractual 'fix', the transition also provided for the supply price control—protecting those customers in the monopoly franchise—to expire in 1993 too. Hence, the back-to-back contractual solution was watertight, the industry remained *contractually* vertically integrated, and politicians could concentrate on other matters, such as the controversy over Britain's role in Europe which split the Conservative Party, through to the next election. The generators, meanwhile, could get on with investing in import facilities for the day when they would no longer be beholden to British Coal, build up stocks, and the RECs could encourage the dash for gas. The market was rigged in favour of coal, but its very protection—higher prices and volumes than dictated by market forces—would be its undoing.

That liberalization of the fuel market failed to be delivered in 1993 came as a great surprise to politicians and many in the industry. Indeed, flush with a somewhat unexpected election victory in May 1992, the new President of the Board of Trade, Michael Heseltine, and his Energy Minister, Tim Eggar, began to consider ways of privatizing the coal industry—what Cecil Parkinson had called 'the ultimate privatization' (1992: 280–1). The coal perspective on the crisis and the privatization are discussed in Chapter 9; here we consider the electricity side. NM Rothschild (see DTI 1993: 22) was commissioned by the government to review in the summer of 1992 the financial prospects for the industry, and a leaked draft report suggested that, when these coal contracts expired in 1993, the demand for coal from the England and Wales electricity supply industry would fall from over 70 million tonnes in 1992/93 to 45–50 million tonnes in 1996/97. Following the Rothschild report, the government announced on 13 October 1992 that thirty-one of British Coal's fifty deep mines would close within six months. It was a matter of arithmetic: there was no market for any more pits to service. This pro-voked a crisis. Ministers seemed paralysed: the Lawson doctrine and the transitional arrangements dictated non-interference, but the politics of coal dictated otherwise (as it was to do again for Labour in 1997). The small parliamentary majority left the government vulnerable to back-bench pressure, and this comprised an odd alliance of members from mining constituencies, advocates of the national champions model, and some of the Heathites, who believed that miners had a place within the one-nation tradition of Eden, Macmillan, Butler, and Heath.

After an initial period of stoicism, the political resistance began to crum-ble. On 19 October, Heseltine announced a moratorium on the closure of twenty-one of the thirty-one pits and the government began its own review of the closure programme, supported by suitably minded consult-ants. Government action led to the other remaining pits being subject to a ninety-day consultation period to end on 29 January 1993. The House of Commons Select Committee on Trade and Industry had in any event launched an inquiry, and it quickly became the focus for the political debate. Chaired by Richard Caborn and including the previous chairman of the House of Commons Select Committee on Energy, Michael Clark, as well as the influential backbenchers, Keith Hampson, Cranley Onslow, and Stan Orme, the government accepted early on that it would have to go with the grain of its recommendations if it was to secure a majority in the House of Commons.

It was not, however, to be a straightforward exercise to rescue coal from its market fate. Privatization meant that ministers now had to 'persuade' generators to buy more coal in the face of shareholder, not public, inter-ests. The scope to persuade generators to buy more British coal at higher prices than those which prevailed on world markets depended, in turn, on the ability of the generators to pass these costs on to final customers. As long as these were within a franchise monopoly, the RECs could pass through the coal 'tax'. These customers were, however, protected by a price cap, set by the *independent* regulator. It was therefore Littlechild who held the key to further protection of the coal industry, and who con-sequently in effect decided policy.

Given that the government was reluctant to legislate in favour of coal, and given, in any event, the limitations to its powers to provide state aid under European law, the task for the government was to 'persuade' the independent regulator to facilitate the circumvention of fuel competition. Given Littlechild's duty to *promote* competition and his free-market cre-dentials, this was far from straightforward. Indeed, so independent was Littlechild that, when asked at a Select Committee Hearing on 4 November about his discussions with Heseltine on these matters, he answered that he had not even met the President of the Board of Trade, providing a salutary reminder of the gulf between political and public understanding of the new relationship between regulators and government, and the reality of what had been unleashed through privatization. To the political audience, it came as a great surprise to learn that regulators no longer saw their domain as political (House of Commons Select Committee on Trade and Industry 1992: paras 457–60, and 526).

Littlechild did, however, realize the danger of a return to planning and, while hostile to limiting coal competition upstream, he could take comfort from the fact that higher coal prices encouraged entry by gas. As Schumpeter (1943) had famously argued, monopoly profits created the carrots to suck in entrants, and hence monopoly was likely to be temporary. Paradoxically, then, limiting upstream fuel competition had the effect of encouraging entry in generation and, hence, adding to the process of slowly eroding PowerGen's and National Power's market share. A temporary fix meant higher prices, which in turn meant more competition. It was a paradox that was to recur throughout the transition to competition—the trade-off between consumer protection in the short run through lower prices, against promoting competition to limit longer-term market power—and one which had been delegated to the regulator.[2]

The government wavered over the Christmas period, and still in early January it toyed with a U-turn on the whole transitionary process—and therefore with legislation, with all the parliamentary difficulties this might create.[3] In hindsight, the sense of a knife edge has been largely forgotten, but it was very real at the time.[4]

---

[2] In the event, the options were set out in Offer (1992*b*) and then the proposals for the new supply price control were set out in Offer (1993*c*). Littlechild stated: 'I have decided against introducing a generation yardstick as a formal determinant of allowed revenue. I propose that the purchase costs of electricity for the franchise market should continue to be passed through to franchise customers' (ibid.: i, para 3; see also paras 3.10 and 3.11). In the earlier 'Review of Economic Purchasing' (Offer 1992*c*), Littlechild stated that he was satisfied that the new five-year contracts met the RECs' obligation to purchase electricity economically. The author recommended that there should be no automatic pass-through, but rather an industry average or index of fuel cost should be used (House of Commons Select Committee on Trade and Industry 1992, p. 57).

[3] Littlechild set out his views in a letter to the government, dated 11 January (Offer 1993*a*). In effect, he conceded the cost pass-through for the coal contracts as the price for allowing the 1994 franchise drop to go ahead.

[4] The author had a meeting with Heseltine, Eggar, and senior officials in early January 1993 to outline his suggestions. Repeatedly, Heseltine asked 'how many pits will this save'? to specific proposals. A sense of short-term expediency prevailed, even as the wider political heat in the debate was gradually dissipating.

The House of Commons Select Committee on Trade and Industry report, 'British Energy Policy and the Market for Coal', appeared on 26 January 1993, concluding that financial help for British Coal should be limited to that necessary to establish a competitive basis, and that a severe imbalance between supply and demand could not be sustained indefinitely. In other words, a further temporary fix should be engineered to buy time for the coal industry to become more competitive. Within these new market constraints, a larger market for coal could, it believed, be found. The recommendations fell into three broad categories: measures to create a bigger market, new subsidized contracts, and reforms to the regulatory regime.

The first group of recommendations to create a bigger market meant essentially biasing the market towards coal and against nuclear and other alternatives. These measures suggested that: a carbon/energy tax should be resisted; the Fossil Fuel Levy (FFL) should be reduced; the nuclear review should be brought forward; the French interconnector should be subject to the FFL and conditional on non-discriminatory access to French markets; flue-gas desulphurization (FGD) should be required for Orimulsion and more FGD should be fitted to coal stations; opencast planning should be restricted and licensed output reduced; the 1 MW limit on opening up the electricity market should be maintained until 1998; the consents policy for new generators should give preference to combined heat and power (CHP); CCGTs should be considered for mid-merit; coal stocks should be held at not less than 20 million tonnes by generators; and clean-coal technology should be supported.

The second group of recommendations was concerned with new contracts from 1993 to 1998, and indeed beyond. The Committee recommended:

The Government should provide a subsidy to the generators of England and Wales to burn up to 15 million tonnes of deep-mined [British Coal] coal per annum above the quantities of 40 million tonnes falling to 30 million tonnes which they already expect to contract for in 1993–98, and the subsidy should be equal to the difference between the delivered costs of the additional [British Coal] coal and imported coal. (1993, ibid.: para. 225)

In addition the non-electricity market could be subsidized by up to 3 million tonnes for the same period. And, finally, in 1994/95 the government should require the generators to buy an extra 5 million tonnes above the 45 million tonnes recommended above. These extra tonnes were to be paid for by the RECs in return for not lowering the franchise below the 1 MW level until 1998. In other words, more room would be created to burn coal by restricting the alternatives, and generators would be required to contract for the extra volume in exchange for REC contracts whose monopoly franchises would be maintained. Customers would then pick up the bill.

The third set of recommendations related to regulation. The Committee thought that the regulator should take a stronger hand in controlling generators' prices, and he should be given a new primary duty of protecting consumers, and a new secondary duty 'to consider the legitimate long-term interests of indigenous fuel producers'. His powers, and those of his colleague at Ofgas, should be subject to greater governmental and parliamentary control. Finally, the Committee suggested that Offer and Ofgas might be merged, and that an energy commission might be considered.[5]

These points on regulation were incidental to the Committee's main preoccupation, but the primary duty to customers and the merging of the two bodies were to eventually figure in the Utilities Act 2000, and the idea of an energy commission has not gone away (although the government was to sidestep this proposal, instead setting up an Energy Advisory Panel).[6]

With this extensive exploration of the options available to hand, and armed with its own consultancy reports, the government had to decide which way it would jump: to work within the new structures; or to abandon the competitive market approach. Fortunately the Select Committee on Trade and Industry gave it enough room for manoeuvre: it could claim to be *both* adhering to the competitive approach *and* putting in place a 'temporary' fix for coal.

The White Paper, 'The Prospects for Coal: Conclusions of the Government's Coal Review', was published in March 1993 (DTI 1993). Its starting point was pure Lawson: 'Competitive markets provide the best means of ensuring that the nation has access to secure, diverse and sustainable supplies of energy in the forms that people and businesses want, and at competitive prices' (para 2.2, p. 3).

But it was one thing to assert such principles, and another to follow them. What followed was a re-run of 1990–93. The government decided to put in place a further 'final', and implicit, transition for coal. The generators would agree to sign contracts for higher volumes at preset prices for the period 1993–98, though not at the level the Committee proposed. The RECs would, in turn, contract to buy coal-backed electricity for the

---

[5] In evidence to the Committee, the author recommended the setting up of an energy agency (House of Commons Select Committee on Trade and Industry 1992: 55–66).

[6] The Performance and Innovation Unit report (PIU 2002) recommended a Sustainable Energy Policy Unit.

same period, and the regulator would ensure that the extra costs to the RECs would be passed on to final customers through the supply price cap, but the franchise would still drop as planned in 1994. Everyone apparently got something: the miners had higher employment; the generators had an assured revenue stream; and the RECs got cost pass-through and greater profits from their first wave of CCGT contracts and equity investments. The regulator could happily see the dash for gas bring more competition, and the government could claim to have saved some of the pits, while providing a secure contract revenue stream for the coal industry until 1998, which would in turn provide the basis for privatization. Only the customers and the environment lost out, but neither had effective political voices in the 1992/93 crisis.

To this new set of coal contracts, other elements of token support were offered for coal. The government offered a subsidy for *additional* tonnages above those in the new contracts to displace imports or other fossil fuels, but this would have little effect, as world prices continued to fall. The government also put pressure on stock levels, and on opencast, but resisted the Select Committee recommendations on French imports and nuclear.

In the end, the outcome of the great coal crisis of 1992/93 was a temporary setback to a longer-term trend. Coal was given a reprieve, and the market was rigged to achieve this. But the reprieve served only to underline the inevitable end for a large-scale coal industry. And it spelt the end of the nationalized coal monopoly, as it provided the basis for its break-up and sale.

Pool Pricing and Generator Competition

The 1990–93 and 1993–98 coal contracts provided the framework within which the transition to competition in generation was designed to evolve. At the time of privatization, the behavioural consequences on the generation market of these contracts had not been fully appreciated. The fundamental assumption made at privatization was that the generators would compete in the Pool, and that, since Pool prices were open and transparent, any abuse of dominance would be immediately apparent to the regulator, who had the statutory duty to promote competition.

A basic difference of view then resulted. The generators themselves, and many investors, had taken the government's intentions seriously: that the generators were only very lightly and passively regulated, free to pursue the normal profit-maximization strategies. In business terms, this could include behaving 'commercially'. On this view, then, Pool prices would be determined by the market. The other view, held by the regulator and large users, assumed that an active strategy of *promoting competition* would lead to a gradual reduction in market share by National Power and PowerGen, and that intervention would follow if Pool prices were 'excessive'. Reduction of market share was then in an important sense an *objective* of regulatory policy from the outset, as it had already become for the gas regulator. 'Competition' and 'loss of market share' were assumed to be synonymous.[7]

This difference led to a long-drawn-out series of skirmishes between the generators and the regulator, and the active policy of encouraging entry into generation by the RECs which was to continue into the next decade. By 2000, the two main fossil-fuel generators, National Power and PowerGen, were to have seen their market share substantially reduced, to have been subjected to a two-year price cap and been forced (twice) to dispose of plant, and to have been threatened with a 'good behaviour' clause. None of this was anticipated at privatization, and if the regulatory objective was 'loss of market share', Offer was remarkably successful. Indeed, by 2001 National Power had been broken up into Innogy and International Power, and in 2002 PowerGen was absorbed by E.ON, and Innogy into RWE. No trace of a national champion was left.

The early years focused on entry and, in particular, the vertical contracts by the RECs with so-called independent power producers (IPPs), which, in turn, took out contracts with North Sea gas producers. The context for that entry was the coal contracts, expectations about the conduct of National Power and PowerGen, fuel price projections, and environmental constraints. In a very real sense, 'bad behaviour'—the exercise of market power to keep prices above costs—was assumed all round, by investors, incumbents, and entrants.

Indeed, even government itself assumed that the duopolists would at least implicitly collude, and this was reflected in its price projections. At privatization, the Department of Energy had produced a series of projections for Pool prices, most of which never saw the light of day. One of these—known as Horton IV after Geoff Horton,[8] then an official in the

---

[7] This second view was held by the more astute City commentators too. A UBS Phillips and Drew report stated that: 'if price competition between National Power and PowerGen locks out new entrants further structural changes to the industry will be made. This is likely to occur through an MMC referral and subsequent break up of the two generators, probably through assets sales' (UBS Phillips and Drew 1991). In fact, the *threat* of an MMC referral was to be enough to trigger such sales.

[8] Horton was to become a key member of Offer's team, under Littlechild, and, eventually, the Director General of Electricity and Gas Regulation for Northern Ireland, before going on to advise Northern Ireland Electricity and a wide range of other energy companies and regulators.

TABLE 8.1 Contracts for differences as a percentage of total capacity

	1991	1992	1993
National Power	84.3	72.7	72.7
PowerGen	89.1	70.6	70.6

Source: Helm and Powell (1992), derived from the privatization prospectus.

Department—became central to subsequent debates. It showed a slow but continuous rise in Pool prices through to 'an equilibrium' in 1993. Events proved this scenario to be very wrong and, for reasons which could have been foreseen in advance; Pool prices actually *fell* following privatization.

Why did the generators with overwhelming dominance permit this? The key fact for the period 1990–93 was that most of their revenues were already fixed through contracts for differences with the RECs to back the coal contracts (as shown in Table 8.1).

Thus, the Pool, far from being the central market in electricity, was actually a sideshow with regard to current revenue. It might have mattered to the large industrial customers (LICs) which were free from the start to choose their supplier, but, in any event, these were initially protected by the LICs' scheme (see Chapter 7).[9]

For the generators, then, Pool prices could be viewed from a medium-term perspective and, in particular, could take account of the threat of entry. By lowering prices initially, the future prospects of the new IPPs might be more uncertain. In addition, the two generators were able to sort out their relative market shares, free from significant revenue costs. Lower Pool prices were, in an important sense, nearly as good as a free lunch.

In practice, there were two problems with this strategy. The first was that it was not credible over the appropriate timeframe for which the IPPs were to operate. After 1993, it was expected that the generators' contracts with the RECs would fall away when the coal contracts expired. Hence, after March 1993, the Pool price would be more important, and was expected to rise. Second, to the extent that RECs were allowed to pass on the costs of the IPPs to their captured customers through the supply price cap, Pool prices did not matter to the economics of the IPP contracts until after 1998 when the RECs' domestic monopoly franchise was due to expire. By that time, the depreciation on the capital costs of the first wave of CCGTs would have been recovered, and the RECs had the comfort of knowing that the IPPs were critical to the regulator's policy of promoting generator competition.

[9] See Allaz and Vila (1993) on the impact of quantity contracts on oligopolistic behaviour in spot markets.

The vertical contractual relations in the first period were, however, complex, and at the end of each year a process of adjustment took place. Gradually, more of the large users could exercise choice, and a strategic game in Pool prices ensued. The generators' initial pricing behaviour, which produced Pool prices in the first year some 25 per cent below Horton IV, was gradually reversed, and, by August of the second year, they were 17 per cent above prices in the August of the first year (Helm and Powell 1992). At the same time, costs (coal) had been falling, as provided in the contracts with the generators. Hence, prices rose as costs fell—a wonderfully profitable scenario. With the expiry of the initial LICs' scheme to protect industrial customers in the first year after privatization, they were now exposed to Pool prices and, hence, to the market power of the generators. Heartened by the success of the agitation against British Gas, which had resulted in the 1988 Monopolies and Mergers Commission (MMC) inquiry, the industrial customers lobbied hard, and Littlechild responded by conducting an inquiry—the first of many, as it turned out, which triggered a sequence of events rather similar to that which the Ofgas inquiry into competition in the industrial gas market had set off in 1987/88.

The first investigation by Offer began in September 1991 into spikes in Pool prices, the level of Pool prices, capacity payment, and uplift. The calls from large users for intervention were rejected, except in regard to capacity payments and uplift. Littlechild found that the generators had been playing games with the Pool rules. For example, 'during the period, PowerGen followed a policy of declaring some plant unavailable which was subsequently declared available.' This, the Director General said, was an abuse of dominance (Offer 1991: 3). Games were also played with uplift, doubling its costs, by increasing the bid prices for constrained-on plant required to balance the system. National Power's conduct with the Fawley plant was particularly criticized.

As to remedies, Littlechild proposed a new licence condition in respect of plant availability and closures, allowing him to appoint an assessor who would opine on whether the closure was reasonable, taking into account, among other things, whether alternative buyers had been sought for mothballed or closed plant, and he also suggested that a relaxation of direct sales limits be considered. The House of Commons Select Committee on Energy considered the proposals for the new licence condition, and went one stage further (House of Commons Select Committee on Energy 1992*a*, paras 62–69), recommending that:

The Director General take steps as soon as possible to reduce the dominance of the two generators, and that when the electricity market has had time to develop further, not later than 1995, he should decide whether the two main generators should be referred to the MMC and explain fully the reasons for his decision. (Para 72)

He had in fact entertained the option in the 1991 report, but not come to such a definite conclusion.[10] Further encouragement to consider structural options came from the evidence on uplift, set out in his 'Report on Constrained-on Plant' in October 1992 (Offer 1992a). In December 1992 a further Offer 'Review of Pool Prices' was published (Offer 1992d), in response to increases in system marginal price after recontracting in April (13 per cent), more pronounced peaks in the summer months (arousing the suspicion that maintenance outages were being manipulated), and more trouble with uplift. Littlechild concluded that 'National Power and PowerGen together have market power and exercised it in a significant way' (ibid.: 2).

Concurrent with the December 1992 'Review of Pool Prices', Offer also published its 'Review of Economic Purchasing' (Offer 1992c), followed by 'Review of Economic Purchasing: Further Statement' in 1993 (Offer 1993b). These dealt with the thorny question of the contracts between the RECs (obliged under licence to purchase 'economically') and IPPs. By this time the conduct of the generators had got conflated with the dash for gas and the coal crisis.

Contracting Out and the Pool

Facilitating competition by ensuring that customers can shop around is a necessary condition for supply competition. To be effective, there needs to be upstream competition. One of the issues raised by large users from the outset had been their right not only to choose their supplier, but also the way that they are supplied. There was from the early days a questioning of the restriction which required all contracting to be directed via the Pool. Some customers demanded the right to be able to contract outside the Pool in direct bilateral contracts with generators—motivated largely by a desire to obtain lower prices for industrial customers.

Such a demand raised the issue of the centrality of the Pool to supply competition. Is it necessary to prescribe the form and structure of the market place? Although, as we shall see in Chapter 17, Littlechild and Eileen Marshall were to take a very different tack later with the review of electricity trading arrangements and NETA, the early debates produced rather different answers. In response to a ministerial request (16 December 1993), Offer duly investigated this issue, publishing a consultation paper on

---

[10] 'I do not rule out the possibility of a reference to the Monopolies and Mergers Commission' (Offer 1991: 2).

3 March 1994 (Offer 1994*a*) and then a 'Report on Trading Outside the Pool', in July 1994 (Offer 1994*b*) Against the obvious libertarian view that parties should be left to contract voluntarily as they choose, to seek the most efficient solutions, two sets of objections were raised: that compuls-ory trading through the Pool ensured transparency, and hence was essen-tial to limit monopoly abuse and to facilitate the development of contract and futures market; and that the need instantly to match demand with supply was a physical requirement for the Pool to provide a despatch mechanism. In the event, Littlechild upheld both arguments and rejected trading outside the Pool. As Littlechild stated in the report:

Allowing trading outside the Pool could have potential benefits to those involved, and arrangements could be made to maintain coordination of the system. But so far there is little tangible evidence of the gains likely to be secured, and it would be time consuming and costly to make necessary arrangements. There are poten-tial detriments to competition and new entry, both from a thinner and less trans-parent market and from placing new entrants and smaller competitors at a disadvantage in securing rights to despatch... I conclude that, at the present time, a sufficient case has not been made for significant changes to existing arrange-ments so as to allow widespread trading outside the Pool. (Offer 1994*b*: iii–iv)

He went on to reject *pay-as-bid* too, on the grounds that 'it seems likely to have disadvantages in terms of increasing risks, particularly for smaller gen-erators, without a strong likelihood that prices will be lower' (ibid.: iv–v). Thus, in 1994, Littlechild rejected two of the main planks of what was to become NETA in due course, and for good reasons which, as we shall see in Chapter 17, remain relevant.

However, Offer's conclusions did not satisfy the critics. On the one hand, industrialists could not gain better terms than RECs in the Pool because the prices were transparent; on the other hand, the loss of load probability/value of lost load mechanism was clearly crude and an imper-fect reward for capacity availability. The pressure for Pool reform therefore continued unabated, and, as the problems with 1998 implementation mounted (in which the Pool and its cumbersome governance structure were intimately involved), eventually a full Pool inquiry was launched in 1997. As long as the answers that emerged from the Pool—the prices—were unsatisfactory, there would continue to be pressure for reform. NETA was the eventual result.

The Dash for Gas

Whether one describes the generators' behaviour as the 'abuse of dom-inance' or 'commercial' depends on the perspective from which it is viewed. Whatever the description, it provided one reason, among many, for probably the most distinctive feature of the early 1990s—the dash for gas. With hindsight, the most dramatic consequence of privatization has been the displacement of coal by gas, something which the architects of privatization had not foreseen in the late 1980s. But it was the product of the coincidence of several necessary conditions and hence a more complex phenomenon than the simplistic explanations subsequently given by politicians, most notably by Peter Mandelson in the 1998 White Paper, 'Conclusions of the Review of Energy Sources for Power Generation and Government' (DTI 1998b), that it resulted from market abuse.

The formal origins of the dash for gas lie in the relaxation first of the interpretation of, and then subsequently formally of, the European constraint on burning gas in power stations. Until the end of the 1980s, gas had been seen as a 'premium fuel', to be used for high value-added, chemical-based activities, and for direct conversion to heat in households. This policy arose in response to the perceived scarcity of natural gas—that it would only last for a short period of time. Burning gas in power stations represented a more profligate use of resources—in terms of both the quantities involved and the thermal efficiencies, once account had been taken of the losses through electricity transmission as well as those in the generation process, rather than transporting gas as near as possible to the point of final consumption.

By the end of the 1980s, it was apparent that much more gas was available than had been assumed, and that, once natural gas ran out, there was plenty to come from Norway, and, indeed, if pipelines were built, from further afield. The removal of the legal constraint and the more optimistic perspective on supplies provided the context for the dash for gas. A further significant feature was the price schedules introduced by British Gas.[11] The market power of the generators created a pricing scenario which would make gas reasonably competitive, but until later in the decade when gas prices collapsed, probably not enough by way of economic returns to justify the large-scale investment that in fact took place. The catalyst was the strategic aim of the RECs to become players in generation and undermine the generators' market power, coupled with the ability to pass on the costs of new gas power stations to captured monopoly customers. In other words, the dash for gas would not have happened on the scale and at the pace that it did in the early 1990s had it not been

---

[11] The 1990 long-term interruptible tariff (LTI2) was set at 17p/therm and triggered the initial dash for gas. British Gas then raised the price to 21.1p/therm in LTI3, when the scale of the demand from the electricity sector was revealed.

facilitated by the regulator's tacit support. Again the regulator effectively determined policy.[12]

To see why this tacit support was necessary, the contractual structure of the early gas stations needs to be explored. They were built on the basis of back-to-back contracts. The IPPs bought North Sea gas on the basis of take-or-pay contracts: the price and quantity were assured. In turn, the gas station sold its power through power purchase contracts (PPAs), which ensured the price and output of the stations to the RECs, which in turn added the IPP contracts to their supply customer base, and the regulator allowed these costs to be included within the price caps. Thus, what appeared to be an increase in new competitive entry turned out to be vertical integration through contracts by the RECs. The main constraint was the limit placed on the percentage of own generation by the RECs—set at 15 per cent initially. There followed a 'dash': all the RECs except Manweb joined in.[13]

---

[12] There was a further reason to encourage gas, which was the 1988 EC Large Combustion Plants Directive and its SOx and NOx targets. Littlechild recognized this early on, but acknowledged that the dash for gas arose primarily for other, non-environmental, reasons (Littlechild 1991).

[13] REC own-generation interests by 1993 were as follows.

REC	Plant	Total declared net capacity (MW)	REC equity stake (%)	Accumulated interest (MW)	Total accumulated interest (MW)
Eastern	Barking	930	13.5	125.5	
	Peterborough	350	50.0	175.0	300.5
East Midlands	Corby	350	40.0	140.0	140.0
London	Barking	930	13.5	125.5	125.5
Manweb		0			0.0
Midlands	Wilton (Teesside)	1,725	19.2	331.2	331.2
Northern	Wilton (Teesside)	1,725	15.4	265.7	265.7
NORWEB	Roosecote	224	20.0	44.8	
	Keadby	680	50.0	340.0	384.8
SEEBOARD	Medway	660	37.5	247.5	247.5
Southern	Barking	930	22.0	204.6	
	Medway	660	37.5	247.5	
	Derwent Cogen	215	49.5	106.4	558.5
South Wales	Wilton (Teesside)	1,725	7.7	132.8	132.8
SWEB	Wilton (Teesside)	1,725	7.7	132.8	132.8
Yorkshire	Brigg	240	75.0	180.0	180.0
Total					**2,799.3**

Source: Offer (1993b: 27).

Why did the regulator encourage this rapid entry of gas? The answers—as so often with Littlechild—have an Austrian flavour. The *promotion of competition* required that the stranglehold which National Power and PowerGen held had to be broken. That meant new power stations, and if the LICs were not prepared to put their money where their loud and effective lobbying pointed and build their own (as both the government and the regulator had hoped), then the only option was the RECs. They might of course be 'uneconomic', but then Littlechild was playing a long game. After 1998, retail supply competition would undermine the back-to-back arrangements; more investment meant excess capacity; and the coal interest would be undermined. The 'temporary monopoly' rents created by passing through the IPP costs were worth paying for by customers who would, in due course, reap the benefits, once full supply competition arrived.

The consequence was that gas came on faster than would have been dictated by competitive markets, and the coal industry contracted more quickly. In the long run, gas would probably have displaced coal, but the economics of energy markets is largely about transitions rather than end states.[14] And, as noted repeatedly throughout the history of the post-war period, the conventional wisdom about end states often—indeed usually—turns out to have been mistaken. Who could have known that gas prices were going to collapse in the mid-1990s? Or that they would be ramped up in 2000?

The architects of privatization had anticipated that the RECs might push for vertical integration, and then exploit that integration with generation through their local monopolies. Some commentators had argued that there should be no vertical integration at all, that supply and generation should be kept separate until 1998 at least. Recognizing the incentive to integrate vertically, but not wishing to constrain behaviour too rigidly, the privatization framework provided two safeguards: the 15 per cent limit and a licence condition (Condition 5) which set an 'economic purchasing' test for the RECs. Condition 5 stated that RECs are required to purchase 'at the least effective price reasonably obtainable, having regard to the sources available'.

---

[14] An additional reason for the dash for gas was advanced that CCGTs were a cheaper way of reducing SO_2 emissions to conform with the EC Large Combustion Plants Directive 1998 (LCPD) than the further fitting of FGDs. Newbery argued that the switch from coal to gas 'was probably inevitable' and 'would eventually have been forced on a vertically integrated but efficiently managed CEGB' (1994: 23–4). Although this was probably true, it was the RECs initially, not the generators, who pursued the CCGT strategy, although PowerGen and National Power subsequently joined in.

The dash for gas elicited controversy from early on, and the conduit for much of this discontent, particularly from coal interests, was the Select Committee on Energy, and then, after the Department was abolished after the 1992 election, the Trade and Industry Select Committee. It looked at the 'Consequences of Electricity Privatization' in 1992 (House of Commons Select Committee on Energy 1992*a* and *b*). The Committee, chaired by Michael Clark, homed in on the economic purchasing condition, and challenged the then Secretary of State for Energy, John Wakeham, on whether the IPP contracts met the test. Wakeham was categorical in his comments to the Committee:

The regional electricity companies have an obligation for economic purchasing. If they have got—I put it absolutely crudely so there is no doubt about it—an interest in a gas-fired power station which gives them electricity which is more expensive than the electricity they can buy from another source, in my judgement they are in breach of their licence condition. They have to buy the cheapest electricity in the market. (House of Commons Select Committee on Energy 1992*a*, vol. 1, para 56)

The Committee recommended in 1992 that Offer investigate, which it duly did. Offer's 'Review of Economic Purchasing' (published in two reports in December 1992 and February 1993—Offer 1992*c* and 1993*b*) provided a comparison of *prices* rather than costs between coal and gas. In the report, the regulator stated that no REC went to full open tender, so that the value of IPP contracts could be tested against (coal-based) alternatives (Offer 1992*c*, para 64). While, for many, that might be sufficient evidence that the RECs had violated Condition 5, the two Offer reports were at great pains to stress that the contracting strategies of the RECs derived from a desire to diversify away from National Power and PowerGen. The contracts were then *strategic* and, hence, *strictly* the price and cost comparisons Offer carried out were not necessary to test conduct against the condition. As the author pointed out at the time, the absence of a requirement for competitive tendering was extremely hard to reconcile with Littlechild's preference for competitive solutions (House of Commons Select Committee on Trade and Industry, 1993: 55–66). In addition, his position clearly contradicted Wakeham's public stance, as quoted above.[15]

---

[15] Offer 1993*b*, paras 87–89, pp. 39–40, provided little justification for the rejection of tendering. Littlechild stated that 'the need for an explicit tendering requirement will depend, in part, on the effectiveness of other incentives to economic purchasing' and 'on the degree of competition in generation'. Wakeham's position privately was believed to be very supportive of the IPPs.

The conclusion in that paper was intended to draw attention to the mismanagement of the dash for gas. The author stated:

The reality, of course, is that the Director General's position would, in practice, probably have been untenable had he found against the REC–IPP contracts: his apparent implicit objective of maximizing the number of competitors would have been abruptly undermined, and some RECs might have questioned the comfort they thought they had got in their earlier discussions with him. The 'Review of Economic Purchasing' was, in many respects, an analysis looking to provide a particular answer. (Helm 1994*a*: 97)

In retrospect, the right answer might have been a two-pronged attack: to demand that RECs tender competitively; but also to reduce the market power of the generators. If the RECs were guilty of hasty investment in gas in order to integrate vertically, the generators could also be accused of holding up prices.

This latter tack was one taken by the DTI Select Committee inquiry into the coal crisis (House of Commons Select Committee on Trade and Industry 1993). As one of its recommendations, it urged the regulator to look into the conduct of the generators more thoroughly and, in particular, to consider a cap on generator prices (pp. 251–7). Offer took up this challenge in 1993 and launched an inquiry into the generators' costs and margins led by Eileen Marshall. This took over six months to complete, and the full report was never to see the light of day. Since the contracts themselves were confidential, there has never been a public inspection of the claims and counterclaims by the parties. Yet the 1993 inquiry did spark off a further round of intervention into the generation market, which was to run on for the rest of the decade. A further 'Pool Price Statement' was issued in July 1993 (Offer 1993*d*) in response to yet more price increases and complaints, and the regulator now actually threatened an MMC reference, with price controls and disposals of plant as options. This in turn led to a continuing investigation into costs and margins.

As with the 'Review of Economic Purchasing', the costs and margins exercise once again exposed the contradictory demands of short-term customer benefits against the longer-term rewards which competition was supposed to bring. For, if the contracts showed excessive margins, then customers were paying too much now. But if the contract prices were lowered, the existing gas IPP contracts would look even more exposed (and should not be allowed in the supply price cap) and entry would be deterred. Faced with political and industrial pressure, it was difficult for the regulator to simply sit on his hands. Late in the process, a solution dawned. Suppose he left the contracts intact. This would be attractive to the generators, whose earnings would thereby be underpinned. In exchange, however, he demanded that plant be divested. That way, competition would be increased, addressing the underlying structural problem. Finally, to assuage the industrial critics, Pool prices would be capped for two years. The 'deal' would then be encapsulated in a 'voluntary' undertaking.

This episode provides a wonderful illustration of the ways in which the new regulatory regime operated. Littlechild did not refer the generators to the MMC over the contracts, but got divestment through. An MMC inquiry into the contracts would have probably reduced current prices, but it is doubtful whether it would have forced divestment. In the process, virtually nothing was exposed to public scrutiny. Finally, the Pool price cap demonstrated beyond doubt that the two generators could control prices—otherwise it would not have been achieved.[16]

The regulator was less competent at ensuring that the details of the 'deal' guaranteed the outcome he wanted. The voluntary undertakings required the generators to use *reasonable* (not *best*, as Littlechild wanted) endeavours to dispose of 6 GW (4 GW National Power and 2 GW PowerGen),[17] *provided* shareholder interests were protected. Although a number of parties showed an interest in purchasing the plant, in the end Eastern Electricity entered into a leasing arrangement with earn-out provisions. The plant was not therefore in a position to provide the competitive challenge Littlechild wanted. The generators had managed to turn what would have been threats to their price-setting ability into a neutered new participant in the duopoly. The duopoly had become a triopoly: but not much else had changed. The stations had simply changed hands. The lack of commercial understanding at Offer is one possible explanation of this outcome.

The MMC did, however, get a chance to look at generation competition when PowerGen bid for Midlands Electricity and National Power for Southern Electric in September and October 1995, respectively. That development is discussed in Chapter 12. For the purposes of this chapter, it is, however, worth summarizing its findings with respect to competition, and, in particular, the effect that gas entry had begun to have.

The MMC concluded that both mergers would be against the public interest, but that this could be remedied by disposal of the RECs' generation interests, and ring-fencing of both IPP contracts and the PES-licensed activities. The reasons why the MMC took a relatively relaxed view—backed up

---

[16] The effects of price caps on competition and entry are ambiguous. For a summary of some of these issues, see Borenstein (2002: 207–8). However, in view of what was to come in the generation market, getting rid of more capacity turned out to be a sensible strategy for the generators.

[17] National Power fared relatively worse than PowerGen, probably due to weaker negotiation.

by the DTI's own evidence to the MMC—were that it was convinced that the divestments and the CCGTs together had created sufficient competition to prevent upstream abuse of market dominance, and *crucially* that the compulsory Pool prevented the exploitation of the vertical links to supply. This role of the Pool in preventing vertical abuse was to be forgotten when NETA was introduced. In the event, however, the Secretary of State, Ian Lang, prohibited the takeovers, as we shall see in Chapter 12.

Opening Up Supply

By 1994, the transition timetable had collapsed for coal, but the government resisted pressure to delay the development of supply competition. The 1994 franchise drop for the over 100 kW market occurred at the specified time. Competition had been restricted to the over 1 MW market since it was felt at the time that the RECs needed some protection.

In principle, the restriction was relatively easy to organise: the LICs had already had the necessary metering, and could load-manage. In an important sense, they had always been the customers of the CEGB rather than the Area Boards under nationalization. In practice, the resulting intense competition proved somewhat difficult to manage. As with any arbitrary regulatory rule, the industrialists sought ways of circumventing it. What constituted 1 MW? Was it a company's total demand or a site? What was a site? Could a site comprise several companies? Dropping the limit in 1994 solved many of these problems.

While supply competition in the over 1 MW market worked well, it was a very different story when the over 100 kW market was opened up. Here, there were real problems of metering, and confusion as to the nature of the interface between RECs and customers. The result can only be described as chaotic (see OXERA 1994). The chaos was predictable in two senses: supply competition required metering which was not readily available across the 100 kW market; and it also required a strong regulatory steer. In the latter regard, the 1994 liberalization was classic Littlechild: set a milestone and broadly leave it to the players to get on with it. It was a strategy he used again in the run-up to 1998 with similar deleterious effects, as we shall see in Chapter 14.

Two Cheers for the Process

The concept of a transition was both an inevitable consequence of the political fudges which privatization necessitated, and of the limited understanding of competition and competitive markets at the end of the

1980s. It simply would not have been politically possible to expose the coal industry to the full forces of competitive markets in 1990. Moreover, although supply competition could have been declared in 1990, it would not have meant much without the associated meters and information technology.[18] What was not inevitable in 1990 was the concentration of generation within a duopoly, and the failure to devise a strategy for quickly reducing this market power, other than giving the regulator the duty to promote competition. That the government did not perceive the duopoly as having market power—and hence the light regulation—indicates a serious lack of analysis.

The transition had the additional merit of increasing the stakes for those forces opposed to competition. It set up a series of what turned out with hindsight to be potential 'crises', and therefore pushed the players, regulators, and government to confront the consequences. Of these, the artificial contract structure propping up the coal industry proved the most contentious, and the coal crisis nearly brought the whole structure crumbling down. But ministers and their officials were heavily constrained by the new structures created in 1990, and the fact that a further temporary fix for the coal industry resulted, rather than a full-scale retreat from the new market structure, was a significant benefit. Ministers had to operate *within* the new market, and that constrained the choices available to them.

The new coal contracts for the period 1993–98 did, however, have a number of serious consequences, notably the further encouragement of the dash for gas, and prices at higher levels than necessary. As fossil-fuel prices fell generally, electricity consumers lost out. It is, however, fair to point out that without the new contracts British Coal could almost certainly not have been broken up and privatized, and that ownership and structural change were further necessary steps to solving the British 'coal problem'.

The more apparent weaknesses in the transition related to the generation market and the failure to address its competition problems. The dash for gas was very badly handled: it came too early, happened too fast, and cost too much. The reasons were various: the corporate strategies of the RECs; the pass-through in the price controls; the Littlechild approach to competition; the coal contracts holding electricity prices up; and the failure to use Condition 5 of the RECs' licence. The dash for gas was multi-causal: it was not simply the result of the abuse of dominance, or, as was to be later alleged, the fault of the Pool design: the price of electricity was high because of *both* the coal contracts *and* market power; the Pool could

[18] Other countries followed the expedient of declaring the market open in advance of the necessary metering and demand profiling, with the result that switching was very limited.

be 'manipulated' *both* because the contracts made the generators almost revenue-independent of the Pool price in the early years, *and* because of their market power.

A transition to supply competition was sensible at the outset, given the lack of experience with it, the understandable desire to bed the new structures down, and the absence of comprehensive metering. That the 1994 franchise drop turned out to be fairly shambolic was a consequence of poor leadership and management by Offer, which failed to appreciate the need to set the rules and coordinate the processes—failures which were to be repeated to a significant degree in the run-up to 1998. But the transitional timetable itself held in 1994, and it is doubtful whether, had this not been set at privatization, this would have happened when it did. Without a hard constraint, delay would have been easy to acquiesce to, and the focus of companies and Offer on 1998 issues would not have been sharpened until later—perhaps much later.

9

Preparing for the End of British
Coal—Privatization and Decline

> Coal will be privatised. By the next Parliament, we will be ready for this, the ultimate privatisation. (Cecil Parkinson, Conservative Party Conference, 1988)[1]

> The coal industry must take its place within a competitive energy market. It must compete with other fuels and other suppliers to meet the needs of its customers at commercial prices. (DTI, *The Prospects for Coal: Conclusions of the Government's Coal Review*, 1993)

Politicians are well acquainted with the virtues of opportunism. The history of energy policy is littered with examples. Before the coal crisis in 1992/93, few in government had any idea how to fulfil what Cecil Parkinson had described as the 'ultimate privatization'. But the new contracts for 1993–98 had a value, and these could now be sold off. The trick, as with nuclear, would be to convince the public that selling off the contracts was equivalent to privatizing the coal industry. The government pulled this off in 1994, though it failed in the process to depoliticize the industry, or indeed to secure its longer-term future.

A Bleak Prospect

The privatization of the electricity industry broke the vertical link with the coal industry. No longer could the civil servants and nationalized industries' managers centrally plan the energy sector. The electricity industry could diversify its sources of fuel supply, into gas and towards imports. As we saw in Chapter 7, the full implications of this structural separation were only weakly understood in 1990.[2] In 1992 the government was forced to hold back from the brink of these implications becoming too obvious by

---

[1] Quoted in Parkinson (1992: 280).

[2] More informed interests in the coal industry were somewhat ahead of the game. See, for example, BACM (1991).

brokering new contracts and promising more subsidies. Even in 1997, the Department of Trade and Industry (DTI) struggled to understand the new realities.

These realities were really little more than the laying bare of the underlying economics of coal, and the continuation of a longer-term trend of decline. Redundancy had become a way of life for the miners from the 1960s onwards. In the 1990s, the industry (and the National Union of Mineworkers, NUM) moved from a place of significance in the economic life of the nation, to one of marginality. And, with the economics deteriorating, its environmental costs were also more to the fore.

The 1992/93 coal crisis had resulted in the new contracts between British Coal and National Power and PowerGen of 160 million tonnes of coal, 40 million tonnes from 1993/94 and 30 million for the rest of the contract period (DTI 1993: 7). These were backed by contracts with the RECs, in turn supported by the new supply price controls.

That this was a generous outcome for the coal industry, in terms of quantity and price, can be seen against the backdrop of the deteriorating market for coal. By the early 1990s, coal was overwhelmingly dependent on the electricity industry. This derived demand depended upon the relative price of coal against gas, and the scale of new gas entry. It also depended upon the performance of the nuclear power stations, at the base of the electricity load curve.

All three factors moved against coal: the gas bubble was gradually beginning to emerge, and gas prices fell. Although the direct link between oil and gas was less pronounced in the 1990s than it was to become once the interconnector joined the British North sea to the Continental market, the downward pressure on oil prices had its effects too. As we saw in Chapter 8, new gas entry was also being encouraged to increase competition. Finally, the nuclear stations began to perform much better, especially the advanced gas-cooled reactors (AGRs) (see Chapter 10). So coal was under pressure within the electricity market and its share would inevitably fall. It was also not helped by the fact that the electricity market itself was not growing—in part because of the recession of the early 1990s, and because the energy ratio was improving.

British coal had to compete for this declining market against imports, and international prices were also falling relative to domestic production costs. The intensity of import competition depended on the location of power stations relative to the ports, the extent of the infrastructure at ports, and transport costs. It had been a deliberate policy of governments in the 1960s and 1970s to construct power stations on inland sites. Even Fiddler's Ferry near Warrington was set just sufficiently inland to make direct supply from ships all but impossible.[3] The privatized generators, aware of the strategic bargaining position that British Coal would have when the fuel supply market was to be liberalized in 1993, immediately began to invest in new ports facilities. There was a parallel here to the RECs' investments in combined-cycle gas turbines (CCGTs). Both of these sets of strategic investments were the consequence of the failure to create competition at the outset. The main investments were planned at Avonmouth and at Immingham.[4]

Given the facilities, the cost of imported coal depended upon the world price and the sterling/dollar exchange rate. In 1993/94, in the run-up to privatization, the price of contract and spot traded coal (the ARA price) was falling, and widely expected to remain weak. There was little reason to expect that the £/$ rate would move much from the $1.50–$1.60 range, and indeed it was to remain remarkably stable for the rest of the decade. As a result, it was also reasonable to conclude that, even on low assumptions about the domestic coal industry's costs, it was unlikely that British coal could be generally competitive at coastal power stations distant from the coalfield (OXERA 1995: 34). Imported coal had a further advantage for the generators: its sulphur content was lower. Given the SO_2 targets that had been adopted as a result of the EC Large Combustion Plants Directive (88/609/EEC), the generators were to meet their commitments by a strategy of low-sulphur coal, fitting flue-gas desulphurization and CCGTs.

Notwithstanding the attraction of imports to the generators, they were effectively squeezed out of the market by the combination of the new contracts for 1993–98 and the high level of stocks built up in anticipation of a liberalized market in 1993.[5] This, however, was a policy with limited life—unless the costs of British coal could be reduced substantially, by 1998 the threat of import competition would inevitably re-emerge.

Other markets for coal continued to be cited by the coal industry, the unions and sympathetic MPs, and the 1993 report by the House of Commons Select Committee on Trade and Industry made encouraging comments on these prospects, but by the time the White Paper appeared in 1993, hopes, except at the margin, had effectively been given up.

Within the residual market left for British coal, competition existed between opencast and the deep mines. The former tended to be profitable, but opencast supply was limited by planning constraints, in turn subject

---

[3] It is widely believed that the location was influenced by pressure from the NUM

[4] The Immingham project was cancelled in 1992 following ABP's withdrawal.

[5] The imports of coal (in thousand tonnes) were as follows: 1990, 14,783; 1991, 19,611; 1992, 20,339; 1993, 18,400; 1994, 15,400 (*Source:* HM Customs and Excise 1995).

to an element of political control. Whereas opencast had supplied over 18 million tonnes for the period 1990–93, thereafter it was held back to between 16 and 17 million tonnes for the next five years, to protect the deep mines.[6]

These considerations determined the market for British coal for the next five years, and this in turn determined the number of deep mines. The level of employment could then be determined too, subject to the increases in productivity that might be expected. Demand was given, and supply would have to adjust. Once the contracts expired in 1998, the full force of gas and imported coal competition could be assumed to reduce the deep-mine output to a small residual, in the absence of political intervention, as long as the nuclear power stations continued to work and gas prices remained low.

Preparing for Privatization

The declining market for coal was but one aspect of the prospects facing government in thinking about its privatization. The total financial assistance to British coal over the period since the Conservatives had come to power was estimated in the 1993 'Prospects for Coal' White Paper at *almost £18 billion*, comprising over £15 billion of grants and £2.5 billion in payments under the Redundant Mineworkers Payments Scheme (DTI 1993: 96). The losses in individual years depended considerably on the accounting conventions used and on the timing of exceptional and restructuring items. Not much should therefore be read into particular years; the sheer scale of the total is what counted.

This bleak background provided the context of the preparations for privatization, on which ministers concentrated in 1994. The basic assumptions in working out the value of the business were the value of the contracts, plus any residual value after 1998, minus the costs and liabilities. The arithmetic was very simple, and Rothschilds, the government's

---

[6] The figures for opencast output versus deep mine are shown below.

Output	Supply production of coal (thousand tonnes)							
	1990	1991	1992	1993	1994	1995	1996	1997
Deep-mined	72,899	73,357	65,800	50,457	31,854	35,150	32,223	30,281
Opencast	18,134	18,636	18,187	17,006	16,804	16,369	16,315	16,700

Source: DTI (1997, 1998), *Digest of United Kingdom Energy Statistics*.

adviser, had already done the preliminary homework for the report in 1992 (the famous twelve pits document).[7]

Ministers assumed that the business must have a positive value to be capable of sale. The contracts provided the revenue line. The next step was to subtract the costs, which fell into two categories: operating costs; and liabilities and the wider externalities of coal mining. The operating costs, on a narrower definition, were less than the revenues in the contracts for 1993/94 to the tune of around £200 million, and hence the operating activities were profitable, and this is where the value was to be found. Of this £200 million operating profit, opencast provided £80 million, and deep mines only £66 million. Against the operating profits, there was around £120 million of interest payments, restructuring costs of £360 million and a provision for liabilities of over £2.1 billion in the 1993/94 accounts, the last before privatization.

These revenues could be projected forward, given the new contracts, so that future operating profits were the difference between committed revenue payments from the generators, minus current and expected production costs.

Here the major innovation in privatization was introduced—soon to be repeated for the nuclear industry. Operations could be separated from assets and/or liabilities. The political and practical question was how much of the current liabilities could be loaded up onto the privatized successors. The task never was to privatize the industry; it was to privatize as much as financially possible, retaining the rest in the state sector. Industries in aggregate might be loss-making, but parts of the business could be profitable.

That left the liabilities, which comprised six main elements: debt; old mines already closed which might subside or cause pollution incidents; the future costs of closing existing mines; health claims from retired and current miners; pensions; and redundancy. These liabilities raised two distinct problems: some of them, such as the cost of servicing the debt, could be estimated, but were simply too big to leave a positive profit; others were uncertain in magnitude and timing, and depended in part on regulatory and political actions.

The interest on existing debts was, as noted above, over £120 million in 1993/94 (British Coal Corporation 1994), and this was addressed by writing them off. The buyers would therefore get the investment made in the public sector without balance-sheet burdens—unlike British Gas and the

---

[7] As noted in Chapter 6 the Rothschild report was confidential, but leaked to the press. See 'New Report Sees More Pit Cuts', The *Times*, 19 January 1992.

electricity generators. The liabilities for subsidence from old mines were transferred to a new public body, the Coal Authority.[8] Health and related liabilities transferred to the government. Pensions were guaranteed. The costs of redundancy were transferred to the private successor companies, but, as much of the slimming down of the industry had been done prior to privatization, the burden was not as great as it might have first appeared (although it was to be an issue in the 1997/98 crisis at the end of the contracts). The Treasury did not rid itself of the burden of the coal industry. And these residual costs would not be remotely approximated by the value of the sale, and hence would fall to taxpayers.

To these must be added the wider environmental damage caused by the coal industry. Coal is one of the most polluting industries in Britain. It takes considerable energy to extract coal. The pits produce methane. Transporting coal to power stations is polluting. Coal at power stations rots, in the sense of losing energy and giving off gases. Burning coal produces CO_2, nitrogen oxides (NO_x), and SO_2. Power stations use lots of water. The ash has to be disposed of, and contains toxic residual elements. Few of the costs had been paid by British Coal and few provisions made, and, after privatization, most of these costs remained with the state. Mines also create waste in great volumes, which despoils the landscape. These waste tips can be made more acceptable by landscaping, but, again, at considerable costs. They can also be unstable, as the people of Aberfan will never forget.[9]

The scale of these costs will, like so much associated with the nationalized industries, probably never be known. The pollution costs show up in the accounts of many different companies, institutions, and individuals. The water pollution, for example, creates costs for the Environment Agency, for industrial companies which use the affected supplies, and for the water companies. Individuals also directly suffer in affected areas.

The Coal Authority's accounts give details of subsidence payments and government accounts for health payments.[10] Health risks are endemic to

---

[8] The Coal Authority assumed responsibility for all outstanding subsidence liabilities resulting from the activities of the National Coal Board and British Coal Corporation. The continuing privatized mining companies were responsible for their coal-recovery activities within legally red-lined locations, known as 'Areas of Responsibility'. The companies are required to provide securities to the Coal Authority to discharge these liabilities in the event of liquidation.

[9] In 1966, a slag heap collapsed onto the village of Aberfan in South Wales, burying its primary school, with the loss of 144 lives.

[10] The figure on subsidence for the year ending March 2002, as stated in the Coal Authority's annual statement to Parliament, was just over £10 million, and its provision for future subsidence claims was £17 million (Coal Authority undated, and 2002).

the coal industry. In the underground environment, miners inhale every day dust, minerals and gases from the rock faces. The air pollution is inescapable, but over much of the history of the industry the consequent disabilities and premature deaths have been ignored. Indeed, it was not until a court case in January 1998[11] finally established liability for lung disease that compensation was to be paid. The costs are uncertain, but likely to be well in excess of £1 billion. A section of the DTI was eventually set up solely to deal with them. Whether this is adequate compensation for the suffering which has been the lot of most retired miners' lives is doubtful.

The Coal Industry Act and the Break-up of British Coal

In order to meet this catalogue of mainly unquantifiable costs, British Coal had to be split up into two parts: the liabilities, which would remain in the public sector; and the operations of the mines, which would be sold off. It is not too much of an exaggeration to describe the resulting privatization as a large operations and maintenance (O&M) contract. The operation of the mines was to be contracted out to the private sector. This logic was underlined by the last set of accounts for British Coal, which, as noted above, reported an operating profit of nearly £200 million for 1993/94 (British Coal Corporation 1994).

Government reflected this logic in the restructuring of the industry. It was determined to eliminate British Coal as an entity, and hence it took two steps in the Coal Industry Act 1994. The first was to create a Coal Authority; the second was to break up British Coal's activities on a regional basis. The Coal Authority was given four functions in the Coal Industry Act. These were: ownership of coal reserves and granting access to them; licensing coal mining; responsibility for subsidence and other physical effects; and providing information. The transfer of ownership of reserves to the Coal Authority replicated aspects of the treatment of the oil and gas regimes. The licensing of preferred bidders was carried out by the Secretary of State ahead of privatization, and hence the Coal Authority's role was limited in this area. Further licences were to be made available on an open-access basis—it was assumed that these would not be auctioned or otherwise sold. Importantly, the Act quite deliberately prohibited the Coal Authority from acting commercially in the market, in producing or selling coal. There was to be no back-door route for the Coal Authority to another nationalized coal industry.

---

[11] Judgement of Mr Justice Turner, The British Coal Respiratory Disease Litigation, 23 January 1998. This was the largest ever personal injury action to date in Britain.

The regionalization was designed to lay the ghost of the NUM forever, making a national strike virtually impossible. The new structure was designed with both geography and (mainly) financial viability in mind. The regions were: Central North, Central South, North East, South Wales, and Scotland.

The new companies would comprise a mix of opencast and deep-mine activities. In contrast to the deep mines, opencast mining had been largely profitable, but, as noted above, was heavily constrained by planning restrictions as a consequence of its all-too-visible environmental impact.

The sell-off then followed quickly. In September 1993, Tim Eggar set out details of the five regional coal companies to be privatized, as well as seven deep-mine pits then under 'care and maintenance'. Pre-qualification applications had to be in by May, and those who passed then received detailed Information Memoranda. Pre-qualifiers could then bid for the companies and pits by mid-September. There were twenty-five pre-qualifiers, some of which, like the electricity generators, were simply interested in getting access to the information. Eighteen bids for regional coal companies were forthcoming.

The process revealed that interest was limited to a small number of UK companies, and that a successful privatization would depend on existing opencast businesses and interest from British Coal employees. RJB Mining dominated the pre-qualifiers, and was to mop up virtually all the English mines, leaving Wales in the hands of Celtic Energy, and Scotland with Mining (Scotland) Limited.

The most notable casualty in this process was Coal Investments, led by Malcolm Edwards, with Union of Democratic Mineworkers (UDM) support. It failed (against expectation) to win either Central North or Central South. Those whom Margaret Thatcher had regarded as 'our boys', the UDM miners, were no longer important enough to need to be pacified. The most significant reason for Coal Investments' failure was price. RJB Mining was prepared to bid over £914 million, compared with £600 million from Coal Investments for three English companies. For a small opencast mining company[12] having a leader with a colourful past[13] to offer over £300 million more than its nearest rival, led by people and at the core of British Coal, took many (including the author) by surprise.

---

[12] About 2 million tonnes in 1993.

[13] Richard Budge was director of the A.F. Budge Group, which went into receivership in December 1992. There was some dispute about the circumstances, and in particular between the receivers and Budge. See RJB Mining (1994: 166).

It was all the more surprising since the valuation problem was relatively simple. The contracts set the revenue line and the costs were fairly predictable. That gave the profit in the contracts which could then be discounted back to yield a capital value. To this, a residual, post-1998 value needed to be attached, dependent on the view taken of the market after it had been liberalized. It was this last component which must have differed significantly, with RJB Mining taking an altogether more optimistic position on prices and volumes (and on the level of implied and actual government support).

RJB Mining could take such a position because, with all three English coal companies, it would have very significant market power—indeed, probably all the greater without the tail of Wales and Scotland. It would have 80 per cent of total UK coal output—around 36 million tonnes (RJB Mining 1994). The future of the coal industry, and all the political capital invested in it, was now likely to be effectively equivalent to the future of RJB. Hence, when 1998 came, the politics of coal might well favour RJB Mining, the residual value once the contracts expired could be expected to be positive, and RJB might be in a good position to maximize it. This turned out to be a shrewd political calculation, as we shall see in Chapter 16 in describing Peter Mandelson's partial surrender to mining pressures in the 1997/98 coal crisis.

RJB, once its bid had succeeded, then sought to negotiate. It got the price reduced by £99 million, to £815 million, and, furthermore, agreed to pay in instalments. Celtic Energy got the South Wales assets for £94.5 million, again to be paid in instalments. Mining (Scotland) Limited paid £34.9 million for the Scottish assets (with Coal Investments taking a 29.6 per cent stake in the company). The Tower Employee Buyout Team bought the Tower Colliery, the last South Wales deep mine. The remainder of the assets were progressively sold off by the residual British Coal Corporation and the Coal Authority. Certain land assets, however, such as potentially unstable tips, are likely to remain in the ownership of the Coal Authority for the foreseeable future, with the British Coal Corporation to then be wound up.[14]

The total revenues raised from the sale were finally in excess of £1 billion (and well in excess of the government's and its advisers' expectations),[15] leading some to conclude that even the most serious of the nationalized 'basket cases' could be turned around through privatization. It was a tempting illusion for those whose primary motivations were

[14] At the time of writing, this is anticipated to be at the end of March 2004.
[15] See NAO (1996), especially p. 5.

ideological rather than rooted in analysis, and one which was to be erroneously claimed for nuclear in due course. Although, as noted above, the final accounts will probably be impossible to create, the known numbers paint a very different picture.

Even the £1 billion presents too rosy a picture: the sale proceeds incorporate a significant implicit 'consumer tax' element, comprising the higher costs paid by electricity companies above the market rate for the coal contracts. In other words, the customers paid an additional premium which was capitalized in the sale proceeds. Other factors to include are the costs of pollution due to the coal-burn which the contracts imposed over and above the market-driven volumes. The future liabilities on the state were much more significant than the value of the privatization. As noted above, over the rest of the decade, over one billion were paid out for health damage, as well as money for subsidence, and untold millions in dealing with the environmental effects.

From this analysis, we can safely conclude that the main achievement of coal privatization was to limit future economic costs and to force government to come to terms with the legacy of coal. Its burden on the economy has been large and negative: it ranks up in the superleague of subsidized activities, with nuclear power and agriculture.

The industry did, for a brief time—and certainly until just after the 1997 election—drop off the political agenda, as had always been intended. It seemed as if the long battle with the industry, dating back to Edward Heath's demise in 1974, had finally ended. The once mighty NUM lost its power and status, no longer capable of creating fear amongst ministers. The last gasps of mining radicalization were to be heard in the brief flutter of Arthur Scargill's Socialist Party in the 1997 election, the ghost which had haunted Thatcher since Heath's defeat was laid to rest, and ministers could get on with finishing off the energy agenda set back in 1982 with Nigel Lawson's famous speech on energy policy (Lawson 1982). Nuclear was to be the last frontier for privatization.

Or so it seemed. But the coal industry did not fade away as intended. It was to have a further fling under Labour, as its powerful grip on the Labour Party's historical identity and the peculiar geographical nature of Labour's electoral base was to trigger another backbench rebellion and another fix for coal. Even in 2002, subsidies continued to be paid, despite the DTI's resistance to the demands to keep the Selby complex open.

10

Nuclear Privatization and the End of the Nuclear Dream

> The government cannot identify *any* reasons why the electricity market should not *of its own accord* provide an appropriate level of diversity [italics added]. (DTI, 'The Prospects for Nuclear Power in the UK', 1995*b*: paras 2.8, 5.74–75)

With coal privatized in 1994, only nuclear remained in the public sector. This unfinished business was the last major task for the heirs of Nigel Lawson's energy policy vision, and throughout 1995 it was to form the main focus of energy policy for Department of Trade and Industry (DTI) ministers and officials. Coal privatization had given them the confidence that virtually anything could be sold. With a review in any event promised by John Wakeham when nuclear had been withdrawn from privatization in 1989, this provided the opportunity to finish off the job.[1]

Privatization of National Power and PowerGen left the nuclear assets unhappily stranded in the public sector—unhappily for the government and the industry managers. As described in Chapters 5 and 7, the nuclear climbdown from the 1988 White Paper was done only under duress, and was a messy process. Cecil Parkinson stood out for the 70/30 model, with the deeply flawed contradiction that National Power would have enough market power to carry the nuclear programme, while, at the same time, the regulator would promote competition.

The process followed a gradual and, for the nuclear industry, demoralizing path: first, the Magnox stations were withdrawn, then the advanced gas-cooled reactors (AGRs) and the Sizewell B pressurized-water reactor (PWR). The government was left with the problems of picking up the pieces—of keeping the nuclear dream afloat in the face of mounting evidence that new stations were hopelessly uneconomic. Withdrawing nuclear, thereby sealing the fate of the future programme, led quickly to another casualty—Walter Marshall. More than any other individual, he was associated with the advocacy of civil nuclear power. As described

---

[1] Wakeham also announced a moratorium on new nuclear build until 1994, effectively shelving the Hinkley and Sizewell C PWR proposals.

in Chapter 2, it had been Marshall, as chief scientist, who had tried to persuade Tony Benn to go for the PWR back in 1978. He had helped persuade Margaret Thatcher of the merits of the programme of at least ten PWRs which formed the basis of David Howell's 1981 programme (see Chapter 3), and had steered the Central Electricity Generating Board (CEGB) through the Sizewell and Hinkley inquiry processes. As a scientist and mathematician of considerable repute, he had never let his vision of a nuclear future be sullied by the dismal scribbling of mere economists. With Marshall gone, the industry lost its champion.

The economists, however, had the upper hand. As described in Chapter 7, when Thatcher was forced to decide between the very different views of the future of Marshall and Parkinson, she decisively rejected Marshall's advice. Even the structure adopted for the remaining nuclear industry paid some lip service to competition, albeit in a regionalized structure. Two separate companies were created: Scottish Nuclear and Nuclear Electric.[2]

Nuclear Electric, by far the dominant player, inherited the CEGB's mantle, and indeed its philosophy. Its chairman, John Collier,[3] was brought in from UKAEA and he was to be joined in 1992 by Robert Hawley from NEI ABB Gas Turbines. The company's immediate priorities were threefold: to complete and commission Sizewell B; to make the case for more PWRs (notably Sizewell C); and to try to match the fossil-fuel generators' efficiency drive.

Scottish Nuclear was an altogether smaller outfit, and was concerned to make the most of its existing stations (including Torness, the last of the AGRs, finally commissioned in 1998), rather than to invest in more stations. It was chaired by James Hann, with Robin Jeffrey as Chief Executive. Always the junior partner in the nuclear camp, Scottish Nuclear was to have a short life before being extinguished at privatization. Jeffrey would, however, prove to be the only major survivor of the 1990 structure until his departure in late 2002, when British Energy had to turn to government for help. He became Chairman and Chief Executive of British Energy in 2001, and the advocate in 2001/02 of a new PWR programme, rather similar to the 1981 Howell proposal. Scottish Nuclear was

---

[2] The stations of the nuclear generators were **Nuclear Electric** Magnox stations— Bradwell, Oldbury, Wylfa, Hinkley A, Dungeness A, Sizewell A, Trawfynydd, Berkeley; AGRs—Heysham 1 and 2, Hartlepool, Hinkley B, and Dungeness B; and PWR—Sizewell B; **Scottish Nuclear** Magnox stations—Hunterston A; AGRs—Hunterston B and Torness; **BNFL** Magnox stations—Calder Hall and Chapel Cross.

[3] John Collier's career was almost entirely in the nuclear sector, and he was recruited by Marshall in 1983 to run the CEGB's power station construction programme. He was appointed Chairman of UKAEA in 1987.

to prove the more innovative and successful of the two. Its performance improved markedly, and it sought to break out of the THORP reprocessing arrangements. Scottish Nuclear advocated a dry-storage facility, with a view to creating a lower cost base.

The Liabilities

The history of nuclear privatization has been the very gradual triumph of economic reality over managerial optimism. Although economics was never the prime rationale for the civil nuclear programme, it was to be its undoing (as described in Chapter 2). Privatization of the electricity industry in 1990 spelt the end of the nuclear industry's future, at least as long as it was built around large-scale technologies, such as the PWR and for as long as markets were liberalized. Despite the many hours of sweat and toil that have been spent by its loyal employees trying to prove the impossible, nuclear needed monopoly, compulsory, long-term, take-or-pay contracts (a nuclear obligation), or state support to survive. It has been left largely to a small group of independent academics to take a more impartial look, and to spell out the consequences.[4]

Before we get into the detail, it is worth pointing out that, although we can be sure that the programme since the 1950s has never shown a positive return, the scale of the losses will probably never be known. The nuclear industry has been surrounded by secrecy, conveniently buried in the aggregated CEGB's accounts. The capital costs have never been separately identified, joint costs were never fully allocated, and, of course, the linkages to the military programme remain state secrets. Furthermore, by placing British Nuclear Fuels (BNFL) *between* the CEGB and the military, and keeping BNFL's public accounts at best rudimentary, the obscurity was reinforced.

This secrecy and its consequences for cost accounting are not unique to the British nuclear industry. They are endemic worldwide. All major developed countries have been secretive in their nuclear programmes, and it is only recently that the Energy Policy Act 1992 in the United States has provided the eventual basis—through the 1996 Federal Energy Regulation Council (FERC Order 888)—for an exposure of its costs. Previously, rate-of-return regulation had lumped all the costs together and passed them on to customers. France is perhaps the extreme example of cost obscurity. Its PWR programme was driven by national prestige,

---

[4] The main contributions were by Gordon MacKerron, George Yarrow, and the author. See, for example, MacKerron (in House of Commons Select Committee on Energy, 1990: 111–22 and 123–9), Yarrow (1988), and Helm (1987c).

national energy self-sufficiency from the Middle East, and defence. At times, the costs of the French programme became confused with the national debt, and, to date, no one has been able to penetrate the fog of official silence and financial confusion. Probably no one knows the true costs. As a result, there are no obvious international benchmarks against which to evaluate the British nuclear industry.

Ignorance may be bliss in a public-sector monopoly. It was not so after the nuclear assets had been put in separate accounts. There now had to be a bottom line. Losses would be explicit. Thus, the creation of Nuclear Electric and Scottish Nuclear proved to be a giant step in terms of public exposure, compared with what had gone on before. Coal and nuclear would no longer be blended in the CEGB's accounts, and the Pool provided a price for nuclear output. Costs would now be nuclear only.

As noted in Chapter 7, ministers claimed that the underlying financial position of nuclear power came as a shock to them (see Lawson 1992: 166–70). Parkinson claimed that the decision in January 1988 to include nuclear within the privatization was based upon acceptance of the advice of the bankers and brokers assisting with the sale, that not only could the existing industry but also the new generation of PWRs be funded in the private sector (1992: 270 and 273). He goes on to claim that, as the privatization bill was in its final parliamentary stages, he 'received disturbing news' from the CEGB's auditors (ibid.: 278). The provisions for nuclear reprocessing and decommissioning 'about which I had sought and received assurances earlier' were inadequate and, worse still, undefined. On this basis, he withdrew Magnox from the sale as one of his last acts as Secretary of State for Energy before he was transferred to the Department of Transport.[5]

Ministers' concerns in 1989/90 were less with the past and more with creating a balance sheet for the new industry and a revenue stream which would make Nuclear Electric and Scottish Nuclear viable. This had two components: funding the liabilities and providing a cash flow to finance the ongoing activities of the companies. The three solutions adopted were: writing off debts, the nuclear tax, and contracts with BNFL.

The first task facing government was to calculate the future liabilities. This turned out to be more of an art than a science, and not surprisingly the numbers kept changing (almost always in an upward direction). While it is tempting to conclude that the industry was responsible for the lack of clarity on these costs by capturing civil servants through its monopoly on the relevant information, it should also be remembered that

---

[5] Statement of the House of Commons, 24 July 1989.

many of the decisions which would shape future costs lay with government and the nuclear regulators. Issues—such as the degree to which stations had to be returned to greenfield sites on decommissioning and over what timescale; the parameters within which safety regulators operated in determining the life of the plants; and the discount rate to be applied—were all very much for ministers to decide. Indeed, it is the fact that so much is politically driven which will always make full privatization of nuclear risk a practical impossibility on cost grounds. As we shall see below, that is why much nuclear risk remains in the public sector after the privatization of British Energy, and why *full* privatization of BNFL has proved impossible.[6]

The prospect of privatization did, however, force these issues to be addressed, first in 1987–9 and then in 1995/96. The first attempt was conducted with at least four interests in mind: those of BNFL, National Power, the City, and the Treasury. BNFL naturally wanted to continue its cost-pass-through arrangements with the CEGB. National Power wanted the best terms for the funding of nuclear, notably with respect to its balance sheet, the fixing of its arrangements with BNFL and the limiting of its future liabilities through guarantees and support (including, at this stage, the Fossil Fuel Levy). The City wanted, above all, certainty, and hence risk minimization. Finally, the Treasury wanted the passing of as much of the liabilities as possible from the public to the private sector.

As we saw in Chapter 7, this was a game which ended in failure for nuclear privatization in 1990. But it also ended in failure to agree what the liabilities actually were, as it proved impossible to sort out the answers when all the players had strategic interests in presenting 'the facts' to their benefit. BNFL's monopoly was backed by its control of information, whilst National Power (or at least its Chief Executive, John Baker) had clear incentives to talk up the numbers.

MacKerron (1996), in 'Nuclear Power under Review', lists the main decommissioning cost increases which were 'discovered' in 1987–9. The main ones were that: decommissioning each Magnox doubled from £312 million to £600 million, and BNFL's own undiscounted decommissioning increased from £138 million to £4,605 million (ibid.: 145). Further nuclear cost shocks applied to the costs of BNFL's fuel services and the capital costs of Sizewell B, which would have been subject to private-sector costs of capital.

---

[6] The 2001 five-year review of UKAEA, and the proposals to set up a Nuclear Decommissioning Authority, merely confirmed this point. In due course, these proposals were enshrined in the 2002 White Paper, 'Managing the Nuclear Legacy: A Strategy for Action' (DTI 2002d) and the subsequent bill in 2003, 'Draft Nuclear Sites and Radioactive Substances Bill' (DTI, 2003d). See Chapter 21.

The important point here is the uncertainty these cost escalations revealed. The numbers were not robust, and any capitalization of National Power would be extremely vulnerable to further cost shocks. Dividends would be small in comparison to potential cost escalations, and hence vulnerable to changes in circumstance beyond management's control (as British Energy would discover in the 2000s). Thus the only way in 1987–9 to privatize nuclear power was to provide insurance to share-holders by government underwriting the risks. The lesson of these years was that the underlying risks simply could not be privatized. But that did not mean that the liabilities would go away. They had to be financed somehow, and the convenient mechanism of cost pass-through in the CEGB's bulk supply tariff would not be available once the Pool was put in place. As competition developed, nuclear risk would be transferred from customers to taxpayers.

So how was the government to meet these liabilities? The first step was—as with coal privatization—to write off its past investments, some-thing which in the private sector would have resulted in bankruptcy. What would otherwise have been stranded costs, and which caused so much difficulty in the United States and European liberalizations of elec-tricity markets, were cancelled. This included not just the investments in past stations, but also the last two AGR stations, and, of course, the capi-tal costs of Sizewell B so far incurred. We will probably never know how big that write-off was, as we will never know what the true capital costs were. Privatization exposed future costs, but not those of the past.

The Fossil Fuel Levy and the Contracts

The next step was to fund future liabilities with a revenue stream. Since the revenue from the sale of electricity from existing generators would not be sufficient, a further income was needed. This was the Fossil Fuel Levy (FFL).[7] But, as MacKerron pointed out, the real purpose of the levy was to make Nuclear Electric 'cash-positive' and in addition to help it pay for back-end liabilities (1996: 153–4). The important point was that its primary purpose was *not* to pay for decommissioning.[8] The FFL was paid for by those with a Non Fossil Fuel Obligation, namely the regional electricity companies (RECs). Thus they would *have* to buy a quantity of electricity at

---

[7] Section 32 of the Electricity Act 1989 gave the Secretary of State the power to issue an order to effect the FFL.

[8] The 1995 White Paper on 'The Prospects for Nuclear Power in the UK' reinforces this point—see DTI (1995a: para 9.3, p. 61).

a premium (initially set at 10.6 per cent) and a nuclear contract between Nuclear Electric and the RECs, relating to about 8 GW of nuclear capacity, was signed on 31 March 1990. The use of a quota was the obvious way to favour a particular source of generation within a notionally competitive market, and it could be done as long as the RECs had a franchise. In effect, it was equivalent to a long-term, take-or-pay contract supported by a back-to-back monopoly franchise. Liberalization in 1998 was to be the undoing of such a mechanism: once customers could switch, they would desert nuclear for cheaper options. It was, however, later to be realized, with renewables, that the licensing of suppliers was the key to imposing technical preferences on customers: once *all* suppliers had to be licensed, *all* suppliers could be forced to buy a fixed proportion of a designated fuel.[9]

This mechanism—of a reserved market and a high premium therein—underlay National Power's thinking on the nuclear negotiations. Indeed, it had since the Hinkley inquiry. The FFL was that mechanism. Its terms could have been invented by George Orwell, and were particularly appropriate to the nuclear industry. Although renewables gained a helpful advantage, the overwhelming bulk of the revenue went to the nuclear industry, and it is therefore appropriate, if slightly inaccurate, to call it a 'nuclear tax'. Indeed, renewables were subject to a separate order, to ensure that the nuclear capacity was fully contracted.

The nuclear tax was not strictly new—customers had been paying for it under the bulk supply tariff, as Wakeham had been keen to point out. Rather, as he told the House in his statement on 12 February 1990: 'the levy simply brings the matter out in the open.'[10] But there was a serious problem: to design this instrument without distorting competition. This was a considerable challenge, aggravated by the need to pass the test of European Commission state-aid approval under Article 93 of the Treaty of Rome, and this effectively required it to be time-limited.

The official position was that the tax was designed to ensure that Nuclear Electric received a sufficient revenue to ensure that it could meet its liabilities in full as they fell due (DTI 1995*b*: para 9.7). Thus, the *rate* of the tax varied to deliver a required revenue. Because the background conditions changed (including the price of electricity), the levy did not fall in the early years as had been anticipated.

The tax was conveniently due to expire in 1998, with the arrival of competition. However, there was no inevitability here: a levy on all electricity sales had much in common with valued-added tax (VAT). It was

---

[9] Both the coal and nuclear lobbies would advocate this route in the 2001/02 Energy Policy Review, as we shall see in Chapter 21.

[10] HC Deb. (session 1989–90) vol. 167, col. 31.

inescapable, and hence indifferent to whom the supplier was. Furthermore, it was highly unlikely that by that date it would conveniently be the case that 'sufficient money' would have been raised 'to enable the cost of discharging all Magnox liabilities to be met without further recourse to the taxpayer' (DTI 1995*b*: para 9.15).

Separate arrangements were made for Scotland, with a contractual framework put in place between Scottish Nuclear, ScottishPower, and Scottish Hydro-Electric. It took the form of a Nuclear Energy Agreement (NEA), which bound the two companies to take all of Scottish Nuclear's output up to 2005, and determined a price which was intended to move towards the competitive level set by the Pool in 1998.[11]

The final parts of the financial arithmetic to make the new companies viable were the supply of fuel, the disposal of spent fuel and the provisions for decommissioning, provided by BNFL through contracts, the details of which have never been made public. These contracts—later revisited when British Energy was being privatized and again in 2002 when British Energy's financial crisis broke—are crucial to risk assignment. If the contracts were fixed-price for complete services, then most of the nuclear risk would be with BNFL; if variable, and reflective of the actual costs as they evolved, the risk would be with Nuclear Electric and Scottish Nuclear.

Performance in the Public Sector

With these financial 'fixes' in place, Nuclear Electric and Scottish Nuclear began their public-sector lives. They both had two related implicit (and sometimes explicit) missions: to get privatized; and to harness the emerging global-warming debate to the wheel of nuclear power. But to achieve these ambitions they first had to prove that the costs could be contained. There began an impressive focus on internal efficiency.

Costs in the nuclear industry are notoriously hard to control. In any industry where safety is paramount, costs are always subservient. Where a well-organized workforce exists with an interest in protecting employment and advancing pay, and where safety is at stake, strikes are much more serious than in other manufacturing activities where plant can simply be shut down. In a very real sense, then, managers' ability to drive down costs is heavily circumvented. The result is inevitably a higher cost structure.

In a monopoly nationalized industry, it may not matter much, since cost pass-through is facilitated. But Nuclear Electric and Scottish Nuclear no

---

[11] When the Pool was replaced by NETA, this became a matter of legal dispute in 2001, resolved in 2002.

longer had this luxury. Competition (by comparator and the market place) from an aggressively cost-cutting PowerGen, and to a lesser extent from National Power, helped to provide the management spur to take on the unions.

The results are impressive. Staffing levels were reduced, the costs of decommissioning fell, and station availability—in particular, the load factor—improved. In the period from 1990 to 1995, the main focus was on the AGRs, which had (as noted above in Chapter 5) had an appalling record. As the load factors increased, output from the AGRs in total increased from 36.9 TWh in 1989/90 to 54.1 TWh in 1994/95, and, as a result, total unit operating costs reduced from 5.2 p/kWh in 1989/90 to 2.7 p/kWh in 1994/95 (DTI 1995b: para 9.13). As the White Paper noted, this was 'by far the most significant change since 1989/90' (ibid.: para 9.14).

Several explanations have been given for this remarkable turnaround, but basically they boil down to two: the result of commercial pressures, and a fortuitous technical fix. Before privatization, the CEGB's incentives were to make the case for a family of new PWRs. Marshall had told Parkinson in 1987 that some 13 GW of new capability would be needed by 2000, and naturally he thought most of this should be nuclear.[12] He was only really interested in PWRs. With this objective in mind, and remembering Marshall's arguments with Benn back in 1978 over the choices of technology (see Chapter 2), it is plausible to argue that the CEGB in the 1980s had little incentive to seriously address the lamentable performance of the AGRs. However, once Nuclear Electric and Scottish Nuclear had the prospect of privatization, provided their performance improved, and with little prospect of any new PWRs in a privatized environment, the logic pointed to a major drive to address the AGR's problems. Management's focus was therefore almost exclusively on solving the AGR's poor load factors, and it is likely to have had an effect.[13]

The other view—advanced, notably, by MacKerron (1996)—is that the AGR's problems were deep-seated and technical, and that it was 'a fortunate coincidence' that they happened to get solved in the early 1990s. MacKerron offers little evidence to support his claim, however, and it is hard to doubt the conclusion that, had the boards of Nuclear Electric and Scottish Nuclear not devoted their attention and technical resources to the problems, it is unlikely that they would have been solved. Technical fixes rarely just 'happen'. It takes incentives to root them out.

[12] This requirement by the CEGB for new investment had been used by the Department of Energy to argue for a higher required return and hence to increase prices.

[13] For the CEGB's scepticism about AGRs, see Marshall's evidence to the House of Commons Select Committee on Energy (1990).

The improvement in the performance of the AGR was reflected in the financial performance of the two companies. For Nuclear Electric, its operating loss (before financing charges, *excluding* the levy income and exceptional items) was £1,101 million in 1990/91. By 1994/95, it was reduced to a loss of £35 million. For Scottish Nuclear, the losses of £32 million in 1990/91 were transformed into a profit of £150 million in 1994/95, such that, even without the NEA contributions, a profit of £31 million would have been realized.

The Nuclear Review

The arrangements put in place in the aftermath of the failure to privatize the nuclear industry in 1990 were seen by politicians and management as temporary, but which could easily become permanent. In recognition of this fact, Wakeham undertook that the government would review the nuclear industry in 1994—after the next election, and after the anticipated liberalization of the coal industry.

The fact that there would be a review created an air of expectation in the industry. If only it could prove its case then the review might herald a new dawn of expansion and privatization. By the end of 1993, Robert Hawley could proclaim that Nuclear Electric was 'highly competitive, commercial, and ready for the nuclear review'. Output had increased, with a market share of 25 per cent in England and Wales, and it was claimed that by 1995 it would be profitable without the levy, ready for privatization. To prove its commercial credentials, the company was granted a second-tier supply licence.[14]

Scottish Nuclear took a rather different tack in its public positioning ahead of the nuclear review. In December 1993 it published a pamphlet, 'The Need for an Energy Policy Framework'. Focusing on the dangers of over-reliance on gas, it wanted an energy agency, with the capacity, location, and type of plant determined by the dictates of security and diversity of supply. This was widely interpreted as a push for a role for nuclear to be defined first, before privatization, and was rightly seen at the time as contrasting with Hawley's privatization priority, even if that meant no more nuclear.[15]

After much wrangling between the DTI (which wanted a narrowly focused review), the Department of the Environment (which wanted

[14] See 'The Elusive Nuclear Review', *Energy Utilities*, January 1994, 18–19.
[15] British Energy, under Jeffrey's leadership in 2001, was to take a remarkably similar line in its approach to the Performance and Innovation Unit (PIU) Energy Policy Review.

a thorough analysis of waste-management and decommissioning costs), and the Treasury (which preferred a detailed audit of the liabilities), the terms of reference for the nuclear review were finally announced in a parliamentary answer by Tim Eggar on 19 May 1994 (see DTI 1995*b*: Annex A). The key considerations were: the future prospects for nuclear power and the economic and commercial viability of new nuclear stations, in particular 'whether any new nuclear station could be built with private-sector finance'; the options for introducing private-sector finance into the nuclear industry; and the financing of the 'full costs' of nuclear power, including the FFL. The DTI review team was led by Christopher Wilcox, widely regarded as hostile on economic grounds to the case for new build, and Timothy Walker.

The industry, which had been gearing up for the review since 1993, responded to the challenge to make the case for privatization and new investment, recognizing that the DTI was more interested in the former than the latter. But it was not a united response and, as a result, three main contributions were made, by Nuclear Electric, Scottish Nuclear, and the Nuclear Utilities Chairmen's Group (NUCG). The structural splits made at privatization had begun to undermine the cohesion of the industry. Nuclear Electric's formal submission was published on 20 June 1994. It distanced itself from future investment. As John Collier, its Chairman, put it:

We made no bones about it. Privatisation is our top priority in the review. As for new construction, it is now for the government to decide whether to retain the UK nuclear option by supporting the construction of a new PWR station.[16]

Nuclear Electric's submission made clear that, as a privatized company, it could not build a new PWR. Rather 'a public/private sector joint venture is an appropriate way to combine such support with private finance' (Nuclear Electric 1994: Vol. 1: Future Nuclear Construction in the United Kingdom, p. 4). Government support would also need to be backed by guarantees to constructors, and a long-term power purchase agreement would be required. All of these Nuclear Electric could be privately confident the Conservative government was unlikely to provide, and hence its future private investors would not be exposed to more PWR risk beyond Sizewell B.

Scottish Nuclear had now also been converted to the cause of privatization. This had partly been spurred on by the refusal of Ian Lang, Scottish Secretary of State, to grant permission to build a dry-storage unit

---

[16] Quoted in *Energy Utilities*, July 1994, 5. See also Nuclear Electric (Vol. 3. Privatization of Nuclear Electric: Benefits and Feasibility 1994: 3), 'Nuclear Electric believes the company can and should be privatized at the earliest opportunity.'

at Torness (as a cheaper alternative to BNFL) and the public-sector restriction on commercial freedom that it implied; and partly by the obvious success of Hawley's campaign at Nuclear Electric.[17] However, Scottish Nuclear could not yet let go of further plans for a nuclear future. It still wanted to build a replacement for Hunterston B by 2011. This was motivated by a continued belief in the superiority of energy policy over a purely market approach. It would have the effect of maintaining sufficient scale to help to justify a separate private Scottish Nuclear approach.

NUCG carried the nuclear industry view forward, and took a more 'nuclear view' as a result. Its report stressed nuclear first, privatization a distant second. It echoed the case which Marshall had raised in the 1980s with Thatcher. 'An early restart programme would be the minimum cost and financial risk option' (NUCG 1994: 4), it argued, playing up the diversity, security, and environmental benefits of nuclear. On the other side, Greenpeace took the challenge of the review seriously. It sought expert advice, and made an attempt to engage in the cost debate. Greenpeace's submission, 'No Case for a Special Case' (1994), concentrated on Sizewell C, and purported to demonstrate that its costs would exceed those of a new combined-cycle gas turbine (CCGT) by a factor of two or three. Perhaps of greater interest was the assertion that nuclear power had little to contribute to environmental objectives. Whilst Greenpeace could hide behind the familiar argument that our energy needs could be met by renewables and energy efficiency, the fact that the former were likely to be every bit as expensive as nuclear meant that less nuclear meant more fossil fuels in the short to medium term. It is also interesting to note that, in the coal crisis in 1992/93, Greenpeace was curiously silent about the environmental case for closing the coal industry down as soon as possible—a fact that Eggar, Minister for Energy, noted wryly.

The debate rumbled on for a year, with the conclusions of the review eventually being published on 9 May 1995, in a White Paper entitled 'The Prospects for Nuclear Power in the United Kingdom' (DTI 1995*b*). The main conclusions were that the AGRs, the PWR and their liabilities should be privatized, with the Magnox stations and their liabilities remaining in state hands (eventually to be subsumed within BNFL); Nuclear Electric and Scottish Nuclear were to be wholly owned subsidiaries of a new holding company with headquarters in Scotland; there was no case for providing further public money for the construction of new nuclear power stations; and, as Nuclear Electric 'should now be able

---

[17] The storage issue was resolved in early 1995 when BNFL offered a complete package for the AGR fuel cycle (see *Energy Utilities*, March: 1995).

to meet the full cost of its liabilities', the nuclear element of the FFL would cease on privatization, as would the premium price in the Nuclear Energy Agreement in Scotland.[18]

In reaching these conclusions, the review had rejected the arguments for nuclear power, which had to be rebutted in order to facilitate privatization—since a commitment to a new build programme would have had to have a public-sector component. The government not only rejected the economic case for a PWR against a CCGT (which was not difficult), but also the environmental and diversity case. Its statements were emphatic:

> The government concludes...that there is at present *no* evidence to support the view that new nuclear build is needed in the near future on emissions abatement grounds (DTI 1995*b*: paras 2.7, 5.26)...The government cannot identify *any* reasons why the electricity market should not *of its own accord* provide an appropriate level of diversity. (ibid.: paras 2.8, 5.74–75) [italics added]

These conclusions supported its overarching energy policy. The government 'believes that, so far as possible, choices about primary energy sources should be left to market participants' and it 'is drawing back from direct involvement in the energy markets' (ibid.). It could do this because it assumed that the market would deliver diversity and *fortunately* (because of the switch from coal to gas) the CO_2 and other environmental targets would be met (and hence no carbon-free premium needed to be taken into account).

The White Paper was very much a privatization package: no investor would be persuaded to buy a company bent on building more PWRs, and the liabilities had to be covered for a viable private entity. Yet the White Paper was based upon the flimsiest arithmetic. There was no real prospect that assets to be purchased would be followed by their full attendant liabilities, as Eggar had promised,[19] or that, without the FFL, the Magnox liabilities would be covered. To make the sums with regard to the Magnoxes add up, the government made a series of assumptions, most of which were open to doubt.

First, it had the monies already set aside by Nuclear Electric. Next, it had the expected future revenues of the Magnox stations (with assumptions about the price of electricity in the Pool and the load factors and lives of the stations). Then, it had the proceeds from the sale of the AGRs

---

[18] See also British Energy's privatization prospectus (British Energy 1996).

[19] 'As I have stated on numerous occasions, we have established the basic principle that assets will be followed by the associated liabilities', HC Written Answers, col. 309, 3 April 1996. A narrower interpretation is that their assets would be followed by their *decommissioning* liabilities.

and the PWR. Against these were set the expected costs of decommissioning. Finally, all numbers had to be discounted back to the present. By making heroic assumptions about the efficiency savings which could be achieved in the decommissioning process, and, using a suitable discount rate, the numbers could always be made to 'add up'. Whether they would or not remained to be seen. In the event, they did not, but there is little doubt that the DTI started with the answer, and worked backwards through the numbers.

Though there was undoubtedly some cynicism about the extent to which the government genuinely tried to come up with the best estimates in the evidence available, in an important sense it did not much matter: either there would be a tax in the form of the FFL or the government would have to pay out of general taxation if the numbers did not add up. In the end, the costs would end up with government and hence be paid by one form of tax or another.

Privatization

With the case for new build dismissed, with the liabilities 'parked' in Magnox, and with the prospects of operating profits from Nuclear Electric and Scottish Nuclear, it remained to decide whether to privatize one company or two. The answer to this structural question was far from obvious. The two companies had functioned effectively in the public sector as separate entities, and indeed the smaller Scottish company had arguably outperformed its bigger southern rival. The two electricity markets were largely distinct. There were separate contractual agreements between Scottish Nuclear and the Scottish electricity suppliers (the NEA) and between Nuclear Electric and the RECs. Finally, no compelling evidence was provided as to economies of scale. Littlechild even canvassed the possibility that the assets could be reshuffled between Scottish Nuclear and Nuclear Electric to create two competing companies of similar size (Littlechild 1994b: 13). In the event, the dominant factor was financial and the advice of the financial institutions. It was thought easier to float one large nuclear company than two. Indeed, had the two continued, the comparator competition might actually have increased regulatory risk.

The final structural element was within British Energy itself. A segregated fund was set up to receive monies set aside for waste management and decommissioning the AGRs and the PWR. These funds were not available for other purposes, such as financing acquisitions or as collateral against borrowings. The fund had first claim on revenues, and directors had a specific responsibility to ensure that the payments were made. This was a major advance in transparency, and it would have a marked effect when British Energy got into financial difficulties in 2001 and 2002.

The government then moved quickly on to complete the privatization. John Robb was appointed Chairman designate (formerly Chairman of Wellcome), with Hawley his Chief Executive, of British Energy. The Scottish interests were institutionalized within the board of the new company with Robin Jeffrey as Deputy Chairman (John Collier was also Deputy Chairman until his death shortly thereafter), and the headquarters were to be in Edinburgh. British Energy was to all intents and purposes a takeover by Nuclear Electric of Scottish Nuclear.[20]

In preparation for flotation, Hawley formally abandoned plans for a new reactor at Sizewell C, with the explanation that: 'At present, the future of UK energy prices is insufficiently certain for British Energy to invest in new nuclear, or indeed any other form, of new generation in the short term' (British Energy press release, 11 December 1995). Risks for investors were further reduced by the contract struck between BNFL and the new entity. Work here started early, with agreements in March 1995 between BNFL, Nuclear Electric and Scottish Nuclear, which were subsequently renegotiated in June 1997, in a £1.5 billion agreement between BNFL and British Energy (BNFL 1997). These contracts, though never made public, pass much of the nuclear risk on to BNFL, translating what at first sight was a nuclear company into more of the form of an operations and maintenance (O&M) business, analogous to the arrangements for coal, where liabilities too remained largely in the public sector.[21]

The sale plans were then scrutinized by the House of Commons Trade and Industry Select Committee, whose report was published on 14 February 1995, with the focus on the way in which the special segregated funds for future liabilities were to be financed.[22] Speculation arose that the DTI was in discussions with Duke Power, an American utility with nuclear experience, over a possible trade sale. Whether this was simply a ruse to gain compliance from British Energy over the DTI's approach to

---

[20] Formerly, Jeffrey was Chairman of the Scottish Nuclear subsidiary, and Collier was Chairman of Nuclear Electric—all within British Energy. James Hann was dropped.

[21] These contracts are described in British Energy's prospectus as mostly on fixed-price terms (British Energy 1996: 13). Such a fixed-price contract had been discussed in 1989–90 as part of the earlier attempt to privatize nuclear within National Power. See Marshall's evidence to the Energy Select Committee (House of Commons Select Committee on Energy 1990: para 28, p. 7).

[22] This aspect of privatization was raised in, 'UK Nuclear Privatization and Public Sector Liabilities', a 1995 report written by Science and Technology Policy Research (SPRU) and partly funded by the Consortium of Opposing Local Authorities and Friends of the Earth, which cast doubts on the adequacy of the provisions and accounting procedures.

privatization (as Hanson had provided with PowerGen's reluctance to take on debt back in 1990—see Chapter 7) cannot be proved but it must have helped the DTI. In any event, both Duke and the DTI flatly denied the stories.

The prospectus was published on 10 June 1996, and British Energy was floated on 15 July at 203p per share. The shares dropped sharply on the first day of trading, but by the end of July had recovered. The announcement just a few days before of temporary shutdowns of one reactor at Hinkley B and at Hunterston B underlay the risk of output interruptions. Yet, admittedly at a price, the government had achieved what had seemed almost impossible in 1990. The AGRs and the PWR were finally in private hands. And it was a remarkable achievement, given the exposures shareholders faced. Not only had the AGRs to carry on working, but the price of electricity in the Pool (and then NETA) had to hold up too. As it turned out, by 2001–2, the revenues were not enough to cover the annual liability contributions, and British Energy only managed to continue meeting its requirements because of profits from its overseas diversification in the United States and Canada. The share price would reflect this, trading well below its issue price. Eventually, even this was not enough, and a financial crisis broke in September 2002.

Magnox Stations Transferred to BNFL

BNFL was far from delighted at the prospect of taking over the Magnox power stations. Though in the public sector, it perceived itself as a public limited company, and had the normal solvency requirements that accompany this status. While the transfer had sound business logic, giving BNFL control over the timing of decommissioning and enabling it to gain station-specific experience, transferring Magnox also meant transferring liabilities, and these required funding if BNFL's balance sheet was to absorb them. Fraught negotiations followed, with an eventual settlement (which included a ministerial letter of comfort with respect to the provision of liabilities for Magnoxes), though like most such nuclear arrangements, it proved temporary. By 2001–2, the Magnox liabilities rendered the company close to insolvency, and the proposed Nuclear Decommissioning Authority to take over the liabilities from BNFL would be seen as a solution (see Chapter 21).

The transfer also provided another difficulty. Under British regulation, transferring nuclear sites from one publicly owned company to another introduced a process of reassessing the licensing arrangements. It took the rest of the decade to complete, so the full transfer was not effected until February 1998.

Life in the Private Sector—Searching for a Strategy

Having achieved the goal of privatization, British Energy turned to consider its future. The AGR stations were ageing and no more PWRs were planned. Therefore, either the company could slowly wind itself down and return cash to shareholders, or it could try to grow in related markets. The obvious choice was the international nuclear market, which was undergoing the traumas of competition in electricity and the exposure of sunk and stranded costs. As Nuclear Electric and Scottish Nuclear were integrated, Jeffrey departed for the United States and set about taking on O&M contracts in the United States and Canada, building up a portfolio which was to prove important in keeping British Energy afloat after 2000. But the opportunities were limited, and British Energy therefore looked to other forms of electricity generation, first contemplating gas[23] and eventually buying the Eggborough coal plant at what turned out to be a substantial premium. It also bought SWALEC's electricity supply business to create a vertical hedge (mimicking the moves by PowerGen and National Power). These electricity market forays proved disastrous, and led to the departure of Hollins, Hawley's successor as Chief Executive. SWALEC was sold and substantial write-downs in asset values were necessitated for Eggborough. By the end of the decade, British Energy was finding the new NETA arrangements hard to cope with. Without a long-term contract, as prices fell and with its output problems, it was experiencing losses, and had recognized that its future lay with a new PWR programme. This in turn needed active government support through compulsory long-term, take-or-pay contracts, and Jeffrey, made Chairman and Chief Executive after the Hollins departure, led the case posited to the PIU review. This however was for the future. Time ran out in 2002, and it had to turn to the DTI for help.

Half a Solution

The privatization of nuclear, like that of coal, was partial, leaving the liabilities question to be sorted out largely in the public sector. Like coal, it was presented as far more comprehensive than the facts supported. But it was nevertheless almost wholly good in its effects. Privatization shed much light on the obscure economics of the nuclear industry, and the

---

[23] In 1997 British Energy took a 12.5% share in Humber Power (CCGT) which it sold in 2001.

prospect of privatization focused management almost exclusively on getting the AGRs to work properly. The FFL further exposed the costs and made the public more aware of nuclear's back-end liabilities.

Of these, by far the most important gain from privatization was managerial. The incentives on profit-seeking managers were overwhelmingly focused on plant availability and load factors. Under the Pool, British Energy was a baseload price-taker. Revenue could only be improved by increasing output, and at the margin reducing the few costs that were not fixed.

Finally, the existence of a segregated fund for future liabilities was the first clear attempt to ring-fence monies in a meaningful way. Although there had been provisions in the past, in the public sector these were always vulnerable to manipulations. British Energy's fund was not so easily interfered with.

However, getting the existing nuclear assets properly managed did not solve the longer-term future of the industry.[24] The absence of long-term supply contracts, of a properly defined decommissioning policy and long-term waste-management strategy, or of a commercial future for THORP and MOX, left much of the nuclear sector in limbo. As the Flowers Report had shown (RCEP 1976), the nuclear industry had little future if there was no agreed solution to its past. By 2003 that solution was not much nearer, although a sense of urgency finally emerged as CO_2 emissions started to rise, renewables proved expensive, and British Energy ran into financial difficulties. The creation of the NDA was, however, a first step in the right direction.

---

[24] In the first five years after privatization, these fundamental questions about nuclear power were left largely to specialists, with the Royal Society providing a focus. See NAPAG (1995) and especially The Royal Society (1999).

11

Regulatory Failure and Financial Engineering—The RECs' First Review

> There is no doubt that REC shareholders have done very well out of electricity privatisation. (Stephen Littlechild, 'The Competitive Electricity Market from 1998', Offer 1995a)

Although the focus of policy and regulation had been the promotion of competition, the privatized electricity industry would always contain an important element of natural monopoly. This, in turn, required regulation to limit prices and to ensure that the network was adequate to the task of securing competitive supplies. As with previous privatizations, the chosen instrument of regulation was licences rather than a contract-based approach,[1] with provision to reset the prices on a periodic basis. The price cap, set through the RPI−X mechanism, was chosen to provide high-powered incentives for efficiency. Indeed, the electricity industry had the architect of RPI−X regulation, Stephen Littlechild, as its regulator. It is therefore ironic that Littlechild proved less able than his fellow regulators to execute periodic reviews. Indeed, his attempt to reset the RECs' distribution price caps in 1994/95 proved sufficiently flawed that the system as a whole nearly faltered. The preference of the Labour opposition for profit-sharing received a considerable boost as a result, and the seeds for the windfall tax were sown.

The Privatization Prospectus and the First Regulatory Period for the RECs

Viewed with hindsight, anyone who had sold all their worldly goods in 1990 and invested in the RECs would, by 1995, have become extremely wealthy. The offer to investors at privatization turned out to be extremely generous. The companies quadrupled their values, as well as paying generous dividends. Compared with the stock market as a whole, this was a staggering return. But once the stability of the RECs' income and

---

[1] The contract approach was later adopted for train operating companies in rail privatization, and was to prove fraught with difficulties.

the relative maturity of their networks are borne in mind, it is all the more remarkable. It would be extraordinary if such returns were thought necessary to entice investors to take the risks of running such apparently dull businesses. Nor were such returns intended by the government that privatized the RECs. How, then, did such a turn of events transpire? The answers are fourfold: the amateur nature of the initial price-setting process; the scale of inefficiency in the public sector; the recession; and regulatory failure.

The government hired Kleinwort Benson Ltd to advise it on the privatization of the RECs. These advisers were not operating in a vacuum. They had the limited experience of regulation in BT,[2] BAA and British Gas from the 1980s to draw upon, as well as parallel work on water privatization. Moreover, the RECs were much simpler businesses than any of the previous cases. There were also lots of them, from which comparisons could be drawn. The Monopolies and Mergers Commission (MMC) had investigated a number of the companies' performance in the 1980s. The networks were mature, using well-known technologies.

Yet, with the advantages that the privatizers of BT, BAA, and British Gas lacked, there were mistakes made in calculating all of the main variables that made up the initial distribution price cap. Most notably, the government provided for around £5 billion of capital expenditure (CAPEX) in the first period, and grossly underestimated the operating expenditure (OPEX) efficiencies which might be reaped (Kleinwort Benson 1990). (In the event, as we shall see below, the RECs spent only £2.5 billion on CAPEX over the first regulatory period.) Subsequent investigations, including by the National Audit Office (NAO 1992a), indicated that the quality of the work done at privatization by the government and its team was poor.[3]

A defence which some have mounted for the scale of these errors is that the City did not seem to have been much better at recognizing the RECs' potential, nor indeed at analysing the new utility sector of the equity market. Share prices did not rise sharply initially, and it was only towards the end of the first period that they began to reflect the underlying economic value of the businesses. Furthermore, golden shares in the RECs meant that they could not be taken over until 1995, and hence the strength of the RECs' balance sheets could not be forcibly exploited through takeovers.

---

[2] See, for example, Oftel (1988a,b). There was also the classic article by Beesley and Littlechild (1989).

[3] It has also been suggested that the overwhelming priority of the Department of Energy was to get the flotation done, and since the value was perceived to be in distribution rather than supply, there were pressures to make the regulatory controls less demanding.

Lack of understanding of the political and regulatory context may have played a part. A cautious investor might reasonably have assumed that, should returns turn out to be high, intervention would follow. The fact that, as we shall see, the regulator strictly adhered to the central principle of RPI−X regulation (i.e. that the regulatory deal at privatization was a fixed price for a fixed period) and therefore kept his hands off until the review, came as a pleasant surprise to the financial markets.

A second possible explanation is that the inefficiency in the public sector was much greater than realized at the time. The argument goes on: only privatization could have revealed the scale of the inefficiency, and RPI−X regulation worked well precisely because it provided incentives to the RECs to drive down costs. The incumbent management may themselves not have realized the potential.

A third explanation is the recession. For most of British industry, recession is a bad thing; the fall in demand has more impact than the reduced pressure on costs. For the RECs, however, the opposite is true. Electricity demand is largely inelastic, so *relative* to the rest of industry, there is an element of demand protection. However, costs fall, reducing the actual OPEX and CAPEX needed to meet the requirements determined at the first price-setting, on the basis of economic boom in the late 1980s. In addition, unlike the rest of British industry, RECs' prices do not adjust in the short run: they are fixed. The RECs' prices are inflexible between reviews (unlike the competitive markets which RPI−X was supposed to imitate). Thus, when the UK economy plunged into a major recession immediately after privatization, the RECs were beneficiaries. The decline in economic activity was reflected in the labour and construction price indices.

All of the above reasons contributed to a much healthier financial performance for the RECs in the first five years. Dividends, projected at around 10 p per share at privatization, turned out much higher by the fourth year, at 16 p per share on average for the RECs. These were, in fact, *underestimates* of overall performance, as much wealth was dissipated on diversifications. Faced with a strong balance sheet, positive cash flows and the absence of a takeover constraint, the RECs embarked on significant diversifications in the first five years following privatization. In principle, there was an industrial logic, insofar as diversification had been prohibited in the public sector, and it was unlikely that, by the 1990s, the structure established after the Second World War in very different circumstances would now reflect the cost conditions of the industry. Some acquisitions and diversifications were therefore likely to be desirable.

The pattern that emerged followed four paths: diversification upstream into gas-fired independent power projects; horizontal diversification into gas supply; international diversification; and, finally, conglomerate diversification into a range of activities from security alarms to hotels. Telecoms—the real money spinner in the 1990s for ScottishPower and National Grid Company (NGC)—did not feature in any of the RECs' plans for the early 1990s, and, in adjusting their portfolios, only slowly did the RECs engage in divestment of retailing activities.[4]

As was to be expected, the paths and speeds of diversification varied from company to company, largely in response to the personalities and ethos of the management teams that emerged from privatization. They ranged from the ambitious failures at East Midlands Electricity on the one hand, to the more cautious approach at Manweb (which kept out of combined-cycle gas turbines CCGTs) and at SWEB (which found little other than Teesside Power to invest in), on the other. Interestingly, it was the cautious companies which fell first to takeovers when the golden shares lapsed in 1995 (see Chapter 12).

Unfortunately, it is impossible to provide any accurate estimate of the scale of shareholder wealth lost through these activities, since the shape of the businesses has changed, the regulatory accounts have been slow to ring-fence the core activities, and the subsequent takeovers have muddied the accounting and market valuation issues. It is, however, hard to conclude other than that the 'dash for acquisitions' reflected the consequences of giving managements with little or no acquisition experience large cash flows free of the normal capital market disciplines.[5]

Thus, the main picture that emerges from the first five years in the private sector is one of very high returns, some of which were squandered on acquisitions, which could not possibly be justified on efficiency grounds alone. The question that follows is how the RECs got away with it: why did Littlechild not intervene? The answer he gave was that intervention would undermine the incentives of the RPI−X regulatory regime. Hence, while an interim price cut would, temporarily, be beneficial to customers, it was bound to lead to higher prices in the long term, as companies no longer strove to minimize costs.

To understand why this answer is mistaken, and why regulatory failure was a contributor to the excess returns, it is necessary to examine the underlying nature of the RPI−X regime. The theory which lies behind its approach relies upon two sets of economic principles: the nature of economic incentives, competition and the superiority of competition to regulation; and the nature of informational problems.

---

[4] ScottishPower's Thus and NGC's Energis were both casualties of the collapse of the telecommunications battle in the early 2000s.

[5] See OXERA (1995) 'Acquisitions and Diversifications: The Record of the Privatized Utilities'.

At the theoretical level, Littlechild's approach emphasized the dynamic view of the way capitalism worked, and, in particular, the importance of profit to incentivize managers. Hayek had argued famously in the 1930s that the price mechanism is superior to that of planning because it economizes on information. Given the price, decentralized choice requires that each individual uses the private knowledge of their own tastes and preferences to choose the best option available. Each only needs to know the price. The planner, on the contrary, needs to know all the prices *and* all the preferences. Hence, the superiority of the price mechanism over planning.[6]

In a perfectly competitive market, each firm is a price-taker and cannot therefore exploit market power. Entry will follow any deviation from marginal cost pricing. Hayek believed that such a perfect state would provide no incentive to compete. In effect, competition would impose a 100 per cent tax on abnormal returns. It is a feature shared with pure rate-of-return regulation.[7] It follows that market imperfections would be necessary to motivate profit-seeking behaviour. But, as noted in Chapter 3, Schumpeter (1943) added to the Austrian debate about capitalism the idea that any exploitation of monopoly would be temporary: the presence of monopoly rents attracts entrants, who then compete away the rents until a normal profit results.

The idea of price-takers and temporary monopoly rents provided two key elements to RPI−X, and, in particular, informed Littlechild's views.[8] The first necessitated that prices had to be set in the case of a natural monopoly for as long as it remained; the second that it would not greatly matter if, in the short term, there were some element of monopoly profits, since the possibility of these rents would provide incentives to managers to improve performance. RPI−X met both of these requirements. It was price-based, not rate-of-return-based, and it permitted abnormal profits within the regulatory period. Properly applied, these abnormal profits within the period would not be clawed back when prices came to be reset after the (typically) five-year period. These periodic reviews would mimic what competitive entry would have done—that is, they would drive returns (eventually) back to normal.

[6] Hayek's work on this price mechanism and planning are brought together in Hayek (1948). His *Road to Serfdom* (1944) greatly influenced the wider political debate, and provided an underpinning for Margaret Thatcher's brand of neo-liberalism. See Helm (1986) for a discussion of the issues.

[7] This is a point Alan Walters recognized about rate-or-return regulation—see DTI (1983: 3).

[8] See also Littlechild (1981a) on the social costs of monopoly.

The second set of principles related to the inherent weakness of the regulator in trying to prejudge the evolving cost structure of the industry. This, in turn, had two parts: the asymmetry between the parties; and the inherent indeterminacy of the capitalist process. As was to become abundantly clear in the RECs' periodic review, the regulator was at a considerable disadvantage to the companies. The latter had the information, and the incentive to reveal it strategically so as to bias the outcome of the review in their favour. As we shall see, the process of strategic information revelation is a subtle one, involving ever more sophisticated games (and armies of advisers). Even the best-resourced regulator cannot hope to win this battle, and is forced to rely on a variety of informational checks and crude mechanisms to guess at the underlying performance.

To this asymmetry, the Austrian school provided a further reason why trying to predict costs accurately would be an impossible task. The process of competition is itself one of information revelation. We cannot know what unexpected consequences will be thrown up. Indeed, it is precisely because we do not know the future that even the most well-intentioned planners will fail. Thus, to the practical difficulties of information asymmetries and game playing must be added an objection to the exercise in principle.

These considerations give rise to a view of RPI−X regulation which is fundamentally different from that pursued by other regulators of utilities, notably Ian Byatt, then Director General of Water Services.[9] On the Littlechild view, the purpose of regulation is to bear down on costs by exploiting the profit motive. The RPI−X regime provides this incentive, as long as it is not interfered with. When it is reset, the forward-looking new price cap will be informed by the past, but *not* determined by it. Better, on the Littlechild view, to set a crude target and let the market reveal the costs in consequence than to try to approximate the cost function of the companies. The justification is simple: on the Littlechild view, the costs will be lower in the longer term. High-powered incentives to minimize costs dominate short-term considerations. The essence of RPI−X regulation is therefore the fixed-price contract for a *fixed period*.

Thus, when the performance over the first period began to signal high abnormal returns, Littlechild's reaction was not to regard this as a necessary sign of failure or to necessitate intervention, even if the returns were embarrassingly high and customers were disadvantaged. On the contrary,

---

[9] The differences between the regulatory approach in water and electricity are a matter of considerable debate. In water, Byatt, too, repeatedly stressed the importance of incentives, but he was also much more intrusive in his intensive efforts to estimate the companies' cost functions, and repeatedly intervened within periods (see Helm and Rajah 1994).

he thought that intervention would be counterproductive. And, indeed, faced with pressure to act as early as 1992, he set out the classic arguments against such a course of action:

Some have suggested that I should accelerate the REC reviews so that new controls can be implemented earlier. I well understand the concerns of users. However, there are disadvantages as well as advantages associated with the premature review of price controls. They were set on the basis that there would be a reasonable period between reviews, giving companies the incentive to improve efficiency and reduce costs during that period. If a regulator is seen to intervene constantly in the operations of a company, there will be an adverse effect on the incentive for that company to improve its efficiency and reduce costs. What is more, the degree of regulatory risk to which it is subject may be perceived as greater. Consequently, there may well be some increase in the rate of return which investors require—that is, in the company's cost of capital—and so a higher level of prices for customers in the longer run. Taking these considerations into account, I do not believe that an earlier review of this price control is warranted at present. (Littlechild 1993b: 136).[10]

It was an argument that was simple and consistent with his wider economic approach, and he would stick to it for as long as he could.

In trying to mimic the incentives of competitive markets, the Littlechild approach is open to a number of criticisms. First, in competitive markets entrants do not arrive at discrete five-year intervals. Second, in competitive markets, prices vary—indeed, in very competitive commodity markets, they can be highly volatile. Intervention, if it is mimicking the market in changing prices, would not need to be confined to the five-year periods. Third, management can only be incentivized to act upon those aspects of the business *within* their control, and much of the returns were *outside* their control. Changing *external* parameters cannot in itself be detrimental to incentives. Fourth, RPI−X provided incentives to reduce CAPEX and delay its delivery, even if this went beyond efficiencies. Not all cost reductions are efficient. Put simply, there is nothing natural or sacrosanct about five-year periods, and incentives can survive carefully crafted interventions when these are based on returns well outside any reasonable expectations.

But perhaps of most importance was Littlechild's failure to take sufficiently into account the political dimension of his approach. For him, regulation was a *technical* exercise, reflected, as we saw in Chapter 8, in his response to the 1992/93 coal crisis. But, in practice, regulation works *within* a political and social context, and, if the returns are high enough to

---

[10] This text was based on a lecture given in summer 1992.

be regarded as 'politically unacceptable', the regime itself comes under pressure. The failures to correct the manifest errors in the original price caps when they became apparent in 1993 cost the industry dear, and sowed the seeds of the windfall tax. A purist approach, based upon a particular school of economic theory, neglected the political dimension of the industry. And when the review itself was conducted, Littlechild failed to properly redress the balance.

The First Periodic Review of the RECs

With the high returns in the first period very much in mind, Littlechild set about the periodic review of the RECs. The process began in October 1993 with the appointment of consultants to gather information on the costs, business plans and CAPEX projections of the companies, to be reviewed by the regulator in spring 1994. In keeping with Littlechild's views on the overall approach, it was not until well into the process that he began to reveal his methodology. In stark contrast to the Treasury-like approach taken by Byatt at Ofwat, the analysis of operating and capital cost projections was less sophisticated, and there were no consultation papers on the key building blocks, such as the cost of capital and asset base. The review got off to a bad start when a letter from Littlechild to the chairmen of the RECs on 22 April 1994 leaked, suggesting that a common X factor would be adopted along with a 10–20 per cent immediate cut in prices (the 'P_0 factor'). A second letter followed on 24 June, again private rather than public, and again subject to rumour and leaks. The results were finally announced on 11 August, leaving only the determinations for the Scottish companies to follow later in the year on 29 September.

The 'solution' for which the regulator opted had three main components: a 50 per cent uplift on the privatization asset valuation; a differential P_0 cut to place the companies on an even footing; and an X factor to reflect future cost trends. In particular, the financial determinants of the returns to shareholders received relatively little attention. For Littlechild, prices and costs were what mattered: how the industry was financed and valued was less his concern. It would be hard to imagine Littlechild following Byatt and Bryan Carsberg, Director General of Telecommunications (1984–92) in checking the share prices regularly. Yet these financial considerations could not be avoided.

Each of these three core components was the subject of both methodological and practical disputes, about both the rationale for each within an incentive regime, and the balance between customers and shareholders.

The 50 per cent Uplift

Despite a wobble at the time of the leaked letter, at the time of the periodic review, share prices for the RECs indicated that the market valued the companies at a much higher level than at privatization. The problem facing Littlechild was to decide what the shareholders' stake in the business should be for the second period, and then what rate of return to provide. There were three options: the privatization value, rolled forward to take account of inflation and the CAPEX in the first period not paid for out of current revenue from customers' bills; the current market value; and some intermediate value to reflect the risk at flotation. The first was deemed at the time to be too severe and unsettling to capital market expectations; and the second was circular, in that it simply validated share prices. Thus, the third option prevailed.

But by how much should the initial flotation value be marked up? The regulator chose an arbitrary 50 per cent, to which a cost of capital of 7 per cent pre-tax was applied. Since it was largely a distributional matter and arguably had little effect on incentives, on Austrian grounds it mattered little what precise number was chosen.[11] But it had significant beneficial consequences for shareholders, who not only benefited from the higher profits due to lower CAPEX and OPEX in the first period, but were also to be rewarded by a 50 per cent mark-up on their initial investment, and would then receive a 7 per cent return on that higher number. This generous treatment was compounded by a failure to consider fully the relationship between the consequential regulatory asset base (RAB) and the balance sheets of the companies. Little reference was made in Littlechild's explanation of his determination of the new price cap to the strong financial position of the companies, an oversight which would soon come to haunt him when Trafalgar House bid for Northern Electric, and Northern Electric demonstrated how far the balance sheet could be geared up with debt.

---

[11] Littlechild's explanation was as follows: 'In using a market valuation for the distribution businesses, some further adjustment to the flotation value is appropriate. It is reasonable to take into account initial expectations of dividend growth which (other things being equal) would imply a rise over time in a company's share value; investment in the distributions business since flotation; and any change in the cost of capital from which investors at flotation might expect to benefit. There has been a fall in Stock Market yields since flotation, and there seems to have been a fall in the overall cost of capital for RECs... To reflect these elements, I based calculations on the flotation value increased by 50% for each company, plus net investment since flotation. The resulting valuations vary across companies, but on average are around 90% of CCA asset value excluding revaluations other than for RPI' (Offer 1994c: paras 5.64 and 5.65, pp. 68–9).

The Differential P_0 Cuts

The second feature of the review was a novel one: a cut in the price *level* or P_0. Until this review, regulators had confined price reviews to setting the X factors to reflect changing expectations of the *future* course of costs—that is, the rate of *change* in prices. This path had been previously used by Carsberg for BT and by Littlechild himself for NGC in April 1993/94.

The rationale for an initial price cut was that the evidence for the previous period indicated a lower cost function. Thus, the past efficiencies were passed on to customers through a lower price. This was a rebasing of the price level. Then the X factor would reflect *future* cost trends. Furthermore, since evidence for the previous periodic review indicated that some companies had improved their efficiency more than others, the scale of the P_0 would vary across companies (whereas the X factor would not). This was the first step in electricity towards the idea that prices would be set on the basis of the *efficient*, not actual, level of costs.

To estimate the efficient frontier, the costs of the RECs were compared. This task should have been straightforward. Unlike the reviews of BT, British Gas, and NGC, there were twelve companies to compare, and, unlike water, the CAPEX programmes were modest and largely driven by maintaining and replacing a mature infrastructure. Arguably, the distribution review for the RECs was therefore easier to conduct than that of any other utility industry. In fact, the comparative exercise was fairly crude. Having assessed the data for each REC separately, the regulator simply placed the companies into three broad bands.[12]

The overall logic of this approach was sound and, indeed, the P_0 cut methodology has been broadly adopted across the utilities in subsequent reviews. The problem lay in its execution. There was much dispute about whether the Offer estimates of the efficiency frontier properly reflected cost differences which were *within* the control of managers, and hence whether the incentives for managers for *future* reviews had been properly set. Next time around, there might be similar arbitrary adjustments too.

The Uniform X Factor

The uniform X factor had the great advantage of simplicity. In effect, Littlechild took a view of the future evolution of cost trends in the sector and assumed that all were equally placed to exploit these opportunities.

---

[12] P_0 cuts for the RECs at the first determination were 11% for Eastern, East Midlands and Southern; 14% for London, Midlands, NORWEB, SEEBOARD, South Western, and Yorkshire; and 17% for Manweb, Northern, and SWALEC.

Furthermore, to the extent that there might be some differences in potential between the RECs, it was far from obvious that Littlechild, given his relatively weak position in accessing the necessary information to make a judgement, could make a good estimate of these differences.

The X factor chosen was based on quite crude and general information. It was widely assumed that the economy was experiencing something like RPI−2, and that the utilities still had some pre-privatization fat to come out. Therefore, RPI−3 looked reasonable (Offer 1994c: para 14, p. vi). This reduced to RPI−2 when rates and non-chargeable costs were included. There was little appreciation at the time of the step change in efficiency that information technology would eventually bring to networks. Indeed, the *added* costs of information technology for the 1998 programme continued to disguise this technical revolution.

The Outcome, the Aftermath, and Northern Electric

Taking the 50 per cent uplift, the cost of capital at 7 per cent and the estimates of OPEX and CAPEX, the regulator determined that the RECs could finance their functions with an average P_0 cut of 14 per cent and a uniform X factor of 2 per cent. The stock market reacted immediately as Fig. 11.1 shows.[13]

The sharp increase in share prices provoked a number of critical comments.[14] In theory, had the review been 'correct', the market value would have approximated the new valuation of the RAB. The cost of capital would have equalled the rate of return, and the expected efficiency would have normalized returns from the operating and investment activities. Thus the sharp rise above the RAB in market value was prima facie evidence that a mistake had been made.

Stung by the criticism, Littlechild moved to defend his position and sought to explain the share-price behaviour as due to two factors: the removal of uncertainty; and the takeover premia associated with the expiry of the golden share (Littlechild 1994a). Both of these explanations were unconvincing. First, the removal of uncertainty could hardly be taken seriously as a reason for share-price rises, unless the outcome was better than market expectations. Otherwise, a Draconian outcome would also lead to share-price *rises*. Second, the expiry of the golden share would

---

[13] It should, however, be noted that the share price had *fallen* after the leaks in April referred to above. The difference between the April and the August reactions can in part be explained by the uncertainty concerning the former, and the much greater understanding analysts had acquired of the REC businesses in the intervening period.

[14] See, for example, *Energy Utilities*, OXERA, September 1994, especially 5–6.

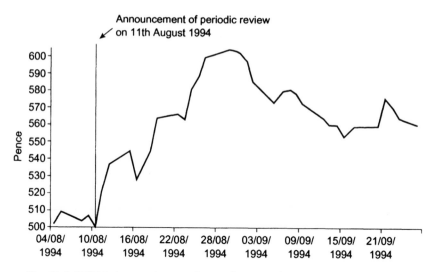

Fig. 11.1 RECs' share-price reaction to the periodic-review announcement
Source: Datastream.

happen *anyway*. There is no reason to suppose that the value of the takeover premium should uniquely enter the share price at the time of the regulator's determination. To these reasons should be added the *scale* of the share-price rise: neither the uncertainty nor the takeover premium for the sector as a whole could be worth the extent of the increases.

That the regulator had got it badly wrong was apparent. It remained for the bid by Trafalgar House for Northern Electric to reveal just how great the error had been. On 19 December 1994 Trafalgar House launched a hostile takeover bid for Northern Electric. Open season on the RECs had begun. Trafalgar House, a construction business in some difficulties (itself to fall prey to a subsequent bid), was attracted by Northern's strong balance sheet. It wanted a secure cash flow and the ability to borrow against Northern's distribution assets. The opening bid was nearly £11 per share (compared with a flotation value of just £2.40 five years earlier).

The hostile bid spurred Northern's advisers to look to its balance sheet to tempt shareholders to resist Trafalgar House's overtures. Given negligible gearing, Northern's second defence document was published on 17 February and proposed borrowing heavily against the assets and then distributing the cash raised directly to shareholders. For every £2.40 share, just over £5 cash would be (and was subsequently) paid out. To put this in perspective, Northern Electric in effect revealed that it could have given its domestic customers a year without paying any bills and still have been able to finance its functions.

This defence strategy let the genie out of the bottle (and Trafalgar retired hurt from the fray, with its own internal difficulties). If Northern could do this, so could all the other RECs. The era of share buy-backs, special dividends and the associated takeovers had dawned, ushering in a shareholder bonanza (see Chapter 12). The inadequacy of Littlechild's price determination was now painfully apparent, and he announced his intention to carry out a re-review on 7 March—probably just in time to avoid direct political intervention:

it is . . . relevant to take into account what appears to be widespread public concern about whether the price control proposals are sufficiently demanding on the RECs and whether they represent an appropriate balance between the interests of customers and shareholders. (Offer, press statement, 7 March 1995)

In the meantime, Scottish Hydro-Electric had appealed against its price determination (the Scottish companies having a separate timetable), and the MMC investigated, publishing its report on 15 June (MMC 1995). Thus, Littlechild was able to draw on its findings to help him solve his problems.[15]

Northern Electric had highlighted not only the weakness of the price cap, but also a more fundamental problem: the balance sheet. It raised a central issue of the privatization arrangements: was the balance sheet set up at privatization with little debt in order to ensure that the flotation was successful; or was it set up to ensure that CAPEX was financed by borrowing, and hence would be paid for by future, not current customers? In other words, was the gearing potential to the benefit of shareholders or customers?

In the case of BT and the water industry, the answer is fairly clear. Both were privatized precisely because the public sector could not (or would not) finance investment programmes—the system X exchanges in the former case, and the European directives in the latter. Privatization was in considerable measure about creating '*private*-sector borrowing requirements' (Helm 2001a). For others, such as gas and the RECs, the investment needs were less apparent. Yet, had any politician told the electorate that the type of financial engineering in which Northern Electric engaged would follow without check, it is hard to see how the legislation could have passed through Parliament.

It is therefore extremely curious that, when Littlechild came to revisit the RECs' periodic review, he again chose to ignore the balance-sheet issue. There was to be no *regulated balance sheet*, rolling forward the privatization

---

[15] The MMC concluded that 'an adjustment to [the initial market value] at the present time, based on an assessment of what investors may rightly or wrongly have assumed about the cost of capital at the time of privatizing, does not seem appropriate to us in this analysis (MMC 1995: para 2.50, quoted by Littlechild in Offer 1995b).

gearing to match the RAB.[16] Instead, Littlechild simply rebased the mark-up on the RAB from 50 to 15 per cent and adjusted the efficiency rankings of the companies. That there was no more apparent rationale for 15 than 50 per cent (or, indeed, any other number) was not addressed.[17] Rather, the price cap had simply been tightened from one arbitrary number to another. For Littlechild, it was more a matter of future incentives, and not the distributional stakes between shareholders and customers.

The damage had, however, been done. For any regulator to have to revisit a price cap is a black mark.[18] But for Littlechild, who had invested so much in creating the reputation for non-intervention and placed so much emphasis on the credibility of the fixed period, the effects were almost fatal. How could investors rely on the maintenance of incentives in the future if high returns resulted? The answer was that they could not in the electricity industry, as they would not elsewhere in the other utilities.[19] Indeed, a few months later, the terms of the review were again revisited when NGC was floated off, and then again with the windfall tax.

The Third Attempt, £50 off and NGC's Flotation

The unprecedented second attempt to get the RECs' distribution prices right should have been the end of the matter, but it was not. Share prices continued to reflect the much higher value that the markets placed on the RECs, and hence the pressure was on to get more customer concessions immediately, rather than wait until 2000, as the incentive approach dictated. The politics of reasonable returns repeatedly put limits on the purity of the RPI − X incentive regime.

The opportunity to revisit the price cap for a third time came up in summer 1995. NGC was to be floated (in December 1995), and hence the RECs would sell their shares in the grid. Once the value of NGC became visible, it was apparent that the valuation assumed for it in setting the RECs' price

[16] This was left to Byatt to address in his second water periodic review, but only with limited success. The flight of equity eventually resulted in pure debt models, such as that of Glas Cymru.

[17] Littlechild accepted that 'the appropriate level of uprate is necessarily a matter of judgement' (para 11.22). See his general explanation in Offer 1995b: paras 11.1–11.24, pp. 13–18.

[18] Only Railtrack's track access agreements price cap in 2000/01 and the initial price cap for National Air Traffic Services in 2001/02 have run into such difficulties once set, and in both cases for exceptional reasons—respectively the Hatfield derailment in October 2000 and the 11 September 2001 attacks.

[19] In the first regulatory period in the water sector, intervention became an annual event (see Helm and Rajah 1994), and 'voluntary' profit-sharing was introduced almost immediately after the first periodic review.

caps was generous. (Alternatively, it could be argued that the price-cap revision of NGC's formula set in 1993/94 was too generous.) Therefore, under political pressure from the Minister for Energy, Tim Eggar, the RECs agreed to pay a one-off rebate to all customers of £50.

In theory (and, in particular, in Littlechild's theory), no such payment was required. Indeed, payment would be counter-productive, since it could only weaken incentives further. If managers had made NGC more efficient, the reward was the higher value when NGC was floated off, and regulators should not intervene within periods—especially not after the re-review. In practice, the rationale was much simpler and more blatant. The public—and, hence, the politicians—would not wait until 2000 to have what were seen as excess profits addressed. Indeed, they did not: the windfall tax was applied after the first three attempts had failed to produce a politically and publicly acceptable answer.

The Windfall Tax

The form and scope of the windfall tax and its implications for the energy sector are explored in greater detail in Chapter 15. However, its relationship to the distribution price controls needs to be noted. If the RECs had been regulated so that they could just, *ex ante,* be expected to finance their functions by the first or even second review, there would have been neither a rationale nor a capacity to levy the windfall tax in 1997.

The ease with which the tax was in fact levied from the RECs is a further condemnation of the periodic reviews.[20] Labour was able to raise around £1.5 billion from the RECs without much by way of consequence. The reason related back—as it always had since Trafalgar House's bid for Northern Electric—to the balance sheets. With gearing potential, the RECs could simply borrow to pay the tax. Instead of borrowing to pay cash to shareholders—as Northern Electric had done—they could borrow to finance public expenditure on the young unemployed instead. Labour had simply recognized the potential of the *private*-sector borrowing requirement.

When the price caps came up for revision at the end of the 1990s, it proved possible to impose price cuts of over 20 per cent, even after the NGC sale rebates and windfall taxes. This could not all be explained by additional efficiency gains, and here provides the final piece of evidence that the 1994/95 regulatory reviews were seriously flawed.[21]

---

[20] The windfall tax was of course applied across all utilities, but its level and the ease of financing varied considerably (see Chapter 15).

[21] The source of these efficiency gains—between OPEX and CAPEX—was affected by the widespread practice of capitalizing OPEX.

Lessons from the RECs' Fiasco

Pure RPI−X regulation—in the form of fixed prices for fixed periods—has only seriously been pursued once in the face of considerable excess profits for the RECs. The returns in the first period were very obviously high, and could not be justified by unanticipated efficiency gains alone. What followed undermined what little public confidence there was in the regulatory regime.

It is tempting to argue that this first period was an aberration—the excess profits were a temporary phenomenon associated with the privatization process, and that, with time, the regime would settle down. Although, after 2000, the regime would be much tighter, as an excuse for the failures in 1994/95, it is too optimistic, partly because these industries will always have a significant political element, but partly also because the philosophy behind RPI−X regulation is itself flawed.

The RPI−X regulation has always been closer to rate-of-return regulation than its inventors claimed. The differences between the regimes are matters of degree, not kind. The RPI−X regulation can be regarded as similar to rate-of-return regulation with a lag (Helm 1994*b*). Both regimes set *prices*, and both use similar information sets *ex ante*. They differ only in relation to the claw-back, and, hence, the scope for shareholders to make significant temporary excess returns.

Applied to the RECs, the scope for genuine unanticipated efficiency gains over the medium term is relatively small. There was a case in the first period for claiming that there was a shakeout of public-sector inefficiencies and that the scale of public-sector failure could only be revealed once private ownership was put in place. But this was more true of OPEX than CAPEX. The incentives for the companies to play regulatory games is great, and there is little agreement as to what constitutes an 'extraordinary' CAPEX efficiency. Even if there were such agreement, a five-year, fixed-price CAPEX contract is not the obvious answer.[22] But the fundamental issues that undermined Littlechild's regulatory credibility were to do with the RAB, the balance sheet and the cost of capital, not OPEX and CAPEX.

Thus, it is hard to avoid the conclusion that, even if Littlechild had used the obvious advantages he had of twelve companies to compare, the task

---

[22] By the end of the decade, there was a growing recognition of the limitations of RPI−X as a mechanism for determining CAPEX. Ofgem, as discussed in Chapter 18, introduced auctions and a new mechanism for varying CAPEX for its 2002 Transco review, and, in its first consultation document on the 2004 distribution review, explicitly recognized the need to change its CAPEX regulation (Ofgem 2002*c*).

he set himself could not have been achieved. As we shall see below, the gas regulator did markedly better—by engaging in those very financial issues which rate-of-return regulation shares, rather than adhering to the pure theory of RPI−X. Pure RPI−X lives only in textbooks: the reality is much more complex and inevitably hedged around with political constraints.

12

Takeover Mania and Capital Market Competition

It was always the intention that, after a short period of protection through special government shares which expired this year, the RECs would be exposed to the normal disciplines and opportunities of the market. That includes the possibility of mergers and acquisitions. I firmly believe that exposing the RECs to such pressures is crucial to keeping management up to scratch and enhancing the efficiency of the industry as a whole. (Ian Lang, 'Don't Be Afraid of Electricity Takeovers', 1995)

Back in 1990, when the electricity industry was privatized, no one imagined that within six or seven years the majority of the regional electricity companies (RECs) would be in foreign hands, and that, by the end of the decade, most would have changed hands at least twice. That the first set of new owners would be predominantly American, where rate-of-return regulation was widely believed to lead to inefficiency and weak management, was particularly ironic. Although the takeover mechanism would eventually play a part after the golden shares expired in 1995, it was widely assumed that the combination of regulators, government and the Monopolies and Mergers Commission (MMC) would limit any major corporate restructuring.

With hindsight, it is easier to see how many of the necessary ingredients for a takeover frenzy were in place. Management had a direct financial interest in the takeovers through their share options and remuneration packages. Investment bankers could see a quick profit, and there was an abundance of cash-rich potential purchasers, many with special reasons for paying a premium. Finally, the regulator himself viewed takeovers in a positive light, regarding this mechanism as an essential check on managerial efficiency (Littlechild 1988). With a fixed-price, fixed-period contract, what could be better than competition between sets of managers to run the assets as efficiently as possible. Competition in the capital market could discipline managers where the natural monopoly in the product market could not.

The Expiry of the Golden Share

Golden shares had been created in many of the privatizations to ensure that companies remained in British hands, or at least that the government could have a direct role in any bids that emerged. They had been used in such diverse cases as Jaguar Cars and British Steel. In the 1980s, it was assumed that the shares would be used to block takeovers, but when Ford bid for Jaguar in 1989, a symbol of national engineering and sporting achievement, the government's decision not to exercise its rights was widely interpreted as a change of direction towards a more *laissez-faire* approach.

In the case of the electricity industry, the generators and the RECs were covered by golden shares. There was a time limit for the RECs, to expire in 1995, but no great significance was placed on this date, since there was always the MMC as a backstop and, indeed, government could always extend the lives of the shares. The golden share is then best seen as a flexible *option*, which could be used as circumstances dictated. As an option, it could be exercised in a pragmatic way, and was perceived as open to short-term political expediency.

What was lacking was any clearly stated *policy* on foreign ownership (other than pure *laissez-faire*, which few believed, rightly, would be rigorously adhered to), or, indeed, any guidance as to who would—and who would not—be deemed acceptable owners. The treatment of regulatory issues which utilities inevitably raised was also confused. Would only those with open liberalized markets be welcome, of which there were very few? Would the closed nature of the US electricity market in many states be an obstacle? Would French and German bidders be excluded? Could foreign state-owned companies bid? Issues such as the location of control with owners in the United States or elsewhere, ring-fencing, the acceptable level of financial gearing, and the characteristics of the individual directors, were not addressed. These mattered, insofar as the utilities in general, and energy industries in particular, were part of the infrastructure of the economy, and hence had a significance far beyond other parts of British manufacturing. If Jaguar Cars had failed under foreign ownership, the damage to the economy would be contained and limited to local job losses. But if a REC failed, then the lights might go out, with a significant multiplier effect on the economy (Table 12.1).[1]

TABLE 12.1 The first takeover wave in the British electricity industry

REC	Takeover company	Country	Bid price (£ billion)	Date of takeover
Eastern Group	Hanson	UK	2.5	9/1995
SWEB	The Southern Company	US	1.1	9/1995
Manweb	ScottishPower	UK	1.1	10/1995
NORWEB	North West Water (United Utilities)	UK	1.8	11/1995
National Grid Company's pumped-storage business	Mission Energy	US	0.7	12/1995
SWALEC	Welsh Water (Hyder)	UK	0.9	1/1996
SEEBOARD	Central & South West Corporation	US	1.6	1/1996
Midlands Electricity	Avon Energy (General Public Utilities Corporation/Cinergy)	US	1.7	8/1996
East Midlands Electricity	Dominion Resources	US	1.3	1/1997
London Electricity	Entergy	US	1.2	2/1997
Northern Electric	CE Electric UK (CalEnergy/Peter Kiewit)	US	0.8	2/1997
Yorkshire Electricity	American Electric Power/PS Colorado	US	1.5	4/1997
Total takeover spend			16.2	

Source: OXERA.

[1] At the time such a failure was thought to be very unlikely. Much later, the failure of Enron as owner of Wessex Water was the first case of a utility parent's bankruptcy (through Azurix), to be followed by the failure of TXU in late 2002. Indeed, it was particularly odd that a Conservative government, prepared to invest so much in defence (from Trident to the Eurofighter) and greatly exercised by sovereignty in European matters, should place so little emphasis on infrastructure control. Without national control of the infrastructure utilities, defence strategy would be seriously weakened, and the difference between sovereignty over the pound and over gas, electricity, and water networks is one of degree not kind.

It is noticeable, too, that other countries (including the United States) took a very different view. When British utilities were eventually to reverse the process and make acquisitions in the United States, they found the regulatory and legal hurdles much higher. Electricity utilities could only be run by companies whose business was energy, and detailed hearings and undertakings were required. In Europe, it was not until Vodafone took over Mannesmann in 2000 that the *idea* of hostile foreign takeovers became accepted, and energy sector acquisitions within Europe have been largely a European matter. Only BEWAG witnessed a significant US entry, but this was short-lived, and a German solution was developed which excluded all but the large European players. In France, foreign acquisition of French energy utilities has been effectively ruled out for public policy reasons.

Domestic Bids

After the curious case of the Hanson interest in PowerGen at privatization (described in Chapter 7), the first REC bid was for Northern Electric by Trafalgar House. Because this had such a regulatory impact, it was considered in some detail in Chapter 11. As described there, after the Northern Electric takeover battle, Trafalgar House retired hurt, and Northern proceeded to carry out the financial engineering at the heart of its second defence document. Stephen Littlechild revisited the periodic review, reducing the mark-up on the RAB from 50 to 15 per cent. While this was in progress, the investment bankers were busy, and a series of acquisitions was being planned.

The first post-Northern bid to test the waters was launched by ScottishPower for Manweb. There followed immediate calls for a reference to the MMC, on the grounds that the concept of multi-utilities raised significant regulatory issues and that the benefits to customers should be taken into account. Whereas the Northern Electric/Trafalgar House bid had involved two companies in different sectors (and, hence, there could be no added concentration), the ScottishPower bid would increase concentration of the supply market, as well as remove a comparator for regulatory purposes.

The case for referral was, however, finely balanced. Manweb was unique among RECs in having no vertical links to generation. It had kept out of the early dash for gas, and hence avoided entering into expensive power purchase contracts with the independent power producers. There was therefore no generation concentration involved. And, even in supply, the introduction of domestic competition was still several years off. Given that, at the time, ScottishPower was widely believed to be a leading player in preparing for the introduction of competition in 1998, its ownership of Manweb might arguably speed up the latter's preparation, as well as provide a more credible competitive threat to the other suppliers in the England and Wales market.

The ScottishPower bid also had a political context, which its supporters were keen to exploit. Scottish Nuclear had just been effectively absorbed into British Energy through a merger with Nuclear Electric, with the latter's Chief Executive, Robert Hawley, clearly in charge. This was widely seen as a setback to the Scottish economy and Scottish business community, and as a result it had a strong negative resonance in Scottish politics at a time when the Conservatives were in electoral difficulty north of the border and viewed as the London party.

To placate these Scottish interests, a cumbersome board structure for British Energy was put in place, with the head office in Edinburgh. However, from the takeover perspective, the import is that the supporters of the ScottishPower bid could wrap it in a tartan flag: if Scottish Nuclear had been stamped out by the English Nuclear Electric, ScottishPower might, they argued, put a Scottish flag on Manweb, and thereby grow Scottish business interests. In a merger system which placed decisions in the hands of politicians with wide discretionary powers, it is hard to know what weight, if any, to place on such considerations in a minister's quasi-judicial decision, and of course it was never put in such nationalistic terms by ministers. Concerns that politics might play a role were to add to the case for independence for the competition authorities in such matters, eventually to be established through the Enterprise Act 2002. In any event, the competition concerns were marginal and ScottishPower escaped an MMC reference.[2]

Such decisions in the British system are made on the particular case in question, but expectations were thereby raised. What was the government's policy on REC takeovers? Could anything now go? Investment bankers began to actively target the RECs, and US interests were clearly aroused. Even National Power and British Gas could be potential targets. Recognizing that the policy was widely seen as confused and that the explanations given in the Scottish case had not convinced, to meet City questioning Lang decided that it would be best to 'explain' government thinking on REC takeovers. He published an article in the *Financial Times*

---

[2] Eggar had a more favourable view of the virtues of vertical integration—as was to be reflected in his differences with Lang over the National Power and PowerGen bids for the RECs (see below).

(*FT*) (Lang 1995),[3] in which he asserted that merger policy remained concerned primarily with competition issues, but that the issue of comparators was important and, if and when the number of companies was so
reduced as to render the regulator's job difficult, a halt might be called.[4]

As so often when ministers seek to 'explain' decisions which inevitably
have a political element, if the intention was to clarify policy, it did little
other than sow confusion, and, if anything, to speed up the takeover
process. If at some point a halt was to be called when too many RECs had
been taken over then some might have thought better to move fast and bid
early. This sense of urgency was reinforced by the fact that the earlier the
takeover, the longer the period until the next periodic review in 1999/2000,
when the high returns which had attracted foreign interest might be
clawed back; also, the longer the period until the next election, which
Labour was already assumed to win. It was expected that the Labour Party
would take a more hostile line on takeovers and introduce tougher
regulation.[5] This was the backdrop to the next moves—from the
United States.

The Americans Arrive

While ScottishPower was pursuing Manweb, Southern Electric
International (subsequently renamed Southern Energy, and then Mirant[6])
was the first American utility to bid for a British REC, the relatively weak
SWEB. SWEB's turnover ranked it among the smallest of the RECs; and
its lack of any other business (other than a stake in the Teesside power station) left it as an easier target. The management team had failed to join the
diversification race after privatization, it was perceived to have little
strategic direction and a lacklustre efficiency record, and ran into difficulties with its information technology investments.[7]

---

[3] This was a highly unusual step to take for ministers involved in competition cases.

[4] Much later, in 2002, Ofgem issued a merger policy paper which said something similar,
but indicated a willingness to surrender the comparators for a one-off benefit to customers
(Ofgem 2002a).

[5] In the event, Labour took an even more relaxed view of takeovers after an initial intervention over the PacifiCorp bid for Eastern, but was to introduce a windfall tax. The latter,
as we shall see in Chapter 15, caused great resentment among the new American owners.

[6] Mirant owned SWEB through its subsidiary, Western Power Distribution (WPD), which
it then sold in part to PPL and then completely in 2002 (after WPD had acquired SWALEC
distribution). Mirant eventually filed for Chapter 11 bankruptcy in July 2003.

[7] Its bid was decided on by Lang simultaneously with the ScottishPower one.

As the first foreign bid, some might expect that the government would refer it to the MMC. Customers in Penzance or Truro would now be managed by a company whose headquarters were in Atlanta, Georgia, and they would be merely one among many of the claims on managers' time, rather than the sole concern under SWEB. There was also the question of the ring-fence: what would happen if the parent failed? Again, Lang resisted the calls for an MMC reference. The Conservative government was more relaxed about US ownership, despite the fact that there were significant barriers to British acquisitions of American electricity utilities and much of the US market was at this time not liberalized. To this was added a belief that ownership was not important, and, in particular, that there was no evidence to suggest that foreign ownership of other parts of British industry had been detrimental. Utilities were, in the spirit of the times, thought not to be 'special', but merely another industry.

Having let Manweb and SWEB go, the pace now quickened. But then for completely unrelated reasons, the political rationale for accepting US takeovers shifted. To the general economic case for the irrelevance of ownership was added a much more specific political one. By now the portrayal of the utility executives as 'fat cats' had caught the public imagination, and the takeovers simply added to the 'telephone number' salaries which the general public could not comprehend. Labour seized on this public discontent by proposing in autumn 1995 a windfall levy on the privatized utilities. From the mid-1990s onwards, the utilities were right at the centre of the political debate.

To the Conservatives, this tax represented a criticism that privatization had not been properly conducted, and an attack on the regulatory regime which was supposed to control monopoly profits. Takeovers had the merit of installing a new set of owners who had not been the beneficiaries of the initial higher returns after privatization, and as they would be the ones who paid, the tax would be unfairly levied on the wrong people. Takeovers therefore rather neatly buried the windfalls, and hence undermined the case for the tax. The US companies were likely to put up the greatest resistance, and in particular use legal and even diplomatic channels to do so. The Conservatives could then hope that the 'special relationship' which had emerged between Bill Clinton and Tony Blair might cool, and the tax itself might prove very hard to levy. Moreover, the Conservatives had a very specific reason for undermining Labour's windfall tax proposal—the windfall tax was necessary to make Labour's public expenditure plans add up with its commitment not to raise general taxes. If the Americans could help to undermine the windfall tax, Labour budgeting credibility might be undermined too. Compared with the minor matters of regulatory comparators and financial controls, this was an altogether more serious political matter. Although it turned out very differently, as we shall see in Chapter 15, this must have been an important factor in how ministers saw the politics of US takeovers back in 1995 and 1996.

Whether these general political considerations had *any* influence on the reference decisions is a moot point, but these doubts in the context of the ScottishPower case were to make the case for independence of major decisions from politicians more pressing. In such circumstances, ministers were in an impossible position. In merger policy, competition might in fact be the prime determinant, but what matters is whether the City and the public at large believe them. In utilities, it is further complicated by the fact that many of the activities are natural monopolies. But regulation must be a factor too, and this was highly political and also technically complicated, especially with respect to ring-fencing and protection of customers in the event of failure (as Enron and Wessex were later to demonstrate).

The ease with which Southern Electric International overcame the British regulatory and political hurdles encouraged others to follow. A bid battle between Houston Industries against North West Water for control of NORWEB followed in August 1995. SEEBOARD fell to Central & South West Corporation (CSW) in January 1996, followed by takeovers of Midlands, East Midlands, London, Northern, and, finally, Yorkshire. Only Southern Electric remained independent, but later merged with Scottish Hydro-Electric to form Scottish & Southern Energy in December 1998.

Before turning to the multi-utilities, the more audacious plans to take over National Power, and the vertical integrating bids by England and Wales generators, a key question needs to be addressed—why did the Americans bid, and why were they apparently prepared to bid more than other potential bidders from Europe and elsewhere? To answer this question, we need to begin in the United States and its own peculiar market place. By the mid-1990s, the US electric utilities were entering a low-investment, cash-rich phase. The regulatory regime was heavily constraining. The rate-of-return element was significant particularly in a period of falling inflation. Rate reviews occur with lags and typically only when one party requests them. The cash surpluses which resulted from low investment and the lags were at risk of regulatory capture, and further down the track the competitive opening of the market threatened the book value of assets which had been written into the rate base. By the mid-1990s, the US market looked much less attractive to managers, and, in consequence, many considered international strategies. Eventually, the big players all went overseas, and those that remained became takeover targets.[8]

[8] These trends were already well established by the end of the 1980s (see Tirello 1990).

The major US companies which turned to overseas investments fell into three broad categories: the generators interested in independent power projects and energy trading; the active mainstream utilities; and the passive overseas investors. No doubt there were other categories, and many straddled more than one category, but the classification serves to illustrate the very different approaches taken.

In the first category, the classic example was Enron. Its investment in Teesside as the largest combined-cycle gas turbine (CCGT) in Europe was typical. The plant was financed on the back of power purchase agreements with four RECs (who also held equity stakes) and long-term, take-or-pay gas contracts.[9] It was followed by others in the independent power producer (IPP) market, and by Mission Energy (part of Edison) in its purchase of the National Grid Company's (NGC) pumped-storage plant.

Southern Electric International is the best example of the second category. Its parent had set itself the aggressive goal of gaining 30 per cent of its revenues from overseas sources by the year 2000. SWEB was the first big overseas acquisition, to be followed by a number of other international acquisitions, the most significant of which was a stake in BEWAG in Germany. It tried, and failed, to go much further by bidding for National Power. Others which might fit this category include American Electric Power (AEP), which acquired 50 per cent of Yorkshire, and then went on to bid for CSW in the USA, the owner of SEEBOARD.

The third category contains many for whom British acquisitions had become a fashion, and who believed that this was a one-off opportunity to diversify their earnings. Many sent very small teams over to Britain, but left the day-to-day management in the hands of the incumbent team. CSW was perhaps the clearest example, with Jim Ellis remaining very much in charge at SEEBOARD. Avon Energy (a combination of General Public Utilities Corporation and Cinergy) left Michael Hughes in control at Midlands, and although Entergy put a new top team in place at London Electricity, it was also largely a passive investor.

If the first two groups had clear strategic objectives, why did those in the third category invest? Various answers have been advanced, including: undervaluation (the bargains theory); the need to acquire experience of competitive markets (the skills theory); and threats to their domestic business (the earnings theory). Although it is impossible to disentangle which factors motivated particular boards at particular points in time, the general outlines can be traced.

---

[9] The gas contract would turn out to be expensive and much subsequent dispute over J block took place from May 1996 through to settlement in June 1997 between Phillips Petroleum, operator of the J block, and Enron.

The *undervaluation theory* has two parts: first, that the cost of capital applied to the regulated assets in the United States was much lower than that used in Britain to establish the market values, and, hence, a financial arbitrage opportunity existed; and, second, that the scope for cost savings was much greater than the incumbent managers were capable of. The cost of capital for British utilities has indeed been much higher than that in the United States. The explanation of the difference is largely regulatory risk: rate-of-return regimes present little up- or downside risk to investors, and utility stocks are treated much like bonds. Price-cap regimes, by contrast, confront investors with high-powered incentives, but also greater political and regulatory risk, as Littlechild's attempts at the distribution review and the windfall tax demonstrated.[10]

To apply US costs of capital to British assets, and thereby come up with a higher valuation, is a convenient way of rationalizing a takeover bid premium. It does not, however, overcome the *fact* of the higher cost of capital in Britain. Regulatory interventions, both blatant, in the case of the windfall tax, and implicit in increasing standards and social and environmental obligations *without* compensation, do not go away.[11]

The other version of undervaluation is *efficiency*. This, at first glance, is a peculiar one. The core regulatory argument which has motivated the British approach to utility regulation has been fostered on the assumption (apparently backed up by empirical evidence) that rate-of-return regulation breeds cost inefficiency and gold-plating. It would seem natural to conclude that management which has grown up in this environment is uniquely badly qualified to drive down operating and capital costs. Much better, one might think, to place investors' trust in managers who have had at least five years' experience of a more efficiency-oriented set of incentives.[12] It remained to be seen whether the new US owners proved any better than their British predecessors in driving down costs, and, in particular, whether those who replaced the incumbent managers did any better than those who have decided to live with them. The evidence from

---

[10] There is much theoretical controversy about regulatory risk and the cost of capital. In the capital asset pricing model, the cost of capital should be independent of regulatory risk, in that it can be diversified. However, comparison of companies under different regulatory regimes and event studies indicate that a regulatory premium exists.

[11] The same mistake was to be made at the end of the decade by water companies which argued that debt-financed companies had a lower cost of capital, when, in fact, the risks had been transferred to customers. See Helm (2001e).

[12] Interestingly, there has been little empirical investigation as to whether *in fact* British utilities are more efficient than US ones, or vice versa.

the second periodic review (described in Chapter 18) is at best ambiguous, and almost all of these US companies were to leave in due course.

The second theory, *skills*, has a superficial appeal. The US utilities might reasonably argue that, faced with the introduction of competition and liberalization in their home markets, their own monopoly/rate-of-return experience might leave them vulnerable as the process of US competition unfolded. Therefore, by acquiring British RECs, it would be possible to tap early competitive experience, and thereby to better prepare their own companies for the onslaught which competition might be expected to unleash. It is an approach that CSW took with SEEBOARD, by including Jim Ellis on its main parent board in the United States. The problem with this argument is the cost. Why pay a 25 per cent premium over the regulatory asset base (RAB) (the going rate at the time) to acquire a set of individuals in order to transfer the skills? Why not buy the individuals? Although, no doubt, access to an organization going through preparation for retail competition is very valuable, there seems little connection between the value of skills and the takeover premium.

The final theory, *earnings*, runs as follows. By using balance-sheet strength or cash surpluses to buy a REC, the purchaser acquires a cash flow which is relatively stable and predictable. In consequence, earnings for the parent company rise. The argument then runs on: since investors are concerned with earnings, this is shareholder-value-enhancing. As a justification to investors, this argument figures prominently in several cases—most notably for Southern Electric International—in US-driven acquisitions. It was also a major reason for the takeovers by British utilities. As an economic rationale, it is nonsense and part of the more general stretching of accounting principles which took place during the great speculative bubble of the second half of the 1990s. Swapping a pile of cash for a cash flow is rather like an individual buying an annuity. It is only worthwhile if the rate of return provided by the cash flow is greater than could have been earned by paying out the cash directly to shareholders and allowing them to invest it themselves. Thus, the question is whether the rate of return exceeds the cost of capital for the acquisition. It was as relevant to United Utilities, PowerGen, ScottishPower, and Hyder as it is to the Americans.

What, then, can we conclude about this first round of US acquisitions? The mark-up on the RAB had to be justified on one of the above grounds, and it is hard to come up with an investor-favourable verdict. Subsequent events paint a harsh judgement: whilst some managed to get out with most of their money—notably Entergy (London) and Dominion (East Midlands)—as the second wave of acquirers made similar valuation mistakes; others hung on long enough to face the falling valuations at the end of the decade, though most did much better than those who ventured into water—notably Enron.

Multi-utilities

The US acquisitions were complemented by utility-wide domestic mergers. North West Water's bid for NORWEB, Welsh Water's bid for SWALEC, and ScottishPower's bid for Southern Water were all motivated by the idea that the core characteristic of management focus was *utilities*, and that the fact that they were in electricity, water or even gas and telecommunications was a secondary consideration. It soon became fashionable to talk about *multi-utilities*, with conferences, City comment and the media taking up the challenge of defining the concept. That exercise proved difficult and often confusing, in part because the companies themselves provided differing rationales, and in part because some of the early ideas proved over-optimistic.

North West Water's bid for NORWEB was the first, and apparently it had the clearest rationale, creating the ambitiously named United Utilities. NORWEB covered a similar franchise area, and, where the overlap was incomplete (in Merseyside), North West Water could give NORWEB an initial help in attacking Manweb's supply area. Geographical overlap provided scope for reducing the network costs of the two infrastructures, and gaining economies of scale in marketing and retail support functions in serving a largely co-extensive set of customers. Rationalizing customer services, network management, and information technology provided the basis for aggressive estimates of synergy savings. To this was added the concept of selling multiple services to the customer base, and NORWEB was soon to launch plans to market gas and telecommunications. Finally, NORWEB would be used as the springboard to nationwide energy sales and, in consequence, was rebranded as Energi.

Such grandiose plans required new ideas of business organization. A new company, Vertex, was set up as a facilities management business outside the regulatory domain. It took over some assets from North West Water, and provided information technology and customer services to the two utilities. In addition, it attempted to market these services to others, although initially with limited success.

Welsh Water's approach was rather different. Although it, too, created a multi-utility based upon geographical coincidence, its approach was to integrate the two businesses as fully as possible within a single operating unit, called Hyder. Ironically, although Hyder was to end up in serious financial difficulty and eventually be broken up, this was the model which United Utilities would eventually adopt after its initial model faltered, and to much better effect.[13]

Finally, ScottishPower's acquisition of Southern Water provided yet another multi-utility model. With no geographical coincidence, focus had been almost exclusively on management. ScottishPower did not create a facilities management company; rather, it concentrated on cost-cutting and efficiency in the early years under the management of Mike Kinski. This model was to be short-lived too, with the decision to sell Southern Water after the 1999 periodic review.

It is possible to disentangle some of the major features of multi-utilities and identify the key questions which have tested their managers. The first, and most important, distinction is between multi-networks and multi-services. Multi-networks (electricity wires, gas pipes and water and sewerage systems) have relatively simple cost structures, and information technology makes a major contribution to their coordination. They were in transition from labour-intensive manual coordination to capital-intensive information technology coordination. Multi-services are quite different: their cost base comprises customer databases, marketing, purchasing portfolios, and brand reputations.

Early multi-utility models combined both. Although the incumbent management might have been able to span both, it should be noted that, as competition developed and supply was split from distribution in the public electricity supply licence, these businesses had very different managerial skill requirements and different risk profiles. The multinetwork business is relatively low-risk, highly capital-intensive, and likely to tend towards debt finance; the multi-service business is much more risky, requires energy trading and marketing skills, and lends itself to equity finance.

Whether there is synergy between multi-networks and multi-services depends in part on customer brand recognition, and the scope for overarching common information technology approaches. So far, none of the multi-utilities established has demonstrated that the two distinct activities can be integrated to the extent that the bid premia might indicate. We can now see with hindsight that none of the original British-based multi-utility

---

[13] It is notable that John Roberts, who had been Chief Executive of Manweb before ScottishPower's takeover, and had kept out of the dash for gas, was in turn responsible for much of Hyder's integration, before moving as Chief Executive to United Utilities where he disposed of NORWEB Supply.

models has survived, and that the search for an integrated multi-network and multi-service model has proved unsuccessful. Multi-network businesses have survived, as have multi-services ones, but the new utilities market has proved that specialism is at least as successful as what is, in effect, a conglomerate model. Synergies between networks and supply activities have not materialized as expected. It remains to be seen whether the European utilities prove any better at the broad approach.[14]

Interestingly, the one arguably successful multi-services business so far has been Centrica, which began life as the supply arm of British Gas, but then grew its supply business in energy organically, and added smaller-scale businesses (such as the Automobile Association) and joint ventures to build a customer-services company. None of the takeover-driven multi-utilities managed this—indeed, it is noticeable that United Utilities and Hyder retreated from an aggressive supply model, with the former concentrating on networks and the latter selling its water business to a not-for-profit company limited by guarantee, while ScottishPower has refocused on energy, and away from financial services, the grander telecommunications vision and water. Centrica itself has gradually refocused, integrating into gas storage and power generation.

Vertical Integration

Alongside the US bids and the creation of the multi-utilities, a third variety surfaced: bids by British generators for RECs. As we saw in Chapter 2, vertical integration has been an enduring feature of British energy markets for most of the post-war period, and has the merit of conventional industrial logic. It is a feature shared with virtually all developed countries. And, as we saw in Chapter 7, privatization did not bring this linkage to an immediate end. Rather, it provided for vertical contracts to replace the bulk supply tariff and supporting arrangements brokered through the Electricity Council, and permitted RECs to begin the process of vertical integration into generation. Scotland remained fully integrated. Only after 1998 was the vertical link with customers broken—by which time consolidation was well under way.

A core problem for National Power and PowerGen had been what would happen when these vertical contracts, from coal through to the RECs' price caps, expired. And, perhaps even more significantly, what would happen when customers were free to shop around in 1998, and,

[14] In Britain, RWE acquired both Thames Water and Innogy. E.ON considered acquiring both Wessex and Southern Water, but in the end acquired only PowerGen. EDF has remained an electricity business.

hence, RECs would be less willing to enter into contracts with generators when it would be unclear whether they would have customers to whom to pass through the costs? An obvious answer was vertical integration, following the example of other industries in similar market positions, such as oil companies and petrol stations, and brewers and pubs.

Although such an approach was clearly not part of the intention behind the original privatization package and, although it would probably be resisted by Littlechild, the power lay with the Secretary of State and the *laissez-faire* approach taken by Lang encouraged the generators to bid. Lang had, in particular, made clear in his *FT* article referred to above that he had no objection to vertical integration *per se*,[15] and the disposal of generators' plant to Eastern (leaving the latter with some 12 per cent of capacity) served to reinforce this more relaxed stance. Finally, Tim Eggar, then Minister for Energy, was widely believed to be supportive. (See Eggar, 2003.)

Given this rather favourable political view, PowerGen launched a bid for Midlands Electricity on 18 September 1995. Rather caught-out, National Power quickly followed suit with a bid for Southern Electric on 2 October 1995. There followed an intense lobbying campaign by supporters to head off an MMC reference, but, contrary to much informed speculation, a reference was in fact made on 23 November 1995. Lang stated that each bid 'raised competition concerns in the generation and supply of electricity', but was anxious not to indicate any desire to reject the bids once the MMC reported back to him. Indeed, he went out of his way to stress that he did 'not believe that vertical integration was inherently objectionable whether in the electricity industry or elsewhere' (DTI 1995c).

The MMC focused on the vertical integration issue, not on the generator–distribution common ownership. In its deliberations, it was encouraged to take a benign view by a submission from the Department of Trade and Industry (DTI). The argument was that the government thought that competition in generation was developing strongly, aided by plant disposal, and that the 1998 supply competition project was coming along well. Since the upstream generation market was becoming increasingly competitive, and, after 1998, the downstream supply market would be too, there was little scope to use the vertical linkages to exploit customers, subject only to a number of safeguards about non-discrimination

---

[15] Lang stated: 'The bid by Scottish Power for Manweb raised different issues [to the bids by Southern Group and Hanson], because it was the first bid by one UK electricity supplier (and a vertically integrated one) for another. In fact, the *only* issue raised by the merger which cannot be fully addressed through licence amendments is the impact on Manweb's relevance as a "comparator" '. [italics added] (Lang 1995).

and transparency in the contracts market. Commenting on the PowerGen/Midlands merger, the DTI argued that: 'provided there were adequate safeguards the present merger would neither increase nor decrease competition in electricity generation'; in addition, 'the proposed merger would be likely to increase competition in electricity supply' and, for good measure, it 'would enhance the status of PowerGen as a world class company' (MMC 1996*b*: para 8.170, p. 207). The same comments were made about National Power too.

Against the DTI's apparent relaxed view of the mergers, Littlechild raised four potential detriments to the public interest. There would be: fewer competitors in the supply market and a thinner contract market; less entry into generation as the two RECs would cease to provide a competitive threat, and this would raise profits and prices in generation; less competition for domestic customers after 1998; and price discrimination might occur. Littlechild seemed to realize that this was a decisive moment in which the disaggregated model of the electricity market was challenged by the vertical integration one which characterized the Scottish market—and indeed Germany too.

The MMC panel broadly agreed with the DTI's argument (and thereby in effect rejected Littlechild's argument), with the exception of Patricia Hodgson, who insisted on a minority report recommending rejection on competition grounds. The counter-case was based largely on the evidence provided by the regulator and independent analysis and comment provided by David Newbery at Cambridge.[16] The majority and minority reports were then submitted to Lang for decision. It was widely assumed that clearance would be given after the public-interest issues raised by the majority reports had been addressed, and this was reflected in the share prices. However, as the MMC reports were leaked to the *Economist*, two ominous developments for the parties emerged: first, preparations for an opportunistic bid from Southern Electric International for National Power leaked out, as Southern Electric International began to raise funds; and, second, Norman Lamont and John Redwood, two key right-wing Eurosceptics, came out strongly against the bids. Gordon Brown then threatened to propose a motion attacking the government for putting monopoly interests ahead of consumers. Suddenly, what had seemed like plain sailing for the bidders looked altogether more politically complex.[17]

Lang, having made clear his belief that foreign (especially United States) ownership was not a problem, and that vertical integration was permissible, was faced with the logic of his position. Southern Electric

---

[16] See MMC (1996*a*: paras 6.290–6.296, pp. 217–18). For a more extensive exploration of the effects of vertical integration, see Newbery (1996).

[17] See *The Economist* (1996), 'Lang Pulling the Plug', 27 April.

International had an offer which would combine these two components in one deal. As owners of SWEB already, SWEB plus National Power was an alternative to National Power plus Southern Electric. What is more, Southern Electric International indicated a willingness to divest more of National Power's power stations, and, hence, it was potentially likely to be less anti-competitive in effect.

The stakes were now much higher. The government balked at the prospect of National Power falling into foreign hands, and the Redwood/Lamont pressure provided a further rationale. As the guardian of the doctrine that competition considerations should drive merger decisions, and with his 'flexible' policy position, as set out in the *FT* article, Lang endorsed the spirit of Hodgson's minority report and declared that the mergers would be anti-competitive. He said that 'in the current state of the market, there would be significant detriments to competition if these mergers proceed' and concluded that he did 'not believe that the remedies proposed by the majority MMC report would be sufficient to address those detriments' (DTI 1996). In the process, he flatly contradicted the recommendations of the Energy Group within his own Department to the MMC.[18]

But, just in case Southern Electric International nevertheless decided to proceed, he indicated that he would be prepared to use the golden shares in Powergen and National Power to protect them from takeover.[19] This last move reveals the inconsistency in policy: why, if foreign ownership did not matter, were golden shares needed at all? And, if foreign ownership did matter, precisely what was the policy? Lang never provided the answers, but carried on allowing US takeovers of the RECs. With the exception of the bids by PowerGen and National Power, Lang allowed all the electricity industry bids without reference to the MMC, and left Labour to face the wrath of the Americans when it came to introduce the windfall tax. The confusion over policy was highlighted by Redwood shortly after the vetoing of the generators' bids. As he put it: 'The Government's competition policy has been far from clear in recent years... It has made a series of piecemeal decisions on bids and deals in the utilities without setting out any principles to make the policy intelligible' (Redwood 1996).

The last of the major acquisitions by the Americans came with the bid by PacifiCorp for Eastern Electricity, now owned by Hanson. The vertical

[18] In his autobiography, Lang (2002) claims that his decision was on competition grounds and that the MMC remedies were inadequate. Curiously, he makes no mention of Tim Eggar, his Minister, in the section of his book dealing with this (pp. 252–6), and indeed only mentions Eggar twice in passing in the whole book.

[19] These golden shares were finally redeemed at the request of both companies in 2001, thus opening the door to the German bids.

integration upstream by Eastern had already been effected by the acquisition of the divested power stations from the main generators, so the PacifiCorp bid apparently raised no new competition issues. However, by this time Labour had won the general election in May 1997, and this was to be the first test of whether New Labour would follow the Conservatives' policy. There was every indication that it would, given not only Labour's new found enthusiasm for competition, but also the fact that it was prepared to proceed immediately with the Competition Bill.

To the surprise of many, Margaret Beckett, the new Secretary of State at the DTI, referred the PacifiCorp bid. There were several reasons why a reference was appropriate: Labour had in opposition called for bids to be referred and this was the first under Labour, and hence the MMC might help to clarify merger policy. There were two important regulatory issues to be considered. In an article in The *Times*, the author argued that the regulatory framework should be adapted to take account of the subsidiary status of the core networks, and in particular that provision should be made in the event of financial difficulties arising for the parent company. Specifically, the author argued the case for a special administrator function to be adopted as was provided for in the water industry (Helm 1997).[20] The MMC looked at a number of financial scenarios for PacifiCorp, one of which displayed financial difficulty, but in the end came down in favour of using credit ratings provided by the credit-rating agencies as the safeguard (MMC 1997c).[21]

In the event, despite MMC clearance, PacifiCorp failed in its bid, and Eastern was acquired by TXU. But this was almost the last gasp of the first phase of the full REC purchases by the Americans. An investment-motivated acquisition of Northern Electric from Warren Buffet added one more. The remaining interest lay with generation assets. Edison Mission acquired power stations to sit alongside its pumped-storage capacity in First Hydro, and toyed with creating a vertical business, and AES acquired the Drax power station in December 1999. The collapse of wholesale prices was to seriously undermine these power station acquisitions in due course.

The Americans Leave and Vertical Integration becomes the Norm

Having purchased RECs at (a typically substantial) premium to their RABs, and having enjoyed the initial boost to earnings that these annuities brought to them, the changing climate in the US electricity and gas

[20] In 2002, an amendment to the Enterprise Bill was proposed to give this effect, but failed to make progress.

[21] In 2003, the DTI consulted on introducing the special administrator, after the failure at TXU, with a view to incorporating such provisions in an energy bill (see DTI, 2003b).

industries led the acquirers to gradually recognize that mistakes had been made, and to begin the retreat. This process had two parts: first, the RECs were loaded with debt which allowed equity to be withdrawn; then the residual interests were sold to the next queue of acquirers—British generators and the Europeans. This next round of acquisitions had one central feature in common: vertical integration had become the normal model to which all the main players aspired. Some would confine this to supply, and generation; others would go for generation, supply, and distribution. Elements of opportunism entered into the calculation, but once the political and regulatory green light had been given, it was only a matter of time before the RECs changed hands again.

The lead in this process was again taken by PowerGen, with National Power following. PowerGen bid for East Midlands, while National Power bid for the supply arm of Midlands Electricity. National Power also split itself into two, floating off its international business to form International Power, leaving Innogy with its British assets. With the two main generators then vertically integrated, and TXU-Eastern and ScottishPower already in this business form, British Energy tried to join with first SWALEC and then the Eggborough power station. Its purchases were, however, poorly managed, and it then sold SWALEC Supply to Scottish & Southern Energy and wrote off much of the Eggborough acquisition. TXU added NORWEB Supply from United Utilities, leaving the latter as a multi-networks business, and made a subsequent acquisition of gas customers. (The British arm of TXU eventually collapsed in late 2002, to be acquired by PowerGen.) Scottish & Southern Energy (founded when Southern and Scottish Hydro-Electric merged) tried to add generation assets, but was hampered by its stated intention of seeking 'no premium mergers'.

This consolidation process mirrored what was already going on in Europe—especially Germany—and, having toyed repeatedly with British acquisitions, the Europeans eventually joined the fray. Electricité de France (EDF) was first, acquiring London Electricity and then SWEB Supply. To these it gradually added generation assets, each time taking incremental steps to avoid regulatory reaction—especially given the hostility of the DTI towards the French blocking of European liberalization measures (see Chapter 20). EDF then entered a joint venture (24Seven) with TXU to run Eastern and London's distribution assets, before eventually taking full control.[22] EDF had thereby built up a formidable vertically

---

[22] 24Seven was set up in April 2000 as the distribution price control came into effect, and planned to seek a stock-market listing by 2003—in effect, splitting off asset ownership from operations. In November 2001, London Electricity announced its acquisition of TXU's 50%, and completed the purchase in January 2002.

integrated business, without ever being referred to the Competition Commission. It then acquired SEEBOARD in 2002, to give it dominance of the south-east of England.[23]

For the British players, with a perceived obstacle to further acquisitions in the home market on competition grounds, the United States became the target. ScottishPower acquired PacifiCorp when the latter got into the financial difficulties which had been feared when PacifiCorp bid for Eastern, and PowerGen acquired LG&E. NGC joined the fray with telecommunications and network acquisitions in Latin America and the United States. Scottish & Southern tried to find a no-premium merger in the United States, but failed to do so in the first wave of British acquisitions.

The vertical integration process was all but completed with the entry of E.ON and RWE, to join EDF in Britain. These three had created dominant businesses across Europe. E.ON itself was the result of a merger between VIAG and VEBA in September 1999, and, with RWE, dominated the German market. E.ON bid for PowerGen in April 2001 and, after a lengthy clearance process in the United States, succeeded in its acquisition in 2002. RWE bid and completed its acquisition of Innogy in 2002 too. Thus, by 2002, the British electricity industry had become in large part an adjunct to the European one, in the hands of the Germans and the French. The consequences were not thought through at the time, but were to have radical ramifications for energy policy. The vision of a disaggregated market with many generators and many suppliers competing in a standardized transparent pool, with a supporting futures market absorbing the risk of long-term contracts, had gone. Politicians and regulators had simply let it happen. The electricity industry had become like the oil industry: dominated by vertically integrated companies with interests that stretched from Russian gas, through the major gas pipelines of Europe to the final customer. The implications will shape energy policy in the next decades, as we shall see in Chapters 20 and 21.

It remained for the other players to try to come to terms with the consolidated European companies. As wholesale prices of electricity fell in the early 2000s, generation-only companies got into difficulties, with British Energy only managing to cover its liabilities because of contracts in the United States and then collapsing. AES, as owner of Drax, became embroiled in detailed negotiations with its bankers, and eventually effectively handed it over to them. ScottishPower rationalized its business and—for reasons outside Britain—Enron went bust. Centrica's only acquisitions slowed down as it found it hard to take its supply-only business model into

---

[23] EDF's overseas acquisition policy eventually came under criticism in France, and was subject to a highly critical review in 2003. See Assemblée National (2003).

Europe, and it quietly acquired greater upstream assets and contracts, and bid for Rough in 2003.[24] Networks consolidated too, with Northern and Yorkshire distribution businesses merging (after Innogy had acquired Yorkshire, and then swapped Yorkshire Distribution for Northern Supply, before RWE acquired Innogy). Then, in 2002, NGC and Lattice merged, bringing the national electricity and gas infrastructures together.

A Weakness of Will with Radical Consequences

There were many reasons for the merger frenzies of the 1990s and early 2000s in the energy sector. Some of these were very general, and had little to do with energy *per se*. The 1990s witnessed a stock-market boom not seen since the 1920s, and inevitably a merger boom too. The 1990s' boom created considerable scope for financial engineering. Managers with cash and balance sheets which could now be geared up had unprecedented opportunities to pursue managerial objectives of growth through acquisitions and, in some cases, empire building. It was a market in which Enron could turn a small pipeline business into America's second-largest company, and E.ON and RWE could afford to buy up assets on an unprecedented scale. In Enron's case, the dubious business practices which are frequently associated with speculative bubbles were painfully exposed, but more generally the pursuit of the shareholders' interests was used as an excuse for a number of questionable activities. The cautious, low-risk, dull business of managing utilities became in the 1990s much more exciting for incumbent managers.

But behind the froth of the speculative bubble lay the search for economically efficient structures, new business models, and market power. The structure of the electricity industry created through privatization in 1990 might have been the best available political fix at the time, but it was not a naturally stable one: it could only be preserved and, in the case of plant divestment from the main generators and the further break-up of British Gas, enhanced by regulatory actions. At any point at which the regulatory guard was relaxed, consolidation was inevitable. The general financial context provided the means, but only regulators and politicians could give the green light.

That regulators—and politicians—failed to defend the initial structure was one of the most curious features of the 1990s. There was no lack of commitment to competition, and all regulators and secretaries of state at

---

[24] The Rough acquisition was referred to the Competition Commission in the face of strong opposition from Ofgem, and only allowed to proceed on condition of demand undertakings on competition. See Competition Commission 2003.

the DTI mouthed this mantra. It had become 'politically incorrect' to suggest anything else. Indeed, so much so that not only was competition made the sole criterion for mergers (finally implemented into law with the Competition Act 1998), but the Enterprise Act 2002 proposed that ministers should no longer have a role in deciding on mergers. So, the reasons why they failed to prevent reintegration are not obvious.

Part of the explanation lies in the incremental ways in which merger decisions are made. Each case is judged on its own merits, with little scope to consider the wider implications. There were also quite serious analytical weaknesses, not least at Offer and more particularly at Ofgem. The implications of financial engineering—as in the Northern Electric defence against Trafalgar—were poorly understood, and indeed remain so (as we shall see in Chapter 18). Then there was the *marginal* aspect to vertical integration. ScottishPower and Manweb together did not add that much more integration. There was the Pool, and the failure to understand that the scope to exploit vertical integration depended on the nature of the spot, contract and futures market. While the Pool provided a compulsory break between generation and supply, NETA facilitated the exploitation of the vertical links (as we shall see in Chapter 17).

There were particular moments when the process of integration could have been halted. Lang had the prime role here, and his early decisions and the attempt to explain them in his *FT* article in 1995 were decisive in letting the first wave of takeovers through. He chose not to intervene, except in the cases of National Power and PowerGen. Here confusion reigned, with his department downplaying the competition and vertical integration issues, and much political speculation. Lang's decision contradicted his own department's evidence to the MMC, while his extension of the golden shares contradicted his relaxed view about foreign ownership of the RECs.

Finally, once Littlechild had gone, the regulatory will to resist collapsed. Indeed, under Callum McCarthy, Chairman and Chief Executive of Ofgem, mergers were all but encouraged as he pointed to the economies of scale in supply, took a more relaxed view of the importance of comparators, and waved through the NGC–Lattice merger. In generation, with his good-behaviour licence condition (as we shall see in Chapter 17) he was more vigilant in both conduct regulation and trying to maintain a disaggregated structure, but by 2002 the reintegration of the industry was well advanced.

But behind weaknesses in regulation and the political process lay economic reasons too. There were economies of scale in supply, and vertical integration allowed risks in contracting to be physically hedged.

In networks, some economies of scale may also exist through the development of the trend towards specialist contracting, and the split between assets and operations complicates the picture considerably. The merit of a market in corporate control is that it allows experimentation with different business structures, and the multi-utility model was one that allowed multi-service and multi-network forms to emerge—with Centrica and United Utilities, respectively, now the two leading examples.

Overarching all these considerations, however, is the search for market power in the face of competition and competitive pressures. Managers and investors do not seek competition: they seek monopoly and what John Hicks called 'the quiet life'. The liberalization of supply in 1998 represented a radical departure from the vertical integration of the post-war period discussed in Chapter 2, and the contractual linkages from 1990 to 1998. After 1998, as described in Chapter 14, there would be no basis for passing through contract costs, and from this point onwards generation and supply became more risky businesses. If generation was in excess supply and there were no long-term contracts to provide stability, prices could collapse, as they did (regardless of NETA). If generation was tight, suppliers without contracts would be exposed to rapidly rising prices, as happened in California. The obvious business solution is vertical integration and scale—which is what EDF, E.ON, and RWE have pursued. If the company is big enough, it can take price risk against equity, as oil companies do. But the consequence of this new model is that the very market power and vertical integration that privatization tried to curtail has re-emerged—and largely without regulators or politicians realizing what they have allowed to happen. That none of the key players is British has been an unintended consequence. The structural experiment which privatization had launched came to an early—and perhaps premature—end within a decade.

13

The Break-up of British Gas

> BG is both a seller of gas, and owner of the transportation system which its competitors have no alternative but to use. In our view, this dual role gives rise to an inherent conflict of interest which makes it impossible to provide the necessary conditions for self-sustaining competition. (MMC report on gas, 1993)[1]

If Denis Rooke, the Chairman of British Gas at privatization, could see little point in restructuring British Gas at privatization, he could see even less point in Ofgas. The new Director General, James McKinnon, was an irritant, but could hardly be taken seriously in determining the future of the mighty British Gas. That view of the regulator and regulation turned out to be a serious strategic mistake on behalf of the management of British Gas. Privatization created a private monopoly, but also contained the seeds of the company's destruction. The critical instrument was the regulator's duty to promote competition.[2] It was as if Peter Walker, Secretary of State for Energy, got the structure for a national champion he wanted, but Nigel Lawson, Chancellor of the Exchequer, won the long-run debate over the future of the industry. The structure of the industry turned out to be a variable, not a given.

The humbling of British Gas by Ofgas and its Directors General was a gradual process. It began slowly, and the campaign was to last over three Monopolies and Mergers Commission (MMC) inquiries. Each was linked in what, in hindsight, was a reasonably coherent and logical chain. Eventually, with the Gas Act in 1995, British Gas was set on a path to full retail competition, the unanticipated consequences of which were to lead the company to break itself up. No one foresaw at the outset that the initial small group of around twenty staff in Ofgas would eventually become more numerous than staff in British Gas's headquarters, nor that Centrica would rival the rest of the business in size.

The structural battle began with the first referral to the MMC of the industrial gas market in 1988, through to the review of the undertakings

---

[1] MMC (1993*b*: vol. 1, para 1.6, p. 2).

[2] This duty was itself something of an afterthought, and its introduction was widely ascribed to Michael Portillo.

which had been given to the Office of Fair Trading (OFT) as a result of the MMC inquiry, to the second MMC inquiry, reporting in 1993, which identified 'the inherent conflict of interest' within the integrated structure. The resulting 'deal' which British Gas did to keep itself intact, at the cost of fast-track competition, led to the Gas Act 1995. That in turn helped to strand its long-term gas contracts and led to the break-up in 1997, with the regulatory arithmetic being sorted out in a 1997 MMC report (MMC 1997*b*).

The First MMC Inquiry

From small beginnings, great consequences can flow. In the case of British Gas, these consequences appear to have crept up upon it, without any serious appreciation of the chain of events to which each event was linked. In 1988, a struggling engineering company, Sheffield Forgemasters Ltd, complained about British Gas's discriminatory pricing in the non-tariff market. British Gas had, it transpired, been engaged in price discrimination. This complaint was soon to become one among many made to the OFT.[3]

The OFT duly investigated and found four matters of concern. There was 'no clear relationship to changes in the price of alternative fuels or British Gas' own costs of gas' (OFT press release, 25 November 1987, reported in MMC 1988: Appendix 1.1, p. 117). There were wide differences in prices paid by customers in similar circumstances. Contracts typically set prices on a short-term basis. Worse still, British Gas was unwilling to quote prices for interruptible supplies until the customer had installed dual-fire equipment, or to offer supplies to companies which would close down if supplies were interrupted rather than switch to alternative fuels (MMC 1988).

It is hard to think of much more that British Gas could have done to abuse its dominance, and in November 1987 the Director General of Fair Trading (DGFT) duly despatched British Gas to the MMC with reference to the supply of gas through pipes to non-tariff customers.[4] The MMC reported, in October 1988, that British Gas was indeed guilty of 'extensive discrimination in the pricing and supply of gas to contract customers' (MMC 1988) and that this resulted from its monopoly position and was against the public interest. In doing so, it agreed with all of the DGFT's concerns.

---

[3] British Gas, in its defence, regarded such discriminatory pricing as part of its 'premium' pricing philosophy towards resource depletion, and this had been applied not only to industrial customers but also to combined heat and power (CHP), to the latter's detriment. However, the competition effects were self-serving, in protecting its market share.

[4] Ofgas also published a report on 'Competition in Gas Supply' in December 1987 (Ofgas 1987).

The report's recommendations were, however, a compromise, and did not withstand the test of time. Its MMC panel's members included Stephen Littlechild, and it was aware of the more radical structural options which might have addressed the monopoly more directly—in particular, those advanced by Colin Robinson and Allen Sykes (MMC 1988: paras 6.112–6.115). Yet it sought a rather complex regulatory solution.

The 'solution' had four components:

(1) to publish a schedule of prices at which [British Gas] is prepared to supply firm and interruptible gas to contract customers and not to discriminate in pricing and supply;
(2) not to refuse to supply interruptible gas on the basis of the use made of the gas or the alternative fuel available;
(3) to publish further information on common carriage terms in sufficient detail to put a potential customer in a position to make a reasonable estimate of the charge that would be sought by British Gas;
(4) to contract initially for no more than 90 per cent of any new gas field (MMC 1988: para 1.6).

The MMC did recognize that these steps might not be sufficient, and ominously for British Gas, it stated that:

If competition in the supply of gas fails to develop over the next five years, further consideration will then be appropriate as to whether changes in the structure of the gas industry are necessary to ensure competition in the supply of gas. (ibid.: para 8.98)[5]

The recommendations led to a series of undertakings to the OFT, the practicalities of which Ofgas and British Gas then agreed. In effect, this conduct approach can be regarded as one of *regulatory handicapping*. British Gas would be compelled to publish its prices, which competitors could in principle then undercut. Furthermore, the competitors would gain access to gas supplies so that they would have the capacity to enter the market.

The rules had considerable affinity with the contestable markets theory, as propounded by Baumol *et al.* (1982), which became fashionable in the mid- to late-1980s. The central idea was that the structure of an industry was irrelevant as a determinant of the conduct of the incumbent, provided that entry and exit were uninhibited by entry barriers. In particular, contestability required that entrants could come into a market, undercut the incumbent, and get out again *before* the incumbent could respond, and without suffering losses associated with the costs of entry which could

---

[5] The MMC, when it returned to these matters in 1993, would quote this.

not be recovered on exit (i.e. no sunk costs). 'Hit-and-run' entry forced the incumbent to price at marginal cost. Making this model a reality in the industrial gas market required tying British Gas to a price list *which it could not revise at will*, and creating a market in gas supplies so that entrants could buy and *sell* gas from the North Sea. The OFT undertakings tied British Gas to publishing the tariffs, but did allow their revision provided they were not discriminatory and subject to a regulatory process. The effect of the undertakings therefore turned on the perceived ability of British Gas to change tariffs—a factor which was to be very important when combined-cycle gas-turbine (CCGT) demand grew in the early 1990s in the dash for gas (see Chapter 8).

The OFT Review of the Undertakings

It was a quirk of the regulatory design for the gas industry that the powers were split between the OFT and Ofgas. The undertakings which British Gas had made were to the OFT, not to Ofgas, so it fell to the general competition body to review compliance. This occurred in 1991, and addressed two core issues: whether British Gas had complied with the undertakings, and whether the undertakings had had the desired effect. The OFT found that British Gas had in fact broadly met the first concern, but that the consequence of this conduct regulation was not that which had been intended (OFT 1991). In particular, British Gas remained the dominant supplier.

Encouraged by Ofgas, the OFT therefore sought further remedies to the public-interest detriment identified in the 1988 MMC report, and moved from conduct to structural regulation. The OFT proposed the release of a significant proportion of British Gas's contracted gas, to relax the tariff monopoly and, most significantly, it took a first shot at breaking up the monopoly structure, recommending that a separate subsidiary be set up for transmission and storage, at arm's length from the rest of British Gas, notably supply. To British Gas's management, the structural remedies raised by the OFT were anathema: the vision of an integrated structure remained at the core of the corporate vision, now led by Bob Evans,[6] who had succeeded Denis Rooke.

The First Review of the Pricing Formula

If the OFT proposals were unpalatable, British Gas quickly found itself fighting on two fronts. This was because, while the competition debate

---

[6] Evans, like Rooke, spent most of his working life in the gas industry and had been Chief Executive under Rooke before becoming Chairman in 1989.

was developing, Ofgas had been carrying out its first price-cap review (see background papers: Ofgas 1991*a–c*). These were early days for periodic reviews. There were a few other examples, which provided some guidance, in particular the review by Bryan Carsberg, Director General of Telecommunications, of British Telecom's price cap in 1988 (Oftel 1988*a,b*) and the setting of the regulatory formulae for the regional electricity companies (RECs) and water at privatization in 1990. There was, not surprisingly, little debate or understanding about the value of the regulatory asset base, comparative efficiency or CAPEX regulation, as there is now, with hindsight, and dozens of periodic reviews later.

In these circumstances, it was understandable that the outcomes would be uncertain, somewhat crude, and that a number of different ones were plausible. Inevitably (and correctly), Ofgas homed in on the rate of return of the Transco network, and proposed that the formula should be moderated to RPI − 5, consistent with a current-cost accounting (CCA) rate of return of between 5 and 7 per cent on the assets allocated to the tariff business (British Gas sought 9.5 per cent). In hindsight, the logic was questionable, but at the time the problem was perceived as being one in which the returns were too high because the cost of capital had been allowed on the full replacement cost of the assets (the CCA value), and not that which investors had paid at privatization. This discount—which became known as the market-to-asset ratio (MAR)—had led McKinnon to propose the lower return on what he deemed to be an inflated valuation.

The Second MMC Inquiry

British Gas now faced threats to both its structural integrity and its returns, and took the brave—and from its perspective, probably mistaken—decision to seek to clear the regulatory uncertainty by appealing to the MMC. It did not take the normal route of just rejecting the proposed price formula (which took the form of a licence amendment). It also sought a full monopolies referral under the Fair Trading Act 1973.

However, it was not within the powers of British Gas to make a reference under this Act. Whereas the Director General had to refer the price cap to the MMC when British Gas rejected it, the Secretary of State did not have to make the Fair Trading Act reference. Here, however, British Gas had what it perceived as an advantage. Peter Walker had by this time joined the board of British Gas,[7] and Michael Heseltine, his long-time political colleague, had become Secretary of State for Trade and Industry.

---

[7] He joined in 1990 and remained until 1996.

A similarity in political outlook could therefore be assumed, although whether it affected the decision to make the full reference, to run concurrently with the Ofgas reference, is unclear. Whatever the pressures, the terms of the reference were drawn very widely, and this was to be British Gas's undoing. It may have thought that the Walker–Heseltine axis would ensure a reasonable outcome—that the reference could be 'managed'.

The MMC panel selected to take on what was, at the time, regarded as the first major challenge to the utility regulatory structure, not one which could be expected to be amenable to British Gas's position. Given the discretion inherent in the MMC's case-by-case approach, it mattered who the individuals were on the panel. It contained two key players in utility regulation: Michael Beesley and Geoffrey Whittington. Together they undermined British Gas's case: Beesley attacked the structure, Whittington the financial arrangements.

Beesley has sometimes been regarded as the 'father of the regulators'. As noted in Chapter 3, he had taught Stephen Littlechild and was a founder of the group of microeconomists in Britain who broadly adhered to Austrian economics. This was the intellectual baggage which Beesley brought to the MMC inquiry. For him, the key was competition. He clearly saw early on in the proceedings that, as the report stated, there was an inherent conflict of interest between owning the pipes and being one of the competitors using them. It followed that break-up was required as a necessary condition for competition to thrive: 'BG is both a seller of gas, and owner of the transportation system which its competitors have no alternative but to use. In our view, this dual role gives rise to an inherent conflict of interest which makes it impossible to provide the necessary conditions for self-sustaining competition' (MMC 1993b: vol. 1, para 1.6, p. 2). The MMC therefore recommended that 'the adverse effects identified be remedied by divestment of BG's trading activities no later than 31 March 1997' (ibid.: para 1.11, p. 3).

But to achieve this objective required a delicate balance. It could only work if British Gas was willing to cooperate and if the Secretary of State was willing to support divestment. The 'price' which the MMC thought worth paying was to give British Gas more money under the pricing formula to pay for restructuring, and to postpone retail competition until after the structural divestment had been achieved. The MMC stated: 'In our view, no decision should be taken as to the timing of the complete removal of the tariff monopoly in gas except after a most careful assessment of the consequences' (ibid.: para 1.9, p. 2).

That left the underlying structure of the price cap, and this is where Whittington came in. At the heart of the case was the treatment of three related financial measures: the cost of capital, the asset valuation, and depreciation. The market value of the company was considerably greater than the flotation value, but considerably less than the CCA value. Whittington's approach to what the report referred to as 'arcane adjustments' was to agree with Ofgas in abating the rate of return rather than providing a normal cost of capital on the full CCA value, but to provide full CCA depreciation. Thus, British Gas had a stream of income sufficient to maintain the value of the shareholders' funds intact overtime *and* to maintain its network investments. In fact, the network was relatively new, and would not need replacing for quite some time. Thus the depreciation arrangement left British Gas with a higher cash flow, and it could therefore support higher returns—a point which was to cause the main controversy at the next review.

British Gas thus lost on both fronts: with the MMC confirming the Ofgas approach to the formula *and* proposing the break-up of the company into a competitive supply business and a monopoly pipeline activity. However, the implementation of the MMC report was split between the regulator and the Department of Trade and Industry (DTI). In the case of the pricing formula, the MMC report was to the Director General, who was required to reach a final decision having taken account of the MMC recommendations (MMC 1993*a*). The Fair Trading Act 1973 reference of the monopoly passed into the Secretary of State's domain for decision. Thus, regulation was dealt with by Ofgas and structure by the DTI.

Towards the end of the process, James McKinnon was replaced by Clare Spottiswoode. New to the office, Spottiswoode accepted the MMC recommendations on the price cap and implemented them. The underlying Whittington methodology was not at this stage questioned, although it was to become the central battleground at the next periodic review, when Spottiswoode rejected the CCA approach to depreciation.

The Deal with the DTI, and the Gas Act 1995

The MMC's structural recommendations posed a serious problem for the government, and politically for Heseltine. British Gas vigorously lobbied against break-up, and was prepared to go to considerable lengths to head it off. However, ministers could not simply back down and reject the MMC report, so some compromise was sought. A 'deal' emerged, although whether this was proposed by Tim Eggar, then Minister for Energy at the DTI, or British Gas is far from clear. Break-up would be avoided, but at a price—bringing forward domestic competition to 1998, in line with electricity, thereby turning the MMC's recommendations on their head.

To Eggar's claimed surprise, British Gas accepted this deal. In addition, it agreed to create Chinese walls between the network monopoly and supply, separating out information, employees, and supply activities, so that the two operated as if they were separate companies. A compliance officer was appointed to ensure that the walls were not breached, and the burden of compliance to this conduct regulation proved onerous.

From the perspective of the shareholders, the deal was perhaps British Gas's greatest mistake. There is no evidence to suggest that it had thought through the full consequences of a fast track to competition in 1998, and what was to emerge as the 'contracts crisis' it entailed. Eventually, as we shall see below, it was forced to write off a significant amount of shareholder value and to break itself up. However, before these dramatic developments unfolded, it became apparent that the deal required legislation. At first, the government (but not the DTI) tried to avoid this conclusion, partly because of a very legitimate fear that there would not be time available in the legislative programme, and partly for fear of the electoral consequences if losers emerged from the competitive process.

In the end, both fears were assuaged: time was found and the fall in gas prices made it possible to begin the gas trials with the assurance that no customers would face real price increases. Indeed, the politics proved benign for the Conservatives: British Gas was compliant and Labour found itself exposed to the charge that it would be the party 'against choice' if it opposed retail competition. Hence, Labour decided not to oppose the second reading of the bill.[8] The Gas Act 1995, which facilitated the deal, also changed the duties of the Director General of Gas Supply from *promoting* to *securing* competition. Spottiswoode rightly attached considerable importance to this. It was no longer sufficient to create a level playing field: competitors now had to succeed, and British Gas had to lose market share. Competition was no longer a means: it was an end in itself.

Unlike the electricity industry, gas now had an appropriate structure and licence amendments in place *before* trials were conducted and before full competition was unleashed. These factors were to be critical and, as competition began to unfold in electricity, the problems created by leaving supply and distribution within the same corporate structure, and not agreeing the key licence amendments until 1998, was to give gas competition a major head start over electricity. It was not until the Utilities Act 2000 that business separation in electricity was to begin to be implemented. Compulsory divestment remains unachieved. The advantages gas held were considerable. The unfolding of competition in retail

---

[8] The Shadow Energy Minister at the time was Martin O'Neill.

supply—and the comparison with developments in electricity—is discussed in Chapter 14.

The Gas Release Scheme, the Contracts Crisis, and Break-up

It gradually began to dawn on British Gas just how radical the implications of retail competition could be. By extending to the retail market the breaking of the link between customers and the supplier in the industrial market, the traditional commitment that customers have to absorb upstream gas costs no longer held. Thus, there was no guarantee that British Gas could recover its gas supply costs (Fig. 13.1).

The difference between British Gas and its rivals lay in its contract portfolio. As described in Chapter 2, its public-sector predecessors had been the instrument of government policy to develop the North Sea gas fields. By signing long-term, take-or-pay contracts, the field development costs could be recovered. These contracts were bequeathed to the privatized British Gas, and, for as long as its monopoly downstream remained, it continued to contract on this basis.

British Gas's grip on the market depended upon the monopoly, and it had already begun to be undermined in the industrial market from the outset, and particularly after the 1988 MMC report and subsequent steps by Ofgas and the OFT to force British Gas to reduce its share of new gas

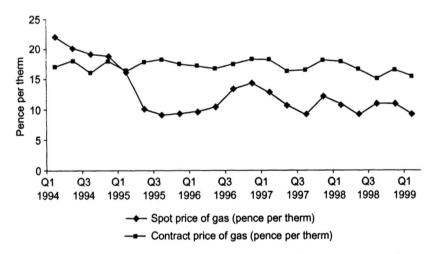

FIG. 13.1 Spot and contract gas prices, 1994–9

Source: Heren Energy Ltd (spot prices); DTI (contract prices).

fields to 90 per cent, and then to release gas to competitors in the supply market. The Gas Release Scheme was proposed by the OFT in 1991. British Gas agreed in March 1991 to reduce its share of the contract market to 40 per cent by 1995, backed by a programme of releasing gas to competitors—500 million therms in October 1992, with further tranches through to 1995 (see Ofgas 1992: 13–14).

If the idea was sound—competition could not be effective without gas suppliers to compete with—the execution was widely viewed as at best unfortunate. Instead of an orderly auction to significant rivals capable of credibly servicing industrial customers, by 1993 over 100 firms bid for the second tranche, of which seventy were 'first-timers', many entirely new businesses. The scheme reached an almost comical state when it emerged that ten of the supposed new entrants into the industrial gas market were all registered at Hestercombe Avenue, London SW6 (see Pease 1993). It was an early example of the importance of regulating markets: creating the conditions for a transition to competition could not be a process of *laissez-faire*, and Ofgas was forced to take a proactive role in subsequent releases.

The Gas Release Scheme was implemented before both the surge in demand from the new market in the generation of electricity got going on a major scale, and before the gas bubble in supply materialized. As a result, British Gas was a reluctant seller. In retrospect, given the subsequent fall in spot prices, British Gas might be thought lucky to have disposed of so much gas at the prices then prevailing. Once the fall had happened, British Gas became exposed to potential losses as its remaining contracts became stranded. What had been regarded as crucial assets turned out to be liabilities. As belatedly the scale of the problem became apparent with the emergence of the gas bubble, British Gas's reaction to the losses was to attempt to renegotiate with the oil companies. The DTI and British Gas discussed various 'solutions' to the contracts problem, including the use of bank loans and a levy. Loans would fund a buyout of existing liabilities and the levy would help to pay for these. A new negotiator, Kenneth Gardener, was appointed, but British Gas was not initially successful and the losses could not easily be stemmed, even if they could be estimated (see *Energy Utilities* January 1996: 4). As long as British Gas had sufficient funds, it could pay, and oil companies had little incentive to reduce their prices. They had been faced by the monopsony for so long, and had had to contract according to the wishes of British Gas. Now the boot was on the other foot. To address this problem, British Gas needed to separate out and protect its transmission and distribution businesses from its supply contracts problem, and the way to do this was to break itself up, and to place the contracts within a separate company, called Centrica, which was formally demerged from British Gas in 1997.

The new company would not, however, be financially viable if it contained only the contracts and the supply business. It was expected to be loss-making, and so could not legally be established. Therefore, assets in the form of Morecambe Bay were thrown in to offset the potential liabilities. In effect, British Gas wrote off Morecambe Bay against the contract losses. Morecambe was Centrica's main asset, worth about £2.5 billion. The importance of this can be seen against Centrica's results for 1996 and 1997. In 1997, the exceptional charges in the annual accounts were £835 million, compared with £822 million in 1996, of which £608 million were related to contract negotiation in 1997, and £705 million in 1996 (Centrica 1998).

These contract renegotiations turned out rather better than had been anticipated. Against the background of the 1996 supply price formula (which had been accepted by British Gas, unlike the Transco formula), by the end of 1997 many of the contracts had been renegotiated and Centrica had begun to realize its market potential. The pressure on margins and the reduction in its gas market through competition forced it to look for volume growth in electricity. As a gas retailer, its market share would decline to a 'natural' market share, and therefore it had to look elsewhere for growth. This was further encouraged by the convergence of the two industries, with gas providing an important input into electricity generation; gas and electricity spot and contract markets beginning to emerge with associated financial markets; and electricity companies entering the gas market. The multi-fuel supply business had arrived, and Centrica was to prove that the retailer model could be carried over to other services.

The Third MMC Inquiry

While British Gas was preoccupied with the contracts crisis and splitting itself up, Ofgas was preparing the next pricing formula for the Transco pipeline business. Ofgas—and Spottiswoode in particular—approached the Transco review with a determination not to repeat the mistakes that Littlechild had made in the 1994/95 RECs' periodic review. Recognizing that Offer and Ofgas might soon be merged, there was considerable interest in the relative performance of the two regulators—both of whom were at the time thought of as potential heads of a merged body. Much was also at stake for the company since the future value of Transco (and, indeed, through the supply review, the value of British Gas Trading, as it was known at the time) depended on the decisions of the regulator (see Helm 1996).

Ofgas's initial approach was somewhat radical, entertaining the notion of profit sharing—having commissioned papers on a sliding-scale element. But by the time its initial proposals were published in May 1996 (Ofgas 1996a), it had focused in on a traditional RPI − X formula. Ofgas proposed an initial price cut of between 20 and 28 per cent, and an X factor of 5. British Gas responded by declaring that it implied 8,000–10,000 job cuts, and one of its directors described it as 'the biggest smash-and-grab raid on shareholders' (*Energy Utilities* June 1996: 9–10).

The central feature of the Ofgas proposals was a revisiting of the financial assumptions determined by the MMC in 1993. Spottiswoode argued that the MMC had got it wrong then, and, in particular, that the asset value should be marked down to a regulatory asset base which would earn the cost of capital. Thus, the existing lower rate on a higher number was replaced by a higher rate on a lower base. In addition, and most controversially, Spottiswoode argued that the depreciation should not be set at the CCA level, but at the abated MAR level. In effect, she argued that Transco did not need the money from depreciation now, since the assets were relatively new. It would be pay-as-you-go depreciation: only when the assets needed renewing would the money be forthcoming—from some future regulator. Thus, what looked like arcane accounting rules turned out to be a fundamental question about who controlled the cash for future renewals, and hence where control of the business lay in this crucial respect. These changes to the methodology would have had dramatic effects on British Gas. The value of the assets in the accounts had to be substantially written down by around £2.3 billion. In addition, a lower depreciation charge meant a lower cash flow. Thus, the dividend, which was already under threat from the contracts, would have to be cut.

Although Spottiswoode clearly thought that the logic of her case would result in British Gas's reluctant acceptance, she misjudged the nature of corporate decision-making. Cutting a dividend was something which any board would find difficult to accept before exhausting all the available appeals mechanisms.

This was probably sufficient to trigger a reference. However, if there was any doubt, two other factors had to be taken into account: the fact that the MMC had clearly provided for full CCA depreciation in 1993 and, hence, would have to accept that it had then acted against the public interest if it now agreed with the regulator's methodology; and the further proposals for unbundling which Spottiswoode threw in for good measure. On the very good grounds that the proposal could not be much worse—except for focusing the discount[9]—British Gas duly rejected the Director General's final proposal published in August (Ofgas 1996*b*),[10] and, hence, the matter was referred to the MMC. The announcement was accompanied by acrimonious exchanges on both sides.

The progress of the MMC case provided considerable theatre as it unfolded. The numbers kept changing, and there was a public row about the exchange of documents. When the conclusions came, the results provided vindication all round (MMC 1997*b*). The basic financial methodology went broadly the Director General's way, but money was found from elsewhere to improve British Gas's lot and, significantly, the unbundling agenda was put back—only to carry over to the next review in 2001. The P_0 was set at 21 per cent, and X at 2.

However, the controversy did not end there. It transpired that the volume forecasts which the MMC had considered had subsequently been raised. Therefore, the regulator decided to amend the recommendations of the MMC report to reduce the returns to British Gas. This produced a final controversy: Spottiswoode had said that the MMC recommendations would be implemented in full, but, in this important respect, they were not.

A Substantial Achievement

With the break-up of British Gas, a more sensible structure emerged, with natural monopoly separated from potentially (and now actually) competitive activities. Public policy could move on to focus on the two rather different tasks: ensuring an efficient provision of the network services; and regulating competition elsewhere. Without the break-up, it is unlikely that management would have had the scope for the specialism and innovation that transpired.

But it was also to transpire that the structural separation, whilst a necessary condition, would not be sufficient to secure the objectives of energy policy. On the network side, Transco would not necessarily have the incentives to invest in its infrastructure, and Ofgem was to return to the question at the 2001/02 periodic review, when it introduced more disaggregation and auctions (see Chapter 18). On the supply side, Centrica would seek to replace its overwhelming dominance in gas supply with

[9] Focusing the discount meant apportioning the initial market value between the Exploration and Production business and Transco, and, hence, rolling forward a lower RAB—an issue which would resurface in the *subsequent* Transco review, discussed in Chapter 18.

[10] These contained minor modifications on the initial proposals, notably a 20% P_0 cut and a hybrid price/revenue cap of RPI − 2.5%. See *Energy Utilities* September 1996, 5.

market power in energy. The question of longer-term, take-or-pay contracts would emerge as an important issue in the 2000s, as North Sea gas declined, the market tightened, and excess demand, rather than excess supply, emerged as the main concern. It remains to be seen whether Centrica's success is largely a function of the gas and electricity surpluses and falling prices of the late 1990s, or a more permanent feature of the new market. Its gradual reintegration after 2002 suggests that it will return to a vertically integrated model—in both gas and electricity.

14

Domestic Competition in Gas and Electricity

> In our view, no decision should be taken as to the timing of the complete removal of the tariff monopoly in gas except after a most careful assessment of the consequences. (MMC report on gas, 1993)[1]

The liberalization of the domestic gas and electricity markets was a policy necessarily driven by theory rather than evidence. There were no examples to draw upon from large industrial economies. The idea of customers choosing their suppliers from a range of competing firms, who in turn would look to a host of competing generators and gas field operators, had enormous appeal in an era of renewed faith in markets. The 1980s had witnessed the rise of Ronald Reagan and Margaret Thatcher's much more robust defence of capitalism. By the end of the decade, the fall of the Berlin Wall symbolized the triumph of capitalism over socialism. In Britain, privatization had been extended into the core monopolies and the idea of turning the state monopolies from producer- to consumer-driven businesses had immense appeal. It was a natural extension to widen the domain of consumer choice.

In this *general* defence of consumer choice and markets, the particular features of energy markets were downplayed. The old assumptions of the post-war period that market failures necessitated a planned approach were inverted: now it was government failure which was the main problem. The economic borders of the state needed to be rolled back to prevent 'crowding out' of the private sector. Electricity and gas could become like other commodity markets, with supply and demand brought into balance by the normal operation of market forces. Failures arose primarily because governments intervened in investments and because state monopolies had allowed inefficiency to go unchecked by competition, and union monopolies (notably in coal) to threaten security of supply.

This *general* presumption in favour of markets led the architects of privatization in electricity and gas to avoid some of the practicalities of introducing domestic competition, and to give virtually no thought to the

---

[1] MMC (1993b: vol. 1, para 1.9, p. 2).

longer-term consequences of liberalization. In electricity, the eight-year transition was designed with politics to the fore. There would be at least two general elections before 1998. Scant regard (and no serious planning) was given to the way the transition would work out. This was the job of the companies themselves, not the regulatory authorities. It was not the regulator's job to 'regulate for competition': the task of the regulator was primarily confined to the 'regulation of monopoly'. In gas, where Peter Walker and Denis Rooke's monopoly model formed the basis of privatization, there was no serious thought about domestic competition at all.

With hindsight, we now know that this lack of a thorough analysis of the consequences of domestic liberalization was a mistake; however, it was one which had the happy background of excess supplies. In time, liberalization would reveal that supply competition required intensive regulatory intervention to define and support the new markets; that it would require the development of financial markets if long-term contracts were to be signed; and that the cross-subsidies inherited from the nationalized industries would be (politically) painfully exposed. All this was, however, in the future: the initial decisions were largely unaffected by such practical considerations.

The Idea of Choice and Consumer Preferences

It is a natural presumption that consumer choice is in general preferable to state planning. Only in *special* circumstances, where there are significant market failures, is this general presumption overruled. These special circumstances can arise on the demand side—people are ill-informed or irrational, or their choices adversely affect others—or on the supply side—costs are such that monopoly supply is more efficient or the firm's activities are damaging to others. And even in these cases, the costs of intervention may exceed those of the failures themselves, and, in any event, market-based instruments can help to alleviate problems such as pollution.

The exercise of choice not only forces firms to reduce costs so that they may be competitive on price, it also affects quality, advertising and product differentiation. As preferences vary across consumers, so too should the nature of the product. People may vary according to the trade-off between price and reliability; and they might have preferences over the sources of electricity generation.

These considerations are given an extra twist by the Austrian economists referred to in Chapter 3, who were prominent in the key decisions on liberalization in both electricity and gas. The advantages of maximizing the domain of individual choice included informational efficiency relative to state planning: the individual need only know their own preferences, the price and the goods on offer for sale; whereas the state planner had to know all the consumers' preferences and the production costs. This could inevitably lead to 'mistakes'. Added to this was the theory of interest group behaviour, and it would be expected that, without choice and with a monopoly onto which costs could be passed, these interests would 'capture' the industry, and lead to the sorts of grandiose 'Plans for Coal' and nuclear programme which this school of thought identified with the post-war consensus and its implications, described in Chapter 2.

Although there is much in these arguments, they are somewhat constrained in the electricity industry, and to a lesser extent, in the gas industry. In electricity, the fundamentals limit the implications of the economics of consumer choice very considerably. Electricity cannot be stored (except in special circumstances). Supply must instantaneously match demand. Therefore, security of supply—the insurance that when the light switch is operated, the lights come on—is a *system* property, with important public-goods characteristics. An unregulated competitive market would need to sell an insurance product or be allowed to charge very high prices when the margin between supply and demand got tight. This insurance product would probably need to have a compulsory element, since the incentives to free-ride would be considerable (*because* security of supply is a system property).[2]

Customer choice also needs to be placed in a dynamic context. Investments in new power stations and gas fields have significant sunk costs. Investors need to be able to manage the risks that these may become stranded. In the 'old world', under monopoly, customers were forced to pay; in the new world, customers are no longer tied to suppliers and, hence, to particular generation contracts.

This dynamic problem was much understated in the 1990s, and to the extent that it was considered, stranding of the legacy gas contracts *was actively encouraged*, as discussed in Chapter 13. The obvious solution—the placing of risk on financial markets—required futures markets of sufficient transparency and liquidity to hedge these price risks. This in turn required an element of standardization and regulatory support—and in fact, the regulatory authorities moved away from this challenge, by de-standardizing the spot market (through replacing the Pool with NETA) and failing to prevent the consolidation of the electricity generation market and its

---

[2] Such free-riding was implicit in the special arrangements for large gas and electricity customers in the 1980s, where 'interruptible' contracts provided marginal-cost electricity and gas, but supplies were rarely interrupted. See Hammond *et al.* (1986), and MMC (1988).

related vertical integration (and failing to do much about concentration in the North Sea gas market).

The limitations to consumer choice were also added to by the distributional effects of pricing in electricity and gas. Energy to domestic customers is typically considered a 'merit good'.[3] It is one of the social primary goods which are necessary to participate in society. Along with housing, education, health, transport and food, heating and light play the role of *necessary* conditions for a minimum standard of living. Rural electrification in the inter-war years and the gradual extension of the natural gas network have been significant factors in the politics of inclusion and the provision of common citizenship, and an element of cross-subsidy has been an inherent part of energy pricing, again supported by the monopolies. 'Fuel poverty' arises not because people are unable to *demand* the supplies of their choice, but because they cannot match their willingness to pay with the ability to do so. And, at the extreme, a number of people die each winter because of damp and cold.

These distributional failures can be addressed *outside* the energy sector. The obvious solution is to use the social-security system to provide sufficient income and then allow people to choose accordingly. But the trouble with this 'first-best' solution is that it tends not to happen, and, indeed, as the sector was liberalized, no significant associated changes in social-security policy took place. Partly, this was because of the happy accident referred to above—of excess supplies and low prices. But partly it was due to wider constraints on the level of public expenditure. The result has been that fuel poverty has remained a significant problem for the sector ever since.[4] The fact that competition tends to make price equal to cost, and that the costs of servicing the poor are often higher than those for the better-off creates an inevitable tension between efficiency and distributional objectives. If and when prices eventually rise, the effects will be significant. Without intervention and regulation, competition may prove politically very unpopular.

Finally, to make competition work, the necessary infrastructure for billing and coping with switching is required. Metering is an essential component. In a monopoly system, much of this is very straightforward, and consequently, in principle, low-cost. There is no switching, bills can be averaged (and cross-subsidized), and bad debts absorbed within the context of total costs. Purchasing strategies by suppliers are not needed—they

---

[3] See Dilnot and Helm (1987).

[4] The Labour government eventually produced a fuel-poverty strategy (see DETR/DTI 2001; see also DTI 2002e: ch. 6 for a survey of fuel-poverty policy instruments).

supply long-term from the generators at cost—and hence portfolio risk management is not needed. Where metering is expensive, it can be avoided through demand profiling and average pricing. A monopoly system should therefore be simple and cheap to run.

By contrast, competition in supply requires very considerable information technology systems, extensive metering and contract-risk management. Thus there are costs as well as benefits to competition. The advocates of liberalization paid too little attention to these at the outset, and cost–benefit assessments were noticeable either by their lack of sophistication or by the almost blind faith placed in the idea that *because* competition was assumed to be more efficient, *therefore* there would be price reductions sufficient to offset these set-up costs *caused* by competition.

The failure of the advocates of supply competition to take account of the limitations arising from the characteristics of the industry—the system nature of supply and demand balancing; the need for contracts; fuel poverty; and the costs of the infrastructure for competition—determined much of what followed. These problems did not go away, and regulators have had to react to them as they have gradually emerged. In practice, almost all the efforts in the run-up to liberalization went into the last one—the infrastructure for competition—whilst the first, second and third have gradually resurfaced and played a core part in the reappraisal of energy policy in 2002.

The Route Map for Electricity and the 1994 Franchise Drop

Until the mid-1990s, it was always assumed that electricity would liberalize first, to be eventually followed by gas. This order arose not just from the way in which the two industries were privatized, but also because the contractual structure of gas was considered more complicated—as it was in Europe, where gas liberalization has lagged electricity.

As we saw in Chapter 8, a transitional process was set up at privatization. Initially the 1 MW market was opened up. Then, in 1994, the intermediate over 100 kW market would be liberalized and, finally, in 1998, the whole market would be opened up. The 1994 drop turned out to be fairly chaotic, as suppliers and customers scrambled to get the necessary infrastructure and contracts in place, with the regulator taking a back-seat, leaving the participants to get on with it. The main requirements for the new market participants were threefold: *metering*, where second-tier customers (those opting for a supplier other than their host regional electricity company (REC)—the first-tier supplier) had to appoint a meter operator; *settlement*, where a system had to be in place for the settling of payments; and *security of information*, where, in the case of the host REC being appointed as meter operator, it must be prevented from using the information obtained for anti-competitive purposes by its trading activities.

In trying to bring these aspects of competition together so that 50,000 customers would have choice of supplier from 1 April 1994, there were likely to be problems. Without a firm guiding regulatory hand on the tiller, these were inevitable. Writing in August 1994, Margaret McKinlay, Chief Executive of the Pool, confirmed that: 'In retrospect, it now seems ambitious to have tried simultaneously on 1 April 1994, to introduce competition amongst meter operators, a new settlement data collection system and an expansion of competition in the supply market' (Letter to *Energy Utilities* 1994: 35).

There were problems with the new meters (called Code 5), not enough telephone lines, and the Electronic Registration System proved difficult to use. Very significantly, McKinlay pointed the finger of blame at Offer: 'I believe that if Offer had taken a more proactive role sooner, then some of the problems that we have encountered with the launch of the 100 kW market might have been reduced' (ibid.). In the aftermath, data sometimes turned out to be missing or inaccurate, and bills were not always settled in an orderly way.

The lessons for the 1998 franchise drop were assimilated into Offer. The year 1998 would be altogether a more difficult process: the customers' demands were smaller, less sophisticated and the transitional costs would be proportionally greater. Yet, despite the initial chaos, the 1994 franchise drop was quickly assimilated into the market. Offer had to claim it was a success, and it was quick to point out the benefits. Interestingly, these had little to do with the second-tier or host suppliers' *direct* costs. The margin on supply was estimated by Offer in the over 100 kW market to be around 2 per cent (Offer 1995a: para 2.5, p. 2), so there was little scope here for significant reductions in customers' bills. The main benefit, Offer claimed, lay in putting pressure on the generators, whose costs comprised about 65 per cent of the over 100 kW customers' bills. Suppliers could compete for customers by contracting for cheaper sources of supply. And it was this element in the generation costs which would, for Offer, be the main target after 1998 (para 2.8).

But what options did suppliers have? They could buy directly from the Pool—on the same terms as everyone else—or they could buy through the contracts for differences and sign contracts with the independent power producers (IPPs). Since, by Offer's own admission, competition in generation remained sufficiently weak that the two main generators—National Power and Powergen—were subject in the mid-1990s to a price cap which they had enough market power to achieve, and such market power did not go away when price caps expired, the scope for significant purchasing gains for suppliers was limited. Furthermore, the first round of gas contracts supporting the IPPs for which the RECs had contracted were beginning to look more and more 'out of the market'.

Offer tended to measure 'success' by the number of customers who switched, as if the fact that businesses incurring the costs of switching was a mark of success. Although, of course, an interesting statistic, what mattered was the *intensity* of competition, and the extent to which the host RECs found it necessary to lower prices to hold on to market share. It could instead be argued that the more customers felt the need to switch, the less intense the competitive pressure had been. There was also an element of management fashion for larger customers: buyers could demonstrate their value to their boards and ultimately shareholders by switching.

Nevertheless, without any serious attempt to assess the costs and benefits of supply competition, Littlechild was convinced of the advantages of pressing on with the liberalization of the electricity market in 1998. He concluded in the classic Austrian style in early 1995 that 'experience to date in electricity, and in other utilities where competition had been introduced, suggests that *all* groups of customers, including domestic customers, will wish to take advantage of the opportunities to exercise choice' [italics added] (Offer 1995a: para 2.5, p. 3).

It remained to determine how much regulation of supply prices might be needed once the liberalization in 1994 had taken place. For Littlechild, liberalization meant deregulation too: once the market had sufficiently developed, price caps would no longer be needed. In the over 100 kW, there was, however, a distinction between the abolition of price cap and deregulation. The suppliers also had an obligation not to discriminate between customers, and domestic customers were still subject to a price cap. Hence, the domestic price provided a benchmark against which to view prices for the over 100 kW market. As these domestic customers bore the brunt of the coal contracts for the period 1993–8, it could be safely assumed that over 100 kW prices would be below those for the below 100 kW market. Hence the price cap would not be needed.

Gas Takes the Lead

Although domestic gas supply competition had not been contemplated at all at privatization, and the Monopolies and Mergers Commission (MMC) in 1993 had recommended a ten-year postponement until at least 2002, the Gas Act 1995 provided a fast-track to full liberalization by 1998, to parallel that in electricity. As we saw in Chapter 13, this turnaround had come about as a result of a series of regulatory inquiries by Ofgas, the OFT, and the MMC, by management miscalculation and by political manoeuvring in the context of a growing gas bubble from the North Sea.

From the outset, Ofgas took an aggressive position in opening up the market, following the point when the Gas Act came into force in March 1996, and the power to issue licences in the supply market came into effect. Considerable thought had been given to the way in which the market would be opened up. Following the announcement by Heseltine in December 1993 of the intention to open up the domestic market from 1996, a joint Department of Trade and Industry–Ofgas consultation document in May 1994 had proposed a transitional approach setting volume limits on the amount of gas supplied to domestic customers of 5 per cent in 1996 and 10 per cent in 1997 across the country (DTI/Ofgas 1994). The 1995 Gas Act provided for competition in phases, and in March 1996 the Secretary of State set out an order defining the phases and dates. The approach was now to open up defined areas (instead of volumes) fully so that the trials might give a more complete picture of the effects of liberalization across all customers—an area of 500,000 premises in 1996 (Phase I) and a further 1.5 million premises in 1997 (Phase II).

The Phase I trial was designated to the south-west. From the outset, it was designed more with a view to demonstrating the benefits of competition than to any serious evaluation of the costs and benefits, and it was therefore crucial that a significant number of customers could benefit from switching supplier. The key to this was the relative competitiveness of British Gas Trading (BGT), the incumbent. BGT had a legacy of (more expensive) long-term contracts, and these had been transferred to the new company, Centrica, precisely so that its market exposure would encourage contract renegotiation with oil and gas producers. Centrica's task was to manage a dual process of recovering as much of the costs as it could from its customer base, and renegotiation. By choosing a regional solution to Phase I, Ofgas must have calculated that BGT would be better off holding up tariffs across the country to protect revenues, even if that meant loss of market share in the south-west trial area. It could not offer different prices in the trial area because that would have been discriminatory. So BGT had its hands tied, and competitors had an obvious advantage.

A second concern for the Phase I trial was to prove that competition would not just be of benefit to the better-off, but to the poor as well. The more profitable customers for suppliers were the direct-debit ones, paying bills automatically and with bigger values to spread the fixed costs of supply. Those on prepayment meters and in disadvantaged groups had

266   *Energy, the State, and the Market*

higher costs. Ofgas did, however, have an advantage in that gas costs were falling as the gas bubble emerged. Hence, although the better-off would see the biggest gains, it was safe to assume that prices would fall for everyone below the RPI−0 level: everyone would be a winner, even if some won much more than others. Furthermore, since the entrants were playing a wider strategic game in gaining brand recognition and market share ahead of full liberalization, at relatively low cost, they could be expected to act in a socially responsible way. By September 1996, Ofgas could claim that the concerns that the better-off would be the main beneficiaries and that disadvantaged customers would not be attractive to suppliers were unfounded. 'Most, if not all, of the new suppliers are offering discounts against British Gas's prices at all levels of consumption and with all payment methods (including prepayment meters)' (Ofgas 1996c: para 46, pp. 12–13). By 1997, Ofgas calculated that 23 per cent of customers had switched during Phase I, with 24 per cent in the Phase II areas (Ofgas 1997b).

Ofgas's approach to BGT's price regulation fitted well with the promotion of competition in supply. Recognizing that the average price in the long-term contracts was well above the spot price, Ofgas proposed that the supply price cap from 1997 should continue to allow a cost pass-through. There would be a price cut of £8 followed by RPI−4, and Ofgas announced that this would probably be the last price cap on supply. Having *proved* that competition was beneficial to customers in Phase I, Ofgas moved swiftly on to Phase II in February 1997 in Dorset and Avon, and to East and West Sussex and Kent in March 1997, and then a series of tranches completed Phase III, to smooth the process of the transfer of customers.

With Phase II producing a similar pattern of market-share loss, BGT recognized that it could no longer afford to hold its line on pricing across the country to protect its contracts, and that it would have to meet the competitive challenge more directly. In March 1997, it announced its new 'ValuePlus' direct-debit tariff, to be introduced in the south-west trial area. Ofgas reluctantly agreed to permit this, after a period of consultation, despite the inevitable protests of the new entrants. ValuePlus was then extended to Phase II in September 1997. Next, also in September 1997, BGT announced a further round of tariff reductions for 'DirectPay', 'OptionPay', and 'Standard' credit customers from January 1998—more than had been anticipated and below the price cap. BGT had decided that tariff rebalancing was the natural consequence of competition. This took the form of a rebalancing application to Ofgas, as part of its price cap, and it came unstuck. BGT 'withdrew' its application in May 1998 since, as Ofgas stated in October 1998, 'if BGT had not withdrawn its application,

Ofgas would have formally rejected the application on the basis of our examination of costs' (Ofgas 1998: para 3.5, p. 14). There would, in Ofgas' view, have been undue preference, and instead a single tariff was proposed. In other words, whilst competitors could set their own tariff structures with only limited interference, BGT could not. As long as it was dominant, it would be constrained.

The result was as expected—or rather, as it was designed to be. By the end of August 1998, Ofgas reported that 15 per cent of all customers had switched to an alternative supplier, and Phases I and II switching had levelled out at around 25 per cent (Ofgas 1998: para 46, p. 49). Centrica would have to come to terms with a market share of between 70 and 80 per cent if this trend continued. It would, however, have one significant benefit: if it had lost out in gas, it could gain in electricity through a dual-fuel offering. And, with a national database of customers and a national brand, it would be in a position to branch out into offering all kinds of domestic services— from the Automobile Association (AA) to financial services and telecommunications. But before we deal with dual fuel, the less happy experience of preparing for 1998 in electricity needs to brought into the frame.

1998 in Electricity

In contrast to the fast track and highly managed transition to competition in gas, the electricity industry's approach to 1998 was altogether more leisurely. It had four years to prepare, and a very different regulator in charge. In January 1995, Offer produced a paper raising some of the issues and options (Offer 1995a). Two sets of issues were identified: the trading arrangements and the associated metering, communications, and settlements; and the licensing price controls and obligations for customer protection. From the outset, the metering problem and supporting information technology infrastructure were the dominant problems. The difference between electricity and gas was that, whilst the latter generally had appropriate metering, the former did not. Therefore, either competition would develop as customers acquired the appropriate metering (as in the over 100 kW market), or some proxy, such as load profiling, would be required. A crucial early decision was to opt for the latter. It was the only possible way to give everyone a choice in 1998, but it would also create major complications and costs. Essentially, an information technology system was required to implement switches with load profiling as a temporary solution, with metering (and its simpler arrangements) gradually taking over.

Littlechild also wanted to hold a trial to test out the process of liberalization, and he even toyed with an earlier opening of the market in

1996 (see *Energy Utilities* 1994: 39–40). In the event, trials were confined to the system, not actual customers—a wise decision, given the problems with the information technology even later in the day. Whilst competition was being brought in, Littlechild took the view that the broad public electricity supply licence conditions—across distribution and supply— should be held in place as a safety net. The advantage of having distribution in play too was that the information technology and other system costs could be absorbed within a monopoly framework, and were controlled within the relevant price caps.

It was already apparent in 1995 that the costs of implementing the 1998 liberalization were likely to be large, and these were likely to be exacerbated by the fact that many parties would be involved. In addition to the RECs and the generators, there was the National Grid Company (NGC), the Pool and potential entrants to take into account. Compounding the costs that the demand profiling decision would impose, a further crucial factor was the decision by Offer to leave it to the Pool and the suppliers to develop the information technology, *without* any significant central direction. This was a typically anti-planning position consistent with Offer's overriding philosophy, but it meant that there was little by way of project leadership. The Pool in turn was a federal institution, with the various interests entrenched through the membership rules, making speedy and effective decision-making very difficult.

In consequence, fourteen RECs *separately* embarked on the development of their own information technology projects, all of which were to interact with the Pool. At the time, these were amongst the largest information technology projects undertaken in the developed world, and all had important first-of-a-kind characteristics, in that nowhere else had full domestic liberalization without comprehensive half-hourly metering been attempted. It had all the features of an information technology disaster, and indeed it is a miracle that there were not more problems as the deadline loomed.

Littlechild did establish a Coordination Group, but it had no specific authority. He stressed that 'my office does not have formal powers to require all the parties to take particular actions or to comply with any timetable that I might establish' (Offer 1995c: para 5.5, p. 15). He could not impose licence conditions without the possibility of an MMC reference, and he could not impose his decisions on the Pool. In retrospect, it was probably a mistake not to seek such powers, replicating the position of Ofgas which had the Gas Act 1995 to rely upon, and the lesson was to be learnt by the time NETA came to be implemented, with the Utilities Act 2000 extending Ofgem's licensing powers.

Yet regulators have considerable discretion and there was scope for Littlechild to impose his views on the process. The players all operated in a regulated framework with a substantial political overlay. Their directors do not like to be publicly criticized, and 'having good relations' with the regulators was a corporate objective for most if not all of them. Being blamed for failure to deliver in 1998 was a serious risk to incumbent management.

In place of the clear leadership from Offer, Littlechild appointed consultants to act as the 'Overall Project Manager' (OPM). In May 1997, Littlechild recognized that the problems the OPM had identified were serious and the April 1998 timetable was already seen to be tight, and he agreed with them that the major requirements were: the stabilization of the legal and commercial framework; the finalization of the interface design between the RECs and the Pool; decision-making on design matters needed to be speeded up; testing arrangements improved; and that the market needed to be managed after 1998 (Offer 1997). Already it looked likely that only some RECs would be ready, and that liberalization might have to start without all the areas open.

The reasons why some RECs were more prepared than others were partly accidental, due to the successes and failures of their own information technology programmes. But there was also the importance of incentives to bear in mind. With no certainty about cost recovery, and with the problems of having information technology ready early, only to find that delays meant extra costs in revisions, there were inevitably differences of views on urgency. Furthermore, for most RECs, liberalization would mean a loss of market share, so that the process had an element of 'turkeys voting for Christmas'. The distribution price control was still some way off, and thus RECs would not know the position on cost recovery until well into 1999.

By January 1998, the OPM was reporting problems in agreeing the baseline of the systems for participants' interface with the Pool. Repeated changes in the specification were being made, each time requiring iterations, testing, and trialling. Unless this could be agreed and frozen, there was little likelihood of being ready to go live. The OPM recommended the date be now set at September 1998 (PA Consulting 1998).

In the meantime, the delays to electricity liberalization were having repercussions elsewhere. RECs could benefit from selling dual fuels—electricity and gas—while Centrica and other gas suppliers could not reciprocate until the electricity market was fully liberalized. Offer and Ofgas issued a joint statement on the matter (Offer/Ofgas 1997), but Ofgas then tried to go further by demanding that RECs stop selling gas to electricity franchise customers, until their markets were open. An MMC reference was threatened, but in the event, Ofgas backed down (see OXERA 1998: 9).

By May, Littlechild announced he would step down in the autumn (at the same time as Spottiswode's appointment at Ofgas expired), facilitating the appointment of a joint energy regulator, ahead of the merger of Offer and Ofgas. The implementation of 1998 would therefore fall in his last months in office, or to his successor. To add to the sense of upheaval, Offer had also begun to get serious about Pool reform, and the early stages of NETA had begun to emerge (see Chapter 17). Thus, having gone through the costs of implementing new information technology to interface with the Pool for the purposes of facilitating customer switching, Littlechild now proposed a utility-run trading system with, as we shall see, very large information technology costs of its own. Finally, for good measure, in May 1998, Offer also published its plans for separating supply from distribution in the public electricity suppliers' (PESs) licences, in line with proposals in the Green Paper on regulatory reform (see Chapter 15).

In the event, market opening was fairly chaotic, as the 1994 franchise drop had been. The initial phase of opening began in September 1998 in four PES areas (Eastern, Manweb, ScottishPower, and Yorkshire) with 10 per cent of customers by postcode and all metered customers. Two more PESs followed in October (SEEBOARD and Midlands), four in November (Scottish Hydro-Electric, Northern, SWEB and NORWEB), two in December (London and East Midlands) and the last two in January 1999 (SWALEC and Southern). The 10 per cent was increased in stages to a further 30 per cent and then to all customers, with the process finally completed in May 1999. Prices continued to be regulated for a further period from the expiry of the price cap in 1998, to last for two years until 2002.

The effect on the market was more muted than in gas. By December 2000, Ofgem reported that PES market shares in the domestic electricity supply market by customers supplied varied between 78 and 89 per cent (Ofgem 2000i: para 10.8, p. 75), whilst BGT's share of the gas market had fallen to 71 per cent. This difference is hardly surprising, given that the electricity industry had none of the contract overhang problems which beset BGT. Indeed, the loss of market share was probably greater because of the dual-fuel offers, which had grown in importance and smeared the price reductions in gas across both markets, leaving customers believing that they had a reduction in the price of both fuels, when in fact it was largely from gas that the price advantages flowed.

Competition was also spurred on by the economies of scale which customer numbers offered. In a game in which not all the players could be winners, and in which consolidation was considered inevitable, an element of disequilibrium characterized the late 1990s and early 2000s as the scramble for customers got under way. With the relaxed view of the regulator to supply consolidation, customers were 'bought' in takeovers—valued anywhere between £150 and £300 each. Quite where the margins would come from to recoup these acquisitions was never clear, but it should be placed in the wider context in which telecommunications companies appeared willing to pay up to £5,000 per customer at the height of the merger boom.

An Act of Faith

The liberalization of the domestic gas and electricity supplies in the 1990s was more an act of faith in markets than a well worked-out policy. The consequences were not thought-out, nor was the process well planned and executed. Rather, liberalization was very much a stab in the dark. It did, however, happen at a particularly opportune moment. There was a window of opportunity in the late 1990s, particularly in gas, with abundant supplies and falling prices. Everyone would be a winner anyway, and price caps could be tightened in any event. That falling prices came to be associated with competition in supply rather than regulation was the consequence of good salesmanship by regulators.

Stripping back the rhetoric and congratulatory statements from regulators and politicians, what actually happened was a combination of the expropriation of British Gas's take-or-pay contracts in gas and a disequilibrium process in electricity supply, which saw an initial burst of competition translate into a merger boom, with the result that a small number of suppliers were able to buy up their rivals. (A similar pattern happened in Germany.) By 2002, supply of electricity and gas was largely in the hands of three large, vertically integrated electricity companies—EDF, E.ON and RWE—and Centrica. In electricity, whilst wholesale prices fell, retail margins in 2002 were between 10 and 15 per cent within the areas of old franchises. The supply price controls had been lifted, so there was little protection for customers.

These developments were facilitated by the absence of any need to engage in long-term contracting. Customers could switch, and suppliers could buy short, in the knowledge that tomorrow's price would probably be lower than today's, as excess capacity in electricity manifested itself—with the dash for gas having added to the capacity margin. There was no real need to worry about risk for future supplies, and hence the fact that the future market did not—and would not—develop to bear the risk of the investment and long-term contracts mattered little. These were problems for the future, when governments would have to work out how to tackle the problems of gas imports, contracts for Russian gas, renewables, and what to do when nuclear stations closed and pollution-control constraints begin to bite on the baseload coal capacity. The liberalization in 1998 may have opened up customer choice, but neither the regulators nor the politicians addressed its consequences. That would in due course require a rethink of energy policy.

15

Regulatory Reform and New Labour

> There is evident public discontent about the levels of profits being
> reported by many regulated companies and a widespread perception
> that the companies are being run only in the interests of their share-
> holders and top executives and are insufficiently sensitive to the
> needs of customers. (Tony Blair, 'Principles for Reform', 1995: 2)

The regulatory regime for both gas and electricity was designed without
much thought to its wider role in energy policy. The architects of privatization believed strongly in their own rhetoric on competition: energy
markets were on a path from monopoly to competition. The job of regulation was to manage that transition, and to ensure that the residual natural monopoly was subject to price controls. Even here, the role of
regulation was limited: regulators would use RPI – X to bear down on
costs, mimicking the competitive market. It was never intended that regulators would be able to accurately model costs—rather the companies'
response to the constraint on prices would reveal them. And, in any event,
large parts of the natural monopoly could be unbundled, and, hence,
deregulated. For those parts which could not, the ideas of competition for
monopoly and auctions might still have a role to play.

As previous chapters have demonstrated, this approach was naive.
Regulation *for* competition proved much more demanding and led to a
growth, not a retreat, of regulatory intervention. Regulation *of* monopoly
proved contentious too, as the high profits and capital gains provoked an
inevitable political response. Far from withering away, the role of the
regulators grew over the period, introducing greater public control over
the businesses.[1] The advent of New Labour, with its much broader social
democratic agenda, merely helped to reinforce the regulatory trend,
introducing social and environmental objectives alongside those of economic efficiency. It is therefore hardly surprising that the 1997 manifesto
committed New Labour to review the regulatory regime and promised
regulatory reform. A review of regulation was duly announced in 1987 by
Margaret Beckett, Secretary of State for Trade and Industry, resulting in

---

[1] The budget for Ofgas's first year (1986/87) was £1.2 million, and for Offer (1990/91), it
was £12.9 million. In 1999/2000, Ofgem's budget excluding NETA was £41.2 million.

a Green Paper in 1998 (DTI 1998), and then legislation in the parliamentary session, 1999–2000, and the Utilities Act 2000.

In order to appreciate the subtleties of the debate, it was first necessary to critique the regime inherited from the Conservatives. This exercise revealed the central dilemma in policy: between the desire to create a more predictable and essentially technical regime with a correspondingly low cost of capital, on the one hand; and to intervene more to ensure that the wider social democratic agenda on social, environmental, and other public concerns is properly taken into account, on the other. This dilemma is a powerful example of what has been described as the 'third way': take what turns out to be two apparently contradictory agendas and try to pursue them both through the same policy instrument—regulation.[2] To decide what type of reform Labour wanted depends on a prior resolution of its objectives. What was euphemistically described as 'joined-up thinking' turned out to require 'joined-up objectives', not something the Labour government found easy to resolve. It was not to be resolved by the Utilities Act, and was carried over to the 2001 Energy Policy Review. To date, no solution has been forthcoming, nor is any in prospect.

What is Wrong with British Regulation?

British regulation, from BT onwards, has had a uniquely British design, and its problems have been as much due to the context within which it has been set, as its architecture. That context is an attempt both to provide flexibility and hence an element of personal discretion; and to come up with 'clever', predictable formulae. The criticisms of British regulation reflect this context, beginning with personalization, and then turning to the flaws in RPI − X. It is, however, the interaction between the two which explains much of the disquiet about the outcome, which Labour tried to capture with its reform programme.

Personalization

British utility regulation is very much in the mould of the more general British approach to administration. It relies heavily on flexibility and discretion: each case, and each industry, is to be judged on its merits and demerits. The British approach is rarely prescriptive, and judicial review is the exception rather than the rule. Regulation is carried out by civil servants and administrative bodies, not lawyers and courts.

---

[2] There have been numerous attempts to define the third way—none of which has proved convincing.

When the gas and electricity industries were privatized, regulation was, in both cases, deemed to be a somewhat temporary affair for much of their activities. Competition would, in due course, take up the strain of ensuring that companies could not exploit market power, and, where a residual natural monopoly remained, regulation was regarded as a technical exercise. All this was consistent within Nigel Lawson's vision. In this vein, the architects did not foresee a conflict between regulation and policy. Policy, in as much as it existed, was largely focused on promoting competition. Regulators implemented policy, and hence, were given duties consistent with it. In both industries, the impact that competition and regulation would have on wider questions—such as the future of the coal industry, the environment and the development of the North Sea—was either ignored, or (in the case of coal) intentionally left to market forces after an initial transitionary period.

As a reflection of the lack of attention to the longer-term regulatory regime in gas, the general duties with regard to competition were secondary and arguably could be inconsistent with other duties. The Gas Act 1986 required the Secretary of State and the Director General of Gas Services (Gas Act 1986: Section 4(1), (2)):

to secure [authorised persons to]...satisfy all reasonable demands for gas;

to secure that such persons are able to finance the provision of gas supply services. (HMSO 1986)

And, subject to these general primary duties, to protect the interests of consumers; promote efficiency and economy; protect the public from dangers; and enable persons to compete effectively in the supply of gas in excess of 25,000 therms per year. This was amended in the Gas Act 1995, such that the regulator had to 'secure competition'.

The Electricity Act 1989 required its regulator:

to secure that all reasonable demands for electricity are satisfied;

to secure that licence holders are able to finance the carrying on of the activities which they are authorised by their licences to carry on;

to promote competition in the generation and supply of electricity (Section 3(1)). (HMSO 1989)

The electricity regulator was also required to pursue secondary duties: to protect the interests of customers in respect of prices, continuity of supply and quality; to promote efficiency and economy; to promote research; to protect the public from dangers arising from the activities of the industry; and to secure health and safety for its employees. Particular regard was to be paid to impacts on the physical environment, rural customers, pensioners, and the disabled. All these duties were held in parallel with the Secretary of State.

Contrary to the intentions to minimize regulation, the scope provided for intervention in both industries was consequentially very great—both in domain and form. Almost anything could be deemed a matter relevant to competition, and competition could conflict with all or any of the other duties. Thus, classically with the British administrative system, it depended on who had the powers to make these choices and what the relationship with government would, in practice, turn out to be. The Utilities Act 2000 would, in due course, make matters worse, both generalizing the general duties even further to the promotion of consumers' interests, and adding a whole raft of 'guidance' to which the regulator would have to have regard, alongside his existing duties.

These regulators were to be free from day-to-day politics and, hence, great play was made of their 'independence'. However, the consequence of independence for the regulator was personalization. With very general duties—which were in any event over-determined—the sort of regulation which resulted depended heavily on the character and interpretation placed upon the duties by the individual in whom they were invested. Thus James McKinnon, Stephen Littlechild, Clare Spottiswoode—and, to a lesser extent, Callum McCarthy—became public figures, and these four were to have enormous influence over the shape of the energy industries—probably more than Citrine, Hinton, Brown, Rooke, and Marshall had had in the great nationalized monopolies. Predicting the course of future regulation became very much a game of regulator watching.

The most compelling examples of personalization come from the experience of changing the people—the change from McKinnon to Spottiswoode, and from Littlechild to McCarthy. When McKinnon left office, Spottiswoode questioned the legality of the gas E factor.[3] Her resistance to intervention on social and fuel-poverty issues was much tougher. She claimed that the E factor was a 'regressive tax' and benefited the wealthy. Her approach to competition was also much more robust, and conflict over the price formula and structure of the industry was inevitable. Spottiswoode did not seek incremental change as McKinnon had done: she wanted to rewrite the whole approach.[4]

[3] In evidence to the Select Committee on the Environment (30 March 1993), she made the claim that her predecessor went beyond his powers, but then had to retract this in a letter to the Committee (7 April 1993) (House of Commons Select Committee on the Environment 1994).

[4] It was left to Tom Winsor, the Rail Regulator, appointed in 1999 to demonstrate just how wide-ranging personalized discretion could be. See Helm (2002c).

Whereas the McKinnon–Spottiswoode transition was very much one of style and aggressiveness, the Littlechild–McCarthy transition was one of more general political content. Littlechild's regulatory approach was always driven by an underlying theoretical conception of how markets work, loosely Austrian in conception. His approach has been to place faith in competitive markets, to pursue a concept of price-cap regulation which avoided detailed cost estimation and focused (in generation at least) on the number of competitors. McCarthy, by contrast, had—at least initially—accommodated much more of the New Labour energy policy, was more interventionist in his approach (see below), and allowed a re-concentration of the industry into vertically integrated blocks—something which Littlechild had opposed from the outset when Northern Electric became a target. However, over time, McCarthy gradually espoused more and more of the Littlechild agenda, supporting the programme advanced by Eileen Marshall and, in 2001, appointing Littlechild as one of his advisers.[5]

These differences can, of course, be exaggerated. All four regulators have (eventually) come to see competition as the principal weapon against incumbents (even if their understanding of what competition means has varied), and most have sought to use their powers to reduce the incumbents' market shares—although this has gradually been reversed under McCarthy, particularly in supply. But the nuances and subtleties of intervention matter greatly, and, as we shall see, contributed to the high cost of capital, and the share-price collapses at the turn of the century.

The Fixed-price Contract and *ex post* Intervention

Littlechild will probably be best remembered for having invented the RPI − X regulatory regime (DTI 1983). In tune with Littlechild's economic approach, the job of the regulation of monopoly is to mimic the market. In a competitive market, it is argued that companies are price-takers; therefore regulation should fix prices so that regulated companies' pursuit of profits is best met by minimizing costs, rather than the rate of return.

However, much of this is, at best, simplistic. The RPI − X regime is not remotely similar to the way in which prices are set in a competitive market. RPI − X does not consider the central question of the 'right' price level. Indeed, in the Austrian view, there is considerable scepticism as to

---

[5] Just how far McCarthy travelled can be seen in his June 2003 lecture to the Institute of Electrical Engineers (McCarthy, 2003), where he claimed to have deregulated supply; created the circumstances in which there was no longer any regulatory risk in generation or supply; to have reduced Ofgem's staffing levels; and that Ofgem would not intervene to prevent prices spikes. The first was true only in respect of the formal price caps; the second is false; the third disingenuous (the number of staff had *risen* before falling); and the fourth far from obvious. See chapter 22 below.

whether it could ever be known. It takes the current price level as given, and addresses what the rate of change should be, on the basis of how much money the companies need to finance their functions. A competitive market is not concerned with the particular cost structure of a company, since each is too small to influence the price through their supply functions, and hence is more concerned to adjust its costs in *response* to the prices set in the market. Furthermore, no company in a competitive market has the right to expect its customers to underwrite its costs.[6]

A further deviation from competitive markets is that RPI − X fixes prices for a *fixed period*. Firms therefore know in advance what prices will be. In a competitive market, there are regular shocks, some exogenous to the market—and, hence passed through directly to customers—and others endogenous within an industry. There is always change and, to the extent that customers buy on a spot basis, the price frequently varies. In competitive markets, contracts spread the risk of price volatility, and the term structure of contracts reflects both the appetite for risk by consumers and the fixed, sunk and variable costs of firms.

Thus, the claim that RPI − X regulation mimics a competitive market is simply wrong. Its supporters, however, have an additional, and separate, argument, which is that RPI − X is a 'high-powered' incentive mechanism, and this, they claim, is the key difference with rate-of-return regulation. Faced with fixed prices, the company maximizes profits by minimizing costs, and hence, has strong incentives to be efficient. Supporters (rightly) claim that the reductions in operating and capital costs since privatization are evidence of this effect.

The incentive turns upon the period being *fixed* in advance, in *forward-looking* price-setting. The necessary conditions for success are: that the period is long enough for shareholders to reap some of the benefits of cost efficiencies; that the base costs set at periodic reviews can distinguish between efficient and super-efficient practices; and that there is no claw-back (Helm 1994*b*). In practice, across the utilities generally, these necessary conditions have been observed more in the breach than in compliance.[7] In electricity and gas, experience has been mixed. As we saw in Chapter 11, the first five-year period for the RECs is probably the leading example of following pure RPI − X principles, but this broke down in late 1994.

---

[6] See Chapter 2 for a discussion of the Rees model, predicting that prices inherited from the public sector were likely to be too low, and Chapter 3 for the attempts to raise these price levels in the early 1980s by the first Conservative government.

[7] See, for example, Helm and Rajah (1994) detailing the within-period interventions in the water sector.

As periodic reviews have progressed, the gradual weakening of the RPI − X regime has continued, such that reviews now bifurcate into two components: the financial variables (cost of capital, regulatory asset base (RAB), and depreciation), and the ongoing revenues to carry out the functions (operating expenditure (OPEX) and capital expenditure (CAPEX)). As we shall see, the scope for further interventions in the 'fixed' period is very considerable, with regulators now anticipating formal *ex post* reviews and error-correction mechanisms.

Inconsistency between Electricity and Gas Regulation

In the energy sector, it is at least as important to get consistency *between* the different fuel sources and network supplies as it is to get the price levels right. Thus, if electricity transmission is priced on a different basis in respect of costs to that of gas transmission, the *relative* costs of generating electricity from gas at the beachhead versus transporting gas to the final market and *then* generating electricity will be distorted, and power stations will end up in the wrong places.

The regulatory regimes for gas and electricity networks were developed separately by different regulators and regulatory offices. Their agendas differed—indeed, Littlechild and Spottiswoode were later to engage in a sort of 'regulatory competition'.[8] This was reflected in different treatments of volume incentives in the National Grid Company (NGC) and Transco price formulae. Losses, geographical de-averaging, the cost of capital and depreciation all were treated differently too. And, even if the two bodies had pursued a consistent approach, which they might have done had they been merged, they started from different financial treatments of the assets at privatization. The market-to-regulatory asset ratios were different, reflecting the embedded effect of the very difficult pricing methodologies adopted in the public sector in the 1970s and 1980s.[9]

These were not mere academic niceties: the effect of the inconsistencies is now cemented into our energy systems, in terms of the location of combined-cycle gas turbines (CCGTs), some of which are almost certainly sited inefficiently. It is therefore hardly surprising that attempts to introduce more cost-effective pricing into transmission have been fraught with difficulty, and evoked strong opposition from the now incumbent

[8] Siebert and Koop (1993) develop the argument that such regulatory competition is desirable in converging on best practice. However, see Helm (1993) for a critique.

[9] Interestingly, once Offer and Ofgas were merged, the regulatory treatments of NGC and Transco's National Transmission System began to converge, most notably with the 2000 and 2001 reviews (see Chapter 18).

generators. This locational outcome is perhaps one of the clearest examples of the importance of institutional design.[10]

Policy Agenda and Politics

The final criticism of the RPI − X framework is that it fails to incorporate aspects of the public interest other than economic efficiency—that there are much broader welfare considerations, such as social and environmental, which need to be taken into account, and which arise within the five-year period.

Whereas the Conservative model envisaged the regulatory task to be one focused almost exclusively on monopoly market failures, and hence on the promotion of competition and the regulation of monopoly, Labour had a much wider social welfare function in mind. In opposition, greater emphasis was already being placed on environmental and social concerns. In adopting sustainable development, these wider considerations were bound to create a tension with the Lawsonian approach, which perceived energy as just another commodity. Whereas, for the Conservatives, energy *policy* had played a role limited to temporary fixes to bail out the coal industry and to support the costs of nuclear decommissioning, Labour would want a much more active policy framework, eventually committing itself to the elimination of fuel poverty and support of renewables and energy efficiency. It would bring to bear a range of instruments, including the windfall tax, the Climate Change Levy, the Renewables Obligation, and emissions trading. Labour would need a host of new institutions to support this more interventionist approach, expanding the Energy Saving Trust, creating a Carbon Trust, an Emissions Trading Group, and eventually entertaining reform of the departmental structures in the DTI and the Department for Environment, Food, and Rural Affairs (DEFRA).

The problem which gradually emerged, given this wider policy remit, was how the boundary between the DTI and the environment ministry in its various guises, on the one hand, and the regulatory bodies, Offer, Ofgas, and then Ofgem, on the other, would be managed. The Conservatives had deliberately created a brick wall between the two, precisely to limit intervention. Labour would need to find a way around this, and, in due course, a very unsatisfactory route was to be attempted through the guidance under the Utilities Act 2000.

---

[10] An important example of the effect of pricing on location and interconnection was the controversy over the extension of the grid over the North York moors to facilitate the Teesside plant's exports of power, to which Michael Heseltine gave provisional approval in May 1994, but which was then subject to planning inquiries.

The Conservatives' model was in practice inevitably somewhat less neatly defined than often presented. A number of duties other than promoting competition and regulating monopoly had been added from the outset, mainly as secondary duties. The relationship between primary and secondary duties was never made clear, and in practice was left to the regulators to adjudicate upon. Early environmental mechanisms included the E factor in gas and Energy Efficiency Standards of Performance (EESOPs) in electricity. Similarly, the weight given to the interests of poorer customers varied between Offer and Ofgas, and over time. Prepayment meters presented special difficulties, as did the cross-subsidies within distribution prices. In the north of Scotland, cross-subsidy was mandated from the outset.

The consequences of the lack of a clear and predictable relationship between political interests and the practice of regulation led to considerable dissonance between the two, and a widespread misunderstanding of the role of regulators. As Labour was to show, much could be achieved by gradually changing the personnel, and, by the turn of the century, a whole raft of measures had been put in place. The regulators liked to argue that policy was for Parliament, not for them, and that ministers were free to subsidize or levy taxes to meet their objectives, as long as these measures passed the European state-aids test. In practice, such measures were hamstrung by their very political visibility, and, in any event, there was nothing in economics that suggested that economic regulators should focus on only one of the multiple market failures in the energy sector. So, by concentrating on getting prices down towards private marginal costs as a remedy to monopoly, they were often in fact driving a greater wedge between the social and private marginal costs. Measures aimed at lowering prices were making the environmental misallocation of resources worse. What looked like a 'technical' economic exercise was far from that: the actions of regulators had a political dimension, weighing lower prices ahead of environmental concerns.

This is not to *blame* regulators, but rather to point out that regulation can never be purely technical. Its efficiency depends on the objectives being pursued, and a key component of the regulatory reform debate focused on what its objectives should be. But what was going badly wrong was the failure to define the trade-offs. New Labour was a broad coalition of political interests—that was one of the reasons for its outstanding electoral majorities. But that was also part of the problem: public success required that the trade-offs were not made too explicit. That, in turn, meant a shifting sand of intervention, with the private sector trying to lobby and second-guess both sides of the interface between the politicians and the regulators.

The Consequences

Regulation is not a costless activity, even if most of the costs are hard to measure. No regulatory system is perfect, and the debate about regulatory reform turns on the costs and benefits of the alternatives. The nationalized industry regime, with regulation exercised through the Treasury and its White Papers, departmental civil servants and the non-executive directors of the state monopolies had, as we saw in Chapter 2, tended to produce engineering-led solutions, white elephants in the shape of much of the nuclear programme, prices which tended to be low, and operational inefficiencies. But against this was to be set the relatively low cost of financing the great post-war expansion of electricity generation and the development of the natural gas infrastructure.

The new privatization system tended to produce the converse of the nationalized one. The impacts on operational efficiency were significant, but the cost of capital was very high. Privatized utilities in Britain turned out to have amongst the highest costs of capital of regulated utilities in the developed world. While the energy industries were, by and large, in excess supply in the 1980s and 1990s, with well-developed network assets, that may not have been too great a burden to bear. If investment was not needed, it did not much matter that it was expensive to finance. But such a happy circumstance could not continue indefinitely. New technologies would one day be needed, and networks would need to be replaced. As the Railtrack debacle in 2001/02 was to demonstrate, once investment became the priority, RPI − X was found to be a very expensive luxury, and was quickly buried in all but name.

The cost of capital is not an uncontroversial concept. Its measurement is contested, depending on the weight put upon the assumption that capital markets are efficient. It also turns upon the debate about the relative costs of equity and debt. In the early years after privatization, the dominant form of finance was equity. Over time, and in particular after the 1994/95 price review of the RECs and the arrival of the Americans (see Chapter 12), debt became a more important component of the cost of capital, sparking off a debate about the optimal gearing of utilities. It was argued (erroneously) that debt was cheaper than equity, whereas, in fact, the greater reliance on debt would gradually push the risk from the companies on to customers. The acquiring (largely American) companies boosted their earnings by buying RECs and then financed the acquisitions by mortgaging the assets to the banks. The cost of debt varied considerably over the period, reflecting changing macroeconomic conditions and the degree to which it was securitized against the assets, and in particular the RAB.

The key question with respect to the regulatory reform debate is how far these observed costs were the result of regulatory uncertainty, and how far particular reform proposals would reduce the cost of capital. If the estimates themselves are subject to debate, assigning a regulatory premium to the cost of capital is even more controversial. There have been various attempts—focusing on cross-country comparisons where different regulatory regimes operate, and event studies which try to identify positive returns around regulatory announcements (see, for example, Connine and Tamarkin 1985: Kolbe and Borucki 1998). The academic consensus is that British regulation has raised the cost of capital, but there is little agreement on how much. Theory suggests that this is likely: evidence says that it probably has.

In addition to the cost of capital effect, there is the question of the level of returns necessary to incentivize companies to reduce costs. In the RECs' case, the returns were high—indeed, by any standard, staggeringly so. As discussed in Chapter 11, in the first regulatory period, the credibility of the fixed-price, fixed-period contract was put to the test. Again, as with the cost of capital effect, whether the returns needed to be this high to maintain incentives is controversial, turning in part on an allocation of the efficiency gains between managerial efforts and developments (such as information technology) outside their control. There is no clear way of adjudicating just how large an incentive needs to be in order to induce efficiencies. But there is an obvious cost: if the rate of return exceeds the cost of capital, customers are paying a premium now for future benefits until prices are reset. By 1993, this was already leading to adverse comment; by 1997 the windfall tax would be brought in as an *ex post* correction, and in the event was easily absorbed.

A third source of regulatory cost was the stewardship of the networks and the incentives within RPI − X to reduce quality and delay investment and maintenance. While the RECs and NGC managed to make very large OPEX and CAPEX savings, there was some early dispute about whether this was at the expense of the robustness of the networks. The benign circumstances—well-invested and reinforced electricity and gas networks— meant that this was not really tested in the 1990s. By the end of the period, however, the concerns were such as to lead to a major extension of RPI − X in the form of Ofgem's Information and Incentives Project (IIP) (see Chapter 18).

Finally, there were the more nebulous costs of the regulatory regime which produced controversy, but little hard evidence. Environmentalists claimed that regulation had sacrificed the climate change agenda in pursuit of competition and lower prices. Green technologies, it was claimed, could not compete with CCGTs without an explicit recognition of the carbon content of fuels (though, as noted in Chapter 9, environmental groups were remarkably silent on the subject of coal closures in 1992/93 and 1997/98). Ever lower prices also meant that energy efficiency schemes were finding it an uphill battle. Consumer groups, particularly those with social objectives, complained that poorer customers were losing out as the promotion of competition led to cherry-picking, forcing a clearer recognition and exposure of the costs of servicing poorer customers. Finally, many on the Left pointed to the 'hollowing out' of government, with the transfer of considerable powers from government to independent regulators, claimed that a democratic deficit was opening up, and demanded greater accountability to Parliament.

These costs—the economics ones relating to the cost of capital, rate of return and prices; and the less measurable costs of network stewardship, social and environmental effects, and democratic accountability—provided the ammunition for reformers, who began to influence the debate from the early 1990s onwards. They were almost successful during the first coal crisis in 1992/93, made a major impact on Labour in opposition, and then eventually induced the Utilities Act in 2000. However, as we shall see, this was not to be the end of the matter, and the regulatory regime remains as controversial now as it was when it was set up.

Regulatory Reform under the Conservatives and the Energy Agency Proposal

The Conservative Party has always been ambivalent about regulation. In general, its ideological preconceptions mean that it is against it. Cutting back on 'red tape' and freeing business to make its own decisions are all good lines for Conservative Party conferences. To be in favour of regulation, or to preside over its growth, is not natural in the Conservative Party. It is therefore hardly surprising that, in office, the Conservatives preferred the rhetoric of liberalization and deregulation, and showed only limited interest in the *context* of regulation or the *design* of regulatory institutions. When BT was privatized, Oftel was an afterthought, and Ofgas and Offer were similarly not matters of high political interest. Getting the right 'chaps' to run them was always more important than careful attention to detail of regulatory design (see Chapter 7).[11]

It therefore came as something of a surprise for ministers to discover that when the first coal crisis erupted in 1992, the power to pass through

[11] The importance of choosing the 'right people' can be seen in Lawson's autobiography (Lawson 1992), and in Thatcher (1995). The phrase which caught on at the time, was 'one of us', to be used by Hugo Young as the title of his biography of Thatcher (Young 1989)—see Chapter 3.

(or not) extra coal costs was not in their hands, but rather in those of a reluctant Littlechild, through control of the supply price review. Energy policy seemed constrained by independent regulatory decision-making, and independent regulators might choose to stick to principles and customer interests, rather than those of the political masters who had chosen them.[12]

This 'discovery' gave rise to the first and only serious debate within the Conservative government about regulatory reform. It was the panic over the coal crisis, not the fundamentals of regulatory performance, which provoked the reconsideration. As discussed in Chapter 8, the House of Commons Select Committee on Trade and Industry, which looked into the coal crisis, considered the case for setting up an energy agency to combine Offer, Ofgas, and aspects of energy policy, and, during the crisis moments over the Christmas 1992/93 period, it was almost adopted.[13] But once Heseltine decided to toughen up the coal position, and the threat of the backbenchers to undermine the government's fragile majority receded, reform went onto the backburner.

The decline in political interest did not, however, dampen the wider debate, egged on by the continued high profits, the share-price boom, and not least Labour's proposal for a windfall tax. In retrospect, it is surprising that the Conservatives did not grasp the nettle—the new regulators had awesome powers, probably more control in practice than secretaries of the state over nationalized industries, and the regulatory regime might enable a future Labour government to exploit this power.

The debate did not, however, die at the academic level. On the contrary, it continued to ferment, through the normal academic channels, through conferences, and through Michael Beesley's Institute of Economic Affairs' annual series of seminars. In response, the Minister for Energy, Tim Eggar did consider what needed to be done, and eventually produced a speech setting out the case against reform.[14] The essence of his argument was that the reform case was not proven. In reality, there was no political will, and much political short-term benefit, in supporting fellow free-market advocates, Littlechild and Spottiswoode (who were, not surprisingly, also opposed to reform).

[12] Littlechild defended the regulatory regime against criticism from the author in April 1993 (see Littlechild 1993a).

[13] The Committee compromised by recommending an energy commission and the government weakened this to an Energy Advisory Panel. See Chapter 8.

[14] Eggar recognized that the principal set of criticisms related to discretionary authority, the 'cult of personality' and consistency—all of which had been addressed by the author in Helm (1994). Though Eggar claimed to have studied recent proposals for reform from outside critics, he concluded that 'they still haven't convinced me that the systems are fundamentally flawed' (DTI 1994). This was aimed very largely at the author.

Labour's Policies in Opposition

The utilities were a rich source of ammunition for Labour in its attacks on the Conservative government. They had all the right ingredients—the household bills directly touched the voter; fat cats were identifiable villains; and industrial customers generally wanted lower bills. Utilities dug up the roads, causing delays, and could even be blamed for the consequences of droughts and storms. And, whereas Labour had to tread carefully on matters of competition and normal markets in the name of its new 'modern' approach, it could attack monopolies and use their profits and pay to play up the perceived inequalities and greed of the Thatcherite philosophy.

The Labour opposition had more difficulty when it came to turning its general line of attack into concrete proposals for reform. Not surprisingly, there were differences in views, and these tended to reflect not only differences in analysis and the interests of trade unions, but also the political ambitions of opposition MPs vying for the key post of Minister of Energy. In the frame were Richard Caborn, Peter Hain, Kim Howells, and John Battle, who was Shadow Minister from 1995 to 1997.

The early contributions took the form of speeches and papers, with the Institute for Public Policy Research (IPPR) providing a platform. The debate had various dimensions, which can be broadly categorized into three: the stakeholders, the reformers, and the status quo. The stakeholders rejected the privatization model, arguing that private profit-maximizing incentives were incompatible with the operation of public services, particularly where these were natural monopolies. Water and rail were the prime targets. There was, however, considerable diversity of opinion within this camp. It ranged from those who wished to return to public control, to advocates of the 'mutuals' model (Holtham 1996), through to a demand for the representatives of the various stakeholders to sit on the boards of the companies.

The difference of opinion turned on whether the public interest would be best furthered by changing the sorts of people taking decisions, or by altering the incentives and constraints surrounding private companies. Much of this debate was terribly confused: advocates of stakeholding in its various guises never explained why the 'right chaps' would in practice follow the public interest, nor how the boardroom could internalize the job of government and regulators. Telling these carefully selected people to look after customers left a wide scope for their personal discretion. The analogy with mutuals elsewhere—notably the building societies—neglected a crucial difference: that building societies operated in competitive, not monopoly markets.[15]

---

[15] This muddle and confusion in the mutuals approach was to be reflected in the model adopted for Glas and for the successor to Railtrack, Network Rail.

The debate between the reformers and the supporters of the status quo had much more substance.[16] The RPI − X regime had its faults, and therefore its critics. But all parties accepted that regulation was imperfect, and, hence, the issue turned on whether there were practical proposals which might improve performance, and particularly lower the cost of capital. The main proposals put forward in the pre-election period were for reforms of the institutional architecture and of the duties of regulators, and changes to the price-cap mechanism. In the energy sector, these boiled down to a merger of Offer and Ofgas; the reforms of the primary duties away from the over-whelming emphasis on promoting competition and financing functions towards a broader (Labour) agenda of customer and social interests (and, for some, environmental duties too); and adjustments between RPI − X fixed periods and elements of error correction, particularly in respect of CAPEX.

The regulatory initiative at the IPPR was led by Dan Corry, who sub-sequently became Margaret Beckett's political adviser at the DTI, and remained in this role under Peter Mandelson and Stephen Byers, seeing through the Utilities Act.[17] Corry transferred to the Department of Transport, Local Government and the Regions with Byers after the 2001 election, resigning with his minister in 2002.[18]

There were three main publications by the IPPR ahead of the 1997 election: *Regulating our Utilities* (Corry et al. 1994), *Regulating in the Public Interest: Looking to the Future* (Corry 1995a), and *Profiting from the Utilities: New Thinking on Regulatory Reform* (Corry 1995b). In the 1994 publication, the thinking was wide-ranging and reflected very great uncertainty as to which path should be followed. The first paper (by Corry) embraced the idea of a predominantly market-driven approach, but with the frame-work set by government. David Souter (Souter 1994) espoused the stake-holder approach, then at the height of fashion within Labour circles, while a more perceptive Michael Waterson predicted that, in electricity and gas: 'regulation of the key monopoly elements will come to resemble rate of return regulation' (1994: 118). He also recognized that there was a case for 'removing certain core elements of the regulated industries into public hands again', on coordination grounds and to control monopoly power. For Waterson, 'the most obvious candidates are the National Grid and its equivalent in gas' (ibid.: 120). It was yet to be realized how much control remained in public hands once ownership had been surrendered, and the extent to which the system operator functions of NGC and the gas

---

[16] See, for example, Hansard Society 1997.

[17] Other key IPPR players included, notably, Patricia Hewitt, who was a deputy director, and Gerry Holtham.

[18] See also Corry (2003) for a retrospective account of Labour's approach once in government.

National Transmission System would become instruments of regulatory discretion (see Chapters 18 and 21).

In the 1995*a* paper, Corry set the scene for the gradual placing of regulation within a policy-driven framework, endorsing the views he had put forward, notably in 'The Regulatory State', BBC, 20/10/94. There would need to be institutional reform, and almost all the themes which were to emerge in the Green Paper in 1998 (DTI 1998) were already in place. It remained for Tony Blair to put his seal of approval on the reform agenda in the IPPR report, itself the product of a scene-setting conference. Blair claimed that:

There is evident public discontent about the levels of profits being reported by many regulated companies and a widespread perception that the companies are being run only in the interests of their shareholders and top executives and are insufficiently sensitive to the needs of customers. (Blair 1995: 2)

In the same IPPR report, the author set out a five-point reform programme (Helm 1995), comprising a profit-sharing mechanism to replace $RPI - X$; a more flexible CAPEX mechanism; the merger of Offer and Ofgas; common methodologies on such matters as the cost of capital across the utilities; and the creation of an appeals mechanism distinct from the Monopolies and Mergers Commission (MMC).

Labour in Power and the Windfall Tax

Labour won the general election with a massive majority and the concomitant high expectations that went with it. But it had achieved its stunning victory by creating a very broad church of support and in particular on a very moderate manifesto. Labour in power had to live with the Conservative inheritance. Renationalization was ruled out as too expensive and, in any event, the legacy of the Clause 4 debate made it politically undesirable. It therefore had to build on the work on reform begun while in opposition. The manifesto committed Labour to 'recognize the need for open and predictable regulation which is fair both to consumers and to shareholders and at the same time provides incentives for managers to innovate and improve efficiency' (Labour 1997: 16). Labour would 'promote competition wherever possible' (p. 15).

None of this spelt radical reform. But Labour's first action was a windfall tax: a 'one-off levy on the excess profits of the privatized utilities', which would fund its 'ambitious programme' to 'attack unemployment and break the spiral of escalating spending on social security' (Labour 1997: 19). This direct hypothecation to Labour's New Deal was the result of the intense controversy at the election about tax, which had forced Labour to guarantee not to raise either the basic or higher rate of income tax, and to bind itself to the Conservatives' spending plans. Hence, these labour market programmes needed a direct hypothecated source of funding, and the utilities provided an ideal *political* target.

This was set out by John Prescott, on 21 November 1996, to Parliament:

the privatised utilities were sold off cheaply, weakly regulated and allowed to make excess profits. Labour plans to raise a levy to help put the unemployed of Britain back to work, because we believe that that is social justice. (HC Deb. col. 1129)

The general idea proved hard to translate into a precise, legally watertight, definition. The new American owners were particularly aggressive in plans to head off the tax, using the offices of the US Ambassador. Eventually, however, the Treasury came up with a formula.[19] This was set out by the Inland Revenue on 2 July 1997:

The Chancellor today announced the introduction of the proposed windfall tax on the excess profits of the privatised utilities. The one-off tax will apply to companies privatised by flotation and regulated by statute. The tax will be charged at a rate of 23 per cent on the difference between company value, calculated by reference to profits over a period of up to four years following privatization and the value placed on the company at the time of flotation. The expected yield is around 5.2 billion pounds. (Inland Revenue, press release, 2 July 1997)

The complexity of the formula reflected the desire on the part of the government to capture all the utilities, and avoid legal challenge.[20] But it was not quite what it seemed: as we saw in Chapter 11, there is little evidence from the first-day premia that the utilities were in fact sold off too cheaply, and the reason for the 'excess' profits arose from a combination of

---

[19] $WT = [\pi(p_e - V_0)]t$, where WT = windfall tax; π = average post-tax profits over the first four years after privatization; p_e = price–earnings ratio; V_0 = flotation value; t = tax rate.

[20] The energy companies were charged as follows:

Company	£m	Company	£m
Eastern Electricity	111.5	National Power	261.0
East Midlands Electricity	95.9	PowerGen	201.3
London Electricity	140.1	Scottish Power	91.9
Manweb	97.0	Scottish Hydro-Electric	43.4
Midlands Electricity	134.2	Northern Ireland Electricity	52.3
Northern Electric	118.4	British Energy	0
NORWEB	155.4	British Gas	708.5
SEEBOARD	109.8		
Southern Electric	165.5		
SWALEC	89.7		
South West Electricity	97.0		
Yorkshire Electricity	134.6		

numerous factors: weak regulation, the 1990–3 recession, the application of information technology, and management initiatives, among others.[21]

The confusion extended to the incidence of the taxes, too. It was claimed that the burden of the tax would be paid by shareholders only, and not by customers. This was, at best, misleading. The companies paid the tax by raising debt—they borrowed to finance the payments. Gearing increased, reducing the scope of balance sheets to be stretched for investment, and eventually they would be exhausted earlier than would otherwise be the case. That, in turn, meant that customers would be paying for current investment sooner.

But the real effect was on the cost of capital. If governments could step in to claw back the profits which the companies claimed were due to efficiencies, then political risk which companies had little power to control was in effect being transferred to shareholders. As Railtrack's shareholders in due course would learn, utilities could be high-risk activities.

The windfall tax was, under these circumstances, a bad tax. It undermined incentives, by providing a claw-back. It raised regulatory uncertainty and thus the cost of capital. It taxed current shareholders, not necessarily those who had reaped the benefits—especially in the case of the US companies which had made their acquisitions after 1995. If the rationale was lax regulation then the right answer was a price cut, since the implication was that customers had paid too much. To open the regulatory reform agenda with a tax hypothecated to an unrelated area of public expenditure was a poor start.

The Beckett Review and the Green Paper

Expectations that Labour would engage in serious regulatory reform were further dampened when Margaret Beckett, the new Secretary of State for Trade and Industry, announced in June 1997 that there would be a review of regulation, rather than immediate reform. Some saw this as an attempt to move the utilities off the political agenda once the political heat had been dissipated through the windfall tax. Others ranked regulatory reform alongside a host of other areas where policy reviews were announced in the early days of the New Labour government, and as an attempt to think through the necessary changes. Probably both factors

---

[21] For estimates of the returns to privatized companies, see Jenkinson and Mayer (1994) and Chennells (1997). See also Robinson (2000, Chapter 6) for a detailed account of how the Treasury team put the tax together, and the problems of making sure British Gas was caught in the net.

played a part, and in any event the DTI's legislative timetable for the autumn of 1997 prioritized the minimum wage and the Competition Bill.

The objectives and terms of reference of the Beckett review gave an insight into the government's wide ambitions for what turned out to be an irreconcilable set of conflicting interests.

The Government's objective for the review is to set a long term stable framework for utility regulation which is seen as fair by all the interest groups involved, particularly by consumers. Without fairness, there can be no long term stability. We want the regulatory framework to deliver value, quality and choice to consumers while providing incentives to managers to innovate and compare efficiency. The guiding principles must be transparency, consistency and predictability of regulation.

The terms of reference for the review are to consider whether changes are required to the system of regulation of the utility industries, in order to ensure open and predictable regulation, fair to all consumers and stakeholders, and which promote the Government's objectives for the environment and sustainable development, whilst providing sufficient incentives to managers to innovate, raise standards and improve efficiency. (DTI 1998a: Annex A, p. 59)

This reflected the all-inclusive nature of the new coalition of interests upon which Labour's landslide victory was based. All the parties had to be winners: there were no losers, no hard choices which regulatory reform would confront.

The review led to a flurry of activity amongst the utilities, the regulators and those involved in environmental and social matters. It revealed what an industry regulation had become. Companies wanted as little reform as possible, and, where necessary, for it to bear down on regulatory risk created by the power and personal discretion of the regulators. Offer and Ofgas might be happy to merge, but otherwise wanted to keep government out—particularly from environmental and social interests. The Department of the Environment, Transport, and the Regions (DETR) wanted its sustainable development ambitions properly recognized, and to bring the regulators to heel. With John Prescott as Secretary of State, and Michael Meacher as Minister, the DETR felt powerful enough to push its case hard. Finally, consumer groups wanted an explicit commitment to their own agenda. Against such lobbies, the small voice of academics and independent critics had little weight, and, in any event, some, like David Currie, were highly defensive of the status quo (Currie 1998: 2–10).

The Green Paper, 'A Fair Deal for Consumers: Modernizing the Framework for Utility Regulation', took nine months to appear (in March 1998, DTI 1998a). It contained forty-two recommendations, the most important of which were: a single primary duty to protect consumer interests; the issuing of statutory guidance on social and environmental objectives; environmental and social policy implementation with significant financial implications should be via specific legal provision, not guidance; an administrator function in energy network businesses to deal with bankruptcy or loss of licence; the merger of Offer and Ofgas; the separate licensing of supply and distribution businesses; social action plans; and boards rather than individual regulators. With the exception of the electricity administrator, all of these were eventually implemented, though not before a long and tortuous path had been followed.

The Utilities Act 2000

After the Green Paper, the DTI's regulatory reform programme drifted throughout 1998 and 1999. In early 1999, rumours circulated that No. 10 was losing any enthusiasm it had for legislation on utility reform. Thought was given to whether a White Paper would be enough (Helm 1999). The Competition Act 1998 gave considerable new powers to regulators. DTI officials therefore had to work hard to make a case for a Utilities Bill in the 1999 Queen's Speech.

Having failed to entirely convince either No. 10 or Beckett, now Leader of the Commons, the DTI shifted its ground from the Green Paper agenda towards its review of electricity trading arrangements (RETA). This had been endorsed in the 1998 White Paper on energy sources (DTI 1998*b*) (see Chapter 16). The DTI dressed up the Utilities Bill case with the argument that, since RETA had been blessed by the White Paper and required legislation, *therefore* legislation was essential. Whether or not the argument stood up, it must have helped to convince those in charge of the legislative timetable, and a slot was duly found for what was now a curious hybrid of utility reform and RETA.

There followed one of the worst examples of poor drafting in recent times. The bill was originally drafted to include telecommunications and water as well as electricity and gas. However, the telecommunications companies revolted, and the DTI caved in, withdrawing it from the bill entirely (to be resurrected in the proposals for the Office of Communications, Ofcom). Water, too, was withdrawn, reflecting the lack of enthusiasm at the DETR. That left only energy, and the Utilities Bill from then on was a *de facto* energy bill. Even this drastic pruning was not enough: at the committee stage around 500 amendments were introduced. Officials privately put some of the failures down to key officials suffering flu over the January 2000 period, but in reality the DTI bill team lacked sufficient resources, and utility experience and expertise, to handle such complex and technical matters.

The bill received Royal Assent in 2000, after the periodic reviews of 1999/2000. Its provisions (outside what has now become known as NETA) did little to address *any* of the fundamental concerns which had prompted the debate in the mid-1990s. It created even greater discretion through the vague overarching consumer-protection duty. Consumers might have been 'put at the heart of regulation', but just exactly what their needs might be was left undefined. Regulatory risk did not fall—indeed, it probably increased. The guidance added a new layer of intervention, but without clarity of purpose or clear financing of its requirements. Indeed, it took until July 2002 for the statutory guidance to be issued in its final draft form (DTI 2002c)—the initial draft, issued in February 2000 (DTI 2000b), having contained a whole host of policies, including notably the sustainable development White Paper (DETR 1999), the fuel-poverty strategy (DETR/DTI 2001), renewables and much else besides. Thus, contrary to the DTI's own regulatory appraisal—which had claimed that 'the cumulative effect of these "better regulation" reforms should help to produce a more certain regulatory regime leading to a lower risk premium being demanded by investors and a lower cost of capital for the companies concerned' (DTI, 2000a: para 11, p. 7)—the Utilities Act 2000 actually made the regime less predictable and probably raised the cost of capital. Not surprisingly, the DTI's appraisal offered no evidence whatsoever to support its claim.[22]

The net effect was to reinforce the flight from equity which had started in the late 1990s. Equity owners faced increased risk and lower returns, and opted to sell out to securitization opportunities and place greater reliance on debt finance. The separation of distribution and supply facilitated this further—with supply vertically integrating with generation, whilst asset owners merged horizontally. In the end, the Utilities Act allowed Labour greater scope to pursue its multiple, social democratic goals without specifying the trade-offs, and Ofgem (as it became) to complete its NETA and unbundling agenda. As we shall see, none of the fundamental underlying problems was thereby solved, and a further Energy Act would be the inevitable consequence. Only when a proper framework for energy policy had been put in place could guidance be given. The DTI seemed to have forgotten the debate in opposition, which Corry had led. Not surprisingly, therefore, energy just refused to go off the political agenda.

---

[22] The Better Regulation Task Force was to highlight the continuing problem of the regulatory regime in a highly critical report in 2001 (BRTF 2001).

16

Energy Sources, Diversity, and Long-term Security of Supply

Doublethink means the power of holding two contradictory beliefs in one's mind simultaneously, and accepting both of them. (George Orwell, *1984*)

While Labour's regulatory reform programme was widely advertised in advance of the 1997 general election, few anticipated that, within a year of coming to office, it would introduce a moratorium on new gas-fired power stations to aid what was left of the coal industry. Labour's renunciation of Clause 4 had presaged an assumption that the expiry of the 1993–8 coal contracts would be the end of the matter, save perhaps for some help over health claims and redundancy terms. Labour might have wanted to slow down the introduction of domestic competition—and, as we have seen, there were some good reasons for doing so—but distorting the market to the degree of interfering in the choice and level of new investment appeared to be a step back into old Labour's past, not something to be expected of the new Blairite party.

Labour's coal crisis and its solution marked the end of the full-blooded Lawson approach to the energy market. Whereas Nigel Lawson had regarded supply and demand to be matters for the market, Labour's foray into licensing policy set it on a course back towards a more activist approach to energy policy more generally. In choosing to pick out the cheapest and (in fossil-fuel terms) the cleanest fuel source for a moratorium, in setting a 10 per cent market share for renewables, and in engineering new coal contracts, the government began to manage capacity. This was not deliberate, but the fix by which Peter Mandelson sought to get over an immediate political problem led to a series of consequences which drove the government into more and more intervention. Each problem was treated largely in isolation, but the trend was clear. Even the laudable attempt to use market mechanisms to aid its climate change strategy ended up with a tax on energy which did not discriminate between carbon and non-carbon fuel sources—for fear of taxing the dirtiest fuel, coal—and the Emissions Trading Scheme which excluded electricity generation, for the same reason.

The muddle and confusion which Labour created in its energy policy began with its ambivalence to competition in opposition. Once in power, the coal crisis began to break in autumn 1997, as the deadline for the expiry of the 1993–8 contracts approached. In April 1998, Mandelson and Geoffrey Robinson, a Treasury Minister, tried—and failed—to do a corporatist 'deal' with the main generators. The crisis rumbled on through the summer of 1998, as Mandelson, having moved from Minister without Portfolio to Secretary of State for Trade and Industry, attempted to put a pro-competition spin on an anti-competition policy to be set out in the White Paper on Energy Sources (DTI 1998b). Stephen Byers, his successor at the Department of Trade and Industry (DTI), then attempted to implement the White Paper. It is a policy episode rich in political strategy, and provides an insight into the interactions between the politics and economics of energy policy.

Labour's Ambivalence to Competition in Opposition

Labour's historical roots lie in monopoly and state ownership. As we saw in Chapter 2, the Labour government in 1945–51 transformed the energy sector, creating the great state monopolies which were responsible for developing the modern electricity and gas industries. At its peak the Central Electricity Generating Board (CEGB) delivered a 7 per cent annual growth rate in capacity, managed the nuclear programme and ensured security of supply. The National Coal Board dug the coal, and the National Union of Mineworkers (NUM) provided a link with the very origins of the Labour Party and the bitter class struggles of the 1930s. Labour, too, could claim credit for the ways in which British Gas built out the National Transmission System, and North Sea oil has been developed. There was, to Labour traditionalists, much to applaud from the nationalized industries' record.[1]

In the long opposition years after 1979, Labour had naturally sided against the Lawson policy agenda. Traditional Labour saw the miners as the target of Thatcherite anti-union policies, and those of a more moderate persuasion were forced to back the miners, even if they balked at embracing Arthur Scargill's rhetoric and tactics. Labour opposed the privatization of both the gas and electricity industries. It argued against break-up of the CEGB, and supported a further deal for coal in the 1992/93 coal crisis. This opposition was carried through by a succession

---

[1] Economists, too, could see the merits of public ownership. In contributing to the Labour utility reform debate, Waterson made the point (Waterson 1994: 120). See Chapter 15.

of energy spokesmen, and included many who were still key players in the second term—from John Prescott, to Tony Blair and Martin O'Neill.[2]

Domestic competition proved a thorny political problem. To be 'against choice' was difficult, and, indeed, the Conservative government was keen to exploit this dilemma for Labour in the run-up to the election. For this reason, Labour had not voted against the second reading of the Gas Bill in September 1995. And when it came to electricity, much of the information technology expenditure was already in place, and a number of the companies had committed themselves to a positive endorsement of the plan. However, there was little doubt that the 1998 electricity programme was not proceeding according to plan, and hence, by the time of the election, there was little chance of meeting the transition timetable. To complicate matters, there was the important matter of the regulators, who were strongly disposed towards delivery.

In the event, Labour proved more enthusiastic than expected, and shortly after the election, John Battle, Energy Minister, was meeting with the regulators and taking responsibility for the timetable: 'the letters will end up on my desk so that's where the buck stops.'[3] This was a politically very risky strategy which he was lucky not to regret. With the endorsement of domestic competition, and regulatory reform at least temporarily kicked into touch by Margaret Beckett's 'review', the energy sector was set to drop off the political agenda, much as the leading political strategists wanted. New Labour's priorities were elsewhere—with health and education—not with the utilities. It was then that the coal crisis broke.

The Coal Crisis Breaks

At the end of December 1997, John Prescott was enjoying playing on the international stage at Kyoto. The Deputy Prime Minister was better known at the time for his domestic role as the guarantor of the Left's support for the Blair government, but his vast new department, combining environment, transport, and regional policy, gave him the international role at the crucial Kyoto round of negotiations on greenhouse gas targets. Even after the DETR empire was broken up, Prescott retained responsibility for international aspects of climate change at the Cabinet Office after the 2001 election. With sustainable development an important component of Labour's election manifesto, Prescott took a leading role at

[2] From 1987, the Shadow Ministers were John Prescott (1987–8); Tony Blair (1988–9); Frank Dobson (1989–92); Martin O'Neill (1993–5); and John Battle (1995–7).
[3] Quoted in *Energy Utilities*, OXERA, July 1997, 10.

Kyoto in pushing (unsuccessfully) the United States towards agreement. Conveniently, because of the dash for gas in the early 1990s, and because the Kyoto targets were for a basket of greenhouse gases and not just CO_2, a very green line could be taken without too serious consequences at least for Labour's first, and probably its second, term of office. And, in any event, the eventual Kyoto target was bound to be soft in comparison with the 1997 Labour Manifesto pledge to reduce CO_2 emissions by 20 per cent from their 1990 levels by 2010.

But a newly green Prescott was also the standard-bearer of the Left, and he owed his position to his support as its champion and his ability to keep the Left on board with the Blair project, which at that stage had proportional representation and ever closer links with the Liberal Democrats firmly in mind. For Blair, Prescott was indispensable. He could tell the first Labour conference after the 1997 election victory that Railtrack could not be renationalized because it would 'make the fat cats even fatter', and, in time, he might be needed to sell even more unpalatable policies to the traditional wing of the party. But to do this he sometimes had to deliver too, and it is in this role that he played a key part in the coal crisis.

Six months after the landslide election victory in May 1997, the Left felt able to begin to flex its muscles, and two issues happened to crop up which met this political requirement: welfare support for lone parents and coal. Both had deep emotional resonance with core Labour values, and both opened the prospect of rebellion. Almost immediately, the key politicians realized that coal was the important one. With the imminent expiry of the 1993–8 coal contracts which had held up both the price and the quantity of coal purchased by the generators, the coal industry faced a further contraction. Events rapidly unfolded, as first Richard Caborn and then Mandelson jumped into the debate. Caborn, as Prescott's long-term ally, and Minister for the Regions at the DETR, took up the issue whilst Prescott was in Kyoto, and Mandelson, at that point Minister without Portfolio, was pictured going down a coal mine. In the early days of Blair's government, Mandelson was a key bell wether of political significance.

The critical point which this discussion illustrates is that the coal crisis was first and foremost a *political* issue which had very little to do with economics. The case for supporting the miners through a major distortion in the energy market was never strong, and, indeed, as we shall see, the mistake of intervention was compounded greatly by the form of distortion needed to present the intervention in a (politically) favourable light. The facts of the case are remarkably simple. First, the scale of the problem was limited to around 5,000 workers in 6–10 pits. These totals were bound to go down, but there was a minimum which would survive the full force of the market. Although the pound was relatively strong, encouraging import substitution, many of the power stations were built in locations which assumed domestic supplies.

Furthermore, although the generators had invested in the early years after privatization in import terminals, the scale was not sufficient to effect an immediate shift, and the 1993–8 contracts had squeezed out this source of supply. The threat from imports was therefore somewhat exaggerated. What the coal industry faced in 1998 was not a collapse, but rather a cut-back followed by the uncertainty of shorter-term contracts.

If the numbers involved were relatively small, so too were the immediate effects on security of supply of the contraction in domestic coal production. The coal would not go away, and the economic issue was really about the costs of keeping uneconomic pits on standby versus the costs of sinking new shafts at some future date and holding stocks in reserve of other fossil fuels. Miners at the time argued that once a pit was closed, it was lost forever.[4] This was reminiscent of the sorts of argument about the impossibility of deep-water drilling in the North Sea two decades earlier. The fact that the technology to dig new holes was not up and running was largely a function of the complete absence of demand for it. If oil and gas prices rose sharply in the future, and if supplies were threatened with interruption, then it might be economic for new mining techniques to be developed. In any event, a threat to *physical* supplies was unlikely to be sudden: the North Sea had storage potential, there was always Norway, and oil stocks were available.

Not that any evidence could be provided that there was an immediate threat to gas supplies. At the end of the 1990s, gas supplies in Europe were probably more secure than at the beginning of the decade. The gas network had become more interconnected, and, in particular, Britain had a direct link to the Continent, and Norwegian reserves were better explored, and, to a certain extent, developed. Supplies appeared relatively secure even in the absence of a full flow from Russia. Over the relevant time period for the building of new power stations, or opening up of old pits, there was no apparent problem.[5] The risks to supply were less physical than price-based.

There were other aspects of security of supply which the coal lobby failed to take into account. The first was the distinction between security gained from fuel diversity and that gained from *British* supplies. The closure of coal

---

[4] See debate in *The Times* (Helm 1997; Callaghan 1997).
[5] The Performance and Innovation Unit report argued that there was little risk of either a shortage of gas supplies or interruptions to them (PIU 2002). Where the problems really lay were in the network infrastructure and in long-term contracts (see Chapter 21).

pits did not close off the coal option; it merely reduced the British supply. There is no shortage of world coal, and, unlike oil and gas, coal reserves are diversely distributed, much in friendly countries. The second was the distinction between fuel source diversity and power station diversity. Multi-fuel power stations could provide a flexibility which single-fuel ones could not. Combined-cycle gas-turbine (CCGT) technology could in theory be multi-fuel, and one possible response would have been to support a bias for this sort of CCGT technology. Third, there was the prospect of new technologies. Diversity could be boosted not just by balancing coal, nuclear, and gas, but by investing in solar, fuel cells, hydrogen and wave power. While renewables appeared expensive compared with gas, once account had been taken of coal's environmental problems, it was not obvious that coal was cheaper than wind. There were also energy efficiency and demand-side measures. On environmental grounds, nuclear might even be competitive.

Notwithstanding that it was very hard to conclude that an economic case could be made for intervention to protect the coal industry, for political reasons the DTI made its best efforts to present one. Armed with a very helpful and convenient letter from the National Grid Company (NGC),[6] which expressed its concern about the growth of gas-fired generation and the implications of this for system stability,[7] the DTI set up a wide-ranging formal 'Review of Energy Sources from Power Generation' in December 1997, which would buy it time, and provide the context in which a moratorium on new gas-fired plant could be introduced.

The right economic path would have been to let the coal industry contract towards a more competitive level. It does not follow that a completely unconstrained licensing policy should have been continued, but that is not necessarily connected to the coal issue. Analysis and empirical evidence have not, however, typically been allowed to stand in the way of political necessity, and it was hardly surprising therefore that Mandelson (with the help of Paymaster General, Geoffrey Robinson) set about concocting a deal in much the same way that Tim Eggar and Michael Heseltine did in 1992. In both cases, the initial deal failed, but not until it had created a number of additional difficulties which proved hard to resolve.

The Mandelson–Robinson Deal

In attempting to solve the coal crisis, Mandelson and Robinson began with much optimism. Unencumbered by a detailed knowledge of the way

[6] Letter to John Battle from David Jones, NGC, 1 December 1997.

[7] The NGC was to be curiously quiet about these issues when the PIU came to investigate these matters again in 2001.

in which the market now worked,[8] and, in particular, the problems that a competitive energy market would pose for implementing any deal, the two politicians were encouraged by the positive response they received from at least some quarters in the industry. Their very approach suggested that they had not fully appreciated that a competitive supply market failed to provide a base on to which costs could easily be passed. Whereas, as we saw in Chapter 8, Heseltine could eventually rely on Littlechild to pass through the 1993–8 coal contracts to the supply price cap in the captured market, that crutch was no longer available.

The key to any *political* bargain is to provide pay-offs to the participants. If the government was to reconcile support for the coal industry with a competitive market, it had to achieve this by ensuring that there were no obvious losers. Because the electricity industry was privatized, it had to 'persuade' the participants to 'agree' to its political solution, without unduly upsetting either the regulator or the customers. Resignations, public rejections, and criticisms were to be avoided. In Labour's very broad coalition, everyone had to be a winner—or at least not too explicitly a loser. In the coal case, RJB Mining had an obvious interest in new contracts. As we saw in Chapter 9, one of the possible explanations as to why RJB Mining bid much more than its rivals at privatization was a different estimate of the residual post-1998 value. RJB had assumed rightly that Labour would not stand idly by while coal collapsed. It also had the stick of redundancy payments to miners (the enhanced terms carried over from the nationalized industry were due to end in 1998).[9] But Richard Budge, as head of RJB Mining, was not politically popular with New Labour, and the government had no desire to allow a windfall to come his way.[10] Hence, whilst government might support higher volumes, it was less keen on keeping up the price. Indeed, a *fall* in electricity prices was a continuing underlying objective. The generators were more difficult. On the one hand, PowerGen wanted to be able to vertically integrate by buying a REC, and that needed DTI support to avoid a Monopolies and Mergers Commission (MMC) reference. On the other hand, National Power claimed (at least initially) not to be interested in RECs, and hence had no

---

[8] By this time the Energy Directorate in the DTI was also much weaker than it had been during the Eggar/Heseltine exercise in 1992/93, when much of the old Department of Energy expertise still existed.

[9] For this reason, RJB had an incentive to play the negotiations 'long' and allow the politics to develop as the deadline approached.

[10] See House of Commons Select Committee on Trade and Industry fourth report on Coal: 'The commercial judgement and negotiating tactics of RJB are open to question', quoted in the 1998 White Paper, para 11.4, p. 104 (DTI 1998*b*).

need to bargain with government. It also had no desire to be lumbered with costs that it could not pass on. (As often had been the case in the past, it was to switch tack in the light of both PowerGen's success and government pressures, as we shall see below.)

Early on, therefore, the ministers' tactics were focused on the objective of getting National Power to play ball on the assumption that PowerGen would comply. For this, it used the carrot-and-stick approach. The carrot was to ban gas entry; the stick was to place the blame for coal's decline at the door of the generators' market power. And, in this approach, the seeds of the White Paper were sown. By April, a deal was almost ready for Cabinet, and was due to be discussed in April, but at the last—and critical—minute Blair went to Northern Ireland, and the opportunity passed.

In the meantime, several factors delayed the process. Presentation was not quite right, and, with Mandelson's move to the DTI in July 1998, he took it upon himself to develop the policy intervention into a broader statement of energy policy. There was also the regulator to be squared. A ban on gas entry could hardly be welcome, given how much regulatory capital had been invested in increasing entry in the 1990s and trying to reduce the market share of National Power and PowerGen. But the prizes of the 1998 liberalization and NETA were of considerable value too, and acquiescence on the new arrangements may have been part of the implicit understanding. In any event, the regulatory setback of the gas moratorium would be temporary, whereas the loss of 1998 (in the early discussions) or NETA might have been permanent.

Spinning the White Paper

The White Paper, published in October 1998, is a curious document when read as a policy statement (DTI 1998b). It is rather best seen as an answer in search of a rationale. It begins with an attempt to state what the objectives of energy policy are:

The Government's central energy policy objective is to ensure secure, diverse and sustainable supplies of energy at competitive prices. (para 2.2, p. 5)

The government, the White Paper goes on to say, has 'three main roles': to 'set the framework'; 'provide for regulation in the consumer interest', and '*monitor* the wider public interest' [italics added] (para 2.4). Quite what all this means, why prices are part of the objective, and why the public interest is something to be monitored, rather than the central objective, is far from clear, and we will return to this below.

Mandelson's White Paper then proceeds to set out the central argument. There is, it claims, a case to support the coal industry, but it is only a temporary one. Coal has, the White Paper argues, been unfairly penalized by the activities of the generators. Their dominance has been exploited through higher prices than justified by coal costs. These prices have sucked in entrants, and thereby caused the artificial dash for gas which is claimed to be the source of coal's problems in 1998. But whereas bygones are bygones—in the sense that the gas plant now generating is a *fact* in the market—the generators' continued dominance will suck in yet more new gas plant. Hence the need to create a level playing field by dealing with market power, and the excuse for the temporary ban on further gas-fired plant.

To create this level playing field, the White Paper proposed two solutions: divestment of plant by PowerGen and National Power, and reform of the Pool. Together these policies were designed to produce a significant fall in wholesale prices—'at least 10 per cent in real terms and possibly more can be expected in the medium term' (para 2.55, p. 16), which presumably would scupper excess new investment, whilst maintaining a revenue stream for the coal industry to keep output up. Once all this had been done, the moratorium could be lifted and a return to the market approach would be reasserted. As the White Paper put it:

The policy will be short-term, temporary and aimed specifically at protecting diversity and security of supply while the distortions in the market are removed, so that the final result is a competitive market that can operate more vigorously and effectively. (para 2.43, p. 12)

This still left the tricky bit about sustainable development. Energy policy was now supposed to be green. As the White Paper put it:

It is important to ensure that these proposals are consistent with sustainable development, which is at the heart of the Government's energy policy, and in particular the Government's environmental targets on greenhouse gases. (para 2.47, p. 14)

Hence, lending support to a dirty fuel source such as coal whilst acting against a cleaner source such as gas required some additional spin. Here, again, Mandelson's White Paper excelled. Having stated the importance of greenhouse gases, the White Paper then *ignores* the implications of supporting coal for the CO_2 problem in its summary and concentrates on sulphur dioxide (SO_2) instead. It argued that the SO_2 problems associated with coal were better addressed by fitting flue-gas desulphurization equipment, and every major generator was now expected to fit one (para 2.51, p. 15).

As the White Paper tries to wriggle off the CO_2 hook, it makes some remarkable claims. For example:

the issue is not...simply whether we should use gas or coal for power generation, but about a range of measures which, in the medium to longer term, can reduce greenhouse gas emissions cost-effectively across the whole economy. (para 9.15, p. 72)

Sir Humphrey would have been proud of this: the choice is widened to a range of measures, the time horizon is stretched to the medium to longer term, cost-effectiveness is introduced, and the whole economy is to be considered for good measure. The fact, however, could not be escaped: protecting coal worsened pollution, and increased CO_2 emissions.[11] Such an argument would not do for the wider air pollution problems of coal, and therefore if coal could not be presented as green, the definition of sustainable development had to be altered to make it compatible with coal. Fortuitously, this had already been done. Whereas sustainable development in the late 1980s was understood to be about the environment, John Major's government had widened the definition to include economic growth (to take account of the politics of the early 1990s' recession) (Department of the Environment 1990). Labour added in the social dimension as well, to create the most plastic of definitions for policy purposes. As Mandelson's White Paper stated, sustainable development now meant: 'social progress which recognizes the needs of everyone'; 'effective protection of the environment'; 'prudent use of natural resources'; and 'maintenance of high and stable levels of economic growth and employment' (DTI 1998*b*: para 9.1, p. 69). It was a simple step to suggest that, in the case of coal, the social and economic development components outweighed the environmental (see Helm 1998), though no cost–benefit analysis nor indeed any empirical evidence was ever presented to support this dubious claim.

In the history of energy policy, the White Paper is one of the best examples of the triumph of spin over substance. It reconciled the irreconcilable, and did it in a sufficiently plausible way that many with only a passing familiarity with the history of the sector believed it. It was perfect 'double think'—perfect in the sense that it was hardly noticed in broader political and public debate.[12]

---

[11] Even the 'Review of the Case for Government Support for Cleaner Coal Technology Demonstration Plant' in December 2001, which provided a comprehensive review of the technological options, was forced to conclude that higher efficiencies would have only a limited effect in reducing CO_2 emissions, and that CO_2 capture and storage technologies would be required (DTI 2001*c*: para 11).

[12] Interestingly, Mandelson's other main contribution at the DTI was the 'solution' to problems at the Post Office—creating 'commercial freedom', but keeping the Post Office in the public sector. This also proved all too temporary, as the Post Office lurched into crisis in 2002.

To make Mandelson's fix 'work', a host of ancillary changes had to be made. The White Paper supported the radical reform of the energy trading market, and, with it, the market institutions and the functions of NGC. It introduced an active licensing policy, and a requirement to change that policy over time as the Pool reforms kicked in. It created a whole ambit of environmental consequences which constrained the options for achieving the greenhouse gas and CO_2 targets. As we shall see, far from being a package of solutions to the diagnosed problems, which could be quickly and effectively implemented, and then 'normality' would be resumed, the White Paper started a process for which there is no obvious end and, indeed, sucked government further down the interventionist path.

Unfinished Business

Once Labour had endorsed full retail competition, it was committed to living with the consequences. As a social democratic government, it had to come up with ways in which its broader social and environmental objectives could be integrated within the market, and, in particular, it had to deal with the uneven benefits across the social classes that would result from an unwinding of cross-subsidies and the search for more lucrative customers by the competitors.

But the really radical problems posed by full competition also had to be tackled. Breaking the link between customers and investment meant that financial markets were more important. The market could not be relied upon to provide an optimal mix of capacity. The energy market could never be perfect, and there would always be failures. Energy policy in the late 1990s had to come to terms with these consequences, and it was inevitable that the Lawsonian conventional wisdom would not be sufficient for the job. A White Paper was certainly needed by the time the coal crisis broke.

The analysis in Mandelson's White Paper of the problem does not stand the test of serious scrutiny, nor do the facts about supply security support it. The dash for gas was an altogether more complicated phenomenon than just the response to the exercise of market power (as discussed in Chapter 8). Much of the rest of this book will be concerned with the unsatisfactory nature of the White Paper's 'solution'. The Pool reforms did not solve the market power problem, nor did they provide stability (as discussed in Chapter 17). The White Paper's environmental credentials were weak, and the ban on gas did not help in this respect (as discussed in Chapter 19). The solution was not temporary, but required a permanent licensing policy. Indeed, in announcing his intention to lift the moratorium, Stephen Byers,

Mandelson's successor, stated that new licences would be conditional on developers having 'explored opportunities' to use CHP.[13] And, finally, the White Paper did not provide a 'positive future' (DTI 1998b: para 11.7). By 2001, the Prime Minister would announce a fundamental review of energy policy.[14] Mandelson's legacy was not to be a happy one.

[13] HC Deb. (session 1999–2000), paras 678–702, 17 April 2000.
[14] Interestingly, the PIU report (2002) does not even mention the 1998 White Paper among its references.

17

NETA and the Consolidation of Generation

Allowing trading outside the Pool could have potential benefits to those involved, and arrangements could be made to maintain coordination of the system. But so far there is little tangible evidence of the gains likely to be secured, and it would be time consuming and costly to make necessary arrangements. There are potential detriments to competition and new entry, both from a thinner and less transparent market and from placing new entrants and smaller competitors at a disadvantage in securing rights to despatch... I conclude that, at the present time, a sufficient case has not been made for significant changes to existing arrangements so as to allow widespread trading outside the Pool. (Stephen Littlechild, Offer 1994c: iii–iv)

The review of the electricity trading arrangements (called RETA) and the implementation of a new system (called NETA) were responses to the failure to develop a sufficiently competitive generation market—and therefore of the original privatization model to deliver what it promised. As set out in Chapter 7, the architects of electricity privatization took the view that, once generation was separated from transmission, split into several companies, and entry was permitted, a competitive market would gradually emerge. Regulation would be 'light', and price caps would protect the supply customers for as long as they were within the franchise. Industrial customers were originally protected by the large industrial companies (LICs) schemes, thereafter able to contract directly.

This view turned out to be remarkably naive. As we saw in Chapter 8, the conduct of the generators was the subject of an almost continuous review by the regulator, resulting in a number of attempts to create a more competitive outcome—from public criticisms, to rules about capacity availability, plant disposals, and temporary price caps. Marginal improvements were made, but, overall, Offer's attempts were largely unsuccessful. Ofgem itself claimed in 1999 that: 'since 1990 wholesale electricity prices have been largely unchanged, while the costs of generation in terms of fuel costs and capital and operating costs have reduced by almost 50 per cent' (Ofgem 1999a). Although the arithmetic is subject to some doubt (see Green 2001), such a conclusion is an indictment of Offer's conduct throughout the 1990s.

In Chapter 8, we noted some of the reasoning behind Offer's approach. Competition was to be promoted by encouraging entry, and high Pool prices would (in classic Schumpeterian style) carry the seeds of the generators' own destruction. The duopoly's market power would be temporary. In the early 1990s, Offer studiously did little to stem the dash for gas. Indeed, Littlechild often appeared actively to encourage it. It was left to Ofgem again to point out the consequences:

To the extent that prices have been higher than they would have been in a more competitive market...it is possible that this has encouraged excess new entry at the expense of existing plant. Entry has been dominated by gas-fired plant whereas the majority of plant closures have been of coal-fired capacity. (Ofgem 1999a: 3)

This view had been more forcefully put in the October 1998 White Paper on energy sources (DTI 1998b), and, even if the environmental constraints would eventually catch up with coal, its contraction in the 1990s was too fast. Customers—and the coal industry—paid a high price whilst waiting for the Austrian medicine to work.

The Structure of Generation and the Pool

The obvious response to the exercise of market power was to address the *structure* of the generation market, and indeed that was probably what Littlechild thought he was doing. But, by 1996/97, a rather different explanation of the source of market power had been identified by Offer. It was the structure of the Pool that, it was now claimed, facilitated the exercise of market power. If only this was reformed, the argument ran, a competitive market might have more of a chance of emerging. Other policies would also continue to be deployed, such as divestment, but as the momentum built up to reform the Pool, all sorts of extravagant claims began to be made about the benefits of the proposed new trading arrangements. In particular, the Department of Trade and Industry (DTI) began to suggest that prices would fall, *as a direct consequence*, by 10 per cent, and after NETA had been introduced, Ofgem and the DTI were both quick to claim that the fall in prices that did occur in 2000 had been at least in part *caused* by the prospect of NETA and that subsequent falls resulted from its implementation.

Amongst the enthusiasts, there appeared to be few doubts about the role and limits of what competition might achieve. These were the heady days when the possibilities of energy trading and the contributions of financial markets seemed almost boundless as the equity markets boomed and companies such as Enron appeared to many to represent the future. The mantra of 'competition' and 'competitive markets' was repeated, almost as if the likelihood of achieving this state depended upon how often the concepts were declared to be the objectives of policy. That there might be *different kinds* of competition, or that electricity generation might have a natural tendency to oligopoly appear not to have been seriously entertained. Of course, many had vested interests in limiting competition, but there remained the possibility that the market might be so limited, and, hence, the design of policy and regulation might have to take this into account. Few in 1996/97, when NETA was first being considered, imagined that within just five years most of England and Wales' electricity industry would be in the hands of three European utilities, themselves overwhelmingly dominant in France and Germany.

The Three Problems with the Pool

The lack of attention to the meaning of competition and competitive markets was to be a blind spot for both Offer (and Ofgem) and the DTI in the commitment to NETA. However, to see how a range of sensible suggestions for Pool reform ended up being translated into a major new market structure (NETA), and to understand some of the consequences, the first step is to consider Offer's and then Ofgem's critique of the Pool. There were essentially three main lines of attack: the payment of the system marginal price (SMP) rather than pay-as-bid; the compulsory and standardized nature of the Pool; and the poor representation of the demand side. There were also other criticisms—such as its governance structures, the way capacity availability was rewarded, and the day-ahead bidding— but these could all have been addressed by modifying the Pool. The first three problems, it was argued, necessitated more radical reform.

SMP versus Pay-as-bid

The concept of an SMP, as the short-run marginal cost (SRMC) of the last station just necessary to meet demand, was grounded in the economic theory of resource allocation, and, as discussed in Chapter 7, was the central concept to ensure economic efficiency in despatch. No one has suggested any other pricing rule with better optimal efficiency characteristics, for the very good reason that, given existing power stations, any deviation from this rule wastes resources.[1] Not surprisingly, the SMP

---

[1] In their conclusions paper, Ofgem and the DTI claimed that: 'When markets are broadly competitive, SMP and pay-as-bid produce similar results, but when market power is evident, pay-as-bid can have advantages' (Ofgem/DTI 1999: 90).

pricing system was easily introduced at privatization by reading across from the Central Electricity Generating Board's (CEGB) least-cost despatch model.

The critique of the SMP mechanism was that it enabled 'gaming'. Generators could bid in prices at which they were willing for their plant to be despatched, in the knowledge that their bid would not determine the price, except where the specific plant was marginal to the system. The gaming then had two dimensions: bidding when *not* setting the price; and bidding for the marginal plant.

The fundamental reason why generators could 'game' was because they had market power. In the 1990s, the two main generators, National Power and PowerGen, set the price most of the time. Furthermore, they had a great deal of common knowledge on plant characteristics, costs and availability, especially in the early days when most of the key managers transferred from the CEGB, where they had all worked together, into the new firms. Nuclear Electric was unimportant in this game because its plants ran at baseload, and hence SMP was above the nuclear SRMCs of each of its stations.[2] In addition, there was a further gaming problem related to capacity, as detailed in Chapter 8.

The advocates of reform argued that if only the generators were *paid* their bids, the scope for gaming would decrease. Bids by generators not setting SMP would now count, in the sense that they were *prices*. Thus, for example, British Energy, which inherited Nuclear Electric's England and Wales nuclear power stations, would be paid its bid. The result was that everyone now entered into a guessing game as to what the SMP would be, and hence the stranglehold of National Power and PowerGen over SMP would be broken. Instead of a tight game between just two players, there would be a much noisier one between many. Overbidding above the real SMP now carried the possibility of being out of the market.

Compulsory Pool versus Voluntary Trading

In itself, pay-as-bid was not a particularly radical step, and could have been grafted onto the Pool. It is merely a different way of arriving at the despatch price, and it is not costless, in that the information contained in each generator's marginal cost bid is now lost—and hence the knowledge to the system operator of the ranking of plant in the marginal cost function. The supply curve is now much harder to construct. But, it was the second line of criticism—and the proposed solution—which was the decisive

---

[2] The main issue was *availability* and hence quantities for nuclear. But, again, Nuclear Electric had every incentive to keep plant on the system.

difference between the Pool and NETA. This was the challenge to the standardized and compulsory nature of the Pool. To economic liberals, the idea that a particular form of contracting could be forced upon traders was anathema. The market was a 'discovery process', in which the participants would each try out new ideas. It could not be known in advance which approach to trading was best, even to those attempting to compete in the market place. *Voluntary* behaviour was, as a matter of principle, deemed superior.

Notwithstanding the fundamental philosophical difficulty amongst those of a more liberal predisposition—that the formal and legal definition of property rights was a *precondition* (and not a consequence) of market functioning—Offer and the DTI decided that, in the new arrangements, generators, suppliers, and customers could contract as and when they chose, and it was left to the market to set up appropriate exchanges for short- and long-term contracting, where the players could refine and hedge their exposure. The new arrangements sought to 'remove unnecessary restrictions' (Ofgem/DTI 1999), as the spin would have it. (If they were '*unnecessary*' then of course they should be removed.) Freed from 'restricture rules', there would be greater opportunities for 'discovery' and 'innovation' in the buying and selling of electricity. Any standardization and any convergence on a particular market structure would be the *outcome* of a competitive and voluntary process, rather than determined in advance.

Such an approach would be the obvious one to follow in most commodity markets.[3] Electricity, however, had some special features. Demand must be instantaneously met by supply, whereas most commodities can be stored. Moreover, for the foreseeable future, the generation market would be oligopolistic and the main oligopolists had been busily attempting to vertically integrate. After the aborted attempts in 1995 by PowerGen and National Power to buy Midlands Electricity and Southern Electric respectively, PowerGen would eventually buy East Midlands, and Innogy (as National Power became) would acquire Midlands Electricity and Yorkshire Electricity supply businesses. The next largest player in the non-nuclear sector, TXU, acquired divested power stations from the two main players (to add to Eastern Electricity) and NORWEB Supply (and then, in a strategic U-turn, TXU began to retreat from generation). London Electricity was bought a second time around by EDF, who added SWEB Supply, TXU Distribution, SEEBOARD, and as many generating assets as it thought it could get past the regulators. Even British Energy entered the

---

[3] The proposals were indeed seen as 'more like those adopted or being adopted in other commodity markets', Offer (1998), para 5.64, p. 75.

game, buying (and subsequently divesting) SWALEC Supply and the Eggborough coal power station. To complete the picture, Southern Electric merged with Scottish Hydro-Electric. As noted in Chapter 12, by 2001, the industry then comprised five main vertically integrated companies: PowerGen, Innogy, London/EDF, ScottishPower, and Scottish & Southern. There were, of course, many additional smaller generation players, as well as Centrica in supply, but the market could not be described as anything other than a vertically integrated oligopoly.

This oligopoly was to be further boosted for a period at the end of the 1990s with the 'temporary' ban on new gas entry. Growth was now more by acquisition of existing plant rather than by new build, and existing (coal) players were protected from entry. Though, as we saw in Chapter 16, this ban was (erroneously) linked with NETA as part of the 'solution' to market power, and was to be lifted on 15 November 2000, it was to become part of a gradual shift towards the managing of generation, to be reinforced by the imposition of a Renewables Obligation—in effect, a duty to contract—a policy preference for combined heat and power (CHP), and even the possibility of quotas for clean coal and nuclear. Licences would be given out on a liberalized basis, but with the strong proviso that government had a preferred ranking of investments. The Energy Policy Review merely served to reinforce this trend (see Chapter 21).

With vertical integration and government interference with entry, the new market structure continued its tendency towards consolidation and concentration. More mergers were expected and not just in England and Wales, but across Europe too. E.ON and RWE gained dominance in Germany, joining EDF amongst the big league players. E.ON acquired Ruhrgas and hence a stake in Gazprom, as well as acquiring PowerGen, whilst RWE acquired Czech gas assets and Innogy. The British consolidation became a part of a much bigger European consolidation (see Chapter 20). Thus, when considering whether the players could be permitted to contract as they wished, the pertinent question was whether, *in the presence* of this sort of oligopoly, NETA provided an appropriate solution. Would not the liberalization of contract forms suit the vertical players, so that different contracts could be set between own-generation and own-supply, from those offered to rival suppliers? Would not the big players also benefit from the lack of liquidity in the market place, which would result from a lack of transparency? And, perhaps most significant of all, would not the combination of a physical and financial hedge prove more advantageous than a mere financial hedge? The value of a physical hedge—that is, owning some generation—depended upon the degree of competition in the spot and contracting market, and the extent of the futures market. If the futures market was sufficiently developed—liquid, transparent and trading well out into the future—*then* pure suppliers could compete with physically hedged (i.e. vertically integrated) players. But these markets were anything but fully developed, and *hence* the physical hedge mattered—as was to become abundantly clear when Enron collapsed. Put simply, the Ofgem/DTI logic could be stood on its head. Whilst it was true that 'without effective trading arrangements, restructuring of the generation, and supply markets will be less effective in producing real benefits to customers' (Ofgem/DTI 1999: 9), the converse was also true. And the wrong sort of trading arrangements would actually make the effects of market power worse. Whereas Ofgem and the DTI saw NETA as the key to reducing market power, it might actually exacerbate the problems.

Why did not Ofgem and the DTI spot this? Poor analysis on the part of the DTI probably played a part, and wishful thinking on the part of Ofgem contributed to an atmosphere in which NETA became more an article of faith than a well-researched policy. An obvious clue was the fact that the main players were all in favour of abolishing the Pool and replacing it with a voluntary framework. Though Offer and Ofgem thought that the Pool created the scope for gaming, to the main players the problem with the Pool was that its very transparency kept them in the regulator's spotlight and limited their scope to exploit vertical integration—hence, the numerous Pool price inquiries, plant divestments, threats of a Monopolies and Mergers Commission (MMC) reference and the price cap. In the early days, the main players might have regarded Offer as having been hamstrung by lack of information, and taken some comfort in Offer's ambivalence to high prices which would help to suck in entrants and encourage the dash for gas, but the repeated interventions spelt a rather depressing future, as the rents from the game were slowly chipped away. Far better from the incumbents' perspective to move to the pluralistic world of NETA.

There was a gradual recognition of the vertical integration problem as the RETA programme translated into NETA. Whilst, initially, the claim was that NETA would *solve* the problem of generator market power (a view set out in the 1998 White Paper—DTI 1998*b*), the complacency would be jolted almost immediately after NETA was introduced, and by 2000 Ofgem was proposing new licence conditions requiring 'good behaviour' from *all* the generators. Whereas, once, NETA was seen as being able to *solve* the problem of market power, by 2001 it was only one part of the jigsaw. (We return to the ill-fated so-called 'good behaviour' proposal below.)

In the run-up to the introduction of NETA, its voluntary nature raised a number of practical issues. These were: the extent to which generators and suppliers would contract; the emergence of new trading markets; and the balancing of the system to ensure short-term security of supply. In the event, it turned out that these three issues were related, but the precise linkages were obscured by the market fundamentals in 2000 and 2001. These included: massive excess capacity (by any historical standard) in the electricity generation as the dash for gas simply added yet more power stations in a situation where demand was static; the gas price shock, which changed the economic balance between combined-cycle gas turbines (CCGTs) and coal; and, crucially, the ending of the coal contracts with the 1998 liberalization (indeed, the absence of *any* significant long-term contracts to underpin the NETA markets).

With excess capacity, generators should scramble to contract, whilst suppliers should go short, creating an imbalance in the contracting market. Thus, in 2000 and 2001, as excess supply continued to be the expected characteristic of the market for some time to come, the non-vertically integrated suppliers appeared to have the strategic advantage. The main players here were Centrica and gradually Innogy. The key asset appeared to be customers rather than power stations. Wholesale prices in such circumstances were set to fall—not because of NETA, but rather as a reflection of the supply–demand balance and the growing consolidation and power of the suppliers. Under the Pool, the Pool price might have fallen too; however, under NETA, generators had to protect their output in the future and, hence, contract forward at lower prices. It appeared that NETA had *caused* the fall in prices, whereas, in fact, in conditions of excess supply, the oligopoly (temporarily) cracked—as it did across Europe, especially in Germany, without any assistance from NETA-type markets. The fall in wholesale prices did not, however, translate into a fall in retail prices. Margins in supply increased into 2002, allowing the vertically integrated companies to offset the upstream loss of revenue. The total price to customers did not fall commensurately: instead, the wholesale generation margin, which had been such a feature of the generation market in the 1990s, migrated downstream.

The response to this situation by the generators would probably have followed the German example—a sharp price fall amongst an oligopoly without either a pool or NETA—had not another factor intervened. This was the sharp rise in the gas price, forcing an output contraction by the CCGTs. What otherwise would have been a reduction in available coal capacity turned into a rise in coal-fired output. The increase in gas prices (on the back of oil prices) did not, however, lead to a significant rebound of wholesale prices. These remained depressed into 2002, before rising strongly in the second half of 2003.

A further pressure on contracting strategies came from the design of the Balancing Mechanism. The idea was a simple one: generators and suppliers would contract with each other, but the amounts of electricity involved would not necessarily be equivalent to the physical values required to keep the lights on. The various contracted parties might be committed to delivering too much or too little power. The *balancing* out of these positions was further complicated by the fact that demand is not known precisely in advance. It matters greatly precisely what rules cover the provision of electricity at the margin, and how market participants are rewarded or penalized for being out of balance. High penalties create strong incentives to contract; weak penalties produce the opposite incentives.

The rules in the Balancing Mechanism were set out in the Balancing and Settlement Code (BSC), which the NGC, as system operator (SO), had an obligation to establish and modify, but subject to strong regulatory oversight.[4] The BSC was envisaged not as a fixed and definitive set of rules (as perhaps the architects of electricity privatization had seen the Pool rules), but rather as an evolving, flexible instrument responding to experience and events. Modification proposals are judged by Ofgem against predefined criteria.

The SO's job is a generic one to every electricity system in developed countries. It requires information, and participants under NETA have to notify their expected physical positions for each half-hour trading period.[5] Balance is, in practice, not restricted to the aggregate supply and demand for electricity, but also its location and 'quality' across the network. In a highly integrated system, such as that in England and Wales, these effects are limited, but a substantial growth in small-scale embedded renewables might magnify the costs considerably. The SO has a monopoly position, in that there is a single SO for England and Wales. This monopoly may also be extended under the British Electricity Trading and Transmission

---

[4] In the initial design, the Balancing Mechanism opens three-and-a-half hours (subsequently reduced) before real time, after the market gate has closed (gate closure). In that final period, the SO must achieve 'balance' and, hence, it accepts offers of, and bids for, electricity. These are then 'settled' between those whose metered take does not equate to their contracted position, and the SO's own costs are recovered through the Settlement Process.

[5] The 'final' notification at the three-and-a-half hour gate was called the final physical notification (FPN). Any signatory of the BSC can then make bids on the demand and supply side to the SO to help achieve balance, but is not compelled to do so. A 'system sell' (for under-contracted generators) and a 'system buy' (for under-contracted buyers) price emerges. These are typically lower or higher than the price that the parties could have contracted for in the pre-balancing markets. The price differences should reflect the costs of the SO in bringing supply and demand into a precise balance. (The SO can also contract for its own reserves.)

Arrangement (BETTA) proposals (see below) to cover all of mainland Britain (and eventually could extend across the gas and electricity industries, following the Lattice–NGC merger). It is therefore regulated, subject to an incentivized price cap.

Balancing is designed to play a residual role, with strong incentives to contract. The case for NETA rests heavily on the emergence of trading markets that are liquid, transparent and extend sufficiently into the future to hedge risks for new investment so that long-term contracts can be facilitated. In the spirit of liberalization, regulators left it to the players to form new trading markets, and for competition to sort out which would emerge as dominant. Although such trading markets display features of natural monopoly, time would tell who would enjoy these benefits.[6]

Since NETA went live, competition between markets has developed, and the extent of trading has increased. These trends, Ofgem contends, fulfil the promise of NETA. In Ofgem's submission to the PIU's Energy Policy Review (Ofgem 2001e: 19–21), the confidence in the new markets is almost unbounded. Though greater liquidity and more price reporting no doubt improve the functioning of markets, they do no more than scratch the surface of the underlying economic issues, concerned with the exercise of market power and, most seriously, the disjuncture between short-term trading and long-term investment. The new markets are very unlikely to trade out into the future over the life of new generation assets, a feature shared with the Pool and the contracts-for-differences. However, there are good reasons for believing that NETA will fare worse, because the absence of a standardized market whose liquidity is guaranteed through compulsion will lead to less transparency.

Market stability is typically provided by the presence of substantial long-term contractual coverage. This was provided between 1990 and 1998 by the coal contracts, back-to-back with the RECs' supply franchises. The absence of such contracts after 1998 did not create immediate problems because of excess supply. But as the market tightens—as it did in California—the results could be severe.[7] The 'solution' within NETA would be a sharp price shock, forcing demand off the system.

---

[6] The over-the-counter (OTC) market operated alongside three power exchanges and a host of bilateral contracts. The OTC has seen the majority of forward trading. The three power exchanges—UKPX, UKAPX, and IPE—offer a range of spot and futures contracts, but mainly the former. Information about prices of longer-term contracts depends upon a market developing for such services.

[7] See Joskow (2001) and Borenstein (2002) for an analysis of the Californian crisis, and in particular the importance of a framework of long-term contracts for the stability of spot markets and prices. By late 2003, wholesale prices had in fact risen very sharply in England and Wales.

Whether in fact this would be 'allowed' without substantial political intervention is a moot point, but the very possibility that such price spikes would be suppressed tends to deter investment in peaking plant.[8]

Demand Side

The third criticism of the Pool and an argument used to advance NETA was the role of the demand side in the market. The idea was not new— that is, that, as prices rise, electricity users could make offers to reduce demand in parallel with generators bidding higher prices for more output. Load management arrangements were a demand-side feature of the CEGB system, as were the interruptible gas contracts in the development of natural gas. Explicit demand-side bidding, Offer and then Ofgem argued, would introduce more competition, and hence a further challenge to the market power of the incumbents (Offer 1998: para 5.65, p. 75). And it would also meet an environmental objective: reducing the demand and hence emissions and transmission losses.

In a normal market, the demand side is represented by the decision to buy or not at quoted prices. Thus, as the price rises, customers buy less. In electricity, it is to be expected that they turn off the lights. But the difference in electricity is that one person's decision to reduce demand needs to be *balanced ex ante* with generation output. Thus, the SO has the key role of inviting bids, rather than simply allowing imbalances to be worked out in the market place. The SO is a *market maker*.

NETA's supporters are undoubtedly right to claim that the demand side was under-represented in the Pool system, despite numerous initiatives in the 1990s. However, it is far from clear that this was *caused* by the Pool's design, or that the Pool could not have been reformed to improve the demand side. The important fact that needs to be taken into account is the presence of excess supply—with the peak demand remaining roughly the same for two decades. Even in a more demand-side friendly system, there may have been little effective demand-side impact on the market, for the simple reason that it was more expensive than using excess supply. To the extent that the Pool led to higher prices (and hence masked the excess supply effect on prices), it should have *increased* the economic value of demand management. Conversely, if NETA reduced prices—as its supporters claimed—then *pari passu* it should reduce the scope for demand-side bidding.

---

[8] This may eventually result in a duty to contract to meet peaks being placed upon the SO or some other party, in effect yet another compulsory take-or-pay contract, recovered through the SO charges (see Chapter 21). See also McCarthy (2003) on Ofgem's likely response.

NETA incorporates demand-side bidding by simply allowing it: anyone can offer to shed demand, either bilaterally or through the SO in the Balancing Mechanism. However, these two options address rather different problems. Shedding demand over time is an odd concept, except insofar as buyers increase their energy efficiency. That simply reduces demand, and it is hard to contract not to buy an amount of electricity over time. Demand bidding really only makes sense at peaks—either by buying electricity on an interruptible basis or by bidding in the very short-term Balancing Mechanism. The former trades on the flexibility of production and consumption versus the flexibility of generation, the latter on sensitivity to (very) high peak pricing.

The value of demand-side responses depends on the structure of energy-consuming capital. In a service-based economy, the scope for shedding demand may be more limited than in manufacturing. One way of measuring this is to consider the costs of supply interruptions, as in California. In times of very tight margins between supply and demand for electricity, the option of demand shedding may be very valuable. At other, more normal, times with a comfortable capacity margin, not surprisingly, NETA's much heralded demand-side bidding gains were much less, and appear to be consistent with the scale of the margin.

Governance

Any new system, invented from scratch, was likely to benefit from reform after experience of its operation. This was as true of the Pool as it is of NETA. From the outset, critics of the Pool proposed reforms and the regulator tried to engineer change, but the Pool's governance structure made it all but impossible to make much progress. The Pool, in effect, provided strong veto powers.

Added to this inflexibility was a separate, but important, problem—its complexity, which made the price-setting process 'opaque'. Its rules were understood by the few—the incumbents—and were almost impenetrable to both entrants and industrial buyers who wished to contract around the Pool. The complexity arose from the combination of the Pool rules and the way in which the information was collated and used to arrive at the SMP, uplift and related prices. The critics of the Pool argued that complexity was not inevitable, and, by implication, that NETA would be less complex.

The inflexibility was not, however, accidental. The architects of electricity privatization did not want to grant the sort of wide-ranging powers that regulators have effectively gained over NETA. The generation sector was to be *lightly* regulated. The market place was compulsory and prices not only open for all to see, but available to all to purchase at. Therefore, the regulator's role was expected to be heavily curtailed—indeed, that is what the prospectuses for National Power and PowerGen offered. Though the way in which the inflexibility in the rules interacted with the complexity and the exercise of market power to produce an undesirable outcome proved a surprise to many of those concerned, the case for greater regulatory discretion rested on the assumption that the market could not be left to its own devices to generate a competitive outcome. Both the designers of the Pool and NETA naively assumed that the markets could achieve such outcomes, but, at least in NETA's case, powers were held in reserve just in case it did not. Regulatory discretion provides safeguards, but it is not costless. Investors, confronted with regulators who can change the rules, face higher costs of capital and may as a result be less willing to invest.[9]

The important point to note here is not, however, the relative merits of the governance of the Pool or NETA, but rather the independence of the governance questions from the market design. The governance rules for the Pool could have been revised without abolishing the Pool. NETA was not necessary to effect such changes. Legislation might still have been required, but this could as easily have been effected through the Utilities Act 2000 as the wholesale abolition of the Pool. Introducing customers into the Pool's governance, giving them voting powers, allowing the regulator to secure changes—all of these were possible as reforms to the Pool.[10]

Implementing NETA and its Costs

The implementation of NETA would have been a daunting task to a well-functioning regulatory body, armed with a large expert staff. In fact, NETA was introduced by a small Ofgem team, dependent to a considerable measure on its consultants. The way it was implemented was greatly influenced by the initial *laissez-faire* views of its design.

The original idea behind NETA developed within Offer was of a step *back* from regulation. The Pool would be dismantled by removing the compulsory element. Trading outside the Pool would be permitted—and as large industrial customers had suggested almost from the Pool's outset. The market would then spontaneously, in true Austrian form, find ways of

---

[9] This negative effect on investment is especially important with respect to peaking plant. If investors expect regulators to intervene to limit price spikes then plant dependent on very high returns very occasionally will not be economic (see Borenstein 2002).

[10] See Ofgem (1999a: 3) for a summary of its criticisms of Pool governance.

trading, and futures and contract frameworks would emerge from the competitive process. Institutions would develop naturally. It was only as Offer began to work on RETA and then Ofgem on NETA, and as the lessons from the gas trading arrangements were carried across, that the complexity of the task—and its costs—began to emerge.

At the heart of implementation lay two (related) problems—the BSC and the information technology to support the Balancing Mechanism. As with the Pool, much of this was first-of-a-kind, complex and understood by the (very) few rather than the many. Those few fell into four groups— the big generators, the new traders, the information technology and consultancy specialists, and a small nucleus within Offer/Ofgem. Remarkably this meant that incumbents with vested interests (PowerGen, National Power/Innogy, Scottish Power and Scottish & Southern, and TXU), together with Enron as the leading trader; NGC as SO; the leading software houses and Offer/Ofgem's consultants; and mainly Eileen Marshall in Ofgem, drove the process, leaving critics to the sidelines.

The complexity of the issues (and the lack of expert resources) closed off much of the necessary scrutiny by the DTI. Few, if any, amongst the Energy Directorate fully understood NETA, and those that did acted as much as advocates of Ofgem's views to government, as impartial critics. Successive ministers of state—John Battle and Helen Liddle for the decisive periods— had only the haziest idea of what they were being asked to agree to. Margaret Beckett, Peter Mandelson, and Stephen Byers—as successive secretaries of state—probably had even less understanding of the detail.

Undermining the naive objective of simplifying the electricity trading arrangements, with each step the complexity increased, requiring more and more regulatory oversight. The market had to be designed, and property rights had to be defined, rather than left to emerge as had been hoped. The information technology systems had to be continually revised, with numerous changes to the required specification. Inevitably the Go Live date had to be put back first to the autumn of 2000, and then to spring 2001.[11] Plans to Go Live in the run-up to Christmas would have been an extraordinarily risky option. Better to wait for the demand–supply balance to ease in the spring, even if this was caused by failures to deliver the information technology programme to timetable rather than foresight.[12]

Once the DTI and Ofgem were committed to NETA, the scope for rational analysis of options and in particular any notion of turning back

[11] The DTI in 2000 required Ofgem to come up with a series of indicators to test the readiness to Go Live. See Ofgem/DTI (2000, 2001).

[12] The author met Helen Liddle soon after she was appointed minister and advised against introduction in the run-up to Christmas—against DTI officials' advice.

became all but impossible. Ministers were politically committed since Mandelson's White Paper, whilst the reputation of the leading Offer and Ofgem figures was at stake. Once Callum McCarthy had endorsed the reforms soon after his appointment as head of Ofgem, and, more importantly, delegated its implementation to Eileen Marshall, the institutional die was cast. From then on, repeating the mantra that the electricity market was 'rigged against coal', and that the Pool was 'flawed', had its effect: it became conventional wisdom to many who had only the faintest idea of what the Pool or NETA were.

From the Mandelson White Paper onwards, there was no *serious* attempt to evaluate the costs against the benefits of NETA. At each stage, Ofgem simply claimed that NETA would reduce wholesale prices by more than the costs of NETA—but without any attempt to evaluate the other option—which was reform *within* the Pool structure. In particular, reform of Pool governance, together with pay-as-bid and demand-side bidding were never seriously entertained after 1998.

The set-up costs of NETA comprised a series of elements, notably: information technology systems for the SO; information technology systems for all the generators and suppliers participating in the BSC; the costs of erecting the BSC—legal and otherwise; consulting costs to the DTI and Ofgem; and Ofgem's direct costs. There will probably never be a full audit of each of these items, but Ofgem did provide a number of estimates of *some* of the components. The RETA proposals included a short section on 'Costs and Benefits of Reform' (Offer 1998). Benefits were 'diverse' and 'to measure them as explicitly quantified components in a cost benefit analysis would be an extremely difficult task' (para 8.62). Offer went on to make the dubious assertion that 'the practical judgement must therefore be whether, if the reforms are beneficial, the costs associated with their proposed realization are such as to cast doubt on the benefit of pursuing them.' Since the proponents at Offer appeared to have no such doubts, the cost estimates were the only serious part of the equation. In the July 1998 document, some hazy components were quoted, notably: hardware and software costs of the balancing, short-term bilateral and options markets, including data collection and settlement of the order of £25–£50 million (para 8.66). Other set-up costs were also assumed to be £25–£50 million, making a total central set-up cost of, say, £50–£100 million, which spread over five years made £10–£20 million a year. Even these estimates might, Offer thought, be on the high side, since 'market operators would have an incentive to reduce these costs.'

To these ballpark assumptions, Offer suggested some further allowance for the continued running of some of the present Pool facilities, particularly the 1998 settlement (para 8.67), but again savings were anticipated. On operating costs, Offer thought that these would not be significantly higher than those of present arrangements, which Offer put at £30 million per annum (para 8.68). Then there were the market participants' own set-up costs. For thirty participants, these might be £60 million a year, but more likely to be less (paras 8.69, 8.70). Their operating costs were expected to be similar to the current ones (para 8.71)—perhaps £30 million more per year.

Adding it all up produced a total of up to £100–£110 million per annum for the first five years (para 8.72), which was less than 1 per cent of the turnover of the total electricity supply industry (para 8.74). Offer satisfied itself that, in any event, 'the key point…is that the proposals have to deliver only a small reduction in prices for the aggregate benefits to exceed the aggregate costs' (para 8.75). What Offer did not add was 'and at a lower cost than any other way of achieving comparative benefits'. Other options were not considered.

A year later, in July 1999, Ofgem returned to the costs in 'New Electricity Trading Arrangements' (Ofgem 1999a). The estimates had now become more precise: Ofgem suggested a range of £136–£146 million per annum, though the operating cost figure was now an estimate stretching beyond five years.[13] These were 'upper-range' (para 17.5), and in any event 'should be adjusted to arrive at estimates that are net of the costs that will be avoided as a result of RETA'.

The House of Commons Select Committee on Trade and Industry inquiry into 'The Work of Ofgem' questioned Ofgem on the breakdown of NETA costs (2000a,b: annex 6, pp. 100–2). Ofgem began by claiming that its 1998 and 1999 reports (Offer 1998; Ofgem 1999a) gave 'total NETA set-up costs of up to £100 million over the life cycle of the Programme' (which is not quite right), and then stated that it would have been £90 million but for the delay in start-up, which added £10 million.

If the cost estimates were crude, and left out the consequential *effects* on the players, with no serious attempt at comparisons, the benefits estimates were even worse. Ofgem made no attempt to quantify these in its 1998 paper, but by October 1999 in the Ofgem/DTI NETA conclusions paper, a series of assertions got bundled together (Ofgem/DTI 1999). These related to the reduction in prices which could be expected *as a result of* NETA. It is worth quoting the Ofgem/DTI paper at some length:

Ofgem/DTI consider that the new arrangements offer the prospect of relatively large and rapidly achieved reductions in wholesale electricity prices and lower

---

[13] Appendix 12 gave a more detailed breakdown of costs—see especially para 12.5.

prices for both industrial and domestic customers. Beyond the immediate change in price level, there is the prospect of continuing pressure to reduce prices. It is estimated that, if wholesale prices are reduced to a level equal to the full costs of new generating capacity, the benefits to consumers could be of the order of £1.5 billion per annum.

This is a staggering claim when taken as a justification of NETA.[14] It begs many questions, not least the performance of Ofgem, its predecessor Offer and the DTI. If Ofgem/DTI knew that the generators were overcharging by £1.5 billion per annum, why had they not acted sooner? The MMC and its successor the Competition Commission should surely have been called in. But what is all the more remarkable is that no other mechanism to rectify this claimed position was considered. If Ofgem knew what the 'right' price ought to be, why not simply impose it? However bad the consequences of price capping generation, were the costs greater than either NETA or £1.5 billion per annum? And how precisely was NETA supposed to *cause* entry pricing so that £1.5 billion would be the answer? Did entry pricing not depend upon the price of gas, and if that increased, should NETA not lead to *higher* prices? Could it really be that the way generators bid and contracted accounted for *all* the £1.5 billion? And if not all, how much?

That NETA was not sufficient was recognized by many of the parties from the outset. Ofgem never claimed it was sufficient, but only necessary. Indeed, it was so concerned that a considerable deviation from entry pricing could persist under NETA that it proposed a major extension of the regulation of generation—the 'good behaviour' clause—which would in turn be based upon the notion that Ofgem knew the 'right' price.

The First Cracks—The Market Abuse Licence Condition

By July 1999, Ofgem had already accepted that, despite its expense, NETA would not of itself *solve* the problems of market power in generation. By then NETA was 'only one aspect, albeit an important aspect, of a wider energy and competition framework, and the benefits that it will produce should be judged in terms of its contribution to the effectiveness of that framework taken as a whole' (Ofgem 1999a: para 14.7, p. 187). In particular, NETA would not solve the gaming which it had been designed to deal with, and Ofgem now proposed that the generators should sign up to a market abuse licence condition (MALC) in their licences.

---

[14] The DTI claimed a reduction of 10% or more in the wholesale price of electricity in the medium term for the whole package of energy reforms, equal to £850 million per annum (DTI 2000a: 21). For a critique by the author, see House of Commons Select Committee on Trade and Industry (2000b).

The MALC was a very badly designed piece of conduct regulation: it gave extra powers to the regulator without a proper appeals process, and, crucially, it required generators to conform to its requirements without specifying what 'bad behaviour' was. Would prices have to be equal to marginal costs in bids? If so, *which* marginal costs? And, if so, would withdrawals of plant have to meet an economic test against *normal* market prices—whatever that might mean? Should it apply to *all* generators, and not just the big ones, to baseload nuclear generators as well as peak providers?

Not surprisingly, the generators resisted. There followed an exercise in behind-the-scenes arm-twisting to gain acceptance of the licence condition. Three tactics were used. First, in order to complete the break-up of National Power, the new entity Innogy required a licence. Ofgem offered a new one which included the MALC, and Innogy was faced with the unenviable choice of the licence *as a whole* or not, and not surprisingly it accepted the MALC by default. The second tactic was divide-and-rule. Each generator was told that, even if they accepted, if any other generator rejected the condition, appealed to the Competition Commission and the Commission rejected the MALC, then it would be withdrawn from all. Since it was widely assumed that Edison Mission would reject, several of the others signed up. The third was to time-limit the MALC with sunset provisions—which, rightly, few generators put much faith in. (What, after all, would happen at the end of the period? Would Ofgem simply propose another licence amendment?)

Ofgem may have felt relaxed about Edison appealing since its pumped-storage system had a significant effect on the price of peak electricity (i.e. it had market power at peaks), and because the business plan on which Edison acquired the plant from NGC in effect assumed that there would be scope for non-marginal pricing. But, if this was Ofgem's calculation, it misfired. Whilst the MALC was under discussion, the head of Edison Mission was replaced and Edison Mission accepted the clause. Meanwhile, AES (the new owners of the Drax power station) and, more surprising to Ofgem, British Energy, rejected the clause. The scene was now set for Ofgem to demonstrate to the Competition Commission that there was a serious detriment to the public interest in the operation of NETA, and that the MALC clause would be an appropriate remedy. Whether this was just for the period over which NETA was supposed to 'bed down', or over the medium term remained somewhat opaque. Clearly, however, NETA would need more regulation to support it—and more than had been available when the much-derided Pool had existed.

As the Competition Commission case proceeded, Ofgem was able to use the clause against Edison Mission. Edison was unable to show that its withdrawal of plant could be supported by an economic calculation, and Ofgem claimed that this withdrawal had resulted in a spike in prices worth more than £30 million.[15]

The Competition Commission decided against the MALC in December 2000, and Ofgem then withdrew the licence condition from *all* the generators (Competition Commission 2001). The Commission had only been able to look at the rationale for applying the condition to AES (where Drax was covered by longer-term contracts) and to British Energy (most of whose output was baseload, with the exception of Eggborough), and *in these cases* found Ofgem's arguments unconvincing.

Ofgem reacted angrily to the Commission's report, and continued to lobby for the inclusion of such a clause in the generators' licences, despite its earlier assurance that it would abide by the Commission's findings. It criticized the Commission analysis, and sought support from the DTI to use the Utilities Act 2000 framework to reintroduce it. In acting in this way, Ofgem was criticized explicitly by the Better Regulation Task Force (2001). The extension of regulation, the form of discretion it created, and the fact that Ofgem would not accept the outcome of the proper appeals mechanism all created further criticism of the direction in which Ofgem's regulation was heading. Indeed, it added further to the wider criticisms of the exercise of regulatory discretion in the utilities generally.

Irrespective of these criticisms,[16] Ofgem pushed ahead with the second attempt in August 2001 with a modified form. This attempt was to be rejected too—this time by the DTI. This left Ofgem in some disarray. Either it was the case that abuse under NETA was possible and could not be dealt with under the Competition Act 1998 powers—in which case the gains for NETA would be reduced—or abuse was not possible, in which case NETA had dealt with gaming. In the short term, the excess capacity and the economic downturn masked the impact of the new freedoms to contract granted to the larger integrated players under NETA. In time, however, as capacity margins tighten, then abuse may become the issue it was in California's crisis. The irony is that the more optimistic one is about NETA, the weaker the case for the MALC is. NETA pessimists, on the other hand, could see all too clearly why conduct regulation might in due course be needed. And they had an example upon which to draw—the way in which,

---

[15] Eileen Marshall, in response to questioning at the Select Committee on Trade and Industry inquiry (House of Commons Select Committee on Trade and Industry 2000a: para 170).

[16] In a letter to the *Financial Times* (17 July 2001), McCarthy was extremely critical of the BRTF Report—both the procedure and the outcome.

after an initial drop in prices, the German market had bounced back as the dominant players began to exploit their market powers. In Germany, the fall in prices facilitated consolidation, which was then exploited. The British market under NETA might in time be similarly vulnerable.[17]

A New Market and All the Old Problems

For Ofgem, NETA represented more than just another regulatory reform. Next to the 1998 liberalization, it was its most important project, from its origins in Offer in 1997 through to its implementation in 2001. Notwithstanding the caveats, the claims made for it were bold. It would 'be less vulnerable to abuse by participants with market power; be more open to innovation; be more conductive to the effective monitoring of anti-competitive practices; strengthen the influence of the demand side on wholesale price formation; be more flexible and adaptable to changing economic conditions' (Ofgem 1999a: para 14.7, p. 188).

None of these claims was open to direct measurement, since they required the specification of a counterfactual (how the Pool would have behaved). By 1998 it had already become an article of faith, not a rational policy, and hence it was easy to prove that its benefits exceeded its costs. Prices would be (much) lower than they would have been under the Pool, precisely because the Pool was assumed inferior to NETA. Monopoly pricing was caused by the Pool. Doubt, empirical scrutiny, and critical analysis never really entered much into the case for NETA after 1998.

Central to Ofgem's claims was the relationship between prices—and particularly the fall in prices in the run-up to NETA's introduction—and NETA. To Ofgem, NETA *caused* prices to fall—and by much more than the costs of introducing and running the new system. As McCarthy said to the Select Committee inquiry into 'The Work of Ofgem' (House of Commons Trade and Industry Select Committee 2000a), NETA was 'already casting its shadow forward in terms of prices for wholesale electricity' (para 144) in the autumn of 2000, and 'I think it is undoubtedly the case that once NETA is there it will be a much more competitive market' (para 146). In subsequent reviews of NETA, Ofgem was quick to point to price falls as part of the justification for NETA (Ofgem 2001b: 37; Ofgem 2002b).

Why, then, did prices fall in the run-up to NETA's introduction—and, indeed, afterwards? The answer is necessarily complex (not uni-causal) as

[17] There is some evidence that Ofgem recognized the specific German dimension. McCarthy told Platts in September 2002: 'One of the things that concerns me very much, and we are looking at this particularly, is that two major companies are owned by German parents where the tradition of competition within the (domestic) market, if I may put it politely, is not well developed' (Platts 2002: 1).

is to be expected in a partially vertically integrated oligopoly. The ingredients start with the obvious fact of excess capacity, which in any oligopoly is usually a cause of weakening scope for collusion, whether cooperative or noncooperative. By far the most important factor is retail competition and the 1998 liberalization, and the ending of the contractual framework which had provided the stability to the market since 1990. Supply competition and vertical integration meant that generators could chase margins up and down the chain. As Innogy, PowerGen, TXU, and Scottish & Southern strove to build up a critical mass in supply, inevitably the upstream pressure built up. Next there was the position of the CCGTs and non-integrated coal plant which the two main generators had sold. After 1998, many of the first batch of CCGTs no longer had the protection of the independent power producer (IPP) contracts with RECs that had recovered the capital and fuel costs through 1990–8. Now market share had to be won, and the high margins upstream in the 1990s, between falling coal and gas prices on the one hand, and steady generation prices on the other, moved downstream. Once the supply market had concentrated, retail margins increased.

The list of factors could be added to.[18] There were lots of reasons why wholesale prices fell. But the central observation is that the critical event was retail supply liberalization in 1998, and its implications were felt over the next few years. Mandelson's White Paper, and the coal fix which went with it, put sticking plaster over the old 1990–8 structure, but it was not enough. Contrary to the intent under NETA to encourage generators to contract, after 1998 there was no long-term contracting structure. It was a short-term market in excess supply. In 2000 and 2001, wholesale prices probably would have fallen anyway, under the Pool or NETA, as suppliers went short, particularly Centrica and then Innogy. And, if they had not, there were many ways they could have been forced down.

There is one further piece of evidence relevant to the hypothesis that 1998 and supply competition were at least important causes of falling wholesale prices—and that again is what happened in Germany, which had neither a Pool nor NETA for the period. The German market was arguably a more concentrated oligopoly than that in England and Wales, and when it liberalized supply, wholesale prices also fell sharply. Thus the form of market bidding, balancing, and contracting cannot be a sole explanation.

None of this is to imply that market design is not important. Market design affects behaviour. But whether it was worth more than half a billion to introduce NETA, and whether NETA is likely in the medium term to be markedly better than a modified Pool, remains very much an open question.

---

[18] See Newbery and McDaniel, 2003, and Evans and Green, 2003.

18

Price Reviews Again: Asset-sweating or Investment?

The regulator has to balance the interests of present and future consumers, both against each other and against the interests of present and future producers. (Michael Beesley and Stephen Littlechild, 'The Regulation of Privatised Monopolies in the United Kingdom', 1989)

Present levels of capacity in the UK in both electricity and gas networks and in electricity generation are healthy. The processes of privatisation and liberalisation seem to have succeeded well. (PIU, 'The Energy Review', 2002)

Whilst government and regulators were focused on the removal of the domestic franchises on electricity and gas supplies, and on NETA, the five-year price caps for the networks were coming up for revision in 1999/2000 for the regional electricity companies (RECs) and in 2001/02 for Transco. There were also the transmission price caps for National Grid Company (NGC) and Scotland and the Northern Ireland Electricity (NIE) transmission and distribution networks to review.

By the end of the 1990s a lot had been learned about utility regulation in general and price caps in particular. The early models of loosely set attempts to replicate a competitive market had given way to a much more complex world of multiple objectives for networks and much less acceptance of the possibility of abnormal returns. Thus the task facing Ofgem at the end of the 1990s was a more difficult one than that facing the Department of Energy in 1989/90. Whereas the Department of Energy had to make educated guesses, Ofgem had to be seen to get the 'right' answers.

Despite the two attempts by Littlechild in 1994/95 to put the RECs on a stable long-term path reflecting the underlying costs, despite the £50 rebate on the sale of NGC, and despite the windfall tax, there remained very considerable fat on the RECs. They could finance their functions on considerably less. The Ofgem approach proved focused and tough, and applied the logic of the building-block approach discussed in Chapter 11.

The RECs' review—and subsequent developments for Transco—also began a process of moving towards a more market-based approach for the determination of capital expenditure (CAPEX), opening up auctioning as a way forward. But the outcomes were not universally regarded as benign: they encouraged the flight from equity towards debt finance, and raised questions about the trade-off between low prices and the level of network renewal and investment. To some, notably engineers, they were a step too far, likely to build up problems for the future.

The Build-up to the RECs' Periodic Review and the Strange Case of NIE

After the first round of periodic reviews had been completed in 1995, the laggard to be considered was NIE, vested in 1992, privatized later in 1993, and subsequently regulated by the Office for the Regulation of Electricity and Gas in Northern Ireland (Ofreg). Its first regulator was Geoff Horton, who had been part of the Department of Energy regulatory team at privatization. Horton was succeeded by Douglas McIldoon, who carried out NIE's first periodic review in 1995 and 1996.

McIldoon was as much concerned with the wider economic development of Northern Ireland as he was with the niceties of electricity regulation. Early on he set himself the objective of closing the gap he perceived between prices in Northern Ireland and those on the mainland as a contribution towards the improvement of the competitiveness of the Northern Ireland economy. Part of this gap related to the peculiar power purchase contracts for the four generators set up at privatization with the single buyer (NIE), and about which he could do little (see Chapter 7). But transmission and distribution prices fell within his ambit, and in the first review, having taken a position on operating expenditure (OPEX) and CAPEX, he was left with the regulatory asset base (RAB) as the primary variable to squeeze down the price level.

This level depended, at the first review, on the view taken of the initial value at privatization and the appropriate mark-up. As we saw in Chapter 11, there is no 'right' answer to its determination. The candidates are: the issue price; the first-day premium; the premium after some initial period (the average over 200 days in the case of water); and the price at the end of the period. None of these is without difficulty: the issue price may turn out to be *higher* than the market price after some period (as, for example, in the Scottish case and subsequently for Railtrack). The first-day price may reflect stock shortages for pension funds and other large investors, while any longer period is essentially arbitrary.

With such uncertainty, investors' expectations turned on precedent, and when McIldoon came to reset the RAB he had the earlier gas, water, and electricity cases to draw upon, and crucially the Monopolies and Mergers Commission (MMC) case on Scottish Hydro-Electric. These precedents pointed to an approach based not on the historic or current-cost accounting value of the assets, but what investors paid for them. McIldoon took the view that this was best approximated by the first-day valuation—that is, the flotation price plus (or minus) the premium on the first day's trading. This was harsher—considerably so—than any other previous case. In 1994/95 the RECs had received first 50 per cent and then, at the second attempt, 15 per cent uplift on the first-day premium. In the Scottish Hydro-Electric case, the MMC opted for 7.5 per cent and water had received an average of 5 per cent. It was therefore inevitable—given the ficundary duty of directors to shareholders and the amount of money involved—that NIE would reject the regulator's final determination and force an appeal to the MMC, which was duly made in September 1996.

The MMC, quite predictably, rejected the Director General's approach to the RAB, and followed its early judgement in respect of Scottish Hydro-Electric—that is, a 7.5 per cent mark-up on the first-day premium (MMC 1997a). The MMC added further modifications to the building blocks, notably changing the depreciation methodology and profile and the cost of capital. The MMC also rejected the claw-back of CAPEX underspend in the first period that McIldoon had adopted, and rejected the operating costs work that Ofreg had commissioned from its consultants. In the rather formal way in which such matters are put, the MMC states that 'we believe the conclusions are not sufficiently robust in themselves to form the basis for the future price control. We have accordingly sought to reach our own assessment' (ibid.: para 2.149, p. 37). This was a serious criticism of Ofreg's competence.

The MMC's approach translated into a new determination which reduced prices by less than the McIldoon proposed, but more than NIE suggested. The MMC had done a markedly better job than Ofreg, it had followed precedent, and reached a decision which, while departing from the Ofreg's methodology in a number of important respects, did provide a basis for the second period.

The expectation of NIE, the rest of the industry, financial institutions, and most outside observers was that this would be the end of the matter, with the MMC outcome determining the licence amendment and hence the new price cap. McIldoon, however, refused to implement the MMC findings and instead imposed his own preferred determination. This action threw into stark relief both the confusing state of the law with respect to the MMC's status, and the imperfections of the appeals process itself. Court action followed, turning on whether the MMC had in effect stated a minimum amount of money required to fulfil the duty to finance functions, and whether this was a public-interest finding. NIE won, although Ofreg never accepted that it would not have been vindicated, had it appealed all the way. (In the 2002 review, McIldoon tried again to reopen the MMC's position, and, after more acrimony between NIE and Ofreg, eventually settled for a glidepath formula which was both opaque and bore little resemblance to precedent.)

Morse's Approach and the Consultation Paper

With NIE's case concluded, and the MMC report to draw upon, the newly formed Ofgem set about its task of carrying out fourteen price reviews of the English and Welsh RECs and the Scottish distribution activities.[1] It was widely believed to be behind in its preparation, in part a reflection of the more relaxed approach under Littlechild. While, in the parallel water reviews under Ian Byatt, work had been under way since 1996, building up the methodology, the business plans, and public consultation, comparatively little had been done before 1998 within Offer. Indeed, there was some consideration at the time as to whether a one-year rollover might be required to buy enough time to do the job properly (as happened in the case of Scottish transmission)—and hence to avoid a reference to the Competition Commission. However, the new Director General, Callum McCarthy, brought in Richard Morse on a two-year secondment from Dresdner Kleinwort Benson, and delegated to him the task of carrying out the reviews. Morse had the obvious advantage of having been involved in the original privatizations of the England and Wales generators and the RECs, as well as having handled the grid demerger. His City background gave him a financial grasp of the businesses which Littlechild and his team did not have the advantage of.

Morse's views on the periodic review were set out in a consultation paper in May 1999 (Offer 1999). It provided a well thought-out analysis of the position, with the intent of finding out what the minimum revenue

---

[1] Scottish transmission was separately regulated, and a rollover was adopted before a new price cap was eventually set, the main aspect of which was a lower cost of capital (see Offer/Ofgas 1999; Ofgem 1999c,d).

requirements would be. Like many new to the regulator's role, Morse began by seriously questioning whether RPI − X was the right approach, and for a time at least, an alternative 'RPI − X Mark 2' was actively discussed, though in the end the priority of getting the job done to timetable meant that more radical approaches had to be left to unfold after the periodic review was completed (we return to this below). The consultation paper reflected what he perceived as the weaknesses in RPI − X, notably the emphasis on periodic negotiation with the regulator, the need to place greater emphasis on outperforming peers, the imbalance between incentives to efficiency in respect of operating costs and capital costs, and the need for clearer incentives in respect of the quality of supply (Offer 1999: para 2.5, p. 9).

As it turned out, the major emphasis in the review was on operating and capital costs. The RAB and the cost of capital conformed to the standard MMC methodology which Morse—unlike McIldoon—was not keen to disturb. The starting point of the cost analysis was to observe how considerable the fall in costs had been since the 1994/95 review. As the consultation paper observed, 'in aggregate, PES distribution business operating costs (excluding depreciation of network assets, NGC exit charges and distribution system business rates) fell by more than one quarter between 1994/95 and 1997/98' (Offer 1999: para 3.10, p. 23).

Costs had fallen dramatically, contrary to what the RECs told the regulator back in 1994 to expect. Either some extraordinary and unexpected efficiencies had been achieved, or regulatory games had been played at the last review. Morse was rightly suspicious therefore of the RECs' estimates of costs for the period 2000–5, which they projected on a comparable basis to rise at the start of the period, only to fall back to the current levels in 1999 by 2004/05. In other words, the RECs claimed that most of the efficiency gains had now been made.

The position on CAPEX was much the same. The consultation paper compared the projections of the companies for the period 1995–6, with Offer's own determination at the time (reductions on some companies' forecasts of up to 25 per cent) and current forecasts of the RECs for the next period (Fig. 18.1).

Having examined the variances between projections and outcomes in the last period on a case-by-case basis (and found they also varied a lot), Morse then turned to the difficult question of how to produce a better forecast for the next period. In the draft determination in August 1999 (Ofgem 1999b), the chosen method was to standardize the costs between companies for differences in accounting policies (which Littlechild, unlike Byatt, had left significantly to the companies' discretion), and then regress

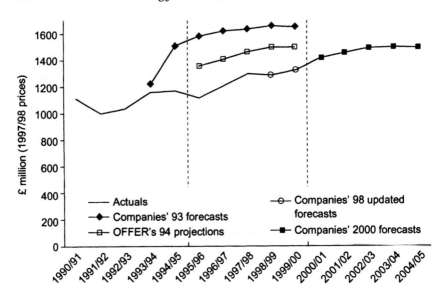

FIG. 18.1 CAPEX actuals, forecasts, and projections
Source: Offer (1999).

these adjusted base costs against a composite scale variable, which was constructed by adjusting customer numbers for differences in units distributed and length of network.[2]

This exercise was carried out for a *sample* of RECs, excluding Eastern and Southern, which were deemed to be on the efficiency frontier. The difference between the scale/cost regression line and the frontier is then used to estimate the 'catch-up' each needed to make to reach the frontier. In the draft proposals, this was around an average P_0 cut of 16–25 per cent, with a forward-looking X factor of 3 per cent. The empirical methodology used was subjected to intense criticism,[3] but much of this missed the central point, which is whether the regulator had a duty to finance the *efficiently* executed functions of the business or just the reasonable costs, and whether the 'best' should be the baseline. For if the frontier was used, then only the frontier company could make normal returns. The possibility of losses—of a return below the cost of capital—was clearly envisaged in the new approach. Since there had been no judicial appeal on the meaning of

---

[2] There had been significant elements of capitalizing what had previously been regarded as operating costs, thereby flattering earnings, although not on the scale that was to be revealed in the WorldCom and other accounting scandals in 2002.

[3] See 'The Final Frontier', *The Utilities Journal*, September 1999, pp. 18–19.

the duty to ensure that companies can finance their functions, penalizing some companies' customers by reflecting differential levels of efficiency against others would be a delicate—and perhaps legally questionable—practice. If Ofgem found a company to be inefficient, it might be regarded as only fair that it be allowed a transitionary period to 'catch up' with its peers—assuming, of course, that Ofgem had measured efficiency properly. It was probably for these reasons that the more 'purist' approach to comparative efficiency and the notion that Ofgem should only have regard to the revenues required to *efficiently* finance *efficiently* carried-out functions was moderated towards a more pragmatic outcome. This more relaxed approach contributed to the acceptance of the review outcomes without appeal—among other factors, discussed below.

In December 1999, the final proposals were published (Ofgem 1999e). Costs had been updated in October, and a number of adjustments made in response to the companies' lobbying on the normalization procedure. Every REC had incentives to present its company in the best light, and there was always an equation which could make each the most efficient. Ofgem used consultants' studies of the efficiency of each REC as a check against the regression analysis, the latter producing somewhat higher estimates of the scope for potential savings.[4]

On CAPEX, a benchmarking exercise in the draft proposals was updated, and Ofgem set allowances midway between the median company and the upper-quartile company performance. Again, an attempt was made to relate allowances to a frontier concept. The scale of gaming by the companies was revealed. For example, for non-load-related CAPEX, adjustments from the modelling to companies' forecasts to NORWEB amounted to over 50 per cent, with half the companies reduced by 30 per cent or more. The *overall* reductions in CAPEX were also significant, NORWEB topping the list with a 41 per cent cut.[5]

Between the draft and final determinations, Ofgem moved very little.[6] The X factor remained at 3. Issues in relation to the wider attempts to relate quality and price were left to be sorted out in the next couple of years—in the form of the Information and Incentives Project (IIP), which is discussed below.

It remains to ask why no REC appealed against these determinations, despite the gap between their projections on OPEX and CAPEX and the amounts allowed by Ofgem. There are a number of possible reasons for

[4] See Ofgem (1999e: 20) for a comparison of the result of the efficiency study and regression analysis for 1997/98.
[5] See also Offer (1994c: paras 5.31–5.33, pp. 54–6) where similar gaming was revealed in the previous price review. [6] See, for comparison, Ofgem (1999c: 52).

this acquiescence. The charitable ones start from the premise that Morse and his team got the right answer, but that the RECs only discovered this through the process. Certainly, a couple of years earlier, there was little expectation that such large price cuts would be imposed, and this was reflected in the valuation placed upon acquisitions. Unless the other assets of RECs were worth significantly more than the share prices reflected, the implied price cuts behind the acquisition valuations were much gentler. Perhaps, once the regression and efficiency analysis had been revealed, and benchmarking of CAPEX published, the managers realized the error of their own forecasts?

A less benign explanation is that the companies deliberately 'overbid', inflating their cost estimates, knowing that these would be negotiated away. This explanation fits with the gaming incentives within RPI − X, confronted with a regulator with asymmetric information. It is hard to avoid the conclusion that much of this was going on. But if this was true, there was also a remedy: a licence condition could have been imposed *requiring* executives to personally certify that they believed the forecasts to be true and accurate, and then to hold them personally to account for them. Monopolists, it could be argued, should—like taxpayers—have a legal duty not to provide inaccurate information.

A third explanation of the reluctance to appeal is a more complex one—that there was a way in which the companies could live with the outcome—but only by replacing equity with debt. In other words, the implied returns—taking both the cost of capital and the allowed operating and capital costs together—were enough to give a return to debt-holders, but not equity. Hence, the determinations were not sufficient to finance the functions of an equity-driven business, but enough to satisfy debt-holders once the business had been mortgaged to the bank—technically securitization.

In fact, the truth probably lies with all three explanations.[7] The Ofgem exercise was not one which is likely to go down as particularly rigorous or robust, and the quality of some of the consultants' work was questionable. Companies, faced with the abyss as they saw it, probably discovered that they could cut costs much more than they had initially thought. But they also played games and were 'economical with the truth'. And securitization did provide a way out, which many of them took, to varying degrees.

---

[7] A fourth explanation has also been suggested: that the companies had considerable freedom to reduce OPEX and CAPEX by taking additional risks with the quality of service—and hoped either not to be found out or to pass on the risks to customers at the next periodic review.

The RECs' Response to the Periodic Review

Reductions in costs and income on the scale required by the final determinations, and the very fact that the uncertainty was now over, led the
RECs to think radically about their futures, and, not surprisingly, a number of models emerged. The common theme was the split between assets
and operations, following on from the separation of supply from distribution which the Utilities Act 2000 had mandated, but which in any event
was becoming the preferred business model.

The reasons for separating out assets from operations were several. The
assets were represented by a RAB which could be securitized, and the
risks to its owners were low—and much lower than those pertaining to
operational and investment activities. Hence an 'asset co' could become
debt-financed. It would, however, need to ensure that the licensed functions were carried out, and this meant it would have to contract out its
activities. By signing fixed-price contracts with suppliers, it could create a
back-to-back cost structure against the price cap, and hence transfer risk
from the distribution business to contractors. Once the risk had been
transferred, securitization would be much easier to achieve.

The pure asset company/operations company split has not to date been
effected in electricity distribution, although several of the elements are in
place. Debt covenants relate to assets, and the use of contractors has
greatly increased. The most radical early model was 24seven, initially a
joint venture between Eastern Electricity (owned by TXU) and London
Electricity (owned by EDF). Such break-up models have given considerable cause for concern amongst regulators, as the core asset owner needed
to ensure that there was sufficient management expertise to monitor performance of contractors and have the capability to step in and deliver the
functions if required. The worry was that 'hollowed-out' distribution
businesses might, over time, prove too empty to sustain their networks.
Thus when the Glas Cymru proposal emerged in the water industry,
Ofgem let its lack of enthusiasm be made very apparent.[8]

Other RECs tried different approaches. Some became distribution-only
businesses and sought out consolidation. Northern Electric merged with

---

[8] Ofgem published two responses to the Dwr Cymru acquisition by Glas (Ofgem 2000c,g),
and went further than any other regulator in commenting on another's business. Its primary
concern was over the financial arrangements. In the second response, Ofgem stated that 'for a
structural change to be acceptable to Ofgem it should bring a net benefit to customers. The additional returns which companies are seeking by structural means can only come from a redistribution of risk. Unless the overall level of risk can be reduced, companies can only gain at the
expense of customers (or possibly other companies)' (Ofgem 2000g: para 2.4).

Yorkshire Distribution, for example. United Utilities made a virtue of its
asset operations skills, whilst trying to maintain an equity profile. Others
were absorbed within vertically integrated utilities, many of these very
large and on a European scale. East Midlands and Midlands Electricity
eventually became part of E.ON, whilst London and SEEBOARD, as well
as Eastern Distribution (and hence 24Seven) were absorbed by EDF.
(ScottishPower had already absorbed Manweb.)

It is too early to tell whether these business and financial restructurings
will prove enduring, but it is already possible to detect the RECs' progress
against the determinations. Evidence on cost performance indicates that
none is overtly struggling to keep within the determination boundaries,
though how far this is at the expense of longer-term investment and maintenance of networks is far from clear. In the short term, sticking plasters
could be attached to the networks.[9] Indeed, it is this concern which has
been one of the motivations behind the IIP project and a greater focus
within Ofgem and the Department of Trade and Industry (DTI) on the
quality and security of supply.

IIP and Other Innovations

As has repeatedly been seen, what started out as a deceptively simple regulatory rule (RPI − X) has turned out to be ever more complex. Very early
on, Oftel recognized that BT could maximize profits in its monopoly business not only by cutting costs, but also quality, and early skirmishing took
place about customer services, rural phone boxes, and other areas where
BT had little incentive to improve its performance. Step by step, more
flesh has had to be put on the bones of RPI − X. But because Littlechild's
approach to regulation, as detailed in Chapter 11, was grounded in the
belief that it was hopeless to try to predict a utility's costs, Offer probably
developed less content to RPI − X regulation than the other regulators in
the early to mid-1990s. In a very real sense, Littlechild did not much
believe in regulation.

Morse's major contribution, in addition to getting the job done to time
and without triggering referrals to the Competition Commission, was to
combine Littlechild's insight with a recognition that the quality of supply
could not be left out of the equation. On the one hand, he recognized that
regulators were unlikely to know what was best for customers, and that
some degree of experiment and variety might better reflect the different

[9] See, for example, 'Concerns over New Rule Hits Engineers', *Financial Times*
9 January 2002.

circumstances of types of customer—and companies should be incent-ivized and rewarded for better performance. On the other hand, deteri-oration of quality needed to be avoided by companies, which would be much more harshly constrained by the price cap.

Time did not permit these matters to be sorted out in the review, and what became known as the IIP project was set up to address these issues. The project rapidly came up against three main problems. The first and most important was that quality is largely a *system* property, rather than easily disaggregated, and hence there was little scope beyond the tradi-tional interruptible contracts and demand management to give different customers different *qualities* of electricity supply. Network investment and maintenance was therefore in large part impervious to such incent-ives. The second problem was that incentives could only meaningfully be provided for things that could be *measured*—and these tended to be such things such as how long it took to answer the telephone and how often customers were interrupted. The third problem was that Ofgem was never clear as to whether the IIP revenue effect was intended to reflect companies' valuations of differences in standards of performance or pro-vide a financial penalty for failing to meet targets.

Once regulators started picking variables on which to focus, and creat-ing incentives to improve performance with respect to these variables, they had (at least implicitly) encroached on management's domain of con-trol. The public–private interface had shifted, making the utilities more like contractors. Managers started to concentrate on these variables, rather than others, keen to demonstrate their superiority to comparator companies, and to gain the rewards from the incentive mechanisms. As was graphically demonstrated in the case of performance targets in the Railtrack situation, the choice of a small number of measurable outputs could seriously distort behaviour.[10] Rather than delegate the objective of running a reliable and well-maintained network—one which requires the allocation of responsibility because elements of judgement are inevitably required—and choosing a series of indicators to *monitor*—the IIP sought to make the relationship between quality and revenue mechanical and deterministic. The IIP had migrated from an incentive-based scheme to a more intrusive regulatory one.

Inevitably, as the IIP exercise developed, some of these difficulties were recognized. Early on, emphasis was placed as much on the information

---

[10] In the case of punctuality targets, their achievement will be affected by the disruption through maintenance, thereby creating an incentive at the margin to reduce maintenance (see Helm 2002c).

regulators collected as on incentives, and, in the end, the outcome was more cosmetic than real, and crude rather than sophisticated.[11] Network security of supply would require other mechanisms—such as the Joint DTI–Ofgem Energy Security of Supply Working Group and subsequent new government initiatives (see Chapter 21).

Although what had started out as an attempt to create a new $RPI - X$ Mark 2 approach turned out a damp squib, the IIP exercise did begin to shift regulatory attention away from network prices and more towards investment and hence security of supply. The quality of electricity supply had a time dimension too. It was therefore perhaps inevitable that Ofgem would get sucked into asset management performance as well, further blurring the distinction between the job of regulators and that of managers. When Ofgem got to the Transco review, this focus had shifted even further from narrower IIP concerns with quality to a broader one of not just asset management but the determination of investment. And again, Ofgem began to flirt with the idea that this might be determined less by the traditional CAPEX game between regulator and regulatee, and more by customers. The idea of using auctions at a point in time—the allocation of existing capacity—had long been around. What was more revolutionary was the idea of auctions *over time*, determining investment. Gas was to prove the guinea pig.[12]

The NGC Review and the Separate Controls for the Transmission and System Operator

The NGC review began in December 1999 in the shadow of the Utilities Bill, which was due to be introduced into Parliament in January 2000, and just as the REC reviews were being concluded and NETA was in the process of being introduced. It therefore provided an opportunity for Ofgem to consider how price-cap regulation should adjust to the new regime, and, within it, how the traditional gaming over CAPEX could be ameliorated, if not avoided. It was also the first time since the merger of Offer and Ofgas that the electricity and gas networks could be considered consecutively within the same institutional structure. The inconsistency between the regulation of NGC and the gas National Transmission System (NTS) noted in Chapter 15 could now be addressed, and indeed, taking the two reviews together, by 2002 a much more coherent regulatory

[11] The two key papers are Ofgem (2000d, 2001g).
[12] The proposal to extend auctions to NGC's transmission system was dropped in early 2002 after strong opposition.

framework emerged. The convergence of the gas and electricity industries, as gas became increasingly dominant as the marginal fuel for power generation, made the need for such a joined-up approach urgent.

By the end of the 1990s, the core issues were already well known, and the review provided an opportunity to resolve many of them. The first, and most important, issue was structural: were the functions of the system operator (SO) sufficiently distinct from those of the transmission asset owner to warrant separate regulatory controls? In effect, this was the assets/operations separation issue discussed above for the RECs, but with the added twist that the SO had the crucial role in making NETA work, particularly in respect of the Balancing Mechanism. This in effect created three separate functions: transmission owner (TO), transmission system operator (SO), and balancing operator. There was also the issue of system services, losses and uplift, for which a separate set of incentives applied, from April 2000. Finally NGC's provision of reactive power and the settlement administrator role for NETA was put out to tender.

Thus, what at privatization had been a simple monopoly transmission system, had by 1999/2000 become a complex bundle of activities, which Ofgem had actively sought to unbundle. Consistent, too, with its overall approach, as much as possible of these functions had been opened up to competition, pruning the natural monopoly back to a minimum. To the question: 'What is the transmission function?', Ofgem's answer was in effect a series of disaggregated activities.

An initial consultation document was produced in December 1999 which raised the possibility of splitting the control in two: a TO and SO control (Ofgem 1999*f*). Further consultation papers followed in 2000, with final proposals for the TO in September 2000 and for the SO in December 2000.[13]

Transco Again

Whereas none of the England and Wales RECs nor NGC had ever challenged a regulator's determination of a price cap—disputes being confined to Scotland and Northern Ireland—most of Ofgas's determinations for British Gas had been challenged. The past was littered with acrimony and disputed positions, as we saw in Chapter 13. The MMC had been called in twice on periodic reviews (and twice on competition matters).

So when the parties approached the 2001/02 review, it was with some trepidation on both sides, and a desire to 'return to normal'. Avoiding another reference was an important consideration on both sides, and the

---

[13] The key consultation papers were: Ofgem (1999*f*, 2000*b,e,f,h*).

process was therefore a careful and professional one. That did not, however, mean that the past was forgotten—on the contrary, at least in the early stages, the core disputes of the earlier MMC inquiries (discussed in Chapter 13) remained very much alive, notably the vexed question of focusing.

Ofgem began the process of the review in May 2000 with its 'Initial Consultation Document' (2000a), in a context in which much else was going on. There were also initiatives in respect of separate price controls for metering; consideration of separate controls for connections; consultation on long-term incentives for investment in transmission capacity on the NTS; and, in the background, the possibility that Lattice (as British Gas had become) might break Transco up into an NTS and a series of local distribution zones (LDZs).[14]

There were three other broader considerations which shaped the review—the Utilities Act 2000; the growing role of gas in electricity generation; and the prospect of a gradual switch from North Sea production towards imports. The Act provided for guidance to be given to regulators in respect of environmental and social matters, and, in summer 2000, there was an expectation that this might widen the remit of reviews beyond their narrow technical and economic content to include such matters as fuel poverty, renewables, and other environmental objectives.[15]

With such a broad range of issues in play, the outcome would inevitably be a 'package', and part of the art of avoiding a reference to the Competition Commission was to offer a sufficient inducement to Transco over the issue of focusing the RAB that it might stomach other, less attractive aspects of the review. The possibility that, in the event of a reference to the Commission, everything would again be up for grabs might then temper the incentive to appeal.

The RAB focusing issue had been dealt with at length in the previous MMC report, and Transco's position was (rightly) that that report should provide the starting point, rolled forward by efficient CAPEX, adjusted for depreciation. It was, in any event, a distributional issue about shareholders' entitlement, and focusing would involve an *ex post* allocation of value from investors to customers.[16]

---

[14] This had first been proposed by Hammond, Helm, and Thompson back in 1985 (see Chapter 6). The break-up option receded with the resignation of Phil Nolan as Lattice's Chief Executive in late 2001, with whom it was widely associated, although the NGC–Lattice merger was widely thought to be likely to precipitate sales of LDZs to reduce debt.

[15] In fact, there was no final guidance before the completion of the review.

[16] At the time, the shareholder issue was becoming one of greater general concern, as the water companies' share prices continued to be depressed, and with the events at Railtrack beginning to unfold.

The initial consultation document set out the debate on whether to focus the RAB—that is, whether the market-to-asset ratio discount should be applied in a uniform way (the unfocused approach) or not, and left the choice open for consultation. In the background, the previous Director General of Gas Supply, Clare Spottiswoode, continued vociferously to argue for focusing, as indeed she had ever since the previous price cap had been set.[17] There was also the City reaction, with shares trading at a discount to the RAB, reflecting uncertainty over this issue.

In the event, Ofgem decided against focusing in its document (Ofgem 2001a), and the share price duly appreciated. That left the ground clear to move on to the other building blocks: the cost of capital, OPEX and CAPEX. Structure was again a core concern, and mimicking the decisions with NGC, the SO was separated from the TO, and five-year controls were set for the NTS TO and the LDZs, though, in the latter case, this was very much 'unfinished business', to be further unbundled during the ensuing period. The building blocks were established in the normal way through a process of engagement between Ofgem and Transco, and with the aid of external consultants' advice.

Between the draft and final proposals Ofgem gave some ground on OPEX and CAPEX.[18] This was partly in response to detailed analyses and further information, but no doubt the wider concerns about asset-sweating and security of supply in the gas network, on which the Performance and Innovation Unit (PIU) Energy Policy Review had already begun to

[17] See, for example, Ofgas (1997).

[18]

	Draft proposals	Final proposals	Transco business plans[a]
Regulatory asset value	Unfocused	Unfocused	Unfocused
Cost of capital	6–6.25%	6.25%	At least 7%
Total controllable OPEX[b]	£4.3 billion	£4.6 billion	£5.9 billion
Controllable OPEX[c]	3.5%	2.5%	1.2%
Total CAPEX[b]	£1.9 billion	£2.3 billion	£3.0 billion
Total replacement expenditure[b]	£1.7 billion	£2 billion	£2.4 billion
Initial revenue reduction	14	4	—
X value	2	2	—

[a] Since the business plan, Transco set out revised forecasts, and updated its replacement and NTS CAPEX.
[b] Five-year totals in 2000 prices.
[c] Compound annual growth rate.

Source: Ofgem (2001c).

focus (see Chapter 21), played a part too. Now was not the time to engage in a major confrontation with Transco at the Competition Commission on security of supply.

In setting CAPEX, Ofgem took what might be described as a 'belt-and-braces' approach. It tried to establish a planning total in the conventional way, but it also wanted to introduce auctions with regard to additional capacity. Finally, to make sure that supply would indeed be secure, it reminded Transco that it had a legal responsibility to provide a secure network, independently of the licence condition price cap. This was to be cemented into the regulatory regime through an additional licence amendment. This 'belt and braces' allowed Ofgem to set a base case below the Transco proposal, and then allowed the *possibility* of more investment through the auction mechanism with a slightly higher return. The alternative would have been to allow rather more CAPEX—perhaps in line with Transco's business plan—but then claw back under-spending, should this arise. The choice between these two options is a matter of balancing the risks of over-investment against those of under-investment. Suppose Ofgem was too generous. The prices would be higher than necessary, but supply would be more secure. Suppose now the opposite—Ofgem allows too little, and there are supply interruptions. The costs then would be very high. In networks, this effect is asymmetrical: at the margin, given uncertainty, over-investment is better than under-investment.

The judgement that Ofgem was required to make needed to be set in the wider context. As discussed in Chapter 2, the gas network had been built to a fairly tight specification, with little storage, and it relied on off-shore field load management, interruptible industrial customers, and the managed (and gradual) expansion of its domestic customer base. Now, it is required to carry electricity generation—perhaps, in time, 50 per cent or more of the total—on the existing system, whilst also catering for the expanding direct demand. It, too, has to adjust to the greater role of imports, and to the interconnector flowing inwards rather than outwards. There is an overwhelming dependence on one terminal, at St Fergus. In these circumstances—different from those of the 1980s and 1990s—there is a strong argument for giving investment the priority.

Ofgem could, however, fall back on the argument that auctions would facilitate this extra investment, if it were in fact needed. But the problems that auctions faced for the creation of sufficient new capacity in networks were very great. The gas network is a public good, and cannot be disaggregated into a series of discrete stand-alone enhancements. The gas shippers are an oligopoly and gaming is inevitable. Auctions over more than a year or two into the future are likely to be very thin—not remotely mapping the asset lives of investments. The network is a natural monopoly, so the incumbent has an incentive to under-provide, especially if it receives the monopoly rents from auctions. There is no obvious link between the auction revenues and the investments.

From an energy policy perspective, this substantive set of objections to the *determination* of investment by auctions needs to be set in the wider context of the network's *complementarity* with the rest of the economy. As noted above, the relative costs of over- and under-supply are asymmetric, and auctions cannot be relied upon to err on the over-supply side. For these and other reasons, Ofgem retreated from its initial ambitions, and the belt-and-braces approach left responsibility squarely with Transco (see Helm 2002*b*).

New Problems, Old Solutions

The periodic reviews of the late 1990s and early 2000s represented the application of the ideas that had evolved since the 1980s about natural monopoly regulation. The job of the regulator—of Ofgem—was to mimic the competitive market, setting a fixed-price, fixed-period contract, constructed from a series of building blocks: cost of capital, RAB, OPEX, CAPEX, and depreciation. This methodology applied to the irreducible core of the monopoly, and was combined with a policy of extending the market and competition as far into that core as possible. Supply had been separated from transmission and distribution, and storage, metering and ancillary services had gradually been unbundled.

There were many mistakes along this path. Inevitably, with so much discretion and so many general duties, some regulators performed better than others. The attempt to depersonalize regulation by adopting a broad structure made less practical difference than many had hoped, as McCarthy assumed both the Chairman and Chief Executive roles at Ofgem. But even if the mistakes had been avoided, the outcome would probably have been similar. RPI $-$ X regulation in the hands of Offer, Ofgas, and Ofgem proved successful at sweating the assets. It gave high-powered incentives to cut OPEX costs, and to cut CAPEX too (once the gaming at reviews had first encouraged overstatement of the requirements). Prices fell as a result, and, as regulators screwed down the returns, the flight of equity and consolidating mergers began. By the early 2000s, most of these cost savings had probably been made.

But whether RPI $-$ X, as interpreted by the regulators, will prove to have served the public interest better than its alternatives in the longer term is less clear. RPI $-$ X does not encourage investment, and truncates the management of the networks into five-year periods, creating a mismatch between the time horizon of asset management and investment decisions, and those which are profit-maximizing under RPI − X.[19]

By the 1999/2000 reviews, these investment and management problems were beginning to be apparent to the regulators. As we have seen, Morse toyed with alternatives to RPI − X in the late 1990s, and thought was already beginning to be given to information and incentives (the IIP project) and asset management plans. But in the end the opportunity to cut prices once again, and to cut sharply into the estimates of OPEX—and (in the case of Transco) CAPEX too—was taken. Faced with P_0 cuts of 20 per cent for the RECs and the uncertainty of auctions for Transco, it is not surprising that many managers simply took the regulators' numbers, wrote them into their budgets, and tried to beat them. However, much as regulators might wave their hands at the responsibility for the outcome in terms of network investment, the fact remains that the *consequence* of these reviews has been to reduce the incentives to invest. And, as debt replaces equity, the interests of banks in security of interest payments and repayment of the principal will encourage managers towards the shorter term.

In the aftermath of these reviews, serious concern began to emerge at the Treasury, No. 10 and, to a lesser extent, at the DTI. Perhaps the networks might not be in such a great shape after all. Perhaps the problems which were more generally manifest across Britain's infrastructure—in roads, railways, and broadband in particular—might also be emerging in gas and electricity networks. These concerns—together with the problems of climate change and the need to facilitate embedded generation, the convergence of gas and electricity, and the prospect of gas imports—triggered the PIU Energy Policy Review, and, with it, a rethink of whether the success of RPI − X regulation in the 1990s might turn out to be more the consequence of the circumstances—excess supply, the inefficiencies in operating terms of the nationalized industries, and the coming of information technology—than a demonstration of the generic superiority of RPI − X *per se*.[20] In Chapter 21 we return to these investment issues.

---

[19] For a more favourable view of RPI − X regulation, see House of Commons Committee of Public Accounts, 2002.

[20] Ofgem, by contrast, had few such doubts. See its initial consultation on 'Developing Network Monopoly Price Control' (Ofgem 2002d).

19

The Environment Moves Centre Stage

There are moments in history when apparently disparate forces or issues come together and take shape. Almost half a century ago that was true of arguments about the welfare state. In the last decade, the case for market economics has emerged, coherent and formidable, as a blueprint for prosperity and a guarantee of freedom. Today it is the environment that captures headlines and excites public concern. (Department of the Environment, 'This Common Inheritance', 1990)

Changes in the energy supply sector over the last decade have been the main reason for the reduction in the UK's greenhouse gas emissions. The significant shift from coal to gas for electricity generation during the 1990s transformed the industry and will continue to have a major impact in the future. However, the UK's energy sector is still largely reliant on fossil fuels and, unless they can be replaced by plant with low or no emissions, this dependence will increase after 2010 as existing nuclear power stations close. The direction of the energy supply sector over the coming decades will be critical to the UK's ability to make deeper emission cuts beyond 2010. (DETR, 'Climate Change: The UK Programme', 2000a)

Through most of the post-war period, energy policy had been designed to match supply to demand, and to do this in a way that ensured a comfortable security of supply margin. Coal output and coal-fired power stations had been the prime instrument, eventually providing almost 80 per cent of Britain's electricity, supported by the nuclear programme (the other 20 per cent).

Little thought was given to the environmental consequences. Acid rain and global warming were problems of which policy-makers were largely unaware. And to the extent that they were, Britain's ability to export pollution gave it a privileged position. With fast-flowing rivers to the marine environment, and with prevailing westerly winds, environmental problems could be disposed of via the river system, or through tall chimneys to the Continent and Scandinavia. Nuclear waste could be dumped directly into the sea in deep trenches, such as the Beaufort Channel, a policy which was to be extended to North Sea oil installations until Greenpeace intervened in the famous Brent Spar case in 1995.

In the 1980s, these convenient (and, in retrospect, complacent) assumptions were exposed to scientific scrutiny and, as they were found wanting, increasingly to political objections. The early environmentalists—led by Carson's *Silent Spring* (1963) and the doom-laden predictions in the early 1970s associated with the Club of Rome (Meadows *et al.* 1972)—had not yet persuaded politicians of the need to change direction, and the worst scenarios had not materialized. Fossil fuels appeared to be much more abundant than had been anticipated (and cheaper too). But scientists had begun to establish first statistical correlations and then causal links between the burning of fossil fuels and pollution. Acid rain was recognized as the cause of forest damage and the destruction of lake faunas, particularly in Scandinavia, and resulted in intense political pressures. Then the first serious evidence of global warming began to surface. The former was taken up by the European Commission and was to be incorporated in European directives. The latter—the focus of this chapter—followed a more torturous international path towards a global attempt at a solution. But, for quite different reasons, the coal industry was contracting fast in Britain, and therefore major new initiatives were not a policy priority until the end of the 1990s. CO_2 emissions fell in the 1990s mainly because the coal industry contracted.

CO_2 Emissions and the 2000 Targets

In the late 1980s, to most environmentalists' surprise, Margaret Thatcher was converted to the idea that emissions of greenhouse gases caused global warming. Whether it was her chemistry background that convinced her; whether it was a shrewd political move for the Conservatives to capture the green vote; or whether it was the personal persuasiveness of Chris Patten, then Secretary of State for the Environment and Crispin Tickell, former British Ambassador to the United States, it was to have a considerable effect on policy (see Thatcher 1995: 640).

The first tangible result of this conversion was a speech she made to the Royal Society in September 1988 (Thatcher 1988), and then more substantially, the 1990 White Paper, 'This Common Inheritance', the most significant change in environmental policy for several decades (Department of the Environment 1990).[1] The government formally endorsed the idea that 'global warming is one of the biggest environmental challenges now facing the world' (para 5.1); that 'this generation has a duty to act'

---

[1] David Pearce, the adviser to the Secretary of State, was a significant influence on the paper, especially its endorsement of economic instruments.

(para 5.14); and that, despite the uncertainty, 'the risks clearly justify action to begin to reduce greenhouse gases' (para 5.17).

The new environmental policy was crystallized by a target to reduce CO_2 emissions to their 1990 level by 2005 (later brought forward to 2000). In 1990, this appeared a tough challenge. Energy Paper 58 projected a significant *increase* over the period (Department of Energy 1989*b*). The White Paper pointed to a number of measures, including energy efficiency, nuclear, and renewables, with passing reference also to the role of combined-cycle gas turbines (CCGTs) (para 5.23). These measures would all contribute, but the overall impression is that the 2005 target was more an aspiration than a well-defined policy objective, and little thought had been given to how it might be achieved. In any event, at least three general elections stood between the target and the outcome.

As it transpired, it was electricity privatization and the implications of that privatization for the coal industry which made the achievement of the targets by 2000 much more straightforward. The architects of privatization knew that coal would contract sharply in the 1990s. Indeed, privatization was in part designed with this objective in mind, as we saw in Chapter 7. It was not, however, something that could be admitted in 'This Common Inheritance', but it cannot have escaped Thatcher's attention, given how much time she had devoted to the coal industry since 1981 and especially during the miners' strike. Coal's contraction could now be justified on *both* economic and environmental grounds.

The contraction of coal translated into a steep fall in CO_2 emissions in the early to mid-1990s, augmented by the effects of the 1990–3 economic recession. The Department of Trade and Industry's Energy Paper 65 published in 1995 projected that CO_2 emissions would continue to fall until 2000 and then start to rise (DTI 1995*a*). By 2000, Energy Paper 68 pictured stability or slight falls to 2005 and then a rising trend, but this was before the impact of rising gas prices produced a switch from gas to coal (DTI 2000*e*).

Early Energy Efficiency and Renewables Policies

In the 1980s, governments were already intervening to support renewables and energy efficiency on the grounds of market failure. Three separate sets of reasons explain these interventions (see Brechling *et al.* 1991). The first of these concerns imperfections in the operation of the markets themselves: problems with R&D and new technological developments, barriers to entry erected by the dominant incumbents and planning constraints in the case of renewables; lack of information available to consumers, imperfections in the landlord/tenant relationship and credit and financial barriers in the case of energy efficiency.

The second set of reasons relates to the failure to take proper account of externalities, and, in particular, concerns over greenhouse gas emissions. The absence of a tax on carbon, for example, creates an artificial distortion between renewables and fossil fuels. The third motivation—social considerations—recognizes that the poor use a larger proportion of their income on energy, and, hence energy efficiency measures are also distributionally attractive.[2]

The first two sets of reasons interact. If the non-environmental distortions are corrected for, we can then see what the level of take-up will be before adding in the environmental benefits. If, for example, corrections of non-environmental market failures made renewables economic relative to fossil fuels, the additional environmental intervention may not be necessary. (An example of the latter effect is that, once the barrier to burning gas in power stations was removed, the share of coal—and hence emissions—fell without the need for an extra carbon tax.) We need therefore to take each market separately, and then jointly consider the impact of environmental policy instruments.

The Market for Renewables

'Renewables' is a term much used, and rarely precisely defined (Helm 2002*a*). The lack of a definition has considerable advantage to policy-makers, since its elasticity enables the measure to be stretched to fulfil targets and to exclude some sources (such as nuclear) which have political difficulties associated with them. To an economist, renewables are resources that are not depleted with use. Wind is an obvious example: using wind to drive turbines does not reduce the availability of wind. Even here, however, there are subtleties: more precisely, although there is a transfer of energy from the wind, it is too small to have any impact on the total resource. Similarly, to tap tidal power is negligible in effect, although really large-scale tidal power schemes might have an impact. So our first definitional point is that all energy production requires some energy transfer. It is the scale that matters: burning coal depletes coal reserves in a fashion that is quite different from that of wind.

The second point is an inter-temporal one: some 'renewables' use up resources, which are then replaced. Biomass is an interesting example.

---

[2] The Home Energy Efficiency Scheme was explicitly designed as a distributional measure under the 1990 Social Security Act (see NAO/DETR 1998).

Willows trap carbon which is then released through burning, and then more willows 'take back' the carbon released. We can think of carbon compensation schemes in this light too: if coal is burnt, but more trees are planted, the effect is similar to the biomass activity. The point of this is not merely pedantic: there is no clear criterion which policy-makers use to decide what is and what is not 'renewable'. Hence, unless policy is directed at pricing the pollutant (i.e. a carbon tax), then technologies for inclusion in the policy framework must be designated. That to date has been highly selective.

Renewables are typically small-scale (with the exception of tidal barrage systems, such as the Severn and Mersey projects)[3] and, hence, are embedded within the electricity distributional networks. Their outputs are usually highly variable—for example, dependent on how windy it is—and therefore necessitate system support through peaking plant that can be brought on when the wind stops. The small scale and variability of output have put them outside the mainstream of power generation engineering, which has, for most of the post-war period, favoured large-scale coal and nuclear plant. It is not so much that such schemes have been regarded as a *threat* to the Central Electricity Generating Board (CEGB) and its successors, as an unnecessary nuisance. After privatization, they also represented a cost for connection and system adjustment to the RECs, and, in consequence, were not encouraged. (As we shall see, these characteristics were to prove very costly, confronted with NETA.)

The early interventions comprised elements of research subsidy and attempts to ease entry through the Energy Act 1983. In terms of entry, the publication of private purchase tariffs (PPTs) under the Energy Act 1983 gave renewables *rights* which had not been previously enjoyed. However, these were largely ineffective for two reasons: first, that the PPTs did not reflect the appropriate balance between capacity and energy elements (see Chapter 3); and, more importantly, because renewables remained hopelessly uneconomic in comparison to coal (and, subsequently, gas).[4] Although the exact scale of the cost disadvantage has always been hard to estimate (since there are no 'standard' plants and projects), it has remained significant (see House of Commons Select Committee on Energy 1991).

---

[3] On both these schemes, see House of Commons Select Committee on Energy 1991.

[4] There was an interesting exception to this dismal record under the 1983 Act—the Lynmouth hydroelectric plant. Visitors to the gorge at Lynmouth will find a plaque on the wall crediting its development to that piece of legislation, although the main economic consideration has clearly become tourist revenue.

Such estimates were, however, hard to validate, since they reflected cost calculations rather than market-tested prices. A much more concrete measure was provided by the introduction of the Non-Fossil Fuel Obligation (NFFO) under the Electricity Act 1989. Although this device was introduced primarily as a nuclear tax (see Chapter 10), it also provided support for renewables. Their inclusion was more a matter of 'spin' than deliberate policy choice: the tax would be the more acceptable if labelled 'non-fossil' rather than the less palatable 'nuclear' at a time when the government was trying to privatize nuclear within National Power. The inclusion of renewables probably also helped obtain clearance in Brussels. The scale of the differential support under the NFFO scheme gives it its true colour: renewables received none of the revenues in 1990/91 and still only 8 per cent of the revenues by 1995/96.

The NFFO was an obligation placed on the RECs' supply businesses to purchase a given proportion of their electricity at a premium price. The Secretary of State was given powers to issue Non-Fossil Fuel *Orders* from time to time. In trying to introduce an element of market discipline into the scheme, renewable generators were asked to make bids under a series of technology bands (wind, small-scale hydro, landfill gas, etc.), which were to run for a number of years to give the project a guaranteed market over a period long enough to spread its investment costs—in effect, an auction for a long-term contract. The difference in costs was made up from some of the proceeds from the Fossil Fuel Levy (FFL).

The FFL was charged at a fixed percentage of fossil-fuel sales, the rate to be reset from time to time. It began life at 11 per cent in 1991/92, falling rapidly away to 3.7 per cent by November 1996, 0.7 per cent by January 1997, 0.3 per cent by October 1999, and zero from April 2002. The scale of the levy reflected overwhelmingly the funding of nuclear liabilities, and its sharp fall at the end of the period was part of the arithmetic—and politics—of nuclear privatization (see Chapter 10).

The FFL was collected by an agent appointed by the electricity regulator, who passed the revenue on to the Non-Fossil Purchasing Agency which, in turn, distributed it to non-fossil-fuel generators as a subsidy on electricity produced.

The scheme effectively ended with the opening up of the domestic market to competition in 1998, and the expiry of the first two NFFOs in December 1998. Its impact on climate change had been negligible—indeed, throughout the 1990s, renewables were not much more than a political lobby. The scheme was replaced by contracts signed directly with RECs, via the Renewable Generators' Consortium. This new version, and its subsequent evolution under Labour's renewables policy, are discussed further below.

The Market for Energy Efficiency

The second strand of early environmental policy was energy efficiency. There has been a curious difference of opinion between the *advocates* of energy efficiency, who typically claim that there are numerous projects which have a positive *private* net present value to business and households, and more sceptical observers, who point to the low take-up of such apparently profitable schemes. The difference between these two positions turns on the *barriers* to take-up. For the advocates, it must be because significant barriers exist that take-up is so slow, and it is the job of policy to reduce or eliminate them.

The net present value of an investment in energy efficiency is, essentially, a balance between three factors: the cost of the investment, its return (the amount saved multiplied by the price), and the discount rate applied. There is little reason to believe that the market for energy efficiency investments (such as double glazing, loft insulation, cavity wall insulation, and other such products) is itself seriously distorted, and no particular reason to suspect any serious distortion to the discount rate. Both factors are typically known by consumers and not subject to much change. However, the variable which does change a great deal is the energy price: specifically, energy prices fell from the mid-1980s onwards, and regulation and competition drove the gas and electricity prices down in the 1990s, especially in the last years of the decade. It follows that, if the investment costs and discount rates have not changed much, many energy efficiency saving measures which might have been economic in the early 1980s are increasingly uneconomic now. The energy efficiency industry has therefore been rowing uphill for some time: an age of cheap energy and rising living standards is not conducive to marketing double glazing (except for noise reduction) and associated energy-saving measures.

The associated failures which may have inhibited take-up around this declining trend are threefold: informational (people who do not know that there are positive net present value projects to be had); the landlord/ tenant relationship (which prevents the tenant from capturing the capital value of the investment); and constraints on borrowing by poorer households. Each has a remedy: in providing information and advice; in tenancy agreements; and in social loans and poverty measures. Energy companies may not have incentives to encourage customers to spend less, so some form of regulation of public information may be required; and similar problems may arise with landlord incentives, again requiring regulation. The final category is probably the most important, and can be viewed as part of social rather than energy policy.

An additional reason for energy efficiency initiatives is to lower energy demand and, to the extent that this is based on fossil-fuel generation, to reduce greenhouse gas emissions. To some, this represents a 'no-regrets' policy—it corrects market failures, and has a pay-off for climate change policy. There are those who believe that, by reducing energy demand, climate change can be ameliorated, and that a demand-side policy might even be almost sufficient to achieve much of the climate change objectives. However, it is one thing to argue that an increase in energy efficiency is desirable, but quite another to think that demand for energy can be held down with continued economic growth by such means.

Over the past two decades, a variety of direct interventions in energy efficiency have been tried, short of using the price mechanism. These have included informational campaigns, business-breakfast initiatives, and other schemes targeted at particular groups.

With gas and electricity privatization, there was intense lobbying to incorporate obligations and duties on both the regulator and the companies with respect to energy efficiency. The RECs were required to offer energy efficiency advice to customers, funded through a £1 per customer levy on the monopoly franchise customers. After the 1994 supply review the Energy Efficiency Standards of Performance (EESOPs) scheme was administered through the Energy Saving Trust (EST), combining the setting of energy-saving targets for each supply licence with detailed prescription as to how these were to be achieved.[5] The schemes were supposed to be cost-effective, with defined environmental benefits, and representing an 'exemplary scheme mix of measures'. Special consideration for the elderly, disabled, and poor reflected the extent to which the schemes were from the outset as much about social policy as about energy market failures. Three types of scheme were to be used: national schemes (originated and managed by the EST on behalf of the public electricity suppliers, PESs); framework schemes (developed by the EST to be implemented in particular PES areas); and regional schemes (operated and designed by the PESs).

Marginal Contributions at Best

Did the energy efficiency schemes achieve their objectives? After two decades, has energy efficiency improved by significantly more than would be expected by changes in the underlying net present values? Or has the

---

[5] Littlechild rejected lobbying to include additional sums in his distribution price-control proposals in 1994. He did, however, reduce the volume incentive in the revenue driver and create further incentives to reduce losses (Offer 1994c: paras 4.9–4.14, pp. 33–7).

policy served merely to keep the energy efficiency lobby at bay, address social policy and keep a small army of civil servants busy? Similarly, has the NFFO resulted in a significant growth in the renewables sector, or merely served to subsidize inefficient generation? Have renewables saved much CO_2, and more than could have been achieved by closing a couple more coal-fired stations and replacing them with more efficient gas plants? Finally, would a carbon tax, or some other instrument have proved more effective?

To draw any tentative conclusions, it is important to get some perspective on what has and has not been achieved. Since 1991, the total renewables capacity contracted under the NFFO and the Renewables Obligation (RO) schemes have been 3,038 MW, of which only 907 MW have turned into actual investments. The share of total electricity generation held by renewables in 1990 was 1.8 per cent, and by 2000, it was 2.7 per cent. If the policy objective was to encourage a new infant industry, it is a poor result.

On energy efficiency, the total spent under the EESOP scheme has been running at over £100 million per annum, and the costs of all the other forms of intervention have not been empirically estimated. It is impossible to calculate how much energy has been saved as a result and, specifically, the fact that domestic energy consumption has increased more slowly than disposable income does not establish a strong causal link. For example, informational provision may have led people to take new initiatives, or it may simply have landed on people who were already minded to act. Nevertheless, the EST concludes that the results have been 'extremely successful' (Lehmann 2002: 88).

These benefits from the policy initiatives pale into insignificance against the impact of price: falling energy prices have reduced the economic attractions of renewables and of energy efficiency measures. The impact of the abolition of value-added tax (VAT) on domestic fuel after the 1997 election, the downward trend of commodity prices, and the harsher regulatory regime, have swamped the direct measures. A serious renewables regime requires a direct price effect (such as a carbon tax) or a binding quota. A serious energy efficiency policy requires an energy or carbon tax too. It was not until 1999/2000 that these issues began to be addressed—with the Climate Change Levy (CCL) and the RO. The most that can be said of the earlier policies was that they were too small-scale to do much good, or much harm.

The Marshall Report and the Search for Economic Instruments

By the late 1990s, the inadequacy of existing climate change policies was beginning to be apparent. The international process of negotiating a climate change agreement was well under way, culminating in the Kyoto Protocol to the UN Framework Convention on Climate Change in December 1997.[6] Labour in opposition was keen to reach out to the green vote, and its 1997 Manifesto went beyond the 2000 target, proposing a 20 per cent cut in CO_2 emissions by 2010 over the 1990 level. But how to achieve the more demanding targets remained elusive, especially given the low fossil-fuel prices which were widely assumed to be a prominent feature of energy markets, and the parallel policy objectives of both political parties to hold electricity and gas prices down.

An early consideration was to use economic instruments. The idea of a carbon tax had been around for some time, and the 1990 White Paper had, under David Pearce's influence, advocated the use of economic instruments (Department of the Environment 1990: Annex A, pp. 271–8), mentioning CO_2 as one example (para A.21). There were, however, formidable obstacles, not least the very explicit and visible nature of a carbon tax. In the context of the 1997 election, New Labour had been very careful to avoid the label of 'tax-and-spend', with only the windfall tax in its manifesto raising new revenue. The debacle over the Conservatives' imposition of VAT on domestic electricity and gas was still in politicians' minds, and Labour was pledged to abolish it. The conflict between short-term political expediency and the need to address the long-term problem of climate change could not have been much starker.

With this difficult political context in mind, in March 1998, Labour set up a task force to look into the case for an energy tax, and asked Lord Marshall to lead it. The specific remit was to consider how best to use new economic instruments to improve the industrial and commercial use of energy and help reduce emissions of greenhouse gases. Marshall had not been previously known for his environmental expertise, but he did have wide industrial experience, and therefore could be regarded as better able to 'sell' an unpopular tax to industry. He also fitted into the New Labour vogue for businessmen, rather than academics or experts in helping to shape policy.[7]

Marshall's task was largely one of process rather than strategy. In effect, the government had already decided that of the two options considered (taxes or permits), the former would be chosen. Furthermore, by making

---

[6] See Grubb *et al.* (1999), *The Kyoto Protocol* (Royal Institute for International Affairs/Earthscan) for the background to the agreement.

[7] Lord Marshall's career included the post of Chief Executive of British Airways from 1983. He was CBI President from 1996 to 1998.

clear the two central constraints—that the tax should not fall on the domestic sector, and that it should respect the competitiveness of British industry—the *carbon* tax option was also effectively ruled out. As Marshall told the Trade and Industry Select Committee in July 1999, the exclusion of the domestic sector meant that the tax had to be applied downstream. He also pointed to the practical difficulty of dealing with imports, where the carbon content of electricity would be hard to judge (House of Commons Trade and Industry Select Committee 1999: para 40, p. 11).

Whether such a constraint did indeed imply the *inevitability* of an energy rather than a carbon tax depends on the nature of the political constraint. A carbon tax would not *formally* fall on domestic users—it could be a *business* carbon tax—however, its economic incidence would (as it would with an energy tax too). The incidence effects would of course be different, but the real reason was coal. Thus, although the report devoted only five paragraphs (paras 115–19) to this question, Marshall did conclude that 'in my view, there is a good case for trying to reflect, at least in broad terms, the carbon content of different fuels in the rates set in order to maximize the emissions savings resulting from the tax' (Marshall Task Force 1998: para 119, p. 21). But coal—which is barely mentioned in the Marshall report (see para 41)—was a central part of Labour's political heritage, and it had just invested considerable political capital in trying to prop up the coal industry in the 1998 White Paper (see Chapter 16). A carbon tax meant a further contraction in the most polluting and inefficient source of energy. To avoid direct damage to the coal industry, the tax would have to be energy-based—and hence almost all its effects would fall on the demand side. Whilst this might be desirable in the short term (since the capital stock is fixed), the medium- to long-term supply-side contribution—crucial to the climate change strategy if economic growth was to continue—would be negligible.

A further political consideration influenced the choice between the energy tax and permits, though again the Marshall report was careful not to spell it out too explicitly. It was that an energy tax raised revenue, whereas a permit system might not, unless permits were auctioned. Indeed, as it turned out, the trade-off was worse from the Treasury's perspective—the permit scheme eventually needed subsidies.

The government was particularly careful in its first term of office to avoid the claim that it was the party likely to put up taxes, and hence was keen to avoid such an accusation in the case of the energy tax—somewhat misleadingly named the Climate Change Levy (CCL). It therefore proposed the full recycling of revenues—targeted primarily at a reduction in employer National Insurance Contributions (NICs),[8] but also to support particular schemes and technologies.

However, with a substantial revenue at stake (estimated in the March 1999 Budget at £1.75 billion—HM Government 1999: para 5.63, p. 77), all was not quite as it seemed, and there were two concerns with the recycling commitment. The first—and probably in the medium term the most important—was that the government would seek to recycle into schemes which it might otherwise have used public expenditure to support. The CCL provided a piggy bank, and it was hardly surprising that all sorts of interests lay claim to it. Like the lottery before it, there was inevitably what might be described as public expenditure substitution. Furthermore, in the event of a crisis in public expenditure at some future date, who could say that the CCL might not become a more general tax? France and Germany had similarly investigated such taxes, and in a *general* tax system, an energy tax has much to recommend it, energy being a relatively inelastically demanded commodity. By the pre-Budget report in November 1999, the proposed 0.5 per cent cut in NICs had been reduced to 0.3 per cent (and the tax reduced to £1 billion). £150 million was to go to energy efficiency measures, 'new' renewables and 'good quality' combined heat and power (CHP) were exempted (para 6.32, p. 40) and enhanced capital allowances for energy-saving technologies were added for good measure. By the Budget in March 2000, which introduced the CCL, the horticulture sector was granted £50 million for an energy efficiency fund and a 50 per cent discount on CCL for five years.

There was a more overtly distributional concern too, between industry groups. As might be expected, the energy-intensive users protested the loudest, on the grounds that the CCL would damage their international competitiveness, and there began an exercise in corporatism, whereby the then Department of the Environment, Transport, and the Regions and large users entered into 'negotiated agreements'. These would commit companies to measures to reduce emissions in exchange for lower CCL burdens. The basis for the discounts of up to 80 per cent was sites covered by the EU's Integrated Pollution and Prevention Control (IPPC) Directive (Council of the European Union 1996).

The negotiated agreements were complex, involved much bureaucracy, and needed to be monitored and enforced. From an environmental perspective, they represent a retrograde step, helping to support the very industries which are most energy intensive. Unless such activities can be

---

[8] Although employer NICs were reduced by about 0.3% as a result, they were then subsequently increased in the 2002 Budget for the tax year beginning April 2003 by 1%.

carried out using non-carbon-based sources then reducing the impact of climate change is incompatible with providing reduced taxes to energy-intensive industries. The rationale for such exemptions was really a conflict of objectives—competitiveness of British industry versus climate change.

It is in this context that a further distortion was introduced through the exemption of renewables and CHP, but *not nuclear*. If the tax was purely an energy tax, then all should be within its domain, but it makes little environmental sense to exclude some non-carbon sources but not others. The reasons were, of course, political: Labour did not, at this stage, favour nuclear technologies.

With all these distortions in place, the CCL was launched in the March 2000 Budget, based on the energy content of different products.[9] The Treasury estimated that the CCL and the negotiated agreements would 'save at least 5 million tonnes of carbon a year by 2010' (HMT 2000: para 6.37, p. 113). Quite what the counterfactual was is very unclear, but the ambiguity at least had the political merit of allowing 'success' to be eventually claimed.

Emissions Trading

Marshall may have been given a very clear political steer, but during the course of his Task Force's work, a concerted campaign was mounted to promote an Emissions Trading Scheme instead—with the great merit to industry, noted above, that it would not raise any revenue at the outset. For industry, a *gradually* developed trading scheme would delay further costs, and allow the incumbents in oligopolistic industries the strategic advantage of grandfathered rights over entrants.

The general case for tradeable permits has been well rehearsed in the economics literature.[10] A fixed-quantity target can be disaggregated into a set of permits. These in turn can be traded, so that the least-cost solution is found as permits are accumulated in the hands of those with the highest costs of pollution abatement. Subject to the way in which the revenue is distributed, the price of a permit may closely mirror the optimal carbon tax.

The fundamental difference between permits and taxes arises when there is uncertainty about the damage caused by the emissions and the costs of abatement, specifically the *marginal* benefits and *marginal* costs. Where the primary consideration is to limit the damage (because marginal increases are very damaging) then it is better to fix the quantity, and

---

[9] Equivalent in 2001–2 to: 0.07 p/kWh for liquid petroleum gas; 0.15 p/kWh for gas and coal; and 0.43 p/kWh for electricity.

[10] See the notable contribution from Tietenberg (1990).

let the price adjust. And where it is costs that matter most at the margin, while the *marginal* damage is less critical, then taxes are better.[11]

This theoretical difference translates into a strong preference for carbon taxes over permits in tackling global warming (see Helm 2001*b*). But there is an important caveat: in order to get international agreement on reductions in emissions, quantities have provided the preferred route. Any collusive agreement requires that performance by the parties is measurable, and an allocation of quotas is much more straightforward than agreeing an international carbon tax.[12] Thus the Kyoto Protocol allocates quantities to each party, and the European Commission has correspondingly begun to design its own (rather different) emissions trading scheme.

A number of large industrial users and energy companies therefore joined forces to form the Emissions Trading Group, and Margaret Mogford was seconded from BG to lead the initiative. It drew on early experience of within-company trading at BP, as well as experience of sulphur trading in the United States, and began in earnest to design a British scheme.[13] The Marshall Report reviewed early progress, and recommended that the government encourage a pilot scheme. It therefore proposed *both* an energy tax and a permits system. The difference was merely one of timing. Britain would therefore try to fix *both* prices and quantities—together with all the myriad of other initiatives.

Designing a permits scheme proved a complex task. In theory, the wider the domain of trading, the greater the efficiency gains and hence the lower the resource costs of achieving a given level of emissions reductions. However, it was immediately apparent to those involved that the cheapest option was to reduce coal burning in power stations—hence undermining the government's policy of supporting coal in the 1998 White Paper on energy sources (DTI 1998*b*). The generators were therefore excluded. The next obstacle was renewables, which were to have their own tradeable credits (see below). But renewables were a very expensive way of reducing emissions, and hence inclusion of the renewable credits in the scheme would have undermined the renewables policy. They were therefore excluded too. In consequence, the Emissions Trading Scheme in the United Kingdom was reduced primarily to a game between large industrial users.

There remained a final obstacle: why should any company voluntarily reduce emissions below the limits already set by the integrated pollution control regulatory regime and hence incur greater costs? To create the

---

[11] The classic article is Weitzman (1974). See also Barrett (1998).

[12] Interestingly, OPEC initially fixed prices, but in the 1970s moved to output quotas.

[13] See Schmalensee *et al.* (1998) on the United States, and Sorrell (1999) on the UK.

permits to be traded, further emissions reductions needed to be made, and to do this the Emissions Trading Group asked for a subsidy. This was not in the Treasury's obvious interests, and the Emissions Trading Group therefore came up with the argument that the justification for a subsidy would be that London could become the world leader in green trading, stealing a march on Frankfurt, and perhaps even the United States. Given the highly constrained nature of the scheme, only if it were to subsequently be enlarged to include the generators and renewables would the volumes traded be considerable. These were, however, the days of trading optimism, before NETA's problems were to emerge and before the collapse of Enron. The lobbying proved successful and the government obliged with a subsidy.

The voluntary scheme was given a framework in August 2001 and the subsidy which became available was set at up to £215 million over the five years of the scheme. The Go Live date was set as 1 April 2002, with a first auction on 11–12 March 2002. Rules had to be defined for eligible reductions so that credits could be gained under the Emissions Trading Scheme and, where relevant, the Climate Change Agreements, which had supported reductions in the CCL.

While the British scheme was being developed, the Commission put forward a proposed directive on emissions trading, which was agreed in July 2003 between the European Commission, Parliament and Council (Commission of the European Communities, 2000a and 2003a). It is an altogether better designed regime, including generators, focused on CO_2, and mandatory, not voluntary. As we shall see in chapter 22, the government was to make a virtue of the necessity of implementing the EU directive in its 2003 White Paper, and now the British system will have to accommodate the European one, with all its consequences for the coal industry.

In the event, the initial auctions led to claims that reductions in emissions were not additional and an acrimonious controversy developed between the *ENDS Report* (which pointed this out) and the Secretary of State, Margaret Beckett.[14] Thus, in addition to the theoretical doubts, the inconsistency with the European Union-wide proposals, and the lack of evidence to support the infant industry/infant market argument, the initial scheme has, so far, achieved very little.

Renewables, the Renewables Target, and Credits

Energy taxes and permits were the two principal economic instruments considered by Marshall, and both were supported and implemented. But

[14] See *ENDS Report* 327, April 2002, p. 3 and DETR (2002) letter from Margaret Beckett to the Editor, 24 April 2002.

Marshall was careful to note their partial role within a wider context of other environmental measures. These were—as they had been since 1979— renewables and energy efficiency. Progress on promoting renewables had been, as we saw above, slow under the NFFO. By 2000, less than 3 per cent of electricity generated came from renewable sources. When the NFFO ended, something else was required to be put in its place. The principal difficulty was that, after the 1998 liberalization of domestic gas and electricity, there was no contractual basis to pass on the (much higher) renewables costs. Some companies had set up green energy tariffs, but demand was muted. Customers would not voluntarily pay for green energy on a sufficient scale. They therefore had to be compelled to pay. The only viable way of achieving this enforced payment was by obliging all electricity suppliers to take a percentage of their electricity from renewable sources—the RO. This was set to rise to 10 per cent by 2010. At a stroke, the objective of 10 per cent renewables generation could be translated into reality through this obligation.

The problem, which was immediately apparent, was that, by fixing the quantity, the price was a variable—and might prove very expensive. The Department of Trade and Industry (DTI), with its industry constituency already confronted with the CCL, balked at such an open-ended contract, and was supported by the Treasury (which had imposed a Public Service Agreement target on the DTI of below-average electricity prices compared with Britain's European competitors). As a result, the obligation became subject to a price cap, or buy-out price.

It was also necessary to define what was—and, more importantly, what was not—included within the target. Would landfill—the cheapest option—be included? What about recoverable energy? What about nuclear? Should it be placed on a similar basis? The DTI was anxious to avoid the criticism that it was picking winners. However, for both the theoretical reasons set out earlier in this chapter (the elusive nature of the renewables definition) and for reasons of political expediency, it was inevitably drawn into choosing technologies. The overall policy objective was as a result based on a different, wider definitional basis to the RO.

Given the buy-out price, there was no necessary connection between the 10 per cent and the outcome of the RO. Renewables might turn out to be more expensive than the buy-out price. Government therefore had to intervene to create yet more favourable conditions to support renewables. This had several facets—including subsidies, exclusions from the CCL, beneficial distribution charges to support embedded generation, help with NETA, and changes in planning law. Renewables had become 'politically correct' and almost all aspects of existing energy policies had to lend support. No cost–benefit analysis supported these interventions.

But even the regulator would be told—through the Utilities Act 2000 guidance—to favour renewables.

The saga of the formulation of renewables policy is a case study in intervention in energy markets based on quantities and technologies, and it is worth setting out this process over and above its impact on this particular environmental objective. There have been a series of steps on this path to the current position, at each stage with a significant political input. Renewables were a manifesto commitment for Labour in 1997. It said:

We are committed to an energy policy designed to promote cleaner, more efficient energy use and production, including a new and strong drive to develop renewable energy sources such as solar and wind energy and combined heat and power. We see no economic case for building any new nuclear power stations. (Labour Party 1997: 17)

Under John Battle's guidance, the DTI instigated an early review of the status and prospects of renewables, and in particular of the necessary and practical steps to achieve the 10 per cent target by 2010. The words of support were reiterated in the 1998 White Paper on energy sources, and in March 1999 the DTI produced its consultation paper 'New and Renewable Energy: Prospects for the 21st Century' (DTI 1999a). It was a paper with the now obligatory pretty pictures of wind turbines and happy people, but rather short on definitive proposals. For example, in a section entitled 'What are new and renewable energy sources'? it tells us that 'renewable sources of energy are those which are continuously and sustainably available in our environment'—whatever that means—but importantly, no definition capable of testing is given (and the word 'nuclear' was not mentioned).

The next section of the 1999 consultation paper is entitled 'Why support renewables'? to which the answer given is circular: because renewables are 'sustainable', and government policy is to ensure 'secure, diverse, and sustainable supplies of energy', they must be a good thing. The caveat to policy—'at competitive prices'—created some difficulties, to which we will return. The important point, however, is that a *relative* calculation of the contribution of different types of energy sources is not carried out. Rather, because renewables are assumed to be sustainable—and help diversity and security—it is argued that *therefore* they should receive special support.

The most important aspect of these arguments is that renewables are a necessary part of the achievement of the 'UK Climate Change Programme', published in October 1998 (DETR 1998). It dealt with the 12.5 per cent Kyoto greenhouse gases target (by 2008 below the 1990 level) and the domestic 'goal' of a 20 per cent CO_2 reduction by 2010. The government wanted 'a range of policy options with all sectors playing a part'. But how much from each? Only 10 per cent from renewables? Such questions were not answered, nor indeed was any attempt made to answer them. Rather, a set of arguments was presented as to why renewables were disadvantaged. Not only did electricity prices not reflect the costs of externalities, but, even if they did, 'there could still be a need to support renewable technologies in the market until they achieved the necessary economies of scale, technological development, and investor confidence. There is therefore an argument for government support for renewables in order to help establish initial market share and demonstrate the viability of renewable sources' (DTI 1999*a*: 16). But why *these* infant industries should be supported, and not others, is not explained, nor is any quantification provided as to the level of this claimed market failure.

There was, of course, nothing new in these rationales—nor any explanation for why the industries had not progressed through this initial infant-industry stage in the 1990s under the NFFO support. As with nuclear, competitive status with other fuels was just around the corner, but sufficiently round the corner to require continuous support.

The March 1999 paper goes on to present a host of possible interventions to support renewables. These range from the planning process, embedded generation and information, through to 'market stimulation measures'. Economic instruments such as taxes and emissions trading are discussed, but the consultation paper concludes that 'unless directed at specific renewables technologies, such support would not be selective and might not bring forth the newer, initially more expensive, technologies needed for the longer term' (DTI 1999*a*: 29). In other words, since the renewables the DTI had in mind might not be the least-cost solution to climate change, a direct policy of obligatory purchase *of these technologies* would be required. Winners would be compulsorily picked. Not that the DTI knew whether these were least-cost solutions since the paper boldly stated that 'No attempt has been made at a detailed costing of such a strategy' (ibid.: 35).

There followed a process of consultation ('New and Renewable Energy: Prospects for the 21st Century: Analysis of the Response to the Consultation Paper', DTI 1999*b*), and then the publication of the government's conclusions in February 2000 to coincide with the introduction of the Utilities Bill (DTI 2000*b*). The conclusions were that a 5 per cent target should be set for the end of 2003, and 10 per cent for 2010. The key instruments were: the RO; exemption from the CCL (excluding large hydro); and demonstrations of technologies, together with a host of supportive activities. The obligation would be subject to a price cap, with a fixed price at which suppliers can buy out their obligation. The Utilities Act would impose the RO by statutory instrument and make provision for transitional arrangements for existing NFFOs (3–5) and the Scottish Renewables Obligations (SRO 1–3). The RO would apply for a period at least until 2025. As to what would be eligible, at this stage it was 'likely to include a wide range of renewable sources of energy' (p. 9). The RO could be traded through green certificates (called Renewables Obligation Certificates, ROCs). Thus suppliers could meet the RO by purchasing qualifying renewables supply; by purchasing ROCs; or by paying the buy-out price to Ofgem. Receipts from the buy-out would be recycled to suppliers.

The next step in this tortuous process was to gain the powers under the Utilities Act and then to consult on the form of the RO. That was presented in October 2000 in 'New and Renewable Energy: Prospects for the 21st Century: The Renewables Obligation: Preliminary Consultation' (DTI 2000*f*). The title had got longer but not much new was added, except that the buy-out price would be 3 p/kWh.

The Utilities Act 2000 had defined the base for the target as 'sources of energy other than fossil fuels or nuclear power'. It would include a host of possible technologies, including energy from waste and landfill. Such a wide definition would make the 10 per cent easier to achieve, but the obligation was to have a narrow definition—excluding large-scale hydro and energy from waste on the grounds that these are already commercially viable. Table 19.1 sets out the technologies picked for the target, the RO, the CCL exemption and capital grants, as set out in the October 2000 paper (DTI 2000*f*: 17, Table B).

TABLE 19.1 Summary of incentives for renewables

Source	10% target	RO	CCL exemption	Capital grants
Landfill gas	✓	✓	✓	
Sewage gas	✓	✓	✓	
Energy from waste	✓		✓	
Hydro >10 MW installed capacity	✓			
Hydro <10 MW, installed capacity	✓	✓	✓	
Onshore wind	✓	✓	✓	
Offshore wind	✓	✓	✓	✓
Agricultural and forestry residues	✓	✓	✓	
Energy crops	✓	✓	✓	✓
Wave power	✓	✓	✓	
Photovoltaics	✓	✓	✓	

Source: DTI (2000*f*).

The October 2000 paper also provided an estimate of the costs of the RO. These additional costs to consumers would peak at around £600 million in 2010—about a 3.7 per cent increase in 1998 bills.

The next stage of policy development was yet another DTI paper, this time with an even longer title, 'New and Renewable Energy: Prospects for the 21st Century: The Renewables Obligation Preliminary Consultation: Analysis of the Responses to the Consultation Paper', in March 2001 (DTI 2001*a*). This reflected the inevitable lobbying pressure which a technology-based policy creates. Interested parties pressed for their pet technology to be included (especially waste-based ones), and for higher capital grants.

By 2001 renewables policy comprised a target, an obligation and a buy-out price, CCL exemption and capital grants. Even this substantive support, however, was to prove insufficient to sustain the projects being advanced—the bulk of which were wind-based. The government, and in particular the newly formed Department for Environment, Food, and Rural Affairs (DEFRA), therefore sought yet more measures to support its chosen technologies. In addition to more subsidies, the renewables lobby was demanding significant changes to NETA.[15]

Although the protection of renewables (and CHP) had been part of the requirements placed on the design of NETA, it was apparent early in the spring of 2001 that the balancing system would impose heavy penalties on generators with intermittent supplies. The renewables lobby complained vociferously, mobilizing a powerful alliance of environmentalists and back-bench MPs. A review was ordered, and Ofgem was charged with reporting on the first three months' experience of NETA's operation. Ofgem duly reported in August (Ofgem 2001*b*) and then the DTI and Ofgem came up with a package of measures—primarily aimed at aggregation—to meet the concerns raised.

At the heart of these concerns were two very different views of the future energy market. To Ofgem, as we saw in Chapter 17, NETA was a market which was designed to maximize competition. In a competitive market, prices reflected costs. Hence the costs of renewables were exposed through NETA, and if it turned out that these were such as to render renewables uncompetitive, then so be it. Ofgem had an overarching duty to promote consumers' interests, and its primary instrument was competition. Therefore, why should Ofgem doctor NETA to suit what was manifest as an uneconomic form of generation? Like Clare Spottiswoode and the E factor (see Chapter 15), Callum McCarthy took the view that, if

---

[15] For a comprehensive list of the host of concessions and support the renewables lobby wanted, see House of Commons Environmental Audit Committee 2002, and PIU 2002.

government wanted to subsidize renewables, then that was its business, but not Ofgem's. Ofgem would do what it could, but by the end of 2001 it had not been formally issued with guidance under the Utilities Act, and so had no duty to have any special regard to renewables.

This 'market' view had considerable merits, and there are obvious dangers in an 'independent' regulator choosing to act in a way to suit the political priorities of the government of the day. However, the reason why renewables suffered under NETA had more substance than their individual plant characteristics.[16] Renewables are typically small-scale and embedded, whereas the electricity system in Britain (both transmission and generation) is geared to large-scale coal and nuclear plants located, respectively, primarily in the north and Midlands coal fields, and in isolated locations to reduce the risk to local populations. It is a system peculiarly ill-suited to the task of servicing a lot of small-scale embedded plants. While the total renewables contribution remained below 3 per cent, there was little point in trying to accommodate it.

Policy, however, is set to achieve a very different outcome, with an *aspirational* target in the 2003 White Paper (DTI, 2003*a*) of a renewables share of 20 per cent by 2020, displacing nuclear, and with gas largely displacing coal. The type of electricity and gas transmission and distribution networks needed are likely to be very different, and to require major government and regulatory input. The scale of the investment required could be considered analogous to that of building the national electricity grid in the 1920s and 1930s, or the gas National Transmission System in the 1970s and 1980s.

The problem with NETA, on this view, is that it provides an approximation to the optimal solution within a sub-optimal system. What is more, by discouraging renewables, the transition is made all the more difficult and costly. This should have mattered to Ofgem for two reasons: first, future customers' interests should be weighed in Ofgem's calculation of promoting consumers' interests; and, second, the government's higher levels of support could have an impact on customers through the RO. Although the buy-out price of 3 p/kWh caps bills for the RO now, if it turns out to be more expensive and to take longer to achieve the target, there would be pressure subsequently to change this buy-out price. Hence, if the target is seriously to be pursued, Ofgem should have had regard to making its implementation as smooth as possible. What looked like principled opposition to intervention by meddling politicians—for McCarthy, mostly the Minister for the Environment, Michael Meacher, and the Minister for Energy, Brian Wilson—was arguably counterproductive.

---

[16] The arguments which follow are set out in greater detail in Helm (2002*b*).

Embedded generation—and the concept of 'transforming networks'—has been pursued by the DTI with a working party composed of industry and regulators. It has produced a number of reports on the consequences of greater penetration of renewables, but has confined itself largely to technical issues. The fundamental questions of devising a *plan* for the network *as a whole*, of financing investments, and coordinating renewables developments with network management have been at best skirted around. The main consequence has been to adopt shallow entry charges, which pass the system costs on to the distribution companies and NGC. But this is at best piecemeal: by October 2002, there has not yet been a large-scale modelling exercise on the part of NGC or the DTI. Ultimately, this is the role of a system operator playing a role similar to that of the Strategic Rail Authority in the rail industry. At present, there is no such institutional focus in the energy sector, and, as a result, the public-good issues related to the network as a whole are likely to be ignored in favour of a gradual development of piecemeal projects coming onto the network. (We return to this issue in discussing the PIU report in Chapter 21.)

More Energy Efficiency

As noted above, like renewables, energy efficiency has developed its own lobbying interests, which combine environmentalists who believe that lower consumption is the route to a greener world; industrial interests with products to sell; those interested in fuel poverty who believe that subsidizing the reduced consumption lowers bills for poorer households; and finally officials with interests in building regulations, product standards, and local authority activities.

The main sources of market failure were reviewed above, and the lack of empirical support remarked upon. But, notwithstanding the somewhat shaky intellectual case for energy efficiency policies, other than social concerns, energy efficiency continued to enjoy considerable political support under Labour after 1997, and the EST led the main lobbying campaign for further support measures and an explicit target, analogous to that for renewables. Energy efficiency measures are politically appealing, being typically local, and directly affecting households. Such measures would 'help the United Kingdom to meet *all* its key energy and environment objectives' [italics added] (EST 2001; see also Lehmann 2002). By reducing demand, 'indigenous resources of gas and oil will be maintained for longer, thus delaying the day when importing these resources will be necessary [and] existing nuclear or coal capacity will represent a higher proportion of demand, which will help maintain supply diversity' (EST 2001: 6).

Like renewables, a whole host of *ad hoc* policies have been developed to support energy efficiency. In the 1990s there were building regulations and support for building research; the DETR's Home Energy Efficiency Scheme and Energy Efficiency Best Practice Programme; product labelling; British Gas's E factor, the Energy Efficiency Commitment (EEC); Energy Efficiency Advice Centres; and local authority schemes.

These initiatives have been set in an institutional context, where the governing department (first the Department of the Environment, followed by the DETR and now DEFRA) has been supported by the EST.[17] The EST is very much in the 'partnership' business, with members comprising the heads of other environmental departments and agencies (including the Carbon Trust, the Environment Agency, and the devolved parliaments), as well as the main companies in the energy sector. All sorts of schemes have been launched under this umbrella, and it is well beyond the scope of this book to detail them.[18]

Here the main focus is on the interaction between energy efficiency and economic regulation, and the role of energy efficiency within the framework of energy policy. It was recognized at privatization that there was a conflict between the desire of energy companies to sell as much of their product as possible, and the public interest in reducing demand for the externality and other reasons detailed above. Thus the question arose as to whether the price-cap formula for supply and distribution should have a volume component. A consideration was the raising of money for energy efficiency schemes, and this could be achieved by allowing regulated companies to charge their customers more, provided they spent the additional revenues *directly* on energy efficiency schemes, or they paid the revenue to some fund or public body, such as the EST. The former route led to the idea of energy efficiency obligations, the latter to the E factor.

At privatization, Offer was given a secondary duty of promoting efficiency in the use of electricity and to take account of the effects of the electricity industry on the environment. The RECs' licences required them to produce codes of practice on the efficient use of electricity and to provide advice on the subject to their customers. In the 1994 periodic reviews, Offer reduced the volume incentives and set the companies specific objectives to achieve given energy savings—the Energy Efficiency Standards of Performance (EESOP) scheme. This was financed through a £1 a year

---

[17] The EST was set up in 1992, against the background of the Rio Earth Summit and the closure of the Department of Energy, and was expected to be funded by contributions from gas and electricity customers and parallel sources of funds via the RECs (see Owen 1996).

[18] Many examples of such partnership schemes are documented on the EST's web site at www.est.co.uk.

additional charge to customers in the RPI − X supply formula to March 1998 (the EESOP 1 Scheme). The scheme was extended for the period 1998–2000 in 1997 (the EESOP 2 Scheme).[19]

Ofgas had its own, rather similar scheme, which was introduced in 1992 running through to 1997. This scheme was more *ad hoc*, in that British Gas proposed projects which would enhance energy efficiency, and the regulator then authorized them, and passed the costs through to final customers (the 'E factor'—as discussed in Chapter 15). On her appointment, Clare Spottiswoode questioned the legitimacy—and indeed the legality— of the E factor, arguing that it was in effect a form of taxation. Counsel's opinion (Jeremy Lever) was obtained in 1994, which failed to support her position, but allowed her to have regard to the effects on prices. Thus, while, in theory, the E factor was legitimate, in practice she could rule out projects on cost grounds.

With both the Offer and Ofgas schemes, the basis of charges was the monopoly, and once the domestic franchises ended in 1998, the scope for extracting revenue through supply price caps was inevitably limited. Thus successor schemes were considered (OXERA 1997). After some considerable debate, the EEC was set up as 'son of EESOPs'—in essence, a further tax on customers. The Utilities Act 2000 Sections 70 and 99, together with 103, made provision for energy efficiency obligations to be set by DEFRA for electricity distributors and suppliers (which it split) and gas transporters and suppliers (energy efficiency matters had been transferred to DEFRA after the 2001 election). The Statutory Instrument[20] came into force on 15 December 2001. This provided the legal framework for the EEC 2002–5 Plan.

DEFRA consulted on the EEC 2002–5 in August 2001.[21] Its proposal was for a 64 TWh target on all suppliers of fuel-weighted energy benefits, and it was crafted with two broad policy objectives in mind: carbon savings (which were estimated at 0.4 million tonnes of carbon a year by 2005) and fuel poverty (which should account for at least 50 per cent of the savings to those on income or disability benefit or working families, or disabled

---

[19] The NAO reported on EESOP 1 in 1998 favourably (NAO 1998). There was also an EESOP 3 Scheme, which included second-tier electricity and gas suppliers, with the equivalent allowance raised to £1.20 per customer for each fuel per year, with bids to be finally submitted in July 2002. Arrangements were made for EESOP 3 to be transferred to the EEC 2002–5.

[20] Formally, the Electricity and Gas (Energy Efficiency Obligation) Statutory Instrument 2001.

[21] DEFRA (2001). This was the culmination of a series of papers: notably 'Energy Efficiency Standards of Performance: The Government's Provisional Conclusions' (DETR 2000b).

person's tax credit). These objectives reflected the respective White Paper on 'Climate Change: The UK Programme' (DETR 2000*a*) and the consultation paper on fuel poverty (DETR/DTI 2001).

Ofgem was charged with the administration of this very micro scheme. The administrative role was far from straightforward, given that supply was now liberalized and each supplier had an incentive to free-ride on other—higher—costs of compliance. Detailed disaggregation of targets and *ex post* scrutiny would be required. And, as with renewables, questions of definition were not merely semantic: what constitutes energy efficiency is far from obvious; what is 'additional' as opposed to 'business-as-usual' is debatable; and auditing and reporting are far from straightforward. An insight into the mass of regulatory support required can be gleaned from the consultation papers produced to describe the administrative procedures (see Ofgem 2001*d,h*). The total number of consultation documents for the EEC approached double figures.

By the time of the election in 2001, energy efficiency and demand-side measures had assumed a more prominent role in energy policy, and it had almost become 'politically incorrect' to question their design, purpose or costs. The EST echoed this new conventional wisdom in its supplementary submission to the PIU (EST 2001) claiming that 'reducing demand for energy must be a first principle in developing the UK's long term sustainable energy policy', and advocated a 12.5 per cent per decade target for reducing energy consumption. No doubt there are 'no-regrets' opportunities which consumers fail to exploit, and even more cases where the social and private benefits jointly exceeded the private costs. But with no price of carbon[22] and no explicit evaluation of the alternative of a more generous social-security system to deal with fuel poverty as against direct energy efficiency subsidies, and with no serious attempts to state the *full* economic costs of the regulatory burden, energy efficiency remained more a matter of social policy than a coherent, efficient set of instruments designed to address market failures.

Policies in Search of a Framework

Over the 1990s, environmental policy crept up the agenda of the energy sector. By 2000, there was a wide, if not unanimous, consensus that global warming was a fact, and that the greenhouse gas emissions projections on the basis of business-as-usual over the first half of the twenty-first century

---

[22] On estimates of the social cost of carbon, see Clarkson and Deyes (2002), and Pearce (2003).

would not be remotely sustainable (DTI 2000c; IPCC 2001). The Royal Commission on Environmental Pollution (RCEP) (2000) report acted as a catalyst, stating the obvious that a radical shift in a non-carbon direction would be required.

But if overriding objectives hardened, policy remained fragmented and limited in effect. Politicians were unwilling to face the unpalatable reality that the costs would be great, and prices would have to rise. Nor did they need to in the 1990s. For quite independent reasons, CO_2 emissions were falling as the coal industry contracted, while nuclear output maintained its share of the electricity market. *Relatively*, the dash for gas reduced emissions compared with coal. That it could not continue this improvement when gas would come to replace the zero carbon emissions of nuclear after 2010 was a matter for the future—and beyond the general election horizon of ministers. Indeed, the DTI could pursue a *low*-price strategy, happy in the knowledge that there would be few green negative reactions.

Low prices, which grew out of asset-sweating, competition, and liberalization, meant that environmentalists were rowing against the tide. No overarching framework was provided until the Climate Change Programme in 2000, and even this was weak set against the sheer scale of the challenge. Instead, the existing integrated pollution control regulatory approach, run by the Environment Agency, operated alongside the evolving energy efficiency programmes. The new innovations proved difficult—first, the imposition of VAT had to be reversed, and then the CCL had to be hedged round with negotiated agreements. The permits scheme was so heavily constrained—by excluding generators and renewables—that it hardly merited its name. That left renewables (and policies designed to 'pick winners' and force customers to pay for the higher costs through the RO, itself a compulsory take-or-pay contract), and energy efficiency measures.

To each of these schemes and obligations, new institutions and old bureaucracies have attached themselves and grown with the scale of the micro-interventions and the overlaps between schemes. The bureaucratization of environmental policy has proceeded apace, with a corresponding growth of regulatory burden on companies. There is DEFRA, the DTI, and the Cabinet Office all deeply involved, with the Sustainable Development Commission (set up in July 2000), the Environment Agency and the EST as well. Then there is the Carbon Trust, set up in April 2001, and a major new part of Ofgem involved in administering the RO and the EEC. Hundreds of agreements have had to be negotiated under the CCL and will require monitoring, as have numerous energy efficiency schemes. There is also the work of the Environment Agency officials, policing the carbon limits on each power station and large industrial plant. As we shall see in Chapter 21, the PIU proposed another—the Sustainable Energy Policy Unit.

Regulations and interventions have a multiplicity of effects, many surprising and unintended. They tend to get capitalized, creating their own vested interests. Once created, schemes tend to become entrenched, and then grow. People's careers and jobs depend on them, and much effort is put into demonstrating their success. The total costs are forgotten, and more radical alternatives are often ignored, described as impractical, or, where credibility grows for them, actively opposed. There is of course no single blueprint or measure which will solve the environmental problem. Market failures are multiple, as are objectives. Nevertheless, as schemes and institutions multiply, the relative advantages of a comprehensive instrument such as the carbon tax correspondingly grow.

The 2003 White Paper, 'Our Energy Future—Creating a Low Carbon Economy' (DTI 2003a) acknowledged that energy policy had become in large measure environmental policy, but, as we shall see in Chapter 22, it had little to add about delivery.

20

The European Dimension

> The European Union is extremely dependent on its external supplies... At present, the European Union is not in a position to respond to the challenge of climate change and to meet its commitments, notably under the Kyoto Protocol. (Commission of the European Communities, 'Towards a European Strategy for the Security of Energy Supply', 2000b)

For most of the period since 1979, Europe has impinged on British energy policy in only a marginal way. Britain is an island with only limited connections. The electricity interconnector with France, installed in 1961, has a capacity of only 1,988 MW, and the gas interconnector between Bacton in the United Kingdom and Zeebrugge in Belgium only came into operation at the end of 1998. The national markets have been treated as just that—national—and whilst successive British governments have urged the liberalization of energy markets upon their often reluctant European partners, this has been as much a policy directed at the competitiveness of the European economy and a desire to have something positive to contribute, as it has been for the energy sector *per se*.

Where there have been significant advances in European policy—for example, in the 1996 and 1998 electricity and gas directives—Britain has typically been ahead of the game, so that the practical impact has been negligible. The focus has correspondingly been on the detail—whether Britain has the same definition of renewables as the European directive requires; whether the domain of emissions trading coincides; and how state-aid policy applies to nuclear, coal, and renewables.

The policy flow in the other direction, *from Britain to Europe*, has been very considerable. The 'British model' of privatization—regulated third-party access, unbundling of transmission operator (TO) and system operator (SO) functions, vertical disaggregation, and liberalization of supply—has been one that the European Commission has typically tried to follow, albeit publicly distancing itself from being seen to be too closely identified with the *British* bit, for fear of offending national sentiment elsewhere.

Subtly and slowly, this detachment has begun to erode over the 1990s. This has been partly a physical development, with the United Kingdom–Continental interconnector joining up the European and British gas markets, and partly corporate, as the European energy market has consolidated into one with a few giant players. It has also been reflected in the erosion of Britain's self-sufficiency derived from abundant fossil fuels. Sooner or later, the North Sea's gas depletion will put Britain in the same boat as Germany—reliant on imported gas. Britain's energy isolation is coming to an end, with an increased need for common positions on imports and energy security; greater interconnection as a European electricity grid emerges and Britain needs France's baseload nuclear as its own closes down; and common ownership as E.ON, RWE, and EDF increasingly take over substantial parts of the British electricity industry.

Self-sufficiency has created a substantial gap in understanding too. For Germany and France, energy security has been a matter of national policy since at least the Second World War. Neither has much economic domestic coal. Germany had started the Second World War trying to gain control of Rumanian oil and ended it trying to manufacture synthetic fuel. Its Ostpolitik with Russia has a complex history, and gas dependency will be set in this context. France has its own reasons for emphasizing security, too, particularly from Arab oil and gas sources, and its nuclear programme in the 1970s–90s had as much to do with national security as it did with energy concerns. Being a nuclear power, being outside NATO and having a strong domestic nuclear industry are all related. Few of these sensitivities has played much part in Britain's energy policy since Winston Churchill advocated a switch to oil to power the navy in 1911 and encouraged British firms to establish a base in Iran—thereby beginning the history of BP.

The history of Britain's engagement with European energy policy in the period since 1979 is therefore rather arm's-length, and for wider policy reasons. It was correspondingly also poorly resourced and often transparently lacked effect. It does, however, illustrate further dimensions of energy policy and it will provide the basis for future policy. Whereas general European statements about security of supply in the 1980s could be safely ignored, the Green Paper, 'Towards a European Strategy for the Security of Energy Supply' in 2000 could not (Commission of the European Communities 2000b). Indeed, like its US Energy Plan counterpart (see National Energy Policy Development Group 2001), it is likely to be the start of a much more coherent—and intrusive—policy framework.

Completing the Internal Energy Market

The Treaty of Rome envisaged the creation of a common, internal market between member states of what was then the European Economic Community, and set a path towards that goal[1] over twelve years (Article 8), in three stages of four years. This approach—a deadline and a series of stages—remains a significant instrument of European policy design, and revisions of Article 8 have been a key mechanism used in subsequent treaties.

The early optimism of the architects of economic integration was deflated by the Gaullist policy of France—first in the 1960s, and then reinforced by the impact of the OPEC shocks in the 1970s, and the stagnation which followed. By the 1980s, failure at the macroeconomic level led the Commission to try the micro tack. Led, ironically, by Lord Cockfield (whom Margaret Thatcher had sent to Brussels to rein in integrationist tendencies), the Commission launched a White Paper in 1985, 'Completing the Internal Market' (Commission of the European Communities 1985), which was in due course enshrined in the Single European Act 1987 (see Helm 1993).

The aim of the 1985 White Paper was to remove all internal barriers by the end of 1992—hence it was widely known as the 1992 Programme. It was primarily a *de*regulation exercise, and initially at least excluded areas where regulation might be required to secure competitive outcomes, and where national interests were sufficiently great that inclusion risked vetoing the whole programme. Most notably, energy and telecommunications fell into this category, and the Commission instead developed sectoral directives to address these, independent of the main 1992 Programme. Thus began the campaign by the Commission to complete the internal energy market.

At the outset, the Commission was keen to stress the gains from a common approach to energy and the promotion of competition. Prices varied widely across Europe,[2] and network interconnections were weak. Transmission interconnection was organized on a bilateral basis between

---

[1] Article 2 sets the objective of creating a common market. Article 3 provides for the elimination of customs duties and quotas on imports and exports between members; a common customs tariff (the customs union); freedom of movement of persons, services, and capital; and 'the institution of a system ensuring that competition in the common market is not distorted'.

[2] See Argyris (1993) for the Commission's detailed price comparisons.

national oligopolies and monopolies, and the European dimension to networks remained not surprisingly weak.[3]

In 1990, the Council of Ministers adopted two parallel directives, one on the transit of electricity and the other on price transparency of electricity and gas. These minor first steps were then followed by major proposals in February 1991, for competition in generation; in the construction of transmission and distribution lines; and third-party access (TPA) to the networks (Commission of the European Communities 1991).

It was the last of these that proved most controversial, since it went to the heart of vertically integrated dominant incumbents' power. The response was powerful, organized, and effective. EDF, Ruhrgas and, to a lesser extent, RWE launched a lobbying campaign to first undermine the draft directives—pointing to the 'weakness' of the British model and raising the security of supply flag—and then to delay. It was, with hindsight, remarkably successful—the 1992 draft directives were emasculated, and put off until 1996 and 1998. The chosen vehicle for the lobbying was Euroelectric, the trade organization of the large European electricity generators.

The debate on the directives focused on two very different types of TPA—negotiated and regulated. Negotiated access left it to the parties to arrive at terms, which could reflect a wide variety of circumstances. Regulated access on the British model fixed non-discriminatory tariffs for the use of networks (and required a regulator). In terms of competition, there was no serious case to debate: only regulated TPA could deliver the possibility of entry in generation and competition in supply. Without a common methodology for fixing tariffs, and without a standardized set of tariffs, distortions unrelated to the underlying cost conditions would inevitably arise.

Not that the difficulties of implementing TPA should have been underestimated—as we shall see below, by 2002 much remained to be done. In the early 1990s there was no common methodology for valuing transmission assets, and indeed, in many cases, no separate accounts existed. Even if the Commission had won the regulated TPA argument, it would still have taken years to have an effect.

The Single-buyer Market and Other Distractions

Incumbent utilities were wary of simply taking a negative line, and EDF in particular added a new front in its debate with the Commission by

---

[3] See Commission of the European Communities (1992a), House of Lords Select Committee on the European Communities (1993).

proposing an alternative model—the single-buyer model. This looked remarkably like the *British* Energy Act 1983 model (see Chapter 3). The downstream monopoly would buy the outputs of generation, thereby allowing new entrants upstream in the generation market to compete with the incumbent's own capacity. In the case of EDF, which had significant excess capacity in baseload nuclear power, the single buyer had the convenient consequence that it would preserve its *de facto* monopoly, whilst apparently conceding *de jure* competition.[4]

To the single-buyer model was attached a wider policy agenda. France wanted a single buyer because it wanted to maintain the concept of planning which had been part of the motivation for its nuclear programme. At the European level, that meant an overarching energy policy. In January 1995, the Commission published a Green Paper: 'For a European Union Energy Policy' followed by a White Paper, 'An Energy Policy for the European Union', in January 1996 (Commission of the European Communities 1995, 1996a). This initiative contained the usual litany of factors to be taken into account—security of supply, diversity, social and environmental factors, the role of nuclear, sustainable development, and renewables—but with little idea of how these were to be reconciled with the competition and liberalization agenda. Nevertheless, they provided hooks upon which those opposed to the internal energy market's development could tie their case. In the Green Paper in 2000, they would find a firmer foundation.

By the mid-1990s, a stalemate had resulted. The Commission stuck to its ambition to liberalize energy, and now had a (relatively) successful telecommunications model to draw upon. The utilities kept up the campaign, and used their significant political influence in France and Germany to block progress. Not everything, however, remained static: much was happening on the ground in domestic markets. Britain had led the field in electricity, with its eight-year transition to competition. In 1995 it had put gas on a fast track to 1998 as well. As we saw in Chapter 14, the British approach to electricity was based on the idea that metering had to be sufficiently developed, or a complex proxy for metered demand created (load profiling), *before* customers should switch. The alternative approach had been adopted in the Nordic countries, to the effect that competition could simply be declared, and switching would emerge as customers acquired the metering technology. So rather than create the detailed market and regulatory structures within which competition

---

[4] It is interesting to note that Northern Ireland Electricity operated as a single buyer, tied to contracts with four initial generators. See Chapter 18.

might flourish—regulating *for* competition—an alternative was to treat competition as something which could emerge *after* liberalization.

Such a model appealed to a number of Continental countries, notably Germany, since it required little direct intervention, was simple to implement, and could be controlled within the framework of the existing integrated oligopoly. It would also allow the German government to claim that it had stolen a march on its critics (notably the British). Crucially, it would not need a special energy regulator or regulatory body. Normal competition law could apply. This was the path that Germany took, with liberalization in 1998 roughly coinciding with the British timetable. Its consequences were dramatic, but not in the way that pro-competition advocates had wanted. It was to lead to major consolidation, with two firms emerging as dominant (see below). France, meanwhile, held out against almost all serious reform proposals, a position it maintained until 2002, when it finally relented.

The 1996 and 1998 Directives, and the Florence and Madrid Processes

By the mid-1990s, the Commission had all but given up hope of energy market reform. To meet French and other objections, the best that could be achieved was a small incremental step, and it was seriously questioned whether weak directives were really worthwhile, or might even be counterproductive.

At the end of the Irish presidency in December 1996, the Directive 96/92/EC covering common rules for the internal market in electricity was adopted (Commission of the European Communities 1996b). Its objective of an internal electricity market was advanced with concessions on public-service objectives (Article 3); the form of new capacity entry (by authorization and/or by tender; Article 4); priority for renewables, waste, and CHP sources (Article 8); transmission operator confidentiality of commercial information (Article 9); and the single-buyer model (Articles 15 and 18). Put crudely, France could be kept on board since it could appeal to 'service publique', could operate as a single buyer and, if it so chose, use authorization for new capacity.

On the Commission's side, there was a sense of having peeled away another (admittedly small) layer of monopoly protection. The two key choices—tenders versus authorization for new generation; and single buyer versus TPA—would have to have the same economic effect (Article 3), and, in the case of system access, must lead 'to a directly comparable level of opening-up of markets and to a directly comparable degree of

access to electricity markets'. A system operator of the transmission network must be designated (Article 7), and must not discriminate in favour
of their subsidiaries or shareholders. There must be unbundling and
transparency of accounts. Separate accounts for generation, transmission,
and distribution must be kept (Article 14), and prices for transmission and
distribution must be published by the system operator (Article 17).
National markets were opened to competition progressively over a
six-year period, from a 40 GWh threshold to 20 GWh three years after the
Directive came into force, and 9 GWh after six years (Article 19).

In the case of gas, progress was even slower, resulting in a Directive in
1998 (98/30/EC) (Commission of the European Communities 1998). It
mirrored the electricity directive in its aims and broad approach, but it
confined its focus largely to the provision of information and to transparency. Though its weakness owed much to lobbying by Ruhrgas and
other vested interests, the gas market in Europe was very much in its
infant stage, and take-or-pay contracts created major obstacles to entry.
Unlike Britain—where, in effect, take-or-pay contracts had been written
off by British Gas's shareholders in the mid-1990s—this distributional settlement would have been much harder to engineer on the Continent.
Moreover, with gas import dependency much higher in the mainland of
Europe, and with the strategies and political relationships between
Gazprom and Ruhrgas seen as crucial to (at least) Germany's interests, it
is not hard to sympathize with Commission officials who found that they
had to settle for a very limited advance towards competition.

Once the directives were in place, the Commission pushed on with its
efforts to open up the electricity and gas markets. These took three related
paths: to work on the methodology and regulatory principles through
meetings of all the national regulators; to encourage reform in the
national legislation required to implement the directives; and to push
for new directives. A series of position papers on methodology were
developed for system access and transmission pricing. These formed
'guidelines' and had the effect of 'soft' legislation: their legal status was
ill-defined, but they could be interpreted as being implied by the transparency and non-discriminatory provisions. Added impetus was created
through forums for electricity and gas regulators who would meet on a
regular basis—respectively, the Florence and Madrid processes.

The Florence process was instituted by the Commission as the
Electricity Regulatory Forum, to meet twice a year at the European
University in Florence. The Madrid process followed a similar pattern
for gas. Both provided for the interchange of mutual experience with
regulation for competition, and gave the Commission added support in

its ambitions. These were never far from the surface, and focused on getting new directives in place to make up for the failure to do this job properly in 1996 and 1998.

The second strand related to national legislation. Perhaps the most successful aspect of the 1996 Directive was that it forced the member countries to pass legislation to comply with it. And since parliamentary time was made available, such legislation could also incorporate other concerns that each country might have. Of all these examples of national legislation, Germany's was the most striking. Its energy law (*Gesetz zur Neuregelang des Energiewirtschaftsrechts*) came into effect in April 1998. It adopted negotiated TPA for transmission and the single buyer for distributors, and abolished existing exemptions from German competition law for the electricity industry. The effect was the immediate 100 per cent opening of the market. The Netherlands also provided for faster market opening. By contrast, France dragged its feet[5] and the Commission had to initiate proceedings against it.

Stockholm and the Green Paper

The third strand of the Commission's approach was to agitate for new directives. The Commission spelt out what was required in its reports to the Council and the European Parliaments on the directives and various statements on the state of competition in energy markets. At the Lisbon Summit in March 2000, heads of state demanded rapid work towards completing the internal energy market, which led to a proposal for a further directive (presented to the Stockholm Summit in March 2001).

The proposal tabled at Stockholm (Commission of the European Communities 2001) was to speed up completion of the internal market, to be achieved by 2005—by 2003 freedom for all non-domestic electricity customers; by 2004 all non-domestic gas customers; and by 2005, all customers. This timetable was to be accompanied by a series of detailed measures, notably non-discriminatory access terms; legally separate management of grids from production and supply; network access tariffs set, published and approved by national regulators; and the requirement that each Member State should have a regulator. There would be adoption of cross-border tariff-setting and congestion management for electricity; infrastructure plans; and negotiation of reciprocal electricity market-opening agreements with other European Union member states. Finally, the pill was to be

---

[5] The French Ministry of Finance set up a task force (the Champsaur Commission) to study tariff rates within EDF, upon which the author served.

sweetened for the French by specific proposals with respect to security of supply of affordable energy, and a universal right to energy to enshrine public-service obligations.

The Commission clearly thought that Stockholm would give it the breakthrough for which the Florence and Madrid processes had been the staging posts. The British thought so too. Under Helen Liddell's period as Minister for Energy and Europe, a series of initiatives were launched to promote European energy market competition. These included support for the Florence and Madrid processes (in practice, through Ofgem), a joint initiative with the Dutch government to look at measures of competition across Europe[6] and, somewhat later, an attempt to demonstrate that social, environmental, and security of supply policies were consistent with a competitive energy market (DTI 2001*b*).

The optimism after Lisbon turned out to be misplaced. Opponents of further liberalization and more regulation had not been idle, and after 1999 they had some solid evidence to work with. Parallel to the Florence and Madrid processes, the Commission had also been working on the broader subject of energy policy—much of which the liberalizers chose to ignore or to complacently argue that competition would be sufficient to meet Europe's needs. Energy policy in Europe—as somewhat later in the United States—focused on two issues: import dependency and CO_2 emissions.

In 2000, the Commission published a Green Paper, 'Towards a European Strategy for the Security of Energy Supply' (Commission of the European Communities 2000*b*). It was altogether more to the liking of France and Germany, in that it spelt out that Europe would be very heavily dependent on gas imports by 2020, and that CO_2 emissions were projected to rise sharply by 2020. Renewables and nuclear—neither of which would be economic in a competitive electricity market—were both given some prominence. They would require protection, through longer-term take-or-pay contracts, and perhaps too by some form of green taxation (see Helm 2001*d*).

The Commission had toyed with a carbon tax as far back as 1991, with its strategy of combining energy efficiency measures, renewables, and an energy/carbon tax. The joint energy/environment council in December 1991 decided that Community-wide taxation would require further study. In 1992, the Commission published 'Energy: Consequences of the Proposed Carbon/Energy Tax' (Commission of the European Communities 1992*b*). The main barriers were political—tax harmonization

---

[6] This work was undertaken by OXERA and published by the DTI and the Dutch Ministry of Affairs (2000).

had been an area of intense debate about national sovereignty and subject to veto. In the end, energy taxes were pursued by national governments in the late 1990s, notably Britain and Germany.

The gas import dependency played to Ruhrgas's strengths. Reliance on Gazprom would necessitate the creation of both an infrastructure and a contractual framework. In such matters, size counted, and only those who could take long-term contractual risks on their balance sheets (such as BP and Shell) or because of their vertically integrated structures, would be able to ensure European supplies. Add to that Ruhrgas's stake in Gazprom, and its seat on its board, and the Commission's security of supply concerns began to sit rather uneasily with its desire to complete the internal market. Not surprisingly, the Green Paper puts more emphasis on *direct intervention* than the *market route* (see Helm 2001c).

Thus, by the Stockholm Summit the Commission had in fact bifurcated its approach—and there was no real coherence or consistency between the elements. In the background, however, changes in the energy markets had begun to dent the optimism of the liberalizers. The oil price shock of 1999 had fed through to gas prices, reminding Europeans of their energy dependency. Evidence on climate change and the challenges it posed had not become any more comforting. And, of more immediate consequence, the Californian crisis had demonstrated that one of the most advanced economies in the world could be vulnerable to power cuts. That California was widely *perceived* to be based upon the British model gave much encouragement to the opponents at Stockholm.

As a result of these disparate forces, the Commission (and especially the British) lost at Stockholm. Against (British) expectation, a French–German alliance defeated the directive, and one more saga in the long series of delays left the Commission with the task of regrouping for another attempt in 2002. At Barcelona in March 2002, the British tried another concerted push for liberalization of energy markets, this time with Italy and Spain as allies. But with the French presidential elections looming, advances were very limited. The proposal from the Stockholm Summit, with complete opening targeted for 2005, was weakened to only the commercial sector by this time (Commission of the European Communities 2002). France was isolated, but it is unlikely that Germany was very disappointed. Indeed, given EDF's desire to continue its wider European acquisitions, without opposition from the European Commission's Competition Directorate, and that, in any event, corporate activity had already undermined much of the scope for competition through rapid consolidation—a trend which the Commission did little to stop—by playing for time, the French were slowly undermining the effect that liberalization would eventually have.

Monopolizing the European Market

Whilst many of the incumbents did what they could to frustrate the Commission's attempts to introduce directives, and to water down those that did make it to legislation, there was in the 1990s a widespread acceptance that competition was inevitable, and that companies should ready themselves for its eventuality. At one level this meant acquiring the necessary skills, studying what was regarded as the 'British experiment', and reducing costs to enhance efficiency. At another, it was to seek to secure markets through the opportunities that liberalization brought.

The most obvious strategy was to consolidate market power through acquisitions. This proved relatively easy to achieve in the 1990s because of the coincidence of benign factors. Capital investment was subdued in all the main markets, and hence companies had a surplus of funds to invest.[7] It was also a period in which the gearing of balance sheets became fashionable, so that large utilities, such RWE and E.ON (itself the result of a merger), had previously undreamt of sums to spend.

British utilities were vulnerable to takeovers, for the very good reason that there was an active market in RECs and generation assets, and European presence began in earnest, with the bid for London Electricity by EDF in November 1998. As described in Chapter 17, EDF was then able to go on to acquire generation assets and SWEB Supply, and eventually Eastern Distribution and SEEBOARD. EDF also made acquisitions across European markets.

For a company with an almost complete monopoly of one national market, with the most significant cross-border interconnectors within Europe, and with the baseload nuclear which had the potential to play a pivotal role in Europe in the 2000s and 2010s, there were from the outset serious objections to these acquisitions. Added to which, EDF had significantly outbid other rivals by virtue of a low (state) cost of capital. Each of its major acquisitions was vetted by the European Commission's Directorate General for Competition on competition grounds, and, in a remarkable set of decisions, the Commission deemed the relevant market to be the national one—not the European one its policies were designed to create. Since EDF's share of the British market prior to its acquisition of London Electricity was limited to the interconnector, once the relevant market was

---

[7] A similar phenomenon had spurred on the US utilities' overseas expansion in the mid-1990s, as described in Chapter 12.

England and Wales, there could be few grounds for objection. When EDF purchased a stake in Energie Baden-Württemberg in Germany, the Commission actually considered that EDF was an *entrant* in the German market, and thereby the acquisition was deemed to *increase* competition.

Thus, whilst the Directorate General for Competition was happily over-seeing a series of acquisitions by EDF which would greatly extend its market reach across the European Union, the Directorate General for Energy and Transport (DG TREN) was pursuing a *European* rather than national internal energy market policy which the acquisitions were undermining. Once developments in the German market are added in, the number of significant players in the potentially competitive market had been radically reduced, to the point that the prospect of a genuinely competitive European market had been undermined (see Helm 2001*d*).

The expansion of EDF was perhaps not surprising, but the extent of consolidation in Germany was, and led to a significant proportion of the market of over 80 million people coming under the control of just two companies. The German 1998 liberalization triggered off this remarkable concentration. It began with a sharp fall in wholesale prices, which in turn threatened the finances of a host of smaller players and the municipalities. The tradition of vertically integrating contracts was no longer viable with customer switching, and the major generators began buying them up. Meanwhile, VEBA and VIAG merged to create E.ON which, in turn, began to shed its non-energy activities. E.ON then bought up PowerGen (which in turn bought TXU and then Midlands Electricity), giving it access to the British market and an entrée into the United States (through PowerGen's ownership of LG&E Energy) and continued with the proposed swap of its petrol stations for a controlling stake in Ruhrgas with BP. After a tortuous process through the German cartel office,[8] this eventually gave E.ON an interest in Gazprom, Ruhrgas, its German electricity interests, British and US electricity companies, and thereby made it one of the largest energy utilities in the world.

RWE, somewhat caught on the back foot by E.ON, followed a similar pattern in Germany, acquiring HEW, and developed its interests in the east, notably in the Czech Republic. It also went down the water route, buying Thames Water and American Water Works, and, mirroring E.ON's Ruhrgas acquisition, it acquired the gas assets too. Together, RWE and E.ON developed their German duopoly, withdrew plant, and, in 2001–2, prices began to rise. The German government tried to create a 'third

[8] The Ruhrgas acquisition by E.ON was blocked by the German cartel office, but the German government overruled it. This in turn led to court action. Very belatedly, Brian Wilson, Minister for Energy, voiced his objections in August 2002, supported by McCarthy at Ofgem in a letter to the *FT* (see McCarthy 2002). With further concessions, the Ruhrgas takeover was completed in February 2003.

force', and encouraged Vattenfall to gain control of BEWAG in Berlin (as Mirant pulled out).[9] The result, however, is one in which competition *de jure* exists, but *de facto* is all but eliminated.

Taken together with the ambitions of Italy's ENEL (which had significant domestic market power) and the consolidation of the British market with E.ON, RWE, and EDF leading the way, the picture that emerges is of a European market dominated by E.ON, EDF, RWE, ENEL, and possibly Vattenfall as well. A number of Dutch, Belgian and Spanish players contribute very limited competition, and, in all the main cases, gas follows a similar concentrated pattern. By 2003, the chances of the sort of competitive market which the Commission had in mind in the later 1980s and early 1990s had all but disappeared. Network access had been significantly opened up—but to a game between a small number of dominant national utilities. The Commission has been busily defining the rules, while failing to notice that there are not enough players in the game, or to do anything positive about it.

Whither Europe?

From a British perspective, the internal energy market programme had been a failure. The Department of Trade and Industry (DTI) had expected that Europe would 'catch up' with Britain, and that energy liberalization would be an example of a policy area where British leadership could be exercised. Instead of opposing European intervention, this was one area where Britain could be ahead of the pack.

In all of this, the DTI simply *assumed* that the British model was the one Europe should follow, and that its superiority would be evident from the results. It would lead to lower prices, making Europe more competitive against the United States. And, because it assumed superiority, it seemed obvious too that Europe would come to its senses at Stockholm and Barcelona. That they did not demonstrated graphically how little the DTI understood about the way European energy markets worked, and how European alliances were constructed. Where the German government was alive to developments with Gazprom, British officials had little idea of what was going on. Where Germany, France, and Italy worried about security of supply, Britain's abundance of natural resources underpinned its disregard for external worries.[10]

---

[9] Mirant was previously known as Southern Energy and before that The Southern Company. It filed for Chapter 11 bankruptcy in the USA in July 2003.

[10] Eventually a liberalization package was agreed at Brussels in November 2002, but with the date for full liberalization extended to 2007 in a compromise with France and Germany.

Britain not only failed to push through the internal market, but it also failed to do much about the consolidation taking place—even in its own market. The failure to prevent EDF's acquisition of London Electricity or its subsequent incremental acquisitions reflected not just an ignorance of how to work the Commission, but also of how to play the system. Whilst RWE, Ruhrgas, and EDF invested in the politics and processes of Brussels, the DTI relied on general principles. Its officials were systematically outclassed, despite a receptive team first at DG Energy and then at DG TREN.

In the new century, Britain is finally joining the European energy market in a physical as well as a policy context. The gas interconnector has carried European prices and contracting as well as gas, and the increased reliance on imports (primarily of gas) gives a new interest in security of supply. The arrival of EDF, E.ON, and RWE joins Britain to the European corporate energy club as well, and, over the next decade, the integration of European companies with British counterparts is likely to continue. Finally, the environmental concerns are overwhelmingly European in domain and jurisdiction. Kyoto had a European definition, and renewables, emissions trading, and related interventions are covered by European directives. When the Cabinet Office's PIU team reviewed energy policy in 2001, not surprisingly it, too, reflected these concerns, and it is interesting that the European Green Paper (2000b), the US Energy Plan (National Energy Policy Development Group 2001), and the PIU report (PIU 2002) are all dominated by the imports question and CO_2 emissions. The answers differ in degree, but not—to the surprise of Ofgem and some of the older guard at the DTI—in kind.

21

The Energy Policy Review

> For the UK, an international agreement...which prevented carbon dioxide concentrations in the atmosphere from exceeding 550 ppmv and achieved convergence by 2050 could imply a reduction of 60% from current annual carbon dioxide emissions by 2050 and perhaps of 80% by 2100. These are massive changes. But the government should implement short, medium and long term strategies which are sufficiently coherent and effective to achieve these reductions. (RCEP, 'Energy: The Changing Climate', 2000)

> Securing cheap, reliable and sustainable sources of energy supply has long been a major concern for governments. (Tony Blair, Foreword to 'The Energy Review', PIU, 2002)

From the early 1980s, British energy policy, and its associated regulatory regime, was designed to transform a state-owned and directed sector into a normal commodity market. Competition and liberalization would, its architects hoped, take energy out of the political arena. After the windfall tax in 1997, Labour shared this vision and hoped that energy would drop off the political agenda, while it focused on 'Education, Education, Education'.

A series of seemingly unrelated events in the early 2000s jolted that complacency. Oil prices tripled, against an expectation of falling prices. That, in turn, triggered fuel price protests in September 2000, leading to the only time that the Conservatives moved above Labour in the opinion polls in Labour's first term in office. It also led to a rise in gas prices against an expectation that oil and gas prices had decoupled as a result of liberalization and competition in Britain.

These changes in fuel prices occurred in the context in which two aspects of the government's energy policy were at variance with the fundamentals. First, the government was committed to low prices as policy objectives—both in Public Service Agreement targets set by the Treasury for the Department of Trade and Industry (DTI) and, explicitly, in the stated policy objectives following the 1998 White Paper (DTI 1998*a*). Second, the environmental constraint was tightening. Not only did emissions of CO_2 start to *rise* as the easy gains from closing much of the coal industry were no longer available, but also the scale of the problem—and hence of the reductions required too—was spelt out by the Royal Commission of Environmental Pollution's (RCEP) report in 2000, which suggested that emissions of CO_2 should be cut by more than half by 2050. These two factors interacted: if CO_2 was to be reduced, this could only be achieved *and* prices kept low through ever greater subsidies. Since subsidies, except at the margin, were not a policy option, the two objectives were incompatible.

A further twist to the renewed interest in energy policy was given by the Californian crisis. At the beginning of the twenty-first century, one of the most advanced economies in the world ground to a halt as a result of power cuts. Not since the brown-outs of the late 1960s in the eastern seaboard of the United States had such an event happened, and what alarmed British politicians and officials was that it occurred in the context of a new market-based system which apparently drew much of its design from Britain. Although the explanation turned out to be complex, at first glance it looked like the first real test of the 'British system' and it had failed badly. The complementary nature of electricity, and the scale of the damage inflicted by failures, political and economic, registered with ministers.

In a context in which it was widely recognized that Britain's infrastructure was sub-standard, and where the rail network appeared close to collapse after the Hatfield rail accident, and little progress was made in the first term of office on the London Underground, the suspicion arose that all might not be well with energy networks too. The gas network, as we saw in Chapter 18, had not been designed to carry gas for baseload electricity generation, was heavily reliant on the St Fergus terminal, and would in the next decade have to handle the switch to imported gas. By 2002, the interruptible gas contracts to combined-cycle gas turbines (CCGTs) were proving problematic, and concerns were being expressed about the possibility of power cuts in the London area. A joint committee between the DTI and Ofgem (called Joint Energy Security of Supply Working Group) found that, in the next few years, the network would come within the one-in-twenty winter test of conventional security of supply requirements (DTI/Ofgem 2002). In electricity, the problems of embedded renewables generation in a system designed for large-scale coal and nuclear plant were also beginning to be recognized.

Perhaps less recognized was the basis on which future gas—and indeed other fuels—would be produced. Inputs from Russia and Norway would require long-term, take-or-pay contracts to back up the upstream sunk costs—just as they had for the development of the North Sea in the 1970s, as described in Chapter 2. But in a liberalized supply market, with customer switching, and with the experience of the stranding of British Gas contracts in the mid-1990s, it was far from clear how such contracts for sufficient quantities would be signed in the British context—unless on the back of the very market power the British model was designed to destroy.

Taken together—the oil and gas price shocks, environmental constraints, network problems, and imports—these 'events' created nervousness in government, and in particular at the No. 10 Policy Unit. As a result, the Cabinet Office's Performance and Innovation Unit (PIU) was asked immediately after the 2001 general election to conduct a review of energy policy. It duly reported in February 2002, but sufficiently inconclusively that the DTI then launched a consultation exercise, covering the same ground yet again, but with the intention of providing a White Paper in autumn 2002—although inevitably the date slipped and it eventually emerged in February 2003 (see Chapter 22). A process of reassessing energy policy had begun, but with no further immediate crisis it gave every appearance of being a long, dragged-out affair.

The Oil Shock

Oil prices collapsed in the mid-1980s from a peak of around $30/bbl at the time of the Iran/Iraq war. This was not widely anticipated, and, as we saw in Chapters 2 and 3, most of the key investment decisions in the energy sector taken in the late 1970s and early 1980s were based upon the assumption that prices would continue upwards. $60/bbl was not thought to be impossible. THORP, the Howell plan for ten pressurized-water reactors (PWRs), and the Plan for Coal were all products of a rising oil price scenario.

By the late 1990s, the conventional wisdom was quite different. It was that oil prices would stay low, and might even fall further. The *Economist* speculated (March 1999) that oil might reach $5/bbl,[1] as OPEC's grip weakened further with Russia and other non-OPEC sources taking a greater market share, and with gas competing with oil. As with the 1970s' conventional wisdom, that of the 1990s produced a series of investment consequences—or rather, lack of investment. If oil was likely to be abundant and cheap, and with it gas too, then investment in marginal oil fields in the North Sea was less justified and more generally exploration and production (E&P) was less attractive. Investment in stocks and storage was also less attractive: if oil was likely to be cheaper tomorrow, then holding stocks today was a costly activity. In the oil industry, asset consolidation and cost reduction were the appropriate business strategy

[1] The *Economist* (1999), 'The Next Shock', 3 March.

response. The oil merger boom was partly in response to the cost-cutting imperative. US refinery and pipeline infrastructure was widely acknowledged to be in a poor state.

As with the 1960s, the era of cheap oil created the conditions for its demise. On the supply side, the contribution of low stocks and low E&P made the market more vulnerable to short-term shocks, and, in the medium term, supplies were not able to respond quickly to price rises as the marginal capacity had been reduced. The dominant role of Saudi Arabia as swing producer had been reinforced, so that the market power of OPEC (through Saudi Arabia) was increased. These supply-side trends were reinforced by those on the demand side. Cheap oil increased demand and reduced the attractiveness of energy-saving and demand-management investments—as it had in the 1960s. Cheap gas led to a boom in CCGTs. What tipped the balance was the scale of demand relative to expectation. Whereas it might reasonably have been assumed that the great economic boom of the 1990s might come to an end in 1998, in fact it carried on until 2001. Demand was correspondingly above expectations. Less marginal supply and more marginal demand, in the presence of increased market power, was a dangerous combination (Fig. 21.1).

The 1999 oil shock took the DTI, and indeed many oil companies, by surprise. Unlike the 1973, 1978/79, and 1990/91 shocks, this time there was no Middle Eastern war to trigger Arab solidarity, and the experience of the 1980s and 1990s suggested that the market would quickly

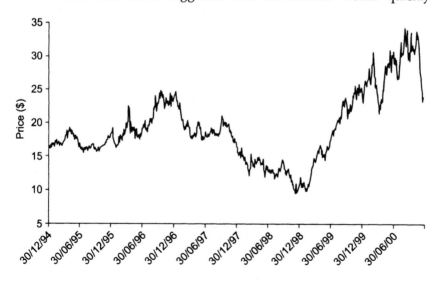

FIG. 21.1 London Brent crude price index, 1995–2000

Source: Databank.

respond—on the supply side with increased Russian exports, and on the demand side as the economic boom cooled down. Both turned out to be right, but crucially *with a lag*. The Russian exports were constrained by Russia's weak oil field and production infrastructure, and the boom did not weaken until 2002. In the meantime, the prospect of war increased, and the market was supported by an 'Iraqi premium', and oil prices remained above $25/bbl throughout most of 2002 and into 2003 through the Iraq War and its aftermath.

The most politically visible consequence of the oil price shock was the fuel protests in September 2000. During the 1990s first the Conservatives and then Labour had raised taxes on petrol. Kenneth Clarke had introduced the fuel price escalator—5 per cent in real terms per annum—on the assumption of weak oil prices. This was presented as a pro-green measure, and later endorsed by John Prescott as part of his integrated transport strategy designed to engineer a significant switch from road to rail. But when the escalator combined with the oil shock, the consequences were explosive, and in September 2000, a loose coalition of interests, centred around truck drivers (complaining about the UK/Continental diesel tax differences), farmers (who had special cheap red diesel anyway), and motorists began a protest. Oil refineries (notably Stanhope) were picketed. What turned a protest into a crisis, however, was the realization that the stocking levels at petrol stations were now much more efficient because the advances in information technology facilitated just-in-time delivery systems. As motorists filled their tanks, and the protests limited some supplies, a tight supply–demand balance resulted in a crisis.

In the event, the crisis proved very short-lived, and the protestors were given a few tax concessions in the subsequent Budget. However, the petrol crisis was to have two more significant consequences. First, the DTI began to recognize that storage and stocks of energy sources would not necessarily be optimally provided by the market. The optimal level of storage and stocks was a *system* property, and the sum of individual decisions by the various companies would not necessarily add up to a level that reflected the economic damage caused by interruptions in supply to the economy as a whole. Second, and perhaps of greater long-term significance, politicians recognized the extent of voters' resistance to paying the costs of action on climate change and pollution. The use of green taxes, dented in the mid-1990s by VAT on domestic fuels, had been dealt a significant blow.

Gas Follows Oil

The oil shock was, from a political and energy policy perspective, limited to the short-term crisis of the fuel protests. Its knock-on consequences for the gas market led to a more substantial response. The DTI and Ofgem had assumed that the oil shock would be short-lived, and that oil and gas prices had decoupled. This mattered because decoupling was seen as a major success of gas liberalization, and because Ofgem was about to remove the price cap on domestic gas prices in April 2000.[2] The DTI and Ofgem might reasonably have expected that prices would continue to fall thereafter, adding to the *perceived* success of the removal of the price cap.

If oil and gas prices were decoupled then the rise in gas prices in parallel to those of oil could only have occurred because of the excesses of market power. The DTI accordingly began an investigation into North Sea pricing behaviour, and encouraged the European Commission to investigate too. These investigations did not, however, produce any conclusive evidence of collusion, and provided an explanation based upon the link between oil and gas prices in Continental contracts and the spread of Continental prices to Britain via the interconnector (which opened in October 1998). It was the first evidence of the likely consequences of Britain's growing imports of gas, and how the market might develop as Britain became dependent on such imports (see Ofgem 2000*b*).

The DTI took the view that the oil/gas contract link reflected the failure to liberalize European gas markets, and hence pushed on with its Stockholm and Barcelona agendas, discussed in Chapter 20. However, the oil/gas link had economic substance: oil and gas were sometimes joint products, and they were sometimes competitor fuels. Neither oil nor gas prices remotely approximated their marginal costs, and hence a reference price was needed. Oil, at least, had some published prices. If not oil, then some other benchmark could be required, and it was far from obvious what this might be (see OXERA 2000).

Convergence between the gas and electricity markets meant that the price shock could not be confined to the industrial and domestic gas market. Gas was now the marginal fuel in electricity generation, and, in a normal market, it might be expected that the link would go from oil to gas to wholesale and retail electricity prices. The electricity market was, however, anything but normal: the dash for gas had produced very considerable excess supply. The price effect thus created a substitution of coal for gas, without raising the wholesale price. Coal burn then rose in 2000 and 2001, with the consequence that CO_2 emissions increased too. Such easy absorption of gas prices could not, however, be guaranteed indefinitely. Once supply and demand came

---

[2] As a rough estimate, upstream gas costs comprise about 40% of the typical domestic gas bill.

into balance, with gas the dominant marginal fuel for electricity generation, and with Continental imports of gas displacing North Sea supplies, the British energy market risked becoming even more sensitive to the oil price.

The Royal Commission Report

Traditional energy policy has focused on the questions of energy security of supply and the role diversity plays in providing an element of insurance against shocks, of which the 1999 oil price increase is a classic example. But in 2000, the government faced an additional problem, which made the design of energy policy altogether more difficult, and complex too. The RCEP produced a detailed report on climate change (RCEP 2000) in which it suggested that if Britain was to make a serious contribution to addressing climate change, it would have to reduce its emissions of CO_2 by some 60 per cent by 2050, and it went on to suggest a number of alternative scenarios—including, most notably, a renewables and energy efficiency approach, and a new nuclear programme. The government—notably Michael Meacher, Environment Minister—promptly welcomed the report.

The political trouble with the RCEP report was not only that it was abundantly clear that Britain did not even have a policy capable of stabilizing CO_2 emissions—since the renewables at best *replace* the nuclear power stations as they come to the end of their lives, but do nothing to meet increases in demand—but that it required a formal government response, since it was a statutory Royal Commission.

Confronted with the report to respond to and little idea of what to say, the government reached for the classic device—a review. This would buy time, allow for the public mood to be tested, and, hopefully, come up with some practical suggestions. Even if the oil price shocks and network issues had not produced much action, the RCEP provided a political imperative.

The Energy Policy Review

In the spring of 2001, these various concerns built up to a sufficient pitch to trigger a substantive review of energy policy. The foot-and-mouth epidemic postponed the election, but once it had occurred, a review was rapidly announced before the summer recess. It was a mark of the decline of the standing of the DTI's Energy Directorate with Downing Street that the Cabinet Office's PIU was charged with the task, not the DTI. Initially, the DTI would not even have the ministerial chair, although this changed as the Prime Minister warmed towards nuclear, and Brian Wilson became Energy Minister.

Once the review was announced, the various lobbies and interest groups began in earnest to campaign for their preferred options. The scale of this activity should have conditioned the PIU team's approach, but in fact the way the team went about the review reinforced this pressure. The PIU set up a web site, and published a list of questions at the outset in July 2001, and invited all the stakeholders to contribute, which many duly did, with over 400 submissions coming in by September 2001.

For the PIU team, there was clearly a choice of methodology at the outset. The obvious approach would have been to treat the exercise as an analytical and factual one, identifying the issues and assessing the efficiency of alternative policy approaches. It could have tried to set out alternative energy policy frameworks and spell out the implications. No doubt it tried to do some of this, but it was hampered in two ways. First, its team inherited quite a lot of work from the study already under way at the PIU on resource productivity, and carried over some of the team from that earlier project. In the early days, there was an attempt to take the renewables agenda as an *assumption* onto the PIU review, which, rightly, the team resisted. Second, any coherent answer in the form of an energy policy framework would have produced clear losers, and within a quasi-political context this was somewhat constrained. For example, any sensible environmental policy would inevitably have nasty consequences for the coal lobby. Building nuclear power stations would offend the green lobby. Too much by way of renewables would impose high costs, and a realistic carbon tax would hurt industry and voters, who might prefer low prices. A more interventionist policy would offend Ofgem,[3] and the DTI/DEFRA conflicts would have had to be managed.

It was therefore perhaps inevitable that the PIU would find it hard to reconcile these conflicting interests and come to definite conclusions, and would end up with a compromise, with something for everyone. The various lobbies all had their shopping lists, and by and large the PIU report kept most of them happy. While recognizing concerns, it broadly defended the status quo of NETA and Ofgem's performance on networks. It argued that climate change should only be addressed in the United Kingdom if other countries did so too, thus assuaging industry, who knew that others probably would not. Whatever the environmental rhetoric, that probably meant that low prices would continue.

---

[3] Ofgem's views were set out as follows: 'Ofgem believes that the future uncertainties with respect to security and diversity of energy supplies are best resolved through the continued operation of competitive markets in electricity and gas. Such markets will ensure that participants face the correct signals and incentives to invest so as to deliver sufficient supplies' (Ofgem 2001e).

The environmental lobby could, however, also take some comfort. A 20 per cent Renewables Obligation (RO) was recommended by 2020—inevitably, given the very limited time the PIU had, without much serious cost analysis of its implications. This was reinforced by an energy efficiency target. A carbon tax was also mooted, but far enough into the future to avoid offending shorter-term political interests. Nuclear was not given the go-ahead, which some environmentalists had feared, but it was nevertheless given some encouragement about 'keeping the options open' and the importance of its contribution.

The PIU did wrestle with the issue of institutional reform, but what it came up with was less radical than it appeared. It recommended that a Sustainable Energy Policy Unit be set up, something which the DTI quickly latched onto, as a way of increasing its resources without ceding its control to a more independent energy agency or to DEFRA. Such a Unit did not appear to pose much of a threat to Ofgem either.

Not surprisingly, the response by most of the lobby groups was supportive. Only the serious press and academics criticized the review publicly in the days after it was published. Ministers, too, could live with the results, picking out the bits that favoured their own predispositions and departmental interests, and, although a White Paper and eventually legislation was promised, in reality there was little immediately to legislate about. The DTI could welcome the report, and eventually (in April 2002) issue a consultation paper asking almost all the main questions again, safe in the knowledge that there was at this stage no political urgency.

In retrospect, then, whatever the intentions and however good the analysis, the PIU process was one which lent itself more to a *political* objective of keeping as many interests happy as possible. The PIU report produced no significant casualties or disaffected parties. But at the end of the process the government was no nearer resolving the two fundamental issues—gas dependency and imports, and CO_2 emissions—nor to having anything which might resemble a coherent energy policy as a result. In the end, there was not enough of an *imminent* crisis to mandate action—or at least not until the British Energy crisis.

Analytical Weaknesses

Although the exercise quickly slipped from the intention of producing a report *of* government to the more modest one, of a report *to* government, the PIU could nevertheless have provided an analytical framework for decisions. That it did not do so reflects the fact that a small team could not possibly produce the level of necessary analysis in a few months. There are three main components to designing an energy policy: a specification of the objectives; an analysis of the nature of the problems; and a coherent set of policy instruments. Not surprisingly, in all three areas, the PIU report did not give clear guidance to government.

The PIU report recommended that the objectives of energy policy meet the objectives of sustainable development—environmental, economic, and social—and 'consistent with this' should be 'the pursuit of secure and competitively priced means of meeting the UK's energy needs, subject to the achievement of an environmentally sustainable energy system' (PIU 2002: 7). Elsewhere, the PIU states in respect of greenhouse gases that 'it would make no sense to incur abatement costs in the United Kingdom and thereby harm our international competitiveness, if others were not contributing' (PIU 2002: 9). Sustainable development is an objective, but only if others pursue it too. The PIU report did not suggest how these overlapping objectives might be traded off against each other. The central tension is between price, security, and the environment. In the Prime Minister's Foreword to the report, more confusion is sown, with the objectives being '*cheap*, reliable, and sustainable sources of energy supply' [italics added] (ibid.).

The difference between a well-designed energy policy and a wish list is that the objectives are clearly specified in such a way as to enable success or failure in meeting them to be identified (and preferably measured). The Conservatives had *reduced* the objectives towards economic efficiency, and used competition as the policy instrument. Labour, after 1997, in the social democratic tradition, *added* objectives to the policy framework, thereby complicating policy design further. It is this step—and the trade-offs required—which was a central challenge for the PIU to address, and little light was shed upon it.

The PIU rightly approached the analysis of the emerging energy policy problems in terms of the challenges of climate change and the security of gas supplies. On the former, the starting point was the RCEP report in 2000 and the reductions it proposes. The science was taken as largely given, and a series of scenarios was envisaged. For the PIU, the 'solutions' were in practice largely confined to three: energy efficiency, renewables, and nuclear. New technologies were referred to, but most of the relevant policy analysis was in terms of these three. The data (to the extent that the PIU had time to engage with the empirical evidence) suggested to the PIU that, of these three options, there are very considerable gains to be made at low cost from energy efficiency; that renewables are (very) expensive but have 'vast potential'; and that nuclear is currently an available technology at costs which developed economies might be able to live with.

But such evidence as was presented did not translate into the conclusions: because the main policy preferences are more renewables and energy efficiency, the report played up the scope for scale economies and other cost savings in these areas—as did the subsequent White Paper when it eventually emerged in 2003.[4] These the PIU did not seriously question: there was no analysis of appraisal optimism, which has been a feature of the lobbying for these options—and indeed nuclear too. Just how a 20 per cent renewables target and a demanding energy efficiency target are to meet the overarching objectives was never made clear. There were no cost–benefit and risk assessments of a substantive empirical kind in the report.

The second dimension of the analysis was the security of gas supplies. This has a number of different dimensions: availability of gas; the network's capability of supplying gas; the interaction of the gas networks with the need to balance the electricity system; and the ability of British suppliers to sign long-term, take-or-pay contracts with Russia and Norway, given the liberalization of supplies and the ability of customers to switch supplier.

The PIU placed overwhelming emphasis on the first of these dimensions, which is probably the least important. It rightly pointed out that there is plenty of gas in Norwegian and Russian hands, but very little follows from this. Indeed, if all these gas reserves were to be burned, the impact on the climate would be serious. What matters is *not* whether there is enough gas, but what it costs, whether the infrastructure exists to transport it, and on what terms. The report contained virtually nothing about the European gas infrastructure except to link this to the question of liberalization of European gas supplies. There were no maps, diagrams, or schemes to show what the pipeline options might be, either in Europe or the North Sea. Whereas German, French, and other European governments would monitor these developments carefully, they appear to have largely escaped the PIU's attention.

Perhaps even more worrying was the failure of the PIU to evaluate the problems of long-term, take-or-pay contracts within the context of the British liberalized markets. The PIU wanted the liberalization of energy and the promotion of competition of the 1980s and 1990s to be the 'cornerstone' of future energy policy, but it failed to explain how this might be compatible with long-term contracts, for gas, or indeed renewables and nuclear. That the RO is a compulsory long-term contract was not mentioned. Indeed, the words 'long-term contract' were noticeably

---

[4] A bold strategy along these lines is proposed by Hewitt (2001), though again lacking a serious cost–benefit assessment against alternatives.

largely absent from the report. There was also little recognition of how vertical integration has changed the way competitive markets work, and the rapid concentration of the European energy market around three dominant electricity companies (EDF, RWE, and E.ON) and the large oil and gas companies. And when it comes to security of supply, there was very little analysis of Gazprom, despite its immense market power.

On the networks, while there were issues raised, the PIU argued that there is no need for immediate concern. All that needed to be done was to 'monitor' the position. The present situation is considered to be 'healthy' and intervention would be 'premature'. This is a bold and indeed heroic claim since there is no evidence of substantial research by the PIU to support this. Presumably it relied on the submissions made by the various parties. But even here it was selective, appearing to disregard those that warned of a more urgent set of problems. It might have reached the conclusion having set out some of the options, listed out the areas of concern and then explained why—preferably with some risk analysis—ministers could be relaxed about the networks. But it did not do this.

The final area of the analysis on which the PIU focused was the institutional structure of energy policy. It rightly identified the weaknesses in the current DTI resources, pointed out the need to address the interface between environmental and economic policy, and indicated the need for better scientific research and support. However, the role of Ofgem was never seriously questioned, probably because the PIU had already concluded that the policy of the 1980s and 1990s should be the cornerstone of future policy. If competition and liberalization are to dominate, if networks are in good shape, and if the United Kingdom should not tackle CO_2 emissions if other countries do not, then there is little need to change the main regulatory and policy arrangements.

Institutional reform for the PIU was incremental, about tagging on a Sustainable Energy Policy Unit to (probably) the DTI, which would be likely to absorb it within its Energy Directorate. No energy agency is required, the remit of Ofgem need not change significantly, and institutional reform boils down to a tidying up of the myriad of environmental bodies that have proliferated in the last few years. A 'radical' change in policy, which the PIU claimed it was recommending, needed only a small amount of institutional change. Whether such a conclusion is warranted is a moot point, but it should at least be based upon an analysis of the alternatives. Although the PIU claims to have considered the options, it is far from clear how it actually did so. Some principles were listed for good institutional design, but how they lead to a Sustainable Energy Policy Unit and not, for example, an energy agency is far from obvious. The result of the PIU's approach would be likely to be a tinkering at the edges of Whitehall, and indeed the state of permanent tension between the DTI and DEFRA shows no sign of abating. The DTI's Public Service Agreement focused on low prices as the priority, which hardly helps to reconcile the various objectives.

As a summary of the commonality that might emerge from the various lobby groups, the PIU report makes interesting political reading. If energy policy is conceived of as an attempt to reconcile a series of interests, the PIU report provided a solution. But as a serious attempt at analysis, the tools of the trade—cost–benefit analysis, risk analysis, cost and demand analysis, contractual design, and risk assignment—are largely (and possibly inevitably, given the time and resources at the PIU's disposal) absent.

The DTI Tries Again

Across government, the weaknesses of the PIU report were widely recognized, but there was no consensus about what to do next. Throughout 2002, the various interest groups carried on their lobbying activities, and a number of facts were beginning to make themselves apparent. First, the renewables target of 10 per cent by 2010 would be challenging to achieve, expensive in its impact on bills, and any increase to 20 per cent would be extremely difficult to achieve without significant technological and efficiency advances. Second, nuclear provided an obvious way of achieving the CO_2 targets at a cost which a most industrialized nation might cope with, but would require a solution to the waste problems which had been ducked since at least the 1976 Flowers Report referred to in Chapter 5. Third, the tensions between Ofgem, the DTI, and DEFRA would grow as none of the central options—renewables, nuclear, and energy efficiency— was cost-competitive within the NETA framework, and at least renewables and nuclear required long-term, take-or-pay contracts, which NETA did not facilitate. Since the government was reluctant to rely on a carbon tax, intervention which went across Ofgem's activities was inevitable. Finally, none of this could be achieved without an effect on prices—and hence the 'low-prices' objective was in jeopardy.

If the PIU review bought time, politically it did not buy enough, and the response was to buy some more. In April 2002, the DTI launched a follow-up consultation exercise (DTI 2002b), which asked the same questions as the PIU had done all over again. It was to last until mid-September 2002, and also involved the testing of public opinion.

The DTI's consultation process did at least provide it with the opportunity to take back control of energy policy which had been passed to the

PIU, but by the summer of 2002, its resources to carry out the necessary analysis were at a low point. The DTI was itself restructuring its activities, and the future of the Energy Directorate was in some doubt. The Minister, Brian Wilson, considered that there was a strong case for a separate Energy Department (see DTI 2002*a*).

It is therefore hardly surprising that the DTI consultation added little—other than time—to the formation of an energy policy. All the main factors—to the extent they were relevant—were known, and policy would in any event need to be robust against developments in the market place. Ever more precise measurements of CO_2 trends, or the precise demand–supply balance in generation and networks, would not change either the questions that an energy White Paper would need to address, nor the answers it provided. The problems lay with the objectives (there were too many and the trade-offs were not defined), and the choice of instrument (between market-based and planned interventions). The DTI could not expect in 2002 to discover anything so new and important as to change the nature of decisions about the future of nuclear, renewables, coal or gas. The questions it asked in its consultation had already been raised by the PIU and answered by the various interested parties. As with the European Union's Green Paper (2000*b*) and the US Energy Plan (National Energy Policy Development Group 2001), the problems were import dependency and CO_2 emissions. None appeared to have much by way of politically acceptable solutions, given the public's addiction to low prices in Europe and especially the United States.

22

A Low-carbon Economy—The White Paper

> Our country needs a new energy policy. Despite the improvements
> we have made over the last five years, today's policy will not meet
> tomorrow's challenges. We need to address the threat of climate
> change. We must deal with the implications of reduced UK oil, gas,
> and coal production, which will make us a net energy importer,
> instead of an energy exporter. And over the next twenty years or so
> we will need to replace or update much of our energy infrastructure.
> (DTI, 2003, 'Our Energy Future—Creating a Low Carbon Economy',
> para 1.1, p. 6)

> it is a general maxim worthy of our attention that no testimony is suf-
> ficient to establish a miracle, unless the testimony be of such a kind,
> that its falsehood would be more miraculous, than the fact, which it
> endeavours to establish (Hume, 1751, *An Enquiry Concerning Human
> Understanding*, Section X, part 1, pp. 109–131).

When the White Paper, 'Our Energy Future—Creating a Low Carbon
Economy', was eventually published in February 2003, it was initially
greeted with considerable enthusiasm, especially by environmentalists
and the new environmental lobbies that had grown up in the 1990s. There
was something for everyone, but not enough for any one sufficient to
cause substantive losses to others. Even the nuclear industry found reasons to be cheerful about keeping the nuclear option 'open'. Within a few
weeks, however, the enthusiasm began to wane, and when the Cabinet
was reshuffled in June 2003, and Labour had its fifth energy minister since
1997 (Stephen Timms) with a very broad remit (including telecoms and
postal services), some claimed that energy policy had been downgraded
to the status meriting only a 'part-time minister'.

To understand how a politically very radical White Paper, in terms of
its demanding objective of reducing CO_2 emissions by 60 per cent by 2050
from current levels, so quickly looked tarnished, it is necessary to see how
it was put together. Such a substantive reduction in CO_2 emissions was
bound to be expensive, not just in price, but also in terms of the political
consequences to powerful lobbies linked to the carbon economy. That the
DTI managed to convince itself that, after an exhaustive process which

had begun with the study by the Cabinet Office Performance and Innovation Unit (PIU, 2002), and had been followed by a further round of consultation,[1] the costs of achieving the 2050 target would be negligible was not only remarkable, but also inevitably led to the conclusion that a radical objective did not need to be immediately followed through with radical policies.

Plans A, B, and C, and the MARKAL Model

The White Paper's development naturally focused on the question of how the 60 per cent CO_2 target could be achieved. The basic choices the DTI identified—in line with the earlier report by the PIU, as discussed in Chapter 21—were between the main carbon-free technologies (renewables, energy efficiency, and nuclear) and market-based instruments (carbon taxes and emissions trading). Although the wording in the White Paper is carefully constructed to include virtually all these options, early on the DTI homed in upon (at least implicitly) a preferred approach, what might be called Plan A—that renewables and energy efficiency would jointly be sufficient.[2] It was what the PIU had recommended. But, whilst, of course, they *could* be sufficient, the secondary objective of cost provided a constraint. Could, then, renewables and energy efficiency achieve the objective without significant increases in prices, especially in the short run?

As the process of the PIU review and the subsequent DTI consultation process had revealed, this question had political as well as economic content. The implied question was whether the 60 per cent reductions could be achieved *without* nuclear. There were those within and outside government opposed on environmental grounds to nuclear (notably Michael Meacher at Defra); those opposed on environmental *and* cost grounds (notably Patricia Hewitt at the DTI); and those who recognized that if there was to be a major new build programme of nuclear power stations, the case for large-scale support and subsidies for renewables and energy efficiency would be weakened. On the other side, the pro-nuclear camp

---

[1] The PIU study's conclusions did not lead to immediate action in the autumn of 2002, but rather the DTI launched a consultation exercise asking very similar questions to those addressed by the PIU. It also involved asking the public for their views in a series of stakeholder meetings, See DEFRA, DTI, DTLR (2002).

[2] A series of high-level seminars was organized by the No. 10 Policy Unit during the process from July 2001 through to a post-mortem in June 2003 on the White Paper. Plan A, as I have described it, was set out in autumn 2002.

included the Energy Minister, Brian Wilson, together with powerful elements of the scientific establishment.

Within the renewables and energy efficiency camps, it was considered very important that Plan A included binding 20 per cent targets for 2020 as the PIU had recommended, and not just support.[3] The Renewables Obligation for 2010 supported the price of Renewables Obligation Certificates (ROCs), and it was argued that a similar market could be developed for energy efficiency. But to get the White Paper to commit to binding targets meant that politicians had to be comfortable with the consequences, and in particular that the price effects would not lead to a customer (and therefore voter) backlash. This included not just the DTI and Defra ministers, but also, crucially, the Treasury and the Prime Minister's office.

The writing of the White Paper therefore, in part, revolved around the politics and economics of this balancing act, between commitment and cost. One of the mechanisms by which the DTI team (and indeed the PIU before it) tried to understand the economics behind the trade-off was the MARKAL model (DTI 2003e), a fairly standard bottom-up technology model, within which a series of scenarios[4] could be explored and the effects of different levels of emissions constraints estimated. The model itself is, not surprisingly, quite complex, and therefore few of the politicians, officials or lobby group interests mastered its technical details. Complexity, however, should not have allowed the White Paper to place much weight on its findings[5] without the need to seriously test its validity—a common problem in political decision-making where analytical expertise is involved.[6]

The findings were indeed very supportive of Plan A. In early versions of the MARKAL modelling, completed for the PIU report, an even more demanding 70 per cent carbon abatement was considered against the three scenarios by the DTI's consultants,[7] and it was concluded that 'the results ... show that without exception, the effects seem likely to be very

---

[3] The main advocates of binding targets were Friends of the Earth (FoE, 2002), the Energy Saving Trust (EST, 2002), and the Institute of Public Policy Research (Hewitt, 2001).

[4] The three scenarios are 'Baseline' (business-as-usual, GDP growth 2.25% pa), 'World Markets' (GDP growth 3% pa, no new environmental policies); and 'Global Sustainability' (GDP growth 2.25% pa, strong collective environmental action).

[5] A section of the DTI's 'Options for a Low Carbon Future' paper is devoted to 'White Paper Modelling: Use of the MARKAL Energy Model' (2003e, pp. 152–60).

[6] See, for example, Heclo and Wildavsky (1974), and Wildavsky (1979).

[7] The consultants were Future Energy Solutions and Imperial College Centre for Energy Policy.

small, and certainly within the measurement errors of both GDP and its growth' (DTI 2003e, Para 4.6, p. 32).[8]

The MARKAL work was then revised by the consultants between the PIU report and the White Paper, but with no substantive changes in the results. Although in some scenarios there was a small increase in the GDP costs, nevertheless 'the estimated effects on economic growth of carbon abatement were generally small (i.e. annual GDP growth reduced by about 0.01 percentage points over a 50 year period).' (DTI 2003e, p. 53.)

How could this be? How could tackling global warming be so cheap— in practical terms, effectively free? And if it was so cheap, why were so many countries reluctant to sign up not just to the Kyoto Protocol, but to much tougher requirements? The philosopher, David Hume, suggested that when people tell us they have seen a miracle, there are two options: to believe them, or to see if the opposite is a more credible claim (see quotation at the start of the chapter). The second approach, which Hume recommends, requires an analysis of the assumption that renewables and energy efficiency are not low-cost options—and, in this case, an analysis of claims made over the 1980s and 1990s and the observed low take-up (see chapter 19 above). Although a range of sensitivities were explored within the MARKAL framework, DTI officials and ministers might have been expected to have interrogated the model much more rigorously, given its radically counter-intuitive results.

The starting point is the old modelling adage, 'garbage in, garbage out'. The MARKAL model's results are only as good as the bottom-up data upon which the model relies—the quality of this data, and whether it comprehensively includes all the costs. In effect, the MARKAL model results upon which the White Paper relies for its prediction that the GDP costs of achieving the 2050 target will be negligible *assume* that renewables and energy efficiency are low cost, and downplay the system and security costs they impose. It does this notably by: excluding the network costs[9] to support renewables with low and variable load factors; ignoring transaction

[8] The numbers for the earlier version were as follows (DTI 2003e, table 6, p. 32).

Impact of 70% carbon abatement on economic growth

Scenario	Reduction in GDP growth (% pa)	Time to recover lost GDP (months)
Baseline	0.018	4.7
World Markets	0.020	3.9
Global Sustainability	0.013	3.3

[9] Indeed, in DTI 2003e, renewables actually get a credit for transmission costs avoided.

costs; taking no account of the higher costs of capital reflected in equity and debt markets, to reflect political and regulatory risk; as well as neglecting the environmental *costs* of some renewables technology and the health effects of reducing air circulation of some energy efficiency measures. And where the costs of renewables and energy efficiency might be significant in the short run, it *assumes* that innovation and technical progress will reduce them in the long run. Remarkably, the DTI *explicitly* recognizes this *assumption* that 'there is a lot of low or nil cost technology or energy efficiency potential' (DTI 2003e, para 18, p. 158).

These cost claims about renewables and energy efficiency may be true, but where departments are predisposed to want them to be so, there is a great premium in avoiding appraisal optimism through demanding critical analysis. The MARKAL model itself tells us virtually nothing about these prior technological costs—in effect, the engineering cost function. The model merely aggregates and integrates these assumptions. Indeed, in the DTI Economics Paper No. 4 (DTI 2003e) there is *no* summary table of precisely what costs assumptions are made for the renewables and energy efficiency technologies—a surprising omission.[10] Nevertheless, the White Paper boldly states that 'the assumptions used reflected expert opinion, informed by workshops with industry experts' (DTI 2003a, p. 28). As with the connection between assumptions and MARKAL's outputs, relying on 'industry experts' depends on which ones are chosen.[11] It is a well-known problem in policy design and appraisal optimism.

MARKAL served its political, as well as analytical, purposes, and although the DTI was careful to avoid explicitly accepting its findings, they supported the DTI's rejection of what might be called Plan B—renewables plus energy efficiency plus nuclear.[12] Despite vigorous support for nuclear from Brian Wilson, the Energy Minister, from a number of leading scientists and, of course, from the nuclear industry, the White Paper concluded that:

Although nuclear power produces no carbon dioxide, its current economics make new nuclear build an unattractive option and there are important issues of nuclear waste to be resolved. Against this background, we conclude it is right to concentrate our efforts on energy efficiency and renewables. We do not, therefore, propose to

[10] Some crude summary cost numbers are tucked in at the back of the report in a section titled 'Key Messages' (pp. 164-8), but their derivation is far from clear.

[11] A clue to how this worked can be found in the workshop attendance list in the DTI Economics Paper No. 4 (DTI 2003e, p. 125) in terms of the small numbers listed (23, of which four were from the DTI). The list is not littered with critics. The role of 'expert selection' in public policy formulation is an under-researched one.

[12] These two options or plans—A and B—were explicitly set out in one of the Downing Street seminars by a DTI official in September 2002.

support new nuclear build now. But we will keep the option open. (DTI 2003*a*, para. 4.3, p. 44)

And that is basically *all* the White Paper says about nuclear. Although many in the industry saw a ray of hope in the White Paper, it is hard to conclude other than that it is a wake rather than a renaissance for nuclear power in Britain—unless renewables and energy efficiency fail to deliver—and it followed the predictable pattern already established in the nuclear review in the mid-1990s (see DTI, 1995*b*).

Whether there is to be some future revival turns in large measure on the waste issues. In July 2002, the DTI published a White Paper, 'Managing the Nuclear Legacy: A Strategy for Action' (DTI 2002*d*). This provided the first plank of a strategy to deal with the decommissioning and waste issues, by proposing the creation of a new authority, the Liabilities Management Authority (LMA), which would take on the main nuclear liabilities and the sites, and focus on developing a coherent long-term contracting strategy. In July 2003, this was taken forward in its 'Draft Nuclear Sites and Radioactive Substance Bill', with the LMA becoming a Nuclear Decommissioning Authority (NDA) (DTI, 2003*d*). But, in itself, the NDA cannot resolve the core issue of nuclear waste—whether to build a deep depository or opt for some other long-term storage option. Nor will it resolve the future of THORP (the thermal-oxide reprocessing plant) and the MOX (mixed-oxide fuel) plant at Sellafield.[13] In July 2003, Margaret Beckett, Secretary of State for Environment, Food and Rural Affairs, announced that NIREX would be put on an independent footing from the industry (but not necessarily the government), so that it could give more robust advice on long-term waste disposal (Defra, 2003). In practice, this may reflect an understandable desire to distance Defra from the final decision-making, with Cumbria the likely site—both politically, and to give greater credibility to the site-selection process.

The further contributing factor to the White Paper's negative views on nuclear power was the unfolding crisis at British Energy. The collapse of British Energy occurred in autumn 2002, with the government providing a loan facility in September, extended in March 2003, while the company tried to restructure its finances.[14] Although the problems were deep-seated and largely associated with advanced gas-cooled reactor (AGR) technology—not the technology of choice for new reactors—and wholesale electricity prices, which had brought a number of the coal power stations close to

---

[13] The closure of THORP once the existing contracts expire in the next decade was actively discussed in autumn 2003.

[14] In July 2003, the European Commission launched a formal investigation into whether the loan constituted an illegitimate state aid (Commission of the European Communities 2003*b*).

bankruptcy too, nevertheless the opponents of nuclear power were quick to point to its history, which, as Chapters 5 and 10 above document, was an unhappy one.

For the next few years, the priorities in the nuclear industry will therefore be focused on the NDA; the restructuring of BNFL; finding a long-term solution to waste disposal; restructuring British Energy; trying to keep the output of the AGRs up; and extending the lives of existing plant. To cement this change of prospects and retreat further from the market-driven agenda for the industry in the 1990s, the government announced in July 2003 that plans for a public–private partnership—ie, an element of privatization—for BNFL had been shelved, and launched a strategic review of BNFL.[15]

With nuclear effectively parked, the government's strategy to achieve the target of the Royal Commission on Environmental Pollution (RCEP) would be left to renewables and energy efficiency. However, comparatively late in the process of writing the energy White Paper, the importance (though not the existence) of the EU Directive on Greenhouse Gas Emissions Trading (Commission of the European Communities, 2003a, discussed in Chapter 19 above) began to dawn.[16] With introduction of the new scheme scheduled for 2005, Britain's coal-fired power stations would come quickly under pressure, even if the UK opted to delay joining until 2008, since the Directive requires that delay has to be accompanied by measures with 'equivalent effect'.[17]

Emissions trading had the attractions of being market-based, modern, and in line with the Treasury thinking since 1997 and the strong political support for the UK's own emissions trading scheme (HMT, 1997, and HMT, 2002, especially paras 6.24–6.35, pp. 29–31). Without much public debate and analysis, the DTI therefore gave the EU Emissions Trading Scheme a central role in the White Paper as part of what might be called Plan C—renewables, energy efficiency *and* emissions trading.[18]

In principle, emissions trading in the European-wide scheme has many attractions. It is international, whereas the UK scheme is not; and it is comprehensive—including generation, whereas the UK scheme excludes it.

[15] House of Commons Hansard Written Ministerial Statements for 3 July 2003, Col 33WS.
[16] See Defra and DTI (2003). The EU Emissions Trading Scheme did not figure prominently in the PIU report (see PIU, 2002, p. 48), nor in the early Downing Street seminars, where the emphasis was on renewables and energy efficiency.
[17] A further pressure on coal will come from the application of the EU Large Combustion Plants Directive (LCPD), with new conditions to be introduced from 2008. See also Defra, Department for the Environment (in Northern Ireland) and Welsh Assembly Government (2003).
[18] It is noteworthy that, while the DTI published a very detailed account of the MARKAL modelling work, there was no parallel document for the EU Emissions Trading Scheme. A consultation paper appeared in late summer (DTI and Defra, 2003).

Whatever the initial permit allocation, trading should ensure abatement from the lowest marginal cost source. However, from the British perspective, the lowest marginal costs of abatement are probably coal, and hence the EU scheme is in effect a mechanism for speeding up coal closures in the short term, with the benefits for non-carbon technologies (on which the energy White Paper focuses) more long-term. In 2005, if the European scheme comes into operation on time, then either more coal-fired plant will close or coal generators will have to be compensated to stay on the system. But, for security-of-supply reasons, given the state of the gas infrastructure and the need to balance more renewables, the coal stations will be increasingly valuable to the system. There was no public evidence to suggest that the DTI had, at the time of the White Paper, linked its intellectual enthusiasm for emissions trading with the practical effects of pushing up coal generation prices in the mid-2000s.

Emissions trading, being market-based, also sat rather uneasily with the renewables and energy efficiency priorities of the White Paper. As a market-based instrument, emissions trading would allow a price for carbon to emerge, and for the market to sort out least-cost solutions. Advocates of market-based mechanisms argue that it is precisely because governments do not know the supply functions of the future—i.e. which technologies will be appropriate, or how much energy efficiency of what sort will be taken up—that using prices is likely to be more efficient. The pervasiveness of uncertainty is central to the market-based approach. The MARKAL approach, by contrast, assumes a set of technology costs and is therefore more akin to the kind of exercises in central planning that the Department of Energy used to pursue, and which Nigel Lawson rejected in setting out the early rationale for the energy market reforms—as discussed in Chapter 3 above. The White Paper tries to combine both approaches, and does quite a lot of 'picking winners' as a result.

Delivery mechanisms

With Plan C the preferred route to achieving the RCEP target, but resting, in part at least, on the very insecure foundations of the MARKAL model, and the relative lack of analysis of the effects of the EU Emissions Trading Scheme, the White Paper then turned to delivery mechanisms, and here the content is at best sketchy—and, not surprisingly, it is here that most of the immediate criticisms focused. Although apparently convinced that the costs of renewables and energy efficiency are negligible over all but the short term, the White Paper does not commit to the PIU recommendations on targets for 2020—a decade and a half ahead, and hence long-term. These are now merely *aspirational*. It proposes little change in the machinery of government, and relies on guidance to Ofgem to align the White Paper with Ofgem's independent status.

This relative neglect of delivery mechanisms has a rationale—though not one the DTI has sought to highlight. If, *pace* MARKAL, the costs of achieving the 2050 target are negligible, then cynics might argue that not much needs to be done to achieve the carbon reductions. If the net present value of most of the required energy efficiency projects is likely to be positive over the timescale to 2050, and, for the Energy Saving Trust at least, even in the short run, then little extra revenue is needed. Similarly, if the costs of renewables are set to fall with innovation and technical progress, and with the premiums available that the EU Emissions Trading Scheme will bring in the second half of the 2000s, then again new initiatives lie more with planning and other related barriers, rather than new government delivery mechanisms. Delivery ought to be largely automatic, cheap, and driven by market forces, in line with the Prime Minister's earlier view that energy policy ought to be based on 'cheap energy' (see the Foreword in PIU, 2002, quoted in Chapter 21 above). But few believe that the market will deliver as cheaply as implied by the MARKAL results. Indeed, the White Paper itself is schizophrenic on this: it 'sets a new direction, and a new determination, to deliver very significant changes in both the short and longer terms. It is a massive challenge' (DTI 2003a, p. 19, para 1.48). 'Massive challenges' are rarely at negligible costs. Furthermore, the lobbying for binding targets in 2020 also suggests a lack of conviction on costs among not only the environmental groups, but also commercial companies, and even parts of Defra too.

The White Paper takes a low-key, evolutionary approach to institutions. According to the DTI, it 'does not believe we need a new organisation' to meet its 'challenging, long-term agenda for change'. 'We want to concentrate our energies on following through the commitments we have made, not on creating new machinery' (DTI, 2003a, p. 112). A *new direction* can therefore be met with *old* institutions. Ofgem will be required to produce regulatory impact assessments, publishing regular statements on the security of supply, and be given new guidance (p. 114), but it will not be reformed. The DTI will promote new offshore wind farms,[19] address planning issues and encourage network investments, but the main source of both effective powers and expertise will rest with Ofgem.

---

[19] Hewitt announced in July 2003 plans for three offshore wind farms (DTI 2003f), and claimed in the process that these would be the equivalent of six nuclear power stations— neglecting to mention the intermittent nature of wind compared with baseload nuclear, and claiming cost comparisons for wind which left out the network and back-up power costs.

In June 2003 the DTI duly issued new draft Guidance to Ofgem which, in effect, told it to take account of the White Paper (DTI 2003c).[20] Whilst, to some, this represented 'joined-up' policy and regulation, the Guidance remains a secondary duty on Ofgem, next to its primary duty to customers, and it is left to Ofgem to set prices for energy networks as it sees fit in the light of its statutory duties. The Guidance is not a direction, it is not prescriptive, and it does not cover specific social or environmental measures which would have significant financial effects—which arguably is what the 2050 CO_2 target would have. Furthermore, since both generation and supply are not subject to price-cap regulation, it is hard to see what its basis is for intervening to deliver the energy White Paper objectives. It is not an *objective* of Ofgem to deliver a low-carbon economy, and it does not have the machinery or powers to promote renewables and energy efficiency. The choice of generation technology is not an Ofgem function. Having ruled out changes to the machinery of government, the DTI will have to rely on itself to deliver—the guidance cannot achieve this objective.

Security of supply: gas, gas, and more gas

The White Paper is careful to put security of supply alongside its environmental and other objectives, and to recognize the challenges from switching to gas and imports. However, having noted these challenges, it does not propose to do much of concrete substance about them. In part, it relies on the relaxed approach in the PIU report noted in Chapter 21 above, and in part, it relies on Ofgem to do the job for it. But Ofgem's stated position is that it 'believes that the future uncertainties with respect to security and diversity of energy supplies are best resolved through the continued operation of competitive markets in electricity and gas' and that 'such markets will ensure that participants face the correct signals and incentives to invest so as to deliver sufficient supplies' (Ofgem 2001d). The DTI apparently has sympathy with this view. The White Paper states that:

For the markets to work, firms need to be confident that the Government will allow them to work. Energy supply problems in other countries have demonstrated the risks of not doing so. We will not intervene in the market except in extreme circumstances, such as to avert, as a last resort, a potentially serious risk to safety (DTI, 2003a, para 6.7, p. 77).

Consistent with this view, the main actions on security of supply are to get Ofgem to 'report on how its regulatory activities impact on energy

---

[20] See Helm (2003b) for a comment. The first Guidance was intended to last for five years, rather than one.

security', to work on 'international infrastructure problems',[21] and to 'give high priority to our new monitoring arrangements to track all aspects of energy reliability' (para 6.6).

Among the actions that could have been taken, a capacity payment had been recommended by a number of generators and commentators.[22] On this, the paper also takes a relaxed view. It states that 'there is currently no need or incentive for significant investment in new generation plant apart from renewables' (para 6.40, p. 86). Indeed, so confident is the White Paper that it boldly states that 'we are unlikely to need significant new invest- ment in non-renewables power stations over the next five years or possi- bly longer' (para 86). Just how this sits with the impact of, and reliance on, the EU Emissions Trading Scheme and on British coal plant, its age profile and maintenance problems is not addressed. By summer 2003, the plant marginal forecasts for the winter 2003/04 had become sufficiently worry- ing for National Grid Transco (NGT) to take steps to introduce greater scope for interruptible contracts, and interruptions in gas supplies were indeed required over the summer, as the system experienced a number of occasions when the supply–demand balance became uncomfortably tight.

A form of capacity-payment-by-default had in fact emerged when NGT was forced to contract directly with the Drax power station in autumn 2002, as events at TXU unfolded, exposing the system to the threat of inter- ruptions in supply. NGT began to act in the role of contractor-of-last-resort, a role that could turn the system operator function into a much more extensive commercial activity, as the plant margins tighten.[23] These con- cerns on the generation side were augmented by worries about the state of distribution networks, which had failed in the storms of autumn 2002, meriting a DTI (rather than Ofgem) inquiry,[24] and on the transmission side with the substantial power cut in London on 28 August 2003. The London power cut came after the major blackout in the USA earlier in the same month. After the US power cut, there were assertions to the effect that, 'it couldn't happen in the UK'. These events and the overoptimistic assur- ances added to the concerns about the state of the energy networks.

Whereas the White Paper places its emphasis on renewables and energy efficiency, the main consequence is in fact likely to be much greater reliance on gas, as the coal and nuclear generation capacity gradually closes. The process, begun in 1990 with electricity privatization, when around 20 per cent of capacity was nuclear and 75 per cent was coal (and overwhelmingly *domestically* sourced), of switching to a predominantly

---

[21] The primary focus here is on Norwegian and Russian gas pipeline negotiations.

[22] See Helm (2003*a*).

[23] See Ofgem (2003*a* and *b*).

[24] The DTI Select Committee began a further inquiry into network security in autumn 2003.

gas-based electricity system is likely to run its course, leaving Britain with
an energy mix in 2020 which is heavily reliant on a single imported fuel
source. This outcome is not one the White Paper chooses to give much
prominence to. Indeed, it describes 'the energy system in 2020' as being
'much more diverse than today. At its heart will be a much greater mix of
energy, especially electricity sources and technologies' (DTI, 2003*a*, p. 18).
In fact, the diversity may end up masking a new mix where gas in 2020
mirrors the role of coal in 1990, with the other 25 per cent made up of
renewables and other technologies. In such a world, the security-of-
supply issues in relation to gas will be much greater than those of coal in
1990: the gas will not only need to be reliable in itself, but also back up the
intermittency of renewables. The White Paper is virtually silent on the
energy policy implications.

Building up trouble for the future

The White Paper's bold objective to reduce carbon emissions by 60 per
cent by 2050 marks one of the first, high-profile, official recognitions in
energy policy that there has been a fundamental shift in priorities. The old
objectives of security of supply and competitive prices are now hedged
with the caveat of carbon-emissions constraints. It is for this that the
White Paper will be remembered.

But as an energy *policy*, the White Paper is more wishful thinking than a
coherent framework for delivery of the target, and it is, like Mandelson's
White Paper in 1998 (DTI, 1998*b*), more political than economic. It envisages
a world in which a radical transformation from a carbon-intensive to a low-
carbon economy can be achieved at little cost. It envisages that the closure of
the nuclear 20 per cent of capacity can be offset by an 'aspiration' to build
20 per cent renewables over the same timescale, and that energy efficiency
can deal with the rest of the demand growth. This *could* be done, but there is
little empirically robust evidence to suggest that it will be anything other
than expensive, and that prices will have to rise significantly in consequence.

But perhaps the most naïve aspect of the White Paper is not its cost
estimates, but rather the failure to recognize that the DTI is ill-equipped
to deal with the scale of the challenges it faces. The reason why it has convinced itself that the costs are low, and that the major switch to gas and
gas imports does not require much more than 'monitoring', is that it lacks
the expertise and resources to think through the issues and undertake
rigorous analysis. And this is, at heart, why changes to the machinery of
government, contrary to the White Paper, are a necessary condition for
delivery of a proper energy *policy*.

23

Reinventing Energy Policy

Two decades on from Nigel Lawson's path-breaking speech on energy policy, which set the tone for an energy policy based upon competition and privatization, there is a widespread recognition that a refocusing of policy is required. Lawson recognized that the old answers which had sufficed for the post-war period, and particularly the 1970s, were no longer appropriate as the 1980s unfolded. Now a similar challenge faces government, in recognizing that the problems of the 2000s, notably gas dependency and imports, and the environment, cannot be properly addressed in the framework of 1980s' and 1990s' policy.

But, for all the calls for a new energy policy, it is also apparent that there is little understanding of what such a policy might mean and how it could be implemented. Some place overwhelming emphasis on climatic change, and argue for an energy system based on renewable energy and energy efficiency. Others argue for a new build programme of nuclear power. Few argue that competition and market forces will in themselves be sufficient. The 1995 White Paper on Nuclear Power assertion to this effect looks complacent: 'The government cannot identify *any* reasons why the electricity market should not *of its own accord* provide an appropriate level of diversity' [italics added] (DTI 1995*b*: paras 2.8, 5.74–75).

Fortunately, in reinventing energy policy, there is a rich history to draw upon. The main themes to emerge from the period provide a basis for designing future energy policy. History matters because we cannot escape from it. It shapes our expectations and our reactions to events. In the energy sector, the connection is physical too. There are no *optimal* networks, sets of power stations or nuclear assets. The economist's model of competition and of *optimal* policy, which formed the basis of Michael Posner's classic statement of energy policy in 1973, provides little guidance as to how to price energy. Investments are incremental to imperfect sets of legacy assets, built against often very different assumptions. Long-run marginal cost is largely irrelevant: costs are always incremental to a sub-optimal system. This is all too apparent in considering the current problems of renewables and embedded generation: the electricity and gas networks were built for large-scale power stations and for industrial and retail gas supply, respectively.

Short-run marginal costs have their place, but few investments are made on the basis of spot prices, and futures markets are thin. Hence the attempt to shift investment risk from customers to financial markets has failed, sometimes spectacularly. Legacy assets come with long-term, take-or-pay contracts, power purchase agreements, or, as with the first wave of combined-cycle gas turbines (CCGTs), a regulated franchise. Such contracts are not only necessary to finance investment, but, as the evidence from California demonstrates, they may also be necessary to the smooth operation of the market.

The legacy comprises a further element—in addition to physical assets and contracts—and that is ideas. Even a cursory glance through the publications of the Department of Energy's statements, reports, and papers in the 1970s, or a reading of the voluminous recent outpourings of Ofgem, reveals a host of unwritten assumptions, which are in large measure the product of what Keynes described as the scribblings of defunct economists. And as Keynes indicated, much of the dependency is unconscious.[1] In the energy sector, the concepts of planning go back to the great debates of the interwar years, and particularly to the writing of Lange and Lerner. Modern welfare economics developed this framework to its current intellectual beauty, with at its heart the idea of the rational civil servant or nationalized industry manager allocating resources according to its precepts. A more practical version was that which formed the core of Denis Rooke's and Walter Marshall's vision of great national institutions developed in the public rather than the private interest; the former for the natural gas infrastructure (successfully) and the latter for a nuclear programme similar to that of France (unsuccessfully). These ideas played their parts too in the development of North Sea oil, and British National Oil Company's role.

Taking the energy sector as a whole, this planning idea had all the main industries linked together and run by enlightened government officials, with the Department of Energy at its centre. These would be 'Plans for Coal', joint understandings and contracts with the CEGB, which would, in turn, set the bulk supply tariff with the distribution and supply Area Boards through the Electricity Council, all within the framework of the economic and financial rules set by Treasury White Papers.

Lawson, Littlechild, McKinnon, Spottiswoode, and McCarthy were similarly caught within their own intellectual frameworks. That they all recognized the failings and inefficiencies of the nationalized and planned

---

[1] Most of the energy ministers since 1979 who have commented on drafts of this book have stressed how little they believed intellectual ideas have shaped their actions and decisions (private correspondence).

system inherited in the 1980s is greatly to their credit. But they too are prisoners of Keynes' defunct economists. The set of the ideas promulgated by Hayek and Friedman, and developed by a clutch of brilliant theorists of the Austrian school—typically outside the mainstream of academic economics—provided an often unwritten and sometimes unrecognized basis for their views and actions. The influence of these ideas was manifest through the extraordinary capture of the regulatory bodies after privatization, through the network of economists who came out of Birmingham University—Michael Beesley, Stephen Littlechild, and Eileen Marshall—together with Colin Robinson at Surrey University.

In both cases, the main actors thought that they were dealing not with intellectual fashions, which might be relevant to particular periods, but with enduring truths. The sheer elegance of the general equilibrium model, on the one hand, and the inherent superiority of markets over planning, on the other, captured imaginations. That planning and its implicit rate-of-return regulation worked reasonably well when the basic requirement was investment to keep up with the post-war boom and to develop the North Sea; and that private ownership and competition worked well when cost reduction rather than investment was the priority in the 1980s and 1990s; these were not recognized as either explanations of the success or otherwise of energy policy, or relevant to its intellectual design. It has been a central theme of this book to argue that this context was both important and relevant.

Such a claim does not imply that there are no lessons to be learnt, nor that the design of energy policy is always relative. The history of the past two decades provides some very powerful clues as to what will and what will not serve well in the next decades—about private and public ownership; about the way markets work; about the role of labour monopoly in security of supply; and about regulation. Although each is dealt with in the separate chapters, it is helpful to draw out the main conclusions before turning to the design of future energy policy.

It is tempting to conclude that public ownership was not a success, in that the 1980s and 1990s have demonstrated that private ownership is always and everywhere superior to public ownership. It was a view which the Austrians held as a matter of principle. Hayek had demonstrated that markets would always be informationally superior to state planning, and that the informational inferiority of the state was bound to have unintended consequences, which he (without any serious theoretical basis) claimed would tend to be negative. Littlechild's 'Ten Steps to Denationalization' in 1981 provided a practical blueprint, much of which was eventually implemented. But further inspection indicates that the argument is neither necessarily correct as an interpretation of what happened, nor theoretically sound. Just why private ownership by share-holders would be superior in the context of competition was not clear: product market competition *on its own* should ensure that prices equalled marginal costs.

The choice between public and private ownership in the energy sector turns out to be more pragmatic than one based on theoretical preconceptions. Private ownership provides capital market discipline on managers, allowing inefficiency in the boardroom to be rooted out through the takeover mechanism. But managers can only be efficient with respect to matters within their control, and in some areas of the energy sector they clearly are not. In the networks, regulation sets many of the key parameters, and, because regulation plays such a central role, politics intrudes too. Where regulatory risk arises outside the control of managers, shareholders tend to demand considerable premia on the cost of capital. As we saw in regard to regulatory failures in the REC reviews in 1994/95, in the writing-off of British Gas's stranded contracts, and with the windfall tax, those premia appear to have some justification.

In periods of excess supply, when investment is neither a priority nor indeed needed, the higher cost of private capital matters little. Indeed, it might even be helpful in choking off marginal investment, although cus-tomers will pay higher bills with respect to existing assets. But in periods of high investment, the cost of capital becomes a key variable. Then the differential cost between Treasury finances and private debt and equity matters greatly. For the energy sector in the 2000s and 2010s, investing in non-carbon technologies, the balance will be a finer one, especially for the electricity and gas system operators.

The difference between private and public ownership is a matter of degree, not kind. The ways in which capital is provided are necessarily shared between private and public sectors, and even public ownership can be supported by largely private provision. Thus, in the nuclear sector, there are risks and liabilities which it is unlikely the private sector will ever bear, but that has not prevented British Energy operating nuclear power stations in the private sector until the absence of long-term con-tracts undermined it. Similarly, the proposed Nuclear Decommissioning Authority will hold liabilities in the public sector, but may enable British Nuclear Fuels (BNFL) to compete with others from the private sector (DTI 2002*d*). Coal presents a similar picture: it can be operated by the private sector, while the Coal Authority discharges important functions from within the public sector. Whether, as Michael Waterson suggested in 1994 (Waterson 1994), the electricity grid and the gas transmission system should come back into the public sector is a moot point, but in any event it is very much controlled already by government and regulators. It is *between* the market and the state, rather than firmly in either camp. New nuclear and renewables are similarly *between* the market and the state, being overwhelmingly dependent on the protection and support of government.

Private ownership of most of the energy sector has had some remarkable effects, many of them benign. Operating efficiency of all the privatized energy companies has improved very considerably to cost levels which were never anticipated in the 1980s. Part, no doubt, of the explanation lies in the application of information technology to infrastructure, but privatization provided the incentives to reap the gains.

Privatization also facilitated the writing-off of the sunk costs of the coal and nuclear industries. Both carried liabilities which would have rendered them bankrupt had they been in the private sector in the 1980s. Instead, both were kept alive with subsidies, sometimes explicit and often implicit. Writing prospectuses and preparing them for privatization meant that the balance sheets had to be wiped clean. Both industries also had to face their inherent lack of economic viability in a more competitive market. In effect, the prospect of, and then the reality of, privatization closed most of the coal industry down, and for the 1990s at least put an end to new nuclear power stations. The result was to switch the generation mix from almost 80 per cent coal and 20 per cent nuclear, to one in which gas would gradually take the lion's share. It is hard to imagine that such a major shift would have happened in the public sector.

These consequences of private ownership—cost efficiency and the winding down of coal and nuclear industries—were largely benign. Other aspects of private ownership were less attractive. Whereas, in the public sector, diversification was heavily curtailed, once privatized, the utilities wasted considerable sums on acquisitions of dubious value. Where the takeover mechanism worked, it is not obvious that the results were in the public interest. The American takeovers of most of the RECs added virtually nothing to the industry's performance, and left a legacy of financial engineering by mortgaging the assets and extracting the cash. They did not start this—Northern Electric did—but they carried it to its logical conclusion. Many of the RECs were left without much balance-sheet capacity, and, whereas it might have been reasonably expected that the balance sheets were ungeared at privatization precisely to finance investment (as a *private*-sector borrowing requirement), by 2000 there was very little left.

Subsequent capital market activities have seen a sharp reversal from the agenda of creating a significant number of competitors—facilitating the incorporation of much of the electricity industry into the folds of the three major European players, E.ON, RWE, and EDF—and permitting NGC and Lattice to merge. The pursuit of profit does not distinguish between efficiencies and market power, and private ownership has recreated the sorts of concentration that the process of electricity privatization and subsequent legislation in the gas sector was designed to reverse.

These more complex consequences of private ownership have arisen as the process of creating liberalized markets has unfolded. The Conservatives left the gas monopoly intact to facilitate what was then the world's largest flotation, and the electricity industry was deliberately given a set of contracts to ease in the introduction of competition over an eight-year period. Whereas it was comparatively easy to set out the Lawson doctrine, it was altogether more difficult to deliver it, given the vested interests and the lack of international examples upon which to draw. Back in 1988 many very sensible commentators wondered whether the grid could be separated from generation, whether indeed the lights would stay on. Although critics rightly pointed to the missed opportunities of breaking British Gas up in 1985 and the Central Electricity Generating Board (CEGB) in 1988, the practicalities of the parliamentary timetable limited the scope for really radical restructurings. Subsequent regulators had to deal with a necessarily imperfect legacy, and inevitably mistakes were made.

Perhaps the most enduring consequence of leaving the transition to competition to the regulators was the dash for gas. Contrary to much ill-informed but widely believed commentary (not least by ministers, notably Peter Mandelson), the Pool was not the cause of the dash for gas. Rather, it was caused by the inflated coal contracts designed to protect the coal industry until after the 1992 election (and then to provide the basis for its privatization), by the failure of the regulator to curtail sufficiently the exercise of market power by National Power and PowerGen (by structural and conduct regulation), the regulator's desire to promote entry, and the RECs' strategic ambitions to integrate vertically. The result was too much investment, eventually resulting in the collapse of wholesale prices at the end of the decade, undermining the remaining nuclear sector, renewables and energy efficiency in the process.

Private ownership is therefore not sufficient to deliver the aims of energy policy, though at least outside the networks it is probably necessary. It operates within a framework of competition and regulation. An early casualty in the market approach was the recognition that promoting competition and deregulation did not go hand in hand. On the contrary, it turned out that, in order to promote competition, very intense *regulation for competition* would be required, which was much more demanding than the regulation *of* monopoly. Markets had to be designed, property rights established and policed, and conduct rules put in place. Designing and operating the Pool—and NETA subsequently—were not *de*regulating activities. Both were costly and demanding. Markets, too, do not naturally remain open—the creation of market power will, if unchecked, undermine such markets. (In the United States, dubious financial practices and even criminality added to the demise of trading markets.) The fact that, for government, the regulation of markets was an afterthought, and, in the case of the Pool, the role of regulator was heavily constrained, was to cause serious difficulties. Liberalization changes the nature of regulatory problems, but it does not eliminate them. Not surprisingly, regulation has grown since the early days when there were around twenty people in Ofgas.

The structural questions which confronted the privatization teams and regulators subsequently were not simply confined to creating enough competitors to have a competition. They had a political context too. Margaret Thatcher's support for the break-up of the CEGB had more to do with her goal of dealing with Arthur Scargill and the National Union of Mineworkers (NUM) than it did with the finer points of competition economics. She could simultaneously support nuclear and the break-up of the CEGB because both limited the power of the miners.

Energy policy, in so far as it was concerned with security of supply, had to have regard to the main threat of supply interruptions, which in the 1980s clearly came from the NUM. The fact that fragmentation of the electricity industry created competition in electricity generation was an additional benefit, over and above the dealing with labour monopoly. It was a major achievement of the 1980s and 1990s that this threat had been neutralized. Had the electricity industry remained in state hands—as it did in France—it would have been politically much harder to resist the mining or other labour market interests.

There were, however, limits to the possibilities of competition in electricity and gas industries, though it took time for these to materialize. The aspiration of turning both fuels into commodities covered by general competition law, and outside the political domain, was to be frustrated. Just as, in the 1970s, great emphasis—perhaps too much—was placed on the market failures, and not enough on government and regulatory ones, in the 1980s and 1990s, the pendulum swung too far the other way. The market enthusiasts failed to recognize just how far the electricity market deviated from the normal commodity model. To recap, supply must instantaneously match demand as there is limited scope for storage; the assets are sunk and long-lived; the networks are natural monopolies; there are very great environmental externalities; and, critically, electricity and gas are complementary to the rest of the economy, in that failure to supply has (extremely) large costs to all economic activity. It is hard to think of any other activity in modern developed economies with quite such a coincidence of major market failures. If the issue of fuel poverty and the distributional implications of electricity and gas pricing and supply are also included, it is extraordinary that anyone could have regarded these as anything other than *political* industries.

After the initial privatizations, the extent of political influence—defined in the broadest sense—gradually reasserted itself. It became apparent that the government had swapped public ownership for significant public control, and that, free from the constraints and responsibilities (notably paying for interventions) that nationalization brought, the regulators had arguably more power and control than secretaries of state had had over the fiefdoms of Rooke and Marshall. Much of this was disguised in the early days after privatization as the Conservative governments and the regulators had a very similar agenda—of driving down prices and costs. Being 'beastly' to the incumbent utilities, screwing down the price caps, and threatening the generators with the Monopolies and Mergers Commission made good political as well as economic sense, when there was little need for investment. Stranding British Gas's contracts could probably have not passed the Treasury had it been in public hands, but in the private sector, the government could let the 'fat cats' and their shareholders suffer.

The British regulatory system, centred around Directors General with very wide personal discretion and the RPI − X fixed-price, fixed-period contracts, was well suited to the task of sweating the assets and, although the application of the price caps and the conduct of the periodic review were at best mixed, and sometimes very poor, the overall effect was largely benign. Utilities were forced to look to the interests of their customers rather than pursue those of producers, and, as noted above, the costs and (some of) the prices fell too. In the 1990s, customers got a better deal than they would have had under continued public-sector ownership. Regulatory reform was needed, and when it did come with the Utilities Act 2000, it did little to address the fundamental problem of generalized duties and the uncertainty within the system, and the cost of capital did not fall. But by then it had begun to matter, as the new agenda began to emerge, with the prospect of investment-driven regulation to meet environmental and network concerns.

By the end of the 1990s, when the asset-sweating had largely run its course, the energy sector was leaner and prices were lower, and it should have been to politicians' liking. Indeed, once the windfall tax had been extracted, it was expected in government circles that energy would simply drop off the agenda, with a junior minister and the regulators dealing with the arcane technicalities of periodic reviews, the 1998 liberalization and the introduction of NETA. In fact, of course, it did not go away, but rather imposed itself repeatedly on the political agenda through a series of crises. To the extent that energy policy had been reduced to crisis management, there were plenty of 'events' to come. The new structures of the energy industries, and the regulatory arrangements and institutions were to prove inadequate to the task, with the result that energy policy failed to 'go away'.

As we have seen, these political events in the late 1990s were numerous and multifarious—including coal and nuclear, the environment and the networks. The first of these was the coal crisis and Mandelson's White Paper in 1998—a fitting triumph of spin over substance. Labour's energy policy was to include more than that of its Conservative predecessors, in the sense that the objectives were to be widened to include the party's traditional loyalties to coal and its wider social democratic traditions too, especially in relation to fuel poverty. Even without its commitment to sustainable development and ameliorating climate change, it was to have difficulty in reconciling all its other objectives with coal. Mandelson managed a brilliant political manoeuvre, claiming that banning gas entry would help to promote competition. More inconsistency was to follow, with the Climate Change Levy and the UK Emissions Trading Scheme both being distorted to protect coal.

This problem of multiple objectives has become a major obstacle to developing a new energy policy. It gradually became apparent that the competitive market would not support renewables or nuclear power, and, of their own accord, suppliers preferred well-off direct-debit customers to poor indebted ones. And when it became apparent that the easy environmental gains which came from closing coal were no longer available—and CO_2 emissions were actually rising again—the tension between cheap energy and all the things Labour wanted delivered became more and more apparent.

Because Labour lacked a coherent energy policy, it dealt with each problem in an *ad hoc* way. The result was an inevitable mess, and considerable wasted resources. There were policies and institutions in abundance, but they were not 'joined up'. Multiple objectives did not necessarily mean that policy had to be inconsistent, but it did make it much harder to design. Trying to please as many interests as possible was not a substitute for rational analysis and efficient resource allocation.

The trouble with multiple objectives is that the trade-offs have to be defined, and the objectives themselves need to be coherent and clearly specified. Being in favour of security of supply means little unless the trade-off with cost is defined. Infinite security is clearly not desirable. Being in favour of reducing greenhouse gas emissions means little unless some target is set. Reducing emissions *in the United Kingdom* to their pre-industrial levels is radically different to stabilizing emissions, and this itself is very different to reducing them to 60 per cent by 2050, as the RCEP suggested (and the 2003 White Paper adopted), or 20 per cent on the 1990 level by 2010 as Labour originally committed itself to. Unless the target is credibly specified, designing an energy policy is all but infeasible.

Then there is the confusion between means and ends. The Prime Minister stated in the introduction to the Performance and Innovation Unit report on energy policy (PIU 2002) that he favoured a policy aimed at '*cheap*, reliable and sustainable sources of energy supply' [italics added]. Prices are, however, an outcome, within the context of the security of supply and environmental objectives. If they were an *objective*, then, short of Treasury subsidies, they may be inconsistent with other aims. The great merit of Conservative energy policy was that the objectives were fairly simple and straightforward. The means were also fairly simple: privatization and competition.

The starting point for a new energy policy is to define the objectives and trade-offs in an explicit way, something politicians are typically very reluctant to do. They will be all the more reluctant, given that the new agenda is likely to require considerable investment and prices will inevitably rise. Something—probably prices—will have to give.

The new agenda is driven largely by the environmental constraints. This is true for Europe and the United States too. If climate change is to be addressed then the overwhelming dependency on fossil fuels will have to be reduced with a switch to non-carbon sources, of which there are two main immediate candidates: renewables and nuclear. The former are typically small-scale and embedded, and a substantial share for renewables would require the re-engineering of the electricity transmission and distribution networks and probably supporting changes in the gas network too. The latter would avoid some of the network issues, but requires major investments in the management of nuclear waste if public opinion is to be supportive. Under either option, if the RCEP agenda is to be fully addressed as the 2003 White Paper requires, almost all of the main electricity assets will need to be replaced.

Some claim that energy efficiency could provide a way forward without nuclear. As we saw in Chapter 19, its advocates have been better at lobbying than in delivery, and it has been largely a social policy over the past two decades. It is a moot question as to whether the energy intensity of economic output can continue its declining path, but it is hard to imagine economic growth over the next decades at 2–3 per cent without a rise in the demand for electricity and gas.

Over the sorts of timescales which climate change is taking place, it is likely that none of the existing technologies will provide much more than temporary stopgaps. New technologies are likely to take up the strain, possibly built around hydrogen. Just as the Sizewell B inquiry compared coal with nuclear and forgot about gas, the current debate about wind, PWRs and energy efficiency tends to ignore the possibility of more radical options.

It is crucial to recognize that neither renewables nor nuclear (nor new technologies) are likely to thrive within the NETA market which regulators and government have created. Both need long-term, take-or-pay contracts, which the market as it has now evolved is unlikely to support. Hence, the Renewables Obligation is a compulsory take-or-pay contract, and similar interventions around NETA will be required if nuclear is to expand. These contracts are a key part of energy policy. They underpinned North Sea gas development and they supported coal. They also play a crucial role in stabilizing markets: without long-term contracts, California was vulnerable to massive price spikes.

The problem of long-term contracts extends to gas, too. As imports grow, Russia faces many of the problems the North Sea faced in the 1970s and 1980s. Sunk investments need long-term contracts. Yet having torn up British Gas's take-or-pay contracts in the mid-1990s, and facilitated customer switching, the liberalized market does not provide a strong basis for writing such contracts in the future. To the extent that they are forthcoming, the risks will tend to be set against equity—as they are in the oil industry. That can only be done by very large companies, with diverse portfolios and market power. Arguably, that is what has emerged with the concentration of the European gas and electricity markets. It is, however, hardly a first-best solution, and it is the antithesis of the competitive market approach that the British government claims to be pursuing.

So a second major building block—after defining objectives—is to provide a framework within which long-term contracts can be written. The third building block is networks. These are the motorways to the market, and over-provision is greatly preferable to under-provision. The optimal level of interconnection will not be developed by private vertically integrated oligopolists and their design and development have system-wide characteristics. An element of planning and a (heavy) dose of regulation is essential. It was a lucky coincidence that the market approach of the 1980s and 1990s was applied in the context of mature and well-invested electricity and gas networks. The assets could be sweated without worrying too much about the cost of capital or supply security. That luxury is no longer available, and hence the regulatory priority, and the appropriate instruments, need to shift towards investment.

Where there are multiple market failures, it is important to ensure that economic regulation addresses these jointly, rather than separately, and gives appropriate weighting to each. Thus, the twin failures of monopoly and externalities are worthy of equal attention. When regulators say that their domain is primarily competition and the regulation of monopoly, and that this is what economic regulation should focus on, there is nothing in economic theory, and no efficiency reason for this view. Indeed, if monopoly leads to prices which are too high, externalities tend to point to them being too low, and therefore solving the former may make the latter worse. This is indeed probably what has happened, worsening the allocation of resources. Low prices are not necessarily efficient prices.

Though there is no a priori reason why market-based instruments will always be better than more traditional forms of intervention, the focus on prices which such instruments bring is likely to be better at integrating the different aspects of policy. For example, utility regulators can deal with monopoly by setting prices, and carbon taxes can reflect the externality. The net effect is the aggregation of these prices.

This is the fourth aspect of a new energy policy. The 1990s moved away from government 'picking winners' among competing technologies—largely because there was little choice to be made, and CCGTs were the overwhelmingly preferred technology. As we saw in Chapter 2, the consequences of picking winners in the nationalized industries has been sometimes dire—notably with the AGRs in the 1960s and 1970s. Now, as non-carbon sources are increasingly required, the issue of picking winners is important again, and the RO displays the dangers, as some technologies are excluded. A carbon tax is a better policy option, though its political aspects are more difficult. It is an explicit environmental tax. Emissions trading, while less explicit, will have a similar effect.

The fifth and final aspect of energy policy is the institutional structure. Energy policy is a process carved out by officials, regulators and specific institutions. In the 1980s and 1990s, when the agenda was one of asset-sweating, the discretionary powers of Directors General, backed up by the new offices, could put pressure on the utilities with scant regard for the effect on the cost of capital. The closure of coal meant that the externalities could be largely ignored, and be left to the Environment Agency and a host of special bodies, such as the Energy Saving Trust and the Carbon Trust. The economic regulators maintained the fiction that they were 'independent'. Now, however, the agenda has changed. Take-or-pay contracts are required, energy and carbon taxes may be required, we have emissions trading and an important European interface. It is not obvious that Ofgem is the right institution to provide the basis for the investment in renewables, nuclear and the networks that may be required.

There are a number of options. Brian Wilson, Minister for Energy for much of the period leading up to the 2003 White Paper, favoured a Department of Energy (see DTI 2002a); though how much thought has gone into addressing its past mistakes (which Lawson emphasized) is far from clear. The Chief Scientist, David King, proposed a broad-based energy research council (PIU 2002: annex 8). Another option is an energy agency. The choice between these options turns on the nature of the problems to be addressed. With environmental priorities to the fore, the relationship between DEFRA and the DTI becomes more important, as the hegemony of the DTI is more questionable. Energy policy under the DTI is an activity more in keeping with the interests of industry, particularly large industrial companies which may be significant polluters.

A further aspect of institutional design is corporate and sectoral knowledge. Lawson's approach dismantled much of the demand modelling and other energy-specific work of the Department of Energy precisely because civil servants did not need to know much about the market when private companies and competition took over. Decisions were transferred from Whitehall to boardrooms and the regulatory offices. Apart from dealing with crises and handling privatizations, there was little for civil servants to do.

New Labour not only added more objectives—such as environmental and fuel-poverty targets—but also faced the interventionist consequences. Once ministers actively wanted to do something, civil servants were required to implement policy. That in turn required expertise. Ofgem's interests were rather different: it had acquired a culture and an interest in a particular focus in the market failures associated with monopoly and market power, and has at times been hostile to interventions to achieve the government's wider agenda.

Rebuilding the expertise within the DTI—which is what the 2003 White Paper relies upon—is likely to be a difficult task, given the broad industrial remit of the department and its historically difficult relations with the environmental department. Trying to change the interests of Ofgem is similarly likely to be difficult, given its history and the way it has developed its own remit. Each set of historical circumstances requires its own institutional structures, but typically governments soldier on with what they have inherited, rather than restructure themselves. Thus in 1982 Lawson recognized the problems of a 1970s-style Department of Energy, and wryly noted that, when Peter Walker took over, it reverted to type. Similarly DTI Energy Ministers, and their counterparts in DEFRA, echo their frustrations with Ofgem, but as yet have not faced up to the need to take a more radical approach. No amount of 'guidance' will solve this problem.

The history of energy policy, while never repeating itself, gives us important insights into the design of energy policy. It tells us that the scope for change is limited by the physical assets, that objectives often conflict, and that the sorts of policies relevant to excess supply are rather different from those where investment is a priority. But it also suggests that it takes time to recognize when the fundamentals have changed, and that policy—and institutional structures—tend to lag rather than lead. The inertia within the industry and in government is very considerable, and energy policy tends to be better designed to solve yesterday's problems rather than today's or tomorrow's. Substantive changes in direction tend to come about as a result of crises, not careful analyses and forethought. The great contribution Lawson made was to break out of these constraints, ushering in a period of profound change. Only the Attlee government in the 1940s managed anything quite as radical. The task now, twenty years later, is to reinvent an energy policy designed to address the new problems of the environment and gas import dependency. It has yet to be delivered.

REFERENCES

ALLAZ, B. and VILA, J. L. 1993. 'Cournot Competition, Forward Markets and Efficiency'. *Journal of Economic Theory* 59: 1–16.

ALLSOPP, C. and RHYS, J. 1989. 'The Macroeconomic Impact of North Sea Oil'. In *The Market for Energy*, eds D. R. Helm, J. Kay, and D. Thompson. Oxford: Clarendon Press.

ARGYRIS, N. 1993. 'Regulatory Reform in the Electricity Sector: An Analysis of the Commission's Internal Market Proposals'. *Oxford Review of Economic Policy* 9(1): 31–44.

ASHWORTH, W. 1986. *The History of the British Coal Industry, vol. 5: The Nationalised Industry*. Oxford: Oxford University Press.

Assemblée Nationale. 2003. 'Rapport Fait au Nom de la Commission D'Enquête sur la Gestion des Entreprises Publiques afin d'Améliorer le Système de Prise de Décision'. 3 July.

BACM. 1991. 'Coal Industry Privatisation: Draft'. April, British Association of Colliery Management, Nottingham.

BAKER, J. 1987. 'How Best to Give Power to the People'. *Financial Times*, 25 November.

BAMBERG, J. 2000. *British Petroleum and Global Oil 1950–1975: The Challenge of Nationalisation*. Cambridge: Cambridge University Press.

Bank of England. 1982. 'North Sea Oil and Gas: A Challenge for the Future'. *Bank of England Quarterly Bulletin* 22.

BARRETT, S. 1998. 'The Political Economy of the Kyoto Protocol'. *Oxford Review of Economic Policy* 14(4): 20–39.

BAUMOL, W., PANZAR, J. C., and WILLIG, R. D. 1982. *Contestable Markets and the Theory of Industrial Structure*. San Diego: Harcourt Brace.

BEESLEY, M. E. and LITTLECHILD, S. C. 1989. 'The Regulation of Privatized Monopolies in the United Kingdom'. *RAND Journal of Economics* 20(3): 454–72.

BENN, T. 1989. *Against the Tide: Diaries, 1973–1976*. London: Hutchinson.

——1990. *Conflicts of Interest: Diaries, 1970–1980*. London: Hutchinson.

BERKOVITCH, I. 1977. *Coal on the Switchback: The Coal Industry since Nationalisation*. London: Allen and Unwin.

BLAIR, T. 1995. 'Principles for Reform'. In *Principles for Reform: New Thinking on Regulatory Reform*, ed. D. Corry. IPPR: 2–4.

BNFL. 1997. 'BNFL Sign New Contracts with British Energy'. Press release, 4 June, British Nuclear Fuels Ltd.

——2002. 'BNFL Announces Shortened Lifetimes for Calder Hall and Chapelcross Power Stations'. Press release, 21 June.

BORENSTEIN, S. 2002. 'The Trouble with Electricity Markets: Understanding California's Restructuring Disaster'. *Journal of Economic Perspectives* 16(1): 191–211.

BRECHLING, V., HELM, D. R., and SMITH, S. 1991. 'Domestic Energy Conservation: Environmental Objectives or Market Failures'. In *Economic Policy Towards the Environment*, ed. D. R. Helm. Oxford: Blackwell Publishers.

British Coal Corporation. 1994. 'Report and Accounts, 1993/94'.

British Energy. 1996. 'British Energy Share Offer', 26 June.

British Gas. 1977. 'Annual Report and Accounts'.

BROWN, S. 1970. 'The Next 25 Years in the Electricity Supply Industry'. Lecture delivered to the Institute of Electrical and Electronic Technical Engineers, 16 November.

BRTF. 2001. 'Economic Regulators'. July, The Haskins Report, Better Regulation Task Force.

CAIRNCROSS, A. 1985. *Years of Recovery: British Economic Policy 1945–51*. London: Methuen.

——1994. 'Economic Policy and Performance 1964–1990'. In *The Economic History of Britain since 1700, vol. 3 1939–1992*, 2nd edn, eds R. Floud and D. McCloskey. Cambridge: Cambridge University Press.

CALLAGHAN, J. 1997. 'Why the Coal Industry should not be Scuttled'. *The Times*, 6 November.

CAMPBELL, J. 2000. *Margaret Thatcher: vol. 1 The Grocer's Daughter*. London: Jonathan Cape.

CARSON, R. 1963. *Silent Spring*. London: Hamish Hamilton.

CASTRO-RODRIGUEZ, R., MARIN, P., and SIOTIS, G. 2002. 'Capacity Choices in Liberalised Electricity Markets'. CEPR Discussion Paper no. 2998, Centre for Economic Policy Research.

Centrica. 1998. 'Annual Report: 1997/98'.

CEGB. 1982. 'Sizewell "B" Power Station Public Enquiry: CEGB Statement of Case, vol. 1'. Central Electricity Generating Board.

CHENNELLS, L. 1997. 'The Windfall Tax'. *Fiscal Studies* 18(3): 279–91.

CLARKSON, R. and DEYES, K. 2002. 'Estimating the Social Cost of Carbon Emissions'. GES Working Paper 140, London: HM Treasury.

Coal Authority. 2002. 'Coal Authority Reports and Accounts, 2001/02'.

——(undated). 'The Coal Authority Report to the Secretary of State for Trade and Industry on the Administration of Coal Mining Subsidence Damage Claims during 2001/02'.

COCKETT, R. 1994. 'The Road to Serfdom——50 Years On'. *History Today*, May.

Commission of the European Communities. 1985. 'Completing the Internal Market'. White Paper from the Commission to the European Council, Luxembourg, Office for Official Publications of the European Communities, COM(1985)310.

——1991. 'Proposal for a European Parliament and Council Directive concerning common rules for the internal market in electricity'. Com(91)548 final.

——1992a. 'Electricity and Natural Gas Transmission Infrastructures in the Community'. SEC(92)553 Final.

—— 1992*b*. 'Energy: Consequences of the Proposed Carbon/Energy Tax'. SEC(92)1996 Final, 23 October, supplement to *Energy in Europe*.

—— 1995. 'Communication from the Commission: For a European Union Energy Policy: Green Paper'. Com(1994)659, 11 January.

Commission of the European Communities 1996*a*. 'An Energy Policy for the European Union: White Paper'. COM(95)682 Final, January.

—— 1996*b*. 'Directive 96/92/EC of the European Parliament and of the Council of 19 December 1996 concerning common rules for the internal market in electricity'.

—— 1998. 'Directive 98/30/EC of the European Parliament and of the Council of 22 June concerning common rules for the internal market in natural gas'.

—— 2000*a*. 'Green Paper on Greenhouse Gas Emissions Trading within the European Union'. COM(2000)87 Final, March.

—— 2000*b*. 'Towards a European Strategy for the Security of Energy Supply'. COM(2000)769, June.

—— 2001. 'Proposal for a Directive of the European Parliament and of the Council amending Directives 96/92/EC and 98/30/EC concerning common rules for the internal market in electricity and gas'.

—— 2002. 'Amended Proposal for a Directive of the European Parliament and of the Council amending Directives 96/92/EC and 98/30/EC concerning common rules for the internal market in electricity and gas'. COM(2002)304 Final.

—— 2003*a*. 'Proposal for a Directive of the European Parliament and of the Council amending the Directive establishing a scheme for greenhouse gas emission allowance trading within the Community, in respect of the Kyoto Protocol's project mechanisms'. COM(2003)403. Final, 23 July.

—— 2003*b*. 'Unnotified State Aid NN 45/03—United Kingdom Aid in Favour of British Energy plc', letter from Mario Monti, Member of the Commission, to Jack Straw MP, Secretary of State for Foreign and Commonwealth Affairs, July.

Competition Commission. 2001. 'AES and British Energy: A Report on References made under Section 12 of the Electricity Act 1989'. CC 453, TSO.

—— 2003. 'Centrica plc and Dynegy Storage Ltd and Dynegy Onshore Processing UK Ltd', Cm 5885, 8 August.

CONNINE, T. and TAMARKIN, M. 1985. 'Implications of Skewness in Returns for Utilities' Cost of Equity Capital'. *Financial Management*.

Conservative Party. 1979. 'Conservative Party General Election Manifesto'.

—— 1983. 'Conservative Party General Election Manifesto'.

COOPER, D. and HOPPER, T. 1988. *Debating Coal Closures*. Cambridge: Cambridge University Press.

CORRY, D. 2003. 'The Regulatory State: Labour and the Utilities 1997–2002'. March, London: Institute of Public Policy Research.

—— ed. 1995*a*. *Regulating in the Public Interest: Looking to the Future*. London: Institute for Public Policy Research.

—— ed. 1995*b*. *Profiting from the Utilities: New Thinking on Regulatory Reform*. London: Institute for Public Policy Research.

CORRY, D., SOUTER, D., and WATERSON, M. 1994. *Regulating our Utilities*. London: Institute for Public Policy Research.

CORTI, G. and FRAZER, F. 1983. *The Nation's Oil: A Story of Control*. London: Graham and Trotman.

Council of the European Communities. 1975. 'Council Directive of 13 February 1975 on the restriction of the use of natural gas in power stations' (75/404/EEC), *Official Journal*, L 178, 9 July 1975, p. 0024.

Council of the European Union. 1996. 'Council directive 96/61/EC of 24 September 1996 concerning integrated pollution prevention and control'.

CURRIE, D. 1998. 'Making the Green Paper a Reality'. Keynote Address, Gas Consumers Council conference, 4 June.

DEFRA. 2001. 'Energy Efficiency Commitment 2002–2005: Consultation Proposals'. August, Department of the Environment, Food and Rural Affairs, London: TSO.

—— 2003. 'Margaret Beckett Announces Way Forward On Radioactive Waste Management'. 16 July, News Release, Department for Environment, Food and Rural Affairs, London: TSO.

——, Department for the Environment (in Northern Ireland) and Welsh Assembly Government. 2003. 'Consultation on Implementation of the Revised Large Combustion Plants Directive'. June, Department for Environment, Food and Rural Affairs, London: TSO.

—— and DTI. 2003. 'Consultation Paper on the Implementation of the EU Emissions Trading Scheme'. August, Department for Environment, Food and Rural Affairs and Department of Trade and Industry, London:TSO.

——, ——, DTLR. 2002. 'Energy Policy: Key Issues for Consultation', 14 May, Department for Environment, Food and Rural Affairs, Department of Trade and Industry, Department for Transport, Local Government and the Regions, London: TSO.

Department of Employment. 1972. 'Report of a Court of Inquiry into a Dispute between the NCB and the NUM under the Chairmanship of the Rt. Hon Lord Wilberforce'. Cmnd 4903, London: HMSO.

Department of Energy. 1974. 'Coal Industry Examination Interim Report'. London: HMSO.

—— 1978. 'Energy Policy: A Consultative Document'. Cmnd 7101, London: HMSO.

—— 1979. 'Coal for the Future—Progress with "Plan for Coal" and Prospects to the Year 2000'. London: HMSO.

—— 1981. 'Nuclear Power: The Government's Response to the Select Committee on Energy's Report on the Nuclear Power Programme'. Cmnd 8317, London: HMSO.

—— 1987. 'Sizewell B Public Inquiry: Report by Sir Frank Layfield', vol. V: The Economic Case, London: HMSO.

—— 1989a. 'Electricity Act 1989: Successor Company Licences in England and Wales, vol. I: Public Electricity Supply Licence'. London: HMSO.

—— 1989b. 'An Evaluation of Energy Related Greenhouse Gas Emissions and Measures to Ameliorate Them'. Energy Paper 58, October, London: HMSO.

Department of Industry. 1983. 'Regulation of British Telecommunications' Profitability'. Department of Industry, London: HMSO.

Department of State and Official Bodies and Ministry of Power. 1964. 'The Second Nuclear Programme'. Cmnd 2335, London: HMSO.

Department of the Environment. 1978. 'The Windscale Inquiry'. March, London: HMSO.

—— 1990. ' This Common Inheritance: Britain's Environmental Strategy'. Cm 1200, London: HMSO.

DETR. 1998. 'UK Climate Change Programme'. Department for the Environment, Transport and the Regions, London: TSO.

—— 1999. 'A Better Quality of Life—A Strategy for Sustainable Development for the UK'. May, Cm 4345, Department for the Environment, Transport and the Regions, London: TSO.

—— 2000a. 'Climate Change: The UK Programme'. Cm 4913, Department for the Environment, Transport and the Regions, London: TSO, November.

—— 2000b. 'Energy Efficiency Standards of Performance (formerly EESOP 4): The Government's Provisional Conclusions'. Department for the Environment, Transport and the Regions, London: TSO, November.

—— 2002. Letter from Margaret Beckett to the Editor of *Ends Report*, 24 April.

DETR/DTI. 2001. 'The UK Fuel Poverty Strategy: A Consultation Paper'. February, London: TSO.

DILNOT, A. and HELM, D. R. 1987. 'Energy Policy, Merit Goods and Social Security'. *Fiscal Studies*. 8(3): 29–48.

DONOUGHUE, B. and JAMES, G. W. 1973. *Herbert Morrison: Portrait of a Politician*. London: Weidenfeld and Nicolson.

——, *Digest of UK Energy Statistics*, annual publication, various, Department of Trade and Industry. London: TSO.

—— 1993. 'Prospects for Coal: Conclusions of the Government's Coal Review'. Cmnd 2235, March, Department of Trade and Industry, London: HMSO.

—— 1994. 'Speech by Mr Eggar, Minister for Industry and Energy on the Role of Regulators, 21 November 1994'. Press release, P/64/699, Department of Trade and Industry.

—— 1995a. 'Energy Projections for the UK: Energy Use and Energy-related Emissions of Carbon Dioxide in the UK 1995–2020'. March, Department of Trade and Industry, London: HMSO.

—— 1995b. 'The Prospects for Nuclear Power in the UK: Conclusions of the Government's Nuclear Review'. Cmnd 2860, May, Department of Trade and Industry with the Scottish Office, London: HMSO.

—— 1995c. 'Ian Lang refers PowerGen and National Power Bids to MMC'. Press release, 23 November, Department of Trade and Industry.

—— 1996. 'Ian Lang blocks Electricity Mergers', press release, 24 April, Department of Trade and Industry.

—— 1998a. 'A Fair Deal for Consumers: Modernising the Framework for Utility Regulation'. Cmnd 3898, March, Department of Trade and Industry, London: TSO.

—— 1998*b*. 'Conclusions of the Review of Energy Sources for Power Generation and Government Response to Fourth and Fifth Reports of the Trade and Industry Committee'. Cm 4071, October, Department of Trade and Industry, London: TSO.

—— 1999*a*. 'New and Renewable Energy: Prospects for the 21st Century'. March, Department of Trade and Industry, London: TSO.

—— 1999*b*. 'New and Renewable Energy: Prospects for the 21st Century: Analysis of the Response to the Consultation Paper'. July, Department of Trade and Industry, London: TSO.

—— 2000*a*. 'A Fair Deal for Consumers: Modernising the Framework for Utility Regulation: Regulatory, Environmental and Equal Treatment Appraisals'. January, para 11, p. 7, Department of Trade and Industry, London: TSO.

—— 2000*b*. 'A Fair Deal for Consumers: Modernising the Framework for Utility Regulation: Draft Statutory Social and Environmental Guidance to the Gas and Electricity Markets Authority'. February, Department of Trade and Industry, London: TSO.

—— 2000*c*. 'New and Renewable Energy: Prospects for the 21st Century: Conclusions in Response to the Public Consultation'. February, Department of Trade and Industry, London: TSO.

—— 2000*d*. 'A Fair Deal for Consumers: Modernising the Framework for Utility Regulation: Regulatory, Environmental and Equal Treatment Appraisals'. April, revised, Department of Trade and Industry, London: TSO.

—— 2000*e*. 'Energy Projections for the UK: Energy Paper 68'. August, Department of Trade and Industry, London: TSO.

—— 2000*f*. 'New and Renewable Energy: Prospects for the 21st Century——The Renewables Obligation Preliminary Consultation'. October, Department of Trade and Industry, London: TSO.

—— 2001*a* 'New and Renewable Energy: Prospects for the 21st Century: Analysis of the Responses to the Consultation Paper'. March, Department of Trade and Industry, London: TSO.

—— 2001*b*. 'Social, Environmental and Security of Supply Policies in a Competitive Energy Market: A Review of Delivery Mechanisms in the United Kingdom'. May, Department of Trade and Industry, London: TSO.

—— 2001*c*. 'Review of the Case for Government Support for Cleaner Coal Technology Demonstration Plant'. Final Report, 13 December, Department of Trade and Industry, London: TSO.

—— 2002*a*. 'Memoranda submitted by the Department of Trade and Industry: Examination of Witnesses'. 24 April, Department of Trade and Industry, London: TSO.

—— 2002*b*. 'Energy Policy: Key Issues for Consultation'. May, Department of Trade and Industry, London: TSO.

—— 2002*c*. 'Social and Environmental Guidance to the Gas and Electricity Markets Authority'. Draft, June, Department of Trade and Industry, London: TSO.

—— 2002*e*. 'Managing the Nuclear Legacy: A Strategy for Action'. July, Department of Trade and Industry, London: TSO.

——2002*f*. 'Energy: Its Impact on the Environment and Society'. July, Department of Trade and Industry, London: TSO.

——2003*a*. 'Our Energy Future—Creating a Low Carbon Economy'. February, Department of Trade and Industry, London: TSO.

——2003*b*. 'Proposals for a Special Administrator Regime for Energy Network Companies', consultation document. 16 April, DTI Energy Markets Unit, Department of Trade and Industry, London: TSO.

——2003*c*. 'Draft Social and Environmental Guidance to the Gas and Electricity Markets Authority: A Consultation Document by the Department of Trade and Industry'. 4 June, Department of Trade and Industry, London: TSO.

——2003*d*. 'Draft Nuclear Sites and Radioactive Substances Bill'. 24 June, Cm 5858, Department of Trade and Industry, London: TSO.

——2003*e*. 'Options for a Low Carbon Future', DTI Economics Paper no. 4. 25 June, Department of Trade and Industry, London: TSO.

——2003*f*. 'Hewitt announces biggest ever expansion in renewable energy', press release. 14 July, P/2003/403, Department of Trade and Industry, London: TSO.

——and Ministry of Economic Affairs. 2000. 'Energy Liberalisation Indicators in Europe'. October, prepared by OXERA.

DTI/Ofgas. 1994. 'Competition and Choice in the Gas Market: A Joint Consultation Document'. May, Department of Trade and Industry, London: TSO.

DTI/Ofgem. 2002. 'Joint Energy Security of Supply Working Group, First Report'. June, Department of Trade and Industry, London: TSO.

EDWARDS, J., KAY, J., and MAYER, C. 1987. 'The Economic Analysis of Accounting Profitability'. Oxford: Oxford University Press.

EGGAR, T. 2003. book review of Helm, D., *Energy, the State and the Market*, in *The Utilities Journal*, March, Oxford: OXERA.

Electricity Consumers' Council. 1987. 'Privatising Electricity: A Chance for Change? The National Grid and the Merit Order'. Privatisation Discussion, Paper 4, October.

ELLIOT, D. *et al*. 1978. *The Politics of Nuclear Power*. London: Pluto Press.

ENDS Report, April 2002.

EST. 2001. 'Towards an Energy Efficient Strategy for Households to 2020: Supplementary Submission to the PIU Energy Policy Review'. 17 October, Energy Saving Trust.

——2002. 'Putting Climate Change at the Heart of Energy Policy: Energy Saving Trust Submission to the Energy White Paper', London: Energy Saving Trust.

EVANS, N. 1984. 'An Economic Evaluation of the Sizewell Decision'. *Energy Policy* 12(3): 288–95.

EVANS, J. and GREEN, R. 2003. 'Why did British Electricity Prices Fall after 1998?', Centre for Economic Policy, Hull: University of Hull Business School.

EZRA, D. 1993. 'A Framework for Energy'. *The Political Quarterly* 64(4): 391–5.

FERC. 1996. 'Order 888'. Federal Energy Regulatory Commission, Washington, DC.

Financial Times. 1987. 'Competition, but with Care', 30 September.

——1988. 'Fair Pricing of Electric Power', 22 February.

FISHLOCK, D. and ROBERTS, L. E. J. 1998. 'Walter Charles Marshall, CBE, Lord Marshall of Goring'. *Biog. Mem. Fell. R. So. Lon.* 44: 297–312.

FoE. 2002. 'Energy Policy Review: Friends of the Earth Submission'. September, London: Friends of the Earth.

FOREMAN-PECK, J. S. and MILLWARD, R. 1994. *Public and Private Ownership of British Industry: 1880–1990.* Oxford: Clarendon Press.

FORSYTH, P. J. and KAY, J. A. 1980. 'The Economic Implications of North Sea Oil Revenues'. *Fiscal Studies* 1(3): 1–28.

FRIEDMAN, M. and FRIEDMAN, R. 1980. *Free to Choose.* London: Secker and Warburg.

GLYN, A. 1984. *The Economic Case Against Pit Closures.* Sheffield: NUM. Reprinted in *Debating Coal Closures*, eds D. Cooper and T. Hopper. 1988. Cambridge: Cambridge University Press.

——and MACHIN, S. 1997. 'Colliery Closures and the Decline of the UK Coal Industry'. *British Journal of Industrial Relations* 35(2).

GOWING, M. 1974. *Independence and Deterrence: Britain and Atomic Energy, 1945–52, vol. 1: Policy Making; vol. 2: Policy Execution.* London: Macmillan.

GREEN, R. 2001. 'Markets for Electricity in Europe'. *Oxford Review of Economic Policy* 17(3): 329–45.

GREENPEACE. 1994. 'No Case for a Special Case'.

GRUBB, M. *et al.* 1999. *The Kyoto Protocol.* Royal Institute for International Affairs/Earthscan.

HALL, T. 1981. *King Coal.* London: Penguin.

——1986. *Nuclear Politics: The History of Nuclear Power in Britain.* London: Penguin.

HAMMOND, E. M., HELM, D. R., and THOMPSON, D. J. 1985. 'Regulation of the Gas Industry: Memorandum 27'. Institute for Fiscal Studies.

——1986. 'Competition in Electricity Supply: Has the Energy Act Failed'? *Fiscal Studies* 7(11): 11–33.

HANNAH, L. 1979. *Electricity Before Nationalisation.* London: Macmillan.

——1982. *Engineers, Managers and Politicians: The First Fifteen Years of Nationalised Electricity Supply in Britain.* London: Macmillan.

Hansard Society. 1997. *The Report of the Commission on the Regulation of Privatised Utilities*, The Hansard Society for Parliamentary Government. London.

HAYEK, F. 1944. *The Road to Serfdom.* London: Routledge and Sons.

——1948. *Individualism and Economic Order.* Chicago: University of Chicago Press.

——1960. *The Constitution of Liberty.* Chicago: University of Chicago Press.

HEALD, D. 1980. 'The Economic and Financial Control of U.K. Nationalised Industries'. *The Economic Journal* 90 (June): 243–65.

HECLO, H. and WILDAVSKY, A.B. 1974, 'The Private Government of Public Money: Community and Policy inside British Politics', Berkeley: University of California Press.

HELM, D. R. 1986. 'The Assessment: The Economic Borders of the State'. *Oxford Review of Economic Policy* 2(2): i–xxiv. Reprinted in *The Economic Borders of the State*, ed. D. R. Helm. 1989. Oxford: Oxford University Press.

——1987a. 'RPI – X and the Newly Privatised Industries: A Deceptively Simple Regulatory Rule'. *Public Money* 7(1): 47–51.

——1987b. 'Competition, but with Care'. *Financial Times*, 30 September.

——1987c. 'Nuclear Power and the Privatisation of Electricity Generation'. *Fiscal Studies* 8(4): 69–73.

——1988. 'Nuclear Switch'. *The Times*, 12 December.

——1993. 'The Assessment: The European Internal Market: The Next Steps'. *Oxford Review of Economic Policy* 9(1): 1–14.

——1994a. 'Regulating the Transition to the Competitive Market'. In *Regulating Utilities: The Way Forward*, ed. M. E. Beesley. IEA Readings 41, Institute of Economic Affairs in association with the London Business School.

——1994b. 'British Utility Regulation: Theory, Practice, and Reform'. *Oxford Review of Economic Policy* 10(3): 17–39.

——1995. 'Regulating in the Public Interest'. In *Profiting from the Utilities: New Thinking on Regulatory Reform*, ed. D. Corry. Institute of Public Policy Research.

——1996. 'British Gas Splits'. *Energy Utilities*, March, p. 3.

——1997. 'Why Coal Should no longer be King. *The Times*, 31 October.

——1998. 'The Assessment: Environmental Policy——Objectives, Instruments, and Institutions'. *Oxford Review of Economic Policy* 14(4): 1–19.

——1999. 'Changing Priorities'. *The Utilities Journal*, April.

——2001a. 'Making Britain More Competitive: A Critique of Regulation and Competition Policy'. *Scottish Journal of Political Economy* 48(5): 471–87.

——2001b. 'Submission to House of Lords on Green Paper'. 12 September.

——2001c. 'Climate Changes, Policies, and the Case for Carbon Tax'. *Turning Point? An Independent Review of UK Energy Policy*, British Energy Publication, October.

——2001d. 'The Assessment: European Networks——Competition, Interconnection, and Regulation'. *Oxford Review of Economic Policy* 17(3): (Autumn): 297–312.

——2001e. 'The Debt Illusions'. December, p. 1.

——2002a. 'A Critique of Renewables Policy in the UK'. *Energy Policy* 30(3): 185–8.

——2002b. 'Investment in Energy Networks: Auctions, Regulation and Planning'. In *Towards an Energy Policy*, ch. 6. ed. D. R. Helm. OXERA, August.

——2002c. 'A Critique of Rail Regulation'. In *Utility Regulation and Competition Policy*, ed. C. Robinson. Cheltenham: Edward Elgar: 19–41.

——2003a. 'The Energy Policy Britain Needs', IEE Maxwell Lecture. 28 April, London.

——2003b. 'Comment on: "Draft Social and Environmental Guidance to the Gas and Electricity Markets Authority"', submission to the Department of Trade and Industry, August.

——and MAYER, C. 1988. 'The Privatisation of the Electricity Supply Industry'. Confederation of British Industry, London.

——and McGOWAN, F. 1989. 'Electricity Supply in Europe: Lessons for the UK'. In *The Market for Energy*, eds D. R. Helm, J. Kay, and D. Thompson. Oxford: Oxford University Press: 237–60.

——and POWELL, A. 1992. 'Pool Prices, Contracts and Regulation in the British Electricity Supply Industry'. *Fiscal Studies* 13(1): 89–105.

——and RAJAH, N. 1994. 'Water Regulation: The Periodic Review'. *Fiscal Studies* 15(2): 74–94.

HELM, D. R., KAY, J., and THOMPSON, D. eds 1989. *The Market for Energy*. Oxford: Clarendon Press.

HENDERSON, D. 1981. 'Nuclear Power in Britain: The Case for a New Approach'. *Public Money*, September.

HENDERSON, P. D. 1977. 'Two British Errors: Their Probable Size and Some Possible Lessons'. *Oxford Economic Papers* 29(2): 159–205.

HENNESSEY, P. 1989. *Whitehall*. London: Secker and Warburg.

HEWITT, C. 2001. 'Power to the People: Delivering a 21st Century Energy System'. Institute of Public Policy Research, London.

HICKS, J. R. 1955. 'Economic Foundations of Wage Policy'. *The Economic Journal* (reprinted as 'Inflation and the Wage Structure'. In *Money, Interest and Wages, Collected Essays*, vol. II. ed. J. R. Hicks, 1982).

HM Customs and Excise. 1995. 'Coal UK', February.

HM Government. 1999. 'Economic and Fiscal Strategy Report and Financial Statement and Budget Report 1999'. HC 298.

HMSO. 1909. 'Electric Lighting Act'. London: HMSO.

——1911. 'Electricity Supply Act'. London: HMSO.

——1944. 'Employment Policy'. Cmnd 6257, London: HMSO.

——1946. 'Coal Industry Act'. London: HMSO.

——1948. 'Gas Act'. London: HMSO.

——1959. 'Nuclear Installations Act'. London: HMSO.

——1964. 'Continental Shelf Act'. London: HMSO.

——1965. 'Gas Act'. London: HMSO.

——1967. 'Fuel Policy'. Cmnd 3438.

——1972. 'Gas Act'. London: HMSO.

——1973. 'Fair Trading Act'. London: HMSO.

——1976. 'Energy Act'. London: HMSO.

——1978. 'The Challenge of North Sea Oil'. Presented to Parliament by the Prime Minister, the Chancellor of the Exchequer, the Lord President of the Council, the Secretary of State for Energy and the Secretary of State for Scotland, Cmnd 7143.

——1980. 'Competition Act'. London: HMSO.

——1980. 'Coal Industry Act'. London: HMSO.

——1980. 'Employment Act'. London: HMSO.

——1980. 'Coal Industry Act'. London: HMSO.

——1981. 'Gas Levy Act'. London: HMSO.

——1982. 'Oil & Gas (Enterprise) Act'. London: HMSO.

——1982. 'Coal Industry Act'. London: HMSO.

——1982. 'Employment Act'. London: HMSO.

——1983. 'Energy Act'. London: HMSO.

——1984. 'Trade Union Act'. London: HMSO.

—— 1986. 'The Gas Act'. London: HMSO.

—— 1987. 'Single European Act'. London: HMSO.

—— 1988. 'Privatising Electricity: The Government's Proposals for the Privatisation of the Electricity Supply Industry in England and Wales'. Cm 322, February, London: HMSO.

—— 1989. 'The Electricity Act'. London: HMSO.

—— 1990. 'The Hinkley Point Public Inquiries: A Report by Michael Barnes to the Secretaries of State for Energy and the Environment'. London: HMSO.

—— 1994. 'Coal Industry Act'. London: HMSO.

—— 1995. 'Gas Act'. London: HMSO.

—— 1998. 'Competition Act'. London: TSO.

—— 2000. 'Utilities Act'. London: TSO.

HMT 1961. 'The Financial and Economic Obligations of the Nationalised Industries'. Cmnd 1337, Her Majesty's Treasury, London: HMSO.

—— 1967. 'Nationalised Industries: A Review of Economic and Financial Objectives'. Cmnd 3437, Her Majesty's Treasury, London: HMSO.

—— 1978. 'The Nationalised Industries'. Cmnd 7131, Her Majesty's Treasury, London: HMSO.

—— 1985. 'The Success of Privatisation'. Speech by J. Moore, Financial Secretary.

—— 1986. 'Accounting for Economic Costs and Changing Prices: A Report to HM Treasury by an Advisory Group (The Byatt Report)'. Her Majesty's Treasury, London: HMSO.

—— 1997. 'Environmental Taxation—Statement of Intent'. 2 July, Press Office, Her Majesty's Treasury, London: TSO.

—— 2000. 'Budget 2000: Prudent for a Purpose: Working for a Stronger and Fairer Britain', March.

—— 2002. 'Tax and the Environment: Using Economic Instruments'. November, Her Majesty's Treasury, London: TSO.

—— and DEFRA. 2003. 'Economic Instruments to Improve Household Energy Efficiency: Consultation Document on Specific Measures'. Her Majesty's Treasury and the Department for Environment, Food and Rural Affairs, London: TSO.

Holtham. 1996. 'Water: Our Mutual Friend'? *New Economy*, December.

House of Commons Committee of Public Accounts. 1973. 'North Sea Oil and Gas'. First Report, Session 1972–73, February, London: HMSO.

—— 2002. 'Pipes and Wires', Fiftieth Report of Session 2001–02, 8 August, HC 831, London: The Stationery Office.

House of Commons Environmental Audit Committee. 2002. 'A Sustainable Energy Strategy? Renewables and the PIU Review'. Fifth Report of Session 2001–02, vol. 1: Report and Proceedings of the Committee, 22 July, London: TSO.

House of Commons Select Committee on Energy. 1981*a*. 'The Government's Statement on the New Nuclear Power Programme'. Session 1980–81, vol. 1: Report and Minutes of Proceedings, HC Paper 114–1, London: HMSO.

—— 1981*b*. 'Energy: Government's Response to the First Report of the Select Committee on Energy'. Session 1980–81, Cmnd 8317, London: HMSO.

—— 1982. 'The Disposal of the British Gas Corporation's Interest in the Wytch Farm Oil-field'. First Report, Session 1981–82), HC138, London: HMSO.

—— 1990. 'Cost of Nuclear Power'. vol. II: Minutes of Evidence and Appendices, 4th report, HC 205-ii, London: HMSO.

—— 1991. 'Renewable Energy: Minutes of Evidence'. Session 1991–92, 20 November, HC 43-ii, London: HMSO.

—— 1992a. 'Consequences of Electricity Privatisation: Second Report from the Energy Committee', vol. I. Report'. HMSO, HC 113-I.

—— 1992b. 'Consequences of Electricity Privatisation: Second Report from the Energy Committee', vol. II. Memoranda of Evidence'. HC 113-II, London: HMSO.

House of Commons Select Committee on Science and Technology. 1974. 'The Choice of a Reactor System'. First Report, Session 1973–74, HMSO, White Paper.

House of Commons Select Committee on the Environment. 1994. 'Energy Efficiency: The Role of Ofgas'. Session 1993/94, HC 328iii, London: HMSO.

House of Commons Select Committee on Trade and Industry. 1992. 'British Energy Policy and the Market for Coal: Minutes of Evidence'. HC 237-iii, 3/4 November, London: HMSO.

—— 1999. 'Impact on Industry of the Climate Change Levy, vol. II. Ninth Report, Minutes of Evidence and Appendices'. 15 July, London: TSO.

—— 2000a. 'The Work of Ofgem'. HC 193-ii, London: TSO, 16 January, London: TSO.

—— 2000b. 'Minutes of Evidence taken before the Trade and Industry Committee: Appendix 6: Memorandum submitted by Dr Dieter Helm, New College, Oxford'. 25 January, London: TSO.

House of Lords Select Committee on Science and Technology. 1999. 'Management of Nuclear Waste'. Third Report, HL 41, Session 1998–99, London: TSO.

House of Lords Select Committee on the European Communities. 1993. 'Structure of the Single Market for Energy'. HL paper 56, London: HMSO.

HUME, D. 1751. *Enquiries Concerning Human Understanding and Concerning the Principles of Morals*. Reprinted from the 1997 edition with introduction and analytical index by L.A. Selby-Bigg. 1975, 3rd edition, Oxford: Clarendon Press.

Industry Department for Scotland. 1988. 'Privatisation of the Scottish Electricity Industry'. March, Cm 327, London: HMSO.

IPCC. 2001. 'Climate Change 2001: Impacts, Adaptation and Vulnerability'. IPCC Working Group II, Summary for Policymakers, Intergovernment Panel on Climate Change.

JACKSON, M. P. 1974. *The Price of Coal*. London: Croom Helm.

JENKINS, R. 1991. *A Life at the Centre*. London: Macmillan.

JENKINSON, T. and MAYER, C. 1994. 'The Costs of Privatisation in the UK and France'. In *Privatisation and Regulation: The UK Experience*, eds Bishop *et al.* Oxford: Oxford University Press: 290–8.

JOSKOW, P. 2001. 'California's Electricity Crisis'. *Oxford Review of Economic Policy* 17(3): 365–88.

KLEINWORT BENSON. 1990. 'The Regional Electricity Companies Share Offers'. 21 November.

KLEMPERER, P. 1999. 'Auction Theory: A Guide to the Literature'. *Journal of Economic Perspectives* 13(3) (July): 227–86.

KOLBE, A. L. and BORUCKI, L. S. 1998. 'The Impact of Stranded-cost Risk on Required Rates of Return for Electric Utilities: Theory and an Example'. *Journal of Regulatory Economics*, May.

Labour Party. 1997. 'New Labour Because Britain Deserves Better'. April.

LANG, I. 1995. 'Don't Be Afraid of Electricity Takeovers'. *Financial Times*, 1 September.

——2002. *Blue Remembered Years: A Political Memoir.* London: Politico's Publishing.

LAWSON, N. 1980. 'The New Conservatism'. London: Center for Policy Studies.

——1982. Speech given at the Fourth Annual International Conference, International Association of Energy Economists, Churchill College, Cambridge, 28 June, reproduced in *The Market for Energy*, eds D. R. Helm, J. Kay, and D. Thompson (1989). Oxford: Clarendon Press.

——1992. *The View from No. 11: Memoirs of a Tory Radical.* London: Bantam.

LEDGER and SALLIS. 1994. *Crisis Management in the Power Industry: An Inside Story.* London: Routledge.

LEHMANN, P. 2002. 'Energy Efficiency'. In *Towards an Energy Policy*, ch. 8. ed. D. Helm. OXERA, August.

LITTLE, I. 1953. *The Price of Fuel.* Oxford: Clarendon Press.

LITTLECHILD, S. C. 1981a. 'Misleading Calculations of the Social Costs of Monopoly Power'. *The Economic Journal* 91(362): 348–63.

——1981b. Ten Steps to Denationalization. *Journal of Economic Affairs* 2(1) reprinted in *Privatisation & Competition: A Market Prospectus*, ed. C. Veljanovski (1989). Institute of Economic Affairs.

——1988. 'Economic Regulation of Privatised Water Authorities and Some Further Reflections'. *Oxford Review of Economic Policy* 4(2): 40–67.

——1991. 'Competition, Efficiency and Emission Reduction: A Regulator's View'. Speech delivered at the 'Energy Policy——Market-led or Government-driven'? Conference of the Royal Institute of International Affairs Energy Committee, 3 December.

——1993a. 'Debate on Regulatory Framework should be Better Informed'. Speech given at the 'Fuels for Power Generation' Conference, 20 April.

——1993b. 'New Developments in Electricity Regulation'. In *Major Issues in Regulation*, ed. M. E. Beesley. IEA Readings 40, Institute of Economic Affairs in association with the London Business School: 119–36.

——1994a. 'Chairman's Comments' (reply to Helm, 1994). In *Regulating Utilities: The Way Forward*, ed. M. E. Beesley, IEA Readings 41, Institute of Economic Affairs in association with the London Business School.

——1994b. 'Competition in Electricity: Retrospect and Prospect'. Speech given at the Institute of Economic Affairs Lectures on Regulation, 15 November.

——2002. 'Michael Beesley's Contribution to Privatization, Competition and Regulation'. In *Utility Regulation and Competition Policy*, ed. C. Robinson. Cheltenham: Edward Elgar.

London Economics. 1987. 'Electricity Privatisation and the Area Boards: The Case for 12: Report Commissioned by the 12 Area Boards of England and Wales'.

LYONS, J. 1987. 'Power Shocks in Store for Parkinson'. *The Times*, 29 July.

—— 1988. 'Intolerable Contractions'. *Financial Times*, 25 January: 14.

MACKERRON, G. 1984. 'Is Sizewell a Good Investment'? *Public Money*, December: 15–19.

—— 1996. 'Nuclear Power under Review'. In *The British Electricity Experiment: Privatisation: The Record, The Issues, The Lessons*, ed. J. Surrey. London: Earthscan: 138–63.

MARSHALL, W. 1989. 'The Future for Nuclear Power'. British Nuclear Energy Society, Annual Lecture, Royal Lancaster Hotel, London, 30 November.

Marshall Task Force. 1998. 'Economic Instruments and the Business Use of Energy: Conclusions'. November, Marshall Task Force on the Industrial Use of Energy.

MCCARTHY, C. 2001. 'Letter to the Editor'. *Financial Times*, 17 July.

—— 2002. 'Energy regulators back call from Brussels to act'. Letter to the Editor, *Financial Times*, 22 August.

—— 2003. 'Regulation, Myth and Reality'. Speech given to the Institute of Electrical Engineers, London, 17 June.

MEADOWS, D. H. *et al.* 1972. 'The Limits to Growth: A Report for the Club of Rome's Project on the Predicament of Mankind'. London: Earth Island.

MILLWARD, R. 1976. 'Price Restraint, Anti-inflation Policy and Public and Private Industry in the UK 1947–1973'. *The Economic Journal* 86 (June): 226–42.

Ministry of Fuel and Power. 1946. 'Domestic Fuel Policy: Report by the Fuel and Power Advisory Council (the Simon Committee)'. Cmnd 6762, London: HMSO.

—— 1955. 'A Programme of Nuclear Power'. Cmnd 9389, London: HMSO.

—— 1965. 'Fuel Policy'. Cmnd 2798, London: HMSO.

MITCHELL, C. 1998. *Renewable Energy in the UK: Policies for the Future*. Council for the Protection of Rural England, London.

MMC. 1980. 'Domestic Gas Appliances: A Report on the Supply of Certain Domestic Gas Appliances in the United Kingdom'. HC 703, 1979–80, July, Monopolies and Mergers Commission, London: HMSO.

MMC. 1981. 'Central Electricity Generating Board: a Report on the Operation by the Board of its System for the Generation and Supply of Electricity in Bulk'. HC 315, 1980–81, May, Monopolies and Mergers Commission, London: HMSO.

—— 1983a. 'London Electricity Board: a Report on the Direction and Management by the London Electricity Board of its Business of Retailing Domestic Electrical Goods, Spare Parts and Ancillary Goods'. Cmnd 8812, March, Monopolies and Mergers Commission, London: HMSO.

—— 1983b. 'National Coal Board: a Report on the Efficiency and Costs in the Development, Production and Supply of Coal by the NCB'. Cmnd 8920, June, Monopolies and Mergers Commission, London: HMSO.

——1983c. 'Yorkshire Electricity Board: a Report on the Efficiency and Costs of the Board'. Cmnd 9014, August, Monopolies and Mergers Commission, London: HMSO.

——1984. 'South Wales Electricity Board: a Report on the Efficiency and Costs of the Board'. Cmnd 9165, February, Monopolies and Mergers Commission, London: HMSO.

——1985a. 'The Revenue Collection Systems of Four Area Electricity Boards: a Report on the Efficiency and Costs of and the Services Provided by the East Midlands, South Eastern, North Eastern and South Western Area Electricity Boards in Relation to their Systems for the Collection of Revenue from the Supply of Energy'. Cmnd 9427, January, Monopolies and Mergers Commission, London: HMSO.

——1985b. 'North of Scotland Hydro-Electric Board: a Report on the Efficiency and Costs of the Board'. Cmnd 9628, October, Monopolies and Mergers Commission, London: HMSO.

——1986. 'South of Scotland Electricity Board: a Report on the Efficiency and Costs of the Board'. Cmnd 9868, August, Monopolies and Mergers Commission, London: HMSO.

——1988. 'Gas: a Report on the Matter of the Existence or Possible Existence of a Monopoly Situation in Relation to the Supply in Great Britain of Gas through Pipes to Persons other than Tariff Customers'. Cm 500, October, Monopolies and Mergers Commission, London: HMSO.

——1993a. 'Gas and British Gas plc'. Cm 2317, July, Monopolies and Mergers Commission, London: HMSO.

——1993b. 'Gas: Volume 1 of Reports under the Fair Trading Act 1973 on the Supply Within Great Britain of Gas Through Pipes to Tariff and Non-tariff Customers, and the Supply Within Great Britain of the Conveyance or Storage of Gas by Public Gas Supplies'. Cm 2314, July, Monopolies and Mergers Commission, London: HMSO.

——1995. 'Scottish Hydro-Electric plc: A Report on a Reference under Section 12 of the Electricity Act 1989'. June, Monopolies and Mergers Commission, London: HMSO.

——1996a. 'National Power plc and Southern Electric plc: A Report on the Proposed Merger'. Cm 3230, April, Monopolies and Mergers Commission, London: HMSO.

——1996b. 'PowerGen plc and Midlands Electricity plc: A Report on the Proposed Merger'. Cm 3231, April, Monopolies and Mergers Commission, London: HMSO.

——1997a. 'Northern Ireland Electricity plc: A Report on a Reference under Article 15 of the Electricity (Northern Ireland) Order 1992'. April, Monopolies and Mergers Commission, London: TSO.

——1997b. 'BG plc: A Report under the Gas Act 1986 on the Restriction of Prices for Gas Transportation and Storage Services'. June, Monopolies and Mergers Commission, London: TSO.

—— 1997*c*. 'PacifiCorp and The Energy Group: A Report on the Proposed Acquisition'. Cm 3816, December, Monopolies and Mergers Commission, London: TSO.

MORGAN, K. O. 1997. *Callaghan: A Life*. Oxford: Oxford University Press.

MORRISON, H. 1933. *Socialisation and Transport*. London: Constable.

NAO. 1992*a*. 'Report by the Comptroller and Auditor General: The Sale of the Twelve Regional Electricity Companies'. May, London: HMSO.

—— 1992*b*. 'Report by the Comptroller and Auditor General: The Sale of National Power and Powergen'. June, London: HMSO.

—— 1992*c*. 'Report by the Comptroller and Auditor General: The Sale of ScottishPower and Hydro-Electric'. July, London: HMSO.

—— 1996. 'Report by the Comptroller and Auditor General: The Sale of the Mining Operations of the British Coal Corporation', 3 May, HC 360, London: HMSO.

—— 1998. 'Improving Energy Efficiency Financed by a Charge on Customers'. July, London: TSO.

NAO and DETR. 1998. 'Report by the Comptroller and Auditor General: The Home Energy Efficiency Scheme'. Session 1997–98, HC 556, February 25th.

NAPAG. 1995. 'Energy and Environment in the 21st Century'. The Royal Society, London, National Academies Policy Analysis Group.

National Energy Policy Development Group. (2001). 'National Energy Policy: Reliable, Affordable and Environmentally Sound Energy for America's Future'. US Government Printing Office.

NCB. 1972. 'Annual Report, 1971/72'. National Coal Board.

NEDO. 1976. 'A Study of UK Nationalised Industries: Their Role in the Economy and Control in the Future'. London: National Economic Development Office.

NEWBERY, D. 1994. 'The Impact of Sulfur Limits on Fuel Demand and Electricity Prices in Britain'. *The Energy Journal* 15(3): 19–41.

—— 1996. 'Vertical Integration in the Electricity Supply Industry'. Mimeo, Department of Applied Economics, Cambridge University, January.

—— and McDANIEL, T. 'Auctions and Trading in Energy Markets—An Economic Analysis', in Centre for Regulated Industries (2003), *Regulatory Review 2002/2003*.

Nirex. 2001. 'Report on the Nirex Internal Inquiry, July'.

NM Rothschild. 1986. 'British Gas plc: Offer for Sale'. On behalf of the Secretary of State for Energy, December.

NUCG. 1994. 'The Future Role of Nuclear Power in the UK. A Background Paper to the Nuclear Review. Prepared by Nuclear Electric, Scottish Nuclear, UKAEA and BNFL'. Nuclear Utilities Chairmens Group.

Nuclear Electric. 1994. 'The Government's Review of Nuclear Energy. Submission from Nuclear Electric plc'. Published in four volumes.

O'RIORDAN, T. *et al.* 1988. *Sizewell B: An Anatomy of the Inquiry*. London: Macmillan Press.

Offer. 1991. 'Report on Pool Price Inquiry'. December, Birmingham, Office of Electricity Regulation.

—— 1992*a*. 'Report on Constrained-on Plant'. October, Birmingham, Office of Electricity Regulation.

—— 1992*b*. 'The Supply Price Control Review: Consultation Paper'. October, Birmingham, Office of Electricity Regulation.

—— 1992*c*. 'Review of Economic Purchasing'. December, Birmingham, Office of Electricity Regulation.

—— 1992*d*. 'Review of Pool Prices'. December, Birmingham, Office of Electricity Regulation.

—— 1993*a*. 'Letter to the Rt Hon. T. Eggar, MP by the Director General'. 11 January, Birmingham, Office of Electricity Regulation.

—— 1993*b*. 'Review of Economic Purchasing: Further Statement'. February, Birmingham, Office of Electricity Regulation.

—— 1993*c*. 'The Supply Price Control Review: Proposals'. July, Birmingham, Office of Electricity Regulation.

—— 1993*d*. 'Pool Price Statement'. July, Birmingham, Office of Electricity Regulation.

—— 1994*a*. 'Consultation on Pool Reform'. 3 March, Birmingham, Office of Electricity Regulation.

—— 1994*b*. 'Report on Trading outside the Pool'. July, Birmingham, Office of Electricity Regulation.

—— 1994*c*. 'The Distribution Price Control: Proposals'. August, Birmingham, Office of Electricity Regulation.

—— 1995*a*. 'The Competitive Electricity Market from 1998'. January, Birmingham, Office of Electricity Regulation.

—— 1995*b*. 'The Distribution Price Control: Revised Proposals'. July, Birmingham, Office of Electricity Regulation.

—— 1995*c*. 'The Competitive Electricity Market from 1998: The Next Steps'. August, Birmingham, Office of Electricity Regulation.

—— 1996. 'The Transmission Price Control Review of the National Grid Company: Proposals'. October, Birmingham, Office of Electricity Regulation.

—— 1997. 'The Competitive Electricity Market from 1998: Opening the Market'. May, Birmingham, Office of Electricity Regulation.

—— 1998. 'Review of Electricity Trading Arrangements: Proposals'. July, Birmingham, Office of Electricity Regulation.

—— 1999. 'Review of Public Electricity Suppliers 1998–2000. Distribution Price Control Review: Consultation Paper'. May, Birmingham, Office of Electricity Regulation.

Offer/Ofgas. 1997. 'Dual Fuel Offers in the Gas and Electricity Markets: An Offer and Ofgas Joint Decision Document'. Birmingham, Office of Electricity Regulation, and London: Office of Gas Supply.

—— 1999. 'Reviews of Public Electricity Suppliers 1998 to 2000: Scottish Transmission Price Control Review: Consultation Paper'. June, Birmingham, Office of Electricity Regulation, and London: Office of Gas Supply.

Ofgas. 1987. 'Competition in Gas Supply'. December, London: Office of Gas Supply.

—— 1990. 'Least Cost Planning in the Gas Industry'. London: Office of Gas Supply.

—— 1991*a*. 'New Gas Tariff Formula: Economic Aspects'. Malcolm Keay, September, London: Office of Gas Supply.

—— 1991*b*. 'New Gas Tariff Formula: Tariff Structures'. James McKinnon, September, London: Office of Gas Supply.

—— 1991*c*. 'New Gas Tariff Formula: Proposed Modifications of British Gas' Authorisation'. London: Office of Gas Supply.

—— 1992. 'Annual Report'. March, London: Office of Gas Supply.

—— 1994. 'Price Controls on Gas Transportation and Storage'. London: Office of Gas Supply.

—— 1996*a*. 'Price Control Review 1997: British Gas' Transportation and Storage. The Director General's Initial Proposals: Consultation Document and Appendices', May.

—— 1996*b*. 'Price Control Review 1997: British Gas' Transportation and Storage. The Director General's Final Proposals', August.

—— 1996*c*. 'Extension of Domestic Competition: A Consultation Document'. September, London: Office of Gas Supply.

—— 1997*a*. 'Annual Report'. London: Office of Gas Supply.

—— 1997*b*. 'Competitive Market Review: Consultation Document'. December, London: Office of Gas Supply.

—— 1998. 'A Review of Competition in the Domestic Gas Market'. October, London: Office of Gas Supply.

Ofgem. 1999*a*. 'The New Electricity Trading Arrangements', vol. 1 and 2. July, London: Office of Gas and Electricity Markets.

—— 1999*b*. 'Reviews of public electricity suppliers 1998 to 2000: distribution price control review: Draft Proposals'. August, London: Office of Gas and Electricity Markets.

—— 1999*c*. 'Reviews of Public Electricity Suppliers 1998 to 2000: Scottish Transmission Price Control Review: Draft Proposals Paper'. October, London: Office of Gas and Electricity Markets.

—— 1999*d*. 'Reviews of Public Electricity Suppliers 1998 to 2000: Scottish Transmission Price Control Review: Final Proposals'. December, London: Office of Gas and Electricity Markets.

—— 1999*e*. 'Review of Public Electricity Suppliers 1998–2000. Distribution Price Control Review: Final Proposals'. December, London: Office of Gas and Electricity Markets.

—— 1999*f*. 'The Transmission Price Control Review of the National Grid Company from 2001: Initial Consultation Document'. December, London: Office of Gas and Electricity Markets.

—— 2000*a*. 'Review of Transco's Price Control from 2002: Initial Consultation Document'. May, London: Office of Gas and Electricity Markets.

—— 2000*b*. 'The Transmission Price Control Review of the National Grid Company from 2001: Draft Proposals'. June, London: Office of Gas and Electricity Markets.

——2000c. 'New Ownership Structures in the Water Industry: A Response to the Director General of Water Services' Consultation Paper'. July, London: Office of Gas and Electricity Markets.

——2000d. 'Information and Incentives Project: Output Measures and Monitoring Delivery between Reviews: Final Proposals'. September, London: Office of Gas and Electricity Markets.

——2000e. 'The Transmission Price Control Review of the National Grid Company from 2001: System Operations: Initial Proposals'. September, London: Office of Gas and Electricity Markets.

——2000f. 'The Transmission Price Control Review of the National Grid Company from 2001: Transmission Asset Owner: Final Proposals'. September, London: Office of Gas and Electricity Markets.

——2000g. 'The Proposed Acquisition of Dwr Cymru Cyfyngedig by Glas Cymru Cyfyngedig: A Response to the Director General of Water Services' Consultation Paper'. December, London: Office of Gas and Electricity Markets.

——2000h. 'National Grid Company System Operator Price Control and Incentive Schemes under NETA'. December, London: Office of Gas and Electricity Markets.

——2000i. 'A Review of the Development of Competition in Domestic Gas and Electricity Supply'. December, London: Office of Gas and Electricity Markets.

——2001a. 'Review of Transco's Price Control from 2002: Draft Proposals'. June, London: Office of Gas and Electricity Markets.

——2001b. 'The New Electricity Trading Arrangements: A Review of the First Three Months'. August, London: Office of Gas and Electricity Markets.

——2001c. 'Review of Transco's Price Control from 2002: Final Proposals'. September, London: Office of Gas and Electricity Markets.

——2001d. 'Energy Efficiency Commitment Administrative Procedures: Working Document'. December, London: Office of Gas and Electricity Markets.

——2001e. 'Performance and Innovation Unit Energy Policy Review: A Submission by the Office of Gas and Electricity Markets', pp. 19–21. October, London: Office of Gas and Electricity Markets.

——2001f. 'Mergers in the Electricity Distribution Sector: Consultation Document'. November, London: Office of Gas and Electricity Markets.

——2001g. 'Information and Incentives Project: Incentive Schemes: Final Proposals'. December, London: Office of Gas and Electricity Markets.

——2001h. 'Energy Efficiency Commitment Administrative Procedures: Working Document'. December, London: Office of Gas and Electricity Markets.

——2002a. 'Mergers in the Electricity Distribution Sector: Policy Statement'. May, London: Office of Gas and Electricity Markets.

——2002b. 'The Review of the First Year of NETA'. July, London: Office of Gas and Electricity Markets.

——2002c. 'Separation of Transco's Distribution Price Control: Initial Consultation Document'. July, London: Office of Gas and Electricity Markets.

——2002*d*. 'Developing Network Monopoly Price Controls: Initial Consultation'. August, London: Office of Gas and Electricity Markets.

——2002*e*. 'Report on the Separation of the Transco LDZ Price Control'. 14 November, London: Office of Gas and Electricity Markets.

——2002*f*. 'Separation of Transco's Distribution Price Control: Draft Proposals'. December, London: Office of Gas and Electricity Markets.

——2003*a*. 'Income Adjusting Event under NGC's 2002/03 System Operator Incentive Scheme: A Consultation Document', May.

——2003*b*. 'Income Adjusting Event under NGC's 2002/03 System Operator Incentive Scheme: A Decision Document', June.

Ofgem/DTI. 1999. 'The New Electricity Trading Arrangements: Conclusions'. October, London: Office of Gas and Electricity Markets and Department of Trade and Industry.

——2000. 'NETA Go Live Decision Making Indicators'. November, London: Office of Gas and Electricity Markets and Department of Trade and Industry.

——2001. 'Go Live Indicators Status Report and Risk Assessment'. March, London: Office of Gas and Electricity Markets and Department of Trade and Industry.

OFT. 1987. press release, 25 November, London: Office of Fair Trading.

OFT. 1991. 'The Gas Review'. London: Office of Fair Trading.

Oftel. 1988*a*. 'The Regulation of British Telecom's Prices: A Consultative Document'. January, London: Office of Telecommunications.

——1988*b*. 'The Control of British Telecom's Prices'. July, London: Office of Telecommunications.

——1992. 'The Regulation of BT's Prices: A Consultation Document'. London: Office of Telecommunications.

——1996. 'The Control of British Telecom's Price Control'. July, London: Office of Telecommunications.

Owen, G. 1996. 'A Market in Efficiency: Promoting Energy Savings Through Competition'. London: Institute of Public Policy Research.

OXERA. 1994. *The Franchise Drop 1994: A Guide to Electricity Purchasing in the 100 kW Market*, Immediate Issues Report, Oxford: The OXERA Press.

——1995*a*. *Coal in the UK*. Oxford: The OXERA Press.

——1995*b*. *Acquisitions and Diversification: The Record of the Privatised Industries*. Oxford: The OXERA Press.

——1997. 'Report to the DETR and DTI on Options for the Future Development of Energy Efficiency Standards of Performance'. Oxford: OXERA.

——1998. *The Utilities Journal*. February, Oxford: The OXERA Press.

——1999. *Guide to the Economic Regulation of the Electricity Industry*. Oxford: The OXERA Press.

——2000. 'Oil and Gas Prices'. *The Utilities Journal*, August, Oxford: OXERA: 22–23.

PA Consulting. 1998. 'Revision of the 1998 Programme, Report to the DGES'. January.

Parker, M. 2000. *Thatcherism and the Fall of Coal*. Oxford: Oxford University Press.

Parkinson, C. 1992. *Right at the Centre*. London: Weidenfeld and Nicholson.

PATTERSON, W. C. 1983. *Nuclear Power*, 2nd edn. London: Penguin.

Pay Board. 1974. 'Special Report: Relative Pay of Mineworkers'. Cmnd 5567, London: HMSO.

PEARCE, D. 2003. 'The Social Cost of Carbon and its Policy Implications'. *Oxford Review of Economic Policy* 19(3).

PEASE, J. 1993. 'Firms Use Rules Loophole to Grab Bigger Share of Cheap Gas'. *The Engineer*, 27 May, Miller Freeman.

PIU. 2002. 'The Energy Review'. February, London: Performance and Innovation Unit.

Platts. 2002. *European Power Daily* 4(168): (1, 2) September.

POPPER, K. 1945. *The Open Society and its Enemies*. London: Routledge and Kegan Paul.

—— 1957. *The Poverty of Historicism*. London: Routledge and Kegan Paul.

POSNER, M. 1972. 'Policy towards Nationalised Industries'. In *The Labour Government's Economic Record: 1964–70*, ed. W. Beckerman. London: Duckworth: 247–61.

—— 1973. *Fuel Policy: A Study in Applied Economics*. London: Macmillan.

PowerGen. 1990. 'Annual Report'.

PRICE, T. 1990. *Political Electricity: What Future for Nuclear Energy?* Oxford: Oxford University Press.

PRYKE, R. 1971. *Public Enterprise in Practice*. London: MacGibbon and Kee.

—— 1981. *The Nationalised Industries*. Oxford: Martin Robertson.

—— 1987. 'Layfield Fails the Coal Price Examination'. *Financial Times*, 4 February.

Radioactive Substances Advisory Committee, Panel on Disposal of Radioactive Wastes. 1959. 'The Control of Radioactive Waste'. White Paper, Cmnd 884, London: HMSO.

RCEP. 1976. 'Nuclear Power and the Environment' (The Flowers Report). 6th Report, Royal Commission on Environmental Pollution, Cmnd. 6618, London: HMSO.

—— 2000. 'Energy: The Changing Climate'. 22nd report, June, Royal Commission on Environmental Pollution, London: HMSO.

REDWOOD, J. 1996. 'Presiding over Utility Monopoly'. *The Times*, 1 June.

REES, R. 1989. 'Modelling Public Enterprise Performance'. In *The Market for Energy*, eds D. R. Helm, J. Kay, and D. Thompson. Oxford: Oxford University Press.

Ridley Committee. 1952. 'Report of the Committee on National Policy for the Use of Fuel and Power Resources'. Cmnd 8647, London: HMSO.

RJB Mining. 1994. 'Acquisition of the Principal Coal Mining Activities of British Coal Corporation in England and Placing and Offer for Sale by Barclays de Zoete Wedd Ltd'.

ROBINSON, C. 1981. 'What Future for British Coal? Optimism or Realism on the Prospects to the Year 2000'. Hobart Paper 89, London: Institutes of Economic Affairs.

—— 1992. 'The Demand for Electricity: A Critical Analysis of Producer Forecasts'. In *Energy Demand: Evidence and Expectations*, ed. D. Hawdon. Surrey: Surrey University Press.

—— and MARSHALL, E. 1985. *Can Coal be Saved?* Institute of Economic Affairs paper 105, London: Institute of Economic Affairs.

ROBINSON, G. 2000. *The Unconventional Minister: My Life Inside New Labour*. London: Penguin.

ROUTLEDGE, P. 1993. *Scargill: The Unauthorised Biography*. London: Harper Collins.

Royal Society. 1999. 'Nuclear Energy: The Future Climate'. London: Royal Society.

SCHMALENSEE, R., JOSKOW, P., ELLERMAN, A., MANTERO, J., and BAILEY, E. 1998. 'An Interim Evaluation of Sulfur Dioxide Emissions Trading'. *Journal of Economic Perspectives* 53–68.

SCHUMPETER, J. 1943. *Capitalism, Socialism and Democracy*, 1st edn. London: George Allen and Unwin.

Scottish Nuclear. 1993. 'The Need for an Energy Policy Framework'.

SIEBERT, H. and KOOP, M. J. 1993. 'Institutional Competition versus Centralization: Quo Vadis Europe'. *Oxford Review of Economic Policy* 9(1): 15–30.

SKIDELSKY, R. 2000. *Fighting for Britain 1937–1945*, vol. 3. London: Macmillan.

SORRELL, S. 1999. 'Why Sulphur Trading Failed in the UK'. In *Pollution for Sale: Emissions Trading and Joint Implementation*. eds S. Sorrell and J. Skea. Cheltenham: Edward Elgar.

SOUTER, D. 1994. 'A Stakeholder Approach to Regulation'. In *Regulating our Utilities*. eds D. Corry, D. Souter, and M. Waterson. London: Institute for Public Policy Research.

SPRU. 1995. 'UK Nuclear Privatisation and Public Sector Liabilities' in association with the Consortium of Opposing Local Authorities and Friends of the Earth, Science and Technology Policy Research, Brighton: Sussex University.

STUART MILL, J. 1909. *Principles of Political Economy*, Book 4, ch. 7, London: Longman, Green and Co.

SUPPLE, B. 1987. *The History of the British Coal Industry, iv: 1913–1946: The Political Economy of Decline*. Oxford: Clarendon Press.

THATCHER, M. 1988. Science and Technology speech to the Royal Society, 27 September at Fishmonger's Hall, City of London, www.margaretthatcher.org/speeches.

—— 1995. *The Downing Street Years*. London: Harper Collins.

The Economist. 1978. 'Appomattox or Civil War'. 27 May, p. 21.

—— 1996. 'Lang Pulling the Plug'. 27 April.

—— 1999. 'The Next Shock'. 27 April.

The Electricity Council. 1981. 'Electricity Supply Industry in England and Wales: Review of the Structure of the Bulk Supply Tariff'. December.

The *Times* 1997a. 'Why Coal Should no Longer be Kept'. D. R. Helm, 31 October.

—— 1997b. 'Why the Coal Industry Should not be Scuttled'. J. Callaghan, 6 November.

—— 1998a. 'Coal Crisis Takes Mandelson Underground'. 9 January.

——1998b. 'Nuclear Switch'. 12 December, p. 12.

TIRELLO, E. 1990. 'And Then There Were 50'. ch. 25. In eds J. L. Plummer and S. Troppman. 'Competition in Electricity: New Markets and New Structures', Public Utilities Reports, Arlington, Virginia, and QED Research, Paulo Alto, California.

TIETENBERG, T. 1990. 'Economic Instruments for Environmental Regulation'. *Oxford Review of Economic Policy* 6:1.

UBS Phillips and Drew. 1991. 'Generating Value'. February.

VON MISES. 1949. *Human Action: A Treatise on Economics*. Yale, USA: Yale University Press.

WALKER, P. 1991. *Staying Power: An Autobiography*. London: Bloomsbury.

WALKER, W. 1999. 'Nuclear Entrapment: THORP and the Politics of Commitment'. Institute of Public Policy Research.

WATERSON, M. 1994. 'The Future for Utility Regulation: Economic Aspects'. In *Regulating Our Utilities*, eds D. Corry, D. Souter and M. Waterson. London: Institute for Public Policy Research: 101–29.

——1996. 'Vertical Integration and Vertical Restraints'. In *Readings in Microeconomics*, ed. T. J. Jenkinson. Oxford: Oxford University Press.

WEITZMAN, M. L. 1974. 'Prices vs Quantities'. *Review of Economic Studies* 41: 477–91.

WILDAVSKY, A.B. 1974. 'Speaking Truth to Power: The Art and Craft of Policy Analysis', Boston: Little Brown.

WILLIAMS, R. 1980. *Nuclear Power Decisions*. London: Croom Helm.

YARROW, G. K. 1988. 'The Price of Nuclear Power, *Economic Policy* 6: 81–132.

——1989. 'Does Ownership Matter'? In *Privatisation and Competition: A Market Prospectus*, ed. C. Veljanovski. Institute of Economic Affairs.

YERGIN, D. 1991. *The Prize*. London: Simon and Schuster.

YOUNG, H. 1989. *One of Us: A Biography of Margaret Thatcher*. London: Macmillan.

INDEX

North East coal region 183
North Sea oil and gas 4, 6, 10, 177, 257,
    340, 345, 373
  state ownership and monopoly 14,
    16–17, 26, 36, 38–41, 43
  British Gas privatization 109–13, 115n, 117
  electricity's transition to competition
    162, 168
  competition 261, 265
  sources and supply 295, 298
  energy policy review 388, 391, 396
  energy policy reinvented 413,
    414, 422
North West Water 223, 228, 232
North Western Electricity Board *see*
    NORWEB
Northern Electric 168n, 277, 416
  first review (RECs) 214–17
  capital market competition 2, 223, 228,
    238, 240
    and Trafalgar 212, 215–16, 218, 224,
    241–2
  market opening 270
  windfall tax 289n
  periodic reviews 335–6
Northern Ireland Electricity *see* NIE
Norway 10, 115, 167, 298, 387, 396
NORWEB (North Western Electricity
    Board) 168, 310, 333
  capital market competition 223, 228,
    232, 233n
  market opening 270
  windfall tax 289n
NORWEB Supply 239
NOx (nitrogen oxides) 181
NTS (National Transmission System—gas)
    5, 14, 134, 249, 295, 365
  British Gas privatization 108, 116, 117
  regulatory reform and New Labour
    279n, 287–8
  periodic reviews 338, 340, 341
NUCG (Nuclear Utilities Chairmen's
    Group) 196–7
Nuclear Electric 18, 142, 225, 309
  privatization 187&n, 189, 191–200
  stations listed 187n
  see also Dungeness; Heysham; Hinkley
Nuclear Energy Agreement 198
Nuclear Industry Radioactive Waste
    Management 96&n
Nuclear Installations Act (1959) 29n
Nuclear Installations Inspectorate 92
nuclear power 2, 177, 299, 360

state ownership and monopoly 15, 16,
    17, 18, 23, 27–30, 37–8, 42
  costs 28&n–9
    decommissioning 29, 42, 90, 189–90,
    194
  Howell's programme 51–2, 56, 58
  option in 1980s 7, **89–107**
    AGRs 90–5, 100, 104, 107n
    electricity privatization 106–7
    PWRs 89, 90–4, 104, 105
      switch to 99–101
    Sizewell Inquiry 52, 90, 101–3, 187
    THORP 90, 96–9, 104
    waste management 90, 95–6
  electricity privatization 106–7, 126,
    126–31 *passim*, 142, 150–1, 188, 201
  privatization 8, **186–203**, 415
    contracts 191–3
    FFL and contracts 191–3
    liabilities and costs 188–91, 202
    performance 193–5
    review 195–9
    strategy, search for 202
  energy policy review 388, 392, 398
  energy policy reinvented 410, 412, 413,
    415–16
  technology, choice of *see* AGRs; PWRs;
    SGHWR
  waste management 5, 29&n, 90, 95–6,
    345
  see also BNFL; UKAEA
Nuclear Waste Disposal Corporation 95
Nuclear Waste Management Advisory
    Committee 95
nuclear weapons 97
NUM (National Union of Mineworkers) 7,
    97, 295
  state ownership and monopoly 16, 37
  market, first steps towards 45, 50, 52–4,
    60, 66
  British Coal privatization and decline
    177, 183, 185
  see also Thatcher versus Scargill
NUR (National Union of Railwaymen) 84,
    85

O&M (operations and maintenance) 182,
    200, 202
Ofcom (Office of Communications) 292
Offer (Office of Electricity Regulation) 8,
    12, 143, 254
  transition to competition 154, 158n, 160,
    162n, 164–6, 170–2, 175

Lightning Source UK Ltd.
Milton Keynes UK
27 July 2010

157485UK00002B/43/P